an unauthorized appreciation of BBC–TV's Doctor Who

UWORP!

.2

by Earl Green

Second Edition

THE LOG BOOK .COM 25 YEARS
1989-2014

Introduction

The First Doctor

Season 1 (1963-64)

Season 2 (1964-65)

Season 3 (1965-66)

Season 4 (1966-67)

The Cushing Movies

The Second Doctor

Season 4 (1966-67)

Season 5 (1967-68)

Season 6 (1968-69)

The Third Doctor

Season 7 (1970)

Series 3 (2006-07)

Series 4 (2007-2010)

The Eleventh Doctor

Series 5 (2010)

Series 6 (2011)

INTRODUCTION
An Early Appointment With The Doctor

I was introduced to the Doctor (in the form of, naturally, Tom Baker), the TARDIS and Sarah Jane Smith at a very young age - I'm pretty sure I was no more than eight years old. *Star Wars* had been flowing through my veins since I was four, and I had become aware of **Star Trek** at the age of six or seven via the first movie and the resulting re-re-re-revival of the original episodes in syndication. But **Doctor Who** was special. Though it would probably get her hauled off in handcuffs in this day and age, for whatever reason, my mother introduced me to **Doctor Who**, **Benny Hill** and **Monty Python**, all around the same time. It was magical. **Python** and **Benny Hill** were - and still are, despite what any highbrow media pundits might have decided in retrospect - hysterically funny, like cartoons with real people in them. (Whether or not it was a great idea to be exposing an eight-year-old kid to this stuff, on the other hand, I leave for you to debate, though I'd argue strongly that there are far worse media-spawned catchphrases for a child to be parroting – or is that ex-parroting? – than "and now for something completely different.") **Doctor Who**, however, was even cooler. To my young mind, it had the outer space stuff, complete with monsters and creatures, that *Star Wars* had, Elisabeth Sladen was way hotter than Carrie Fisher (there, I said it!), and nobody around me in Arkansas talked like these people did. Sure, Grand Moff Tarkin spoke with a British accent, but *he* was a *bad guy*.

If you thought my mother was just asking for trouble by introducing me to **Doctor Who** (and, well, mainly the other stuff) at the impressionable age of eight, consider this: at only a few months old, my son was drawn – almost hypnotically – to the sight of my official BBC **Doctor Who** "time vortex" screensaver. If Daddy deactivated that screensaver by doing boring stuff like doing more work on this book, to cite just one example, quite a vocal complaint would be made.

Perhaps humblingly, he seemed incapable of caring about the body of the show itself. He just liked the time vortex.

But when the time comes, if he's even remotely interested, I will have absolutely no qualms about introducing my son to the Doctor. Because the Doctor is a hero who isn't in love with the power he bears for its own sake. He doesn't advocate violence as a solution to every problem. And he's a friend to the downtrodden, the different, and the unpopular. Even if you think you're on your own against overwhelming forces, *the Doctor will try to help you*. More than any caped or cowled crusader, more than any graduate of Starfleet Academy, it's that rooting-for-the-underdog thing that practically makes the Doctor the patron saint of nerdy kids (of all ages) like me. If it looks like the Doctor isn't being particularly helpful, it's probably because he's trying to force you to learn how to help yourself.

I can't think of a better imaginary friend or hero for a child to have.

Now for the big question...why should I write this book? And why should you read it? Why should you put money on the table for yet another book chronicling the Doctor's adventures, when there are already so many of them crowding your shelf, both BBC-sanctioned and otherwise? That's a good question. I hope that what I'm about to come up with is a good answer.

Fair warning: this book is written from a distinctly American perspective, because I'm an American approaching it from that perspective. I won't insult your intelligence by trying to adopt British spellings or lingo (though a few may sneak in because, as an Anglophile, I tend to use them in my own everyday conversation and writing, much to the chagrin of those listening and/or reading). But I won't be talking about how "this programme got the colour of Dalek armour wrong," because that isn't how I write in real life, and basically, I think you'd know better. I'm not a Brit, nor am I trying to pass myself off as one. I didn't grow up watching **Doctor Who** on BBC1 or BSB; I grew up watching it on usually stormy Sunday mornings on the Arkansas PBS channel, where they'd show it as 90-minute "movies" (though my first exposure to **Doctor Who** came through a late '70s run on KTVT in Dallas, which ran it in its original episodic form, so I already knew that the movie edits weren't how the show was intended to be seen). I also didn't grow up watching **Doctor Who** alongside **Fireball XL-1** or **Space: 1999**; I grew up watching it alongside **Buck Rogers In The 25ᵗʰ Century** and **Battlestar Galactica** (the original series, that is) and the glorious, can't-take-your-eyes-off-of-it train wreck that was *The Star Wars Holiday Special*. Even as I entered my cynical teenage years and early 20s, and stuff like **Star Trek: The Next Generation** and **Babylon 5** entered the picture, **Doctor Who** always retained its special magic for me. I'm not sure anyone was more delighted than I to see it return again and again and again, as novels, as audio plays, and finally back to television.

VWORP!, over what I'm hoping won't be more than three volumes, will chronicle all of these media — television, audio, prose and comics - and try to treat them as a whole entity with a reconcilable timeline. (Given that "reconcilable timeline" is always a relative term with **Doctor Who**, which has presented multiple incompatible scenarios for the birth and death of the human race, the fall of the continent of Atlantis, and so many "final ends" of the Daleks that I've lost count, be prepared to take all this with a dose of retcon that would leave any retired Torchwood employee reeling.)

As such, this book is written with a basic assumption: that the author likes **Doctor Who**, and tries to find something to like in any given stop that the TARDIS makes, and that you, as the reader, either like **Doctor Who**, or like it enough that you want to learn more. This book is predisposed toward being friendly to the show and its personnel. I'm not afraid to level some honest criticism, but even then there's almost always some value to be gleaned from even those installments that seem the least noteworthy. I've also taken the opportunity, with the realization that many of you reading this have only been exposed to the new series, to tell you why certain adventures from the "classic" series are relevant to what you're seeing now. In some cases, like *The War Games, Genesis Of The Daleks* and so on, they're hugely, no-brainer relevant; in others, I'm just letting you know if some relatively obscure Hartnell story has become an even more obscure verbal reference in a David Tennant episode.

As much as I love **Doctor Who**, even I will be the first to admit that it will be a rare and brave soul who should even remotely consider trying to track down and watch (or listen to) every single one of the Doctor's televised adventures. While I did state above that every story has its own rewarding point, even if that good point is a dose of pure **Mystery Science Theater 3000**-worthy goofiness, there are two things to consider: "classic" **Doctor Who** stories take much longer to play out (there are vast oceans of difference in the pacing of a television story of any kind between the 1960s and '70s and television produced now), and there are an awful lot of them to wade through. Beyond that, many stories are either partially or completely missing, and must be watched either via fan-made audiovisual reconstructions (which currently fall into a bit of a legal grey area, so I can't point you in the direction of how to find or acquire them) or the BBC's excellent range of narrated audio transcriptions of those missing adventures. Or, to give you another example, the material in this book originated from my web site, and covers nearly 20 years' worth of writing and viewing and listening. It takes a long time to experience **Doctor Who** from start to finish, and those who have been weaned on the breakneck pace of the new series may not have the stomach for that particular marathon (though if you set out to prove me wrong, good luck to you, enjoy the show, and let me know if this book has been of any help whatsoever). Also, for those wishing to embark on that journey, every story's synopsis includes a note about whether that particular adventure is available on DVD, videotape, audio CD, or what have you.

In the same spirit, I'm going to refer to those Hartnell-era stories – whose individual episodes each have their own titles – by the collective titles to which they are *most frequently referred*. I respect the fan researchers who have found compelling archival evidence to refer to *An Unearthly Child* as *100,000 B.C.*, or *Edge Of Destruction* as *Inside The Spaceship*, and so forth; but however accurate those titles may be from that perspective, they're <u>not</u> what's found on the DVD, CD and book covers. These alternate titles have almost become an in-joke among fandom, a way to tell the old-school *cognoscenti* from casual fans and/or the new-series-only crowd – however, as this book is intended to be of help to casual fans and new series fans, I'm using the titles by which they'll be able to find these classic stories in various officially released media.

My synopses and summaries of the stories themselves usually leave out one important thing: *the ending*. This is a long-standing, unspoken rule of theLogBook.com's style guide: don't spoil the ending, let people watch stuff for themselves because it's usually more fun that way. I intentionally leave most of the summaries open-ended so you can explore and experience the Doctor's travels for yourself. I sincerely feel I would be doing you a disservice otherwise.

Finally, there's one more regard in which I'm *not* going out of my way to please die-hard fandom here. There's a lot of what I call "received wisdom" in fandom, a fickle thing which decides that, for example, the 1996 TV movie starring Paul McGann was great for a short while after its premiere, and then at some point after its initial broadcast, despite not having been edited or changed since then, suddenly became crap. Actors, writers, and producers have come into fashion and fallen out of favor so many times in my years of reading fanzines, forums and newsgroups that I've given up on trying to keep track of who's "in" or "out." Indeed, I've really ceased to care about which direction fandom's prevailing winds are blowing. I'll make a note of it now and again, usually when I'm frustrated with a perfectly good storyline, actor or episode that has been collectively tossed into the trash, but I feel no great need to try to bend my own opinion to meet that of the majority (whether in terms of **Doctor Who** or real life, for that matter). So be prepared: this is a book written by a fan who still thinks that the Paul McGann movie is a great slice of **Who**, liked the Sylvester McCoy era just fine, thinks the existing Hartnell and Troughton stories should be required viewing, and thinks that *Underworld* and *Love & Monsters* aren't as bad as a great many people seem to insist that they are.

All of that being said, there's so much time (and space) to cover in so little space (and time). Let's get this show on the road.

What's different?
This is the second edition of VWORP!1, and the chief differences can be summed up as follows:

- New reviews of recently-recovered episodes (*Galaxy Four, Enemy Of The World, The Web Of Fear*)
- Revised cross-references pertaining to the 2012/2013 episodes and specials
- A few additional photos and illustrations
- New essay material related to the recently-recovered episodes
- More in-depth notes on stock library music used in 1960s episodes
- An index (based on comments from those who bought the first edition)
- New cover artwork (also based on comments from first edition customers)
- Some grammatical, spelling and punctuation corrections

Notes On This Book

Here are some quick notes on how this book is organized. For most of the episode guide/review material, I am using a slightly modified version of the standard format of theLogBook.com episode guides, upon which much of this material is based. Now, before you ask why you've just bought a book of which large chunks would seem to be available online, please understand that I, too, have had an item in theLogBook.com's FAQ for years, arguing strenuously against cutting down trees to present, at best, an incomplete chronicle of something that's still being made. There are many passages of this book that are completely new, written just for this volume. This *isn't* the web site on paper.

A few episode reviews have been completely rewritten from the ground up; though already covered on the web site, the online reviews for these stories were written by other authors. The intention, in replacing those pieces with completely new material, was to unify the book with a single point of view and a single voice, but it has the beneficial side effect of making some material exclusive to either the book or the web site. Even the material that *has* appeared on the site has undergone extensive rewrites. Much of theLogBook.com's **Doctor Who** episode guide is almost a journal chronicling its author's scattershot viewing of the series, and the site preserves that – in the original reviews of both *Survival* and the 1996 TV movie, I made dire predictions about any hope for the Doctor to return to television. I was wildly wrong in both cases, but I like to preserve that, at least online, as a snapshot of a moment in time. Such "present tense" references have been eliminated or heavily reworked for this book, which has to be a little more cohesive.

To make it easier to discern story synopses from my comments, after much trial and error I decided to use two distinctly different (but hopefully easily readable) fonts. The typeface you're seeing now (which, incidentally, was actually used in the on-screen credits for the latter half of the 1970s) will be used for story synopses. My own comments will follow each synopsis in this somewhat more condensed typeface. Separating the two is a section detailing the cast and major creative crew of the adventure in question, its airdate(s), individual weekly episode titles for Hartnell-era stories, any other interesting notes, and the availability of that story on DVD or CD. If you see an episode or story title in an outlined font instead of a solid one, then there's a question as to whether or not the adventure is "official."

Despite my original intentions to cram it all into a single book, it quickly became apparent that I wouldn't be able to include **Torchwood** or **The Sarah Jane Adventures** in VWORP!1. Here's a quick road map to what will be covered where:

VWORP!2 – **Doctor Who** episodes aired in 2012/2013, **Torchwood, Sarah Jane Adventures, K-9,** fan-made video productions, Big Finish main range, eighth and fourth Doctor audio stories

VWORP!3 – **Doctor Who** episodes aired between 2014 and the time of publication; Big Finish Companion Chronicles, Stageplays and Lost Stories, audio spinoffs (Dalek Empire, Jago & Litefoot, Gallifrey, etc.), and Big Finish main range and eighth and fourth Doctor audios released between 2014 and the time of publication.

VWORP!4 - **Doctor Who** novels (New Adventures, Missing Adventures, BBC Eighth Doctor Adventures, BBC Past Doctor Adventures, modern series fiction), **Doctor Who** comics, as well as coverage of TV and Big Finish **Doctor Who** produced after the release of VWORP!3.

I should stress at this juncture that neither the BBC nor Big Finish should feel any need to bring things to a grinding halt so I can catch up. You guys just keep making **Doctor Who**, and I'll keep watching, listening – and writing.

Beneath the cast/crew/trivia section, where applicable, are "Connections," either tying original series episodes forward to the new series, or vice-versa, footnotes on whether or not a given story has missing episodes (a malady, caused by a storage crunch at the BBC, general disorganization and a forehead-slapping lack of foresight in the early 1970s, which affects the 1960s episodes badly), and other footnotes that may enhance your enjoyment of the show. Well, at least that's the idea.

Why Who?

One question that probably readily comes to the mind of anyone looking at this book is: Why a whole book about **Doctor Who**? Or, if you're already an avid fan, why *yet another* book about **Doctor Who**?

To put it simply, it's not the Doctor's longevity on television or in other media alone that makes his adventures worthy of revisiting, analyzing and following. There are lots of shows on the air that have been around for a good while, that have transitioned into other media, and have attracted a large (if cultish) fan following. But **Doctor Who** has something they don't have - the Doctor himself.

A 900+ year old Time Lord capable of "regenerating" into a new body (with a new personality) in the event that grievous bodily harm - of a kind which would kill most of us mere mortals - occurs, the Doctor is an unconventional hero. Though his personalities range from the polite to the eccentric to the occasionally downright rude, he has a love of life, and is a staunch defender of the defenseless and the downtrodden. A renegade who technically broke the laws of his fellow Time Lords when he "misappropriated" his time machine and began using it to intervene in time and space rather than sitting back and watching events unfold, the Doctor is not sanctioned by any other person or agency when he meddles in events to tweak their outcome. Though there are a few entities on Earth who recognize him as a helpful influence, they seem to do so warily, aware that chaos almost always seems to follow him. And yet the Doctor doesn't bring an arsenal of weapons or an army of allies with him. Usually traveling with one, two or three close friends, the Doctor improvises on the spot, avoids violence until it has become the last and only resort, and nearly always gives his adversaries an opportunity to yield and reconsider their actions.

His adversaries seldom do this, of course, but that's hardly the Doctor's problem. He doesn't just blow them away. The people who travel with him in the TARDIS get to see history unfold, invariably gain a greater understanding of cause/effect and the heights and the lowest depths of human (and alien) nature. When their travels inevitably end, they're better people for the experience, more likely to intervene in history themselves - albeit on a smaller scale - on behalf of those less fortunate. They also inevitably face the sometimes heartbreaking reality that while the Doctor might be able to put things right, he can't undo all the damage that has been done in the course of doing so. His traveling companions have included everyone from schoolteachers to a Scottish highlander from the 1700s to journalists and aliens and stowaways, robot dogs, battle-hardened soldiers, and fellow Time Lords. All have left the TARDIS with a new perspective on their own lives and on everything that goes on around them. Well, almost all — very few TARDIS travelers have stepped out of the time machine's doors for the last time with any kind of pettiness intact from their former lives, and those who show a tendency toward doing so usually aren't aboard the TARDIS for very long (see the ninth Doctor story *The Long Game* for a good example of this).

Perhaps the most perfect summation of the Doctor's character, throughout his many lives, was penned by Terrance Dicks, former writer and script editor during the third Doctor's era (and frequently quoted by Paul Cornell), who summed the Doctor up succinctly in The Making Of **Doctor Who** (1972):

He is never cruel or cowardly. Although he is caught up in violent events, he is a man of peace.

The Doctor does not shy away from confrontation, despite knowing that it may cost him one of his precious, almost cat-like lives, and that a serious enough injury could even preclude his ability to regenerate. He does not shy away from defending those in need, no matter how unpopular it might be, and regardless of how their persecution and mistreatment might be built into in the law of some distant world or time. He doesn't always set world-changing events into motion, but often helps to win one battle in a larger war, inspiring the underdogs to rise up and keep fighting. And every so often he inadvertently makes things worse with the best of intentions.

Doctor Who - the show, not the character (who is virtually never referred to as "**Doctor Who**" as a proper name) - is a unique phenomenon in pop culture. The new series on the air right now is not a "reimagining" of the original, rebooting the continuity from scratch (*a la* **Battlestar Galactica**), or a passing-of-the-torch (*a la* **Star Trek: The Next Generation**, etc.). The Doctor we see now on TV is, after a few regenerations, the same man we first met with the long white hair, furtively trying to conceal his existence in a police box in a London junkyard in 1963, rather than a descendant or a protegé of that man. It's almost unique in modern mythology to have the longevity, the range and the depth of stories that have revolved around a single character. Though not impervious to harm, the Doctor does have a kind of immortality. Unlike Tarzan, the Lone Ranger, Hercules and even the heroes of all-pervading mythological pop culture such as *Star Wars*, the Doctor is rooted in no one place and time. Even the fact that he visits modern-day England frequently doesn't limit him, because modern-day England means something completely different in 1963, 1989, and 2010.

Doctor Who has always had a curious morality at its core, one which invites its viewers - via their hero - to be respectful of authority, but wary of it at the same time, always questioning how that authority came to be in power to begin with, and whether or not that authority deserves to remain in power. And while the Doctor is well-known – and indeed, in some circles, feared – for his regime-toppling prowess (indeed, in both the 2010 and 2011 seasons of the show, cabals of evil-doers stop fighting one another and join forces in an attempt to trap the Doctor and put him out of the way once and for all), he seldom puts a gun to anyone's head to do it (he seldom needs to), which is quite remarkable in and of itself. In popular culture, especially the visual media, the gun is very useful storytelling shorthand, telling you without saying a word that the hero (or villain) is prepared to do anything, up to and including taking lives, to achieve his or her desired outcome. It saves a lot of time on character study: the writer doesn't have to explore how fiercely and deeply-felt a character's motivations are when the gun frequently says it all. The Doctor does not resort to this, and yet leaves no doubt that he's capable of bringing down mayhem upon his adversaries.

With the possible exception of **McGyver**, the idea of a *non*-gun-toting action hero is almost unheard of in the popular western media. Even **Kung-Fu**'s Kwai-Chang Caine, who offered many a platitude about peace, could become a blur of flying fists at a moment's notice; much was made of Starfleet's peaceful mission in **Star Trek**, but let's face it, you couldn't have gotten five live-action series and an animated show out of Starfleet going around shaking pseudopodia and kissing babies - so *of course* they had to get into scuffles. The Doctor's use of martial arts (a trait limited to his third incarnation) or weaponry is outstanding simply because of its scarcity: when the fourth Doctor brandishes a gun (which, to be fair, he wasn't carrying until he relieved one of his assailants of it in a scuffle) in *The Seeds Of Doom*, or when the tenth Doctor does so in *The Doctor's Daughter*, it's not something he does every other week. It's an extraordinary moment that shows he's been pushed to the brink of his own self-control, usually because someone else seems hell-bent on harming the innocent. (What is perhaps even more ironic is that **Torchwood**, the highest-profile **Doctor Who** spinoff to date, is *very* trigger-happy.)

More often, one finds that the Doctor is almost directing traffic among the characters already on the scene wherever and whenever he arrives: with a word or a suggestion, he seems to be pushing people to better themselves and find the better angels of their nature – or to stand up for themselves in the face of oppression. This character trait has manifested itself both harmlessly and as a sign of an almost self-destructive deviousness (the latter chiefly seen in some of the seventh Doctor's later TV stories and many of the novels centered around him). His companions may wind up becoming pawns in the game as much as anyone else. And before things even get to that point, it's the Doctor's own curiosity that lands him in these situations. For someone who once had access to the vast archives of the Time Lords, there are a great many episodes in past and future history that he seems not to know about – or just wants to see unfold for himself. He didn't want that knowledge spoon-fed to him, and he's not likely to let his companions on his travels sit back either. One of the series' original missions in the 1960s was to educate young viewers about history, and somewhere along the way this has become the character's mission as well.

Doctor Who is a show that defies the narrative conventions of nearly any other series that has come along before or since. Its reputation for having fifty years of tangled continuity is a misnomer. The show is, in fact, very easy to fall in love with at just about any stop along the way. VWORP!1 is your guide to that history should you decide to pursue the series' internal history on a deeper level. **Doctor Who** has always been a dazzling, unpredictable journey through time and space, and while the episodes that were being broadcast in 1972 are wildly different in structure, style and production values from episodes being broadcast in 2012, it's almost always enjoyable – the show becomes its own time capsule.

Sit back and enjoy the ride; I'll do my best to be a reliable guide.

LEGEND

This story involves the DALEKS	This story involves the CYBERMEN	This story involves the SONTARANS	This story involves the TIME LORDS	This story involves the MASTER	This story involves UNIT
This story involves the SILENTS	This story involves the SILURIANS	This story involves the SLITHEEN	This story involves the AUTONS	This story involves ICE WARRIORS	This story involves the YETI

LEGEND

⓿ **NEW WHO CONNECTIONS**: These will point you toward later episodes (either classic or new series) referenced by the episode you're reading about. How vital is this story to the overall **Doctor Who** mythos? This is where you'll find out.

⓿ **CLASSIC CALLBACKS**: These will point you toward classic series episodes referenced by the new **Doctor Who**. Feel like you missed something in a throwaway reference rattled off by someone? This will point you to the source material.

⓿ **BEHIND THE SCENES**: Interesting facts that have more of an impact on the show's TV studio reality than its ongoing fiction.

⓿ **A.K.A.**: Familiar faces crop up in the show's cast from time to time, as well as faces who would become better known for later works.

⓿ **STOCK MUSIC**: A more thorough listing of the "library" or "stock" music licensed by the BBC for certain 1960s episodes, drawn directly from the BBC's records.

⓿ **MISSING**: Almost 100 episodes of 1960s Doctor Who are missing from the BBC archives. This will let you know if the story you're reading about is "incomplete"; be sure to check to see if any surviving footage has been released on DVD. Audio recordings of all of the missing episodes still exist and have been released in narrated form on CD by the BBC.

⓿ **SJA CONNECTION**: This indicates a reference that crops up later in the spinoff series **The Sarah Jane Adventures**, which will be covered fully in VWORP!2.

⓿ **TORCHWOOD CONNECTION**: This indicates a reference that crops up later in the spinoff series **Torchwood**, which will be covered fully in VWORP!2.

⓿ **K-9 CONNECTION**: This indicates a reference that crops up later in the K-9 series; while not strictly speaking a BBC-recognized **Doctor Who** spinoff, it does feature the character of K-9 so any crossovers will be mentioned here. The K-9 series will be covered fully in VWORP!2.

⓿ **AUDIO CONNECTION**: This indicates a reference that crops up later in the BBC or Big Finish **Doctor Who** and **Doctor Who**-related audio adventures.

⓿ **BOOK CONNECTION**: This indicates a reference that crops up later in the **Doctor Who** books published by Virgin Publishing and BBC Books.

⓿ **COMICS CONNECTION**: This indicates a reference that crops up later in the **Doctor Who** comics and graphic novels.

UWÔRP!

THE CLASSIC SERIES

1963 – 1989

The First Doctor
(William Hartnell: 1963-66)

Launched on November 23rd, 1963 on the BBC's television service (back when there was only one BBC channel, and thus no need to refer to it as "BBC1"), after a full day of coverage of the Kennedy assassination, **Doctor Who**'s travels through time were originally conceived as a family-friendly adventure series aimed at acquainting children with history. The basic concept of an old man - "possibly Oriental" according to the original character sketch - traveling through space and time in a fantastic ship bigger on the inside than the outside was originally delivered to the BBC by Sydney Newman. A Canadian-born producer who had recently defected to the BBC from an Australian network, Newman had struck an immediate nerve in British television with the modern-day drama **Armchair Theatre**. For an encore, Newman wanted to venture into the realm of science fiction, but his aim there was also Earthbound: **Doctor Who** would take his timeship full of companions on journeys through our own history, not on voyages to other worlds. In fact, Newman wasn't against any visits to futuristic Earth, so long as they had some redeeming educational value and didn't feature - as he put it - "bug-eyed monsters."

To this end, Newman and the BBC entrusted the **Doctor Who** concept to Verity Lambert, a young producer (and, atypically at the time for that job, a woman) with the drive and vision to shepherd the series through the then-normal 52-week production schedule, effectively keeping the show on the air year-round. Lambert latched onto the more fantastical concepts of her new project, seeking the highest technical expertise that the British Broadcasting Corporation had to offer. Finding scripts to keep the show fueled for a year-long production run, however, was a formidable task. So was the casting of the lead role of the Doctor, now envisioned as an eccentric, temperamental old man whose origins were unknown. At this stage, none of the staples of the show's mythology had been developed, especially not the character's origins among a race known as the Time Lords (something which wouldn't even be hinted at until six years into the show's run), though early drafts of the pilot script indicated that the Doctor and his granddaughter Susan were probably not human - or, if they were, they were from the distant future, and not a very pleasant one at that. But no further exploration of the character's background was anticipated at the time.

Nor was a sudden dearth of scripts. Historical briefs were assigned to writers: the Doctor would visit the cavemen and watch humans discover fire. He would witness the epic journey of Marco Polo, and visit the savage yet advanced tribe of the Aztecs, but a looming production schedule and a writer failing to complete his assignment left Lambert and script editor Dennis Spooner in a bind. A call for a new script to fill the sudden seven-episode gap resulted in new work for an out-of-work comedy writer named Terry Nation. Keen to write something serious for a change, and to provide something to fill the series' brief for educationally and socially redeeming adventures, Nation turned in a script set in the distant future of a planet called Skaro, where a Nazi-like alien race meted out unjustified retribution against a smaller, peaceful population. The parallels to Nazi Germany and the Holocaust didn't go unnoticed, but what caused Sydney Newman to balk at Nation's script was his description of the aggressors: the Daleks were, in Newman's mind, the very bug-eyed monsters he sought to avoid. But Verity Lambert was adamant and overrode his objections to prevent a costly production delay that could have ended the series prematurely. Nation's Daleks would appear five weeks into **Doctor Who**'s broadcast run.

The pilot episode, *An Unearthly Child*, was not without its own problems. The core cast of veteran stage/TV/film actor William Hartnell (the Doctor), Carole Ann Ford (Susan), William Russell (Ian Chesterton) and Jacqueline Hill (Barbara Wright) had been assembled, and the pilot had been taped. But neither Verity

Lambert nor Sydney Newman were happy with the result. Hartnell's portrayal of the Doctor was too ill-tempered, and more frustratingly, numerous technical difficulties occurred which fell short of the BBC's standards. But the premise was sound enough that the BBC ordered an unprecedented remount of the pilot: it would be recorded anew from scratch. Hartnell's portrayal became more crotchety and less mean-spirited in rehearsals, and the script was adjusted as well. Perhaps most importantly, the revised script pegged the Doctor and Susan's origins as "from another time...another world" instead of a line from an early draft of the pilot script indicating that they came from 49th century Earth.

With a masterfully-arranged Ron Grainer theme tune, brought to life in the BBC Radiophonic Workshop studios by Delia Derbyshire without the use of a single conventional musical instrument, and a mysterious swirl of video feedback, **Doctor Who** premiered at 5:15pm on November 23rd - and went mostly ignored due to the lingering shock of the news of the assassination of President John F. Kennedy. To protect its investment in what was becoming a technically advanced and therefore costly production, the BBC aired a repeat of *An Unearthly Child*, attracting a decent but not overwhelming audience to the series before the second episode aired. (In those days, each weekly episode had a different title; for reference purposes, these early stories are generally referred to by a blanket title which may or may not also be the title of the story's first episode.)

In its fifth week, **Doctor Who** started a new seven-part story, Terry Nation's *The Daleks*. At the end of part one, TARDIS traveler Barbara was seen cornered by the famous plunger-tipped arm, and it would be the following Saturday night before the Daleks were revealed in full. In only its second story, **Doctor Who** had ventured into the future on a planet other than Earth, complete with bug-eyed monsters - but the audience figures from *The Daleks* led Sydney Newman to drop his objections. And if Newman had tried to veto future visits to strange new worlds? The BBC was already deluged with license requests from toy companies, candymakers, children's clothing manufacturers...and the series' ratings more than doubled. Dalekmania was, for a brief time, as all-pervading as Beatlemania. Another set of Terry Nation scripts was quickly commissioned - and they were set in the future and featured unearthly creatures too.

They weren't the only ones, either. In his first year of TV adventures, the Doctor, with Susan, Ian and Barbara, witnessed the French Revolution and the brutal nobility of the Aztecs, but he also met the telepathic Sensorites. On average, the futuristic voyages of the TARDIS scored higher in the ratings than historical explorations. As Verity Lambert made plans for the second year of the series, she discussed a return of the Daleks with Terry Nation, and in general tipped the scales toward science fiction instead of history. Other changes were afoot as well. The second season opener, *Planet Of Giants*, dealt with an unscrupulous scientist unleashing an untested pesticide on the world, mindless of its deadly side-effects. So far, **Doctor Who** had only been faced with the theoretical dilemma of time travelers meddling in history. This was but the first sign of a growing sense of the lead character's social conscience on a more relatable level.

The Daleks did indeed return in the next adventure, *The Dalek Invasion Of Earth*, but when they were beaten back this time, a member of the TARDIS crew stayed behind as well, as the Doctor left his granddaughter Susan on Earth to help rebuild after the invasion. In the very next adventure, the two-part *The Rescue*, the TARDIS crew status quo was returned with the introduction of Vicki. Later that season, Ian and Barbara stayed on modern-day Earth after another brush with the Daleks in *The Chase*, which also saw a new companion arrive in the form of astronaut Steven Taylor. The story after *The Chase*, *The Time Meddler*, closed the season after pitting the Doctor against the Monk, a member of the same advanced society who possessed his own time-traveling TARDIS.

For its third season, a massive Dalek epic was in the works for **Doctor Who**. Of the nine multi-episode stories shown, only three were firmly rooted in Earth history, with a fourth, set in the modern day, foreshadowing the UNIT stories of the 1970s. Companions again came and went, with the 12-episode *Daleks' Masterplan* introducing the previously unthinkable plot development of some of the Doctor's companions being killed during their adventures. This season also provided **Doctor Who** with its lowest ebb thus far: *The Gunfighters*, a low-rated Western set during the gunfight at the OK Corral. But series star William Hartnell, who had tirelessly made public appearances in character to promote the show for three years, was also hitting his own low ebb. He was suffering from the onset of multiple sclerosis, taking its toll on his physical and mental endurance. A fiercely opinionated individual in his own right, Hartnell also objected to the increasingly dark storylines. The Doctor himself, it seemed, no longer felt the series was suitable for children.

By this time, Verity Lambert had vacated the producer's seat, and Innes Lloyd had taken over. Unable to come to an agreement with Hartnell over the show's content, and fully aware that the actor's physical condition would eventually prevent him from playing the part, Lloyd made unprecedented plans to replace the lead actor with someone who looked nothing like him. Not sure of the "scientific" explanation that would be given for this transformation, and unsure if the series would even survive it, Lloyd relentlessly pursued character actor Patrick Troughton to take over the role. After several refusals, Troughton finally gave in when more money was offered - and he was certain that the public's reaction to the jarring change of casting would mean it would be a very short gig.

During planning for the show's fourth season, script editor Gerry Davis - along with Dr. Kit Pedler, an imaginative scientist tapped as the show's science advisor for its increasingly futuristic stories - brainstormed with series creator Sydney Newman to find an explanation for a change in the Doctor's appearance and character. It was finally settled that the transformation was a kind of renewal, probably a function of the TARDIS (and something that couldn't possibly take place outside of it), and something that the Doctor's now decidedly alien race did whenever mortally wounded or exhausted. Troughton was convinced not to insist on heavy makeup or costumes. And a new adversary was invented to see the original Doctor out in style.

Davis and Pedler imagined a race very much like human beings who, after progressively replacing more and more of their bodies with prosthetic limbs and artificial organs, would be more computer than man. 22 years before the Borg was invented for **Star Trek: The Next Generation**, the Doctor's new arch nemesis would be the Cybermen. And like their latter day counterparts, the Cybermen sought to enslave humanity to convert every man, woman and child into more Cybermen. At the end of their debut adventure, *The Tenth Planet*, the Cybermen were of course fended off from their planned invasion of Earth. But the Doctor, exhausted, staggered back to the TARDIS and literally changed into a new man. It was October 29th, 1966, not even two months after the U.S. premiere of a science fiction series called **Star Trek**, and the Doctor had just regenerated for the first time - though nobody called it that yet. And to make sure that the change stuck (and to ensure that the viewing public stuck around despite the change), Innes Lloyd had arranged for the "new" Doctor's first adventure to feature the Daleks.

SEASON 1: 1963-64
AN UNEARTHLY CHILD

In London, 1963, teachers Ian Chesterton and Barbara Wright discuss their most problematic student at Coal Hill School, one Susan Foreman. Susan's knowledge vastly exceeds that of her instructors in science, but she has also been known to challenge long-standing historical facts...yet she also has some things completely wrong, including one occasion where she notes that British currency isn't on the decimal system "yet." Ian and Barbara follow Susan discreetly when she walks home one night, and the teachers are puzzled when home seems to be a junkyard. When they follow her into the junkyard, Susan has disappeared, and the only place she could have gone is a police call box which is emitting a strange hum.

Moments later, an elderly man appears, apparently determined to enter the police box himself. Ian and Barbara force their way in, along with the old man, and find that the police box is actually a time-space vehicle, bigger on the inside than out. They also discover that neither Susan nor her grandfather, a mysterious and irritable man known only as the Doctor, are human beings.

The Doctor, worried that Ian and Barbara will draw unwelcome mass attention to the presence of his ship (called the TARDIS), hastily sets it into motion over everyone's protests, and when Ian and Barbara next step out of the doors of the TARDIS, they are no longer on Earth as they know it.

William Hartnell . . . . The Doctor
William Russell . . . . Ian Chesterton
Jacqueline Hill . . . . Barbara Wright
Carole Ann Ford . . . . Susan Foreman
Althea Charlton . . . . Hur
Howard Lang . . . . Horg
Derek Newark . . . . Za
Eileen Way .Old Mother
Jeremy Young . . . . Kal

This story has been released on DVD

written by Anthony Coburn
directed by Waris Hussein
music by Norman Kay

An Unearthly Child aired on Nov. 23, 1963
The Cave Of Skulls aired on Nov. 30, 1963
The Forest Of Fear aired on Dec. 7, 1963
The Firemaker aired on Dec. 14, 1963

NEW SERIES CONNECTIONS: This story is *vitally important* to any fan of **Doctor Who** - even if you're not keen on the cavemen's story, the first twenty-five minutes are essential viewing, and from there you can almost skip to part one of *The Daleks* (a narrative shortcut that the Peter Cushing movies *did*, in fact, use — see page 60). And even with all of the various styles of storytelling that followed it, there was never anything remotely like the first episode of *An Unearthly Child* in the history of the series. *The Name Of The Doctor* (2013) reveals how the Doctor came to choose the particular TARDIS that he stole.

A.K.A.: In addition to a later appearance in the Tom Baker four-parter *The Creature From The Pit* (1979), actress **Eileen Way** (1911-1994) was a regular in the spooky 1993 kids' show **Century Falls**, written by an up-and-coming television writer by the name of Russell T. Davies.

STOCK MUSIC: The song attributed to "John Smith and the Common Men" is actually the instrumental "Three Guitars Mood 2", performed by the Arthur Nelson Group.

K-9 CONNECTIONS: Intriguingly, the K-9 episode *The Cambridge Spy* catapults one of that show's young characters into 1963, meaning that, depending on whether or not the fork in history resulting in the **K-9** series' alternate future London had already happened in 1963, *The Cambridge Spy*'s "past" scenes happen simultaneously with the first episode of **Doctor Who** (and, arguably, with the events of 1988's *Remembrance Of The Daleks* as well).

An Unearthly Child's first twenty-five minutes are beautifully self-contained, and still stand as one of the best and most important episodes in **Doctor Who**'s history. Some might even say *the* most important, and I find it difficult to argue with that. The entire internal mythology of the series is built upon a few scant, vague bits of dialogue in part one: the Doctor and Susan are from "another world, another time." They're on the run from unspecified people or circumstances. And one day, they intend to return.

William Hartnell is magnificent as the Doctor in this first installment, and Carole Ann Ford was never better as Susan. Ian and Barbara are two of the best companions ever seen in the show, and much of this is owed to their maturity; seldom, unless one counts Romana, did the Doctor travel with anyone who was clearly into his or her thirties. It wasn't until the fourth season of the new series, with Catherine Tate as Donna — or the <u>New Adventures</u> novels, with the introduction of Bernice and then Roz — that more mature companions were given a chance again.

The latter ¾ of the story are practically a self-contained three-parter, and there are numerous oddities in the show as well. Most of the time I can accept that most every alien creature in **Doctor Who** speaks with a British accent, but in this case, the "cavemen" in question shouldn't even have been speaking anything remotely resembling English. There's also the unusual scene which gets the Doctor's party involved with the cavemen in the first place - they see him lighting up a pipe, and therefore believe he can make fire. This is thankfully the only instance we ever see of the Doctor smoking...keep in mind, while **Doctor Who** was originally conceived as a children's series, this was a different day and age.

THE DALEKS

The TARDIS arrives on the distant planet Skaro, which seems at first to be uninhabited, except for fossilized animals. When the Doctor, Susan, Ian and Barbara discover a city constructed by an advanced civilization, there is a difference of opinion on whether or not to explore it. But the Doctor deems it necessary due to a shortage of mercury in the TARDIS' fluid link system. After wandering aimlessly in the city for a while, the travelers discover two horrifying things - their growing fatigue is a sign of radiation sickness from Skaro's toxic environment, and there are still living creatures inhabiting Skaro. One race, the pacifist humanoid Thals, try to maintain their primitive culture in the face of adversity. The other race, metallic monstrosities known as the Daleks, intend to wipe the Thals out - along with the Doctor and his companions, unless they assist the Daleks in their genocidal plan.

William Hartnell . . . . The Doctor
William Russell . . . . Ian Chesterton
Jacqueline Hill . . . . Barbara Wright
Carole Ann Ford . . . . .Susan Foreman
Robert Jewell . . . . Dalek
Kevin Manser . . . . Dalek
Michael Summerton . . . . Dalek
Gerald Taylor . . . . Dalek
Peter Murphy . . . . Dalek
Peter Hawkins, David Graham . . . .Dalek voices
Philip Bond . . . . .Ganatus
Jonathan Crane . . . . .Kristas

This story has been released on DVD

written by Terry Nation
directed by Christopher Barry
and Richard Martin
music by Tristram Cary

The Dead Planet aired on Dec. 21,1963
The Survivors aired on Dec. 28, 1963
The Escape aired on Jan. 4, 1964
The Ambush aired on Jan. 11, 1964
The Expedition aired on Jan. 18, 1964

UWORP!

The Ordeal aired on Jan. 25, 1964
The Rescue aired on Feb. 1, 1964

NEW WHO CONNECTIONS: This is another story to file under "You're kidding, right?" Though it's not the "origin story" for the Daleks (to borrow a term from comics), *The Daleks* lays out so much of what the metal monstrosities would become — and future stories stuck to it to varying degrees, but the basics were always there. Even with its occasionally punishing pacing, you should seek out *The Daleks* at least once, sit back, and imagine what it was like for kids in the early '60s to see them for the first time, *not* knowing all the backstory and continuity baggage that the Daleks carry around now.

One of the best William Hartnell stories, *The Daleks* not only introduced the alien creatures which put the show on the map, but it's a good story in its own right. At nearly twice the length of *An Unearthly Child*, *The Daleks* is an intelligent introduction for the Doctor's mortal foes, though many fans find the very 60s pseudo-science of this seven-parter laughable (what with the TARDIS requiring mercury to travel, and a mere vinyl jacket being the only weapon necessary to incapacitate the Daleks).

I also have to single out Tristram Cary's musical score: very creepy yet not dated. It's also very electronic, but not in the swooping-oscillator way that characterizes the show's theme tune as a thing of the 60s. Given appropriate visuals, Cary's music could be lifted out of this episode and would feel perfect in any current thriller.

At seven 25-minute episodes, *The Daleks* bogs down a bit in the middle, especially with the almost-too-lengthy trek back to the Dalek city. But the story also contains some surprisingly mature concepts and moments, including Ian's effective demonstration of the danger facing the Thals if they refuse to fight for their survival, the Doctor's insistence that the Thals must follow their own destiny without any further assistance from him, and the hints of potential romance between Barbara and a Thal leader (and some slightly less obvious hints that Susan is fully capable of developing a typical teenage crush, too). The Doctor also provides an anti-heroic surprise when he reveals that the mercury "problem" was in fact a ruse so he could satisfy his curiosity about the city.

The Daleks would return again…and again…and again. And by striking such a chord with viewers - especially kids - in Britain, they transformed **Doctor Who** forever.

THE EDGE OF DESTRUCTION

The Doctor, Susan, Ian and Barbara find themselves sprawled across the floor of the TARDIS console room after some kind of accident, scarcely able to remember each other (or, for that matter, whether they can trust one another). The TARDIS itself won't let them exit, and gives very vague readings as to what may be outside - readings indicating inescapable danger. Even within the timeship, strange signs of danger are making themselves known. And something appears to be affecting the minds of its occupants…could that something be the TARDIS itself, trying to warn them of their own impending doom?

William Hartnell . . . . The Doctor
William Russell . . . . Ian Chesterton
Jacqueline Hill . . . . Barbara Wright
Carole Ann Ford . . . . Susan Foreman

This story has been released on DVD

written by David Whitaker
directed by Richard Martin and Frank Cox
stock library music - see credits below

The Edge Of Destruction aired on Feb. 8, 1964
The Brink Of Disaster aired on Feb. 15, 1964

NEW WHO CONNECTIONS: We hear a lot about the TARDIS as a sentient being in its own right; this is really the starting point of that element of the **Doctor Who** mythos. Much later in the series, this element becomes a handy *deus ex machina*, (see *Doctor Who*, 1996 and *The Parting Of The Ways*, 2005) but here the TARDIS isn't doing much to help its occupants understand what the message is. It proves to be similarly cryptic when dealing with some of the Doctor's companions later on as well (*Hide*, 2013).

STOCK MUSIC: "Musique Electronique" (Eric Siday); "The Day The Sky Fell In" (Desmond Leslie); "Musique Concrete Part II" (Buxton Orr).

A nice, simple little story, this two-parter (what a relief after *The Daleks*!) is sidetracked by some occasional over-the-top acting (at least by today's standards), especially from Carole Ann Ford, who as Susan seems to shriek at almost anything that moves over the course of the story. Though many later **Doctor Who** stories spent a lot of time - in a few cases, *too much* time - aboard the TARDIS, this one is famous for *never even leaving* the TARDIS. Normally, "stuck aboard the ship" episodes of science fiction series are used to develop the characters, but in this case, it's hard to pick any characterization out of the show because the stars have all been possessed, or they're in shock, or something, and they don't even know who they are. In some respects, this helps to point up the alien nature of the Doctor and Susan, and Ian and Barbara's unease with them is brought firmly to the foreground here. That the characters are able to come to an uneasy truce and work together is a key character moment in the early part of the series.

MARCO POLO

The TARDIS lands in the Himalayas in 1289, and promptly breaks down, stranding the Doctor, Ian, Susan and Barbara. Fortunately for them, a caravan is passing through and they are able to secure shelter. Ian and Barbara are impressed to learn that their new benefactor is none other than Marco Polo himself, on his latest passage to Cathay from Venice. But they are less enthused when Marco reveals that he intends to take the Doctor's "flying caravan" to Peking as a gift for Kublai Khan, who will hopefully be impressed enough to continue to grant Marco safe passage. The Doctor and his companions continue traveling with Marco and his own suspicious companion, the Mongol warlord Tegana. Susan befriends a young girl named Ping-Cho, who is being transported to meet her future husband in an arranged marriage. The Doctor doesn't give up hope that he will have an opportunity to recover the TARDIS, but he may have to travel with Marco for months to seize it.

William Hartnell . . . . The Doctor
William Russell . . . . Ian Chesterton
Jacqueline Hill . . . . Barbara Wright
Carole Ann Ford . . . . Susan Foreman
Gabor Baraker . . . . Wang-Lo
Paul Carson . . . . Ling-Tau
Philip Crest . . . . Bandit
Claire Davenport . . . . Empress
Mark Eden . . . . Marco Polo
Jimmy Gardener . . . . Chenchu

This story has been released on audio CD

written by John Lucarotti
directed by Waris Hussein and John Crockett
music by Tristram Cary

The Roof Of The World aired on Feb. 22, 1964
The Singing Sands aired on Feb. 29, 1964
Five Hundred Eyes aired on March 7, 1964
The Wall Of Lies aired on March 14, 1964
Rider From Shang Tu aired on March 21, 1964
Mighty Kublai Khan aired on March 28, 1964

O. Ikeda	Yeng
Peter Lawrence	Vizier
Tutte Lemkow	Kuiju
Zienia Merton	Ping-Cho
Martin Miller	Kublai Khan
Derren Nesbitt	Tegana
Basil Tang	Foreman
Philip Voss	Acomat
Charles Wade	Malik

Assassin At Peking aired on April 4, 1964

A *very* condensed (approximately 30 minutes) reconstruction of *Marco Polo*, using surviving photos and excerpts from the audio recording of the soundtrack, is available as an extra on the *Edge Of Destruction* DVD.

MISSING: All seven episodes of *Marco Polo* are missing from the BBC archives. Only still photos and complete sound recordings of all seven episodes remain. It is also a very frequent subject of "recovered episode" rumors.

A.K.A.: Actress **Zienia Merton** has been cast as just about every "exotic" nationality imaginable, but is probably best known to science fiction TV fans as Sandra Benes, one of the few crew members of Gerry Anderson's **Space: 1999** series to survive the cast turnover that occurred at the end of that show's first season. She also officiated over Sarah Jane Smith's wedding in **The Sarah Jane Adventures:** *The Wedding Of Sarah Jane Smith* (2009).

The earliest **Doctor Who** story to have been wiped from the BBC's archives, *Marco Polo* is an extended historical epic with jeopardy and suspense aplenty, though when the whole premise of the Doctor and company staying with Marco is the long wait for an opportunity to escape in the TARDIS, one wonders if viewers in 1964 thought of this seven-parter as one long wait to reach the end of the serial.

In terms of casting, *Marco Polo* comes up aces. Mark Eden does an excellent job - at least judging by the existing sound recordings of the story - of playing Marco as reluctantly ruthless. He comes across as a normally decent man forced into a more cutthroat way of thinking by circumstances, though it could also be argued that since he makes that transition so easily, Marco doesn't get an entirely heroic portrayal here - an interesting early example of a historic figure being painted in shades of grey in **Doctor Who**. (He later plays another pivotal figure in the Doctor's history, BBC programming executive Donald Baverstock, in 2013's docu-drama *An Adventure In Space And Time*.

We also see here one of the first examples of the Doctor vanishing from the story for a while, on this occasion to rest in the TARDIS. (In future stories, it would be almost common for the Doctor to require rest, or to be knocked out cold, in order to get the character out of sight so William Hartnell could get some rest of his own; this trick also turned up during Patrick Troughton's era from time to time.) Ian and Barbara are proactive enough in the story, and Susan's relationship with Ping-Cho is vital enough to the plot, that it works.

A fine example of a historical adventure, it's a shame that *Marco Polo* is now something only to be heard, and not seen; even if the story dragged on a bit, the surviving photos leave little doubt that no expense was spared on the period costumes and sets.

THE KEYS OF MARINUS

The TARDIS lands on the planet Marinus, a world whose seas are filled with acid and whose beaches are sand fused into glass. They investigate a fantastic building, but at the same time something else is investigating the TARDIS - a tall creature in what appears to be a black skinsuit. Inside the building, more of these creatures are encountered, and Ian saves a man who's being threatened by one of the beings. The man, Arbitan, tells the Doctor and his friends the story of the Conscience, a machine that was built to be the perfect impartial judge and evolved into a device that eliminated crime from Arbitan's society by controlling the thoughts of the population. But when a rebel group aided by the Voords arrived, four of the Conscience's five keys were hidden to prevent the Voord from ruling over Marinus with its mind control. Arbitan enlists the Doctor's help to search for the missing keys, and to make sure he has the time travelers' help, he prevents them from reaching the TARDIS. They undertake a lengthy quest across Marinus, through lawless frozen wastelands, enduring moving vegetation, and visiting a ruined city whose inhabitants use hypnotic means to trick visitors into seeing an opulent palace. They even find a counterfeit Conscience key. But when they return with the four keys, they find Arbitan dead and the Voords in control.

William Hartnell . . . . The Doctor
William Russell . . . . Ian Chesterton
Jacqueline Hill . . . . Barbara Wright
Carole Ann Ford . . . . Susan Foreman
Michael Allaby . . . . Larn / Ice Soldier
Heron Carvic . . . . voice of Morpho
Martin Cort . . . . Aydan / Voord
George Couloris . . . . Arbitan
Alan James . . . . Ice Soldier
Robin Phillips . . . . Altos
Donald Pickering . . . . Eyesen
Katharine Schofield . . . . Sabetha
Peter Stenson . . . . Voord / Ice Soldier
Henley Thomas . . . . Tarron
Anthony Verner . . . . Ice Soldier

This story has been released on DVD

written by Terry Nation
directed by John Gorrie
music by Norman Kay

The Sea Of Death aired on April 11, 1964
The Velvet Web aired on April 18, 1964
The Screaming Jungle aired on April 25, 1964
The Snows Of Terror aired on May 2, 1964
Sentence Of Death aired on May 9, 1964
The Keys Of Marinus aired on May 16, 1964

Gordon Wales . . . . Voord
Fiona Walker . . . . Kala
Edmund Warwick . . . . Darrius

A.K.A.: Actor **George Couloris** (1903-1989) has a far more iconic claim to science fiction fame than playing Arbitan in **Doctor Who**. As a member of Orson Welles' Mercury Theatre Players, he also took part in Welles' **Mercury Theatre Of The Air** radio program, including the infamous panic-inducing 1938 broadcast of *The War Of The Worlds*. Couloris and Welles continued working together, with Couloris also appearing in Welles' 1941 big-screen magnum opus, *Citizen Kane*.

COMICS CONNECTION: A 1987 <u>Doctor Who Magazine</u> comics adventure featuring the sixth Doctor, *The World Shapers* (written by comics great Grant Morrison), posits that the Voord would someday evolve into the Cybermen, and that Marinus would be renamed Mondas. While this is an interesting extrapolation (and a neat way to make the Voords' "head handles" less of a design throwaway), it's been contradicted by nearly every other account of the Cybermen's origins since then.

An early precursor to such "quest" stories as season 16's Key To Time story arc and new series story arcs like the crack in Amy's bedroom wall, *The Keys Of Marinus* is one of the few times Dalek creator Terry Nation got a shot at creating other adversaries for the Doctor. The story is essentially a series of one-episode vignettes connected by an over-arching story

With stabbings in the back, accusations of murder and a rogue who may have rapacious intentions toward Barbara, *Keys* is also a surprisingly dark installment of early **Who**, from a time when the show was unreservedly meant for a younger audience. Almost more disturbing is the backstory of Marinus itself, a world whose population apparently submitted to mind control as a means to controlling crime. (From a 21st century perspective, however, that seems less like science fiction and more like a cautionary tale.) Though the end of the story quietly assures us that this is no longer the case due to the destruction of the Conscience, until that is mentioned we're seeing the Doctor and friends working toward *restoring that state of affairs* - something that one can scarcely imagine *any* of the Doctors doing. (The series' slightly anti-authoritarian underpinnings were nowhere to be seen just yet.)

It's left a little unclear if the Voords are aliens, mutated natives of Marinus, or men in rubber suits (which is certainly what they appear to be). There's a hint that they're just suited rebels, but there's no explanation for the oddball costume if that's the case. The Voords were briefly the stars of ancillary **Doctor Who** merchandising efforts, especially as they were the first alien race to feature on **Doctor Who** after the Daleks (and were created by the same writer), but they've faded into obscurity since then.

THE AZTECS

The TARDIS lands in the ancient empire of the Aztecs, a culture that has always fascinated Barbara for its mix of scientific and technological achievement and brutal savagery. Exploring with Susan in tow, Barbara quickly discovers that the Aztecs aren't in the past tense here - the time machine has brought its passengers to the height of that civilization, a time when being caught in the temple vaults is punishable by death. When the Aztecs do discover the two women there, Barbara takes advantage of her and Susan's "futuristic" appearance by explaining that they are the embodiment of the god Yetaxa and his handmaiden. Quickly installed as a god in the temple, Barbara decides to push history along a different course, declaring the Aztecs' bloody human sacrifices will no longer be needed - over the Doctor's protests.

William Hartnell . . . . The Doctor
William Russell . . . . Ian Chesterton
Jacqueline Hill . . . . Barbara Wright
Carole Ann Ford . . . . Susan Foreman
David Anderson . . . . Captain
Tom Booth . . . . Victim
Andre Boulay . . . . Perfect Victim
Ian Cullen . . . . Ixta
Keith Pyott . . . . Autloc
Walter Randall . . . . Tonila
John Ringham . . . . Tlotoxl
Margot van der Burgh . . . . Cameca

This story has been released on DVD

written by John Lucarotti
directed by John Crockett
music by Richard Rodney Bennett

The Temple Of Evil aired on May 23, 1964
The Warriors Of Death aired on May 30, 1964
The Bride Of Sacrifice aired on June 6, 1964
The Day Of Darkness aired on June 13, 1964

NEW WHO CONNECTIONS: Nothing concrete, but for fans of new series episodes like *Father's Day*, this presents another take on the basic premise of not interfering with history. Also, for anyone who thought it was out of place for the eighth, ninth and tenth Doctors to flirt with anyone like Grace, Jabe or Madame du Pompadour, the Doctor apparently needed a chaperone much earlier than that — here he uses his Time Lord charms on Aztec maiden Cameca, all the way back in his first incarnation. Out of character? Nah — he's a romantic at heart.

An intriguing and engrossing four-parter from the series' first season, *The Aztecs* poses some of **Doctor Who**'s best-ever moral dilemmas concerning changing history, and does so without any technobabble or cheap plotting. The only science fiction element in *The Aztecs* is that the TARDIS has deposited its crew in this situation - from that point on, they're on their own as far as getting out of it.

Anyone wanting to question *The Aztecs'* credibility can bring up the fact that this ancient civilization is speaking English with British accents, but the guest characters are quite rich and varied. And frankly, I've always found that the dichotomy is heightened by the presence of those somewhat incongruous accents - it's not authentic by a long shot, but helps to point up the advanced, cultured side of the Aztecs. The regular cast members are at their absolute best here, possibly the best ensemble performance they would give until *The Dalek Invasion Of Earth*, with William Hartnell once again turning in a superb take on the

Doctor. You can feel the searing indignation toward Barbara's attempt to rewrite the history books - one of the least-contrived moments of tension among the TARDIS crew that the series would ever produce.

THE SENSORITES

In the distant future, the TARDIS lands aboard a human spacecraft whose crew claims that they are under siege by creatures called the Sensorites, who can influence their thoughts. Captain Maitland warns the Doctor and his friends to leave immediately and assures the time travelers that they can do nothing for the ship's crew, but by the time they return to the TARDIS, it's too late - the lock has been removed and the doors cannot be opened. The Doctor resolves to help the human crew fight the influence of the Sensorites. The ship is boarded by spacewalking Sensorites, who are able to exert mental control over Maitland and his crew, though the Doctor and his companions are able to fight off that control, and they begin to show the humans how to do the same. But the Sensorites quickly detect that someone aboard has powerful telepathic abilities of their own, and they use that mind-link to open peaceful negotiations - through Susan. The Doctor and his friends, and the ship's human crew, are invited to visit the Sensorites' home planet, Sense-Sphere, where the Sensorites reveal their fear of humanity visiting their world to exploit it for the molybdenum on its surface. Worse yet, a previous human expedition to Sense-Sphere has come and gone, but many of its crew died after leaving the planet. When Ian falls ill, the Doctor discovers that the water is poisoned - and Ian is only the latest victim. But are the Sensorites - who claim that they are peaceful - behind the plot? Time is running out for the Doctor to find out.

William Hartnell . . . . The Doctor
William Russell . . . . Ian Chesterton
Jacqueline Hill . . . . Barbara Wright
Carole Ann Ford . . . . Susan Foreman
John Bailey . . . . Commander
Lorne Cossette . . . . Captain Maitland
Stephen Dartnell . . . . John
Eric Francise . . . . Elder
Peter Glaze . . . . Sensorite
Joe Grieg . . . . Sensorite
Martyn Huntley . . . . Survivor
Bartlett Mullins . . . . Elder
Arthur Newell . . . . Sensorite
Giles Phibbs . . . . Survivor
Ilona Rogers . . . . Carol
Ken Tyllson . . . . Sensorite

This story has been released on DVD

written by John Lucarotti
directed by John Crockett
music by Richard Rodney Bennett

Strangers In Space aired on June 20, 1964
The Unwilling Warriors aired on June 27, 1964
Hidden Danger aired on July 11, 1964
A Race Against Death aired on July 18, 1964
Kidnap aired on July 25, 1964
A Desperate Venture aired on Aug. 1, 1964

A complete audio recording of this entire story is available on CD, although the complete story exists in visual form as well.

NEW WHO CONNECTIONS: The first story to feature a verbal description of the Doctor and Susan's home planet as having orange skies and silver leaves, *The Sensorites* left a bit of a problem for future production teams when later stories actually visited the yet-unnamed Gallifrey. Most future Gallifrey stories took place indoors and avoided the planet's surface, at least until *The Invasion Of Time* (1977) and *The Five Doctors* (1983). Numerous novels repeated *The Sensorites'* description of Gallifrey, and finally the planet's orange sky was seen, thanks to effects technology undreamt of in 1964, in *The Sound Of Drums* (2007).

BEHIND THE SCENES: Again due to actress Jacqueline Hill being on vacation, the character of Barbara is absent for much of *The Sensorites*.

A.K.A.: Actor **Lorne Cossette** later crossed the Atlantic, appearing in a recurring role in **Captain Power And The Soldiers Of The Future** (a show whose writers and effects experts later went on to create the sprawling 1990s space opera **Babylon 5**) and an episode of the 1980s revival of **The Twilight Zone** (coincidentally *also* written by **B5** creator J. Michael Straczynski).

One of the earliest iterations of the classic **Doctor Who** story in which the creatures who appear to be the most alien and terrifying are not the true monsters, *The Sensorites* is another '60s story that creaks under the sheer number of episodes it takes to tell the story. It's a clever enough story, but even the first Doctor's era would do a better job of the "don't tell a book by its cover" storyline with *Galaxy Four*, to say nothing of the number of times later eras of the show would make a plot point of judging by appearances.

The Sensorites - for their not-so-threatening appearance - are a truly alien race, well-presented, though they've often been left on the scrapheap of Who history because they weren't actually "monsters". In keeping with the show's preoccupation with its monsters, few other alien creatures would be presented so sympathetically during William Hartnell's tenure, and indeed for the remainder of the '60s. In this respect, '60s **Doctor Who** is much like its American contemporary, **The Outer Limits**, whose producers were under constant pressure to make sure each episode had a "bear" (network executives' pet name for **The Outer Limits**' endless parade of horrifying alien creatures) to threaten the protagonists and draw the audience in. *The Sensorites* is a welcome - and early - exception to the rule that anything Not Human was a threat.

THE REIGN OF TERROR

Offended by Ian's insistence that he isn't in control of the TARDIS, the Doctor is determined to return his two passengers to their rightful place and time. But while they do manage to return to Earth, the TARDIS has put them in the path of history again, this time bringing them to the eve of the French Revolution. The time travelers stumble into a farmhouse being used as a staging area for opponents of the Revolution, where they are captured by the Revolutionary soldiers - except for the Doctor, who's left for dead when the barn is burned down. A scraggly youngster helps the Doctor to escape, but his companions are rounded up and scheduled for execution. Ian learns of the presence of a British spy among the Revolutionaries, and this knowledge saves his life; Barbara and Susan are eventually liberated by forces fighting against the Revolution. The Doctor adopts a disguise to free his friends from prison, but by the time he arrives, they have all already gone their separate ways; the Doctor tries to convince Robespierre to halt the executions. Eventually, all of the time travelers are rounded up and returned to prison to await execution once more - unless, of course, Napoleon's uprising provides a distraction...

William Hartnell . . . . The Doctor
William Russell . . . . Ian Chesterton
Jacqueline Hill . . . . Barbara Wright
Carole Ann Ford . . . . Susan Foreman
Keith Anderson . . . . Robespierre
Terry Bale . . . . Soldier
John Barrard . . . . Shopkeeper
Edward Brayshaw . . . . Colbert
James Cairncross . . . . Lemaitre
Dallas Cavell . . . . Overseer
Howard Charlton . . . . Judge
Denis Cleary . . . . Peasant
Jack Cunningham . . . . Jailer
Laidlaw Dalling . . . . Rouvray

This story has been released on DVD

written by John Lucarotti
directed by John Crockett
music by Richard Rodney Bennett

A Land Of Fear aired on Aug. 8, 1964
Guests Of Madame Guillotine aired on Aug. 15
A Change Of Identity aired on Aug. 22, 1964
The Tyrant Of France aired on Aug. 29, 1964
A Bargain Of Necessity aired on Sep. 5, 1964
Prisoners Of Conciergerie aired on Sep. 12

Patrick Marley . . . . Soldier
Donald Morley . . . . Renan
Ronald Pickup . . . .Physician
Neville Smith . . . . d'Argenson

James Hall	. . . . Soldier		Pete Walker	. . . . Small Boy
Roy Herrick	. . . . Jean		Tony Wall	. . . . Bonaparte
Caroline Hunt	. . . . Danielle		Jeffrey Wickham	. . . . Webster
Robert Hunter	. . . . Sergeant			
John Law	. . . . Barrass			
Ken Lawrence	. . . . Lieutenant			

MISSING: Episodes 4 and 5 of *The Reign Of Terror* are missing from the BBC archives.

BEHIND THE SCENES: The scenes of the Doctor making his way to Paris on foot are the first-ever location footage shot outside the studio for **Doctor Who**. But these filmed sequences don't feature William Hartnell: it's a costumed extra made up to look like him. *The Reign Of Terror* was released on DVD in 2013 with animation replacing the missing episodes.

The Reign Of Terror suffers from one primary problem - it should be gripping and exciting, but somehow, for long stretches, it's a snoozer. Four of the six episodes still exist, so it's not as if we have to watch an entire reconstructed six-part serial whose visuals move at the snail's pace of a still-photo slide show. Two-thirds of the show are there - and it just doesn't help. The idea of the Doctor butting heads with Napoleon and Robespierre is a fascinating one, but *The Reign Of Terror* barely does it justice. Sadly, even when I try to be gracious and make allowances for the difference between television then and now, the pace at which this story is told is what makes *Reign* a real terror.

The palace intrigue, so to speak, is at least carried off well...if somewhat tediously. After the events of *The Aztecs*, the Doctor's attempt to sway Robespierre away from his spree of politically-motivated executions is a startling turnaround, but perhaps understandable when one considers that the Doctor's friends and his granddaughter are at stake. (In an indication that an evolving mythology is consciously on the minds of the writers, Barbara is said to have learned not to try to change the course of history after *The Aztecs*.) Also, in terms of **Doctor Who** history, *Reign* is the first in a long line of a grand tradition of misadventures that start with the Doctor trying to return one of his companions to their original place in time and space.

This six-part story wrapped up **Doctor Who**'s first season, and the show's makers already knew they'd be back. The lengthy epilogue at the end of part six - over an ahead-of-its-time moving starfield - promises that the next adventure would be *Planet Of Giants*. It seems as though, by the time the Doctor's saber-rattling with the French Revolution came to an end, all involved knew that the TARDIS might be better used to journey to other worlds and other times. Historical adventures continued to be part of the show's fabric for the remainder of the first Doctor's tenure, but with twists to hook the viewers, including all-out comedy (*The Romans, The Myth Makers*), the use of science fiction elements in otherwise historical situations (*The Time Meddler*), and even "evil twin" plot devices (*The Massacre*). The days of the straight historical story were numbered before the show was even into its second season.

SEASON 2: 1964-65
PLANET OF GIANTS

Just prior to materialization, the TARDIS main doors open prematurely. Ian, Susan and Barbara struggle to close them, and the ship seems to make a smooth landing. Outside, the time travelers find the remains of an enormous earthworm and ants at least a foot in length. When Ian and

Susan find a huge sign which is clearly from present-day Earth, and a gigantic matchstick almost crushes the Doctor and Barbara, the conclusion is obvious - the in-flight accident has reduced the crew of the TARDIS in size. The planet on which they have landed is modern-day Earth, and everything from a normal human being's footsteps to an ordinary (but hungry) housecat is a potentially lethal danger to the time travelers.

William Hartnell . . . . The Doctor		written by Louis Marks
William Russell . . . . Ian Chesterton		directed by Mervyn Pinfield
Jacqueline Hill . . . . Barbara Wright		and Douglas Camfield
Carole Ann Ford . . . . Susan Foreman		music by Dudley Simpson
Reginald Barratt . . . . Smithers	This story	
Frank Cranshaw . . . . Farrow	has been	
Fred Ferris . . . . Bert	released	*Planet Of Giants* aired on Oct. 31, 1964
Rosemary Johnson . . . . Hilda	on DVD	*Dangerous Journey* aired on Nov. 7, 1964
Alan Tilvern . . . . Forester		*Crisis* aired on Nov. 14, 1964

One can see Irwin Allen's influence on this three-parter (the first story of that length in **Who** history). Sadly, the emphasis is solidly on Allen-esque spectacle, so the attempt at an environmental message becomes a bit of a misfire.

Still, it proves that the makers of **Doctor Who** had done their homework and learned something from the first year of the series - they knew who was watching, and *Planet Of Giants* is squarely aimed at that decidedly young audience. Silly, yes, but still a fun romp, with all of the prerequisite threats that you'd expect an Incredible Shrinking TARDIS Crew to face.

Planet Of Giants is also a major first for an unsung player in the **Doctor Who** legacy; it was the first story scored by Australian composer Dudley Simpson, whose influence would grow until he became the show's *de facto* full-time composer throughout the 1970s. To many longtime fans, the sound of Dudley Simpson's small acoustic ensemble *is* the sound of **Doctor Who**, full stop.

SHORT HOPS

**...in which the author kept circulating the tapes,
shortly after everything had been circulating in the air around him.**

As novel an idea as it may be for an American to try to write an exhaustive guide to **Doctor Who** – well, it's not that novel, several such endeavours have been undertaken from this side of the pond by now. But I'd be willing to bet that you've never seen such a book emerge from the American state of Arkansas, a sometimes lovely and sometimes scary place about whom most people know little, apart from it being the setting of all the bad stuff that happens in the movie ***Deliverance***.

It's really not like that, by the way. I live out in the country, and while one does run into one's share of folks who qualify as stereotypical hillbillies, they're not so much terrifying as slightly unkempt. I've got all of my teeth, give or take a little bit of dental surgery (long story), and while I do run around barefoot a lot, it's usually – get this – *in my own house*. So, in a nutshell: ***Deliverance***, it ain't.

It's also not a place you'd associate with being a hotbed of **Doctor Who** activity, but thanks to the persistence of AETN (Arkansas Educational Television Network, the statewide Public Broadcasting Service outlet) in showing **Doctor Who** on Sunday mornings, there was a time in the '80s when you could actually mention **Doctor Who** and find that people knew what you were talking about. I had friends who watched it, and understood that I was Not To Be Disturbed on Sunday mornings. *The Doctor was on, man.*

In the late spring months, Arkansas is also a hotbed of bad weather – *really bad* weather. With the neighboring plains states of Oklahoma and Kansas to its immediate west and northwest, respectively, powerful storms that would form in those states due to the dangerously favorable weather conditions would regularly slam into western Arkansas like clockwork. The National Weather Service would dutifully issue watches to keep everyone on their toes when the conditions were reaching that perfect dangerous boiling point, leading to a somewhat tiring kind of "combat readiness" for those covered by the watches. No one questioned me staying inside to watch **Doctor Who** on Sunday mornings, because there was a better-than-even chance that we were probably under a tornado watch by that time of the day.

One typically stormy night in April 1996, I was on the phone with my friend Mark, who hails from Sacramento. He and I had been brothers-in-modem-arms since co-moderating a **Star Trek: Voyager** "echo" on Fidonet, a network of bulletin board systems that predated wide access to the internet. My weather alert radio – a device which would emit a shrill, wailing alarm upon picking up a special signal from the radio network operated by the National Weather Service – had been going off repeatedly during the phone call. I had the TV on, watching one of the local stations' weather coverage, which was admittedly looking bleak. In eastern Oklahoma, violent tornadoes were forming with the frequency of popcorn popping. This was actually a storm system to be reckoned with. "Not to worry," I told Mark, "I live just a few blocks from the Arkansas River. *Tornadoes never jump the river.*"

Part of his concern about this unfolding weather scenario was that he'd just sent me a rather large shipping container full of videotapes. His local PBS affiliate had shown every **Doctor Who** story that had ever been made available to American stations; AETN, sadly, had dropped the show after a single showing of *Time And The Rani* shortly after its British premiere in 1987. I had seen everything from Pertwee forward, and a handful of isolated B&W stories from the first two Doctors. Mark was setting out to rectify that for me (and probably got a bit of house cleaning done at the same time). He was understandably worried that his box

Life before Doctor Who on DVD: the entire shelf at far right holds VHS tapes of Doctor Who. (The far left and center shelves were mostly taken up by the equally-sprawling Star Trek saga, all lovingly taped from first syndicated broadcast or straight from satellite.)

of videotapes – which really shouldn't be getting wet under *any* circumstances – might be getting soaked on some loading dock right about now, though his concern was gradually shifting to "Is the weather going to try to kill you tonight?"

Turns out Mark was asking the valid question, and I'd given him a staggeringly stupid answer based on "local wisdom," an "old wives' tale," and absolutely no basis in scientific fact. My apartment was a few blocks away from the riverfront, but only a parking lot away from the television station where I worked at the time, and shortly after a panic call from the control room after 11:00 that night, I found myself sprinting across that parking lot, being pelted by baseball-sized hail, trying to race to work. This was more than a storm to be reckoned with, this was a storm that was going to *kill people*. I looked over my shoulder at one point and saw the indistinct, shifting silhouette of the storm coming across the river, apparently oblivious to the fact that I had decreed that no such thing should or could take place. I got inside to safety, but the tornado flattened a good portion of the historic downtown Fort Smith area, much of which had been standing for at least a hundred years. My apartment building got a good kick, and a bit of baking from a huge explosion a few days later when the gas lines were turned back on, but it still stood. (Which is more than can be said for the building where the gas lines were turned on.)

And it was in this borderline-intact building where I heard a knock at the door the following day. Some public safety official checking on me? Or worse, someone letting me know that the building had been condemned as unsafe and I had mere hours to vacate? No. It was a man delivering a giant box of videotapes from Sacramento, all intact and dry and full of **Doctor Who** stories about which I had read, but had never seen. While various police, fire and medical officials were combing over the uncomfortably close ruins of destroyed century-old buildings, walking gingerly through wind-blown debris, this guy was *just making a routine delivery*.

The Doctor makes house calls after all.

The only problem now was that I had no electrical power (for some reason, the whole building-across-the-street-exploding thing had made the authorities nervous about "turning stuff back on"), and wouldn't have power for a week to come. Talk about keeping the suspense intact.

But what *else* was on those tapes? Stay tuned, for I will tell you about one of the best examples of *applied Doctor Who fandom* that I've ever seen.

THE DALEK INVASION OF EARTH

The TARDIS arrives on the edge of the Thames, but when the Doctor and his friends step outside and look around, it's obvious that London has seen better days. Susan hurts herself while climbing onto a crumbling bridge to look around, and Barbara stays to tend to her as Ian and the Doctor investigate a nearby warehouse, where they find a murdered man with a strange device attached to his head. A pair of desperate-looking men take Susan and Barbara to their hiding place, telling them it's not safe to wander around London. The Doctor and Ian encounter a group of men wearing the same unusual headgear, commanded by Daleks. The Daleks have dominated Earth for over ten years, enslaving humanity in an effort to mine something of vital importance under the Earth's crust. A resistance movement is fighting against the Daleks, but they need outside help from someone who has experience in beating the Daleks.

William Hartnell . . . . The Doctor
William Russell . . . . Ian Chesterton
Jacqueline Hill . . . . Barbara Wright
Carole Ann Ford . . . . Susan Foreman
Robert Aldous . . . . Rebel
Peter Badger . . . . Roboman
Ann Davies . . . . Jenny
Michael Davis . . . . Thomson
Nick Evans . . . . Dalek / Slyther
Peter Fraser . . . . David Campbell
Michael Goldie . . . . Craddock
Peter Hawkins, David Graham . . . . Dalek voices
Martyn Huntley . . . . Roboman
Robert Jewell . . . . Dalek
Alan Judd . . . . Dortmun
Bernard Kay . . . . Carl Tyler
Kevin Manser . . . . Dalek
Richard McNeff . . . . Baker
Bill Moss . . . . Roboman

This story has been released on DVD

written by Terry Nation
directed by Richard Martin
music by Francis Chagrin

World's End aired on Nov. 21, 1964
The Daleks aired on Nov. 28, 1964
Day Of Reckoning aired on Dec. 5, 1964
The End Of Tomorrow aired on Dec. 12, 1964
The Waking Ally aired on Dec. 19, 1964
Flashpoint aired on Dec. 26, 1964

Peter Murphy . . . . Dalek
Patrick O'Connell . . . . Ashton
Graham Rigby . . . . Larry Madison
Nicholas Smith . . . . Wells
Gerald Taylor . . . . Dalek
Reg Tyler . . . . Roboman

NEW WHO CONNECTIONS: "Daleks are the masters of Earth!" Heard in the 2008 episode *The Stolen Earth*, this long-running phrase actually originated in this 1964 story, which was the first of many Dalek invasions of Earth. Interestingly, this story may take place at roughly the same time as the Dalek-ruled future seen in 1972's *Day Of The Daleks*, which presents the intriguing possibility that two different Doctors were in two different locales during the same invasion, each fostering rebellions and creating headaches for the Daleks.

A.K.A.: Actor **Bernard Kay** was a **Doctor Who** mainstay; mere months after this story wrapped up, he appeared again in *The Crusade* (1965) as Saladin, and put in two further **Doctor Who** appearances in *The Faceless Ones* (1967) and *The Colony In Space* (1971). Let it never be said that Kay has no time to see a doctor: he was dividing his time between filming the *Dalek Invasion Of Earth* episodes of **Doctor Who** and his scenes for the movie *Doctor Zhivago* during the same period of 1964. He also went on to appear in the 1993 series **Century Falls**, the second TV series written by Russell T. Davies.

This outstanding six-parter is one of the darkest and most violent shows of the William Hartnell era, with shootings and stabbings aplenty, and corpses - along with large signs asking the public not to dump them in the river. There are also some really fast-moving Daleks seen here, certainly the fastest I've ever seen. These Daleks zip down ramps and roar through London with the greatest of ease. I pity the poor operators who were locked inside the Dalek props, roaring around at breakneck speeds like that...

One of the most charming aspects of the story is the dynamic between Susan and David the rebel. One of the most convenient ways to write out a female companion in **Doctor Who** was to marry her off, and this was one of the best examples of handling that plotline well - as opposed to, for example, 1977's *The Invasion Of Time*, where Leela stays on Gallifrey with Andred with little or no preamble. A bond is shown to be growing between Susan and David as early as the third episode, until finally she's faced with the decision between continuing to travel with the Doctor, or rebuilding Earth with David. And the Doctor finally makes the decision for her, and not without regret. The "one day, I shall come back" speech will probably be the most familiar part of the entire show, as it was used to open *The Five Doctors* in 1983 and to close *An Adventure In Space And Time* in 2013. It truly is a sad ending, and must have been quite a shock to viewers at the time - Susan was the first companion to leave the series.

Susan also gets one of the cleverest lines of the entire story. When Tyler and David ask Barbara if she can cook, she replies yes; when they ask Susan what she does, she responds "I eat." In other humorous moments, a Dalek bellies up to a radio transmitter to deliver another edict of terror to the rebels, and it sounds like it's clearing its throat just before it speaks. And on the Dalek ship, the Doctor delivers a withering verbal assault - worthy of Pertwee or Colin Baker, two of the most acerbic Doctors - on a sarcastic, less-than-helpful fellow prisoner.

Certainly worth a watch, and one of the best Hartnell adventures.

THE RESCUE

The TARDIS comes to rest on the planet Dido, where its arrival is detected by the sensors of a crashed ship from Earth. The shipwreck's only two survivors, a girl named Vicki and a man named Bennett, disagree on whether or not rescue is coming or is even possible. Vicki insists that the sensor reading should be investigated, but Bennett insists that any exploration won't be looked kindly upon by a spiny creature called Koquillion, who has already killed the rest of the surviving crew. After attacking Ian and Barbara the moment they emerge from the TARDIS, Koquillion does indeed put in an appearance at the crashed ship, unaware that Vicki has rescued Barbara and nursed her back to health. As soon as Koquillion leaves, Vicki reveals Barbara to Bennett and seems puzzled by his reaction - he seems displeased that they will have another set of hands and eyes to use in their struggle against Koquillion. The Doctor, who has taken to an uncharacteristic bout of sulking in the wake of Susan's departure, is energized by the mystery and goes with Ian to search for Barbara, braving Dido's treacherous landscape and local life forms until they reach the crashed ship. The Doctor demands to speak to Bennett, but finds him curiously absent, which is odd, since Bennett has been described as nearly bed-ridden. The Doctor discovers and explores a trap door, concealing evidence of the horrible truth: Bennett and Koquillion share a link that nobody expected, and Vicki will be in terrible danger if she doesn't leave Dido with the TARDIS.

William Hartnell . . . . The Doctor		written by David Whitaker
William Russell . . . . Ian Chesterton		directed by Christopher Barry
Jacqueline Hill . . . . Barbara Wright		music by Francis Chagrin
Maureen O'Brien . . . . Vicki	This story has been	
Ray Barrett . . . . Bennett / Koquillion	released	*The Powerful Enemy* aired on Jan. 2, 1965
Tom Sheridan . . . . Space Captain	on DVD	*Desperate Measures* aired on Jan. 9, 1965

NEW WHO CONNECTIONS: One astounding thing about *The Rescue* is that we see here, for the first time, the Doctor lash out violently at an enemy. He isn't provoked, he isn't defending himself - he's simply reached a breaking point where Koquillion's murderous intent is concerned and can no longer bear to let the killer go free. This may seem like an odd place for it to happen, **but this is a massive shift in the character of the Doctor,** or perhaps a revelation of a part of his character that has always been there. There are some injustices for which he simply cannot contain his fury.

A.K.A.: Actor **Ray Barrett** has been seen in numerous TV projects over the years, and even the 2008 movie *Australia*, but you may know the sound of his voice better: he was a part of the "repertory company" that voiced numerous Gerry Anderson Supermarionation series; Barrett was the voice of John Tracy in **Thunderbirds** and Commander Sam Shore in **Stingray.**

One of the things I was on the lookout for in *The Rescue* was what I call "New Companion Syndrome," or an instance where a guest character is so well developed in their initial story that you can spot them as the new TARDIS crew member from a mile off. Indeed, *The Rescue* does suffer from this somewhat, though at the time it aired - right after the somewhat shockingly quick departure of Susan, the first member of the original TARDIS team - I'm sure it didn't stick out *that* much. It does, however, accomplish what the New Companion Syndrome usually sets out to do. It's there to make sure we're sympathetic to the new character and see why they would make a good addition to the show. In the case of Vicki, it's interesting - but in the end almost inconsequential - that she's from the future, making it a bit more plausible than just going and picking up another girl in 1963 or 1964. That's inconsequential largely because very little use was made of the plot point of Vicki hailing from the 25th century, especially given that, for all the grief she gave Ian and Barbara for their "primitive" ways, she eventually left the TARDIS to take up life in an era that was even further into the past.

The production design, for a "mere" two-part story, is exceptionally good, with the interior of Vicki's crashed ship and the opening exterior model shot that pans across the wrecked hulk of that ship. Koquillion's mask is a bit menacing too, and the monster's first appearance as it lurks near the TARDIS is truly unnerving, taking place as it does in a flash of lightning. A few elements fall a bit short - the native critters of Dido are unintentionally cuddly, and then there's that ray gun that Barbara uses to shoot one of these creatures - but for the most part, *The Rescue* is a visual treat married to a marvelously compact piece of storytelling. Both halves of the story together take about as long to watch as any given episode of the new series, and it all just works quite nicely. *The Rescue* is an oft-overlooked gem from the Hartnell era which helped to ease viewers into a casting change that, with respect to even more major casting changes that would take place in a couple of years, seems almost minor in retrospect.

THE ROMANS

Vicki, thus far unimpressed with the promise of adventure aboard the TARDIS, gets more than she bargained for when the time machine touches down on a steep ledge and takes a tumble with its time travelers inside. When they come to, they find themselves in the Roman Empire at its height, and take advantage of the hospitality and indolence offered to them - for weeks. The Doctor and Vicki go to explore Rome itself, but in their absence, Ian and Barbara are captured and sold as slaves. Ian manages to escape, but he is recaptured and dragged back to the dungeon, where he learns that Barbara has been sold while he was gone. The Doctor and Vicki happen upon the body of a murdered man, but before they can do anything more than pick up the victim's lyre, a centurion appears and assumes that the Doctor is a musician en route to Rome. When the Doctor and Vicki arrive, they find that the Doctor has assumed the identity of a court musician whose personal patron is the Emperor Nero - who, unbeknownst to them, has bought Barbara as his newest slave. And unknown to any of the others, Ian awaits his fate as a gladiator...

William Hartnell . . . . The Doctor
William Russell . . . . Ian Chesterton
Jacqueline Hill . . . . Barbara Wright
Maureen O'Brien . . . . Vicki
Bart Allison . . . . Maximus Petullian
John Caesar . . . . Man in market
Peter Diamond . . . . Delos
Nicholas Evans . . . . Didius
Dennis Edwards . . . . Centurion
Derek Francis . . . . Nero
Dorothy-Rose Gribble . . . . Woman slave
Barry Jackson . . . . Ascaris
Ernest Jennings . . . . Man in market
Edward Kelsey . . . . Slavebuyer
Gertan Klauber . . . . Galley Master
Michael Peake . . . . Tavius

This story has been released on DVD

written by Dennis Spooner
directed by Christopher Barry
music by Raymond Jones

The Slave Traders aired on Jan. 16, 1965
All Roads Lead To Rome aired on Jan. 23, 1965
Conspiracy aired on Jan. 30, 1965
Inferno aired on Feb. 6, 1965

Tony Lambden . . . . Messenger
Kay Patrick . . . . Poppaea
Brian Proudfoot . . . . Tigilinus
Derek Sydney . . . . Sevcheria
Margot Thomas . . . . Stallholder
Ann Tirard . . . . Locusta

NEW WHO CONNECTIONS: This early adventure is alluded to very vaguely by the tenth Doctor, who tells Donna - in *The Fires Of Pompeii* (2008) - that he had nothing to do with Rome burning; he then backpedals a little bit from that statement...

One of the first attempts in the history of televised **Doctor Who** to do an all-out comedy as the primary storyline, *The Romans* can be quite a crafty story to get one's head around. It puts the characters in dramatic, potentially life-or-death scenarios...and then proceeds to poke fun at the utter absurdity of those scenarios. There's also a comedy-of-errors element running through the plot, in which one or more of our intrepid time traveling heroes exits a scene just as another appears, whom they would surely help if they only knew the dire straits their friends were in. It's light years away from the slapstick comedy that would overtake **Doctor Who** some 22 years later.

It helps that the regulars are certainly up to the task, and the guest stars are as well. There are priceless comedic moments where William Hartnell's facial expression speaks volumes. Unlike the deadly serious avoid-involvement-in-history message of *The Aztecs, The Romans* puts the TARDIS crew hip-deep into history, and watches them try to wade out of it for laughs.

The Romans probably isn't going to top the favorites list of any modern **Doctor Who** fans, but it's quite sophisticated in its own way, with a nod to the humor of the *Carry On...* film series, and fine moments in a more dramatic vein. Pretty entertaining stuff.

THE WEB PLANET

After the TARDIS leaves Rome behind, it's dragged off course to the planet Vortis, where some force keeps the time machine trapped. The Doctor's attempts to take off again are futile, and he and Ian leave the TARDIS as Vicki recovers from hearing a strange noise that has an unusual effect on her. Aboard the TARDIS, Babara also experiences something odd, as though she's being drawn out of the time machine and onto the planet's surface. There, she encounters the butterfly-like Menoptera, who are desperately planning the last battle of a war against the ant-like Zarbi, who have the advantage in their sheer numbers. Controlled by a malevolent consciousness called the Animus, the Zarbi move the TARDIS from its landing site, capture the Doctor, Ian and Vicki, and make a deal with the Doctor: his friends' lives will only be spared if he helps to defeat the Menoptera.

William Hartnell	. . . .	The Doctor
William Russell	. . . .	Ian Chesterton
Jacqueline Hill	. . . .	Barbara Wright
Maureen O'Brien	. . . .	Vicki
Jocelyn Birdsall	. . . .	Hlynia
Arthur Blake	. . . .	Hrhoonda
Jolyon Booth	. . . .	Prapilius
Roslyn de Winter	. . . .	Vrestin
Catherine Fleming	. . . . .	voice of the Animus
Arne Gordon	. . . .	Hrostar
Martin Jarvis	. . . .	Captain Hilio
Robert Jewell	. . . .	Zarbi
Barbara Joss	. . . .	Nemini
Hugh Lund	. . . .	Zarbi
Kevin Manser	. . . .	Zarbi
John Scott Martin	. . . .	Zarbi

This story has been released on DVD

written by Bill Strutton
directed by Richard Martin
insect movement directed by
Roslyn de Winter
stock library music - see credits below

The Web Planet aired on Feb. 13, 1965
The Zarbi aired on Feb. 20, 1965
Escape To Danger aired on Feb. 27, 1965
Crater Of Needles aired on March 6, 1965
Invasion aired on March 13, 1965
The Centre aired on March 20, 1965

Gerald Taylor . . . . Zarbi

Jack Pitt . . . . Zarbi	Ian Thompson . . . . Hetra

A.K.A.: Actor **Martin Jarvis'** TV and film career was just getting underway when he donned one of the unwieldly alien costumes for *The Web Planet*. He appeared in later **Doctor Who** stories (*Invasion Of The Dinosaurs*, 1973; *Vengeance On Varos*, 1985) and a **Doctor Who** audio story for Big Finish (*Jubilee*, 2003); after conquering British TV, he crossed the pond to appear in such American shows as **Murder, She Wrote, Space: Above And Beyond, Walker, Texas Ranger**, and **Numb3rs**. He's also found a lucrative sideline in animation voice work, lending his voice to **The Tick, Extreme Ghostbusters**, and **The Grim Adventures Of Billy & Mandy**. In 1997, he and his wife Rosalind Ayres appeared in *Titanic*.

STOCK MUSIC: "Marche" (Jacques Lasry and Francois Daschet/Les Structures Sonores), "Pieces Nouvelles" (Jacques Lasry and Francois Daschet/Les Structures Sonores), "Rapsodie de Budapest" (Jacques Lasry and Francois Daschet/Les Structures Sonores), "Sonatine" (Jacques Lasry and Francois Daschet/Les Structures Sonores), "Suite" (Jacques Lasry and Francois Daschet/Les Structures Sonores). During pre-production for the first season, producer Verity Lambert had used the works of French experimental music act Les Structures Sonores as an example of how she envisioned **Doctor Who**'s (at the time, yet to be composed) theme music.

If there's anything that everyone can agree on when it comes to *The Web Planet*, it's this: it was a brave attempt. For 1965, on a studio-bound BBC-TV budget, *The Web Planet* is an extraordinarily bold attempt to do large-scale science fiction, telling a story with imagination unfettered by the chains of budget and other production realities. The problem, of course, being that the end result was completely, woefully fettered with those very things; *The Web Planet* comes off as a great idea hindered by its own budget…or something so trippy that it's entertaining in a bad B-movie way.

To be fair, neither *The Web Planet* nor any other **Doctor Who** adventure from this phase of the show's history was expected to be repeated many times, let alone cleaned up and put under the relatively high-resolution microscope of a medium like DVD. I can forgive the obvious painted background of the planet surface, admire the sometimes bizarre insectoid costumes, and bask in the truly alien atmosphere of the setting. I can get a big laugh out of sometimes unintentionally funny scenes such as a Zarbi "larva gun" creature being smashed up against the scenery like a giant cockroach, much in the same way that affectionate fans forgive the occasionally bouncy styrofoam rocks that littered the surface of many a studio-bound alien planet in the original **Star Trek**. But I do puzzle over such things as the "Vaseline-smeared-on-the-camera-lens" look of the exterior scenes on Vortis, and the distracting but elaborately worked-out body language choreography of the various alien races.

In the end, what you take into *The Web Planet* will determine what you leave with. If you're expecting an epic tale to rival the modern revival of the series, just go home now. But if you're expecting an ambitious-but-flawed story that, if you're in the right frame of mind, is still strangely enjoyable, *The Web Planet* is a completely unique adventure. Even in later years, when there was more money to spend on creating alien environments for **Doctor Who**, the show never quite produced anything else like *The Web Planet* again. Never mind its reputation, try to watch through the whole thing at least once.

THE CRUSADE

The TARDIS brings the Doctor and his friends to 12th century Palestine during the time of King Richard's Crusade into the Muslim holy lands. Barbara is abducted by the Saracens and is held prisoner. The Doctor, Vicki and Ian fend off a Saracen attack, and are found by King Richard the Lionhearted and his men. Ian is infuriated when his request for help in rescuing Barbara is met with King Richard's refusal, but the Doctor smooths things over with the King. He winds up becoming a member of the royal court, while Ian is knighted and sent on his way to save Barbara and the King's brother - and to offer the hand of the King's sister, Joanna, to Saladin in the hopes that their marriage would end the ongoing conflict. The Doctor and Vicki try to keep their necks out of the court intrigue as they discover that King Richard has told his sister nothing of her role in his plan for peace. In Saladin's court, Barbara finds an ally who has his pledged vengeance upon the Emir...but this new ally leaves it to Barbara to carry out his murderous revenge for him.

William Hartnell . . . . The Doctor
William Russell . . . . Ian Chesterton
Jacqueline Hill . . . . Barbara Wright
Maureen O'Brien . . . . Vicki
David Anderson . . . . Reynier de Marun
Roger Avon . . . . Saphadin
Gabor Baraker . . . . Luigi Ferrigo
John Bay . . . . Earl of Leicester
Tony Caunter . . . . Thatcher
Anthony Colby . . . . Saracen Guard
Billy Cornelius . . . . Soldier
John Flint . . . . William des Preaux
Julian Glover . . . . Richard the Lionheart
Sandra Hampton . . . . Maimuna
Bernard Kay . . . . Saladin
Chris Konyils . . . . Saracen Guard
Robert Lankesheer . . . . Chamberlain
Tutte Lemkow . . . . Ibrahim
George Little . . . . Haroun
Pera Markham . . . . Safiya
Jean Marsh . . . . Joanna
Diane McKenzie . . . . Hafsa
Valentino Musetti . . . . Saracen Guard

This story has been released on audio CD

written by David Whitaker
directed by Douglas Camfield
music by Dudley Simpson

The Lion aired on March 27, 1965
The Knight Of Jaffa aired on April 3, 1965
The Wheel Of Fortune aired on April 10, 1965
The Warlords aired on April 17, 1965

The Crusade is partially available on DVD; the existing video is presented, along with audio recordings of the missing episodes, in the "Lost In Time" box set

Raymond Novak . . . . Saracen Guard
Reg Pritchard . . . . Ben Daheer
Walter Randall . . . . El Akir
Zohra Segal . . . . Sheyrah
Viviane Sorrel . . . . Fatima
Derek Ware . . . . Saracen Guard
Bruce Wightman . . . . .William de Tornebu

MISSING: Episodes 2 and 4 of *The Crusade* are missing from the BBC archives.

A.K.A.: Two actors in *The Crusade* raise this story to a whole level above most **Doctor Who** of this era: guest star **Jean Marsh** is probably best known as the co-creator of international hit series **Upstairs, Downstairs** and **The House Of Elliott**; she also won an Emmy for her starring role in the former (a rarity for the American-centric Emmy awards). Before appearing in **Doctor Who**, she had already appeared in an episode of **The Twilight Zone**'s first season in 1959 during a three-year Broadway gig. Other TV appearances include **I Spy, UFO, Hawaii Five-O, The Love Boat**, and **Tales From The Darkside**, and a big-screen turn as baddie Bavmorda in 1988's George Lucas-produced *Willow*. She returns in the following season, in the role of one-time TARDIS traveler Sara Kingdom in *The Daleks' Masterplan* (a role she revived in audio form for Big Finish's Companion Chronicles audio series) and again as Morgaine in 1989's *Battlefield*. She was also married to Jon Pertwee in the 1950s. **Julian Glover** has been in *everything* - seriously. On the UK side, he appeared in **The Saint, The Avengers, Space: 1999, Blake's 7**, and he would also appear in **Doctor Who** again, as the villain of the all-time-classic 1979 Tom Baker story *City Of Death*. But big-screen villainy marked the apex of his career: he played General Veers in *The Empire Strikes Back*, Kristatos in the James Bond movie *For Your Eyes Only*, and Walter Donovan in *Indiana Jones And The Last Crusade*, all while making regular TV appearances on both sides of the Atlantic (including the **Magnum P.I.** episode that also guest starred Peter Davison). You've seen him most recently as Grand Maester Pycelle in HBO's **Game Of Thrones** series.

A surprisingly mature adventure from an era when **Doctor Who** was unquestionably considered to be children's programming, *The Crusade* takes a remarkably even-handed approach to both sides of the conflict around which the story revolves. King Richard and his men are not portrayed as flawless, nor are Saladin and the Muslims portrayed as brutish savages. With the Doctor once again struggling mightily - as in *The Aztecs* - to keep out of history's way, *The Crusade* achieves a kind of storytelling sophistication that was occasionally missing from the more futuristic SF tales made at around the same time.

Julian Glover, Jean Marsh and Bernard Kay help to elevate the material even further with their performances, not chewing on the scenery but becoming full participants in the even-handed treatment of the story. Glover's King Richard alternates between the expected prerequisite nobility and moments of petulance, while Jean Marsh gives Joanna a steely resolve that serves her in good stead when she discovers that she's about to be bartered for a peace agreement. For this period of **Doctor Who**, where the acting even among the regulars could often be very stagey (though that was the fashion of the time), *The Crusade* is also one of the best-acted stories.

Sadly, the second and fourth episodes are missing from the BBC archives, though of course the entire story is available in audio form and the first and third episodes are included - along with the missing segments in audio form - on the "Lost In Time" DVD box set. *The Crusade* was one of the last 1960s stories to be archived in audio form, as off-air sound recordings of all four episodes weren't found until the mid-1990s. Even in audio form, however, the performances and the story shine. This really is one of the best "historical" stories from the series' early years, and hopefully those two missing episodes will come to light someday.

THE SPACE MUSEUM

The Doctor, Vicki, Ian and Barbara experience a number of completely inexplicable phenomena. Their clothes are suddenly different, and broken glasses instantly leap back into one piece. The TARDIS has arrived on a bleak planet whose only sign of civilization is a museum of space vehicles and hardware - and, as they discover to their horror, travelers. At first, no one else in the museum can see, hear or touch the Doctor or his friends, and they soon find out why - they're already exhibits in the museum, a fate they must now try to escape.

William Hartnell . . . . The Doctor
William Russell . . . . Ian Chesterton
Jacqueline Hill . . . . Barbara Wright
Maureen O'Brien . . . . Vicki
Jeremy Bulloch . . . . Tor
Billy Cornelius . . . . Guard
Peter Craze . . . . Dako
Peter Diamond . . . . Technician
Murphy Grumbar . . . . Dalek
Peter Hawkins . . . . Dalek voice
Ivor Salter . . . . Commander
Peter Sanders . . . . Sita
Richard Shaw . . . . Lobos
Salvin Stewart . . . . Messenger

This story has been released on DVD

written by Glyn Jones
directed by Mervyn Pinfield
stock library music - see credits below

The Space Museum aired on April 24, 1965
The Dimensions Of Time aired on May 1, 1965
The Search aired on May 8, 1965
The Final Phase aired on May 15, 1965

A.K.A.: Jeremy Bulloch later became known for wearing the armor of Boba Fett in *The Empire Strikes Back* and *Return Of The Jedi*; he's also appeared in the James Bond film *Octopussy*, the TV series **Robin Of Sherwood**, **Spooks** (retitled **MI-5** for American consumption), **Law & Order UK**, and the short-lived, direct-to-DVD sci-fi spoof **Starhyke** (alongside former **Babylon 5** star Claudia Christian). He also appears in 1973's *The Time Warrior*. Peter Craze, in addition to being the brother of actor Michael Craze (who played the first Doctor's companion Ben), later appeared in 1969's *The War Games* — the last **Doctor Who** story made in black & white — and 1979's *The Nightmare Of Eden*.

STOCK MUSIC: "The Laboratory" (Eric Siday), "Mood 7 B2" (Eric Siday), "Space Age B2" (Eric Siday), "Space Agitato" (Eric Siday), "Space Time" (Eric Siday), and "Threat Attack" (Eric Siday), "Mutations" (Trevor Duncan), "Synchro Stings" (Trevor Duncan), "Bathysphere" (Eric Nordgren); "Dramatic Bridges" (Denis Ryooth); "Asyndeton" (Robert Gerhard), "Ultimate Moonscape" (Eric Siday), "The Ultra Sonic Perception" (Eric Siday), "World Of Planets" (Jack Trombey),

"Astronautics Suite" (Erich Sendel), "Six Short Dramas" (Roger Roger and the Champs Elysees Orchestra), "Musique Concrete Part II" (Buxton Orr), "Quick Sand" (Buxton Orr), "Dramatic Brass Chords" (Wolf Droyson), "Scene Shifts" (Don Banks), "Atoms and Mushrooms" (Frank Tailey), "Panic In The Streets" (Frank Tailey), "Kaputt" (Desmond Leslie), "Sting Tintabuloid" (Desmond Leslie), "Brass Chords — Staccato Ending" (Wolf Droyson).

Though there are a number of interesting moments - including the amusing sight of the Doctor popping out of a Dalek casing and Ian demonstrating his hand-to-hand combat expertise - these moments are peppered throughout a story that may not make a lot of sense on first viewing. Other movies, books and shows, including future **Doctor Who** stories, made much better use of the potential paradox of time travelers interfering in events in which they've already participated (*Back To The Future Part II* springs immediately to mind as one of my favorite examples) but this one just doesn't come together for me. Why should the Doctor and friends become ghost-like because they've crossed their own time lines? On that pseudo-scientific basis, none of the many later classic "multiple Doctor" stories would have happened.

In a rare instance of irreconcilable continuity, the Doctor says that he has always found comprehending the fourth dimension extremely difficult - but remember that, at this time, no one had even imagined his Time Lord origins, a plot point that wouldn't be written for four more years.

THE CHASE

The Doctor, Ian, Barbara and Vicki take a rare opportunity to relax. The TARDIS arrives on the desert planet Aridius, where the Doctor shows off his time-space visualizer screen — allowing him to peek in on any moment in history without being there — and the others hope to do a little bit of sunbathing. But the visualizer warns the time travelers of an imminent event in their own history: the Daleks have perfected their own time machine and are preparing to hunt down the Doctor to keep him from interfering in their plans any further. After a number of brief skirmishes taking place at random locations in time and space, ranging from the Empire State Building to the *Marie Celeste* to a haunted house full of robots, the Doctor is forced to make his last stand against the Daleks on the planet Mechanus. Though most of its surface is a dense jungle, Mechanus is also home to the Mechonoids, a single-minded series of robots who occupy a vast city. The Mechonoids have also nursed a crashed human space pilot, Steven Taylor, back to health, and he sees the time travelers as his only means of returning to civilization as he knows it. But if they can wrest it from the Daleks, Ian and Barbara see the metal monstrosities' time machine as their own ticket back to Earth.

William Hartnell . . . . The Doctor
William Russell . . . . Ian Chesterton
Jacqueline Hill . . . . Barbara Wright
Maureen O'Brien . . . . Vicki
Hywel Bennett . . . . Rynian
Vivienne Bennett . . . . Queen Elizabeth I
Patrick Carter . . . . Bosun
Dennis Chinnery . . . . Albert Richardson
Richard Coe . . . . TV announcer
Roslyn de Winter . . . . Grey Lady
Douglas Ditta . . . . Willoughby
Arne Gordon . . . . Guide
David Graham . . . . Mechonoid voices
Murphy Grumbar . . . . Mechonoid
Roger Hammond . . . . Francis Bacon

This story has been released on DVD

written by Terry Nation
directed by Richard Martin
music by Dudley Simpson

The Executioners aired on May 22, 1965
The Death Of Time aired on May 29, 1965
Flight Through Eternity aired on June 5, 1965
Journey Into Terror aired on June 12, 1965
The Death Of Doctor Who aired on June 19
The Planet Of Decision aired on June 26, 1965

Jack Pitt . . . . Stewart / Mire Beast / Mechonoid
Peter Purves . . . . . Steven Taylor / Morton Dill
Al Raymond . . . . Prondyn

Peter Hawkins, David Graham . . . Dalek voices		Malcolm Rogers . . . . Dracula	
Robert Jewell . . . . Dalek		Gerald Taylor . . . . Dalek	
David Blake Kelly . . . . Captain Briggs		Ian Thompson . . . . Malsan	
Kevin Manser . . . . Dalek		Ken Tyllsen . . . . Mechonoid	
Robert Marsden . . . . Abraham Lincoln		Hugh Walters . . . . William Shakespeare	
John Scott Martin . . . . . . Dalek / Mechonoid		Derek Ware . . . . Bus Conductor	
John Maxim . . . . Frankenstein's Monster		Edmund Warwick . . . . Robot Doctor	
		The Beatles . . . . themselves	

NEW WHO CONNECTIONS: Considering that the time-traveling Daleks seen here are hunting down the Doctor in only their third appearance, is it possible that these Daleks — who appear to be significantly upgraded from previous appearances (note the vertical "slats" on their midsections, intended to represent solar panels) — are from the Doctor's far future, in which several of his incarnations have thwarted their plans? **This could even be one of the Daleks' earliest forays into the Time War.** Additionally, the time-space visualizer may have just missed a glimpse of one of the Doctor's future incarnations: the fourth Doctor talked about transcribing Hamlet from Shakespeare's dictation in *City Of Death* (1979), while the tenth Doctor and Martha visited the Bard in *The Shakespeare Code* (2007).

BEHIND THE SCENES: It wasn't uncommon for actors to double up in more than one role in early **Doctor Who**, but this was usually done with stunt personnel or "monster operators" such as the men who frequently found themselves sweating away inside Dalek or Mechonoid casings. In a rare instance of an unmasked double role *within the same story*, Peter Purves plays the part of Morton Dill in an early episode of this serial, but then later joins the regular cast in the role of stranded astronaut Steven Taylor. Due to prohibitive music licensing costs, the Beatles' brief appearance (an existing film clip rather than a scene shot especially for **Doctor Who**) was excised from *The Chase* prior to its North American DVD release; the UK DVD still includes the scene with the song.

The Chase is home to a number of bizarre sequences, including in part one a brief shot of the Doctor from the TARDIS console's point of view, the almost disturbingly funny shot of Ian dancing around the TARDIS, lip-syncing "Ticket To Ride", and last but not least, the Doctor warbling something that sounds like opera while he's catching a suntan. But it is amusing to see the Doctor and friends vacationing instead of dropping into the middle of some kind of trouble. It's also a rarity in **Doctor Who** that the Doctor is not drawing attention to himself and isn't interfering in any way: this series of misadventures begins when he finds himself hunted by the Daleks. It's also a little bit of evolution for the character of the Doctor himself, as he is seen to be relaxed and perhaps a little fun-loving, instead of Hartnell's usual deadly-serious portrayal, and that trait carries on to all of the Doctor's future incarnations, as does his sadness when Ian and Barbara leave. The final episode fails to make clear that Steven is joining the crew, however — he could just as easily have been dropped off on Earth by the next episode.

Another funny thing which persists in *The Chase*, as well as many later Dalek stories, is the fact that the stubby metal ones must be deaf in one ear and legally blind. How many times, over the years, has someone said "Quick, they're coming!" and hidden behind a convenient obstruction *just as the camera zooms out* to show that the Dalek was heading in *that precise direction*, presumably able to see and hear them from yards away? Later, aboard the *Marie Celeste*, one of the Daleks falls overboard and actually *yells*. The length of time that it takes for a room full of Daleks to utter even a simple sentence to one another presages the mammoth Dalek story that would spread out over 12 Dalek-dialogue-filled episodes later in 1965.

The Chase jumps back and forth between comedy and drama at a breakneck pace — sometimes sacrificing the seriousness of the Dalek threat for the sake of plunging the creatures into unlikely situations. And yet for all of this rapid change of mood, parts two and three move along far too slowly. The Mechonoids were carefully calculated creations to rival the Daleks themselves in both on-screen threat and marketability; they made a minor merchandising splash at the time, as the huge, geodesic-domed robots translated into toys and even became a recurring foil for the Daleks in comic strip adventures. In hindsight, perhaps it's best to group *The Chase* with *Delta And The Bannermen* and *Love & Monsters* - later adventures that were less than deadly serious, but still enjoyable.

THE TIME MEDDLER

The Doctor seems to calmly accept that Earth space pilot Steven Taylor, stranded on the planet Mechanus, has stowed away aboard the TARDIS following their harrowing adventure with the Daleks. The TARDIS arrives on 11th century Earth, and despite all evidence to the contrary, Steven refuses to believe that he is now traveling in a time machine. The Doctor receives a warm welcome from the locals and quickly determines that he has arrived in 1066 A.D., just prior to a Viking invasion of Northumbria. But something is amiss - the chanting of the monks in a nearby monastery seems to slow down, as if it has been recorded. Steven and Vicki have a run-in with another local, finding a 20th century watch on his wrist. It soon becomes apparent that someone else capable of time travel is here, someone who has no qualms about a little bit of historical tampering. The Doctor sneaks into the monastery and finds that a tape player is indeed responsible for the music...but he is then trapped, a prisoner of a lone Monk who seems to have a wide array of anachronistic technology, including his own TARDIS. Now, in the shadow of a great historic battle, the Doctor and his friends must try to stop the Monk's machinations.

William Hartnell	. . . .	The Doctor
Peter Purves	. . . .	Steven Taylor
Maureen O'Brien	. . . .	Vicki
David Anderson	. . . .	Sven
Peter Butterworth	. . . .	Monk
Alethea Charlton	. . . .	Edith
Geoffrey Cheshire	. . . .	Viking Leader
Michael Guest	. . . .	Hunter
Norman Hartley	. . . .	Ulf
Michael Miller	. . . .	Wulnoth
Ronald Rich	. . . .	Gunnar
Peter Russell	. . . .	Eldred

This story has been released on DVD

written by Dennis Spooner
directed by Douglas Camfield
stock library music - see credits below

The Watcher aired on July 3, 1965
The Meddling Monk aired on July 10, 1965
A Battle Of Wits aired on July 17, 1965
Checkmate aired on July 24, 1965

NEW WHO CONNECTIONS: A major turning point for old series and new, *The Time Meddler* sees us meeting another of the Doctor and Susan's people for the first time in the entire series. Even so, at the time of this story's premiere, we still didn't know that the Doctor or the Monk were Time Lords, but it seemed to put to rest any possibility that the Doctor was a mere human — perhaps he was a human from the future, or something else entirely. The Monk also claims to have assisted in the construction of Stonehenge; could he have been aware of the Pandorica?

BEHIND THE SCENES: *The Time Meddler* was a turning point behind the scenes: it was the final story produced by Verity Lambert, the pioneering BBC producer who launched the show.

STOCK MUSIC: "Suspended Animation" (Eric Siday), "Medieval Drama" (Lawrence Leonard and his Orchestra), "Nuvane" (Light Symphonia), "Secundae Vesperae In Nativitate" (Choir der Monche der Benediktiner), "Scorched Earth" (Trevor Duncan), "Drum Effects" (Charles Botterill), "November Fog" (Peter Hope / Landsdowne Light Orchestra), "Twelve Tone Links" (Henry Dexter), "Magnetic Field Mood Seven" (Eric Siday), "Meteoroids" (Robert Gerhard),

This rather modest four-parter is an absolutely vital entry in the **Doctor Who** mythos, for it finally puts beyond any doubt that the Doctor is *not* human (or, depending on your interpretation of a line of dialogue in the 1996 TV movie, not *entirely* human at any rate). The Monk is an interloper, like the Doctor, and the fact that he has an identical time machine puts an end to any possibility that the Doctor himself invented the TARDIS. (Though such an assertion was made in the Peter Cushing Dalek movies, the only hint of the Doctor being the inventor of the TARDIS occurs in *An Unearthly Child*, the series premiere in which Susan claims to have given the TARDIS its acronym name.)

The Time Meddler is an amusing little adventure which makes good use of the show's time travel premise. It takes advantage of known historical events without becoming so bogged down in them as not to have a little fun, and that fun doesn't come at the expense of real live drama. The Viking invasion is a big deal, as is the fact that the Monk plans to derail that vital point in history with an atomic cannon (!). It's a nice little romp, rather than the overly serious time travel epics of later years. There are some immensely funny scenes, though - the Doctor holding up the Monk with a stick (which he claims is a loaded Winchester!) stands out as one of them, to say nothing of the legendary bovine space helmet.

Peter Butterworth puts in a nice comic performance as the Monk, and I wonder if I'm the only one who notes a slight resemblance between Butterworth and Patrick Troughton, the second Doctor. Hartnell didn't vacate the role of the Doctor for another year, but the fact that the Monk was brought back in the later epic *The Daleks' Masterplan* (the bulk of which, sadly, is missing from the BBC's vaults today) indicates that the character and the actor made some sort of impression. One wonders...

An unusual time-filler at the end of this story's final episode anticipates the series' future title sequences; Steven, Vicki and the Doctor's faces are superimposed briefly over a starfield before the credits roll. Once again, the BBC was ahead of its time. It wasn't until several stories into the Patrick Troughton era that the Doctor's face was featured in the opening titles at all.

SHORT HOPS

...in which the author ponders the Monk as an early incarnation of the Master and other role-playing-game-spawned oddities.

In pre-internet 1980s **Doctor Who** fandom, there was a unique experience to be had on the American side of the Atlantic: a few companies actually secured licenses from the BBC to turn out uniquely American **Doctor Who** merchandise.

A great many more companies and individuals didn't bother with a license at all, and as they were dealing on a regional basis, with classifieds in the back pages of Starlog Magazine as the nearest they could afford to national advertising, few if any of them ever got a cease-and-desist from the BBC.

One of the most high-profile products that *did* have the BBC's blessing, however, made one wonder just how much leeway the BBC had given its creators. Throughout the 1980s and '90s, FASA Corporation produced numerous original and licensed wargames and role-playing games, including the obsessively detailed and much-loved paper-and-dice RPG based on the original **Star Trek** series. In 1985, FASA issued a **Doctor Who** RPG starter set which was – to the extreme delight of my friends and me – *compatible with the Star Trek game!* (This probably just seems like a weird and improbable cross-universe mess waiting to happen now; at the time, when we were in our early teens, this was *pure geek nirvana.*)

Three supplemental rule sets were issued – one each for the Big Three enemies of the time (Daleks, Cybermen, the Master) – along with seven add-on adventures featuring both familiar **Doctor Who** adversaries and enemies original to FASA's team of veteran game designers. As with FASA's **Trek** game books, the **Doctor Who** RPG was illustrated with a mixture of licensed photos and original artwork. The latter often provided unintentional amusement (a pre-mutation Davros as a goateed, gloved mad scientist still stuck in more or less the same pose as post-mutation, gnarled Davros from the series) and drool-worthy sights (all-out Dalek-Cybermen-Sontaran warfare) in equal measure.

One of the *strangest* supplements, hands-down, was that devoted to the Master. This packaged two game books together: one for the game master's eyes only and one, supposedly the docket prepared on the Master by Gallifrey's Celestial Intervention Agency (which, in the game's universe, was the authority granting so much freedom to so many rogue Time Lord player characters), which could be distributed to players. Both of these booklets offered the absolutely bizarre theory that *the Monk was an early incarnation of the Master*.

Wait, *what?* Back that type 40 time travel capsule up.

Time to fetch the Dubious Canonicity Sceptre of Rassilon: FASA's questionable-but-still-fun RPG sourcebooks and the (probably equally official) <u>Doctor Who Technical Manual</u>

Despite the fact that FASA's **Doctor Who** RPG had Tom Baker-centric artwork on the box, it was released during the *Colin* Baker era. At this point, it was very well-established that the Master was a murderous genius with few or no scruples about holding the entire universe hostage to his whims (*Logopolis* was recent history at that time for American viewers, including the FASA game writers). It also made sense, therefore, that it was *highly unlikely* that the Master would just screw around with history for the sheer chaotic *fun* of it.

FASA's Master manual didn't really offer much in the way of connecting tissue to justify the connection. Frankly, it's much easier to read something into the scene in *The Evil Of The Daleks* in which the *second* Doctor reacts with uncharacteristic alarm when a house servant mentions that he's going to fetch the master. Not *the* Master, mind you, but the master of the house. Still, Troughton places an unusual emphasis on his response: "*The Master?!?*" You'd almost think the show's writers somehow had it all planned out.

Throughout the pre-**Star Trek: The Next Generation** 1980s, FASA's **Star Trek** game supplements — *especially* the much-prized ones that divulged the technical details of new, never-before-seen ship classes employed by the Federation, the Klingons and the Romulans — were considered gospel, simply because Paramount *wasn't doing anything* other than the occasional movie to add any new material to the **Star Trek** universe. At least until the next movie came along that might contradict something in the recent supplements, the sky was the limit in the final frontier. Perhaps wisely, FASA's gamesmiths steered clear of the major ongoing plot threads inherent in the **Star Trek** movies of the '80s and filled in the gaps around those developments. In other words, they *wouldn't* try to predict the next move that Kirk and his increasingly-at-odds-with-Starfleet crew would make in the next movie, but the next gamebook could *happily* fill in the blanks that, say, brought a Klingon ambassador to Earth to protest the existence of the Genesis device.

Nightmare in silver...well, okay, nightmare in malleable white metal: FASA's 35mm Doctor Who miniature Daleks, Cybermen and Sontarans prepare to do battle with the fourth Doctor and the Brigadier. Eat your heart(s) out, Game of Rassilon.

Doctor Who, at the time, was still a going concern at a rate of more than just two hours of new story per year. And of course, once Picard-era **Star Trek** got going, FASA's two biggest licensed properties were off the map: there were too many new developments to keep up with any more frequently than an end-of-season sourcebook. And by the time FASA issued only its second **Star Trek: The Next Generation** supplement, it had given up on the **Doctor Who** RPG — prematurely, as it turns out, because just a few years later, **Doctor Who** would be in the same void of new material that had once made FASA's **Star Trek** RPG such a hot ticket for that series' fandom.

And even then, the Monk still wouldn't have been the Master. Not by a long shot.

SEASON 3: 1965-66
GALAXY FOUR

The Doctor, Steven and Vicki, exploring the latest destination to which the TARDIS has brought them, encounter a primitive robot which Vicki nicknames a Chumblie. While it seems harmless enough, it soon indicates that it wishes the time travelers to follow it - and makes its wishes even more clear by demonstrating its ability to vaporize a nearby bush. Two statuesque, armed women ambush the Chumblie, and then take the Doctor and his friends prisoner for themselves. The TARDIS travelers are brought before Maaga, the self-proclaimed leader of the Drahvins. Maaga tells the Doctor that the Chumblies are the robotic servants of the vicious Rills, another alien expedition visiting this planet. Ever since the Rills revealed that the planet is just fourteen dawns away from destroying itself, the Rills and the Drahvins have been at war. The Rills' ship is the only vehicle capable of leaving the planet in time, and the Drahvins intend to take it for themselves - with the Doctor's help, which they secure by holding Vicki hostage. When the Doctor visits the TARDIS to see how much time this planet has left, however, he discovers that the Rills and Drahvins have less time than they thought to settle their differences.

William Hartnell	The Doctor
Peter Purves	Steven Taylor
Maureen O'Brien	Vicki
Lyn Ashley	Drahvin
Stephanie Bidmead	Maaga
Marina Martin	Drahvin
Susanna Carroll	Drahvin
Robert Cartland, Anthony Paul	Rill voices
Barry Jackson	Garvey
Jimmy Kaye	Chumbley
Angelo Muscat	Chumbley
Pepi Poupee	Chumbley
Tommy Reynolds	Chumbley
William Shearer	Chumbley

This story has been released on audio CD

written by William Emms
directed by Derek Martinus
stock library music - see credits below

Four Hundred Dawns aired on Sep. 11, 1965
Trap Of Steel aired on Sep. 18, 1965
Air Lock aired on Sep. 25, 1965
The Exploding Planet aired on Oct. 2, 1965

The third episode, *Air Lock*, was discovered intact at the end of 2011; it was restored and included with reconstructions and other surviving clips on the Special Edition DVD re-release of *The Aztecs*.

MISSING: Episodes 1, 2 and 4 of *Galaxy Four* are missing from the BBC archives.

NEW WHO CONNECTIONS: The Drahvins are name-checked (but not seen) as one of the many alien enemies of the Doctor gathering in the skies above Stonehenge in *The Pandorica Opens* (2010).

STOCK MUSIC: "Sonatine" (Jacques Lasry / Les Structures Sonores), "Mister Blues" (Jacques Lasry and Francois Daschet/Les Structures Sonores), "Pieces Nouvelles" (Jacques Lasry and Francois Daschet/Les Structures Sonores), "Marche" (Daniel Ouzonnoff / Les Structures Sonores), "Spontaneite" (Jacques Lasry / Les Structures Sonores), "Moelle de Lion" (Jacques Lasry / Les Structures Sonores), "Rapsodie de Budapest" (Jacques Lasry and Francois Daschet/Les Structures Sonores), "Suite" (Jacques Lasry / Les Structures Sonores), "Invention a 2 Viox en Re Mineur" (Jacques Lasry and Francois Daschet/Les Structures Sonores)

❀ **The following review was written prior to the discovery of the missing episode three.** ❀

One of the better specimens of real SF in the first Doctor's era, most of *Galaxy Four* is sadly missing from the archive of **Doctor Who** episodes that still exist on video. Hence, this story has been reviewed by listening to the commercially available soundtrack recording and examining the scant remaining video and still material. But in a way, that's not a bad trade-off - the story itself is imaginative enough that it deserves the kind of special effects that exist in the mind's eye. *Galaxy Four* truly stands alongside some of the sophisticated conceptual SF that most people only associate with **Doctor Who**'s later years. (That being said, I won't kick the Restoration Team out of bed for cleaning up the recently-rediscovered third episode.)

While the style of some of the performances clearly dates *Galaxy Four* to the '60s, the dialogue is mostly believable - but there are occasional moments of clumsy dialogue and even a few hints of what would be viewed today, some four decades later, as outrageous sexism. (But no better and no worse than what one might find in the average *Austin Powers* movie, to be truthful.) There's something interesting hinted at with Maaga, the Drahvins' leader - she appears to be superior to them, and is withholding something from them, but aside from hints to that effect, we learn nothing more. (Perhaps William Emms thought there might be room for a rematch of some sort if he dropped a few vague hints like that.) But overall, the "don't judge a book by its cover" motif at work in *Galaxy Four* is not only commendable, it's carried off with a surprising degree of sophistication for this point in **Doctor Who**'s history. It's truly disappointing that so much of this story is missing; the discovery of the intact third episode in late 2011 was a huge find. Very highly recommended.

> **The following review was written after the missing episode was recovered and made available in 2013.**

Discovered in late 2011, part three of *Galaxy Four* promptly went into its own time warp, not to be seen until a nicely-put-together reconstruction was assembled and released by the BBC as a bonus feature on the DVD re-release of *The Aztecs* in 2013. A few minutes of part one had been discovered some time earlier, and of course the soundtrack survived. Things were made somewhat easier by the fact that visual filler material standing in for the missing segments had already been prepared for inclusion on a previous DVD release and then dropped – a curious decision, considering that the DVD in question predated the discovery of the missing episode.

Rather than taking the "cel animation style" approach to reconstructing well over half the story, the reconstruction is condensed down to a somewhat simplified, bare-bones telling of the story for those parts of it that are missing actual footage of any length. (*Air Lock* and the six extant minutes of *Four Hundred Dawns* play out in full.) Slideshows of still photos are the meat of any reconstructed **Doctor Who** episode, but in this case the photos are enhanced by subtle animation and even surprisingly decent CGI Chumbleys trundling across simple 3-D landscapes.

While this is no substitute for having all four episodes to view, the newly discovered episode and the above-average reconstruction of the rest of the story only reinforce my initial impression of *Galaxy Four* as an overlooked and surprisingly sophisticated **Doctor Who** classic. Whether or not this makes the purchase of the "special edition" *Aztecs* DVD a must will depend on the individual, but for my money, it's one of the best incentives yet to step up to a revised/enhanced edition of one of the existing classic series stories on DVD.

MISSION TO THE UNKNOWN

A ship from Earth, piloted by three Space Security Agents, lands on the jungle world of Kembel for a scouting mission. Their stop soon turns into more than they'd bargained for - the local flora is capable of infecting humans and turning them into mindless killers, and one of the Agents is gunned down by his fellow officers in self-defense. Worse yet, they learn that the Daleks are massing a secret strike force on Kembel. The metallic monstrosities are planning to overrun

Earth's entire solar system, subjugate the human race, and from there take over the entire universe. In the end, only Space Security Agent Marc Cory is left alive, and he's dying, infected by the mind-controlling vegetation of Kembel. He manages to fire off a distress signal to Earth - not a plea for help, since he will be dead by the time help can arrive, but a warning: prepare for an invasion.

Robert Cartland . . . . Malpha
Edward de Souza . . . . Marc Cory
Peter Hawkins, David Graham . . . Dalek voices
Barry Jackson . . . . Garvey
Robert Jewell . . . . Dalek
Kevin Manser . . . . Dalek
John Scott Martin . . . . Dalek
Ronald Rich . . . . Trantis
Gerald Taylor . . . . Dalek
Jeremy Young . . . . Gordon Lowery

This story has been released on audio CD

written by Terry Nation
directed by Derek Martinus
stock library music - see credits below

Mission To The Unknown aired on Oct. 9, 1965

The third episode, *Air Lock*, was discovered intact at the end of 2011; it will be restored and included on a future DVD release.

MISSING: *Mission To The Unknown* is missing from the BBC archives.

NEW WHO CONNECTIONS: New series devotees may be accustomed to the single-episode format, but this was the first complete **Doctor Who** story to be told in a single episode during the original series (the only other single-episode stories were *The Five Doctors* and the 1996 TV movie). *Mission To The Unknown* also paved the way for "Doctor-light" episodes such as *Love & Monsters*, *Blink* and *Turn Left*: it stars *none* of the regular cast members, and the Doctor does not appear and is not mentioned.

STOCK MUSIC: "Synchro-Stings" (Trevor Duncan)

The unique one-part adventure was forced onto the production slate by the trimming of a previous episode from four parts to three. But there was only one hitch: no story was written, and with other episodes already in front of the cameras, a way had to be figured out to excuse the regular cast from the action.

By the time *Mission To The Unknown*, also referred to by fan historians as "Dalek Cutaway," was conceived, the epic-scale *Daleks' Masterplan* 12-parter was already in the works. To fill the gap, the **Doctor Who** production team essentially turned the open slot in the schedule into a 25-minute teaser for the upcoming Dalek story. Dalek creator Terry Nation makes it interesting, if obvious, and one can also sense that he was feeling his way around the possibilty of a Doctorless Dalek series, an ambition he harbored but failed to realize in his own lifetime. To some degree, Big Finish - the modern-day holders of the **Doctor Who** audio drama license - has closed the circle with the Dalek Empire audio series.

Naturally, *Mission To The Unknown* was wiped from the archives, just like most of *The Daleks' Masterplan*. Enterprising fans who tape-recorded the audio of these episodes from their TV sets, however, have made this and other BBC audio-only **Doctor Who** releases possible. *Mission To The Unknown* was released as a bonus disc, rounding out the 5-CD set necessary to present *The Daleks' Masterplan* in its entirety in audio form. On its own, *Mission* is intriguing, though as a teaser story it's a little less than subtle.

THE MYTH MAKERS

The Doctor is suitably bemused when the TARDIS lands him in the middle of a fight on the plains of Greece, where his appearance fatally distracts one of the two combatants and convinces the other that he is Zeus. Vicki and Steven watch helplessly as the surviving warrior, Achilles, tries to recruit "Zeus" in his quest to topple the city of Troy. More of Achilles' countrymen appear, led by Odysseus, who doesn't believe that the Doctor is Zeus, and he is taken prisoner. Steven insists that Vicki, still nursing a sprained ankle, remain in the TARDIS while he goes to help the Doctor. Faced with no choice, the Doctor decides to masquerade as a god, proving his "powers" with foreknowledge of events to come in the Trojan War. The ruse works too well, though - his captors decide that he's too valuable to let go, but at least they grant him some hospitality. When Steven tries to come to the Doctor's rescue, he is captured and brought before Agamemnon; to save Steven's life, the Doctor claims him as his own personal "sacrifice to Olympus", promising to make him disappear at the dawn of the next day at his "blue temple"…but when the appointed hour comes, the temple - the TARDIS - has vanished. The Doctor and Steven are declared spies, and fast talking is required to save their necks from Agamemnon's sword for impersonating a god. The TARDIS has in fact been spirited away, and now lies within the walls of Troy. Cassandra admonishes the Trojan soldiers for bringing an unknown object into the city, warning that she has foreseen that a "gift" from the Greeks will result in the fall of Troy. Vicki emerges from the TARDIS, where she too claims to have knowledge of the future. She is given the name Cressida, and Cassandra immediately objects to having competition in the prophecy field. To recover the TARDIS and Vicki intact, the Doctor must propose an outlandish plan that may just prove Cassandra's grim predictions correct…

William Hartnell . . . . The Doctor	
Peter Purves . . . . Steven Taylor	
Maureen O'Brien . . . . Vicki	
Max Adrian . . . . Priam	
Francis de Wolff . . . . Agamemnon	
Alan Haywood . . . . Hector	
Adrienne Hill . . . . Katarina	
Barrie Ingham . . . . Paris	
Cavan Kendall . . . . Achilles	
Tutte Lemkow . . . . Cyclops	
Jon Luxton . . . . Messenger	
James Lynn . . . . Troilus	

This story has been released on audio CD

written by Donald Cotton
directed by Michael Leeston-Smith
music by Humphrey Searle

Temple Of Secrets aired on Oct. 16, 1965
Small Prophet Quick Return aired on Oct. 23
Death Of A Spy aired on Oct. 30, 1965
Horse Of Destruction aired on Nov. 6, 1965

Jack Melford . . . . Menelaus	
Ivor Salter . . . . Odysseus	
Frances White . . . . Cassandra	

MISSING: All four episodes of *The Myth Makers* are missing from the BBC archives.

NEW WHO CONNECTIONS: It would seem that none of the Doctor's companions have ever gotten along with anyone named Cassandra…

BEHIND THE SCENES: This story marks the exit of Maureen O'Brien as Vicki, whose age is finally nailed down in this story as being in her late teens.

If the name wasn't already taken, I'd say this story should be renamed *Mythbusters*. It's quite refreshing to see - or, sadly, since it exists only in a series of audio recordings of the missing TV episodes, hear - how "postmodern" *The Myth Makers* is. The heroes of myth are reinterpreted with modern foibles, and some thirty years before **The Princess Bride** or **Hercules** and **Xena** came along to do the same thing.

Sharp, funny dialogue keeps the whole thing thundering along, bringing new dimensions to a story that everyone knows - or at least they think they know it. There are a few bizarre moments, such as Vicki abandoning the shelter of the TARDIS because the Trojans are about to burn it as a sacrifice - something that in future years would be established as an impossibility. But obviously **Doctor Who**'s mythology was still just beginning to evolve at this point, and the Time Lords hadn't been invented yet, along with many of the TARDIS' less obvious attributes. That can be overlooked in favor of *The Myth Makers*' wickedly funny dialogue, though - my favorite example being Cassandra's "Woe to try!" followed by King Priam's "You might as well say whoa to the horse." There aren't many classic **Doctor Who** stories that have me laughing out loud while I'm listening to the audio recordings, but this is an exception.

If there's anything disconcerting or out-of-place with *The Myth Makers*, it's the sudden and seemingly tacked-on arrival of the quite literally short-lived TARDIS traveler, Katarina. She's the show's first companion from a distant past, but that idea wouldn't find a real expression until the arrival of Jamie during Patrick Troughton's era. The fundamental problem, from a standpoint of character, is that Katarina is from *too* far in the past to relate to anyone else in the TARDIS at all; to her, the Doctor is a god and the TARDIS is his temple. But given that her demise just a few weeks later in an early installment of the 12-episode epic *The Daleks' Masterplan* is prophesied here, it would seem that she wasn't destined to be much of a character anyway - just enough of a character to sacrifice to raise the next story's stakes. As such, I don't consider Katarina as a "companion" at all, any more than I would consider Adam from 2005's *Dalek* and *The Long Game* a true companion. She simply wasn't around long enough, and I get the impression that the producer and writers knew that would be the case.

That aside, *The Myth Makers* is a delightful listen. It's sad that the video component of this story is forever lost, but it's filled with such witty dialogue and characterization than it survives into a purely audio medium.

THE DALEKS' MASTERPLAN

As Space Security Agent Bret Vyon and a fatalistic colleague search for their missing comrade Marc Cory on the planet Kembel, little do they realize they're about to become the first witnesses to the beginning of a Dalek invasion of Earth's galaxy and solar system. Vyon escapes with his life, but his radio transmitter is destroyed, leaving him unable to warn Earth of the impending danger. The TARDIS lands on Kembel, and when the Doctor steps outside to explore, he is ambushed by Vyon, who takes the key to his timeship. Vyon enters the TARDIS and tries to coerce Katarina into operating the controls, but Katarina - still new to the TARDIS - can't help him, and Steven attacks Vyon and lets the Doctor back in. The Doctor secures Vyon in a magnetic security chair which holds him immoble, and returns to his explorations outside, spotting Daleks nearby and infiltrating a nearby spaceport where the Daleks are gathering. He impersonates one of several visiting delegates, and discovers that the Daleks - with help from the traitorous Mavic Chen, guardian of the solar system - plan to unleash a weapon called the Time Destructor. When they find the TARDIS door ajar, the Daleks force Katarina, Steven and Bret Vyon out of the time machine, and the former TARDIS travelers have to steal a ship from the spaceport. Vyon intends to leave the Doctor behind, but the Doctor manages to get aboard as the ship takes off - having stolen the valuable taranium core that would power the Time Destructor. The Daleks pursue, forcing the ship down on the prison planet Desperus, where two prisoners hijack the ship as it takes off again. The criminals take Katarina hostage and barricade themselves into an airlock, but the girl bravely sacrifices her own life to open the airlock, killing the hijackers in the process. The Doctor and Steven are stunned, but continue racing toward Earth to warn humanity of the Daleks' plan.

Mavic Chen beats them back to Earth and has the Space Security Service declare Vyon, Steven and the Doctor traitors to the human race, but the three travelers haven't taken the escape route

Chen expected, and elude capture. Chen assigns special agent Sara Kingdom to track them down and eliminate them, unaware that she is Vyon's sister. Vyon leads the Doctor and Steven to a friend of his, only to discover that this friend is in Chen's employ and is also in on the conspiracy to hand Earth over to the Daleks. Sara Kingdom arrives at the scene and guns down her brother in cold blood, continuing the pursue the other two. She pursues them into a laboratory where a matter-transmission experiment is taking place, and all three are transported through space to the planet Mira. The Daleks follow the travelers to Mira, where Sara experiences a change of heart as the murder of her brother sinks in. But her realization is almost cut short by a new threat - Mira's invisible and lethal indigenous life forms. When the Daleks corner the time travelers, those creatures offer an opportunity to escape. The Doctor, Sara and Steven commandeer the Dalek ship and leave Mira. As the Dalek ship follows a pre-programmed course back to Kembel, the Doctor makes a fake taranium core. He uses it to bluff his way back into the TARDIS on Kembel, handing it over to the Daleks at the last minute. But despite the fact that the travelers still have the real taranium core, the TARDIS takes them someplace else inhospitable, with a poisonous atmosphere: 20th century Earth.

When the Doctor investigates, he is mistaken for a homeless man, discovering that the "poisonous atmosphere" is merely that of polluted 1966 London. Steven and Sara have to act fast to rescue the Doctor from police (who are, after all, merely looking after "their" police box) and escape back to the TARDIS. They then wind up materializing in a Hollywood studio during a film shoot, and a brief but maddening chase ensues between the time travelers and the filmmakers. The TARDIS then takes them to the volcanic planet of Tigus. Not only are the Daleks lying in wait, having discovered that they do not possess a real taranium core, but so too is the Meddling Monk, an interfering fellow time traveler the Doctor and Steven left stranded in 1066 A.D. The Monk tries to exact his revenge by locking the Doctor out of his own TARDIS, but the Doctor uses a special property of his ring to gain entry. With both the Monk and the Daleks in hot pursuit, the Doctor and his companions make a quick escape to ancient Egypt, but their reception is anything but friendly there - a possessive Pharaoh lays claim to the TARDIS.

Followed to Egypt by the Monk, the Doctor realizes that the stakes are now higher and he'll have to use the real taranium core as a bargaining chip. When the Monk ensures that Steven and Sara are captured by the Daleks and suggests they use the two humans as hostages, the Doctor is forced to hand over the core to the Daleks. His friends returned to him (and having once again sabotaged the Monk's TARDIS), the Doctor races back to Kembel, where Mavic Chen's ambition grows to the point where the corrupt leader no longer thinks he needs the Daleks. They solve this problem by swiftly exterminating Chen and activating the Time Destructor. When the Doctor realizes how the Daleks' ultimate weapon will work, he decides to run for the safety of the TARDIS to wait out its effects, for the weapon will quickly destroy itself and all those around it. Tragically, Sara does not live to see the Daleks' grandiose plan fail.

William Hartnell . . . . The Doctor
Peter Purves . . . . Steven Taylor
Adrienne Hill . . . . Katarina
Philip Anthony . . . . Roald
Roger Avon . . . . Daxtar
Albert Barrington . . . . Professor Webster
Roger Brierly . . . . Trevor
Maurice Browning . . . . Karlton
Peter Butterworth . . . . Monk
Brian Cant . . . . Kert Gantry

This story has been released on audio CD

written by Terry Nation and Dennis Spooner
directed by Douglas Camfield
music by Tristram Cary

The Nightmare Begins aired on Nov. 13, 1965
Day Of Armageddon aired on Nov. 20, 1965
Devil's Planet aired on Nov. 27, 1965
The Traitors aired on Dec. 4, 1965
Counter Plot aired on Dec. 11, 1965
Coronas Of The Sun aired on Dec. 18, 1965
The Feast Of Steven aired on Dec. 25, 1965

Dallas Cavell . . . . Bors
Geoffrey Cheshire . . . . Garge
Nicholas Courtney . . . . Bret Vyon
Harry Davies . . . . Make-up Man
Sheila Dunn . . . . Blossom Lefavre
Clifford Earl . . . . Sergeant
Roy Evans . . . . Trantis
David Graham . . . . Dalek voices
Leonard Grahame . . . . Darcy Tranton
Pamela Greer . . . . Lizan
Michael Guest . . . . Interviewer
James Hall . . . . Borkar
William Hall . . . . Cowboy
Peter Hawkins . . . . Dalek voices
John Herrington . . . . Rhynmal
Jeffrey Isaac . . . . Khepren
David James . . . . Arab Sheik
Robert Jewell . . . . Dalek / Clown
Jack le White . . . . Cameraman
Malcolm Leopold . . . . Keystone Cop
Steven Machin . . . . Cameraman
Kevin Manser . . . . Dalek
Jean Marsh . . . . Sara Kingdom
John Scott Martin . . . . Dalek
M.J. Matthews . . . . Chaplain
Bill Meilen . . . . Froyn
Conrad Monk . . . . Assistant Director
Bryan Mosley . . . . Malpha
Jean Pastell . . . . Saloon Girl
Jack Pitt . . . . Gearon
Walter Randall . . . . Hyksos
Douglas Sheldon . . . . Kirksen
Julian Sherrier . . . . Zephon

Volcano aired on Jan. 1, 1966
Golden Death aired on Jan. 8, 1966
Escape Switch aired on Jan. 15, 1966
The Abandoned Planet aired on Jan. 22, 1966
The Destruction Of Time aired on Jan. 29, 1966

The second, fifth and tenth episodes of *The Daleks' Masterplan* are all that remains of this story in the BBC archives, and along with a few very brief surviving clips from other episodes of this story, were released as part of the "Lost In Time" DVD box set.

This story's music is on the BBC's *Doctor Who: Devils' Planets* compilation CD, released in 2003 (now out of print).

Gerald Taylor . . . . Dalek
Norman Mitchell . . . . Policeman
Reg Pritchard . . . . Man in mackintosh
Malcolm Rogers . . . . Policeman
Mark Ross . . . . Ingmar Knopf
Paul Sarony . . . . Keystone Cop
Kevin Stoney . . . . Mavic Chen
Kenneth Thornett . . . . Inspector
Royston Tickner . . . . . . Steinberger P. Green
Paula Topham . . . . Vamp
Derek Ware . . . . Tuthmos
Bruce Wightman . . . . Scott
Buddy Windrush . . . . Prop Man
Terence Woodfield . . . . Celation

MISSING: Episodes 1, 3, 4, 6, 7, 8, 9, 11 and 12 of *The Daleks' Masterplan* are missing from the BBC archives.

NEW WHO CONNECTIONS: Though it's almost entirely disconnected from the rest of the 12-episode plotline, *The Feast Of Steven* (the seventh episode of *The Daleks' Masterplan*) is **the first-ever Doctor Who Christmas special**, broadcast on Christmas Day and even featuring the Doctor breaking the fourth wall and directly addressing viewers (a tradition in British holiday TV at the time) to wish them a merry Christmas!

In its day, where - as legend would have it - it was the product of a BBC controller's wish to placate his mother (reportedly a fan of the Daleks) and the Dalek-hungry public, *The Daleks' Masterplan* tested the metal monstrosities' popularity to the breaking point. The only episode of the dozen-week saga in which the Daleks do *not* appear is the goofy part 7, *The Feast Of Steven*, an almost self-parodying Christmas pantomime episode designed to lighten the mood for the holidays. Otherwise, it was three solid months of Dalek dialogue, delivered at a deathly dull clip. One wonders if the audience ever started pining for scenes in which the Daleks *didn't* appear.

Overall, an exhausting epic, but there's a very good story at the heart of it - **Doctor Who**'s first attempt at a major story arc. There are some ripping good cliffhangers here in William Hartnell's final tussle with the Daleks, and the jeopardy escalates throughout the story, though there's also a lot of padding: running around, being caught, and escaping in the nick of time.

THE MASSACRE

The Doctor and Steven arrive in Paris, 1572. The Doctor is eager to visit apothecary and scientist Charles Preslin, whose early research into germs fascinates him, but doesn't want to bring Steven along. Steven is loathe to stay in the TARDIS, and promises not to mingle with the locals, but is alarmed when he thinks he sees a man following the Doctor. Steven tries to follow, but runs afoul of the tavern keep (whom he has forgotten to pay). A man helps Steven out of his predicament and then brings him up to speed on the events into which the time travelers have emerged: the bloody fighting between Catholics and Protestants. Steven becomes very worried indeed when the Doctor vanishes, and is even more alarmed when a servant girl named Anne Chaplet bursts into the home of Admiral de Coligny, where he is staying. Anne claims to have overheard what could be a large-scale plot to rid Paris of all Protestants by any means necessary. Steven sees a man he believes to be the Doctor, but his new friends suddenly regard him coldly — they know this man as the Abbot of Amboise, one of the most fanatical Catholic crusaders in France. Not only does Steven not know whether the Doctor is safe, but he now has no backup. He's a foreigner in a decidedly hostile situation, trapped between fanatical elements among both the Catholics and the Hugenots, and if he can't find the Doctor, he'll be stuck there.

William Hartnell..The Doctor / Abbot of Amboise
Peter Purves . . . . Steven Taylor
Jackie Lane . . . . Dodo Chaplet
Clive Cazes . . . . Captain
Eric Chitty . . . . Preslin
Cynthia Etherington . . . . Old Lady
Edwin Fenn . . . . Landlord
Reginald Jessup . . . . Servant
Barry Justice . . . . Charles IX
Andre Morell . . . . Tavannes
Annette Robertson . . . . Anne Chaplet
Leonard Sachs . . . . Admiral de Coligny
Eric Thompson . . . . Gaston
John Tillinger . . . . Simon

This story has been released on audio CD

written by John Lucarotti
directed by Paddy Russell
stock library music - see credits below

War Of God aired on Feb. 5, 1966
The Sea Beggar aired on Feb. 12, 1966
Priest Of Death aired on Feb. 19, 1966
Bell Of Doom aired on Feb. 26, 1966

Christopher Tranchell . . . . Roger
David Weston . . . . Nicholas
Joan Young . . . . Catherine de Medici

MISSING: All four episodes of *The Massacre* are missing from the BBC archives.

NEW WHO CONNECTIONS: Though the idea became common in Big Finish audios, and in David Tennant's final few stories in 2009, this story marks the first time we see the Doctor (temporarily) companionless — at least until Steven changes his mind and returns to the TARDIS.

STOCK MUSIC: "Illustrations No. 4: Hunted Man" (Pierre Arvay), "Illustrations No. 4: Frightened Man" (Pierre Arvay), "Illustrations No. 4: Little Prelude" (Pierre Arvay)

AUDIO CONNECTIONS: *The Massacre* was the first "lost" television story to be released in audio CD form in the 1990s; its popularity kick-started a series of releases that eventually included all of the lost stories from the first two Doctors' eras, thanks to the tireless efforts of some of **Doctor Who**'s earliest fans, who sought to preserve a record of the show through amateur tape recordings.

One of the final "historicals" in the first half of **Doctor Who**'s televised existence, this period adventure is pretty sophisticated fare. The story is complicated and densely layered, and if you don't already have a passing acquaintance with the historical events portrayed, you'd do well to gain one soon afterward.

The Massacre is a true rarity: a story that makes *good* use of the dreaded "evil twin" plot device. The Abbot of Amboise is the first Doctor's exact double, and is played with chilling precision by William Hartnell. However, Steven is dead certain that the Abbot is the Doctor in disguise – after all, Steven rationalizes, this is exactly the sort of thing the Doctor would do if there was a good reason. That reasoning quickly causes Steven's allies to turn their backs on him – and puts him in a position where he could easily get himself killed.

The climax of this four-parter is grisly, and is one of the original series' hardest-hitting examples of the Doctor's insistence that history must run its course. Steven's rage that the Doctor left to her fate a girl who helped them both results in his pledge to leave the Doctor at the TARDIS' next stop – which, in fact, he does. This leads into a somber and eloquent monologue delivered by Hartnell. It's a very nice piece – the Doctor reflects on how all of his companions have left, going down a laundry list all the way back to his granddaughter Susan, and even contemplates "going back home, back to my own planet." But this most interesting moment is brought to an abrupt end when a young woman named Dodo Chaplet – possibly a descendant of the girl who helped the Doctor and Steven in 16th-century France – bolts into the TARDIS, thinking it to be a real police box. Thus we are introduced to a new female companion in what has to be the most inelegant and arbitrary introduction of a new lead actor in the series until the introduction-less introduction of Melanie in 1986 – and just when I was enjoying Hartnell's impassioned performance, too.

THE ARK

The TARDIS arrives in a verdant forest, which the Doctor, Dodo and Steven assume must be on Earth. They are soon proven wrong when alarms sound in the "forest," which turns out to be part of a vast spaceship carrying the last remnants of the human race away from a doomed Earth, ten million years in the future when the sun is slowly edging toward its nova stage. The Doctor and his friends also meet the one-eyed alien Monoids, peaceful creatures which seem to languish in a benevolent servitude to the ship's human crew. But the travelers' arrival becomes a bad omen when Dodo, suffering from the common cold, accidentally transmits it to the commander of the ship – unaware that the human race ten million years hence lacks her immune system. Condemned for what is perceived to be biological warfare, the Doctor races to immunize the future humans against the cold. Having cleared his name, the Doctor and his friends depart in the TARDIS – but accidentally return to the same place seven centuries later, finding the Monoids in control and the last of the human race in the chains of slavery.

William Hartnell . . . . The Doctor
Peter Purves . . . . Steven Taylor
Jackie Lane . . . . Dodo Chaplet
Terence Bayler . . . . Yendom
Richard Beale . . . . Refusian voice
John Caesar . . . . Monoid Four
Ralph Carrigan . . . . Monoid Two
Edmund Coulter . . . . Monoid One
Eric Elliott . . . . Commander
Ian Frost . . . . Baccu
Frank George . . . . Monoid Three
Paul Greenhalgh . . . . Guardian
John Halstead . . . . Monoid voice
Eileen Helsby . . . . Venussa
Inigo Jackson . . . . Zentos

This story has been released on DVD

written by Paul Erickson & Lesley Scott
directed by Michael Imison
music by Tristram Cary

The Steel Sky aired on March 5, 1966
The Plague aired on March 12, 1966
The Return aired on March 19, 1966
The Bomb aired on March 26, 1966

Michael Sheard . . . . Rhos
Roy Skelton . . . . Monoid voice
Roy Spencer . . . . Manyak
Terence Woodfield . . . . Maharis
Brian Wright . . . . Dassuk

NEW WHO CONNECTIONS: In some respects, this story presages the thread connecting the ninth Doctor stories *The Long Game* and *Bad Wolf*: they both mark a rare instance in which the Doctor actually has to deal with the results of his own interference in future events, realizing that perhaps his actions during the first adventure in question haven't made things better. *The Ark's* notion of a human diaspora scattering outward from the doomed solar system squares nicely with similarly-themed original series episodes such as *The Ark In Space* (1975), but it's slightly difficult to match up with the end of the Earth as seen in *The End Of The World* (2005), unless there's a huge class divide between the haves (partying it up on Platform One with the ninth Doctor) and the have-nots (slumming through deep space here, or sleeping it out aboard Nerva Beacon).

A very clever and unique story in the history of **Doctor Who**, *The Ark* is one of the few tales that follows up on the consequences of the Doctor's travels instead of – as often happens – leaving the guest characters to clean up the mess. Though relatively simple, *The Ark* is rooted in solid science fiction, and could be considered eerily prescient for its "prediction" – more creative coincidence than clairvoyance – of the decline of the human immune system. There's also a certain charm to the unabashed '60s-ness of this segment; in one scene, when Dodo says "okay," the Doctor pledges to teach her to speak proper English!

William Hartnell is, as always, serious and believable as the original Doctor, and the high stakes in both halves of the story are a good showcase for his talents. Though I don't often see any indication that this **Doctor Who** story is particularly well-remembered, it *should* be – it's one of the best of the Hartnell era.

SHORT HOPS

...in which the author recalls one of the best products of applied Doctor Who fandom.

As I mentioned earlier in the book, a large box of Hartnell and Troughton-era **Doctor Who**, on videotape, wound up in my possession under some unusual circumstances (to say the least; see page 29). When the electricity was finally restored, I dove into the first and second Doctors' adventures in earnest for the first time, discovering that the older **Doctor Who** stories had both delights (tremendous performances) and a few strikes against them (the occasional letdown on the production end of things) that made them significantly different from the Target novelizations I'd read.

But these tapes had other delights as well. Originating from Sacramento Public TV affiliate KVIE, each of the first and second Doctor adventures were prefaced with an original introduction produced in 1988, reportedly in the course of a single day-long shoot in the KVIE studio. The stage was mostly empty, save for a few expertly-built props – a Dalek, a Police Box, and the most beautiful fan-made TARDIS console I've ever seen – and one of the three hosts would offer trivia and context from an epoch of **Doctor Who** when not every contiguous adventure was available for KVIE to show. In short, they were doing more or less what this book is trying to do now. But with better props.

If there was a story missing in between the show being introduced and its predecessor, it would be mentioned (and fans would be encouraged to visit their local library to check out the novelization of the absent story). If significant events unfolded between this story and the next existing story (such as, say, the quantum leap between *The War Machines* and *The Dominators*, due to the incomplete or totally AWOL status of the final Hartnell story and two *seasons* of Patrick Troughton in between those stories), viewers would be warned that the show wouldn't quite look the same next week. Missing companion exits and introductions were noted, and significant behind-the-scenes details were revealed. In the case of "historical" stories whose details diverged from actual history, the public education remit of the PBS station was fulfilled by the hosts pointing this out.

All of which may seem like yesterday's news to most people reading this, except that it was aimed at casual viewers who, perhaps, *didn't* know this stuff. It was fascinating: value-added material, years before any DVDs existed to carry DVD extras, and much like the entry-level documentaries accompanying virtually every classic **Doctor Who** DVD in recent memory, it was aimed at viewers who weren't familiar with the show, rather than trying to appeal to the hardcore insiders. In 1988, a Sacramento PBS station was making the forerunners of today's **Doctor Who** DVD bonus features.

And as much as I hate to completely geek-out over it, the prop console was one of the slickest fan-made pieces I have ever seen. Obviously it was ready for considerably scrutiny on TV, as it dominated quite a few of the shots. It wasn't an exact replica of the TARDIS console from a specific "era," but was instead a kind of "greatest hits" – the coolest stuff about all of the original series consoles, all in one place.

One can imagine this same strategy being adopted now, but covering the entire original series, some of which is nearly inpenetrable to viewers who have only been exposed to 21st century **Doctor Who**. We're in the 21st century – all of this shot-on-video, standard-definition stuff is ancient history to today's audience. Perhaps someone needs to call the KVIE hosts out of retirement to take on the task – judging by the quality and homespun charm of their 1988 intros, I can think of no one better qualified.

THE CELESTIAL TOYMAKER

After leaving the Ark behind, the Doctor shows signs of having picked up Dodo's sneeze, but he then exhibits a startling behavior that can't be attributed to the common cold: he vanishes completely for a few moments. The TARDIS lands in a realm populated by toys, games and clowns, and a man in Mandarin clothes whom the Doctor instantly recognizes as the Celestial Toymaker. The Toymaker whisks the Doctor away, forcing him to play the lengthy, unforgiving Tri-Logic game with deadly stakes, while Steven and Dodo are trapped with the Toymaker's minions and a host of characters whose only motivations seem to be to deceive the time travelers to lure them into making the wrong moves in their own deadly games. With his TARDIS, his companion's lives and his own life up for grabs, the Doctor must play to win, but he'll have to start playing dirty to stay ahead of an opponent who has no qualms about cheating.

William Hartnell . . . . The Doctor
Peter Purves . . . . Steven Taylor
Jackie Lane . . . . Dodo Chaplet
Michael Gough . . . . Toymaker
Reg Lever . . . . Joker
Carmen Silvera . . Clara / Mrs. Wiggs / Queen of Hearts

Campbell Singer . . . . . Joey / Sgt. Rugg / King of Hearts
Peter Stephens . . . . Knave of Hearts / Kitchen boy / Cyril

This story has been released on audio CD

written by Brian Hayles
directed by Bill Sellars
music by Dudley Simpson

The Celestial Toyroom aired on April 2, 1966
The Hall Of Dolls aired on April 9, 1966
The Dancing Floor aired on April 16, 1966
The Final Test aired on April 23, 1966

The Celestial Toymaker is partially available on DVD; the existing episode is in the "Lost In Time" box set.

MISSING: Episodes 1, 2 and 3 of *The Celestial Toymaker* are missing from the BBC archives.

AUDIO CONNECTIONS: The Toymaker faces off against the sixth Doctor in *The Nightmare Fair*, the first release in Big Finish's Lost Stories range recreating written-but-never-produced TV scripts in audio form (*The Nightmare Fair* was originally written to kick off the 1986 season before the stories originally penned for that season were nixed in favor of *The Trial Of A Time Lord*), the seventh Doctor audio story *The Magic Mousetrap*, and the eighth-Doctor-era Companion Chronicles story *Solitaire*; in all of his Big Finish appearances to date, the role originally played by the late Michael Gough is voiced by David Bailie.

Rightly held up as an example of the Hartnell era's ability to evoke an intensely creepy atmosphere, *The Celestial Toymaker* is an intriguing and spooky four-parter that ultimately asks more questions than it answers. On its own merits, the whole thing is actually rather simplistic in its treatment of the various games and challenges, and in places it seems deliberately vague in explaining everything. We know no more about the Toymaker, his origins and his domain at the end of the proceedings than we do at the beginning; he and the Doctor are apparently well acquainted (if not terribly well disposed to one another), and all that we find out in the course of the story is that he's an immortal being who can assemble a powerful space (strong enough to trap a TARDIS?) around himself, where he holds sway over the laws of nature, by sheer force of will. In retrospect, it's a wonder that no reunion with this character was planned until Colin Baker's era (*The Nightmare Fair*, a four-parter written for season 23 but abandoned when a publicly-decried attempt to cancel the series resulted in the *Trial Of A Time Lord* season instead).

Could *The Celestial Toymaker* be done today? Part of me wants to say yes, but in truth, so many of the reversals of our heroes' fortune come about simply because someone takes advantage of Steven and Dodo's decidedly gentle manners. But, though it pains me to suggest recasting the Toymaker (although Big Finish has since done precisely that for audio purposes), perhaps a rematch with the current TV Doctor is in order.

THE GUNFIGHTERS

His tooth broken by a booby-trapped piece of candy leftover from his struggle with the Celestial Toymaker, the Doctor seeks dental help in the old west – from none other than Doc Holliday himself, in Tombstone, Arizona. But when the Doctor, Steven and Dodo go to seek his help, the Doctor is mistaken for Holliday…and this threatens to plunge the time travellers into the legendary, bloody shootout at the OK Corral, not as observers, but as participants.

William Hartnell . . . . The Doctor
Peter Purves . . . . Steven Taylor
Jackie Lane . . . . Dodo Chaplet
John Alderson . . . . Wyatt Earp
Richard Beale . . . . Bat Masterson
Victor Carin . . . . Virgil Earp
David Cole . . . . Billy Clanton
Reed de Rouen . . . . Pa Clanton
Maurice Good . . . . Phineas Clanton
David Graham . . . . Charlie
Martyn Huntley . . . . Warren Earp
William Hurndell . . . . Ike Clanton
Anthony Jacobs . . . . Doc Holliday
Sheena Marshe . . . . Kate
Laurence Payne . . . . Johnny Ringo
Shane Rimmer . . . . Seth Harper

This story has been released on DVD

written by Donald Cotton
directed by Rex Tucker
music by Tristram Cary

A Holiday For The Doctor aired April 30, 1966
Don't Shoot The Pianist aired on May 7, 1966
Johnny Ringo aired on May 14, 1966
The OK Corral aired on May 21, 1966

This was the final original series story whose individual episodes had unique episode titles.

A complete audio recording of this entire story is available on CD, although the complete story exists in visual form as well.

BEHIND THE SCENES: The ballad that runs throughout all four parts of the story is sung by Lynda Baron, who would appear later in the series, guest starring as Captain Wrack in *Enlightenment* (1983) opposite Peter Davison's Doctor and as Val in *Closing Time* (2011) starring Matt Smith. Guest star Anthony Jacobs was the father of writer Matthew Jacobs, who wrote the script for the 1996 TV movie starring Paul McGann, which premiered exactly 30 years after the third episode of *The Gunfighters*.

Until the 1980s and *The Trial Of A Time Lord* rolled around, *The Gunfighters* earned a dubious distinction in **Doctor Who** history: the lowest-rated story up to that point in the series' history. Granted, that low rating was eclipsed by an even lower rating in 1986, though – to be fair – *The Gunfighters* didn't face competition from video games, computers, cable television, and VCRs. *The Gunfighters'* record-setting low ranking in the viewing figures wasn't due to distractions for the viewing audience, but because they weren't interested in seeing William Hartnell and company go through the motions of retelling the story of the gunfight at the OK Corral.

Going back and watching *The Gunfighters* again, it's hard to blame the audience. But in fairness, perhaps the collective memory of fandom has been rather hard on this one, expecting a bit too much from it. On a purely escapist level, if you can check your brain at the door, **Doctor Who**'s one and only western is light-hearted, light-headed fun. The sad thing is, the production crew really did try to pull it off, but in the end it all has about as much credibility as, oh, say, Kevin Costner's shaky accent in ***Robin Hood: Prince Of Thieves***. Not the finest outing for the first Doctor, and frankly, **Star Trek**'s *Spectre Of The Gun*, **Red Dwarf**'s *Gunmen Of The Apocalypse* and virtually the entire run of **Firefly** point to the kinds of storytelling opportunities that a **Doctor Who** western completely missed. It was a setting and a style that Doctor Who wouldn't return to until 2012.

THE SAVAGES

The Doctor brings the TARDIS in for a landing on a world whose inhabitants have, according to him, achieved peace and balance. As the Doctor surveys the planet, Steven grows impatient and goes to look for him, but he and Dodo run into stone-age primitives – hardly an advanced civilization. The TARDIS travelers are saved by the Elders, who welcome them to their city and offer the Doctor a seat among their most revered leaders. The Doctor is honored, but continues to ask questions about his hosts. But the more questions he asks, it becomes clearer that there's trouble in paradise: the Elders and their guards capture the "Savages" and drag them into the city, where they are subjected to a process that extracts their life energy and transfers that vitality to recipients in the city. When Dodo discovers the process, the time travelers are suddenly less welcome, and instead of a place of honor, the Doctor becomes the next in line to have his life force drained.

William Hartnell . . . . The Doctor
Peter Purves . . . . Steven Taylor
Jackie Lane . . . . Dodo Chaplet
Edward Caddick . . . . Wylda
Christopher Denham . . . . Assistant
John Dillon . . . . Savage
Geoffrey Frederick . . . . Exorse
Patrick Godfrey . . . . Tor
Tim Goodman . . . . Guard
Norman Henry . . . . Senta
Tony Holland . . . . Assistant

This story has been released on audio CD

written by Ian Stuart Black
directed by Christopher Barry
music by Raymond Jones

Part 1 aired on May 28, 1966
Part 2 aired on June 4, 1966
Part 3 aired on June 11, 1966
Part 4 aired on June 18, 1966

The Savages was the first **Doctor Who** story to simply

Frederick Jaeger	Jano
Clare Jenkins	Nanina
Andrew Lodge	Assistant
Kay Patrick	Flower
John Raven	Savage
Robert Sidaway	Avon
Ewen Solon	Chal
Peter Thomas	Edal

use the overall story title followed by "Part One", etc., instead of individual story titles for each episode.

MISSING: All four episodes of *The Savages* are missing from the BBC archives.

One of the more intriguing adventures of William Hartnell's era, *The Savages* is surprisingly mature and sophisticated. And if that's not enough, it also provides a plausible exit for Peter Purves as Steven, who, while occasionally a walking cliché, really was the first Doctor's most effective male sidekick.

The script delves into some quite advanced concepts for a show that was, at the time, aimed squarely at children. The relationship of hunter and prey, and the concept that no society thrives without exploiting someone to ensure its level of comfort, are brought up, and while the story doesn't get bogged down by those ideas, they're clearly being flagged so that they'll be in the viewers' mind when watching the rest of the story. Or, in our case these days, listening – *The Savages* is a fascinating story, and yet it's represented by a mere handful of photos (and a very brief surviving film clip of Steven's departure), barely enough to get a taste of what it looked like upon its first broadcast.

It's also a retcon dream come true: long before Time Lords or regeneration ever became part of the **Doctor Who** mythos, this story makes clear that whatever life force the Elders can extract from their victims, they're able to get *even more of it* from the Doctor (which, in hindsight, makes absolutely perfect sense – also see *Mawdryn Undead*). Almost more intriguing than that bit of future-proof plotting is the revelation that the Elders have tracked the Doctor's travels through time extensively, but what I can't let go of is the fact that the Doctor winds up there in the first place. Though not implicit in the script, I wonder if the Doctor was seeking this advanced, "peaceful" civilization out as a possible new home to settle down, away from the Time Lords. That he seems receptive to joining the Elders (before he knows their terrible secret, of course) makes this a very interesting possibility indeed.

At first I rolled my eyes at the somewhat corny twist that brings things to an end – in addition to the Doctor's life force, Jano also winds up with some of the Doctor's conscience and wisdom – but the more I thought about it, the more I realized that this made for a more satisfying ending than just blowing the problem to smithereens. And Steven winds up with the winner of the award for a companion whose departure makes the most narrative sense in the entire Hartnell era, staying behind as the only person who both the Elders and Savages will trust to help rebuild their society into one civilization. Of all the companions' departures in the first Doctor's era, I found Steven's to be the most effective, and the most genuinely emotional. More consistently written than Ian, and all-around more useful than Ben, Steven was a great foil for Hartnell's Doctor, even when the writers fell back on his hotheaded impetuosity as the character's only defining feature.

THE WAR MACHINES

The Doctor and Dodo arrive in 1966 London, finding that the city has undergone some changes since they were last there. The Post Office Tower has been completed, and something about it makes the Doctor suspicious. He and Dodo visit the Tower and find that an immense computer called WOTAN has been constructed, and its designers intend for it to take over functions that normally occupy the time of human beings. But WOTAN's vast artificial intelligence has already decided that it can take over *all* of humanity's functions – and those who refuse to follow its orders will be eliminated. WOTAN also realizes that it requires the Doctor's expertise – and so it takes control of Dodo and a secretary named Polly to lure him into a trap.

William Hartnell . . . . The Doctor	
Jackie Lane . . . . Dodo Chaplet	
Michael Craze . . . . Ben	
Anneke Wills . . . . Polly	
John Boyd-Brent . . . . Sergeant	
Sandra Bryant . . . . Kitty	
Desmond Callum-Jones . . . . Worker	
John Cater . . . . Professor Krimpton	
Edward Colliver . . . . Mechanic	
Carl Conway . . . . U.S. Correspondent	
George Cross . . . . Minister	
Alan Curtis . . . . Major Green	
Eddie David . . . . Worker	
Robin Dawson . . . . Soldier	
John Doye . . . . Interviewer	
Frank Jarvis . . . . Corporal	
Kenneth Kendall . . . . himself	
Ric Felgate . . . . American journalist	

This story has been released on DVD

written by Ian Stuart Black
directed by Michael Ferguson
stock library music - see credits below

Part 1 aired on June 25, 1966
Part 2 aired on July 2, 1966
Part 3 aired on July 9, 1966
Part 4 aired on July 16, 1966

Roy Godfrey . . . . Tramp	
John Harvey . . . . Professor Brett	
William Mervyn . . . . Sir Charles Summer	
Ewan Proctor . . . . Flash	
Michael Rathbone . . . . Taxi Driver	
John Rolfe . . . . Captain	
John Slavid . . . . Man in phone box	
Gerald Taylor . . War Machine / voice of WOTAN	
Dwight Whylie . . . . Announcer	

NEW WHO CONNECTIONS: Is WOTAN, in calling the Doctor "**Doctor Who**," somehow aware of the question that, if answered, will have dire consequences (*The Wedding Of River Song*, 2011; *The Time Of The Doctor*, 2013)?

STOCK MUSIC: "Frantic Fracas" (Johnny Hawksworth), "The Eyelash" (Johnny Hawksworth), "Beat To Begin" (Johnny Hawksworth), "Browbeater" (Johnny Hawksworth), "Latin Gear" (Johnny Hawksworth), "Rhythm n'Beat" (Johnny Hawksworth), "Musique Electronique: Hypnotic" (Eric Siday)

This tremendously intelligent and often-imitated story is easily the most modern of William Hartnell's **Doctor Who** adventures – it could have, with only the most minor of script adjustments, been tailored to any of the later Doctors. It's a four-parter, we see the Doctor experiencing a premonition of great evil, a huge computer decides that the human race is redundant, and the Doctor lends his support to the government and the military. In other words, expand this story by two episodes, put Jon Pertwee in the lead role, and you have *The Green Death*. *The War Machines* is a template for what **Doctor Who** became in the '70s.

Ben (Michael Craze) and Polly (Anneke Wills) also stumble into the TARDIS at the end of the story to become the first Doctor's final companions, after Dodo decides to stay on Earth, possibly traumatized after her takeover by WOTAN. Though Polly isn't a terribly distinctive character in this story, Ben is immediately very likeable and ready for action, and he's one of my favorite Hartnell companions – but sadly, this is the only story with Ben and Polly which is complete and available on video.

This story features the infamous line, spoken repeatedly throughout by WOTAN's sinister hissing voice: "Doc-tor *WHO* is required!" Many fans have panned this show since then simply because of this one amusing flaw that slipped through the fingers of the script editor – after all, we all know that William Hartnell and his successors are known only as the Doctor, never "Doctor Who" – but then again, until Tom Baker's era, the lead actor of the show was, without fail, credited as "Doctor Who." And aside from that, didn't anyone ever wonder how WOTAN knew of the Doctor's presence and knew what the initials of the TARDIS stand for? It seems that, depending on whether or not you want to attach some retroactive continuity to it (especially in light of the conclusion of 2011's *The Wedding Of River Song*), there may have been a lot more going on in *The War Machines* than anyone suspects...

SEASON 4: 1966-67
THE SMUGGLERS

The Doctor is infuriated when Ben and Polly burst into his TARDIS just before he takes off; they were merely trying to return Dodo's TARDIS key to the Doctor, but now find themselves on the coast in Cornwall in the 1600s. While the two were instrumental in helping the Doctor defeat the War Machines in 1966, they're utterly lost in their first time trip – which is not a good thing when they find themselves in the midst of pirates' search for a lost treasure, and the pirates' feud with contraband smugglers. The local church warden seems to know something about the whereabouts of the treasure, but he's killed not long after divulging this secret to the Doctor, who now becomes the pirates' target. It seems that everyone in this seemingly quiet seaside town is on the take somehow – but the time travelers simply want to get home.

William Hartnell . . . . The Doctor
Michael Craze . . . . Ben
Anneke Wills . . . . Polly
Jack Bingh . . . . Gaptooth
George A. Cooper . . . . Cherub
Terence de Marney . . . . Churchwarden
Michael Godfrey . . . . Pike
Elroy Josephs . . . . Jamaica
Paul Whitsun-Jones . . . . Squire
David Blake Kelly . . . . Jacob Kewper
Mike Lucas . . . . Tom
John Ringham . . . . Blake
Derek Ware . . . . .Spaniard

This story has been released on audio CD

written by Brian Hayles
directed by Julia Smith
no incidental music

Part 1 aired on September 10, 1966
Part 2 aired on September 17, 1966
Part 3 aired on September 24, 1966
Part 4 aired on October 1, 1966

MISSING: All four episodes of *The Smugglers* are missing from the BBC archives.

Not the greatest **Doctor Who** adventure ever to hit the air during William Hartnell's reign, *The Smugglers* is a surprisingly average tale from the pen of Brian Hayles, who had already given **Who** fans the incredibly imaginative *Celestial Toymaker* and would, in Patrick Troughton's era, introduce the Ice Warriors to the pantheon of all-time great **Doctor Who** monsters. But here, we get a very tame series of chases, double-crosses, fights, captures, and escapes, with hints of plot slipped in via dialogue.

Arguably the most engaging feature of *The Smugglers* is Ben and Polly's reactions to their first time trip, but little is made of this opportunity for developing those characters here; all too quickly, they're swept into a situation where their actions and dialogue could've been done and said by nearly any companion. Ben and Polly, as lively as they seem to be, are insert-random-placeholder-companion-here characters with little development (which may explain a lot about why they were shuffled back out of the TARDIS in the course of this same season, a decision apparently handed down from higher up in the BBC). That said, Michael Craze and Anneke Wills do the best they can here with a scarcity of actual character to work with – the fact that these characters have a following at all within **Doctor Who** fandom is really down to their efforts.

That context – of being Hartnell's penultimate story as the Doctor – is important in hindsight. After the thoroughly (almost jarringly) modern *War Machines, The Smugglers* probably lulled many a viewer into a false sense of security before the next story not only introduced the Cybermen, but stunned everybody with the first change of the Doctor's face. In that sense, *The Smugglers* is the last time that **Doctor Who** was the same show that the first generation of fans had been watching since 1963.

THE TENTH PLANET

The TARDIS arrives at a military base on the South Pole in 1986. The base is routinely tracking a spacecraft in orbit when odd things begin to occur. A trio of oddly-dressed people suddenly appears outside, emerging from a police box, and observatories (and the orbiting capsule) spot the approach of a planet which is identical in mass to Earth. A spaceship from that planet lands at the polar base, and cybernetically augmented humans – Cybermen – emerge to take control. Their world, Mondas, was thrown out of its orbit around the sun long ago, forcing its inhabitants to turn to cybernetics to preserve their species. Having succumbed to the machinery that was only intended to extend their lives, the Cybermen now face another kind of extinction. Mondas is a dying planet, and the Cybermen hope to colonize Earth for its resources, including converting the human population into more Cybermen. The Doctor seems to know about Mondas and its people already…but he also seems to have a premonition of something else, a momentous change that could render him helpless in the ensuing battle with the emotionless Cybermen.

William Hartnell . . . . The Doctor
Michael Craze . . . . Ben
Anneke Wills . . . . Polly
Callen Angelo . . . . Terry Cutler
Robert Beatty . . . . General Cutler
Glenn Beck . . . . Announcer
John Brandon . . . . Sergeant
Harry Brooks . . . . Krang / Talon
Earl Cameron . . . . Williams
Ellen Cullen . . . . Technician
David Dodinhead . . . . Barclay
Christopher Dunham . . . . Radar Technician
Nicholas Edwards . . . . Radar Technician
John Haines . . . . Cyberman
Peter Hawkins . . . . Cyberman voices
Dudley Jones . . . . Dyson
Sheila Knight . . . . Secretary
John Knott . . . . Cyberman

written by Kit Pedler, Pat Dunlap and Gerry Davis
directed by Derek Martinus
stock library music - see credits below

This story has been released on DVD

Part 1 aired on October 8, 1966
Part 2 aired on October 15, 1966
Part 3 aired on October 22, 1966
Part 4 aired on October 29, 1966

Christopher Matthews . . . . . . Radar Technician
Gregg Palmer . . . . Gern / Shav
Steve Plytas . . . . Wigner
Shane Shelton . . . . Tito
Roy Skelton . . . . Cyberman voices
Bruce Wells . . . . Cyberman
Alan White . . . . Schultz
Reg Whitehead . . . . Krail / Jarl

MISSING: Episode 4 of *The Tenth Planet* is missing from the BBC archives, although a copy of the all-important regeneration scene was retained.

STOCK MUSIC: "Blast Off" (Roger Roger and his Champes Elysees Orchestra), "Music For Technology" (Walter Stott), "Power Drill" (Douglas Gamley), "Space Adventure" (Martin Slavin), "Drama In Miniature Part 2" (John Denis), "Machine Room" (Douglas Gamley), "Drumdramatics No. 7" (Robert Farnon), "Drumdramatics No. 10" (Robert Farnon). A (now long out of print) 20-minute compact disc featuring these stock music pieces was released in 2000 by Ochre Records to coincide with BBC Video's VHS release of *The Tenth Planet.*

The final adventure of William Hartnell's Doctor packs quite a punch and stands up well. Now, yes, this is the one where the Cybermen are basically guys in body stockings with floodlights on their heads, and their voices are almost laughable at times. But other than the production values (and remember that this was top-of-the-line stuff in 1966) *Tenth Planet* is an exciting and tense slice of vintage **Doctor Who**.

One startling preview of things to come: the Doctor arrives out of nowhere just before things get hectic, with extensive foreknowledge of the situation. This is the sort of thing that Sylvester McCoy often did as the seventh incarnation of the Doctor toward the end of the original show's run. That element of the story is extremely intriguing, particularly in light of the foreknowledge that the Doctor also seems to have about his impending regeneration late in the story.

Another compelling reason to revisit *Tenth Planet* – perhaps even moreso than the debut of the Cybermen – is the regeneration. At the end of part four, almost without warning (as opposed to later years, when virtually everyone watching knew when the outgoing Doctor would hand the torch to his successor onscreeen), the Doctor rushes back to the TARDIS, weakened by the recent struggle. He falls to the floor and changes with no warning or explanation – try putting yourself in the shoes of the 1966 audience for that unexpected, game-changing surprise.

With the arrival of the Cybermen, and the startling change of the Doctor's appearance, *Tenth Planet* is one of those watershed stories that changes everything that came later. If there's a drawback to it, it's not one that the makers of the series could have done anything about: in what should be his magnificent swan song, William Hartnell's screen presence is reduced (and, for one of the four episodes, eliminated altogether) to accommodate the actor's advancing illness. Remember the scene in *The War Machines* where the Doctor implacably faces down the oncoming War Machine as everyone behind him – even well-armed soldiers – scurry for cover? His exit should have been something like that: defending Earth to the last. Sadly, and due to tragic circumstances beyond the cast and crew's control, it wasn't to be.

THE MOVIES: 1965-66
DR. WHO AND THE DALEKS

Well-meaning (but slightly bumbling) bachelor Ian Chesterton arrives at the doorstep of his girlfriend, Barbara, where he also meets her younger sister Susan and their father, an enigmatic inventor who calls himself Doctor Who. While Barbara is eager to go see a movie with Ian, Doctor Who is eager to show her suitor his proudest creation: a time machine in the form of a Police Box, which he calls Tardis. A skeptical Ian accidentally activates the controls of the machine, and when he next opens the door, he's astounded to find that Tardis has apparently arrived on another planet. Doctor Who, his daughters and Ian explore a nearby city, whose fantastic metallic design seems to be evidence of brilliant alien minds. At first they find no one in the city, but then they meet its inhabitants: armored metallic beings called Daleks. The Daleks introduce themselves as survivors of an atomic war, horribly mutated and forced to live in their metallic shells to survive; they also reveal that Doctor Who and the other time travelers are suffering from radiation poisoning. Susan, the youngest and healthiest of the four time travelers, is selected to "volunteer" for a mission to retrieve anti-radiation drugs from the Thals, the race of statuesque blond humanoids with whom the Daleks were once at war. While the remedy is given to the time travelers, the Daleks also keep a quantity for their own study, never having perfected a means to survive emerging from their life support machines. An invitation to discuss a truce with the Thals turns into a trap, and now Doctor Who and his fellow travelers must quickly decide which side has their sympathies, though witnessing the Daleks' murderous tendencies first-hand makes it an easy decision. What may prove harder, however, is convincing the pacifistic Thals to save themselves by resuming their war with the Daleks.

Peter Cushing . . . . Doctor Who
Roy Castle . . . . Ian
Jennie Linden . . . . Barbara
Roberta Tovey . . . . Susan
Yvonne Antrobus . . . . Dyoni
John Bown . . . . Antodus
Barrie Ingham . . . . Alydon
Bruno Castagnoli . . . . Dalek
Michael Coles . . . . Ganatus
Michael Dillon . . . . Dalek
Ken Garady . . . . Thal
Martin Grace . . . . Thal
Brian Hands . . . . Dalek
Nicholas Head . . . . Thal
Robert Jewell . . . . Dalek
Jane Lamb . . . . Thal
Kevin Manser . . . . Dalek
Eric McKay . . . . Dalek
Mark Petersen . . . . Elyon
Michael Lennox . . . . Thal
Len Saunders . . . . Dalek

This movie has been released on DVD

written by Milton Subotsky
based on the television serial by Terry Nation
directed by Gordon Flemyng
music by Malcolm Lockyer
electronic music by Barry Gray

Premiered on August 23, 1965

This movie's music is included on the Silva Screen "Dr. Who & The Daleks" / "Daleks: Invasion Earth 2150 A.D." CD.

Gerald Taylor . . . . Dalek
Virginia Tyler . . . . Thal
Geoffrey Toone . . . . Temmosus
Jack Waters . . . . Thal
Bruce Wells . . . . Thal
Garry Wyler . . . . Thal
Sharon Young . . . . Thal

NEW WHO CONNECTIONS: Before you dismiss the Cushing movies entirely from having any influence on the future of **Doctor Who** at all, think again — the colorful, taller, more menacing Daleks seen here were a key influence on the decision to radically remodel the Daleks in 2010's *Victory Of The Daleks*.

Dr. Who And The Daleks is a "condensed books" version of *The Daleks*, with a rapid-fire helping of *An Unearthly Child* thrown in for good measure, but in some ways that brevity and condensing of material works wonders for this movie. At some point in the 1990s, the realization hit me that one could jump from the end of part one of *An Unearthly Child* straight into the beginning of *The Daleks* with little indication that the former story's three episodes of cavemen had ever existed in between. So in that respect, and in the not-so-small matter of pacing, ***Dr. Who And The Daleks*** is a big improvement on the corresponding episodes of the original series.

Of course, there's the small matter that it runs completely counter to what little backstory had been established in the original series thus far. Doctor Who is certainly not the Doctor; Doctor Who is a doddering human inventor with two granddaughters, as opposed to an enigmatic alien explorer with one. In a move that almost certainly wouldn't happen today, the Doctor and the entire TARDIS crew were recast with names considered more bankable on the big screen. Just about the only things that didn't change, aside from the broad strokes of the story, were the TARDIS' police box exterior and the Daleks themselves (and even there, larger, more colorful Daleks were constructed for the movie, as opposed to the BBC's Dalek casings, which might not have withstood big-screen scrutiny). There's simply no way to retrofit this story into the series continuity proper.

But is that such a bad thing? By distancing itself from what little continuity there was to date, ***Dr. Who And The Daleks*** was a marvelously colorful, self-contained adventure with plenty of action, humor and a look that, for whatever ways the original series episodes may have been superior, the television version of **Doctor Who** simply couldn't achieve. In particular, the Daleks are shot in a variety of ways that the BBC's large studio cameras (which weren't unlike Daleks themselves, at least in terms of sheer physical bulk and clumsiness) simply couldn't photograph them. The new angles, especially those looking up at the Daleks from near the floor, work incredibly well in establishing them as a threat. (At the same time, for every visual step forward that the movie makes, there's a step back - the movie's producers somehow missed the small detail that the lights atop each Dalek's head denoted which Dalek was speaking, and had the lights wired to blink like turn signals instead; the voice actors charged with providing the Daleks' voices had to go back and re-record their dialogue in a decidedly un-Dalek-like robotic rhythm to match the footage that had already been shot with this flaw.)

DALEKS: INVASION EARTH 2150 A.D.

London beat cop Tom Campbell fails to stop a smash-and-grab robbery, knocked out by the burglars before there's even an alarm to respond to. He comes to and opens the door of the nearest police box, finding not police equipment but a vast, laboratory-like space before he loses consciousness again. When he awakens, an old man introduces himself as time traveler Doctor Who and informs Tom that the police box he stumbled into was a time machine that has now traveled to London in the year 2150. London is in ruins, with little human activity – and the time travelers soon find that the entire world has been overrun by Daleks. Susan and the Doctor's niece, Louise, are sheltered by desperate human resistance fighters, while Doctor Who and Tom are captured by the Daleks and taken aboard one of their spaceships. An escape attempt that seems a little too easy turns out to be a trap: the Doctor and Tom are selected to be turned into Dalek-controlled Robomen due to their intelligence. The conversion process is thwarted by the resistance cell, but Louise is knocked out while hiding on the ship; Tom stays on board, disguised as a Roboman, to protect her. Susan and Doctor Who separately make their way to an enormous mine at Bedfordshire, where the Daleks are using human slave labor to dig a shaft to the Earth's magnetic core – a task that they can't undertake themselves due to the magnetic forces. They plan to destroy that core and replace it with a means of controlling the Earth like a gigantic spaceship, enabling them to take the planet back to Dalek territory to be strip-mined, and any human survivors enslaved. The Doctor realizes what must be done to stop the Dalek plan, but it falls to Tom, the least experienced of the time travelers, to single-handedly rid the world of Dalek domination.

Peter Cushing	. . . .	Doctor Who
Bernard Cribbins	. . . .	Tom Campbell
Ray Brooks	. . . .	David
Andrew Keir	. . . .	Wyler
Roberta Tovey	. . . .	Susan
Jill Curzon	. . . .	Louise
Roger Avon	. . . .	Wells
Geoffrey Cheshire	. . . .	Roboman
Robert Jewell	. . . .	Leader Dalek Operator
Keith Marsh	. . . .	Conway
Philip Madoc	. . . .	Brockley
Steve Peters	. . . .	Leader Roboman
Eddie Powell	. . . .	Thompson
Godfrey Quigley	. . . .	Dortmun
Peter Reynolds	. . . .	Man on Bicycle
Bernard Spear	. . . .	Man with Carrier Bag
Sheila Steafel	. . . .	Young Woman

This movie has been released on DVD

written by Milton Subotsky
additional material by David Whitaker
based on the television serial by Terry Nation
directed by Gordon Flemyng
music by Bill McGuffie
electronic music by Barry Gray

Premiered on August 5, 1966

This movie's music is included on the Silva Screen "Dr. Who & The Daleks" / "Daleks: Invasion Earth 2150 A.D." CD.

Eileen Way	. . . .	Old Woman
Kenneth Watson	. . . .	Craddock
John Wreford	. . . .	Robber

CLASSIC WHO CONNECTIONS: Several actors in this film have also appeared in the television series (in very different roles, naturally): **Eileen Way** appeared in *An Unearthly Child* (1963), while the late **Philip Madoc** made multiple appearances (*The Krotons, The War Games, The Brain Of Morbius, The Power Of Kroll* and even the Big Finish audio plays *Master* and *Return Of The Krotons*). **Geoffrey Cheshire** appeared in *The Time Meddler* (1965) and *The Daleks' Masterplan* (1965-66), while **Kenneth Watson** guest starred in *The Wheel In Space* (1968). **Roger Avon** also appeared in *The Daleks' Masterplan* and *The Crusade* (1965). The only Dalek operator credited, **Robert Jewell**, could also be found inside Dalek casings from their very first TV appearance through their final cameo appearance in the show's black-and-white years (*The War Games*, 1969).

NEW WHO CONNECTIONS: Doctor Who says that his time-and-space machine, Tardis, can take its occupants to "any time, on any planet, *in any universe,*" a line of dialogue inadvertently leaving the door open – if any writers are bold enough to step through it – to actually connect the two Cushing films to the TV series by way of the old "parallel universe" standby. Tom should probably steer clear of Donna's grandfather, Wilfred Mott, since both TARDIS travelers are played by comedian **Bernard Cribbins**. The Dalek units of time measurement, rels, have been mentioned in many a Dalek episode since the series' revival, but the first use of rels was in this movie.

With the lessons of **Dr. Who And The Daleks** learned, **Daleks: Invasion Earth 2150 A.D.** is a vast improvement. The Daleks sound and act more like the Daleks viewers were familiar with from TV, and they actually appear more formidable in many scenes here by the simple virtue that a movie budget could afford to make more Dalek casings than the BBC ever could. The Daleks here appear in *swarms*, making for a fairly intimidating sight in some scenes, and their livery is a bit less ridiculously colorful; most of the Dalek patrols bear the silver-and-blue colors of their television counterparts (as revealed by behind-the-scenes photos; naturally this color scheme couldn't really be seen in black & white). The quotient of action and violence is upped considerably, and the gritty deserted-future-London setting is a bit easier to swallow than the more fantastic environs of the first movie.

Sadly, for every element that this movie gets right, it also gets another thing wrong. The patent leather Roboman suits don't do anyone any favors, and the helmets and their faceplates are even worse, embarrassingly misaligned in many (if not *most*) scenes. It would perhaps be even sillier if every Roboman suit was obviously tailored to the wearer, but somewhere there must be some middle ground between bespoke tailoring and crumpled-and-dumpy. There's a scene of wordless, purely physical comedy, beautifully played by Bernard Cribbins, where the ill-fitting outfits are just a little bit distracting.

And then there's the far-too-quick resolution of the story: in a control room fitted with wheel valves, toggle switches and a radio-studio-style condenser microphone (why would Daleks have *any of these things* installed on their own ship, especially when they're so badly suited to Dalek appendages?), **Doctor Who** grabs the microphone and places a non-countermandable order for all Robomen to turn on their Dalek masters, creating a diversion. As unstoppable and all-conquering as the Daleks have been shown to be in the rest of the film, this is simply silly. To be sure, it's a plot point copied from the original TV version of the same story (see page 31), but the big honking radio microphone makes it inadvertently funny. Also unintentionally hilarious is the death of some of the Daleks as they're drawn to their doom by the magnetic forces beneath Earth's crust. There are impressive Dalek exits (the Dalek that's crushed by an unseen force) and chuckle-inducing ones (the ones that power-dive the mineshaft, breaking off every possible appendage en route).

At only 80 minutes, though it's possible that ***Daleks: Invasion Earth 2150 A.D.*** does the audience a favor by dispensing with some of the padding present in the six 25-minute episodes of *The Dalek Invasion Of Earth*. And it's also possible that the second and final Cushing movie served another useful purpose: premiering in the precise center of the "off-season" between the third and fourth seasons of the TV series, this movie debuted almost exactly three months before the television Doctor's first regeneration. Peter Cushing's portrayal of – admittedly – another time traveler known as Doctor Who may have helped to seed the idea that the TARDIS could be piloted by someone other than William Hartnell. It was an idea that audiences would have to get their heads around just a few months after the premiere of the second film.

The Second Doctor
(Patrick Troughton: 1966-69)

After weeks of persuasive offers from the BBC, Patrick Troughton took over the lead role of **Doctor Who** mere weeks into the series' fourth season on the air. The public was mystified and intrigued, as even TARDIS travelers Ben and Polly didn't know what to make of the Doctor's transformation. But the Doctor didn't leave much time to ponder the issue: he was plunged into a sinister Dalek plot immediately after the change, and quickly made it clear that, even with a slightly different personality, he had the same mind as his predecessor, if not necessarily the same personality. The following adventure, *The Highlanders*, had three major distinctions: the introduction of Scotsman Jamie McCrimmon (Frazer Hines), one of the longest-serving companions in the series' history (he stayed until Troughton's final episode); and the last story for many years to meet the historical mandate that Sydney Newman had originally devised. The third, and most dubious, distinction was that the master tapes of *The Highlanders* were erased mere months after its broadcast premiere: the first **Doctor Who** episodes to be destroyed, lost from the BBC's archives permanently. The episodes, like so many others from Troughton's era, have never been recovered.

As the fourth season carried on, it was clear that the scales had now been tipped solidly in the direction of science fiction, modern-day thrillers, and the occasional heavily-embellished trip into Earth's history - usually only to discover that aliens had been influencing humans for decades and centuries. The Cybermen returned immediately in *The Moonbase*, but with relatively sleek redesigned costumes and a much more futuristic setting. Troughton quickly cemented his portrayal of the Doctor as a genius who *knew* full well that he was a genius, and though this new Doctor was generally more amiable than Hartnell's portrayal, he was fully capable of exploding into temperamental rants, belittling those who insulted his intelligence. And behind it all was the occasional feeling that the Doctor was, if not actively scheming, then gently manipulating events to his favor - all the while pretending to be little more than a buffoon.

At the end of the season, Ben and Polly left the Doctor and Jamie when events in *The Faceless Ones* gave them the opportunity to return to modern-day Britain, but the following story, *The Evil Of The Daleks*, introduced a new companion in Victoria Waterfield (Deborah Watling), the daughter of a 19th century scientist whose primitive time travel experiments brought him into contact with the Daleks. As had been the case with their very first story, *The Evil Of The Daleks* was intended to be the end of the road for Terry Nation's metallic creations - they were a source of great nostalgia, but the current team of producer Innes Lloyd and script editor Gerry Davis favored the continuing use of the Cybermen, not least of which was because a fee had to be paid to Nation for any use of the Daleks; Davis had co-created the Cybermen while in the employ of the BBC, and the series therefore had free use of them without any pesky royalty payments.

With the team of the second Doctor, Jamie and Victoria, **Doctor Who** entered what many fans felt was its golden age; new villains were introduced which would recur through many future stories and later Doctors: the Ice Warriors, the Yeti, and more appearances by the all-conquering Cybermen. It was during this period also that **Doctor Who** became a target of TV violence watchdogs, complaining about classic horror-movie-inspired elements and even what passed for gore in the time (a scene from the 1967 classic *Tomb Of The Cybermen* was much criticized for the destruction and apparent disembowelment of a Cybermen, represented not by blood, but by shaving cream and foam). These early concerns over **Doctor Who's** increasingly adult direction seemed to blow over quickly - the show was now more popular than ever before, especially with children.

1968's *The Web Of Fear* was a sequel to the previous year's *The Abominable Snowmen*, bringing back that story's robotic Yeti in an even more frightening form. This story introduced a new character, Colonel Lethbridge-Stewart, played by Nicholas Courtney (who only got the role in a pinch when another actor had to back out at the last minute). Unsure of the Doctor's origins or motivations, Lethbridge-Stewart quickly came to trust the quirky scientist during a Yeti siege of London's Underground. What few people realized was that this character's appearance planted a seed for the show's future. The cost of the Doctor's more futuristic travels were becoming prohibitively expensive, and plans were being made for a yet-undecided story device that would limit the TARDIS's traveling range to modern-day Britain. Locations were plentiful and convincing, while studio-bound spaceships and alien worlds were difficult to design and build, and sometimes didn't stand up to scrutiny.

Victoria left the TARDIS crew in the following story, *Fury From The Deep*, another episode which raised eyebrows for some of its scarier scenes. In the following story, closing **Doctor Who**'s landmark fifth year on the air, Wendy Padbury joined the cast as Zoe, a brilliant but naive mathematician from *The Wheel In Space* - a space station where the Doctor and Jamie thwarted a Cyberman invasion with her help.

As the sixth season began, Patrick Troughton made it clear that three years were enough for him in the role of the Doctor. New producer Derrick Sherwin continued making plans for the future, including a return of Lethbridge-Stewart, now promoted to Brigadier and placed in charge of the top-secret United Nations Intelligence Taskforce (UNIT), a military force devoted to repelling alien invasions from space and paranormal threats from the Earth itself. That story, *The Invasion*, pitted the Doctor and his friends, with UNIT's help, against yet another Cyberman incursion. *The Invasion* laid the groundwork for much of the reign of Troughton's successor.

But just making it to the end of the sixth season proved to be a major challenge. Two major scripts had fallen through, and new script editor Terrance Dicks teamed up with writer Malcolm Hulke to create a massive ten-week epic, *The War Games*, to fill the resulting gap. Not completely plotted out from the beginning, *The War Games* certainly plodded in the middle, until episode eight, in which the Doctor admitted that he would have to call his home planet for help. With little of the Doctor's origins explored, the ninth and tenth episodes of *The War Games* added thick layers of new mythology to the series: the Doctor was a Time Lord, a member of a race devoted to observing in history - but never interfering. The Doctor's escapades in time and space made him a criminal on his own world, as if the theft of his TARDIS didn't already merit that status, and he was held accountable by the Time Lords.

Found guilty of meddling in the web of history, the Doctor was sentenced to exile on Earth, a plot device fulfilling Derrick Sherwin's budget-mandated directive to strand the series in modern-day England. (Sherwin later revealed that the Doctor's exile to Earth and his collaboration with / employment by UNIT would have happened *even if Troughton had been persuaded to stay with the show*, but the condition the actor demanded for his continued services – a more forgiving shooting schedule with fewer episodes per year – was not approved until after his departure.) Jamie and Zoe were returned to their points of origin in space and time, their minds wiped of all but their first adventures with the Doctor. And before being sent to Earth, the Doctor was also sentenced to a forced change of appearance. Patrick Troughton's seminal reign as the Doctor was officially over, and the way was paved for the show to be produced less expensively - if the BBC's changeover to all-color programming in January 1970 didn't negate the savings. And in any event, **Doctor Who**'s return in 1970 was far from certain.

SEASON 4 CONTINUED
THE POWER OF THE DALEKS

The Doctor recovers from his first regeneration quickly, only to find himself trying to reassure Ben and Polly that the diminutive person who now shares the TARDIS with them is, in fact, their time-traveling companion. The TARDIS takes them from the South Pole to the planet Vulcan in the distant future, where an Earth expedition has made a disturbing discovery in the planet's mercury pools – deactivated, but perfectly preserved, Daleks. The chief scientist of the human colony on Vulcan reactivates the Daleks, who promptly vow obedience and subservience…but even after a traumatic regeneration, the Doctor doesn't believe this for a second. But someone in the colony may know the Daleks' true colors – and may be using them to achieve a sinister objective anyway.

Patrick Troughton . . . . The Doctor
Michael Craze . . . . Ben
Anneke Wills . . . . Polly
Bernard Archard . . . . Bragen
Peter Bathurst . . . . Hensell
Pamela Ann Davy . . . . Janley
Peter Forbes-Robertson . . . . Guard
Peter Hawkins . . . . Dalek voice
Nicholas Hawtrey . . . . Quinn
Robert James . . . . Lesterson
Robert Jewell . . . . Dalek
Richard Kane . . . . Valmar
Edward Kelsey . . . . Resno
Martin King . . . . Examiner
Robert Luckham . . . . Guard
Kevin Manser . . . . Dalek

This story has been released on audio CD

written by David Whitaker
directed by Christopher Barry
music by Tristram Cary

Part 1 aired on November 5, 1966
Part 2 aired on November 12, 1966
Part 3 aired on November 19, 1966
Part 4 aired on November 26, 1966
Part 5 aired on December 3, 1966
Part 6 aired on December 10, 1966

John Scott Martin . . . . Dalek
Robert Russell . . . . Guard
Steven Scott . . . . Kebble
Gerald Taylor . . . . Dalek

MISSING: All six episodes of *The Power Of The Daleks* are missing from the BBC archives.

NEW WHO CONNECTIONS: The Daleks again pretended to be servants of humanity in 2010's *Victory Of The Daleks* – a story which saw a massive makeover not for the Doctor, but for his worst enemies.

Oh, how I wish more than a few scant clips of this six-parter existed; it can now be experienced only in audio form instead. But the most compelling conflict of the entire story is undoubtedly that between the Doctor and his companions, who are a little bit skeptical after his first change of body. And considering that this was the first time the Doctor had changed his appearance in the then-short history of the show, this was played to maximum effect for the shocked audience as well.

In this era of the show, it was wise – no, almost necessary – to include the Daleks to ensure that the audience wouldn't desert the show in droves, especially as Dalekmania was still alive and well, even if recent Hartnell era missteps such as *The Gunfighters* had diminished the luster of the series that spawned them. And what an interesting and atypical appearance for the Daleks! They actually exercise something not unlike cunning and guile in this story, qualities which would gradually be excised from the most popular of the Doctor's villains in the 1970s and '80s (though many elements of the story would be unearthed for 2010's *Victory Of The Daleks*). The reuse of Tristram Cary's memorable music from their first appearance in the show was an inspired touch, coming dangerously close to cementing a specific musical theme for the Daleks.

It's an intriguing story overall, one which stands up well as a purely auditory experience…but given its pivotal place in **Doctor Who** history, I could still harbor a few dreams of the entire video component being found intact somewhere overseas.

SHORT HOPS

…in which the author is torn about the recent fan "remake" of *Power Of The Daleks*.

As you've already gathered from the little "missing" bar beneath the *Power Of The Daleks* entry, we're running low on *Power* and have been for a very long time. As with many other '60s stories, *Power Of The Daleks* hasn't been seen since its original airdate. The first post-regeneration story is AWOL.

In 2012, a fan group known for mounting stage productions recreating lost classic episodes set out to bring its unique approach to video. Recasting and significantly rewriting David Whitaker's original scripts (perhaps most noticeably by relocating the action from the planet Vulcan — **Star Trek** fans can breathe a sigh of relief — to an isolated outpost in the Falkland Islands), this new version of *Power* does away with Ben, Polly, any mention of regeneration, and reformats the story to present us with a previously lost tale of the Doctor vs. the Daleks. Only this time the Daleks look like Russell T. Davies-era Daleks, and the Doctor looks like writer and actor Nick Scovell. More modern styles of mounting the production are in play — it's shot in widescreen, the language is more modern, characters have cell phones. It's not an attempt to recreate *Power Of The Daleks* so much as it is an attempt to reinterpret it by the standards of modern **Who**. Or, to put it in context, the fan remount of *Power* is to the original 1966 story what **West Side Story** is to Shakespeare's <u>Romeo & Juliet</u>, or what **Forbidden Planet** is to <u>The Tempest</u>.

It's an interesting notion, and a bold experiment, just one that I'm not sure everyone's ready for. At a time when the compact disc was starting to be seen as past its shelf life as a viable commercial medium, the BBC Radio Collection CDs of meticulously-cleaned-up audio recordings of missing **Doctor Who** stories were selling well enough to justify their continued existence, because the loyal audience *craved* any original source material they could get their hands on. But will they gravitate toward projects like this?

To be fair, it's not a new debate: ask any of the fan groups who have built elaborate sets and costumes in the pursuit of producing "new adventures" for Captain Kirk and crew. They operate under the same basic idea: Kirk, Spock, and company are classic characters, much like Shakespeare's timeless characters; the basic character traits endure and new actors will bring new nuances to their interpretations. But it could also be argued that **Doctor Who** is even more intimately tied into the lead actors who have played the Doctor than **Star Trek** is to its actors. After all, there have already been several **Star Treks** with completely different casts and characters. Whereas *Power Of The Daleks* is the beginning of the Troughton era of **Doctor Who**, which is something that gives it considerable historic weight — a weight that may well be best summed up in terms of "accept no substitutes."

With so many options for experiencing the story, from "as the writers, director, cast and producers intended" to the "DIY" end of the spectrum, *Power Of The Daleks* may be the one classic story that's more open to interpretation than any other. If that sparks interest in the original material, however — or, in a best case scenario, sparks a more intense search for the originals that eventually leads to a find that allows us to compare the fan creations to the real episodes — it can't be a bad thing.

THE HIGHLANDERS

The TARDIS arrives in Scotland, 1745, plunging the Doctor, Ben and Polly into the aftermath of the battle of Culloden. They encounter some fleeing Scots who are trying to escape the Redcoats with their injured Laird in tow. The Doctor tends to the Laird's injuries, despite the suspicions of the others. However, his aid comes too late – the entire group is captured by English soldiers. Polly befriends a woman named Kirsty, and they manage to stay on dry land while the men are hauled off to a ship. Englishman Trask plans to take the captives to be sold into slave labor, including Ben and piper Jamie McCrimmon. But when Polly is fighting to protect herself in an era which isn't even remotely emancipated for women, and Ben is sentenced to death as an object lesson to keep his fellow prisoners in line, where is the Doctor?

Patrick Troughton . . . . The Doctor
Michael Craze . . . . Ben
Anneke Wills . . . . Polly
Frazer Hines . . . . Jamie McCrimmon
Sydney Arnold . . . . Perkins
Donald Bisset . . . . Colin McLaren
Tom Bowman . . . . Sentry
Barbara Bruce . . . . Mollie
Dallas Cavell . . . . Trask
Peter Diamond . . . . Sailor
Andrew Downie . . . . MacKay
William Dysart . . . . Alexander
Michael Elwyn . . . . Ffinch

This story has been released on audio CD

written by Gerry Davis and Elwyn Jones
directed by Hugh David
stock library music - see credits below

Part 1 aired on December 17, 1966
Part 2 aired on December 24, 1966
Part 3 aired on December 31, 1966
Part 4 aired on January 7, 1967

David Garth . . . . Gray
Hannah Gordon . . . . Kristy
Guy Middleton . . . . Attwood
Peter Welch . . . . Sergeant

MISSING: All four episodes of *The Highlanders* are missing from the BBC archives.

NEW WHO CONNECTIONS: When the tenth Doctor and Rose visit Scotland in *Tooth And Claw* (2006), the Doctor uses Jamie's full name – James Robert McCrimmon – as his alias.

STOCK MUSIC: "Pibroch" (traditional, performed by Seamus MacNeill)

"Where is the Doctor?" is a good question. The Doctor appears in what seem to be only fleeting moments, and even those moments are a bit confusing, as he disguises himself as a German doctor, a serving wench, and even an English soldier. Though it would be another four years before the concept of post-regenerative amnesia and confusion would be introduced (when Patrick Troughton handed the role of the Doctor over to Jon Pertwee), maybe the Doctor's antics here can be attributed to the recent trauma of his first regeneration. It's as good an explanation as any, to be honest.

On the other hand, the Doctor's odd mental state gives Michael Craze and Anneke Wills the chance to shine as Ben and Polly, and it also allows time for Frazer Hines to establish himself as Jamie. When *The Highlanders* was originally filmed, it was unknown whether Jamie would be joining the TARDIS crew, though apparently that decision was made by someone in the production staff over the course of making the four episodes. In the second Doctor's sophomore adventure, Jamie becomes a regular, staying with the Doctor until Troughton's final story (and returning in both *The Five Doctors* and *The Two Doctors*). Jamie's introduction in this story is more a function of the story than one expects after seeing some of the late '70s and '80s serials, in which the incoming companion can be spotted from a mile off.

The Highlanders has been lost in its filmed form for decades, and is available as one of the audio releases in the BBC Radio Collection. There aren't even very many surviving photos from this four-parter, making it all the more mysterious. As it introduces the beloved Jamie McCrimmon to the series, *The Highlanders* continues this season's gradual process of rewriting the DNA of **Doctor Who**, but as a purely historical story with the time travelers as the only science fiction element, it may not appeal to everyone.

THE UNDERWATER MENACE

Jamie's first trip in the TARDIS is anything but uneventful, as the timeship brings the Doctor and friends to a volcanic outcropping in the middle of an ocean on Earth. The time travelers are quickly captured taken to an underground city, which they soon realize is Atlantis. The somewhat backward natives seem friendly enough, but they also seem intent on sacrificing the newcomers to the patron goddess of their island. Salvation comes from an unlikely source – a scientist called Zaroff rescues them, but then reveals his plan to cause the Earth to explode by draining the world's oceans into a shaft leading straight to the planet's molten core. Zaroff has also been performing horrific experiments to turn the locals into an enslaved population of Fish People. Now on the run from both Zaroff and the Atlanteans, the Doctor and his friends realize that their only hope of escape – and of stopping Zaroff's mad scheme – may lie with liberating the Fish People. But when Zaroff is so intent on destroying the world, can anything *really* be a deterrent to his plan?

Patrick Troughton	The Doctor
Michael Craze	Ben
Anneke Wills	Polly
Frazer Hines	Jamie McCrimmon
Paul Anil	Jacko
Graham Ashley	Overseer
Bill Burridge	Executioner Priest
Joseph Furst	Professor Zaroff
Catherine Howe	Ara
Colin Jeavons	Damon
Noel Johnson	Thous
Jimmy Mack	Refugee Priest
P.G. Stephens	Sean

This story is due to be released on DVD

written by Geoffrey Orme
directed by Julia Smith
music by Dudley Simpson

Part 1 aired on January 14, 1967
Part 2 aired on January 21, 1967
Part 3 aired on January 28, 1967
Part 4 aired on February 4, 1967

Peter Stephens	Lolem
Gerald Taylor	Damon's Assistant Tom
Watson	Ramo
Roma Woodnutt	Nola

MISSING: Episodes 1 and 4 of *The Underwater Menace* are missing from the BBC archives.

NEW WHO CONNECTIONS: While the Doctor wasn't mad about Zaroff's mad idea to drain the oceans of the Earth into the core of the planet, he was much more *sympatico* with the idea of draining at least the Thames River into the Earth's core to destroy the emerging children of the Empress of Racnoss in 2006's *The Runaway Bride*. The Jon Pertwee story *The Time Monster* offers a completely different story of the destruction of Atlantis.

If *The Underwater Menace* isn't a shoo-in for the low point of the Troughton era, it's at the very least a strong contender. Despite the shock change of the regeneration, the audience gradually took the new Doctor on board following his unprecedented change of features and personality in *The Tenth Planet*, but after watching the reconstructed edition of this mostly-lost four-parter, and then listening to the BBC Radio Collection narrated audio CD of the same story for clarification, one wonders if more viewers didn't defect in the wake of Hartnell's departure than many histories of **Doctor Who** would lead us to believe.

Not to put too fine a point on it, but *The Underwater Menace* is just plain silly - we're talking **Scooby Doo** silly. Part of this is due to the fact that the production team, still trying to find their footing after the change of lead actor, hadn't really nailed down what they wanted the second Doctor to be. In this story he's still doing slapstick costume gags, using his recorder to temporarily disable his enemies (!), and generally being more comical than dramatic. His adversary for this story is the wacky, over-the-top Professor Zaroff, whose vaguely Teutonic accent appears and disappears almost at random while he's hatching wildly implausible schemes to destroy the Earth (for reasons that are never really adequately explained), and making grand proclamations - example: *"Nothing in ze world can stop me now!"* - straight into the camera.

And then there's episode 3's trippy interlude with the Fish People "swimming" under "water". It's a pity that this story isn't intact, but by God, if only one episode could survive, I'm glad it was the third one. If the whole thing was still in existence, that's one **Doctor Who** adventure that I'd want to get Joel, Crow T. Robot and Tom Servo on, *stat*. There have been moments of intentional comedy gold in **Doctor Who** both old and new, but I'm not sure I've ever laughed quite as hard at any of the Time Lord's travels as I did here.

The Doctor's newly-crowded TARDIS crew doesn't fare much better here; Jamie gets some action scenes in, but there's little hint of the fan favorite that the character will shortly become. This may well be Polly's worst outing during her brief stint on the show, with the character used as nothing more than a screaming damsel waiting to be rescued.

It's probably better that *The Underwater Menace* is one of the stories that has sunk (sorry, couldn't resist it) into hazy still-photos-and-audio memory (so of course, perversely, the missing episode two is one of the most recent "lost episodes" recovered).

THE MOONBASE

The TARDIS lands on the surface of the moon in the year 2070, and the Doctor provides Ben, Polly and Jamie with pressure suits so they can explore outside the TARDIS. They spot a massive lunar base in the distance, but when Jamie damages his space suit, reaching the base becomes a matter of urgency. Inside the base, the Doctor and his friends are shocked to find that Jamie won't be alone in the sick bay – a plague is sweeping through the moonbase's population seemingly at random, leaving those it strikes comatose. Worse yet, even the comatose patients have been disappearing without a trace, leaving the base and its gigantic Gravitron, which controls the tides and governs Earth's weather, dangerously short-staffed. The Doctor tries to find out what disease is slowly claiming the moonbase's crew, only to find that the base has been deliberately infected by the Cybermen, who intend to take control of the base and use it as a staging area for an invasion of Earth.

Patrick Troughton . . . . The Doctor
Michael Craze . . . . Ben
Anneke Wills . . . . Polly
Frazer Hines . . . . Jamie McCrimmon
Barry Ashton . . . . Crewmember
Patrick Barr . . . . Hobson
Derek Calder . . . . Crewmember
Arnold Chazen . . . . Crewmember
John Clifford . . . . Cyberman
Keith Goodman . . . . Cyberman
Peter Greene . . . . Cyberman
Peter Hawkins . . . . Cyberman voice

This story has been released on DVD

written by Kit Pedler
directed by Morris Barry
stock library music - see credits below

Part 1 aired on February 11, 1967
Part 2 aired on February 18, 1967
Part 3 aired on February 25, 1967
Part 4 aired on March 4, 1967

Mark Heath	. . . .	Ralph
Ronald Lee	. . . .	Cyberman
Andre Maranne	. . . .	Benoit
Leon Maybank	. . . .	Crewmember
Denis McCarthy	. . . .	Controller Rinberg's voice
Barry Noble	. . . .	Cyberman
Victor Pemberton	. . . .	Crewmember
Edward Phillips	. . . .	Crewmember
Ron Pinnell	. . . .	Crewmember
John Rolfe	. . . .	Sam

Episodes 2 and 3 of *The Moonbase* appear in the *Lost In Time* DVD set.

Alan Rowe	. . . .	Dr. Evans / Space Control voice
Robin Scott	. . . .	Crewmember
Alan Wells	. . . .	Crewmember
Reg Whitehead	. . . .	Cyberman
Sonnie Willis	. . . .	Cyberman
John Wills	. . . .	Cyberman
Michael Wolf	. . . .	Nils

MISSING: Episodes 1 and 4 of *The Moonbase* are missing from the BBC archives.

NEW WHO CONNECTIONS: The electronic, monotone voices of the new series Cybermen are directly evolved from the Cybermen voices of this story (which, like their outward appearance, is drastically different from their first appearance). Voice artist Peter Hawkins created this voice with a vibrating metal palate held in his mouth while performing the Cybermen's lines in post-production; these days it's done with digital post-production tricks... and probably less of a metallic aftertaste.

BEHIND THE SCENES: Actor **Victor Pemberton** would also contribute to the series as a writer in the following season, penning *Fury From The Deep*, the story which introduced the sonic screwdriver.

STOCK MUSIC: "Musique Electronique: Sabre Dance" (Eric Siday), "Electronic Sound Pictures" (Desmond Briscoe), "Group Shapes" (Desmond Briscoe), "Space Adventure" (Martin Slavin), "Moonscape" (Eric Siday), "Musique Electronique: Anaesthesia" (Eric Siday), "Suspended Animation" (Eric Siday), "Musique Electronique: Hypnosis" (Eric Siday), "Musique Electronique: Conflict No. 1" (Eric Siday). The use of Martin Slavin's "Space Adventure" pieces in both *The Moonbase* and *The Tenth Planet* established it as an unofficial "theme tune" for the Cybermen. Desmond Briscoe was a founding member of the BBC Raidophonic Workshop, but contributed pieces to stock music libraries both prior to and (under various pseudonyms) during his association with the BBC.

Though not perfect by any stretch, *The Moonbase* is a standout adventure for the new Doctor, and it's a reintroduction for the improved Cyberman as well. Fresh from their first outing in *The Tenth Planet*, the Cybermen now look metallic (and sound like it too, thanks to a completely different voice treatment), silver-spray-painted boots notwithstanding. Due to the unfortunate 1970s purging of the BBC archives, parts 2 and 4 are all that remain of *The Moonbase* (available on the Troughton portion of the *Lost In Time* DVD set); the other parts are available in audio form.

It's a pity, because *The Moonbase* is, by the standards and budget of the time, quite the science fiction spectacular. For a BBC budget of the mid-1960s, the lunar weightlessness effect is done rather well (though the slide-whistle sound effects accompanying those scenes do much to rob them of their credibility). The sets, and the Gravitron setpiece, are impressive in their scope, and the new Cyberman design does much to make them a much more credible threat than their appearance in *Tenth Planet* did.

The character of Jamie, in only his second adventure aboard the TARDIS, winds up in a hospital bed, thrashing around deliriously and believing a Cyberman he sees to be the equivalent of the grim reaper in his clan's lore. Polly, in the meantime, isn't helped much by this story, as she is seen to scream at the merest glimpse of a Cyberman (and yet she had unflinchingly helped to fight them at the South Pole base just weeks before). Ben is shuffled into the background to make way for the large number of incidental characters on the moonbase.

The real star here, however, is the Doctor. In a far, far cry from his goofy, disguise-assuming persona from *The Highlanders*, the Doctor here offers his famous quote, "There are corners of the universe that have bred the most horrible things. They must be fought." Though it seems like an innocuous enough statement on the surface, *this marks a huge shift in the portrayal of the Doctor, and indeed in the rest of the entire series.* No longer an aimless, passive wanderer whose companions often get him into situations that he has to react to and resolve, the Doctor now seems to be actively seeking out wrongs to right and battles to fight. It could be argued that this creates a through-line that takes you straight through the McCoy era and into the post-TV novels of the 1990s, where this almost vigilante-like approach to the Doctor's wanderings is resolved to a certain extent, but more importantly, it serves as a clear notice of what Patrick Troughton's Doctor is all about.

What remains of *The Moonbase* visually is a tantalizing glimpse of an era of **Doctor Who** that is sadly incomplete in the archives. That it's an interesting and exciting story, even stripped of the visuals, certainly doesn't hurt it.

THE MACRA TERROR

In the future, the Doctor, Jamie, Ben and Polly arrive at a human colony, whose people find them just as they catch up with a refugee named Medok. Medok is treated like a criminal, and even as the colonists show the time travelers their miraculous machines, Medok warns of creatures that stalk the colony. The Doctor later sets him free, much to the consternation of the colony's leaders. He follows Medok to a construction site outside the colony, where he discovers enormous, crab-like creatures called Macra. As the Doctor's friends sleep, a hypnotic voice extolls the virtues of obeying the colony rules; when they awaken, Ben betrays the Doctor to the colony authorities. Polly flees and Ben pursues her, but once they catch a glimpse of the Macra, even Ben can no longer deny that this colony is under the control of aliens. Jamie escapes into a shaft where the colonists mine a poisonous gas that none of them can breathe – but the Macra can breathe it, and they've seized control of the colonists' minds to ensure that their supply of gas continues. But the Doctor can convince the innocent colonists of none of this.

Patrick Troughton	. . . .	The Doctor
Michael Craze	. . . .	Ben
Anneke Wills	. . . .	Polly
Frazer Hines	. . . .	Jamie McCrimmon
Graham Armitage	. . . .	Barney
Richard Beale	. . . .	Broadcast voice
Sandra Bryant	. . . .	Chicki
Ralph Carrigan	. . . .	Cheerleader
John Caesar	. . . .	Guard
Steve Emerson	. . . .	Guard
Jane Enshawe	. . . .	Sunnae
Ian Fairburn	. . . .	Questa
Anthony Gardner	. . . .	Alvis
Denis Goacher	. . . .	Control voice
John Harvey	. . . .	Official
Nina Huby	. . . .	Girl
Peter Jeffrey	. . . .	Pilot
Robert Jewell	. . . .	Macra
Roger Jerome	. . . .	Cheerleader

This story has been released on audio CD

written by Ian Stuart Black
directed by John Davies
music by Dudley Simpson

Part 1 aired on March 11, 1967
Part 2 aired on March 18, 1967
Part 3 aired on March 25, 1967
Part 4 aired on April 1, 1967

Karol Keyes	. . . .	Chicki
Gertan Klauber	. . . .	Ola
Maureen Lane	. . . .	Majorette
Graham Leaman	. . . .	Controller
Terence Lodge	. . . .	Medok
Paul Phillips	. . . .	Scientist
Danny Rae	. . . .	Guard
Linda Reynolds	. . . .	Pilot's secretary
Terry Wright	. . . .	Cheerleader

MISSING: All four episodes of *The Macra Terror* are missing from the BBC archives.

NEW WHO CONNECTIONS: The tenth Doctor encountered a less-evolved version of the Macra, skulking in the ground-hugging clouds of pollution on New Earth in *Gridlock* (2007).

Yet another Troughton-era episode lost to the ravages of (1) time, and (2) the purge at the BBC archives, *The Macra Terror* gained slightly more interest for many fans in hindsight due to the bizarre reappearance of the Macra in 2007's new series episode *Gridlock*. Did the new episode mesh with how the Macra had appeared before, especially with the tenth Doctor's claim that they had devolved?

Truth be told, they're not really used any differently as villains here as they are in *Gridlock* – in both cases, they're all but incidental to the plot, the engine that keeps the human guest characters acting strangely. (How strangely, you ask? Just wait until you get a load of the "cheerleading" session in episode 4!) Though they seem to be forcing the humans to do their bidding here in their first appearance, what I wasn't totally clear on by the end of the story was how this came about. If anything, the Macra in *Gridlock* are more proactive – they're still lurking down in the noxious gases, sure, but once you're down there with them, they'll do you some damage. In *The Macra Terror*, our heroes practically have to walk into pincer range to actually be in danger. How these critters took over a whole human colony without winding up as the prize catch in the 3,987th season of **The Deadliest Catch** is a bit baffling, frankly.

A little more refreshing is that Ben gets brainwashed and turns his back on the Doctor and the others; setting up a nice contrast, the simpler (and still new to the TARDIS) Jamie doesn't fall for the subliminal reprogramming at all; once he realizes on a gut level that something's wrong with the colonists, Jamie throws his lot in with the Doctor regardless of the risks, and even giant crabs can't dissuade him. Character development was haphazard in these days of the series, but with hindsight, one can see why the Doctor valued Jamie's company so much in later stories, even after Ben and Polly's departure.

SHORT HOPS

...in which the author thanks the reconstruction makers.

In the course of my project to watch or listen to all of classic **Doctor Who**, there were some enormous potholes to overcome, not the least of which is that a lot of this era of the show simply doesn't exist anymore. On what basis does one review the stories or individual episodes that fall into that chasm? The novelizations? The narrated audio soundtracks from the BBC? The fan-made reconstructions?

Quite a few missing stories or stories-with-missing-segments, particularly the longer ones, I chose to listen to the official BBC audio releases, often on Sunday mornings spent at my in-laws' horse farm, where it was my solemn duty to scoop horse poop out of stalls and paddocks. Trust me when I say that there's something fitting about experiencing *The Underwater Menace* in the middle of what seems like the world's biggest litterbox.

Later, as I became a stay-at-home dad with an infant who spent long stretches of the day either sleeping or eating (wait a minute, is he a baby or a cat?), I became a fan of the visual reconstructions. Often assembled by fans, these amateur productions use two sources of material: fan-recorded audio recordings of the original (and in many cases, only) broadcast, and the "telesnaps" shot by photographer John Cura (1902-1969) as a service to actors and producers who had no other record of their work in the pre-home-video market of the '60s. The telesnaps have been reprinted in <u>Doctor Who Magazine</u> and various fanzines over the years, and in many cases the source material is – by modern standards – fairly low-resolution scans. Sometimes there's a little bit of a zoom-in or zoom-out effect to keep things from becoming *completely* static, but even that can become a little grating.

The reconstruction of *The Macra Terror* that I watched was a bit of a revelation, however. The fan-made reconstruction of this story is outstanding, with enough animated effects and extra touches to help elevate it beyond a mere slide show. Sure, it's no professionally-animated episode, *a la* the DVD reconstruction of *The Invasion*, but it's lively enough to hold a viewer's attention. Monitors have animated static and animated scan lines. The mines are filled with animated smoke. The abundance of available photos from *The Macra Terror* is also a big help in bringing the story (back) to life.

It's the next best thing to having the original tapes back.

Not every story is so lucky, so the reconstructions are a mixed bag. But they give us a chance to get at least a taste of what it was like to watch these stories, not just hear them, so I've become a bit of a fan.

The BBC has quietly turned a blind eye to these projects in much the same way that American studios have made no comment on fan films based on copyrighted productions. In both games, the ground rules are the same: the product is to be distributed freely, and the lawyers won't swoop in until money changes hands. Considering that the BBC maintained a steady schedule of releases of "lost" stories in audio form until all of the missing Hartnell and Troughton era material was available, this can be described as nothing less than magnanimous.

It would be dandy, as the show hits 50 years old, to see the BBC give some of the reconstruction artists access to digital editing/animation suites and the best available source material (remastered audio tracks and as close to the original telesnaps as possible – dare I hope for the original negatives?), to rebuild – best as possible – the lost episodes for a DVD release. I'm not holding my breath waiting for this to happen, naturally, but tapping into the passion that some of these artists and editors have shown for the Doctor's missing adventures would be far from the worst idea that anyone at the BBC has ever had.

THE FACELESS ONES

The moment they step out of the doors of the just-landed TARDIS, the Doctor and his friends must contend with one rather major problem – their time machine has parked itself on a runway at Gatwick Airport and, as Jamie puts it, there's a "flying beastie" coming in for a landing. A policeman spots the four time travelers and chases them. The Doctor and Jamie go one way, and Ben and Polly in another; eventually Polly is separated from Ben, but while she's hiding in a hangar warehouse building, she witnesses a gruesome murder committed with a futuristic weapon that doesn't belong on Earth in 1967. Worse yet, the killers have seen her face, and eventually trap her. At the airport terminal, the Doctor and Jamie own up to being responsible for the strangely out-of-place police box on the tarmac, but they also realize that something else is even more amiss. Reunited with Ben, and with the help of a young woman who is searching for her missing brother, the Doctor goes to investigate the hangar where Polly disappeared, belonging to Chameleon Tours. He finds more evidence of otherworldly equipment, and proof that wherever passengers are booking their flights to aboard Chameleon Tours' planes, they aren't arriving there. The airline is being run by a race of displaced aliens who have lost their identities due to a disaster on their home planet – and the solution they're pursuing is a kind of identity theft that could eventually rob Earth of its entire population.

Patrick Troughton . . . . The Doctor
Michael Craze . . . . Ben
Anneke Wills . . . . Polly
Frazer Hines . . . . Jamie McCrimmon
James Appleby . . . . Policeman
Pauline Collins . . . . Samantha Briggs
Robin Dawson . . . . Chameleon
Barry du Pre . . . . Chameleon
Gilly Fraser . . . . Ann Davidson
Colin Gordon . . . . Commandant
Bernard Kay . . . . Crossland
Michael Ladkin . . . . Pilot
Pat Leclere . . . . Chameleon
Madalena Nicol . . . . Pinto
Brigit Paul . . . . Announcer
Roy Pearce . . . . Chameleon
Donald Pickering . . . . Blade
George Selway . . . . Meadows
Christopher Tranchell . . . . Jenkins
Leonard Trolley . . . . Reynolds

This story has been released on audio CD

written by David Ellis & Malcolm Hulke
directed by Gerry Mill
stock library music - see credits below

Part 1 aired on April 8, 1967
Part 2 aired on April 15, 1967
Part 3 aired on April 22, 1967
Part 4 aired on April 29, 1967
Part 5 aired on May 6, 1967
Part 6 aired on May 13, 1967
Episodes 1 and 3 appear in the *Lost In Time* DVD set.

Wanda Ventham . . . . Jean Rock
Peter Whitaker . . . . Gascoigne
Victor Winding . . . . Spencer
Barry Wilsher . . . . Heslington

MISSING: Episodes 2, 4, 5 and 6 of *The Faceless Ones* are missing from the BBC archives.

A.K.A.: Actors **Donald Pickering** and **Wanda Ventham** were reunited as guest stars of another **Doctor Who** story 20 years later, *Time And The Rani*, the first story featuring the seventh Doctor. **Pauline Collins'** next **Doctor Who** appearance would come nearly four decades later in the David Tennant episode *Tooth And Claw*, in which she guest starred as Queen Victoria. Her character in *The Faceless Ones*, Samantha Briggs, had been considered as a potential companion but the show's producers decided in favor of Victoria Waterfield instead. Ventham also appeared in *The Image Of The Fendahl* during Tom Baker's TARDIS tenure.

BEHIND THE SCENES: Ironically, despite the story's title, *The Faceless Ones* marked the introduction of a new title sequence which prominently featured the new Doctor's face, an element that would remain a tradition through the end of Sylvester McCoy's era. "Spangly" sounds were added to the theme music to go along with the visual changes.

STOCK MUSIC: "Nigerian Drums" (from an in-house BBC source), "Fantasy In Orbit" (Pacific Dawn Orchestra), "Hindu Funeral Drumming" (John Levy)

Where *The War Machines*, at the tail end of William Hartnell's era, started bringing **Doctor Who** into the modern day with a serious storyline, *The Faceless Ones* does the same, except that its serious storyline is executed in a way that occasionally approaches *Austin Powers* levels of trippy. A race of aliens that preys almost exclusively on attractive young people almost sounds like a godsend for a modern-day sci-fi series; in this case, judging by the two surviving episodes (and the complete audio recordings of the missing installments), it seemed to be an attempt to add some glamour to **Doctor Who**.

This was the final outing for Ben and Polly, who joined the first Doctor in *The War Machines* and thus became the first "regeneration companions". But the way the two were written most of the time, they didn't work well in anything that wasn't a present-day or "15 minutes into the future" (i.e. *Tenth Planet*). And despite that, they barely make a showing in *The Faceless Ones*, which is unusual — and perhaps and indicator of the lack of enthusiasm that **Doctor Who**'s scriptwriters had for the increasingly crowded TARDIS. (Another indicator is the fact that Michael Craze and Anneke Wills were contracted to appear through part two of *The Evil Of The Daleks*, the following story, and were indeed paid, though they were written out after appearing in only the first, second and last episodes of *The Faceless Ones*.) With the arrival of Victoria in *Evil Of The Daleks*, the real salad days of Patrick Troughton's reign would kick in.

It's also refreshing to see a story whose alien baddies show remorse for their actions, and seek (and get) the Doctor's forgiveness and help, rather than needing to be blown to bits or otherwise shown to the door.

Though it seems insignificant, this helps to really establish the Doctor's "root for the underdog" nature that would become central to the character in later years and incarnations.

THE EVIL OF THE DALEKS

No sooner have the Doctor and Jamie seen off Ben and Polly, then the TARDIS is loaded into the back of a truck and whisked away. The Doctor and Jamie try to track down the missing time machine, encountering a man who claims to know nothing about the theft, but the Doctor knows better. The trail of clues leads to an antique store owned by a Mr. Edward Waterfield, whose antiques are remarkably well-preserved, and hides a room in the back full of technology that has no place on 1966 Earth. The time travelers discover a body near this technology, but before they can investigate further, they're gassed by Waterfield and taken back in time to 1866. After Waterfield's employer, Professor Theodore Maxtible, reveals that he has been conducting experiments in time travel, the Doctor learns that his experiments have given a foothold to an invading force: the Daleks. Holding Waterfield's daughter Victoria hostage, the Daleks want to isolate "the human factor" - something that has enabled humans to throw off the shackles of Dalek domination again and again - and transplant it into future generations of Daleks. Using Victoria as bait, they intend to study Jamie's attempts to rescue her to learn more about the human factor. With lives and history itself hanging in the balance, the Doctor can only watch and cooperate with the Daleks' plan… all while preparing one of his own.

Patrick Troughton . . . . The Doctor
Frazer Hines . . . . Jamie McCrimmon
Deborah Watling . . . . Victoria Waterfield
John Bailey . . . . Edward Waterfield
Sonny Caldinez . . . . Kemel
Geoffrey Colville . . . . Perry
Griffith Davies . . . . Kennedy
Windsor Davies . . . . Toby
Brigit Forsyth . . . . Ruth Maxtible
Marius Goring . . . . Theodore Maxtible
Murphy Grumbar . . . . Dalek
Peter Hawkins . . . . Dalek Voice
Robert Jewell . . . . Dalek
John Scott Martin . . . . Dalek
Alec Ross . . . . Bob Hall
Jo Rowbottom . . . . Mollie Dawson
Roy Skelton . . . . Dalek Voice
Gerald Taylor . . . . Dalek
Ken Tyllsen . . . . Dalek
Gary Watson . . . . Arthur Terrall

This story
has been
released
on audio
CD

written by David Whitaker
directed by Derek Martinus & Timothy Combe
music by Dudley Simpson

Part 1 aired on May 20, 1967
Part 2 aired on May 27, 1967
Part 3 aired on June 3, 1967
Part 4 aired on June 10, 1967
Part 5 aired on June 17, 1967
Part 6 aired on June 24, 1967
Part 7 aired on July 1, 1967

Episode 2 of *The Evil Of The Daleks* appears in the *Lost In Time* DVD set.

Two complete audio recordings of this entire story are available: a CD edition narrated by Frazer Hines, and a cassette-only edition (now out of print) featuring Tom Baker narrating the story (but not in character first-person, as he did with *Fury From The Deep*).

MISSING: Episodes 1, 3, 4, 5, 6 and 7 of *The Evil Of The Daleks* are missing from the BBC archives.

NEW WHO CONNECTIONS: The Doctor says that this adventure represents "the final end" of the Daleks (which it was intended to be, as Terry Nation was withdrawing permission for the BBC to use them further in **Doctor Who** so he could attempt to launch them in their own series). In 2010's *Victory Of The Daleks*, the eleventh Doctor threatens to bring about "the final end" of the Daleks. Again.

Possibly the strangest Dalek story in the history of the original series, *The Evil Of The Daleks* sees more of the deviousness that the Daleks exhibited in *Power Of The Daleks*, though this time it's put to an even more sinister use: the Daleks finally admit that they want to improve themselves. Not to be better galactic citizens, mind you, but to be better killing machines. Presaging such future stories as *Destiny Of The Daleks* and *Evolution Of The Daleks*, the metal monsters admitted that they lacked creativity and instinct. The real beauty of *Evil*, however, is the atmosphere that's built up over the course of the story. And this is a story with real scope: by the end of episode seven, when you're witnessing the outbreak of a Dalek civil war on Skaro, it's almost easy to forget that this whole adventure started with the theft of the TARDIS on the back of a truck from an airport.

Evil Of The Daleks is also remarkably forward-looking in a dramatic sense: in episode five, Jamie announces that he's ready to leave the Doctor, fed up with his bizarrely callous attitude toward the mounting body count. It's a moment that wouldn't seem out of place with future Doctors, but here it is, happening this early in the show's history. (It's also hardly the first such instance: Steven is ready to part ways with the Doctor in *The Massacre*.) Frazer Hines gets a lot to do here, and he starts the story as the sole companion, his inexperience occasionally grating on the Doctor's nerves. Victoria gets one of the best companion entrances in the series' history up to this point; where past companions have seldom given viewers a sense of what sort of family they came from, here we meet Victoria's father and see him meet a tragic end, begging the Doctor to look after his daughter. That Victoria winds up rising above this tumultuous introduction and becoming a vital member of the TARDIS team is, quite frankly, remarkable. (And in the modern series, the tragedy built into the character's background would've been revisited until it was *over*done.)

This is also the first appearance of the Emperor Dalek, appearing in a very different form here than the Emperor seen in *The Parting Of The Ways* (2005) or *Remembrance Of The Daleks* (1988), though the Emperor seen in the latter of these two is actually is disguise for another character. The only episodes featuring the Emperor (he doesn't appear until episode six) exist as audio recordings only, but the Emperor makes a huge impact in audio alone thanks to the voice treatment, which combines the ring-modulated Dalek "stutter" with a descending-harmonic effect that's just dripping with menace. In actuality, on the stage, the Emperor was a large, static prop with even less movement than a "normal" Dalek, but its voice alone conjures images of a huge Dalek towering over the Doctor as it gloats. The modern series has tried to echo this effect with its own Emperor (*Parting Of The Ways*) and the Supreme Dalek (*Journey's End*), but somehow it hasn't come close to the unique sound of the Emperor Dalek in this story. On the opposite end of the scale, but no less unnerving, are the "humanized" Daleks reprogrammed by the Doctor to exhibit playful and rebellious streaks. There's something just unnatural about Daleks with singsong voices.

If only one more story can be miraculously be found complete someday, it urgently needs to be *The Evil Of The Daleks*. The performances alone keep even an audio recording gripping; seeing them in video form would probably reveal to us the finest hour(s) of black & white **Doctor Who**.

SEASON 5: 1967-68
TOMB OF THE CYBERMEN

The TARDIS brings the Doctor, Jamie and Victoria to the wasteland of the planet Telos, where they spot a human expedition on a journey to unearth the lost tombs of the Cybermen, a threat thought to be long extinct. Despite the Doctor's vocal misgivings, Professor Parry and his fellow explorers insist on breaching the enormous doors and venturing into the apparently vacant tombs. But when automatic defense systems begin to pick off Parry's team one by one, the expedition begins to look like a doomed one. When someone in the expedition reveals their true purpose – to reactivate and take control of the Cybermen – the entire galaxy may be doomed unless the Doctor can confine the Cybermen once more.

Patrick Troughton	The Doctor
Frazer Hines	Jamie
Deborah Watling	Victoria
Cyril Shaps	Viner
Shirley Cooklin	Kaftan
Hans De Vries	Cyberman
Ray Grover	Crewman
Tony Harwood	Cyberman
Peter Hawkins	Cybermen voices
John Hogan	Cyberman
Bernard Holley	Haydon
Richard Kerley	Cyberman
Alan Johns	Rogers
Michael Kilgarriff	Cyber Controller
Ronald Lee	Cyberman
Clive Merrison	Callum
George Pastell	Kleig
Charles Pemberton	Cyberman
Aubrey Richards	Professor Parry

This story has been released on DVD

written by Kit Pedler & Gerry Davis
directed by Morris Barry
stock library music - see credits below

Part 1 aired on September 2, 1967
Part 2 aired on September 9, 1967
Part 3 aired on September 16, 1967
Part 4 aired on September 23, 1967

George Roubicek	Hopper
Kenneth Seeger	Cyberman
Roy Stewart	Toberman
Reg Whitehead	Cyberman

NEW WHO CONNECTIONS: The menacing Cyber-catchphrase "You will be like us" is repeated in 2006's two-parter *Rise Of The Cybermen / The Age Of Steel*, and presages the assimilating action of **Star Trek**'s Borg by over 20 years.

STOCK MUSIC: "Universe Sideral" (Paul Bonneau and his Orchestra), "Josef Weinberger Library Music JW233B: Band 7" (Desmond Leslie), "Josef Weinberger Library Music JW232B: Band 8" (Desmond Leslie), "Space Adventure" (Martin Slavin), "Palpitations" (Johnny Scott), "Impress Music Library IA144A" (track unknown) (Steve Race), "Galaxy" (composer not credited), "Dark Pursuit" (The New Concert Orchestra), "Off Centre" (Frank Talley), "Astronautics Suite" (Erich Sendel), Desert Storm (Heinrich Feischner)

"This story," said so many of the books written on **Doctor Who** during the show's peak of 1980s popularity, "is a classic." Those same books would invariably go on to lament the fact that all four parts of this 1968 black-and-white adventure featuring Patrick Troughton as the second Doctor were lost forever, so we'd have to take it on trust from those who professed to be there when it happened.

In 1992, all four 25-minute episodes were located in watchable condition in, of all places, Hong Kong, and of course, being the year before **Doctor Who**'s 30th anniversary, the whole thing was rushed into release as quickly as possible. Not everyone, upon finally getting to see it for themselves, thought it a classic. They were spoiled by video releases which had, for the most part, made the full-color episodes available, and by the splashier special effects, sets and costumes of more recent **Who** episodes. Not everyone is right, however – this *is* a classic, and it's a classy one. Let no one give you the "old cheap black-and-white show" argument – *Tomb Of The Cybermen* draws most of its tense atmosphere from that very factor.

The Cybermen here are a menace to be reckoned with. Unlike the posturing mini-posse of Cybermen of many later stories, there are a *lot* of them in this story, swarming like insects, and they don't give a flip if they have to break the neck of every non-Cyberman in the room to ensure their command of the situation. Only in 1982's *Earthshock* did the Cybermen even come within shouting distance of the ability to evoke this kind of terror again in the original series. And why are they out to ensnare human expeditions? Why, to assimilate them, of course – eat your heart out, Locutus.

And let's not forget the Doctor and his traveling companions while we're at it. Patrick Troughton turns in easily the best performance as the Doctor which is still on record, and the combination of Frazer Hines' unflappable Jamie McCrimmon and Deborah Watling as Victoria – who had, in **Who** terms, only joined the TARDIS crew in the previous story – makes for some memorable moments. In one of the best scenes between any of the Doctors and any of their companions in the show's 26 years on the air, Victoria confides to the Doctor her protectiveness of him if he is indeed an elderly 400+ years old, a rare and touching exception in comparison to the later norm of Doctors and companions arguing at one another. The supporting cast isn't shabby either, with George Pastell standing out as the maniacal logician Kleig, whose motivation for reviving the Cybermen is to control them – and who better to do such a thing but a logician?

If any motivation is needed to continue the search for further missing **Doctor Who** adventures, particularly those starring Troughton, simply watching *Tomb Of The Cybermen* – which previously languished in the "lost forever" list until the whole thing turned up unexpectedly – should do the trick. Troughton's reign as the Doctor is still missing many entire stories, others which will, if we're lucky, turn out to be as good as *Tomb Of The Cybermen* when they're found…because this story is a classic.

THE ABOMINABLE SNOWMEN

The Doctor, Jamie and Victoria discover that the TARDIS has brought them to present-day Tibet, high in the Himalayas, which the Doctor sees as a perfect opportunity to return a holy relic to the Det-Sen Monastery – an item that has been in his possession since the 1600s. He decides to step outside to explore, leaving Jamie and Victoria in the safety of the TARDIS to find the misplaced relic, and discovers a mangled rifle, a dead body, and enormous footprints. The Doctor returns to his timeship to collect the relic and return it to the monks at Det-Sen personally, but tells his companions that he thinks it best that they remain in the TARDIS. After he leaves again, Victoria's curiosity gets the best of her and she goes outside to look around, and Jamie's chivalry gets the best of him and he goes along to protect her. They're exploring a cave when a huge furry beast traps them inside, and they find a collection of silver spheres there. At the monastery, the Doctor doesn't get the reception he's been expecting, and the warrior monks who protect their more peaceful brethren accuse him of murder; Professor Travers, who is searching the mountainside for signs of the legendary Yeti, witnesses his partner's death and thinks the Doctor is responsible, thinking him to be the leader of a rival expedition. It turns out that Yeti are on the move, but not the reclusive creatures of lore – when they appear and attack the monastery, the Doctor discovers that they are robotic in nature, each containing a cavity custom-made for the spheres discovered by Jamie and Victoria. But the Yeti are being controlled by something else, somewhere – and they may be the greatest challenge ever faced by the Det-Sen monks and even the Doctor himself.

Patrick Troughton . . . . The Doctor
Frazer Hines . . . . Jamie
Deborah Watling . . . . Victoria
David Baron . . . . Ralpachan
David Grey . . . . Rinchen
Tony Harwood . . . . Yeti
John Hogan . . . . Yeti
Norman Jones . . . . Khrisong
Richard Kerley . . . . Yeti

This story has been released on audio CD

written by Mervyn Haisman & Henry Lincoln
directed by Gerald Blake
stock library music - see credits below

Part 1 aired on September 30, 1967
Part 2 aired on October 7, 1967
Part 3 aired on October 14, 1967
Part 4 aired on October 21, 1967
Part 5 aired on October 28, 1967

Raymond Llewellyn	. . . .	Sapan
Charles Morgan	. . . .	Songsten
Wolfe Morris	. . . .	Padmasambhava
David Spencer	. . . .	Thonmi

Part 6 aired on November 4, 1967

Jack Watling	. . . .	Professor Travers
Reg Whitehead	. . . .	Yeti

MISSING: Episodes 1, 3, 4, 5 and 6 of *The Abominable Snowmen* are missing from the BBC archives.

NEW WHO CONNECTIONS: *The Sensorites* showed the Doctor and Susan to have mental abilities beyond those of mere humans. *The Abominable Snowmen* is the first **Doctor Who** adventure to make it clear beyond the shadow of a doubt that the Doctor's psi powers are quite formidable, as he holds the Great Intelligence at bay. The Yeti would be seen again in *The Web Of Fear*, and fleetingly in *The Five Doctors*; they also appear in the fan-made video production *Downtime*, which chronicles a third attempt by the Great Intelligence to seize Earth as its new homeworld. The Great Intelligence first encounters the Doctor much later in the Doctor's timeline in 2013's *The Snowmen*.

STOCK MUSIC: "Morning Prayer" (Monks of Sakya Set), "Offering To God Of Sakya" (Monks of Sakya Set). Also credited in the BBC's paperwork is a rendition of the traditional song "Twinkle, Twinkle, Little Star", credited to "Patrick Troughton and his Recorder"!

Though on the surface it would appear to suffer from the same "confined space full of humans under siege from an outside force" plotline as a great many other second Doctor adventures, *The Abominable Snowmen* was afforded a great deal of extra scope via location filming. Though the location in question was obviously not something one would ever mistake for the real Himalayas, it's also obviously a little further afield, not somewhere just down the highway from the BBC's London base of operations, so it works quite well. The whole six-part adventure is dripping with atmosphere, mystery and menace – if *The Abominable Snowmen* existed in whole, rather than a single orphaned episode and five episodes worth of audio, it might well be remembered and revered even more than *Tomb Of The Cybermen*.

As with most disembodied menaces faced by the Doctor down through the years, it's all down to vocal performances here, and even in the majority of the story that's represented only by audio recordings, the voice of monastery master Padmasambhava and the malevolent tones of the Great Intelligence are striking. I listened to this entire story in broad daylight, wide awake, and found some of the voices unnerving. This story also shows Victoria at her best – it may well be that character's best appearance, as she's inquisitive and yet fearful at the same time. But when push comes to shove and her friends are at stake, Victoria isn't too scared to explore further. (But as is typical with female sidekicks from Troughton's era, she's also unashamed to let rip with a shrill scream when confronted by a Yeti, as you do.) And while Victoria soars in this story, Jamie suffers a bit, spending much of the latter half of the proceedings being preoccupied with worrying about Victoria, who in the meantime is getting by just fine, apart from the whole bit about being hypnotized by the Great Intelligence.

The Abominable Snowmen may well be the height of the Troughton era, and it's an adventure on an unusually large canvas for this budget-conscious era of the show. When I listen to the stories that exist either entirely or mostly in audio form, I tend to picture them in black & white, on BBC sets, with BBC props and makeup jobs. As I listened to this one, I found myself picturing it in color, in widescreen, in even grander and more forbidding settings – because it's such a great story that it inspires that kind of imagination. If we can find no other Troughton adventures complete, we must find this one in its entirety.

THE ICE WARRIORS

The TARDIS tumbles into the world's new ice age, in the third millennium. The Doctor, Jamie and Victoria find themselves surrounded by snow and ice, in a human outpost led by a man named Clent. Clent's staff is Britain's last defense against an advancing ice shelf, but some of his men are preoccupied with something else they've found in the ice – an enormous armored body, larger than most humans. They bring it into the outpost to thaw it out, and when it does, it turns out that the creature is still alive. The so-called Ice Warrior, an alien native to Mars who was trapped on Earth as part of a previous expedition, has little interest in being studied by the humans, preferring to take control of the situation by any means at its disposal.

Patrick Troughton	. . . .	The Doctor
Frazer Hines	. . . .	Jamie
Deborah Watling	. . . .	Victoria
Michael Attwell	. . . .	Ishur
Peter Barkworth	. . . .	Clent
Bernard Bresslaw	. . . .	Varga
Sonny Caldinez	. . . .	Turoc
Peter Diamond	. . . .	Davis
Wendy Gifford	. . . .	Miss Garrett
Tony Harwood	. . . .	Rintan
Roger Jones	. . . .	Zondal
Angus Lennie	. . . .	Storr
Peter Sallis	. . . .	Penley
Roy Skelton	. . . .	Computer voice

This story has been released on DVD

written by Brian Hayles
directed by Gerald Blake
music by Dudley Simpson

Part 1 aired on November 11, 1967
Part 2 aired on November 18, 1967
Part 3 aired on November 25, 1967
Part 4 aired on December 2, 1967
Part 5 aired on December 9, 1967
Part 6 aired on December 16, 1967

Malcolm Taylor	. . . .	Walters
George Waring	. . . .	Arden

MISSING: Episodes 2 and 3 of *The Ice Warriors* are missing from the BBC archives.

By this point in Troughton's era, it wasn't a matter of *which* episodes were going to feature a small group of humans besieged by an even smaller group of alien menaces who were merely the first hint of a foothold before an invasion – almost *all* of the stories from this era followed that basic framework. The real question was: who would the baddies be? In this case, it was the creation for which writer Brian Hayles is best remembered by **Doctor Who** fans: the towering, hissing Ice Warriors. As tall as a refrigerator, about as bulky and about as cold, the Ice Warriors are one of the very few **Doctor Who** monsters to have made the jump from the show's B&W years to the color era, appearing one more time alongside Troughton and then twice with Jon Pertwee's Doctor before remaining in the realm of spinoff media for decades and reappearing in 2013's *Cold War*.

I've always thought that a big part of the Ice Warrior mystique is down to their voices. Rather than the variety of electromechanical audio treatments that have graced the Daleks and the Cybermen, the Ice Warriors speak in a good old-fashioned menacing stage hiss. The Ice Warriors have inspired everything from novels to audio dramas to action figures, and yet on screen they're almost laughable in their lumbering around that one wonders how they caught on – I'm sticking by my theory that it's all about the voice.

In their introductory story, it's certainly not about the supporting cast. As with many a Troughton siege story, you've got stock characters aplenty, and here they're all wearing heavy duty "futuristic" tunics with abstract paisley-esque patterns that say "1960s" more than they say "31st century". From the Hardass Base Commander Who Refuses To Believe Anything's Wrong to the other archetypes of this kind of story, they're all here.

In the 1990s, the BBC released this story on VHS with an incredibly inventive device for covering the action of the two missing segments. In addition to a CD containing the audio of the two missing episodes, the most important plot points and dialogue scenes are condensed into a 15-minute selection of stills with minor animation effects, introduced with an ingenious device that works the lack of full video into the storyline. Considering that, at its original six-part length, this cuts down on the Troughton-era staples of Escaping And Getting Captured, and the other old standby, Characters Arguing Among Themselves, it's actually a bit of a mercy. *The Ice Warriors* really comes across as a middle-of-the-road story…with some great monsters.

SHORT HOPS

…in which the author shakes his head about 2013's Attack of the Omnirumor …and its surprising outcome.

For a couple of weeks during the summer of 2013, one could have been forgiven for forgetting that all of the excitement surrounding the casting of a new Doctor was still to come. During this short span of time, it was all about the *original* Doctors – the first two – and an incredible rumor that something like 90 out of 106 missing black & white episodes had been found, somewhere in Africa.

If you're a fan who's relatively new to the series and not versed in the lore of classic **Doctor Who**, all you really need to know is this: during the 1960s, **Doctor Who** was produced in black & white on video, and the series was made almost year-round to the tune of one 25-minute episode per week. The videotapes were transferred to a more universal medium – film – and sold abroad, often dubbed into the local language. From various points in Europe to the Middle East and beyond, these films were "bicycled" from broadcaster to broadcaster, a practice that was still in force as recently as my early years in the TV biz (I distinctly remember that, at the midwestern American station where I worked in the early '90s, episodes of **Mama's Family** were bicycled from station to station).

And then, in the late '60s, staring down the barrel of an impending change of video format with little reasonable expectation that programs recorded in the older, lower-resolution format could ever be exploited commercially, and knowing that yet a further new format would be introduced in due course (namely, color television), the British Broadcasting Corporation issued internal instructions to its videotape archive: *get rid of these old shows. Get rid of everything that isn't of obvious historic value* (such as footage of the Queen's coronation). In the BBC's view, there was no point in wasting all of that valuable space to preserve programming which had no commercial future.

If only they'd known. This would be the equivalent of Hollywood shrugging and throwing every standard-definition TV series ever made onto the burn pile unless its original film negatives existed and could be rescanned at HD resolution, all while UHD/4K loomed in the distance.

If one ignores the ever-shifting lengths of episodes (25 minutes for most of the original series' 26 years on the air, except for that one season where episodes were 50 minutes, and that pair of 90 minute TV movies, and the more recent 45 minute episodes…), **the 50th anniversary special is the 800th individual episode of Doctor Who.** But due to the BBC's quest to save archive space, which was a reasonable practice at the time, 106 episodes from the 1960s were missing as of the summer of 2013, all but wiping out the era of the late and much-loved Patrick Troughton.

But there were other things they didn't know: not all of the films sold overseas had been returned in a timely manner as per the terms of sale. A handful of members of the viewing public who latched onto the series very early as being something special recorded every episode in audio form in English, enabling any re-dubbed episodes to be re-re-dubbed into their native tongue. And not even the BBC's own archivists had necessarily wiped out every episode due for erasure; there's a degree of *dis*organization in any large organization, and that worked in the Doctor's favor. The left hand often didn't know what the right hand was holding. And thank goodness for that. Thanks to the BBC's "inefficiency," we have much of the Hartnell era, and a fair, though not-as-large-as-anyone-would-like representative cross-section of Patrick Troughton's era.

Then, in June 2013, a series of developments — all of them in the "rumor" column — suggested that the number of missing episodes could soon drop to a mere astonishing **16 episodes** thanks to an incredible find that was rumored to have taken place. Relatively big-name fans began jockeying for position in the unfolding drama, first denying and then apparently confirming everything that we hoped was true. The rumor quickly sprouted an itemized list: we'd soon be able to see *everything* except *The Daleks' Masterplan*, *The Ice Warriors* and *The Invasion*, complete. We would get to see the Doctor's first regeneration (and his first recovery from the same), we would get to see the second Doctor meet Jamie for the first time, we would get to see the legendary *Evil Of The Daleks*, we would get to see the Doctor meet Alistair Gordon Lethbridge-Stewart for the first time (*before* his promotion to Brigadier), we would see Victoria's tearful farewell... can you get a sense of how exciting this all was?

I can't claim to have been immune to hoping that all of this was true. Part of me was quietly thinking, *"Yeah, this would be the ultimate vindication of **Doctor Who**'s 50th anniversary – that the ghosts of William Hartnell and Patrick Troughton and Innes Lloyd and Derrick Sherwin might arise and show everyone how awesome the show had been on a shoestring budget in relatively low-resolution black & white, and remind us of exactly why we're celebrating this show's history."*

In the meantime, the more vague parts of the rapidly-morphing rumor pointed toward a hunter of missing television archives, not just **Doctor Who**, possibly having found 90 (or, according to the rumor's latest iteration, *perhaps even more!*) episodes somewhere in Africa. Nigeria, maybe...

...wait, *Nigeria?* Oh.

As in "Oh, my giddy aunt."

I have no racial or cultural beef with Nigeria, but for whatever reason, the internet seems to have decided that every scam artist who spams everyone's inbox needs to hail from Nigeria. Maybe it's because it's a land so far and so distant from the western world that it's nugh-on-impossible to verify all of those spam e-mails you get offering untold and untraceable bajillions of dollars (or pounds), if only you'll help some war-scarred refugee set up an American bank account? Won't you? Please? God bless you in this, our most trying time.

Poor Nigeria. It almost certainly doesn't deserve this reputation.

And yet there it is.

I could just see it...

DEAR RESPECTED ONE,

GREETINGS,

PERMIT ME TO INFORM YOU OF MY DESIRE OF GOING INTO BUSINESS RELATIONSHIP WITH YOU. I GOT YOUR CONTACT FROM THE INTERNATIONAL WEB SITE DIRECTORY. I PRAYED OVER IT AND SELECTED YOUR NAME AMONG OTHER NAMES DUE TO IT'S ESTEEMING NATURE AND THE RECOMMENDATIONS GIVEN TO ME AS A REPUTABLE AND TRUST WORTHY COMPANY I CAN DO BUSINESS WITH AND BY THE RECOMMENDATIONS I MUST NOT HESITATE TO CONFIDE IN YOU FOR THIS SIMPLE AND SINCERE BUSINESS.

I AM WUMI ABDUL; THE ONLY DAUGHTER OF LATE MR AND MRS GEORGE ABDUL. MY FATHER WAS A VERY WEALTHY COCOA MERCHANT IN ABIDJAN, THE ECONOMIC CAPITAL OF IVORY COAST BEFORE HE WAS POISONED TO DEATH BY HIS BUSINESS ASSOCIATES ON ONE OF THEIR OUTING TO DISCUS ON A BUSINESS DEAL. WHEN MY MOTHER DIED ON THE 21ST OCTOBER 1984. MY FATHER TOOK ME AND MY YOUNGER BROTHER HASSAN SPECIAL BECAUSE WE ARE MOTHERLESS. BEFORE THE DEATH OF MY FATHER ON 30TH JUNE 2002 IN A PRIVATE HOSPITAL HERE IN ABIDJAN. HE SECRETLY CALLED ME ON HIS BEDSIDE AND TOLD ME THAT HE HAS A CACHE OF VERY OLD DR. WHO BROADCAST TAPES LEFT IN A VAULT IN A LOCAL BANK HERE IN ABIDJAN. THAT HE USED MY NAME AS HIS FIRST DAUGHTER FOR THE NEXT OF KIN IN DEPOSIT OF THE FILMS.

HE ALSO EXPLAINED TO ME THAT IT WAS BECAUSE OF THIS WEALTH AND SOME HUGE NUMBER OF OTHER PROGRAMS HIS BUSINESS ASSOCIATES SUPPOSED TO BALANCE HIS FROM THE DEAL THEY HAD THAT HE WAS POISONED BY HIS BUSINESS ASSOCIATES, THAT I SHOULD SEEK FOR A GOD FEARING FOREIGN PARTNER IN A COUNTRY OF MY CHOICE WHERE I WILL TRANSFER THESE TAPES AND USE THEM FOR PURPOSE OF HELPING MANKIND, (SUCH AS REAL ESTATE MANAGEMENT). SIR, WE ARE HONOURABLY SEEKING YOUR ASSISTANCE IN THE FOLLOWING WAYS.

1) TO PROVIDE A BANK WHERE THESE PROGRAMS WOULD BE TRANSFERRED TO.

2) TO SERVE AS THE GUARDIAN OF THEM SINCE I AM A GIRL OF 26 YEARS.

MOREOVER SIR, WE ARE WILLING TO OFFER YOU 15% OF THE FINANCIAL GAIN FROM THESE PROGRAMS AS COMPENSATION FOR EFFORT INPUT AFTER THE SUCCESSFUL TRANSFER OF THESE PROGRAMS TO YOUR DESIGNATE ACCOUNT OVERSEAS. PLEASE FEEL FREE TO CONTACT ME VIA THIS EMAIL ADDRESS

ANTICIPATING TO HEAR FROM YOU SOON.
THANKS AND GOD BLESS.
BEST REGARDS,
MISS WUMI ABDUL

PLEASE FOR PRIVATE AND SECURITY REASONS, REPLY ME VIA EMAIL!

Somewhere around the first mention of Nigeria is when I lost all faith in the rumors. And sure enough, the missing-TV-tape hunter whose name was being attached to this rumor – apparently much to his chagrin – surfaced on Facebook within days, just long enough to issue a terse statement that, while some of the mentioned episodes *had* been bicycled into Africa at one point, they had been destroyed and were no longer in existence, at least not in that particular venue.

Then, of course, the pointless recriminations began, but they were pointless because *everyone wanted this to be true and everyone was holding their breath*. And we were all guilty – fandom as a whole – of mutating and morphing the rumor into something that we *desperately wanted to be true*.

Curiously, none of this made the "omnirumor" go away; the ever-helpful anonymous "inside sources" kept feeding the rumor machine, until British tabloids revived the hearsay that wouldn't go away in October, dragging the omnirumor out of geek circulation and into the mainstream. Just as fandom rolled its eyes collectively and criticized the tabloids for merely recirculating already-debunked gossip, the BBC did something nobody was expecting: it confirmed that something had indeed been found and scheduled a press conference.

The rest, of course, is history: *The Enemy Of The World* went from being a single orphan episode to a complete six-part story, and *The Web Of Fear* – also completely missing except for its first episode, which merely set the stage for the next five episodes – had regained all but its third episode. A carefully coordinated and stage-managed rollout ensued, making all of the episodes available to fans as soon as the news broke (and, obviously, making the BBC a fair amount of cash into the bargain).

It's interesting to look at the context of the modern series with relation to this sudden eruption of rumor about the original series. We'd just had a single season that took *two years* to watch. And we were in the midst of a six-month wait between the most recent finale and the anniversary special, and had just found out that the incumbent Doctor was leaving. And, as always, there was dissatisfaction in some corners with how the current production team went about the business of telling stories (though on the whole, I thought the 2012-13 season was Moffat's strongest to date).

\I think we all wanted the rumors to be true because we were tired of the half-a-season-per-year schtick, which was basically window dressing for the BBC having decided to make fewer episodes per year. And I think, having just recently seen William Hartnell appear in *The Name Of The Doctor* a few weeks before (a sight that would have been impossible if not for previous missing episode discoveries), we were all primed – even the segment of fandom that has only seen the new series and isn't well acquainted with the old – to bask in the retro glory years in lieu of new episodes starring Matt Smith.

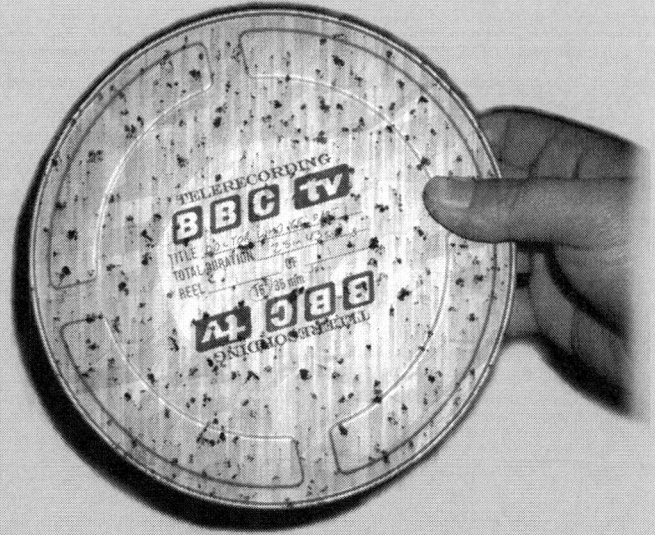

Of course, the omnirumor hasn't died yet. It's merely mutated: more episodes were found in northern Africa than have actually been revealed. Or an enigmatic *über*-fan from the show's earliest days pointed a silent film camera at his television to record *Marco Polo*. Or there are tapes in Taiwan. Or... something like that. Insinuations, allegations, accusations and other things ending in –ations have followed, spinning a sprawling epic saga to rival any storyline that has ever graced **Doctor Who** itself.

But for all of that drama, for now, *The Enemy Of The World* and *The Web Of Fear* are back – and they were well worth the wait.

THE ENEMY OF THE WORLD

The TARDIS materializes in the Australian surf in the future, and the Doctor excitedly tries to get Jamie and Victoria to help him build a sand castle or two. When a hovercraft teeming with armed guards appears, though, the time travelers become less relaxed – especially when the hovercraft starts firing at the Doctor in particular. The time travelers are rescued when a helicopter piloted by a woman named Astrid appears, offering them a ride back to her base, but the Doctor and his friends are no safer there. Astrid works for a man named Giles Kent, who says he's leading a resistance movement against the ruthless dictator known as Salamander – a man who looks exactly like the Doctor. Kent wants the Doctor to impersonate Salamander in an effort to discredit and topple the man's corrupt regime, but the Doctor is certain he hasn't been told the whole story. When Kent also hatches a plan that involves Jamie and Victoria going undercover, the stakes are even higher. But can Salamander's opponents prove that he is the monster that they say he is? And do they even know the whole story?

Patrick Troughton . . . . The Doctor
Frazer Hines . . . . Jamie
Deborah Watling . . . . Victoria
Bob Anderson . . . . Guard
Christopher Burgess . . . . Swann
Simon Cain . . . . Curly
Elliott Cairnes . . . . Guard Captain
Colin Douglas . . . . Bruce
Gordon Faith . . . . Guard Captain
Margaret Hickey . . . . Mary
Milton Johns . . . . Benik
Bill Kerr . . . . Kent
Reg Lye . . . . Griffin
Bill Lyons . . . . Guard
Dibbs Mather . . . . Guard
Rhys McConnochie . . . . Rod
William McGuirk . . . . Guard
Carmen Munroe . . . . Fariah
David Nettheim . . . . Fedorin

This story has been released on DVD

written by David Whitaker
directed by Barry Letts
stock library music - see credits below

Part 1 aired on December 23, 1967
Part 2 aired on December 30, 1967
Part 3 aired on January 6, 1968
Part 4 aired on January 13, 1968
Part 5 aired on January 20, 1968
Part 6 aired on January 27, 1968

Mary Peach . . . . Astrid
George Pravda . . . . Denes
Andrew Staines . . . . Sergeant
Henry Stamper . . . . Anton
Patrick Troughton . . . . Ramon Salamander
Adam Verney . . . . Colin

BEHIND THE SCENES: Previously missing except for episode three, *The Enemy Of The World* was miraculously restored in its entirety and released on DVD in 2013 thanks to the fortuitous discovery of all five missing episodes in a hut owned by a Nigerian broadcast company. The search that led to the missing episode discovery also returned four previously missing installments of *The Web Of Fear*.

NEW WHO CONNECTIONS: The new series would show on more than one occasion that the TARDIS' doors could be open in space (*The Runaway Bride, The Beast Below*); in part 6 of *The Enemy Of The World*, the hazard in the TARDIS doors being open is presumably due to the vehicle already being in the time vortex; unshielded travel through the vortex has been shown on many occasions — in both the old series (*Inferno*) and the new series (*Utopia*) — to be far from the safest way to travel.

STOCK MUSIC: "Miraculous Mandarin" (Bela Bartok), "Music For String Instruments, Percussion & Celesta" (Bela Bartok)

> ⚙ **The following review was written prior to the discovery of the missing episodes.** ⚙

For years, I've read descriptions and summaries of this six-part story that seemed convoluted and confusing; I thought that maybe the absence of everything except part 3 from the BBC's video archives was a factor. For this story, much hailed as a *tour de force* performance by Patrick Troughton as both the Doctor and his "evil twin" of sorts, I sought out a "reconstruction" of the missing footage. Some scant visual record existed of the missing episodes 1, 2 and 4-6. Did they help? Sometimes.

Sadly, I came to realize that *Enemy Of The World* is an overlong, overcomplicated *faux* epic that attempts to push the Time Lord and friends into James Bond territory — unsuccessfully. *Enemy* wouldn't be memorable at all if not for the aforementioned dual performance by Mr. Troughton and the notoriety of being AWOL from the archives. To make matters worse, a fairly major (and completely bizarre) plot strand about Salamander subjugating a *whole other population* that he keeps underground pops up out of nowhere halfway through the story, feeling like nothing so much as a late-in-the-day attempt to pad the story out to six parts. Several characters switch sides, and these various betrayals come across as the same thing — something to fill six 25-minute scripts. *Enemy* could have been told in a much more economical four episode format.

Troughton's performance as Salamander is quite interesting, though, and almost manages to keep the whole thing afloat. It's about 50% "outrageous accent!" (as **Monty Python** would've put it) and 50% just being everything terrible that the Doctor isn't. Troughton was, first and foremost, a character actor, and there are numerous shades of subtlety within his performance. In part six, when Salamander tries to turn the table and infiltrate the TARDIS, it's actually more than a little bit chilling.

Enemy is also notable for being the first **Doctor Who** stint for a director named Barry Letts. He would become the show's producer mere seasons later, and would institute major changes to the show during the Jon Pertwee era.

I can hear an argument that **Doctor Who**, then and now, shouldn't shy away from purely human, non-alien-influenced foibles, but I could just as easily make an argument that there are other shows I watch for that sort of thing, and would like **Who** to remain relatively escapist. I'm still not sure I can even resolve that debate with myself, let alone with anyone else. But *Enemy Of The World* is one example to cite here – by dragging things out to an improbable length, it makes plain old human evil seem boring.

The following review was written after the missing episodes were recovered and made available in 2013.

If there's anything to be learned from the recovery of *The Enemy Of The World*, it is the following equation:

> The best narrated, remastered soundtrack in the world
> + the best telesnap slide show in the world
> + the finest Target novelization that money can buy
> $\neq$ **the show.**

This really should be common sense, but in the case of *The Enemy Of The World*, missing the actual episodes means that we've been missing the whole experience. Here is an episode that rides on Patrick Troughton's meticulous, menacing performance as Salamander, in addition to his usual expert portrayal of the Doctor. Other, later stories in the show's history have given us evil twins aplenty - Tom Baker's vaguely menacing android double in *The Android Invasion* or covered in cactus as *Meglos*, Peter Davison as Omega in *Arc Of Infinity*, and on the more recent end of the spectrum, Matt Smith as both the Doctor and the "flesh Doctor" in *The Almost People*, or as the mind of the Cyber Controller in *Nightmare In Silver*. None of these, however, are on a par with Patrick Troughton's dual role here.

Salamander is a ruthless, mercenary killer with no affection or loyalty toward anyone. Late in the story, when he gets to wield a gun himself rather than relying on armed flunkies, Salamander is genuinely enjoying himself without an ounce of remorse. In a story that was derided at the time for having no monster to speak of, Salamander <u>is</u> a monster, merely of a different kind - a kind that one is, frankly, more likely to meet in real life than, say, a Dalek or an Ice Warrior. This simply wouldn't work if not for Troughton's disturbingly enthusiastic performance. He also deserves praise for developing a *second* characterization of Salamander - that of the uncertain Doctor trying to impersonate him. A few times the two are indistinguishable, but sometimes there are subtle cues. The audience *isn't* always in on the gag (in fact, the final scene of the story depends on the audience not being entirely certain who's who, any more than Jamie and Victoria are).

The supporting players prop the story up for those scenes in which Salamander is not present, at least for the first half of the story, but halfway through the story we learn that Salamander has been keeping an entire bomb shelter full of people slaving away for him incessantly, laboring under the misconception (provided and perpetuated by Salamander himself) that Earth's surface has been rendered uninhabitable due to atomic warfare. Borrowed from Philip K. Dick's 1964 novel <u>The Penultimate Truth</u> (and, by extension, Dick's 1953 short story <u>The Defenders</u>), this plot device is completely ineffectual because *no reason is ever given for Salamander to be doing this to these people.* Nothing they do is providing *any* tactical advantage for Salamander's choke-hold on the world, whereas, between the futuristic base and its occupants, surely some resources are being diverted from the surface to Salamander's seemingly surplus society of subsurface servants. Even a single mention of Salamander planning to nuke the entire surface and wait it out below would've fixed this; the lack of any such clear-cut story justification for the sudden plot twist instead reeks of "Oh crap, I have to stretch this out to *six* episodes!?"

The great thing about the dual story discovery is that *The Enemy Of The World* dovetails very deliberately into part one of *The Web Of Fear;* there is *no* between-story breathing room. And against all possible odds, we now have both stories almost in their entirety, so the links are clear and unambiguous. *Enemy* is loaded with continuity references, whether to the previous story (Jamie mentions the ionizer from *The Ice Warriors*) or clever wink-and-nod references to the next story ("A disused *Yeti!?*").

The Enemy Of The World is *not* an era-defining classic; in some structural areas, in fact, it's a deeply flawed story. But if you can temporarily forgive it those trespasses and imperfections, it's a tremendous showcase for Patrick Troughton, Actor. The last two and a half minutes of part six are spine-tingling stuff as the Doctor interrupts Salamander's attempt to hijack the TARDIS, and the results are as action-packed and scary as anything modern **Doctor Who** could manage. This story deserves a fresh viewing – and a reassessment – after decades of being unviewable in any form.

SHORT HOPS

...in which the author presents just a bit of a wish list. Not that he's being demanding or anything...

It's way too easy to just say "I'll have them all back, please," almost like you're contemplating a side order of fries with that. The following list was jotted down just after the BBC had only just confirmed a missing episode find, its hand having been forced somewhat by the Daily Mirror articles and the Radio Times - and, one suspects, by a fandom that, while known for being demanding from time to time, had probably reached a fever pitch.

The chances of every missing episode of **Doctor Who** returning to the BBC's vaults are nigh-on impossible. Some episodes were never sold overseas. And let's assume that only a handful are coming back intact. Just for fun, I decided to list three "finds" per Doctor as my "wish list", for wildly different reasons.

The Two First Doctor Episodes I'd Most Like To See Returned: *Marco Polo* - the missing gem of the first season, this is by all accounts a lavish costume extravaganza. But more to the point, it's where - having been put through the wringer on Skaro and then trapped in the TARDIS - the Doctor, Ian, Susan and Barbara gel as a team and realize that, whether the strangeness they encounter is on another world or on Earth, they need each other to survive. The following historical Earth adventure, *The Aztecs,* would test that new dependency and loyalty to its limits, a test that doesn't have quite the same meaning with all seven episodes of *Marco Polo* missing. After a fashion, with the release of *The Reign Of Terror* with its two animated missing episodes, the rest of **Doctor Who's** first season on the air exists, marred only by the absence of this, the first story to go missing in its entirety.

The Savages - I almost couldn't decide between this story and more missing episodes of *Galaxy Four*. Both are solid attempts to do "hard" science fiction in the **Doctor Who** format, and both are solid attempts to slip a moral into the story as well. But *The Savages* has something that *Galaxy Four* doesn't (the departure of the first Doctor's loyal companion, Steven Taylor), and as of 2011, *Galaxy Four* has something that *The Savages* doesn't (one full episode safe and sound in the BBC archives at last). We can now see that lone episode of *Galaxy Four*; of *The Savages*, we have seen nothing.

The First Doctor Story In Which I'm *Least* Interested: *The Smugglers* - Ben and Polly's first trip in the TARDIS takes them to an adventure on the Cornish coast! With pirates! In audio form, this story barely maintains my interest, but is that because it's a bad story, or is that because all that swashbuckling just can't be conveyed by the medium of sound? As uninterested in the story as I am, I would be up for sitting through it against for a reassessment. *The Smugglers* is also the last time that **Doctor Who** was a show that could only be fronted by William Hartnell; at the end of the following story, *The Tenth Planet*, the entire structure of the series changed forever.

The Two Second Doctor Stories I'd Most Like To See Returned: *Power Of The Daleks* - the entirety of the history of this show that I love hinges heavily on this story, which is completely lost to the ages. If this hadn't been an effective story - and from its audio recordings and the slideshow reconstruction, it certainly seems like it had to be effective - we would not now be celebrating **Doctor Who**'s 50th anniversary; we might instead be musing on this little show, **Doctor Who**, that dared to recast its main character in its fourth year on the air and suffered an ignominious loss of audience and swift cancellation as a result. But that didn't happen. Patrick Troughton picked up the ball and ran for his life. And when he said run, the audience ran too. This was the biggest risk that **Doctor Who** ever took, with the Daleks riding shotgun as a surefire ratings draw for an insurance policy. I want to see it, not just hear it.

The Abominable Snowmen – I know that segments of fandom would have me up against the wall facing a firing squad for not wishing both *Power* and *Evil Of The Daleks* back into existence, but follow my logic here: *Power* and *Evil* are both very atypical Dalek stories, detours in the overall Dalek mythology. *The Abominable Snowmen*, on the other hand, is the beginning of an ongoing plotline with a much more limited number of available stories (the Great Intelligence story plays out across this story, *The Web Of Fear*, the video production *Downtime*, and the 2012-2013 season episodes *The Snowmen*, *The Bells Of Saint Johns*, and *The Name Of The Doctor*) And even with only the audio by which to judge it, it's eerie and atmospheric – it *sounds* like a classic. It'd be nice to have the opportunity to see if it looks like one too.

The Second Doctor Story In Which I'm *Least* Interested: *The Space Pirates* - I nominate the six-part yawner *The Space Pirates* as possibly the worst second Doctor serial, if not the worst storyline in the series' history. Even slideshow reconstructions and audio recordings fail to make it thrilling, but again, it was a *tour de force* for the BBC's in-house space model shop, whose time was usually taken up by painstakingly recreating American space missions in miniature for BBC News. Is there, in fact, some thrilling element we're missing by not seeing the entire thing in motion as originally filmed? I'd be willing to sit through it again in its entirety to find out. Considering how much I love later BBC space operas like **Blake's 7** and **Moonbase 3**, you'd think I would be all over this one.

As you can see, I got at least one present from my wish list. At the time of its October 2013 announcement, the BBC was willing only to say that it had recovered "a number" of episodes - and that number could've been anywhere between 0 and 106. Even though the final number was nine episodes, this find was a gift, timed almost impossibly right. If, in the future, 20 episodes or more are returned in a single haul, it would be a treasure on a scale for which we could never have dared to hope. If either of the series' "eras" impacted by episode erasures over the years could be fully restored to the archives, you would almost think that perhaps a mad man in a blue box left these somewhere for us as a thank you for keeping an eye out for him for the past half-century.

The credit, of course, properly belongs with fans who have *never* been satisfied with the notion that so many episodes are gone from the show's history. If you think I've devoted a ridiculous chunk of my life to a show from another country by writing a book or two about it, imagine devoting years of your life and very real resources, often including visits to parts of the world that have much weightier issues demanding their attention, to looking for something that may simply no longer exist.

THE WEB OF FEAR

The Doctor, Jamie and Victoria are nearly sucked out into the time vortex when Salamander takes off with the TARDIS doors open. Salamander is ejected from the TARDIS, and the ship lands safely in the London Underground circa 1968. But all is not well in central London: a deadly mist hovers above ground over the Circle Line, and an even deadlier web is filling the tunnels of the Underground. Yeti patrol the tunnels, trapping a batallion of Army soldiers in the tunnels. The Great Intelligence has trapped the Doctor and his friends in a scheme to take over the Doctor's mind, using the Time Lord's immense knowledge for evil. Professor Travers, the scientist who the Doctor saved from the Yeti in 1930s Tibet, is able to vouch for the time travelers' good intensions, though some of the soldiers aren't so trusting. The Doctor races against time to wrest control of the robotic Yeti from the Great Intelligence and to find a traitor among the contingent of soldiers in the Underground. And perhaps most importantly of all, the Doctor must gain the trust of an unusually open-minded Army officer, Colonel Lethbridge-Stewart.

Patrick Troughton . . . . The Doctor
Frazer Hines . . . . Jamie
Deborah Watling . . . . Victoria
Rod Beacham . . . . Lane
Nicholas Courtney . . Colonel Lethbridge-Stewart
Bernard G. High . . . . Soldier
Roger Jacombs . . . . Yeti
Jeremy King . . . . Yeti
John Levene . . . . Yeti
John Lord . . . . Yeti
Richardson Morgan . . . . Blake
Joseph O' Connell . . . . Soldier
Tina Packer . . . . Anne Travers
Derek Pollitt . . . . Evans
Jon Rollason . . . . Chorley
Frederick Schrecker . . . . Julius Silverstein
Gordon Stothard . . . . Yeti
Colin Warman . . . . Yeti

This story has been released on DVD

written by Mervyn Haisman & Henry Lincoln
directed by Gerald Blake
stock library music - see credits below

Part 1 aired on February 3, 1968
Part 2 aired on February 10, 1968
Part 3 aired on February 17, 1968
Part 4 aired on February 24, 1968
Part 5 aired on March 2, 1968
Part 6 aired on March 9, 1968

Jack Watling . . . . Professor Travers
Ralph Watson . . . . Knight
Stephen Whittaker . . . . Weams
Jack Woolgar . . . . Arnold

MISSING: Episode 3 of *The Web Of Fear* is missing from the BBC archives.

BEHIND THE SCENES: Nicholas Courtney was originally hired to play the part of Knight, but when the actor hired to play Lethbridge-Stewart had to bow out, Knight was recast and Courtney was "promoted" to the Colonel's role; had this not happened, **Doctor Who** history might have turned out very differently! Also, though you can't really "see" him, future UNIT regular **John Levene** makes his first appearance here, not as Sgt. Benton but as one of the Yeti. The Great

Intelligence first encounters the Doctor much later in the Doctor's timeline in 2013's *The Snowmen*, during which the eleventh Doctor shows it a map of the London Underground. For decades, the only surviving episode of this story was part one, until four missing episodes of *The Web Of Fear* were discovered in a hut owned by a Nigerian broadcast company in 2013. The search that led to the missing episode discovery also returned the previous Troughton serial, *The Enemy Of The World*, in its entirety.

STOCK MUSIC: "Music For Strings, Percussion & Celeste" (Bela Bartok), "Lunar Probe: Andromeda" (Francois Bayle), Space Time Music, Parts 1 & 2" (Wilfred Josephs), "Impending Danger" (Syd Dale), "Spine Chillers" (Edwin Braden)

The following review was written prior to the discovery of the missing episodes.

There almost aren't words to describe how pivotal this six-part adventure from Patrick Troughton's reign is. The introduction of the future Brigadier Lethbridge-Stewart — initially a red herring for the story as the search begins for a suspected traitor working for the Great Intelligence — is only the most visible reason of this story's significance. Its (then) present-day Earth setting — a little bit easier to create in the studio or shoot on location than any futuristic, otherworldly locale — also plays a big part in determining the direction of the early '70s episodes. *The Web Of Fear* is almost, in these regards, as important as, say, a regeneration episode, or the first episode featuring a popular monster. As it was, it turned out to be the final appearance of the Yeti as the main villains in a BBC-produced **Doctor Who** story, though the Great Intelligence and its minions would rear their heads again in such spin-off videos as *Downtime* and the sixth Doctor Missing Adventures novel Millennial Rites.

It's therefore perversely inevitable that most of the story — including Lethbridge-Stewart's debut — is missing, available only in audio form. Go figure.

The cast is uniformly excellent, and Nicholas Courtney shines in his introductory story as Lethbridge-Stewart. One wonders if the intention was always to bring Lethbridge-Stewart in as a recurring character — an inordinate amount of attention is focused on the Colonel from his first appearance, in very much the same way that incoming companion characters such as Zoe, Peri, Turlough, and Adric received a lot of quality screen time before stowing away aboard the TARDIS for themselves. Particularly intriguing is that the Colonel never seems to completely *doubt* the Doctor. There is suspicion, there is curiosity, but there's never an outright refusal to believe that the Doctor is an otherworldly genius whose police box can travel in time and space.

Thanks to the excellent remastered 3-CD audio version from the BBC Radio Collection, we can at least hear *Web* again with rapid-fire narration of visual scenes by Frazer "Jamie" Hines. It's actually quite effective, and one can almost see the entire thing — good old fashioned radio drama. Even if you're not a big fan of listening to **Doctor Who** as opposed to seeing **Doctor Who**, I recommend this six-parter to you.

The following review was written after the missing episodes were recovered and made available in 2013.

Already regarded as a classic deserving of at least the same amount of admiration as *Tomb Of The Cybermen*, and topping many a fan's missing episode wish list, *The Web Of Fear* had quite an impressive reputation to live up to in the event that it was located. And then, of course, it *was* located, and suddenly it was on iTunes (minus epiosde three, which remained in the realm of "audio with photo slideshow reconstruction"), and we could see if it measured up to expectations. (Of course, even if it did, there's no guarantee that a re-*re*-assessment wouldn't occur down the road - since it was miraculously recovered in its entirety in 1992, *Tomb Of The Cybermen* has been in and out of favor so many times that I forget where fannish "received wisdom" puts it on the scale these days.)

Though the third episode sadly remains missing - denying us the chance to see the first meeting of the Doctor and Colonel Lethbridge-Stewart (though it can at least be heard) - *Web Of Fear* richly deserves its good reputation. It's a dark, scary thriller that may, in fact, work all the better for the almost *noir*-ish look of its black & white footage. **Doctor Who** gained a reputation for being overlit to the point of tackiness in later years, but here it's positively atmospheric, and Douglas Camfield not only makes the action convincing, but he gets some crackling performances out of the cast. Jack Watling is chilling as the Great Intelligence's unfortunate host body, and his showdown with the Doctor may just assume its place in the pantheon of the classic series' most memorable scenes.

And it's important to not undersell Nicholas Courtney's debut as Lethbridge-Stewart. Here we're presented with a man who's never met the Doctor before, or heard of his seemingly magical vehicle, knows nothing of the Doctor's origins or intentions, and has absolutely no reason to take the Doctor at his word... and yet has a mind open enough that he can't completely discount the Doctor's claims to have some kind of spacecraft stashed away near the London Underground. It's known by now that Courtney was "promoted to Colonel" - he was originally engaged to play Captain Knight when the actor contracted to play Lethbridge-Stewart had to drop out of that role - but he's astonishingly good as Lethbridge-Stewart here. You can watch his eyes and see the wheels turning: there's nothing to lose in believing this strange little man's claims of traveling through space and time, and given how outside the realm of human experience the whole event is, there may be survival to gain. But is he out to save his regiment, or just his own skin? (Keep in mind that the audience didn't know whether the Colonel was to be trusted or not at this stage.) Whatever long-range plans may have existed for Lethbridge-Stewart beyond *The Web Of Fear* on paper, Nick Courtney's portrayal of the character almost certainly made his return (and his promotion, to both Brigadier and series regular) a very easy decision for **Doctor Who**'s production team.

The staging of the Coventry Garden battle between the Colonel's Army troops and the Yeti isn't as epic as some accounts had led me to believe, but it's still a very competently staged action piece. (Some of the "contemporary accounts" circulated in the years that these episodes were missing might've led you to believe that **Doctor Who** had exhausted its budget for the next three *years* on this scene alone. Obviously, it didn't, but it's still quite the battle scene by **Doctor Who** and BBC standards.

Finally, kudos to the BBC for its skillful stage-managing of the rollout of *Enemy Of The World* and *Web Of Fear*. The unprecedented iTunes release - within 24 hours of the press conference confirming the episodes' recovery - had no negative impact on future DVD release of the same material (in fact, *The Web Of Fear* turned out to be the best-selling title in the history of the BBC's classic **Doctor Who** DVD range). Perhaps more importantly, it forestalled a lot of grousing and speculation. By comparison, look at the discovery of one episode each from *Galaxy Four* and *The Underwater Menace* in late 2011: As of the end of 2013, the missing *Galaxy Four* episode was woven into a nicely-made reconstruction of the entire story (released on DVD as a bonus feature with the revised "special edition" of *The Aztecs* on DVD), while *The Underwater Menace* - destined for a semi-reconstructed DVD release with two episodes animated and two episodes of restored live-action footage (much like the recent DVD of *The Moonbase*) - still awaits release two years later. The BBC obviously picked up on dissatisfaction with this, and by keeping things firmly under wraps in collusion with TIEA, the DVD Restoration Team, and its own internal publicity machinery, got the word out and got the product into fans' hands, all in time for the 50th anniversary.

Was that worth all of the ebb and flow and *sturm und drang* of the infamous "omnirumor" over the course of 2013? To finally see the second Doctor (who made bow ties cool long before Matt Smith) face off against the Great Intelligence (recently revived in the modern series)... *yes*. Yes, it was.

SHORT HOPS

...in which the author, pondering *Enemy* and *Web*, thinks fandom
on the web has better things to do than be its own worst enemy

In October 2013, fandom collectively did the same thing for once - hovered over the internet waiting for news of the nine recovered episodes, and then swarmed iTunes to download them all at once.

And then, having devoured a few hours' worth of episodes not seen in 45 years, fandom collectively did what fandom is wont to do: we began craving more.

It wasn't really hard to do, considering that we'd just been given access to most of what's generally considered one of the best Troughton adventures, alongside another full story which, while not so highly regarded, turned out to be more entertaining than many expected. Rumors began swirling of other finds, focusing primarily on the Hartnell story *Marco Polo*, and the entire "omnirumor" that had been making the rounds, claiming that anywhere from one to 106 of the 106 missing episodes had been miraculously located, was back with a vengeance. If, indeed, it had ever gone away.

Instant gratification: With a carefully staged iTunes rollout and DVD releases some months later, the BBC talked more than a few of us into buying the freshly unearthed episodes twice.

The find made a celebrity of Philip Morris, head of Television International Enterprises Archives (TIEA), who found the missing episodes in a seldom-visited broadcast relay hut in northern Africa; as soon as the novelty of the find wore off, the hunger for more made Morris a target of speculation, rumor, and more than a few tweets of a surprisingly demanding nature. The man has to have wondered at some point if he wasn't better off when all he was finding was old episodes of Sir Patrick Moore's venerable astronomy series, **The Sky At Night.**

Even the slightest hiccup in the DVD release schedules of partially-reconstructed stories such as *The Moonbase* and *The Underwater Menace* has inspired new rounds of rumors: see? *See?* They've *found another episode* of that story and they're restoring it for DVD! Otherwise why would the schedule have slipped?

Not that anyone's really asked, but my own take on the un-killable omnirumor follows.

As things stand right now, we have access to audio of *every episode* of **Doctor Who** ever broadcast, and photographic reference material to most of those episodes, in many cases enough material for artists to create animated reconstructions of the missing video to match the existing audio. In short, **Doctor Who**'s got it better than a great many series which have just as many missing episodes. Nobody's rushing to create cartoon versions of missing installments of **Dad's Army**, nor is there a complete archive of the full audio from each episode that no longer exists on film or video. (Even well-known series that you'd think would exist in their entirety are missing significant portions of their history; the beloved Patrick Macnee series **The Avengers** is complete only from its second season onward, and Big Finish, the makers of original audio **Doctor Who**, recently undertook the mammoth task of recreating **The Avengers**' entire first season in audio form with a new cast working from the original scripts.)

If Philip Morris is unable to find and return anything else, we're already nine episodes richer for his efforts - and certainly no poorer. Badgering him via Twitter and Facebook does nothing, and there's no evidence that he is hoarding missing episodes or holding them hostage, at least no evidence that doesn't exist entirely in the realm of rumor (omni or otherwise) and insinuation.

It could be that we'll <u>never</u> see *The Massacre* or *The Savages* or *Power Of The Daleks* or *The Highlanders* as they were originally broadcast.

And — here's the part to brace yourself for - *that's okay.* It really is okay. It's perhaps not as good as having the originals, but it's okay. Much fan creativity has sprung from these gaps in the show's history, from animated reconstructions to condensed adaptations ramped up to the speed of modern television (Nick Scovell's remount of *Power Of The Daleks*) to comics (Rick Lundeen's impressive fan-made comic version of *The Daleks' Masterplan*) to full theatrical productions (the on-stage recreation of *The Evil Of The Daleks* mounted by Nick Scovell and Rob Thrush). *It's okay.*

Not that we'd kick TIEA, Ian Levine, or anyone else off the planet if further missing episodes or stories were returned, mind you. But the point is that **Doctor Who** fandom, when it's not busy arguing or grousing over minutiae, is as adaptable and impressive an entity as the show around which it has formed. Thanks to the astounding creativity and resourcefulness of some corners of fandom, workarounds and repairs have been made to these gaping open wounds in the show's history.

And that should be celebrated as much as the series itself. It's fandom at its best.

FURY FROM THE DEEP

The TARDIS deposits the Doctor, Victoria and Jamie near a North Sea natural gas refinery, whose pipelines radiate a disturbing, heartbeat-like sound. When refinery personnel find the Doctor trying to diagnose the problem, the head of the refinery operation assumes that the Doctor is trying to sabotage their operation. But once they're at the refinery itself, the time travelers quickly learn that something is dangerously amiss. Drilling rigs at sea have dropped out of communication, samples of strange seaweed enshrouded in a pulsating foam have been found, and those who have come in contact with the seaweed have never been the same again. The Doctor offers his help, but when it is refused it puts he and his companions in even greater risk. When the Doctor encounters the seaweed, it takes time for him to realize that one of his companions has the best defense against it.

Patrick Troughton . . . . The Doctor
Frazer Hines . . . . Jamie
Deborah Watling . . . . Victoria
John Abineri . . . . Van Lutyens
Bill Burridge . . . . Quill
Brian Cullingford . . . . Perkins
Peter Ducrom . . . . Guard
John Garvin . . . . Carney
John Gill . . . . Oak
Margaret John . . . . Megan Jones
Graham Leaman . . . . Price
Victor Maddern . . . . Robson
Richard Mayes . . . . Baxter
June Murphy . . . . Maggie Harris

This story has been released on audio CD

written by Victor Pemberton
directed by Hugh David
music by Dudley Simpson

Part 1 aired on March 16, 1968
Part 2 aired on March 23, 1968
Part 3 aired on March 30, 1968
Part 4 aired on April 6, 1968
Part 5 aired on April 13, 1968
Part 6 aired on April 20, 1968

Hubert Rees . . . . Chief Engineer
Roy Spencer . . . . Harris

MISSING: All six episodes of *Fury From The Deep* are missing from the BBC archives.

NEW WHO CONNECTIONS: *Fury From The Deep* was the very first story to feature the sonic screwdriver, a tool used by every Doctor except the first and sixth incarnations, and the Doctor prophetically points out that it'll "work on anything". While later versions of the screwdriver seen in the classic series reformatted its shape into a device that emitted energy at a right angle to its handle, the second Doctor's sonic screwdriver — seen here and in *The War Games* — is obviously a penlight; it's also the only classic series sonic screwdriver to match the new series' depiction of the device as something aimed directly at its target. There's an eerie similarity between the behavior of Mr. Quill and Mr. Oak — opening their mouths disturbingly wide and seeming to vomit the alien seaweed toward its next victim — and the Bowie Base One crewmembers infected by *The Waters Of Mars* (2009). Given that real Martian meteorites have turned up in Antarctica, could some of the sentient Martian water have reached ordinary Earth seaweed (perhaps in frozen form riding on another meteorite) and used it as a host?

As effective as it was, *Fury From The Deep* is very much a typical Troughton-era **Doctor Who** story: a confined, isolated setting, a tense crew (complete with a leader who's cracking under the pressure of command and endangering everyone in the process), and a monster that gradually thins the ranks of the besieged, Ten Little Indians-style. While the fifth season is generally regarded as one of the original series' high points, most of its stories clung tightly to that basic formula. By the time we get to *Fury*, a sense of "been there, done that" has set in. Fortunately, *Fury* is one of the better examples of that basic paint-by-numbers plotline.

Where *Fury* succeeds is in pure atmosphere. What little footage survives shows two things this story had going for it: the rapid surge of foam (what we mere non-time-traveling mortals would call "soap suds") heralding the arrival of the seaweed, and the darkly comic duo of Mr. Oak and Mr. Quill, who are very creepy indeed. One of composer Dudley Simpson's earliest collaborations with the BBC Radiophonic

Workshop can be heard here in a piece of music which serves as a theme for Oak and Quill, which helps to make their appearances that much creepier. Sadly, there's not much more footage than that to go by, leaving us – as with many Troughton-era stories – with the audio.

In audio form, *Fury From The Deep* has been issued twice, with very different presentations. It was released on cassette in 1993, with Tom Baker narrating the story in character – i.e. the fourth Doctor looking back on the second Doctor's adventure – and again more recently with Frazer "Jamie" Hines serving as an impartial third-party narrator. While the 1993 cassette release is undoubtedly lower quality – the sound recordings of the original episodes being not only edited down but left untouched, with very poor sound quality and points at which you can tell that you've switched to an even more inferior copy of the source material – there's something refreshing about hearing the story from the Doctor's perspective, even if it means hearing gems like Baker describing Mr. Oak and Mr. Quill as "a psychotic Laurel & Hardy". On the other hand, the narration script for the Baker edition is completely bizarre in terms of what it chooses to describe and what it doesn't. Still, it's an interesting and enjoyable peek into what might have been for the missing stories in audio form.

THE WHEEL IN SPACE

After leaving Victoria on Earth, the Doctor and Jamie find themselves aboard a drifting spacecraft. A fault in the TARDIS' mercury fluid link creates a dangerous malfunction, which the Doctor resorts to drastic measures to stop, removing the timeship's time vector generator and folding down its internal dimensions until it literally is a police box. The Doctor is knocked out as the spacecraft lurches suddenly, leaving Jamie on his own. When the ship comes dangerously close to space station W3, the station's commander prepares to blast the ship out of the sky, over his crew's objections. Jamie manages to signal the space station, which sends astronauts across to retrieve the two time travelers, who find themselves hard-pressed to explain their presence. The ship is millions of miles off course and shouldn't have been anywhere near W3 at all. When a Cybermat appears, the Doctor realizes that the Cybermen can't be far behind, and they've used the ship to smuggle themselves aboard the wheel. But what is the Cybermen's real goal?

Patrick Troughton	. . . .	The Doctor
Frazer Hines	. . . .	Jamie
Wendy Padbury	. . . .	Zoe
Eric Flynn	. . . .	Ryan
Freddie Foote	. . . .	Servo-Robot
Derrick Gilbert	. . . .	Vallance
Michael Goldie	. . . .	Laleham
Peter Hawkins	. . . .	Cyberman voice
Jerry Holmes	. . . .	Cyberman
Clare Jenkins	. . . .	Tanya Lernov
Peter Laird	. . . .	Chang
Kevork Malikyan	. . . .	Rudkin
James Mellor	. . . .	Flannigan
Anne Ridler	. . . .	Dr. Corwyn
Roy Skelton	. . . .	Cyberman voice
Gordon Stothard	. . . .	Cyberman

This story has been released on audio CD

written by David Whitaker
based on a story by Kit Pedler
directed by Tristan de Vere Cole
music by Brian Hodgson and the
BBC Radiophonic Workshop

Part 1 aired on April 27, 1968
Part 2 aired on May 4, 1968
Part 3 aired on May 11, 1968
Part 4 aired on May 18, 1968
Part 5 aired on May 25, 1968
Part 6 aired on June 1, 1968

Donald Sumpter	. . . .	Enrico Casali
Michael Turner	. . . .	Bennett
Kenneth Watson	. . . .	Duggan

MISSING: Episodes 1, 2, 4 and 5 of *The Wheel In Space* are missing from the BBC archives.

BEHIND THE SCENES: Zoe joins the TARDIS crew in this story, and the end of episode six the Doctor sets up a device to replay a recent adventure with the Daleks to her, which was an inspired way to lead into a rare rerun (in this case, *The Evil Of The Daleks*) to fill time between seasons. This marked the final appearance of the *Moonbase*-style Cybermen; in their next appearance, in *The Invasion*, they would undergo a major redesign.

NEW WHO CONNECTIONS: This episode marks the first appearance of the Doctor's psuedonym "John Smith", which would be used more frequently in the Pertwee era and would reappear in everything from the 1996 TV movie through David Tennant's tenure. Jamie coined the name in a bit of a pinch, and perhaps as a payback, the tenth Doctor instead uses the alias "James McCrimmon" during a visit to Scotland in *Tooth And Claw*.

The last gasp of the sleek "Golden Age" Cybermen, *The Wheel In Space* is a curious throwback to an earlier era of **Doctor Who**. In large part, this is thanks to a script by the show's original script editor, David Whitaker, who falls back on the kind of bizarre pseudoscience that was woven into the earlier scripts he oversaw. As with *The Daleks*, the TARDIS is crippled by a lack of liquid mercury (an oddly mundane dependency for such a fantastic craft), and while I give *Wheel* big points for its early filmed portrayal of a torus-style space station, as imagined by space visionary Gerard K. O'Neill, the story leans heavily on talk of wayward rockets and dialogue and characters that, even by the standards of late '60s **Doctor Who**, are absurdly cliched and sexist. It's almost a throwback to 1950s pulp sci-fi, giving us such howlers as "All spacemen are protected from brain control by drugs!" (*Wheel* is also the source of the infamous made-it-into-the-finished-edit blooper in which the Doctor mentions the "sexual air supply" when he means "sectional"... I wouldn't inhale if I were you.)

It's also a throwback to the early, produced-year-round days of **Doctor Who**, with the Doctor out of commission for much of the first half of the story, apparently due to little more than a tap on the head (a plot development inspired more by Patrick Troughton's request for some time off than anything). Jamie carries this half of the story, though it seems like there's wasted potential in following him as he tries to make his own way in the distant future to which he is unaccustomed. The Cybermen are used strangely here too, having suddenly developed the ability to control human minds and utilizing an invasion plan that seems to depend on coincidence as much as anything. And in any case, the story waits until it's almost over to nail down the importance, strategic or otherwise, of the station, and therefore why the Cybermen would go to such lengths to take it over – and even when it is explained, it's nonsense. The story's logic falls down in other places as well, namely in the case of a character who spots a Cybermat on the space station, and bizarrely tries to snag it as a pet, but tells no one about it until it's had a chance to sabotage the station. This could've been explained away simply by allowing the Cybermats to share the Cybermen's newfound drug-resistant brain control ability, but nope: somebody just wants a metal rat to keep him company.

Only two of the six episodes of *Wheel* survive in video form, and they don't necessarily improve things. The Cybermen's spacewalk to, and their subsequent repulsion from, the station is the product of an addled budget, and simply looks silly. Even *The Moonbase* made a better show of low gravity than this.

Wheel may be inordinately fondly remembered for introducing Zoe and for just being a Cybermen story, but this is easily the nadir of their 1960s appearances, and numerous elements of *Wheel* are so outlandishly silly that it's hard for me to avoid dismissing it as one of the biggest clunkers of Troughton's era. I can almost justify this story's existence for the surviving scene of the Doctor turning slowly to face the Cybermen and saying "I imagine you have orders to destroy me," a classic clip if ever there was one, but *The Wheel In Space* is best left rolling into obscurity.

SEASON 6: 1968-69
THE DOMINATORS

The TARDIS brings the Doctor, Zoe and Jamie to the planet Dulkis, which the Doctor knows as a peaceful world that has abandoned war. But the travelers find themselves on an island strewn with the remnants of an ancient war and contaminated with radiation – the legacy of nuclear weapons tests, according to a small number of researchers encountered by the Doctor. What the Time Lord doesn't realize is that the native Dulcians are not the only people visiting the island. Another Dulcian expedition meets with disaster, its only survivor claiming that his shipmates were killed by well-armed robots. The Doctor and Jamie go to investigate these claims, and find themselves taken prisoner by a group of aggressive aliens who call themselves the Dominators. These would-be invaders, backed up by their powerful Quark robots, intend to mine the radioactive minerals on Dulkis to make their own nuclear weapons...and they also wish to use the pacifist Dulcians as their slaves. The Doctor scrambles to find a way to undermine the Dominators when it becomes obvious that the Dulcians are unwilling to rediscover the aggression necessary to protect themselves.

Patrick Troughton . . . . The Doctor
Frazer Hines . . . . Jamie
Wendy Padbury . . . . Zoe
Ronald Allen . . . . Rago
Johnson Bayly . . . . Balan
Giles Block . . . . Teel
Brian Cant . . . . Tensa
Arthur Cox . . . . Cully
John Cross . . . . Council Member
Walter Fitzgerald . . . . Senex
Alan Gerrard . . . . Bovem
Felicity Gibson . . . . Kando
Sheila Grant . . . . Quark voices
John Hicks . . . . Quark
Kenneth Ives . . . . Toba
Ronald Mansell . . . . Council Member
Nicolette Pendrell . . . . Tolata
Gary Smith . . . . Quark

written by Mervyn Haisman & Henry Lincoln
directed by Morris Barry
no incidental music

This story has been released on DVD

Part 1 aired on August 10, 1968
Part 2 aired on August 17, 1968
Part 3 aired on August 24, 1968
Part 4 aired on August 31, 1968
Part 5 aired on September 7, 1968

Malcolm Terris . . . . Etnin
Philip Voss . . . . Wahed
Aubrey Danvers Walker . . . . . . Council Member
Malcolm Watson . . . . Council Member
Freddie Wilson . . . . Quark

Not the best adventure of Troughton's era, perhaps what bogs down *The Dominators* most precariously is – and I hate making this argument – the lack of a "monster," at least one of any effectively threatening posture. The chirpy-voiced Quarks are hardly menacing. As a result, the story becomes an exercise in rather drab political allegory...something which **Doctor Who** can do well, but that just wasn't what one expects of the Troughton era. Put it in the Pertwee or Davison eras, and it might just work.

The slow pace also sucks the urgency out of the story, pretty much ensuring that by the time something finally happens, no one really cares. I hate to say it, because on the face of it, *The Dominators* has a truly intriguing premise, but that same theme – pacifism in the face of extinction – was much more effectively explored in *The Daleks*. Drab is the best word I can think of for this story. Not one of my favorites.

THE MIND ROBBER

The Doctor is faced with an emergency that forces him to yank the TARDIS out of the dimension of reality. The TARDIS arrives in a seemingly empty space outside of time, but the Doctor, Jamie and Zoe are not alone – someone wants them there and intends to force them to stay if necessary. The empty space is filled by the fiction that comes from human imagination – and the very tired human abductee, whose mind is being constantly tapped to keep the Land of Fiction alive, nominates the Doctor as his replacement for a job that can never be vacated.

Patrick Troughton . . . . The Doctor
Frazer Hines . . . . Jamie
Wendy Padbury . . . . Zoe
Paul Alexander . . . . Clockwork Soldier
John Atterbury . . . . White Robot
David Cannon . . . . Cyrano
Ralph Carrigan . . . . White Robot
John Greenwood . . . . D'Artagnan / Lancelot
Ian Hines . . . . Clockwork Soldier
Bernard Horsfall . . . . Gulliver
Timothy Horton . . . . Child
Richard Ireson . . . . Clockwork Soldier / Minotaur
Emrys Jones . . . . The Master
Martin Langley . . . . Child
Sylvestra Le Tozel . . . . Child
Barbara Loft . . . . Child
Christine Pirie . . . . . Rapunzel / Book Narrator
Sue Pulford . . . . Medusa

This story has been released on DVD

written by Peter Ling and Derrick Sherwin
directed by David Maloney
stock library music - see credits below

Part 1 aired on September 14, 1968
Part 2 aired on September 21, 1968
Part 3 aired on September 28, 1968
Part 4 aired on October 5, 1968
Part 5 aired on October 12, 1968

Christopher Reynolds . . . . Child
David Reynolds . . . . Child
Christopher Robbie . . . . Karkus
Philip Ryan . . . . Redcoat
Gerry Wain . . . . Blackbeard
Bill Weisener . . . . White Robot
Hamish Wilson . . . . Jamie
Terry Wright . . . . White Robot

STOCK MUSIC: "Symphony No. 7 In E Major: Scherzo" (Anton Bruckner)

This surreal, fantasy-based five-parter sometimes gets a little silly toward the middle, but the first half-hour episode is probably my favorite single episode of Patrick Troughton's tenure as the Doctor. There's mystery, danger, and a very abstract sense of the unknown. The idea of people wandering around in a shapeless white void was probably quite novel and unsettling, long before it became a visual sci-fi cliché. In parts two and three, things become rather silly as the Doctor is surrounded by a herd of sinister schoolchildren, and Jamie's face is stolen, forcing the Doctor to restore his friend's appearance. In order to give Frazer Hines a break from **Doctor Who**'s hectic, almost-year-round production schedule in those days, the story dictated that the Doctor would accidentally give Jamie the wrong face, allowing Hamish Wilson to take over the part for a couple of episodes. It's a rather strange little twist, even if you understand the real-life necessity behind it.

One often-overlooked scene in part four redresses, at least in a token manner, the accusation of sexism frequently leveled at **Doctor Who**. It's rather amusing when Zoe beats up a comic strip villain from her own time. *The Mind Robber* is a good little adventure, entertaining for all ages in much the same way as the scary fairy tales of the Brothers Grimm.

THE INVASION

The TARDIS reforms itself after what appears to be a cataclysmic explosion in space, only to become the target of a missile fired from the dark side of Earth's moon. The timeship finally materializes in a nondescript field on Earth, but instead of a police box, it's completely invisible. The Doctor, Zoe and Jamie set off for London on foot to seek Professor Travers' help with the TARDIS' visual stabilizer circuit, but soon hitch a ride on a passing truck, whose worried driver informs them that they're in danger as long as they're on International Electromatics property. He gets them safely out of IE's corporate compound, but is then gunned down in cold blood by armed IE guards.

In London, the Doctor and friends discover that Professor Travers has gone to America with his Yeti findings, but his friend Professor Watkins might be able to help. But Watkins has gone missing – he's never returned from International Electromatics – and his niece waits worriedly. The Doctor and Jamie return to IE's headquarters building, where they cause just enough trouble to get a personal audience with the head of the company, Tobias Vaughn. The Doctor immediately suspects that Vaughn is up to no good, but he and Jamie don't have time to think about it before they're intercepted by two cars that have been following their movements. They're taken to the mobile headquarters of a military organization called UNIT – the United Nations Intelligence Taskforce – whose British branch is headed up by their old friend Lethbridge-Stewart, now promoted to Brigadier. The Brigadier and his troops are monitoring IE closely: many brilliant, prominent scientific minds have entered, but none have left. The Doctor suspects that Tobias Vaughn wants control of more than just the world's largest maker of electronic devices...but whose help does Vaughn have to pull off such a coup?

Patrick Troughton	The Doctor
Frazer Hines	Jamie
Wendy Padbury	Zoe
Nicholas Courtney	Brigadier Lethbridge-Stewart
Dominic Allan	Policeman
Edward Burnham	Professor Watkins
Ralph Carrigan	Cyberman
Geoffrey Cheshire	Tracy
Stacy Davies	Perkins
Edward Dentith	Rutlidge
Sheila Dunn	Operator
Clifford Earl	Branswell
Murray Evans	Lorry Driver
Ian Fairburn	Gregory
Sally Faulkner	Isobel Watkins
Charles Finch	Cyberman
Pat Gorman	Cyberman
Peter Halliday	Packer / Cyber Director voice
Norman Hartley	Peters
Richard King	Cyberman
John Levene	Corporal Benton
Walter Randall	Patrolman
Robert Sidaway	Captain Turner
John Spradbury	Cyberman
Kevin Stoney	Tobias Vaughn
Peter Thompson	Workman
James Thornhill	Sergeant Walters
Peter Thornton	Cyberman

This story has been released on DVD

written by David Whitaker
based on a story by Kit Pedler
directed by Douglas Camfield
music by Don Harper

Part 1 aired on November 2, 1968
Part 2 aired on November 9, 1968
Part 3 aired on November 16, 1968
Part 4 aired on November 23, 1968
Part 5 aired on November 30, 1968
Part 6 aired on December 7, 1968
Part 7 aired on December 14, 1968
Part 8 aired on December 21, 1968

In 1993, BBC Video released *The Invasion* in incomplete form with Nicholas Courtney narrating encapsulated versions of the missing episodes. The 2006 DVD release took the unprecedented step of completely reconstructing the missing segments with cartoon-style animation.

MISSING: Episodes 1 and 5 of *The Invasion* are missing from the BBC archives.

BEHIND THE SCENES: Ironically, part one of 1974's *Invasion Of The Dinosaurs*, a Jon Pertwee story, was simply titled *Invasion* to preserve the surprise appearance of that story's adversaries at the end of the first episode; it was later mistaken for part of this story and junked, rendering an otherwise intact full-color story incomplete. A B&W copy of part one of that story was recovered later.

STOCK MUSIC: Though Don Harper did compose original music for this story, stock music was still used, specifically an "enhanced" version of the BBC Radiophonic Workshop track "Time In Advance", composed in 1965 by longtime Workshop member (and non-radiophonic jazzman) John Baker (1937-1997). Harper re-recorded his own music from *The Invasion* for the de Wolfe Music Library, giving the tracks cheeky in-joke titles such as "Auntie's Army" (referring to the popular nickname for the BBC, "Auntie Beeb"); these re-recordings were themselves released on CD in 2014 on the album *Cold Worlds,* which also includes Harper's stock music contributions to George Romero's film *Dawn Of The Dead.*

NEW WHO CONNECTIONS: Tobias Vaughn's company, International Electromatics, stills exists (at least in name) in the alternate universe visited by the tenth Doctor, Rose and Mickey in *Rise Of The Cybermen* and *The Age Of Steel* (2006); the trucks used by Lumic to deploy his Cyber-army bear the company's logo. A Cyber-Planner is next seen in 2013's *Nightmare In Silver.*

Though it's a bit top-heavy at eight parts, *The Invasion* was definitely the shape of things to come for **Doctor Who**. With its modern-day setting, a bit of applied mad science, and UNIT making its first appearance, this is virtually a pilot for the Jon Pertwee years. Even the show's then-producers have admitted that, had Patrick Troughton stayed with **Doctor Who** long enough for the show to be broadcast in color, some story development still would have ensued to effectively exile the Time Lord to contemporary Earth.

As the last Cybermen TV story until Tom Baker's first season, *The Invasion* uses the silver monsters in an interesting and unexpected way. Here, they're subservient to humans (at least at first), mere pawns in a meticulously plotted invasion plan that only begins to fly by the seat of its pants when the Doctor and UNIT intervene repeatedly. (There are similarities between *The Invasion* and *Power Of The Daleks*, also written by David Whitaker, which used the Daleks in a similar context, first presenting them as subservient before revealing their ulterior motives.) When the Cybermen do make their presence known, though, it's one of the most memorable sequences the series has ever shown us, with the Cyber army (well, all six of them, as a major redesign of their headgear meant that older Cyberman costumes couldn't be used to fatten the ranks) walking down the steps of St. Paul's Cathedral. The UNIT battle with the Cybermen really should be equally iconic in most fans' minds, because unlike later years where this international alien-fighting organization is reduced to a Brigadier, a Captain and a Sergeant, here it's shown to be an effective fighting force (thanks to the participation of an actual battallion of Army troops). After seeing this story, I now understand better why so many viewers were disappointed with *Revenge Of The Cybermen*; it's easy to be disappointed if you compare it to one of the few stories that paints the Cybermen as a major threat rather than a budget-addled trio of costumed actors. Derrick Sherwin and Kit Pedler should've been credited with inspiring the tenth Doctor two-parter that reintroduced the Cybermen to the new series, because it owes a lot to *The Invasion*.

A very odd factor in *The Invasion* is a strange, almost James-Bond-esque musical score by Don Harper. The more sinister passages are more contemporary with the '60s than most of Dudley Simpson's electronic/orchestral pieces of that period of the show's history. Some of the music accompanying the appearance of UNIT troops is strangely cheerful. As the years have passed, I've found the music from *The Invasion* more compelling and interesting with repeat viewing/listening.

It's a bit ponderous in terms of total running time, but *The Invasion* is a tremendously enjoyable (and influential) story, and a true classic.

THE KROTONS

Moments after the Doctor, Zoe and Jamie leave the safe confines of the TARDIS to explore a seemingly hospitable planet, a hulking robotic attacker assails the time machine – causing it to disappear on its own! The Doctor reassures his companions that it's merely the TARDIS' automatic defense system in operation, and they continue exploring until they find a peaceful people known as the Gonds. At a certain age, young Gonds undergo an intelligence test; those who pass are permitted to serve the Krotons, a crystalline-based species that rules over them – and the same creatures who attacked the TARDIS. On a whim, Zoe takes the test and ranks highly, assuring her of a place among the Krotons. The Doctor, fearing for her life, takes the same test, naturally scoring off the scale. Once they are taken to the Krotons, the Doctor and Zoe must figure out how to rid the Gonds of their "benevolent" overlords, for not everyone who has passed the intelligence test has lived to tell the tale – keeping the general populace docile, and robbing them of the curiosity that could lead them to defeat the Krotons.

Patrick Troughton	The Doctor
Frazer Hines	Jamie
Wendy Padbury	Zoe
Terence Brown	Abu
James Cairncross	Beta
James Copeland	Selris
Robert Grant	Kroton
Richard Ireson	Axus
Robert La Bassiere	Kroton
Philip Madoc	Eelek
Madeleine Mills	Vana
Miles Northover	Kroton
Maurice Selwyn	Custodian

This story has been released on DVD

written by Robert Holmes
directed by David Maloney
music by Brian Hodgson

Part 1 aired on December 28, 1968
Part 2 aired on January 4, 1969
Part 3 aired on January 11, 1969
Part 4 aired on January 18, 1969

Bronson Shaw	Student
Roy Skelton	Kroton voice
Patrick Tull	Kroton voice
Gilbert Wynne	Thara

It's a fairly tame little story, full of the kind of offbeat humor that marks the best Troughton episodes, but in **Doctor Who** history *The Krotons* is actually worth a mention if only for one thing: it was the first script contributed by writer **Robert Holmes**, who would later serve as script editor during Tom Baker's mold-breaking early seasons, and contributed some of the series' most high-profile stories from the Pertwee era through the end of Colin Baker's reign.

There's something to be said for the simple charm and simple menace of *The Krotons*, though – sure, the main baddies were even more cumbersome than Daleks, and considerably less threatening overall, but the thought of what they're doing to their enslaved minions is pretty sinister. Really not a bad story at all.

THE SEEDS OF DEATH

In the 21st century, mankind has given up rocket-based travel in favor of the T-mat teleportation system – even to the extent of not maintaining any space vehicles in case they're needed. This almost turns into a fatal mistake when a vital T-mat installation based on the moon loses contact with Earth, after a terrified final message from one of the moonbase crew mentioning a takeover. Even when the T-mat administrators find a barely spaceworthy rocket in the workshop of a sentimental space travel hobbyist, they need one more thing – someone who has the experience necessary to fly the rocket. The Doctor, with Jamie and Zoe in tow, arrives just in time to take on the hazardous mission, discovering that the moonbase is just the first step in another Ice Warrior attempt to colonize Earth by brute force.

Patrick Troughton . . . . The Doctor
Frazer Hines . . . . Jamie
Wendy Padbury . . . . Zoe
Alan Bennion . . . . Slaar
Sonny Caldinez . . . . Ice Warrior
Christopher Coll . . . . Phipps
Martin Cort . . . . Locke
Ric Felgate . . . . Brent
Tony Harwood . . . . Ice Warrior
Graham Leaman . . . . Marshal
Ronald Leigh-Hunt . . . . Radnor
Hugh Morton . . . . Sir James Gregson
Louise Pajo . . . . Gia Kelly
Steve Peters . . . . Ice Warrior
Philip Ray . . . . Eldred
Terry Scully . . . . Fewsham

This story has been released on DVD

written by Brian Hayles
directed by Michael Ferguson
music by Dudley Simpson

Part 1 aired on January 25, 1969
Part 2 aired on February 1, 1969
Part 3 aired on February 8, 1969
Part 4 aired on February 15, 1969
Part 5 aired on February 22, 1969
Part 6 aired on March 1, 1969

Derrick Slater . . . . Guard
Harry Towb . . . . Osgood
Peter Whittaker . . . . . Weather station operator
John Witty . . . . Computer voice

Another story which shows the Troughton era's great skill in handling classic horror tales, this six-parter drags a bit, particularly in the scenes involving the Doctor's rocket flight. The actors portraying the crew of the moonbase do a very good job, even if they occasionally overdose on the hand-wringing and terrified sobbing. The first scenes in which the Ice Warriors take over the moonbase are all done in first-person camera shots, a very effective and unusual way of heightening the tension and concealing the hostile force from the audience, at least for a little while (especially since the title, in those days, didn't always give away the big bad from five miles away). And one has to admire the many ways in which the BBC special effects designers managed to manipulate images to show all kinds of different alien death rays, back in the days before digital editing and even serious optical effects. Of the few second Doctor stories remaining fully intact, this is one of the better ones.

THE SPACE PIRATES

With raids on defenseless cargo beacon stations on the rise in the intergalactic spaceway, the authorities and their minnow ships are placed on high alert. Caven and his motley crew of space pirates have been systematically stealing argonite and escaping aboard their sleek Beta Dart ship. General Hermack, aboard the V-Ship, lays a trap for Caven's pirates by placing a full team of armed guards on the next cargo station...but to their surprise, their first visitors aren't pirates, but three odd people who arrive in, of all things, an ancient police box. When the real pirates arrive and the shooting starts, the Doctor, Jamie and Zoe take shelter. Caven's men slaughter the guards, take the argonie and follow their usual procedure of planting charges to blow the beacon's wedge-shaped cargo containers apart from each other. Trapped in a different container from the one in which the TARDIS landed, and left with limited oxygen, the Doctor and his friends are rescued by crusty old-time space prospector Milo Clancey – who is unaware that he's been assigned the rescue mission by Hermack, as a test to see if he is allied to Caven's pirates.

Patrick Troughton . . . . The Doctor
Frazer Hines . . . . Jamie
Wendy Padbury . . . . Zoe
Lisa Daniely . . . . Madeleine
Anthony Donovan . . . . Guard
Dudley Foster . . . . Caven
Donald Gee . . . . Warne
Gordon Gostelow . . . . Milo Clancey
Esmond Knight . . . . Dom Issigri
George Layton . . . . Penn
Jack May . . . . Hermack
Briant Peck . . . . Dervish
Steve Peters . . . . Guard
Nick Zaran . . . . Sorba

This story
has been
released
on audio
CD

written by Robert Holmes
directed by Michael Hart
music by Dudley Simpson

Part 1 aired on March 8, 1969
Part 2 aired on March 15, 1969
Part 3 aired on March 22, 1969
Part 4 aired on March 29, 1969
Part 5 aired on April 5, 1969
Part 6 aired on April 12, 1969

MISSING: Episodes 1, 3, 4, 5 and 6 of *The Space Pirates* are missing from the BBC archives.

I'm almost sad to say it, but after reviewing and re-reviewing the sole surviving episode (out of six) that exists in video form, and watching the rest in reconstructed form, we may finally have here, in *The Space Pirates*, an missing story whose absence is mourned only by the most hardcore fans of **Doctor Who**. Even when absorbed in the form of the reconstructions created by fans with still photos and surviving audio recordings of all six parts, *The Space Pirates* is tediously slow – this would've been slow with only *four* episodes. The BBC modelmakers who constructed and filmed the meticulously accurate models of the Apollo spacecraft for BBC News were contracted for this story, providing perhaps the most realistic vision of space travel seen in **Doctor Who** up to this point. *Too* realistic – the almost slow-motion of zero gravity translates to incredibly slow space sequences, bringing the story to a crawl. The model work is impressive for 1969 on a television budget, probably the closest that B&W **Who** ever came to parity with **Star Trek**, which was in production at roughly the same time…but *man*, is it up on the screen for a *long time*.

Speaking of **Star Trek** connections, it apparently fell to composer Dudley Simpson to pull it out of the hat and do something to sonically salvage the glut of effects sequences – shades of the task that fell to Jerry Goldsmith ten years later with the first **Trek** movie. Simpson employs an unusual-for-its-time operatic female vocal in addition to his usual ensemble (begging further **Star Trek** comparison, thought that series didn't debut in England until after this season of **Doctor Who** wrapped up), but the singer's voice was processed so much that she sounds like she's only a couple of steps removed from becoming more theremin than human. The result is mysterious-going-on-goofy, and makes even the audio-only version of the story a trying listen.

Even attempting to take *The Space Pirates* seriously can induce a headache. Coming so soon on the heels of much more sophisticated fare like *The Invasion*, this story is old-fashioned even by **Doctor Who** standards. With all the characters worrying about the differences between their "rocketships," and the central female character sporting a gigantic metal helmet custom-molded to protect her towering beehive hairdo, *The Space Pirates* is an exercise in revisiting the kind of filmed SF cliches that were on their way out of style when **Doctor Who** premiered. Some 30 years later, **Star Trek: Voyager** proved that you could be hip by making gentle fun of such elements, but here, **Doctor Who** was taking it deadly seriously, and even Patrick Troughton and the other cast regulars couldn't keep it from sinking. *The Space Pirates* is, in my estimation, a strong contender for the worst of the second Doctor's era and possibly the entire original series. Perhaps even more embarrassing than all of the above is that this story was wriiten by Robert Holmes, generally acknowledged to be one of the best writers of the original series' heyday.

SHORT HOPS

...in which the author ponders the most MST-worthy TARDIS travels.

Now that **Doctor Who** has been resurrected from cancellation, the one *other* show that I wish I could "un-cancel" just by sheer force of will is **Mystery Science Theater 3000**. I'm not sure any other show - perhaps not even **Doctor Who** itself - has brought me as much joy as **MST3K** in terms of pure belly laughs. Beating the DVD commentary craze to the punch by over a decade, **MST3K**'s formula was simple: a guy and two robots (actually puppets manned by their voice artists) sit in the corner of the screen and hurl an endless barrage of wisecracks at whatever movie or hilariously out-of-date B&W safety film they're lampooning that week. Every so often I've encountered a **Doctor Who** story that instantly made me wish that the Satellite of Love received BBC1.

For the show's black and white years, there's a wealth of borderline-silly goodness to be mined. But easily the most **MST**-worthy William Hartnell adventure is *The Web Planet*. Somewhere between its mind-bogglingly large insect life, dancing folks in bee suits, and evil-brain-in-a-jar overlords (shades of Jan in the Pan!), *The Web Planet* is perfect MSTie fodder. It's practically custom-tailored to be watched by a guy and two robots.

Running a close second would be *The Chase*. The third Dalek adventure was never meant to be taken as deadly seriously as its predecessors and its antecedents, and with its daffy detours into haunted houses, the *Marie Celeste* and an ersatz Empire State Building, it too is a likely candidate.

An honorary mention has to go out to either or both of the Peter Cushing movies. The first one, in particular, is almost trippy.

From the rather slim pickings of the second Doctor's reign, *The Mind Robber* is probably the best candidate, also trippy in its own way, with *The Dominators* running a close second - it isn't particularly funny in and of itself, and that's precisely the point: it could use the Satellite of Love touch.

A special shout-out should go to the extant segments of *The Underwater Menace*. There really needs to be a showdown between the Fish People and Joel's Channel Cat puppet from *The Magic Voyage Of Sinbad*.

THE WAR GAMES

The TARDIS brings the Doctor, Jamie and Zoe to a World War I battlefield, but upon closer examination they find that the battlegrounds have been recreated on an alien planet. For the next several episodes, the Doctor and company wander through various different simulated wars in Earth history, finally discovering the alien War Lords at the heart of a plot to create an all-powerful army from the most powerful ranks of Earth history's greatest military forces. Left with the task of stopping the War Lords, as well as returning all of the abducted Earth soldiers to their native times and places, the Doctor reluctantly summons the help of his own people, the Time Lords – and in so doing draws their attention to himself as well. After dealing with the War

Lords, the Time Lords put the Doctor on trial, the verdict of which will cost him another of his precious lives.

Patrick Troughton . . . . The Doctor
Frazer Hines . . . . Jamie
Wendy Padbury . . . . Zoe
Terry Adams . . . . Riley
John Atterbury . . . . Alien
Terence Bayler . . . . Barrington
Edward Brayshaw . . . . War Chief
James Bree . . . . Security Chief
Noel Coleman . . . . General Smythe
Peter Craze . . . . Du Pont
Bernard Davies . . . . German Soldier
Vernon Dobtcheff . . . . Scientist
Brian Forster . . . . Willis
David Garfield . . . . Von Weich
Pat Gorman . . . . Policeman
Tony Harwood . . . . Ice Warrior
Bernard Horsfall . . . . Time Lord
Stephen Hubay . . . . Petrov
Bill Hutchinson . . . . Thompson
Clare Jenkins . . . . Tanya
Robert Jewell . . . . Dalek
John Levene . . . . Yeti
John Livesly . . . . German Soldier
Michael Lynch . . . . Spencer
Philip Madoc . . . . War Lord
Trevor Martin . . . . Time Lord
Tony McEwan . . . . Redcoat
Michael Napier-Brown . . . . Villar
Gregg Palmer . . . . Lucke
Roy Pearce . . . . Cyberman

This story has been released on DVD

written by Malcolm Hulke & Terrance Dicks
directed by David Maloney
music by Dudley Simpson

Part 1 aired on April 19, 1969
Part 2 aired on April 26, 1969
Part 3 aired on May 3, 1969
Part 4 aired on May 10, 1969
Part 5 aired on May 17, 1969
Part 6 aired on May 24, 1969
Part 7 aired on May 31, 1969
Part 8 aired on June 7, 1969
Part 9 aired on June 14, 1969
Part 10 aired on June 21, 1969

Charles Pemberton . . . . Alien
Clyde Pollitt . . . . Time Lord
Hubert Rees . . . . Captain Ransom
David Savile . . . . Carstairs
Leslie Schofield . . . . Leroy
Jane Sherwin . . . . Lady Buckingham
Peter Stanton . . . . Chauffeur
Richard Steele . . . . Gorton
David Troughton . . . . Moor
David Valla . . . . Crane
Rudolph Walker . . . . Harper
Esmond Webb . . . . Burns
Graham Weston . . . . Russell
Freddie Wilson . . . . Quark

A.K.A.: David Troughton, who makes a fleeting appearance in *The War Games*, is the son of Patrick Troughton and would make further appearances in both the classic series (*The Curse Of Peladon*, 1972) and the new series (*Midnight*, 2008). He also lent his voice — which sounds uncannily like his father's these days — to a recreation of the second Doctor in the BBC audio stories *The Hexford Invasion* and *Survivors In Space* (2011).

NEW WHO CONNECTIONS: In addition to showing the Doctor's exile to Earth, which would inform the entire Pertwee era (and, according to producers, would have happened even if Patrick Troughton had stayed on board for a fourth season and the transition into color filming), this episode also introduces the "psychic container" used by Time Lords to send distress signals (seen again in 2011's *The Doctor's Wife*). The Time Lord costumes seen here are unlike anything we ever see the Time Lords wearing again — at least until the young Master is glimpsed in a similar outfit in the flashback scene in 2007's *The Sound Of Drums*, in which it's implied that they're the robes of a Time Lord initiate. Could it be that, at this time, the Doctor was just a mild annoyance whose first trial handled by junior Time Lords?

In places, this is a torturously long dose of **Doctor Who** — the third longest-running story in the show's history, necessitated by another script falling through, leaving the producers of the show with no choice but to keep extending *The War Games* week after week.

The worst part about *The War Games*' exhausting length is that it's really a clever story. Despite the exercise in padding out the story length that it represents, *The War Games* has fairly interesting characters and some of the recreations of historical wars are decent; that it keeps changing time periods is its saving grace. For viewers accustomed to the rapid-fire pacing of the new series, however, at ten episodes *The War Games* may just be too much. I've never made it through *The War Games* in its entirety in a single sitting, and I don't recommend trying. (It's not how it was originally shown, if nothing else.) One you complete the marathon sprint to part eight, things start to get interesting and the Time Lords enter the picture for the first time in the show's history. The Time Lords are given a very interesting treatment here, seen as almost all-powerful. The story has a lot to recommend it, but its running time may make it look like a daunting prospect.

The Third Doctor
(Jon Pertwee: 1970-74)

1969: production on **Doctor Who** had come to a full stop with the exit of Patrick Troughton and his co-stars, Frazer Hines and Wendy Padbury. The series was without a star or even continuing companions. Furthermore, the exhausting ten-week epic that was *The War Games*, Troughton's final adventure, didn't produce inspiring ratings where the BBC brass was concerned, despite introducing the Time Lords, firmly establishing the Doctor's background, and promising yet another miraculous change of appearance.

With those elements, and a Time Lord sentence of exile to Earth, producer Derrick Sherwin was already laying the foundation for the series' future. And his blueprint for the Doctor's (hopefully most cost-effective) Earthbound adventures had been on display for some time, even though no one noticed at the time: *The Invasion*, an eight-part modern-day adventure reintroducing *The Web Of Fear*'s Brigadier (formerly Colonel) Lethbridge-Stewart as the head of a top secret military organization called UNIT, was a test run for Sherwin's idea. The Brigadier would return as a regular member of the cast, and the Doctor would be working for UNIT in the capacity of its scientific advisor.

If, that is, the BBC didn't cancel **Doctor Who** first. BBC1 was relaunching in full color in January 1970, and the BBC had already purchased a package of reruns of a recently-cancelled American science fiction series called **Star Trek** to fill its need for color programming. **Doctor Who** had always been shot in black & white, and in many ways took advantage of that limitation and made a virtue of it. With its increasingly complex special effects, the show would be a formidable challenge to produce in color. But in the end, with fans clamoring for more, and no other alternative programming proving to be as promising, the BBC greenlit a seventh season. Now Sherwin had to find a new Doctor.

After an exhaustive search and audition process, the producer chose radio comedian Jon Pertwee, famous for his multi-voiced talents in **The Navy Lark**. The British press, beginning to show its fascination with the selection process of a new **Doctor Who** star, latched onto this as proof that the sometimes whimsical tone of Patrick Troughton's era would now be expanded to full-throttle silliness. But with James Bond and other slick heroes firmly in vogue, Sherwin and Pertwee surprised the speculators with a decidedly dramatic Doctor. Serious but with flashes of humor and eccentricity, there was seldom any doubt that Jon Pertwee was playing the third Doctor as a serious dramatic role. Nicholas Courtney rejoined the cast for the entire seventh season, and Caroline John was cast as a new companion, Cambridge scientist Dr. Liz Shaw.

The third Doctor's first year was serious, somber and spectacular: one four-part introductory story followed by three seven-part epics - and those stories were among the most intense in the series' history, dealing with subjects ranging from biological warfare to ecological disasters that would end the world. Pertwee's Doctor stood his ground against plastic Autons, reptilian Silurians, obsessed scientists, and a group of captive alien ambassadors whose touch was deadly to any human. All four stories were set in modern-day Britain, with the Autons terrorizing the heart of London and the Silurians storming the English countryside.

Early in that season, Sherwin handed the reins over to a new producer, Barry Letts. Keen to leave his own stamp on the show, Letts made changes going into the 1971 season: he brightened up the feel of the series, dropped Liz Shaw (and actress Caroline John) with nothing more than a line of dialogue indicating that she had resumed her research at Cambridge, and introducing a younger, peppier assistant in the form of Jo Grant (Katy Manning). A semi-regular retinue of UNIT soldiers was kept in rotation, with Sergeant Benton (John Levene, a veteran of UNIT stories all the way back to *The Invasion*) and Captain Mike Yates (Richard Franklin) quickly gaining favor with the fans. And perhaps most importantly of all, Letts, script editor Terrance Dicks and writer Robert Holmes created a new arch nemesis for the Doctor: the Master.

Doctor Who's entire eighth season was devoted to introducing this new character, played by the lean and sinister Roger Delgado. The Master was another rogue Time Lord, but unlike the Doctor, he had escaped the Time Lords' justice - and his goals and methods were decidedly evil. The Master repeatedly tried to assist aliens hell-bent on invading Earth, and the Doctor fought him in a close duel of moves and counter-moves. A worthy adversary, the Master employed hypnotism, disguise, bribery, and a matter-compression gun that would reduce its victims to the size of dolls (killing them in the process). Soon, the audience was looking for the Master at the beginning of every new story, as it was a given that he was involved with the foul deeds that were afoot. The Master wasn't above associating with energy-leeching Axons, the Autons, a deadly psychic creature feeding from humans' basest violent impulses, and even - apparently - the devil himself.

And for the first time during Pertwee's reign, the TARDIS left Earth for pastures new - at least in one episode, *Colony In Space* - but only on a mission prescribed by the Time Lords. (Naturally, they wanted the Master brought to justice too, but they seemed only concerned enough to dispatch another renegade Time Lord - presumably an expendable one - to do the job.) Other forces were trying to influence the Doctor's travels as well: *Terror Of The Autons*, the Master's debut story, drew heavy criticism from many corners, including self-appointed TV violence watchdog Mary Whitehouse. But serious concerns were also voiced by Scotland Yard, over scenes where policemen were unmasked to reveal killer Autons. Any further plans for a rematch with Robert Holmes' plastic predators were quickly nixed.

1972 saw the beginning of **Doctor Who**'s ninth year on the air, and the return - for the first time since the Patrick Troughton era - of Terry Nation's Daleks. *Day Of The Daleks* wasn't the first time the metallic monsters had been seen in color (that honor went to the two Peter Cushing theatrical films of the 1960s), but it was their first appearance in five years - and some fans were disappointed as what seemed to be a reduced role in the action. The Master also made two return appearances in the ninth season, and the TARDIS continued to take the Doctor away from present-day Earth...when the Time Lords (and the even more powerful demands of ratings) deemed it necessary.

For the tenth season, Letts and Dicks used a storyline that had been submitted to the **Doctor Who** production office by countless fans: a teaming-up of the three Doctors thus far. This tenth anniversary four-parter, *The Three Doctors*, was hampered by rewrites to accomodate the ailing William Hartnell. Though back in costume and back in character, Hartnell's deteriorating condition limited what was originally meant to be a more dynamic role. This was also the first time either of the first two Doctors had appeared in color, and Troughton in particular seemed to enjoy the experience immensely, building a friendly-insult rapport with Pertwee that the two actors carried on into convention appearances years later. At the end of *The Three Doctors*, the Time Lords - and the makers of the series - lifted all limitations on the Doctor's travels.

In addition to the end of the Doctor's exile, there were other plans afoot, including a definitive confrontation with the Master that promised to reveal, once and for all, the true nature of his relationship with the Doctor - a story which would have also seen the end of the Master, as Roger Delgado was ready to seek other work. The seeds for this were planted in the six-part story *Frontier In Space*, in which the Doctor's rival Time Lord pooled his resources with the Daleks, leading directly into a further six-part story, *Planet Of The Daleks*. The TARDIS brought the Doctor and Jo back to modern-day Earth at the end of the season with *The Green Death*, in which Jo was written out to accomodate Katy Manning's desire to work on other projects. But this wasn't the only storyline brought to an end: Roger Delgado was killed in a car crash while filming a movie in Turkey, putting an end to Letts and Dicks' plans to wrap up the Master's story in the final story of the following season (Delgado had already expressed a desire to move on).

Jon Pertwee, at this point, was in negotiations to renew his contract. About to begin production on his fifth season in the role, Pertwee was the longest-serving Doctor to date - and he felt this entitled him to greater compensation. The BBC's Head of Drama disagreed and declined Pertwee's request for a raise, and between that refusal and the shock of his close friend Roger Delgado's death, Pertwee made it clear that the new season would be his last.

A new companion, Sarah Jane Smith (Elisabeth Sladen), was introduced, and Barry Letts and Terrance Dicks deliberately designed the character in response to complaints about sexism in the series: too many female sidekicks screamed helplessly, some complained, and too few of them truly fought evil alongside the Doctor. Sarah Jane's debut story, *The Time Warrior*, addressed this character trait almost too directly, with the show's new heroine openly proclaiming herself to be an advocate for women's lib. This four-parter also introduced a completely new title sequence - a complex animation showing Pertwee and a new **Doctor Who** logo traveling through a seemingly endless tunnel of colorful swirling patterns - and a new villain in the form of the militaristic Sontarans. Devised by Holmes, the Sontarans were an army of identical clones, gifted with enormous strength, tactical genius, and no remorse whatsoever for killing anyone who got in their way.

Season 11 continued with another Dalek tale, *Death To The Daleks*, a sequel to season 9's *Curse Of Peladon*, and finally a six-part epic, replete with Buddhist symbolism of rebirth and enlightenment, to see the third Doctor out. *Planet Of The Spiders*, reflecting Letts' Buddhist beliefs, was let down on the production value end, but culminated in yet another change of body for the Doctor. A fellow Time Lord hiding on Earth in the guise of a Tibetan monk, K'anpo Ripoche, finally gave this process a name - regeneration - shortly before Pertwee's visage faded into that of his replacement, actor Tom Baker. Could this relatively unknown, eccentric actor match Pertwee's longevity or popularity in the role?

SEASON 7: 1970
SPEARHEAD FROM SPACE

Dr. Liz Shaw is uprooted from her research at Cambridge to serve as the scientific advisor for the recently formed United Nations Intelligence Taskforce, headed by Brigadier Lethbridge-Stewart. The Brigadier seeks Liz's help in the investigation of two mysteriously precise meteor showers which could be signs of alien interference with Earth. But the Brigadier's luck improves with the arrival of a police box in the midst of the most recent meteor shower, though its sole occupant is a man he's never seen before. The Doctor, however, does recognize the Brigadier despite recovering from the trauma of his forced regeneration at the hands of the Time Lords, and the two join forces – with a somewhat bewildered Dr. Shaw in tow – to fight an alien menace which can inhabit and control one of the most common substances manufactured on Earth...plastic.

Jon Pertwee . . . . The Doctor
Caroline John . . . . Liz Shaw
Nicholas Courtney . . . Brig. Lethbridge-Stewart
Edmund Bailey . . . . Waxworks Attendant
Betty Bowden . . . . Meg Seeley
John Breslin . . . . Captain Munro
Hugh Burden . . . . Channing
Clifford Cox . . . . Soldier
Helen Dorward . . . . Nurse
Hamilton Dyce . . . . General Scobie
Prentis Hancock . . . . Reporter
Ellis Jones . . . . UNIT personnel
George Lee . . . . Corporal Forbes
Henry McCarthy . . . . Dr. Beavis
Allan Mitchell . . . . Wagstaffe
Tessa Shaw . . . . UNIT personnel

This story has been released on DVD

written by Robert Holmes
directed by Derek Martinus
music by Dudley Simpson

Part 1 aired on January 3, 1970
Part 2 aired on January 10, 1970
Part 3 aired on January 17, 1970
Part 4 aired on January 24. 1970

Iain Smith . . . . UNIT personnel
Derek Smee . . . . Ransome
Talfryn Thomas . . . . Mullins
Antony Webb . . . . Dr. Henderson
Neil Wilson . . . . Seeley
John Woodnutt . . . . Hibbert

A.K.A.: See if you can spot future **Space: 1999** regular **Prentis Hancock** in a brief scene as a reporter. When the Doctor arrives at UNIT HQ, the reluctant valet upon whom he vents his frustration is outgoing **Doctor Who** producer **Derrick Sherwin**!

NEW WHO CONNECTIONS: For the first time in the series, the Doctor's regeneration has occured off-screen; the only other time this has happened in the series' history was the presumed transformation of Paul McGann's eighth Doctor into Christopher Eccleston's ninth Doctor... at least until *Night Of The Doctor* and *Day Of The Doctor* revealed that the eighth Doctor had regenerated into a previously unknown incarnation played by John Hurt, and the John Hurt Doctor had then regenerated into the ninth Doctor.

Jon Pertwee's first adventure as the Doctor, as well as the first **Doctor Who** story shot in color (not counting the two Dalek movies starring Peter Cushing in the 1960s), gleans a lot of its atmosphere from being shot entirely on film thanks to a strike at the BBC's studio facilities in 1969. Hugh Burden is truly sinister as the seemingly human head villain, especially in some scenes where the camera is practically sitting right on top of his nose as he telepathically orders the plastic Autons around.

If you find the scenes of physicians puzzling over the Doctor's curious x-rays to be a little bit familiar, it's no coincidence – so effective was this introduction to the Doctor, that the character was worked into the story in 1996's TV movie in much the same way, right down to the x-ray showing the Doctor's two hearts. This also makes for a wonderfully strong introduction for Brigadier Lethbridge-Stewart and Liz Shaw, who are the only characters the audience really is sure of until the Doctor gets to his feet two episodes into the story. There's also a vaguely sinister air about UNIT in the early scenes where it appears that Liz is being coerced into working for the Brigadier, and later when one of UNIT's soldiers grills local poacher Seeley for the whereabouts of one of the artificial meteors. This hint of skullduggery helps to lend Pertwee's first year as the Doctor a very **X-Files**-ish feel.

Little things to look for: Jon Pertwee, in this show, bares more of the Doctor than either of his predecessors or any of his successors in the infamous "singing in the shower" scene, though one wonders where the recently-regenerated Time Lord got a tattoo on his right forearm (!). The intense Dudley Simpson musical score is very good, though it gets rather wacky in the scene where the Doctor appropriates a car from one of the hospital doctors and drives it to UNIT – the music doesn't change in and of itself, but it sounds like someone was gradually speeding up the tape on which it was recorded.

And just remember, plastics make it possible!

DOCTOR WHO AND THE SILURIANS

UNIT and the Doctor are summoned to a nuclear power research center located near a complex of caves; something has been slowly driving members of the center's staff mad, one by one, and at least one spelunker has been killed in the caves. The Doctor investigates the caves for himself, uninterested in what initially seem like personnel problems at the center, and finds a living dinosaur inside them; he also discovers evidence of a bipedal reptile species, both in the caves and outside. The center's director doesn't believe the story he's being told, but the Brigadier prepares UNIT to defend against a possible invasion. The Doctor is convinced that the reptile humanoids are Silurians, the original inhabitants of the Earth before a mass extinction wiped out most of the large reptile species and allowed humans to evolve and thrive. The few survivors of the event went into underground shelters, and the energy released by the research center is slowly awakening them. The Doctor is determined to contact them and try to talk them into coexisting peacefully with humans on the surface, only to find that warlike factions exist among the Silurians as well – and some of them will be satisfied with nothing less than wiping out humanity.

Jon Pertwee . . . . The Doctor
Caroline John . . . . Liz Shaw
Nicholas Courtney . . . Brig. Lethbridge-Stewart
Brendan Barry . . . . Doctor
Paul Barton . . . . Silurian
Roy Branigan . . . . Roberts
Simon Cain . . . . Silurian
Dave Carter . . . . Old Silurian
John Churchill . . . . Silurian
Ian Cunningham . . . . Dr. Meredith
Paul Darrow . . . . Hawkins
Pat Gorman . . . . Silurian Scientist
Peter Halliday . . . . Silurian voice
Thomasine Heiner . . . . Miss Dawson
Nancie Jackson . . . . Doris Squire
Nigel Johns . . . . Young Silurian
Norman Jones . . . . Baker

This story has been released on DVD

written by Malcolm Hulke
directed by Timothy Combe
music by Carey Blyton

Part 1 aired on January 31, 1970
Part 2 aired on February 7, 1970
Part 3 aired on February 14, 1970
Part 4 aired on February 21. 1970
Part 5 aired on February 28, 1970
Part 6 aired on March 7, 1970
Part 7 aired on March 14, 1970

John Newman . . . . Spencer
Geoffrey Palmer . . . . Masters
Derek Pollitt . . . . Wright
Gordon Richardson . . . . Squire

Fulton Mackay	. . . . Dr. Quinn	Richard Steele	. . . . Hart
Alan Mason	. . . . Corporal Nutting	Harry Swift	. . . . Robins
Bill Matthews	. . . . Davis	Ian Talbot	. . . . Travis
Peter Miles	. . . . Dr. Lawrence		

A.K.A.: Peter Miles would return several times in **Doctor Who**, almost always as a sinister villain (*Invasion Of The Dinosaurs*, 1974; *Genesis Of The Daleks*, 1975), a feat that he would repeat in audio form after the cancellation of the original TV series (*The Paradise Of Death*, 1993; *Whispers Of Terror*, 1999). He also had recurring roles in **Moonbase 3** (created by Barry Letts and Terrance Dicks) and Terry Nation's **Blake's 7**. Speaking of **Blake's 7**, a young **Paul Darrow** can be seen as the Brigadier's right hand man when the UNIT search team is trapped in the underground caves. **Geoffrey Palmer** returned to play the captain of the spaceship *Titanic* in 2007's *Voyage Of The Damned*.

NEW WHO CONNECTIONS: The Silurians appear in the new series as well, beginning in Matt Smith's first season in *The Hungry Earth*. Though they look nothing like the Silurians introduced here, the existence of a related species known as the Sea Devils (introduced in a later third Doctor story of the same name) leaves room for multiple species of Silurians.

BOOK CONNECTIONS: The 1993 **Doctor Who** New Adventures novel <u>Blood Heat</u> takes place in an alternate, Silurian-dominated timeline in which the Brigadier and Liz lead a human resistance against reptilian dictators who took over when — thanks to interference in the timeline by a third party seeking revenge on the Doctor — the third Doctor was killed by the Silurians before finding the antidote to their plague.

In 1984, after years of running through all of the Tom Baker and Peter Davison episodes available, OETA (Oklahoma's Public TV network, which we could get on cable just across the border in Arkansas) began broadcasting the Jon Pertwee era of **Doctor Who** at long last. Pertwee began appearing every night for 25 minutes at a time, and though I was simply intrigued at first, my mother had made up her mind — Jon Pertwee was *her* Doctor, and I could keep my Peter Davison and Tom Baker. Still, I was thrilled to be watching new-to-me **Who**, and what adventures they were! This one in particular, I recall, stopped just short of giving me nightmares, despite the fact that I was just entering my teens. It *still* gives me the willies, through the combination of one of the best-scripted stories in the entire **Doctor Who** canon, Jon Pertwee's emerging command of his portrayal of the Time Lord, and some of the all-time best latex and rubber creations ever to emerge from the BBC's makeup and wardrobe departments. And see if you can spot young Paul Darrow, still seven years away from filming his first scenes as **Blake's 7** anti-hero Avon, taking orders as the Brigadier's "number one," Captain Hawkins. Those who can ignore the very '60s set dressings and sound effects, spooky creatures who speak in broad rural English accents, kooky music and the primitive special effects (*The Silurians* saw the first ever use of blue screen in **Doctor Who**) are rewarded with a combination mystery/horror/science fiction/suspense thriller. The acting ages very well, including the omnipresent Peter Miles, often cast as a nasty; you may recall he also played the part of Davros' sneaky right-hand man in 1975's Tom Baker classic *Genesis Of The Daleks*. Another welcome appearance is made by the Doctor's scientist sidekick Liz Shaw, a female physicist whose character was allowed to be a lot more intelligent and decisive than most of the Doctor's prior or later companions. An example: when the Silurians abduct the Doctor from the lab where he is working on an antidote to a plague the Silurians have released to eradicate humankind, Liz continues working on the cure until she finds the formula herself. Unfortunately, viewers at the time didn't seem to react to her very well since she didn't cower in the corner at the first sign of trouble, nor did the 1970 production team seem to want to stop actress Caroline John from allowing her contract to expire quietly and uneventfully. A pity. This story in particular shows the Doctor and Liz working together not unlike Mulder and Scully.

If you're looking for some of the best **Doctor Who** from this point in the series' history, jump straight to this one. If you've got almost three hours to kill — or half an hour nightly for seven days — this is a story that will do more than thrill you. In a way seldom equalled by other **Doctor Who** stories, it will scare the hell out of you. With Pertwee's first story *Spearhead From Space*, **Doctor Who** settled firmly on Earth, but it is with *The Silurians* that the show entered the world of more mature storytelling. Here we have prehistoric reptiles attempting to infect the entire human race with bubonic plague, the prospect of the Brigadier and his soldiers reciprocating genocide upon the Silurians, the government repsonding clumsily to an epidemic of the Black Death, martial law, and other trappings of armageddon. If you thought **Doctor Who** was a silly kids' show, you need to check out *The Silurians*…but don't do so in a darkened room.

THE AMBASSADORS OF DEATH

A British manned Mars mission has fallen silent, its crew incommunicado for months. A second manned space vehicle is launched to recover the first, but it too loses contact with Earth. Strange, piercing signals are heard in Space Command on Earth, and the Doctor quickly realizes that they may be messages from whoever took the astronauts – only to hear a similar coded reply being sent from somewhere on Earth moments later. The Brigadier is able to trace the source of the reply and finds that the people who transmitted it are better organized and better armed than anyone suspected, and they even have allies within Space Command who try to sabotage the Doctor's analysis of the original message. The recovery mission returns to Earth, but when the hatch is opened, the crew is nowhere to be found. Three astronauts did, in fact, arrive safely, but they aren't from Earth. When Liz is kidnapped and forced to experiment on the alien visitors, and the military suddenly becomes reluctant to aid the Brigadier, the Doctor finds himself racing against time to avert an interplanetary war sparked by one paranoid man.

Jon Pertwee	The Doctor	
Caroline John	Liz Shaw	
Nicholas Courtney	Brig. Lethbridge-Stewart	
John Abineri	Carrington	
Ronald Allen	Ralph Cornish	
Ray Armstrong	Grey	
Geoffrey Beevers	Johnson	
Dallas Cavell	Quinlan	
James Clayton	Parker	
Carl Conway	Second Assistant	
Peter Noel Cook	Alien	
Robert Crawdon	Taltalian	
William Dysart	Reegan	
Max Faulkner	Soldier	
Ric Felgate	Van Lyden	
Peter Halliday	Alien voice	
Tony Harwood	Flynn	
James Haswell	Champion	
John Levene	Sergeant Benton	
John Lord	Masters	
Bernard Martin	Control Room Assistant	
Cheryl Molineaux	Miss Rutherford	

UNIT

This story has been released on DVD

written by David Whitaker
directed by Michael Ferguson
music by Dudley Simpson

Part 1 aired on March 21, 1970
Part 2 aired on March 28, 1970
Part 3 aired on April 4, 1970
Part 4 aired on April 11. 1970
Part 5 aired on April 18, 1970
Part 6 aired on April 25, 1970
Part 7 aired on May 2, 1970

Juan Moreno	Dobson
Steve Peters	Lefee
Robert Robertson	Collinson
Joanna Ross	First Assistant
Roy Scammell	Peterson
Cyril Shaps	Lennox
Neville Simons	Astronaut / Michaels
Gordon Sterne	Heldorf
Michael Wisher	John Wakefield

A.K.A.: Future **Doctor Who** bad guys abound in this story; **Michael Wisher** would originate the role of Davros a few years later in *Genesis Of The Daleks* (1975), while **Geoffrey Beevers** would eventually inherit the role of the Master for a single TV story (*The Keeper Of Traken*, 1981), returning to play the role several times for Big Finish's **Doctor Who** audio stories. Beevers is also the husband of Caroline "Liz Shaw" John.

Of the three seven-parters in this season, *Ambassadors Of Death* feels like the longest. There are numerous car chase, hijacking, and military action scenes that could've been pared down to make this a six-parter at most, but for the most part, *Ambassadors* is a complex story that needs that time to unravel, even if it drags on a bit slower than *The Silurians* or *Inferno* (though some may disagree with me there). This is also one of the most **X-Files**-ish **Doctor Who** stories of them all, with renegade conspiracies within the government, kidnappings, black ops of all kinds, and paranoia to spare. Adding to the fun is what might just be the best Dudley Simpson music score ever, with one gently undulating cue recurring throughout the seven episodes, often coinciding with the ethereal appearance of the spacesuit-clad aliens.

INFERNO

Joining the Brigadier's team at a hazardous research site where Dr. Stahlman plans to drill through the Earth's crust to tap its core as a new source of energy, the Doctor is annoyed when Stahlman rejects most of his expert scientific advice. But this isn't enough to prevent to Doctor from availing himself of power from Stahlman's nuclear reactor for his own experiments – yet another attempt to restore the TARDIS to full function. But during one such experiment, the TARDIS console shoots the Doctor sideways in time, depositing him in another dimension where Britain is a fascist state. In this alternate Earth, the Doctor can only watch in horror as Stahlman's experiment progresses to the point where it destroys the world. The Doctor barely escapes, only to find that he may be too late from saving the Earth he knows from the same fate.

Jon Pertwee	The Doctor
Caroline John	Liz Shaw
Nicholas Courtney	Brig. Lethbridge-Stewart
Christopher Benjamin	Sir Keith Gold
Dave Carter	Primord
Sheila Dunn	Petra Williams
Ian Fairburn	Bromley
Pat Gorman	Primord
Walter Henry	Primord
Keith James	Patterson
John Levene	Sergeant Benton
Derek Newark	Greg Sutton
Olaf Pooley	Professor Stahlman
Walter Randall	Slocum
Philip Ryan	Primord
Roy Scammell	Sentry

UNIT

This story has been released on DVD

written by Don Houghton
directed by Douglas Camfield and Barry Letts
music by Delia Derbyshire

Part 1 aired on May 9, 1970
Part 2 aired on May 16, 1970
Part 3 aired on May 23, 1970
Part 4 aired on May 30. 1970
Part 5 aired on June 6, 1970
Part 6 aired on June 13, 1970
Part 7 aired on June 20, 1970

David Simeon	Latimer
Peter Thompson	Primord
Derek Ware	Wyatt

A.K.A.: Sir Keith Gold barely survived this story, but actor **Christopher Benjamin** would return in the Tom Baker era to play the popular character of theater impresario Henry Gordon Jago in *The Talons Of Weng-Chiang* (1977). So enduring was the popularity of that story's double-act of Jago and Litefoot that they eventually returned in audio form for their own spinoff series courtesy of Big Finish. Benjamin has also appeared in the new series, playing the wheelchair-bound Colonel Hugh in *The Unicorn And The Wasp* (2008).

Rounding out season seven is yet another seven-part epic, this one breaks ground in the "alternate universe" mold about a quarter of a century before Fox's **Sliders** ever hit the airwaves. One of the best **Doctor Who** stories ever, and tied with *Doctor Who And The Silurians* as my favorite of the Jon Pertwee era, *Inferno* is a dark, intense installment, if perhaps one or two half-hour segments too long. Pertwee plays the Doctor in his typically serious manner, though in this one he gets to display shock and terror as well, especially at the thought that many of his friends from his own dimension could, under different circumstances, evolve into goose-stepping uniformed thugs. *Inferno* also marks – an illusory cameo in *The Five Doctors* notwithstanding – the final appearance of Caroline John as Liz Shaw. Liz didn't get a sendoff scene at all, nor was there even so much as a mention of her departing the show. (A very brief explanation that she had returned to her research at Cambridge was dropped into the opening scenes of *Terror Of The Autons* the following season.) The character, not to mention the actress, deserved a lot more than that, though many an original novel and audio adventure has sought to redress the balance, inferring that the third Doctor and Liz had more than four adventures together.

SEASON 8: 1971
TERROR OF THE AUTONS

As the Doctor begins investigating the theft of the last remaining Nestene energy sphere (left behind in the previous Auton invasion) and the disappearance of a radio astronomer, a Time Lord appears and warns him that the Master – the Doctor's arch rival Time Lord – has come to Earth. The Doctor deduces that the Master's plan is to reawaken the Nestene Consciousness, giving it the opportunity to invade Earth once more. The Master has already set up production of the lethal plastic Autons at a nearby plastic factory – and knows exactly how he wants to rid the universe of the human race...and the Doctor.

Jon Pertwee . . . . The Doctor
Katy Manning . . . . Jo Grant
Roger Delgado . . . . The Master
Nicholas Courtney . . . Brig. Lethbridge-Stewart
John Baskcomb . . . . Rossini
Christopher Burgess . . . . Professor Phillips
Dave Carter . . . . Museum Attendant
Richard Franklin . . . . Captain Mike Yates
David Garth . . . . Time Lord
Pat Gorman . . . . Auton
Stephen Jack . . . . Rex Farrel Sr.
Haydn Jones . . . . Auton voice
Barbara Leake . . . . Mrs. Farrel
John Levene . . . . Sergeant Benton
Frank Mills . . . . Radio Telescope Director
Andrew Staine . . . . Goodge
Norman Stanley . . . . Telephone Man

This story has been released on DVD

written by Robert Holmes
directed by Barry Letts
music by Dudley Simpson

Part 1 aired on January 2, 1971
Part 2 aired on January 9, 1971
Part 3 aired on January 16, 1971
Part 4 aired on January 23. 1971

Roy Stewart . . . . Strong Man
Harry Towb . . . . McDermott
Dermot Tuohy . . . . Brownrose
Terry Walsh . . . . Auton
Michael Wisher . . . . Rex Farrel

NEW WHO CONNECTIONS: The Autons' ability to eliminate victims with even a small amount of plastic would return to haunt the ninth Doctor in *Rose* (2005).

This story's chief claim to fame is the introduction of the Master, an evil Time Lord with an intellect and powers equal to the Doctor's. Roger Delgado made a tremendous impact in the part, and despite later actors such as Tony Ainley and Eric Roberts having a go, they never quite matched Delgado's air of calculated ruthlessness. Katy Manning also debuts here as the Doctor's new assistant for the next three years, Jo Grant, a bubbly (and occasionally bubble-headed) young lady with a knack for getting into trouble. Jo proves to be resourceful as well as clumsy in this story, more or less establishing the entirety of her character in one shot. Richard Franklin also makes his first appearance as Captain Mike Yates of UNIT, and would serve as the Brigadier's right-hand man through most of the Pertwee era.

Thanks to the infamous BBC videotape purge that wiped out so much of **Doctor Who**'s '60s history, several Jon Pertwee stories were also eliminated, only to be recovered through the discovery of black and white copies sold to other countries in Europe and the eastern hemisphere prior to the brief flashpoint of interest in **Doctor Who** in the U.S. during the 80's. *Terror Of The Autons* is one of the Pertwee adventures which existed only in black and white as a result, though the DVD release (and a VHS release in the '90s) presented a restored, re-colorized version.

THE MIND OF EVIL

The Doctor and Jo pay a visit to Stangmoor Prison to witness a test of a revolutionary new device that promises to reform criminals permanently by entirely extracting the evil impulses from their brains. But in this case, the test subject – a hardened convict named Barnham – is not only relieved of the darkness in his mind, but most of his mind's contents as well, rendering him mentally childlike. Not long afterward, Professor Kettering, checking the machine to find out why it overreacted so harshly, dies mysteriously. The Doctor becomes increasingly suspicious and decides to close off the room and check the Keller device himself…only to realize – too late – that it's an alien life form that feeds on fear, that his arch enemy is behind its presence on Earth, and that the device is only a small part of a much larger plan to plunge the world into chaos.

Jon Pertwee . . . . The Doctor
Katy Manning . . . . Jo Grant
Roger Delgado . . . . The Master
Nicholas Courtney . . . Brig. Lethbridge-Stewart
Richard Atherton . . . . Police Inspector
Johnny Barrs . . . . Fuller
Paul Blomley . . . . Police Superintendent
David Calderisi . . . . Charlie
Dave Carter . . . . Officer
Les Clark . . . . Officer
Les Conrad . . . . Officer
Jim Delaney . . . . Passer-by
Tommy Duggan . . . . Alcott
Michael Ely . . . . UNIT chauffeur
Richard Franklin . . . . Captain Mike Yates
Patrick Godfrey . . . . Cosworth
Martin Gordon . . . . Officer
Laurence Harrington . . . . Voices
Nick Hobbs . . . . American aide
Billy Horrigan . . . . UNIT corporal
Tony Jenkins . . . . Officer
Haydn Jones . . . . Vosper
Kristopher Kum . . . . Fu Peng
Simon Lack . . . . Professor Kettering
John Levene . . . . Sergeant Benton
Pik-Sen Lim . . . . Chin Lee
Fernanda Marlowe . . . . Corporal Bell
William Marlowe . . . . Mailer
Eric Mason . . . . Green

written by Don Houghton
directed by Timothy Combe
music by Dudley Simpson

Part 1 aired on January 30, 1971
Part 2 aired on February 6, 1971
Part 3 aired on February 13, 1971
Part 4 aired on February 20. 1971
Part 5 aired on February 27, 1971
Part 6 aired on March 6, 1971

Bill Matthews . . . . Officer
Neil McCarthy . . . . Barnham
Roy Purcell . . . . Powers
Maureen Race . . . . Student
Peter Roy . . . . Policeman
Charles Saynor . . . . Commissionaire
Clive Scott . . . . Linwood
Michael Sheard . . . . Dr. Summers
Gordon Stothard . . . . Officer
Basil Tang . . . . Chinese chauffeur
Paul Tann . . . . Chinese aide
Barry Wade . . . . Officer
Matthew Walters . . . . Prisoner
Leslie Weekes . . . . Officer
Raymond Westwell . . . . Governor
Francise Williams . . . . Master's chauffeur

I remember as a kid, the cliffhanger in part one had quite an effect on me. The Doctor being almost literally scared to death of something? Even though I'd already seen the "more fallible" fifth Doctor in the person of Peter Davison, I found that scene shocking. It went a long way toward wiping out the nearly-infallible impression of the Doctor left behind by the fourth Doctor's era.

As with many six-parters of its era, *The Mind Of Evil* suffers from a certain amount of padding in the form of characters being captured, escaping, being recaptured, and so on. But it also contains the largest-scale demonstration of UNIT in action that the series mustered until *Battlefield* in 1989, with some excellent action sequences, stunts and directing.

The Master continues to establish that he's a Really Evil Guy here, what with the oddity of him sitting around and smoking cigars in an evil way – a trait which was done away with just as quickly. Evil or not, smoking was apparently a little too far for the Master. (Hijacking nuclear missiles, though? *That's* okay.)

THE CLAWS OF AXOS

Freak weather conditions mark the arrival of an unidentified flying object which lands near a power station. The Doctor, Jo and UNIT enter the ship, with an officious bureaucrat named Chinn in tow, finding that the ship's organic nature is closely tied to its inhabitants, the Axons. Though they can appear in humanoid form, the Axons' true shape is an amorphous blob of tentacles – and they have a passenger on board: the Master. The Axons strike up a bargain with Chinn for Britain to serve as the worldwide distribution hub for Axonite, a miraculous substance the Axons are only too happy to provide freely as a gift of peace in all good faith. The Doctor discovers, only too late, that Axonite is a Trojan horse from space – and it will allow the Axons to feed on Earth's resources until the planet is drained.

Jon Pertwee . . . . The Doctor
Katy Manning . . . . Jo Grant
Roger Delgado . . . . The Master
Nicholas Courtney . . . Brig. Lethbridge-Stewart
David Aldridge . . . . Humanoid Axon
Peter Bathurst . . . . Chinn
Kenneth Benda . . . . Minister
Marc Boyle . . . . Axon monster
Royston Farrell . . . . Technician
Richard Franklin . . . . Captain Mike Yates
Patricia Gordino . . . . Axon woman
Paul Grist . . . . Bill Filer
Donald Hewlett . . . . Sir George Hardiman
Nick Hobbs . . . . Driver
Bernard Holley . . . . Axon man / Axos voice
Peter Holmes . . . . Axon monster
Steve King . . . . Humanoid Axon
John Levene . . . . Sergeant Benton
Debbie Lee London . . . . Axon girl
David G. March . . . . Radar Operator

This story has been released on DVD

written by Bob Baker & Dave Martin
directed by Michael Ferguson
music by Dudley Simpson

Part 1 aired on March 13, 1971
Part 2 aired on March 20, 1971
Part 3 aired on March 27, 1971
Part 4 aired on April 3. 1971

Fernanda Marlowe . . . . Corporal Bell
Roger Minnice . . . . Humanoid Axon
Clinton Morris . . . . Corporal
Geoff Righty . . . . Humanoid Axon
Tim Piggott-Smith . . . . Harker
David Saville . . . . Winser
Steve Smart . . . . Axon monster
Gloria Walker . . . . Secretary/Nurse
Michael Walker . . . . Radar Operator
Derek Ware . . . . Pigbin Josh

BEHIND THE SCENES: This was the first **Doctor Who** script written by the team of **Dave Martin** (1935-2007) and **Bob Baker**, known collectively (but informally) as the Bristol Boys. Though they would go on to write many further scripts for the series during the Pertwee and Tom Baker eras, their most lasting contribution to the **Doctor Who** mythos was the creation of K-9, who returned not only in the 21st century **Doctor Who** revival but all of its spinoffs with the exception of **Torchwood**. Baker, with his business partner Paul Tams, is still overseeing the Australian-made K-9 spinoff series, and Baker and Martin are both credited on-screen every time K-9 reappeared in **Doctor Who** or **The Sarah Jane Adventures**.

A very typical Pertwee-era story, this one is probably notable chiefly for being the first Master story whose original color recording is available (even though it's sourced from a PAL-to-NTSC videotape conversion that was recovered from the United States). But other than that, it's classic early 70's **Doctor Who** – the Master is up to no good, Jo is tagging along right into trouble, and the Brigadier and UNIT are doing their best to clean up the Master's latest evil scheme. And, as always, the third Doctor tries to warn humanity of its own mistakes, and watches as human ambition and greed play right into the hands of the Master and his latest cohorts.

All of these elements are textbook ingredients of the Pertwee era, but in *Claws Of Axos* there really isn't much that's new – the Master collaborates with an isolated alien race whose organic technology can bleed the Earth's natural resources dry at an accelerated rate. And as usual, the aliens have chosen Britain as their point of contact with the entire human race. (Though this constant feature of **Doctor Who** was necessitated by production, they could have at least attempted to *mention* the aliens landing elsewhere on Earth; though it's a funny constant in-joke, it strained credibility tremendously.) The political avarice of a particularly nasty (and porky) British public servant allows the aliens to spread components of their organic technology around the world, spreading the potential disaster to global proportions. This time, the Doctor has to enlist the Master's help in fighting the very aliens the Master has invited to Earth – and then turn the tables on the evil Time Lord at the last minute to save himself.

Roger Delgado, as always, is *The* Master. He's rather underused in this story, but his menace is always portrayed in a believable manner. It's hard to believe that the Master has fallen for the "oh, so the Doctor's on my side now" ruse so many times over the years, but this being only the third Master episode in the show's history, it was still relatively new. And the idea that the two Time Lords might slip away and leave Earth to its fate seems, at least momentarily, like a distinct possibility here. Guest star Paul Grist assumes an American accent and huge sideburns as an American agent visiting UNIT to learn more about the Master – a very reasonable idea, making UNIT seem for once like a truly international organization and not just a British one, though as humorously noted before, when has the Master ever threatened any part of the world other than the UK?

The then-new-to-the-BBC miracle of color television is quite a sight to behold, with the interiors of the Axos spaceship – a combination of brightly painted, cushiony "organic" setpieces, rear projection screens, and video overlays – seem downright trippy and psychedelic. Indeed, in numerous "escape" scenes, actors seem to take odd zig-zagging courses through the Axos sets, though if you concentrate on the set and not the overlaid patterns, it's easy to imagine much quicker escape routes! Even more ludicrous is the finale, in which Jo, the Brigadier, and UNIT's finest observe the explosive destruction of a nuclear power plant from what must be the safe distance of very nearly two or three miles away...

COLONY IN SPACE

The Doctor is startled when his latest work on the TARDIS seems to have some measurable results – it suddenly whisks them away to an alien planet several centuries in Earth's future where a small group of determined settlers are engaged in an ongoing battle with an unscrupulous mining company for the rights to the land, and the native population are fighting both parties for their very survival. The Doctor quickly learns that the IMC miners are willing to use any and all means at their disposal to solidify their claim to this world, and the miners' solution to this problem is to call an Adjudicator from Earth to arbitrate the dispute. But two major problems crop up: the "Adjudicator" is, in fact, the Master – and the primitives of Exarius aren't quite as primitive as they seem, since they're sitting on a weapon that could turn the entire planet into a charred cinder.

Jon Pertwee	. . . .	The Doctor
Katy Manning	. . . .	Jo Grant
Roger Delgado	. . . .	The Master
Nicholas Courtney	. . .	Brig. Lethbridge-Stewart
Norman Atkyns	. . . .	Guardian
John Baker	. . . .	Time Lord
Tony Caunter	. . . .	Morgan
Peter Forbes-Robertson	. . . .	Time Lord
Pat Gorman	. . . .	Primitive / Long
Sheila Grant	. . . .	Jane
John Herrington	. . . .	Holden
Roy Heymann	. . . .	Alien Priest
Bernard Kay	. . . .	Caldwell
Graham Leaman	. . . .	Time Lord
John Line	. . . .	Martin
Stanley Mason	. . . .	Alien priest
Stanley McGeagh	. . . .	Allen
Antonia Moss	. . . .	Alien priest
Nicholas Pennell	. . . .	Winton
John Scott Martin	. . . .	Robot

UNIT

This story has been released on DVD

written by Malcolm Hulke
directed by Michael Briant
music by Dudley Simpson

Part 1 aired on April 10, 1971
Part 2 aired on April 17, 1971
Part 3 aired on April 24, 1971
Part 4 aired on May 1. 1971
Part 5 aired on May 8, 1971
Part 6 aired on May 15, 1971

Morris Perry	. . . .	Dent
John Ringham	. . . .	Ashe
Roy Skelton	. . . .	Norton
John Tordoff	. . . .	Leeson
David Webb	. . . .	Leeson
Mitzi Webster	. . . .	Mrs. Martin
Helen Worth	. . . .	Mary Ashe

BOOK CONNECTIONS: For the New Adventures and Missing Adventures, *Colony In Space* seems to be one of the most seminal reference points in all of **Doctor Who**'s fictional history — IMC appeared or was at least mentioned numerous times in the books, practically becoming shorthand for "corrupt corporation" anytime a story demanded such an entity. The rank of Adjudictator was shared by the seventh Doctor's companions, Roz Forrester and Chris Cwej, in the later New Adventures novels.

Another of those rare six-episode stories that fills up most of that time meaningfully, *Colony In Space* is one of the better stories of the eighth season, and it's no coincidence that this is helped by the Doctor's first chance to leave Earth since the beginning of the seventh season, even if it was at the behest of the Time Lords. The supporting cast is mostly good, though there are some hams among both the miners and the IMC crew. With the tiny, shriveled alien puppet, one must occasionally stifle a giggle, but the overriding point of the story — that developing weapons whose destructive power far outweighs the maturity of their owners could reduce any race to mere primitives — is as timely as ever.

THE DÆMONS

A live television broadcast from an archaeological dig at Devil's End — which Dr. Reeves plans to excavate at midnight — draws the interest of the villagers and of UNIT, though the Doctor is unconvinced that there is any supernatural significance to these events until a local woman, claiming to be a white witch, interrupts the broadcast to protest the dig. Miss Hawthorne believes that the dig could unearth the devil himself. The Doctor and Jo rush to Devil's End, arriving just as Dr. Reeves opens the barrow — and brings it crashing down on everyone inside. When the Doctor recovers, all hell has quite literally broken loose in the village, thanks to the new vicar — the Master in disguise — who is calling upon the powers of what most people could only describe as the devil.

Jon Pertwee	. . . .	The Doctor
Katy Manning	. . . .	Jo Grant
Roger Delgado	. . . .	The Master
Nicholas Courtney	. . .	Brig. Lethbridge-Stewart
Matthew Corbett	. . . .	Jones
John Croft	. . . .	Tom Girton

written by Guy Leopold
(pseudonym for Barry Letts & Robert Sloman)
directed by Christopher Barry
music by Dudley Simpson

Part 1 aired on May 22, 1971

Richard Franklin . . . . Captain Mike Yates
Rollo Gamble . . . . Winstanley
Damaris Hayman . . . . Miss Hawthrone
Eric Hillyard . . . . Dr. Reeves
Jon Joyce . . . . Garvin
John Levene . . . . Sergeant Benton
Alec Linstead . . . . Osgood
Stanley Mason . . . . Bok
Don McKillop . . . . Bert
Patrick Milner . . . . Corporal
John Owens . . . . Thorpe
David Simeon . . . . Alastair Fergus

UNIT

This story
has been
released
on DVD

Part 2 aired on May 29, 1971
Part 3 aired on June 5, 1971
Part 4 aired on June 12. 1971
Part 5 aired on June 19, 1971

James Snell . . . . Harry
Robin Squire . . . . TV cameraman
Gerald Taylor . . . . Baker's man
Stephen Thorne . . . . Azal
Robin Wentworth . . . . Professor Horner
Christopher Wray . . . . Groom

NEW WHO CONNECTIONS: The tenth Doctor mentions Azal's home planet, Dæmos, in *The Satan Pit* (2006), while contemplating the possibility that The Beast in the pit may be another Dæmon. Another Osgood is working for UNIT in 2013's *Day Of The Doctor*; could Sgt. Osgood's daughter or granddaughter be working with the daughter of Brigadier Lethbridge-Stewart?

This wonderfully atmospheric five-parter builds brilliantly upon legends both Pagan and Christian, and those roots lend the story a lot of its impact. It's also a rare chance for the UNIT regulars to shine on their own as both Benton and Yates scuffle with the unruly locals (who are under the hypnotic influence of the Master), and the Brigadier is forced to deal with the situation on his own while the Doctor is locked inside a lethal thermal barrier. (After poor Sgt. Osgood blows up a vital piece of equipment, the Brigadier probably realizes how lucky he is to have the Doctor as his scientific advisor…)

The Dæmons could well be Roger Delgado's best outing as the Master, what with all of the vibes of pure evil that are conjured up by the plot elements of devil worship, witchcraft, and the occult, and Delgado's appearance is perfectly suited to that sort of thing. If this had been the Master's *first* appearance, we still would've been pretty sure that he was up to no good.

For several years, especially for those of us who saw this one on PBS, *The Dæmons* was in black & white, which in some scenes added to the creepy atmosphere. It has since been restored to full color.

SEASON 9: 1972
DAY OF THE DALEKS

Sir Reginald Styles, a diplomat whose efforts could keep the world away from the brink of war in the coming days, claims to have seen a ghost stalking Auderly House, his country mansion. UNIT troops search the nearby grounds and find a lone man in combat fatigues and carrying a weapon of a futuristic design. The Doctor and Jo spend a night in Auderly House, and in the morning are taken hostage by three soldiers armed with the same 22nd-century weapons, who claim they're on a mission to kill Styles – a man who, in their history, failed to prevent a world war that left Earth vulnerable to domination by the Daleks. The Doctor and Jo are accidentally transported to the 22nd century themselves, where they find that their attackers are attempting to change history by assassinating a key figure whose role in creating the future has been misinterpreted badly.

UWORP!

Jon Pertwee . . . . The Doctor
Katy Manning . . . . Jo Grant
Nicholas Courtney . . . Brig. Lethbridge-Stewart
Anna Barry . . . . Anat
Deborah Brayshaw . . . . Technician
Maurice Bush . . . . Ogron
Andrew Carr . . . . Guard
Wilfrid Carter . . . . Sir Reginald Styles
Tim Condren . . . . Guerilla
Richard Franklin . . . . Captain Mike Yates
Scott Fredericks . . . . Boaz
Oliver Gilbert . . . . Dalek voice
Murphy Grumbar . . . . Dalek
Peter Hill . . . . Manager
David Joyce . . . . Ogron
Gypsie Kemp . . . . Radio Operator
Rick Lester . . . . Ogron
John Levene . . . . Sergeant Benton
Alex MacIntosh . . . . TV Reporter
John Scott Martin . . . . Chief Dalek

written by Louis Marks
directed by Paul Bernard
music by Dudley Simpson

Part 1 aired on January 1, 1972
Part 2 aired on January 8, 1972
Part 3 aired on January 15, 1972
Part 4 aired on January 22. 1972

This story has been released on DVD

Jean McFarlane . . . . Miss Paget
Frank Menzies . . . . Ogron
Peter Messaline . . . . Dalek voice
Ricky Newby . . . . Dalek
Valentine Palmer . . . . Monia
George Raistrick . . . . Guard
Geoffrey Todd . . . . Ogron
Jimmy Winston . . . . Shura
Aubrey Woods . . . . Controller
Bruce Wells . . . . Ogron

NEW WHO CONNECTIONS: The Dalek leader in its gold casing obviously had an influence on someone; when it came time to reintroduce the Daleks in the new series, suddenly *all* Daleks had a gold/bronze finish.

The first Dalek TV story filmed in color, as well as one of the very first commercial video releases of a **Doctor Who** story, *Day Of The Daleks* begins a trend that later culminated in the creation of Davros. The Daleks themselves appeared to help deliver a little bit of staccato exposition, and mainly to increase the ratings for four weeks. But their dirty work was handled by the more agile Ogrons, and most of their threatening was handled by the Controller. After several years, perhaps as a result of the very long Dalek serials of the 1960s, someone realized that the Daleks take forever to utter a simple sentence, and so maybe someone more articulate would be better suited to that kind of exposition. And since this story's Dalek voice artists were new to the job, they seemed to be more monosyllabic than usual.

Day Of The Daleks is also among the funniest **Doctor Who** episodes of Jon Pertwee's era, particularly in the scenes where the Doctor chows down on the cheese and knocks back the wine at Auderly House, and not long afterward as Sgt. Benton and then Mike Yates hit Jo up for some food too. Even when the guerillas from the future first storm the house, the Doctor dispatches his attacker in an almost comically effortless way.

There are quite a few other interesting or just plain curious elements to the story. The sets for the Daleks' future headquarters are an oddly open and non-specific space, and the set for the adjacent control room is similarly nebulous. When we first see the Doctor and Jo, they're hovering around the TARDIS console in a large room with doors that automatically open. Given the signature "hum" sound effect of the TARDIS and the automatic doors, one might assume – as I did for many years – that the Doctor and Jo were, in fact, standing in yet another remodeled TARDIS control room. However, there is also a phone installed, and the Brigadier strolls in quite casually, so this rules out the possibility of this being the TARDIS interior – he was amazed upon his apparent first visit to the TARDIS a year later in *The Three Doctors*. But you can see where I might have been confused.

The story's time frame raises the intriguing possibility that the Dalek-dominated 22nd century future visited by the Doctor and Jo could easily be the same future seen in 1964's *The Dalek Invasion Of Earth*, which is also dated in the mid to late 22nd century.

SHORT HOPS

...in which the author states cases for and against modernizing classic Doctor Who.

Day Of The Daleks was one of the earliest **Doctor Who** stories released in the burgeoning age of commercial video releases. It was ten years into the extensive release schedule of classic **Doctor Who** on DVD before this story reappeared, and when it did, it reappeared in style: one disc contained the original four-part story as originally broadcast, warts and all, while the second disc reinvents the wheel somewhat: the stilted, robotic Dalek voices are replaced by more traditional Dalek voices courtesy of Nicholas Briggs, there are new CGI "exterior" shots of the Dalek-conquered future, and the climactic battle in episode four includes entire new sequences, shot on 16mm film at the original location, with fan-made UNIT and Ogron costumes and fan-made Daleks battling it out on a grander scale than the BBC could afford in 1971.

On the budget of a DVD bonus feature (with just a dash of free fan labor of love, in all likelihood).

It's hardly the first time that classic Who has been treated to a facelift for DVD. *The Dalek Invasion Of Earth, The Ark In Space, Earthshock, Enlightenment, Planet Of Fire* and *The Curse Of Fenric* are just a few of the more notable classic series releases to include significantly updated visuals. And always with these releases, the "remade" episodes are an *option*, with the original, as-broadcast versions remastered and always presented as the *default* viewing option (George Lucas, please take note). The new versions are never foisted upon the fans buying the DVDs as "the definitive new version" – even the early release of *The Five Doctors* was eventually replaced by a two-disc version that took the restoration-plus-revision approach.

One of the biggest fanboy-pleasing moments in *Day Of The Daleks* is the end of episode three, when – even in the original version transmitted in 1972 – the faces of William Hartnell and Patrick Troughton were glimpsed in a screen hanging over the third Doctor as he is interrogated by the Daleks. While watching the "special edition" of *Day Of The Daleks* on DVD for the first time, I felt a little bit of a tingle. How far would the producers of the new version go? Might the screen show *every* incarnation of the Doctor, as both homage and expansion of that moment in the original show? Was I about to see Matt Smith's face in a Jon Pertwee episode?

As they often do, the makers of the new version chose a purist approach: the scene was recreated and enhanced, with episode footage of the first two Doctors rather than still photos, but only the first two Doctors. I don't blame them a bit – it's the option that best fits the story logic. If the Daleks are performing an interrogation on some kind of neurological level, the third Doctor won't know what his future incarnations look like.

But how far *should* the revising of the original series go?

Let's look at another specimen of classic SF TV remastering and revision: the original **Star Trek**. In 2006, CBS – now the rights holders to Paramount's TV library including the **Star Trek** series – began to embark on a project to rescan the original negatives of every classic Shatner-era **Star Trek** episode for HD, and opted to replace the original visuals with new CGI creations. Some fans loved it, some fans loathed it. Debates broke out on the internet as to how much *texture* the *Enterprise*'s hull should have, or how fast the lights in the warp engines should rotate.

But where one could revise the original **Star Trek** and not have to worry too much about whether or not it's violating the visual lexicon of the franchise's later "generations", with **Doctor Who**, you're playing in the same sandbox, all the time. Most **Doctor Who** stories happen in the same "universe," unless otherwise noted (*Inferno, Rise Of The Cybermen*, the cancelled-out timeline of *The Last Of The Time Lords*). Why *not* shake things up a bit more?

On a purely technical level, restoring **Doctor Who** in the way that CBS restored **Star Trek** simply can't happen due to the limitations of the original media. Where most classic **Doctor Who** stories include location scenes shot on 16mm film, not every story's original film footage is intact, having been transferred to video long ago. And that's the real killer: for those stories whose 16mm film survives and could conceivably be rescanned at a high-definition resolution, you can't do the same with footage originally shot on PAL analog videotape, whose maximum resolution is 625 lines. It could be upscaled to 720p (at the likely cost of looking terrible, amplifying any electronic artifacts of the original footage until they look like crap), or downscaled to the not-really-HD 480i, a picture resolution reserved for "legacy" video shot before the HD age. A restoration of the entire series to HD specs on the scale of what was done with **Star Trek** is impossible.

And just as you couldn't get **Trek** fans to agree on the texture of the *Enterprise*, any proposal to do something like inserting the faces of future Doctors into a classic series episode would be wandering into a minefield. In a strictly chronological sense, the Daleks have been aware of the Doctor's existence since the fourth Doctor tried to prevent them from coming into existence (*Genesis Of The Daleks*, 1975), and there's no reason to assume that the Doctor and the Daleks continue to encounter each other in perfect chronological order. By that same logic, the Cybermen in *Earthshock* should've seen the sixth and seventh Doctors in their historical record search.

In the end, a more realistic re-entry and crash for *Earthshock*'s freighter, or more fluid scenes of Nerva Beacon, or watching Fenric's runes being blasted out of stone by pure psychic energy, or seeing the war-torn vista of Earth under Dalek rule are for the fans only. They're a treat for those of us who have seen the original shows often enough that we know what they look like, and they're a treat because someone finally put them in the grander context that we always envisaged. The heavily-revised fourth episode of *Day Of The Daleks* came about simply because fandom seems to collectively remember the singular '70s battle between UNIT and Daleks as a more elaborate event. Now it finally can be. Just watch disc two.

It's a shame that the remastered-for-DVD episodes aren't getting a wider audience than the DVDs themselves, but in the end, restoration is probably the less-hackle-raising option than revisionism. Part of the charm of **Doctor Who** is that, despite the vast number of people involved with making the show and guiding the Doctor's story over a relatively vast number of years for a fictional character (without a continuity-wiping reboot to be found), the whole thing has held together as well as it has.

THE CURSE OF PELADON

The Doctor, with Jo in tow, tries another of his experiments in getting the TARDIS working – and to both of their astonishment, the time machine roars into life and dematerializes, taking the two to the stormy planet of Peladon. On the eve of its admission into the Federation that includes Earth, Peladon receives delegates from Federation member planets Arcturus, Alpha Centauri – and Earth itself, a delegation for which the Doctor and Jo are mistaken. Also present are the Doctor's old enemies, the Ice Warriors, though the motives for their presence may not be as sinister as the Doctor fears – and yet when both the delegates and the royal house of Peladon come under attack, the Doctor can suspect no one else.

Jon Pertwee	. . . .	The Doctor
Katy Manning	. . . .	Jo Grant
Terry Bale	. . . .	voice of Arcturus
Alan Bennion	. . . .	Izlyr
Sonny Caldinez	. . . .	Sworg
Ysanne Churchman	. . . . .	voice of Alpha Centauri
Wendy Danvers	. . . .	Amazonia
Stuart Fell	. . . .	Alpha Centauri
Henry Gilbert	. . . .	Torbis
George Giles	. . . .	Captain
Murphy Grumbar	. . . .	Arcturus
Nick Hobbs	. . . .	Aggedor

This story has been released on DVD

written by Brian Hayles
directed by Lennie Mayne
music by Dudley Simpson

Part 1 aired on January 29, 1972
Part 2 aired on February 5, 1972
Part 3 aired on February 12, 1972
Part 4 aired on February 19. 1972

Gordon St. Clair	. . . .	Grun
Geoffrey Toone	. . . .	Hepesh
David Troughton	. . . .	Peladon

A.K.A.: David Troughton (son of second Doctor Patrick Troughton) returns in the new series episode *Midnight* (2008), but again he's not quite sure of the Doctor's intentions. He also takes over his father's role in the 2011 BBC audiobooks *The Hexford Invasion* and *Survivors In Space*.

AUDIO CONNECTIONS: Peladon is a favorite destination of **Doctor Who** writers who grew up on the '70s episodes. David Troughton reprises the role of King Peladon (quite a bit older) in *Prisoner Of Peladon* (2009), while the fifth Doctor and his companions revisit Peladon later in its history in *The Bride Of Peladon* (2008).

K-9 CONNECTIONS: A member of the Alpha Centauri race is depicted in the K-9 episode *The Curse Of Anubis* (2010) as a species that Anubis' species has conquered. Given Alpha Centauri's behavior in this story, one can only imagine that it was quite a fight...

Surely one of the defining moments in the Pertwee era and a sign of **Doctor Who**'s evolving moral compass, *The Curse Of Peladon* turns the tables and makes a long-standing adversary a good guy – and all without resorting to a been-there, done-that retread of the already well-worn <u>Enemy Mine</u> formula. Now, I have nothing but love for the aforementioned story/movie, but it's been used as the basis for so many other stories down through the years, especially in TV, that I loved how Brian Hayles – who did, after all, create the Ice Warriors – managed to give his creations credibility, honor, and benevolence here.

David Troughton is the other jewel in the crown here, literally. As the confused young King, he shines, exuding worry, confidence, and at appropriate times a complete lack of confidence. He's a young man thrust into a difficult position – and surely the son of the previous Doctor, Patrick Troughton, can appreciate that. (He also roomed with future **Doctor Who** star Colin Baker, but that's a whole set of ribald tales best left to Mr. Baker's numerous convention appearances!)

The other alien creations are just as inspired – Aggedor is one of the best man-in-suit creatures ever put together by the BBC costume department, Alpha Centauri is a delightful character, and Arcturus, while hideous to look at, is well-executed – and since he's ugly he's naturally the perfect red herring. Or is he?

THE SEA DEVILS

The Doctor and Jo pay a visit to the Master, who has been languishing in an isolated top-security prison since he was arrested by UNIT. But in reality, the Master has already gained control of his jailkeepers, and is simply biding his time as he constructs a device that will summon the Sea Devils, a species of bipedal Earth reptiles related to the Silurians, who once walked the Earth before man. The Sea Devils have already been attacking ships at sea, but the Master has promised them the means to revive all of their people and regain their position as the rulers of Earth – even if it means eliminating the human race. As the Doctor tries to intervene, suggesting a peace between man and reptile, he finds himself fighting not only the Master, but the warlike impulses of homo sapiens.

Jon Pertwee	The Doctor
Katy Manning	Jo Grant
Roger Delgado	The Master
Norman Atkyns	Rear Admiral
Colin Bell	Summers
Martin Boddey	Walker
John Caesar	Myers
Peter Forbes-Robertson	Chief Sea Devil
Hugh Futcher	Hickman
Pat Gorman	Sea Devil
David Griffin	Mitchell
Steven Ismay	Sea Devil
Brian Justice	Wilson
Eric Mason	Smedley
Stanley McGeagh	Drew
Clive Morton	Trenchard
Declan Mulholland	Clark
June Murphy	Jane Blythe
Brian Nolan	Sea Devil
Edwin Richfield	Hart
Rex Rowland	Girton
Neil Seiler	Radio Operator

This story has been released on DVD

written by Malcolm Hulke
directed by Michael Briant
music by Malcolm Clarke

Part 1 aired on February 26, 1972
Part 2 aired on March 4, 1972
Part 3 aired on March 11, 1972
Part 4 aired on March 18. 1972
Part 5 aired on March 25, 1972
Part 6 aired on April 1, 1972

Frank Seton	Sea Devil
Donald Sumpter	Ridgway
Royston Tickner	Robbins
Brian Vaughn	Watts
Alec Wallis	Bowman
Terry Walsh	Barclay
Jeff Witherick	Sea Devil
Christopher Wray	Lovell

A.K.A.: Actor **Declan Mulholland**, who appears in both this story and the Tom Baker-era four-parter *The Androids Of Tara*, had the strange honor of providing **the first on-screen portrayal of Jabba The Hutt in *Star Wars***. His scenes were left on the cutting room floor until they were re-inserted into the controversially revised "Special Edition" of *Star Wars* in 1997, though Mulholland fur-coated appearance and his voice were replaced by a CGI version of the vile intergalactic gangster. Even though his moment of *Star Wars* fame was restored, he still doesn't get to appear in it, though the original footage as shot with Mulholland does appear in numerous behind-the-scenes documentaries on the making and restoration of the original *Star Wars* trilogy.

NEW WHO CONNECTIONS: The design of the new series Silurians (*The Hungry Earth / Cold Blood*, 2010) would seem to show a third Silurian species that has elements of both Silurians and their Sea Devil cousins. A rejected design is glimpsed in an episode of **Doctor Who Confidential**, depicting a more obvious hybridization of classic series Silurians and Sea Devils, but this was passed up in favor of a more "human" face.

K-9 CONNECTIONS: In *The Curse Of Anubis* (2010), Anubis and his people show off a record of species that they've subjugated, including an image of a Sea-Devil, which would seem to imply that they conquered (perhaps in the past), or will conquer, Earth at a time when Sea-Devils and Silurians are the dominant form of life.

One of those rare beasts – a six-parter which actually needed most of that airtime to tell its story – *The Sea Devils* is an effective sequel to 1970's *Doctor Who And The Silurians*. It treads over much of the same ground in terms of the story, but supplants the 1970 story's philosophical debates about indigenous populations in favor of action and set pieces, namely some real naval hardware. The various hovercraft and jet-ski scenes are well-done, even though filming conditions weren't ideal – it's easy to see that the sea was really restless.

This story could well be Roger Delgado's most vicious portrayal of the Master, who normally pulls strings from the sidelines. But in this case, the Master is forced into more hand-to-hand fights, at one point drawing a gun and then engaging in a swordfight with the Doctor, one of the only times that the Master and the Doctor grappled physically in the '70s. At the same time, Delgado also plays up the humility very well in the early scenes where the audience is meant to consider him a prisoner. Fellow cast members have singled Delgado out for praise in this episode, for refusing to use a stunt double in the jet-ski chase with the Doctor; Delgado was reportedly afraid of water, so taking to the open sea must have been a tremendous challenge for him.

On the downside, there's Malcolm Clarke's avant-garde synthesized music, which delves further into abstraction than most **Doctor Who** music. Think of the more unusual synthesizer passages of Jerry Goldsmith's music from *Logan's Run* – and then crank up the weird knob all the way to 11. There's also the amusing government bureaucrat character who is more than willing to start a war from behind a desk, but cowers *under* that desk when the Sea Devils bring the fight to his office.

THE MUTANTS

The Doctor and Jo are sent on a Time Lord-mandated courier mission, shrouded in secrecy, to the 30th century. His cargo is a small container keyed to the bio-readings of a single being. The TARDIS – temporarily cleared for a single flight to the destination of the Time Lords' choice – takes them to an Imperial Earth Skybase orbiting the planet Solos, a world whose poisonous atmosphere and proud natives are the only things that have kept the Earth Empire from completely overrunning it. As it turns out, the container the Doctor has brought is intended for Ky, a Solonian national who is on the wrong side of the law, wanted dead or alive by the tyrannical Marshal of the Skybase. Not only is the Doctor fighting the Marshal's forces from the moment he arrives, but years of the Marshal's dictatorship have made it unlikely that the Solonians will trust an outsider either – even if the future of their entire species depends on it.

Jon Pertwee	The Doctor
Katy Manning	Jo Grant
David Arlen	Guard
Christopher Coll	Stubbs
David J. Graham	Old Man
Garrick Hagon	Ky
John Hollis	Sondergaard
Peter Howell	Investigator
Rick James	Cotton
Sidney Johnson	Old Man
James Mellor	Varan
Geoffrey Palmer	Administrator
Roy Pearce	Solos Guard
George Pravda	Jaeger
Damon Sanders	Guard

This story has been released on DVD

written by Bob Baker & Dave Martin
directed by Christopher Barry
music by Dudley Simpson

Part 1 aired on April 8, 1972
Part 2 aired on April 15, 1972
Part 3 aired on April 22, 1972
Part 4 aired on April 29. 1972
Part 5 aired on May 6, 1972
Part 6 aired on May 13, 1972

Jonathan Sherwood	Varan's son
Martin Taylor	Guard
Paul Whitsun-Jones	Marshal

A.K.A.: For the next two stories, this season of **Doctor Who** becomes a game of "spot the future *Star Wars* actor." **Garrick Hagon**, guest starring in *The Mutants* as Ky, would go on to fly alongside Luke Skywalker – briefly and tragically – as ill-fated Rebel pilot Biggs Darklighter, even though the majority of his scenes early in the movie wound up on the cutting room floor. Hagon returned to **Doctor Who** in *A Town Called Mercy* (2012), as well as providing a disturbing voice for Big Finish's **Doctor Who** audio story *Axis Of Insanity* (2004). **John Hollis** would have to wait for *The Empire Strikes Back* to make his appearance as Lando Calrissian's nameless mute henchman, a character that the movie's action figure line dubbed Lobot.

The Mutants is a classic "they're not like us, we don't want them here" tale whose basic plot outline was later appropriated by **Star Trek: The Next Generation**.

If you thought the 1990 **TNG** episode *Transfigurations*, which hijacked *The Mutants'* plot of a race on the brink of a major evolutionary leap, was aimless, beware of this six-parter. But, to be fair, *The Mutants* is far more intelligently written. The only thing working against it is its sheer length, much of which is occupied by chase scenes. *The Mutants* also succeeds in setting up an elaborate political background for the story, allowing easy comparisons between the Earth Empire's rule of Solos and very real situations of oppression, such as apartheid.

Future **Star Wars** actors John Hollis and Garrick Hagon anchor the story with their believable portrayals, but some of the other cast members – primarily among those no-good Earth colonists – go over the top, making it a little hard in places to take *The Mutants* seriously. But if you like a story that allows the third Doctor to give full vent to his "power to the common man" spiels, with righteous indignation dialed up to 10, you can't go wrong with this one.

THE TIME MONSTER

The Doctor is disturbed by a recent series of dreams whose imagery has included the destruction of the world and the laughing face of the Master. But with no concrete basis for these visions, he ignores them and accompanies Jo as UNIT's observers to the demonstration of the new TOM-TIT device – standing for Transmission Of Matter Through Interstitial Time. But things go wrong from the start, especially when the Doctor sees that the TOM-TIT research program is actually being run by the Master. The Master demonstrates a mere fraction of TOM-TIT's potential by snatching soldiers and artillery from World Wars I & II and launching them at UNIT troops. But the Doctor realizes that TOM-TIT's true power is still largely untapped. The Master plans to capture a Chronovore – a creature which lives outside of the dimension of time and feeds upon temporal energy – harness its power for his continual conquests. The Doctor pursues the Master through time and the lost continent of Atlantis to prevent the Chronovore's incredible powers from falling into the Master's hands...but the only way to stop that from happening may be mutual destruction for both Time Lords.

Jon Pertwee	. . . .	The Doctor
Katy Manning	. . . .	Jo Grant
Roger Delgado	. . . .	The Master
Nicholas Courtney	. . .	Brig. Lethbridge-Stewart
Barry Ashton	. . . .	Proctor
Neville Barber	. . . .	Dr. Cook
Ingrid Bower	. . . .	face of Kronos
Marc Boyle	. . . .	Kronos
Dave Carter	. . . .	Officer
Ian Collier	. . . .	Stuart Hyde
George Cormack	. . . .	Dalios
Keith Dalton	. . . .	Neophite
Donald Eccles	. . . .	Krasis
Richard Franklin	. . . .	Captain Yates
Melville Jones	. . . .	Guard
George Lee	. . . .	Farmworker
Simon Legree	. . . .	Sergeant

written by Robert Sloman
directed by Paul Bernard
music by Dudley Simpson

This story has been released on DVD

Part 1 aired on May 20, 1972
Part 2 aired on May 27, 1972
Part 3 aired on June 3, 1972
Part 4 aired on June 10. 1972
Part 5 aired on June 17, 1972
Part 6 aired on June 24, 1972

Aidan Murphy	. . . .	Hippias
Susan Penhaligon	. . . .	Lakis
Ingrid Pitt	. . . .	Galleia
Gregory Powell	. . . .	Knight
Dave Prowse	. . . .	Minotaur

John Levene	Sergeant Benton	Michael Walker	Miseus
Wanda Moore	Dr. Ingram	Terry Walsh	Window cleaner
Derek Murcott	Crito	John Wyse	Dr. Percival

A.K.A.: You probably won't recognize him with the monster head on, but **David Prowse** shows up here – years before his reign as the man wearing the body armor of Darth Vader throughout the original *Star Wars* trilogy – as the legendary Minotaur. He was a frequent fixture in hulking monster suits on such series as **Space: 1999**, though he did appear in the flesh in the 1981 BBC-TV adaptation of Douglas Adams' **Hitchhiker's Guide To The Galaxy**.

NEW WHO CONNECTIONS: The winged Kronos creature, a chronovore or "time eater", appears when the fabric of time is disturbed by the Master, and later devours the ancient city of Atlantis. The reapers in *Father's Day* (2005) seem to exhibit similar behavior – they're also winged creatures who feed on the oldest living things they can reach – and they may be related to the chronovore.

This six-parter is a little more far-fetched than your average **Doctor Who**, delving into such fanciful realms as Atlantis (which has its own Minotaur, no less!), but it has a quirky appeal. I almost wish there'd been more opening sequences like the Doctor's nightmare in part one – a scene made particularly effective by the fact that the rivalry between the Doctor and the Master, despite the considerable talents of such actors as Anthony Ainley and Eric Roberts, was never more intense or frightening as it was in the Pertwee era, at least where the classic series was concerned. I can almost forgive every moment of silliness in the remainder of the story for that unique opening.

Oh, but it does get silly. Sergeant Benton turning into a baby? David "Darth Vader" Prowse as the BBC bargain-basement interpretation of the Minotaur? And Ingrid Pitt's eye-rolling overacting as Galleia – not to mention a rare slice of overcooked ham from Roger Delgado as the Master pleads with the Chronovore for his life? Even Katy Manning gets in on the (overacting) act as the Doctor and the Master play chicken in their respective time machines.

Thankfully, there are some moments of genuine tension and SF weirdness – the sudden reappearance of weapons from past World Wars, the freezing of time, and the whole Time Ram sequence (despite the aforementioned twice-baked hamminess). Somehow, if you can suspend your disbelief a little more than usual, it all holds together.

One more thing: the TARDIS interior set was really cool in this one. (Yes, the round indentations in the walls suddenly look like giant salad bowls for the duration of this story only, but it's a better look than the black & white cardboard photo backdrop that had been in use since the '60s.)

SEASON 10: 1972-73
THE THREE DOCTORS

UNIT is called in by a radio astronomer whose studies have turned up distinctly unearthly results of late, but even the Doctor can't imagine the magnitude of the threat. Somewhere within a black hole, a gateway to an antimatter universe, a malevolent being seeks one of his own race to assume his place as the master of a doomed world – and locates a fellow Time Lord on Earth. When the Doctor realizes the nature of the threat, he sends a distress call to the Time Lords, but their power source is also being drained by the black hole, and they can spare no help – aside from sending the Doctor's earlier incarnations into his own present. The first Doctor is trapped in a time eddy, barely able to contact his future selves, who travel into the black hole – along with Jo, the Brigadier, and Sergeant Benton – to defy the wrath of Omega…the first Time Lord.

Jon Pertwee . . . . The Doctor
Patrick Troughton . . . . The Doctor
William Hartnell . . . . The Doctor
Katy Manning . . . . Jo Grant
Nicholas Courtney . . . Brig. Lethbridge-Stewart
Alan Chuntz . . . . Omega's Champion
Peter Evans . . . . Time Lord
Murphy Grumbar . . . . Gell-Guard
Tony Lang . . . . Time Lord
Graham Leaman . . . . Time Lord
John Levene . . . . Sergeant Benton
John Scott Martin . . . . Gell-Guard
Ricky Newby . . . . Gell-Guard
Richard Orme . . . . Time Lord
Denys Palmer . . . . Palmer
Clyde Pollitt . . . . Chancellor

UNIT

This story has been released on DVD

written by Bob Baker & Dave Martin
directed by Lennie Mayne
music by Dudley Simpson

Part 1 aired on December 30, 1972
Part 2 aired on January 6, 1973
Part 3 aired on January 13, 1973
Part 4 aired on January 20, 1973

Patricia Pryor . . . . Mrs. Ollis
Roy Purcell . . . . President
Rex Robinson . . . . Dr. Tyler
Stephen Thorne . . . . Omega
Cy Town . . . . Gell-Guard
Laurie Webb . . . . Ollis
Lincoln Wright . . . . Time Lord

BEHIND THE SCENES: The first Doctor may have been confined to a "time bubble", but actor William Hartnell's predicament was much worse. Severely debilitated, Hartnell was filmed at a location near his home, reading his lines from cue cards with a black backdrop behind him, inside the hastily assembled "time bubble" prop. *The Three Doctors* was his final performance before his death in 1975 at the age of 67.

As much of a must-see story as *The Five Doctors* a decade later, *The Three Doctors* was the first anniversary special in the history of **Doctor Who**, and featured the rather inevitable storyline of the various Doctors teaming up to fight a common enemy. Patrick Troughton stole much of the show, but my biggest peeve is with the fact that William Hartnell's final performance – given under the strain of suffering from arteriosclerosis which took his life two years later – is obscured behind the glare of a television monitor. Surely his brief scenes could have been edited directly into the show, rather than appearing on fuzzy TV screens in the TARDIS? There's also a priceless reaction from Sergeant Benton, and later the Brigadier, as both are seen walking into the TARDIS for the first time.

The Three Doctors also sports one of the most traditional-sounding musical underscores Dudley Simpson created during the Pertwee era, but thanks to whoever edited the show, the music is chopped to bits repeatedly, cutting in and out abruptly in a way that reminds me of good old-fashioned cassette tape "pause button" editing. It's some of the more interesting third-Doctor-era music, and seems to begin and end jarringly throughout the show, epsecially the eerie bits which set the mood on Omega's world.

Omega himself is the Pertwee era's most significant contribution to the Time Lord mythos (aside from the Master), and his legend would be built upon in later years, and especially in the New Adventures. The Time Lords were seen much as they were in *The War Games* in 1969 – inhabitants of a glittering, hi-tech world, still bristling with contempt of the Doctor in all of his incarnations but still grudgingly calling on his help.

CARNIVAL OF MONSTERS

The Doctor and Jo land on a ship traveling the Indian Ocean at the turn of the 20th century, and the boat's passengers seem to take the time travelers' arrival in stride at first, though the

Doctor steers clear of the crew. But one event that no one takes calmly is the emergence of an enormous creature from the sea - something that the Doctor immediately recognizes is not from Earth. These unexpected events cast the pair of "stowaways" in a different light, and they're on the run from the crew; worse yet, the TARDIS has been moved by an unknown force. A mysterious hatch – far too futuristic for a ship of this era - leads not to the bowels of the ship, but into the bowels of a massive computer system. Other hatches lead to other environments: the oceanfaring ship is trapped in a simulated ocean, its passengers going through the motions of an endless voyage, unaware of where they are. The alien Drashigs that have been menacing the boat have escaped their own swampy environment and gone rogue. Only when the Doctor finds the exit does he realize the truth: the environments and their occupants are real beings, reduced to microscopic size and stored in isolated environments in a Miniscope operated by Vorg, who offers others the chance to observe those beings as a roving sideshow. On the planet Inter Minor, Vorg and his assistant Shirna are simply plying their trade, but the Drashigs' escape from their Miniscope environment is only the first sign that Vorg's Miniscope is about to become a pawn in this planet's political intrigue. Whether in the Miniscope or outside of it, the Drashigs are a danger to everyone nearby, unless the Doctor can save the day.

Jon Pertwee	The Doctor
Katy Manning	Jo Grant
Leslie Dwyer	Vorg
Tenniel Evans	Major Daly
Stuart Fell	Functionary
Cheryl Hall	Shirna
Peter Halliday	Pletrac
Terence Lodge	Orum
Ian Marter	Andrews
Jenny McCracken	Claire Daly
Andrew Staines	Captain
Michael Wisher	Kalik

This story has been released on DVD

written by Robert Holmes
directed by Barry Letts
music by Dudley Simpson

Part 1 aired on January 27, 1973
Part 2 aired on February 3, 1973
Part 3 aired on February 10, 1973
Part 4 aired on February 17. 1973

A.K.A.: Future Tom Baker companion **Ian Marter** makes his **Doctor Who** debut here; he made enough of an impression on Barry Letts that, as Letts was considering casting an older actor as the fourth Doctor, Letts created the role of Harry Sullivan with Marter in mind: a younger male lead who could handle action scenes if the older Doctor envisioned by Letts was physically incapable of doing so.

BEHIND THE SCENES: *Carnival Of Monsters* marks the second and final appearance of a Cyberman during the Jon Pertwee era, making Pertwee and Christopher Eccleston the only Doctors who never fought them onscreen. The other Pertwee-era Cyberman sighting occurs in *The Mind Of Evil*, where a still photo of a Cyberman appears as part of the third Doctor's Keller-Machine-induced visions of horror. For *Carnival*, a Cyberman costume from *The Invasion* was dusted off and worn by an actor for a very short scene shown on Vorg's Miniscope screen – the first Cyberman sighting in color.

Positively surreal compared to most third Doctor stories, *Carnival Of Monsters* is a brilliantly off-format adventure that keeps you guessing the first time you watch it. Once you know what the story's "gag" is, it holds up to repeat viewing as you go looking for clues that you missed the first time. A brilliant cast is led by Jon Pertwee's **Navy Lark** co-star Tenniel Evans, who plays a stiff-upper-lip specimen of that era of the British Empire during which the sun never set on British soil. Evans' character could almost be considered a silly stereotype, except that as the world begins changing around him, he becomes a little less sure of himself - but keeps up his bluster to keep anyone else from noticing, a brilliant comic-going-on-dramatic performance. In the same vein, Ian Marter makes his **Doctor Who** debut as the Lt. Andrews and nearly steals the show - it's not for nothing that Barry Letts and Terrance Dicks remembered Marter when later casting a younger male companion to assist a still-unspecified fourth Doctor.

Carnival is also a refreshing change of pace in that it deliberately plays to Pertwee's not-inconsiderable comedic chops, and puts him in a position to engage in witty verbal sparring with Evans without making that pairing a fourth-wall-bending wink-and-a-nudge to the audience. (To put it in context: Pertwee and Evans plied their comedy trade on **The Navy Lark** both on radio and television, and Pertwee was associated with that series even longer than he was with **Doctor Who**. **The Navy Lark** also served as a launching point for the career of Ronnie Corbett of **The Two Ronnies** fame, who would later appear in a Red Nose Day special mini-episode of **The Sarah Jane Adventures**.) It might throw some fans off who are most accustomed to Pertwee's usual self-assured, super-serious portrayal of the Doctor, but as stunt casting goes, it was a Big Deal, and it really doesn't *feel* like stunt casting. That Jo Grant manages to *avoid* being upstaged for much of *Carnival* is a testament to Katy Manning's skills as well.

Every so often, a story comes along which breaks out of the parameters of most **Doctor Who** stories without breaking the show. I'm not putting *Carnival Of Monsters* in the same league as *Blink*, to be sure, but it's up there with other format-bending experiments as *The Happiness Patrol, The Romans* and *Vincent And The Doctor*, and it's still very entertaining. Robert Holmes wrote the scripts, so its plotting also holds up to close scrutiny: it's classic oddball Who.

FRONTIER IN SPACE

After months of seething suspicion, Earth and Draconia are on the brink of all-out war, with small skirmishes and raids already taking place. As the TARDIS brings the Doctor and Jo into the fray, they discover that those raids are not all that they seem; the attacks are being carried out by neither Earth nor Draconia, but a third party trying to force the two worlds closer to the beginning of war. The Doctor is outraged to discover that this third party is the Master, working with a hired band of Ogron mercenaries, but the Doctor's attempts to warn both the president of Earth and the royal house on Draconia go largely unheeded – until it is too late. The Doctor, Jo, and several skeptical humans and Draconians track the Master down, discovering that the war is only part of his plan. For the Master has enlisted the help of his deadliest allies yet: the Daleks.

Jon Pertwee . . . . The Doctor
Katy Manning . . . . Jo Grant
Roger Delgado . . . . The Master
Ray Lonn Ashton . . . . Kemp
Peter Birrel . . . . Draconian Prince
Dennis Bowen . . . . Governor
Timothy Craven . . . . Guard
James Culliford . . . . Stewart
Lawrence Davidson . . . Draconian First Secretary
Clifford Elkin . . . . Earth Cruiser Captain
Ian Frost . . . . Draconian Messenger
Vera Fusek . . . . President
Harold Goldblatt . . . . Professor Dale
Murphy Grumbar . . . . Dalek
Karol Hagar . . . . Secretary
Laurence Harrington . . . . Guard
Michael Hawkins . . . . Williams
Caroline Hunt . . . . Technician
Michael Kilgarriff . . . . Ogron
Rick Lester . . . . Ogron
Louis Mahoney . . . . Newscaster
John Scott Martin . . . . Dalek
Bill Mitchell . . . . Newscaster
Roy Pattison . . . . Draconian Pilot

This story has been released on DVD

written by Malcolm Hulke
directed by Paul Bernard
music by Dudley Simpson

Part 1 aired on February 24, 1973
Part 2 aired on March 3, 1973
Part 3 aired on March 10, 1973
Part 4 aired on March 17. 1973
Part 5 aired on March 24, 1973
Part 6 aired on March 31. 1973

Luan Peters . . . . Sheila
Stanley Price . . . . Pilot
John Rees . . . . Hardy
Madhav Sharma . . . . Patel
Richard Shaw . . . . Cross
Stephen Thorne . . . . Ogron
Cy Town . . . . Dalek
Bill Wilde . . . . Draconian Captain
Ramsay Williams . . . . Brook
Michael Wisher . . . . Dalek voices
John Woodnutt . . . . Emperor

A.K.A.: As if the Master and the Daleks working together wasn't scary enough, here's a frightening thought: some of the Doctor's mightiest enemies are allied against him in this story... in the guise of lowly Ogrons! **Stephen Thorne** played Omega in the season opener *The Three Doctors*, as well as the devilish Azal in *The Dæmons*. **Michael Kilgarriff** was the hulking embodiment of the Cyber Controller in *Tomb Of The Cybermen* (1967) and *Attack Of The Cybermen* (1985). Kilgarriff also played the title character in Tom Baker's debut story *Robot* (1974).

Frontier In Space is Space Opera with capital letters, a genre that usually isn't associated with the more eccentric tendencies of most eras of **Doctor Who**; with its political machinations and brinksmanship, it bears a closer resemblance to the later BBC SF series **Blake's 7** than it does to most **Who**. It's full of textured characters, lots of chases and captures and escapes (it wouldn't be a Pertwee six-parter without 'em, you know), and the introduction of one of **Doctor Who**'s most interesting races: the Draconians. Funny thing is, the tall, dignified bearded lizards have made but one appearance in the entire history of the series – this story - but this story apparently intrigued enough fans that video and audio spinoffs, comics and novels aplenty, have been inspired by that singular appearance. In hindsight, it's easy to lose the Draconians in the very crowded category of "fictional alien races who live by a Samurai code of honor," also inhabited by such other SF aliens as the Minbari, Klingons, and countless others, but in 1973 the Draconians were truly unique.

Despite all these commendable qualities, *Frontier* boasts a tragic footnote in **Doctor Who** history: Roger Delgado's final magnificent turn in the role of the Master. It really wasn't planned that way, though the character's exit *was* in the works – Terrance Dicks has since revealed that a "final confrontation" was already being planned to give the Master a rest, and that unwritten, unproduced story might even have seen Jon Pertwee out of the role of the Doctor. Roger Delgado died in a car crash *en route* to a film location in Turkey on June 18, 1973, and his death dealt a serious blow to the show – the late Jon Pertwee even cited the death of his dear friend and on-screen nemesis as a primary reason for relinquishing the role of the Doctor.

Frontier In Space can be a bit plodding at times, but if you get the chance to see it in its original six-part format, perhaps taking in only one or two episodes at a time, you may find that it's more fascinating than you might have thought. Certainly all those fans of the Draconians thought so.

PLANET OF THE DALEKS

The TARDIS continues toward the planet Spiridon, the location of the hidden Dalek army that could overrun the entire galaxy. The injured Doctor falls into a self-induced healing coma, leaving Jo few instructions. When the TARDIS lands, Jo ventures out into the poisonous jungle on Spiridon, eventually encountering a military expedition of Thals, the Daleks' mortal enemies from Skaro. The Thals manage to get the Doctor to safety and join him on a mission to keep the Dalek army from launching its offensive. The invisible natives of Spiridon, enslaved by the Daleks, are another hazard, along with the lethal vegetation. When the Dalek Supreme arrives to lead its army into battle, it appears that the Doctor may be too late to stop his old rivals.

Jon Pertwee	. . . .	The Doctor
Katy Manning	. . . .	Jo Grant
Murphy Grumbar	. . . .	Dalek
Prentis Hancock	. . . .	Vaber
Bernard Horsfall	. . . .	Taron
Jane How	. . . .	Rebec

This story has been released

written by Terry Nation
directed by David Maloney
music by Dudley Simpson

Part 1 aired on April 7, 1973

UWORP!

on DVD

John Scott Martin . . . . Dalek		Part 2 aired on April 14, 1973
Hilary Minster . . . . Marat		Part 3 aired on April 21, 1973
Tim Preece . . . . Codal		Part 4 aired on April 28. 1973
Roy Skelton . . . . Wester / Dalek voices		Part 5 aired on May 5, 1973
Tony Starr . . . . Dalek Supreme		Part 6 aired on May 12. 1973
Cy Town . . . . Dalek		
Alan Tucker . . . . Latep		
Michael Wisher . . . . Dalek voices		

BEHIND THE SCENES: Debuting in some of the final scenes of *Frontier In Space*, and "appearing" throughout *Planet Of The Daleks*, **Michael Wisher** — no stranger to Pertwee-era **Doctor Who** in a variety of roles — provided Dalek voices for this season. In just two seasons, he would become a much more literal mouthpiece for the Daleks, originating the role of Dalek creator Davros in 1975's *Genesis Of The Daleks*.

Until recently, it was hard to find this story in a complete state, since its third episode exists only in black & white. (The "fix" decided upon by the BBC's American syndicator was to edit together the customary all-in-one-shot "movie," completely *skipping over* the B&W episode!) But the plot is a slow build as it is, and for all the set-up of *Frontier In Space*, I couldn't help but feel a bit disappointed that the Dalek army could be stopped with such relative ease. And though the actors playing the Thals – including Bernard Horsfall, who later made a much bigger impression in *The Deadly Assassin* – are appealing, they don't steal the show nearly as much as the actors in *Frontier* did, and the linking of the two stories seems to beg that perhaps otherwise unfair comparison.

The DVD, however, demands a revisitation of this story for its miraculous restoration of the third episode to full color, thanks to a combination of colorization technology and a remarkable process for extracting workable original color information out of B&W film copies of video originally shot in color. I don't even pretend to fully understand the "chroma-dot" process, no matter how many times I read up on the technology behind it, but the results it produced for this DVD were impressive.

Not that this really helps the pacing the story – in color or not, you're still dealing with a Pertwee six-parter: lots of chasing, lots of getting caught, lots of escaping and running away, rinse and repeat. There's a bit of a callback to *The Daleks*, with mentions of both the first Doctor (very unusual, though perhaps taking of the advantage that he'd just been seen a few months before this story) and the "take up arms or be crushed" message he delivered to the Thals on that occasion, and that's the point at which I realized that this was only the second time we'd even seen the Thals on TV. (They're seen once more, in *Genesis Of The Daleks*, for anyone who's counting.)

THE GREEN DEATH

Problems at a Welsh mining operation draw the attention of UNIT. The Brigadier is frustrated by the usual lack of cooperation from the mining company, Global Chemicals, but the Doctor is more interested in the rash of mysterious deaths among Global's miners. He goes down into the mine himself to learn more about the glowing green ooze that has killed almost every miner who has touched it, and discovers a horrifying sight – giant maggots, mutated to a grotesque size by Global's waste chemicals, are secreting the deadly substance and may even be growing hostile enough to attack humans. Despite this revelation (and the well-meaning interference of local environmental protesters), however, Global Chemicals' chairman refuses to shut down the mines – and it soon becomes evident that someone else is in charge of the operation, someone or something whose sinister motives may include allowing the poisonous insect larvae to reach the surface and hatch into equally deadly giant insects.

Jon Pertwee	The Doctor
Katy Manning	Jo Grant
Tony Adams	Elgin
Richard Beale	Minister of Ecology
Stewart Bevan	Professor Clifford Jones
Jean Burgess	Cleaner
Alan Chuntz	Guard
Nicholas Courtney	Brig. Lethbridge-Stewart
John Dearth	voice of BOSS
Mostyn Evans	Dai Evans
Roy Evans	Bert
Richard Franklin	Captain Yates
Ray Handy	Milkman
Billy Horrigan	Guard
Ben Howard	Hinks
Brian Justice	Guard
John Levene	Sergeant Benton
John Scott Martin	Hughes

UNIT

This story has been released on DVD

written by Robert Sloman
directed by Michael Briant
music by Dudley Simpson

Part 1 aired on May 19, 1973
Part 2 aired on May 26, 1973
Part 3 aired on June 2, 1973
Part 4 aired on June 9. 1973
Part 5 aired on June 16, 1973
Part 6 aired on June 23. 1973

Mitzi McKenzie	Nancy
John Rolfe	Fell
Roy Skelton	James
Talfryn Thomas	Dave
Terry Walsh	Guard
Jerome Willis	Stevens

A.K.A.: Talfryn Thomas (1922-1982) had already made an appearance in Jon Pertwee's debut story, *Spearhead From Space*, and would later appear in Dalek creator Terry Nation's grim post-apocalyptic series **Survivors** as the shifty poacher Tom Price, a recurring character who was eventually found guilty of murder in one of that show's darkest plot turns. He appeared in a variety of other series in both dramatic and comedy roles.

BEHIND THE SCENES: *The Green Death* marks the last appearance of the "red swirly patterns" title sequence that had been a trademark of the Pertwee era; those graphics would be retired in favor of the definitive "tunnel" titles in Pertwee's last season, a look which would remain through Tom Baker's penultimate season.

NEW WHO CONNECTIONS: The Doctor would seem to have acquired more than one Metebilis crystal; he also has one on hand in the 2013 episode *Hide*.

I've seen haemovores, dismantled Cybermen, Dalek innards, and dreadful mutations, but nothing, for me, has the sheer *ick* factor in **Doctor Who** history that this six-part adventure holds. Depending on my mood, I can barely watch this one at times. Maggots? Ick! *Giant* maggots? *Giant* ick! I'll hand this to the designers though – the damned things *look* just real enough to merit that giant ick.

On the upside, there's a lot to commend this story. Jo Grant gets a proper send-off, probably the best example in the entire series of the companion-gets-married-off departure. It doesn't seem all that rushed or forced – it reads as natural, and you can see where Jo would fall for the environmentalists' leader, and the point she makes early on – that the man she's attracted to reminds her of the Doctor – goes completely unaddressed, possibly because the age difference between the Doctor and Jo might've raised another ick factor. The whole environmental angle gives *The Green Death* a 70s feel that doesn't help the whole "UNIT happened in the 1980s" continuity argument (as if *Mawdryn Undead* didn't muddy the waters enough). While the maniacal computers and corrupt corporations of the Pertwee era are becoming a little bit old hat by this point, they're at least pulled off with some finesse.

SHORT HOPS

...in which the author admires the forgotten science fiction opus by the creative minds behind Pertwee-era Who.

*This just in: impressed with their creative renaissance of **Doctor Who**, and eager to see if the same creative minds can catch lightning in a bottle a second time, the BBC has given the series' showrunners the task of launching another science fiction TV drama, which will air in between seasons of **Doctor Who**. It will be aimed at a more sophisticated adult audience, and will be backed by the full technical and special effects capabilities of the BBC. There is already interest, and a possibility of a co-production deal, from an American television network.*

Are you thinking **Torchwood**? Think again: though the setup sounds very similar, in 1973 the result was the short-lived BBC "hard SF" series **Moonbase 3**, created by Barry Letts and Terrance Dicks. It did indeed air between the 1973 and 1974 seasons of **Doctor Who**, at a time when both men were already thinking that they'd done as much as they could with the **Doctor Who** format. In hindsight, the BBC was smart to offer them another show and another timeslot of their choosing: if they were already mulling their departure from the TARDIS, it would be best to make sure that the next Letts / Dicks blockbuster didn't wind up being broadcast on, oh, say, ITV.

Moonbase 3 was *not* a spinoff from **Doctor Who**, and was never intended to be. But it was an attempt to mine a more serious vein of politically aware science fiction, something that **Doctor Who** could only do so much of at the time. (The series' then-recent environmental message, in the form of *The Green Death*, was about as overtly political as **Doctor Who** could manage to be in 1973.) It was also an attempt to do less "magical" SF, in favor of stories rooted in an extrapolation of the actual state of space technology in 1973. (The awesome powers of foresight brought to bear on this futurism only went so far, however: **Moonbase 3**, with its moon populated by several nations and political blocs each with their own self-contained lunar stations, is set in 2003.) But the state of the art in manned spaceflight in 1973 was Skylab and Soyuz, and in the name of making production practical, this meant that **Moonbase 3** had comfortable quarters, Earthlike gravity, and corridors wide enough to accomodate a camera crew – in other words, it still wound up *looking* an awful lot like the average **Doctor Who** "future" episode. Familiar faces like Michael Gough and Peter Miles cropped up as guest stars, writer John Lucarotti penned a couple of scripts, and frequent **Doctor Who** director Christopher Barry was behind the camera for half of its six episodes. Dudley Simpson provided the series' theme music and scores, though his contributions to **Moonbase 3** bear a far stronger resemblance to his later work on **Blake's 7** - complete with grand organ flourishes and timpanis - than to his **Doctor Who** music. The lunar "exteriors" and model work, shot at Ealing Film Studios, are above par for 1973 vintage BBC, though they'd be blown away in two years' time by **Space: 1999**.

So what's the biggest difference between **Moonbase 3** and **Doctor Who**? Its outlook is stark, bleak and depressing. Though expressed in terms of some slightly hammy acting histrionics (though that can be blamed more on the flavor in vogue at the time than on any one show), **Moonbase 3** does an excellent job of portraying the stresses, fears and isolated feel likely to crop up on a real long-duration space mission. There is an alarming number of suicides or suicide attempts throughout the series, and **Moonbase 3** beats **Star Trek: The Next Generation** to the punch of having a full-time counselor on staff. In the last episode, an incident occurs which obscures Earth's atmosphere in a haze that cuts off all communication. All hell breaks loose inside Moonbase 3 when the crew believes that not only has home has been wiped out, but the routine resupply flights upon which everyone's lives depend will no longer be coming. It's a great plotline for any space station series, but on **Moonbase 3** it took an already grim atmosphere and poisoned it even further (almost literally, as the base's commander weighs the possibility of putting the entire crew out of their misery with a lethal dose of an airborne anesthetic rather than forcing them to endure starvation). Throughout the series, the enclosed environment of the moonbase is a crucible that heats up every possible foible of its crew, until all of the tension bubbles explosively to the surface. It's possibly the most depressing science fiction that's ever made it to television. Even the darkest hours of **The Outer Limits** and **The Twilight Zone** don't compare to the grindingly relentless, somber tone of **Moonbase 3**... and *that's* probably why it went no further than its initial six-episode order.

SEASON 11: 1973-74
THE TIME WARRIOR

A battle-scarred Sontaran spaceship crashes in medieval England near the castle of Irongron, a plundering pirate who intends to overrun the nearby castle belonging to Sir Edward of Wessex. Linx, the Sontaran warrior, strikes an agreement with Irongron – Linx can repair his ship in Irongron's castle, in exchange for giving him advanced weapons which are centuries ahead of the times. But Linx finds it impossible to conduct his repairs with nothing more advanced than Irongron's forge, so he used what's left of his ship's technology to abduct scientists and materials from the 20th century. UNIT is called in to investigate, and the Brigadier isolates all of the remaining scientists who are likely to vanish in one securely guarded premise. But when another scientist disappears under the Doctor's nose, he follows the trail to Irongron's castle, where he finds himself up against the much more powerful and warlike Linx.

Jon Pertwee . . . . The Doctor
Elisabeth Sladen . . . . Sarah Jane Smith
June Brown . . . . Lady Eleanor
Steve Brunswick . . . . Sentry
Jeremy Bulloch . . . . Hal
John J. Carney . . . . Bloodaxe
Nicholas Courtney . . . . . Brig. Lethbridge-Stewart
David Daker . . . . Irongron
Sheila Fay . . . . Meg
Kevin Lindsay . . . . Linx
Donald Pelmear . . . . Professor Rubeish
Gordon Pitt . . . . Eric

This story has been released on DVD

written by Robert Holmes
directed by Alan Bromly
music by Dudley Simpson

Part 1 aired on December 15, 1973
Part 2 aired on December 22, 1973
Part 3 aired on December 29, 1973
Part 4 aired on January 5. 1974

Alan Rowe . . . . Edward of Wessex
Jacqueline Stanbury . . . . Mary

A.K.A.: Jeremy Bulloch later became known for wearing the armor of Boba Fett in *The Empire Strikes Back* and *Return Of The Jedi*; he's also appeared in the James Bond film *Octopussy*, the TV series **Robin Of Sherwood**, **Spooks** (retitled **MI-5** for American consumption), **Law & Order UK**, and the short-lived, direct-to-DVD sci-fi spoof **Starhyke** (alongside former **Babylon 5** star Claudia Christian). He had already made one **Doctor Who** appearance (in the 1965 story *The Space Museum*). **David Daker**, making his first **Doctor Who** appearance here, would be both seen and heard in later stories: 1979's *The Nightmare Of Eden* and the 2003 Big Finish **Doctor Who** audio story *Creatures Of Beauty*. Daker was a mainstay of British TV, with regular roles in the police series **Z Cars**, soap opera **Coronation Street**, and the relatively long-lived series **Boon**; big-screen appearances included **Monty Python** alum Terry Gilliam's *Time Bandits*.

BEHIND THE SCENES: With Jo having left UNIT and the Doctor at the end of the previous season, *The Time Warrior* was always meant to introduce a new character, but things came close to happening very differently. The production notes of the DVD release of the following story, *Invasion Of The Dinosaurs*, reveal that the first choice of actress to portray Sarah Jane was **April Walker**, a busy actress who would later put in guest appearances in such series as **Fawlty Towers** and **The Two Ronnies**. This piece of information was something of a major find when it was uncovered in 2012 – all the more remarkable when one considers that, between 1973 and 2012, *no one had ever revealed the* *identity of the original actress chosen.* That may have been a deliberate attempt to avoid damage to the reputation of the series' leading man: Jon Pertwee was apparently displeased with the casting of an actress who was taller and decidedly more well-endowed (a calculated casting choice by producer Barry Letts, who wanted to make sure there was a strong visual contrast to Jo Grant); Pertwee felt that his new companion should be a "smaller" female who would require the Doctor's protection. Pertwee's considerable clout resulted in an expensive recasting: April Walker was ousted from the role of Sarah Jane (reportedly causing her a great deal of distress, as it cost her the income of a steady series regular gig, with the career boost of a regular role with high visibility, to say nothing of the payday that many other past companions have accumulated from their association with **Doctor Who**), but still had to be paid out her contract for every episode of the season, a significant payday for *not* showing up. Pertwee also had a more direct hand in casting Walker's replacement, and personally approved the hire of Elisabeth Sladen. Though it was known that Sladen was not "the first Sarah Jane," Pertwee and Letts both went to their graves without divulging any more details, and none of their living colleagues revealed anything in the intervening years; for the star of a hugely popular television series to essentially throw the same kind of hissy fit in ths current era of celebrity-obsessed news would cause a huge uproar, and probably wouldn't have done Jon Pertwee any favors in 1973 either.

A largely light-hearted romp into the Middle Ages, *The Time Warrior* is a bit of a preview of Tom Baker's era. In this story, the Doctor doesn't seem terribly concerned with Irongron as a threat – he's far more worried about the presence of Linx. But to give some credit where it is due, this story is probably the best portrayal of a medieval setting in **Doctor Who**, with some excellent sets and costumes (though the knaves inhabiting these sets and costumes were, as always, far too clean-cut – darn those showbiz knaves!).

The Time Warrior also introduces us to Sarah Jane Smith, played by the always competent Elisabeth Sladen, though even her debut isn't without its problems. The third Doctor has often been held up as an example of the Doctor as a very sexist character, with his assumption, in *Terror Of The Autons*, that Jo – then in her first episode – was the UNIT HQ *tea lady*. That somewhat ridiculous angle was played up again here, mainly to give Sarah a kind of pro-feminist platform speech. I have nothing against this, and indeed the introduction of a more independent female companion was long overdue, but this first insight into Sarah's character seemed a bit forced, and had no subtlety whatsoever. It could have caused a backlash against the character. But it was worth it to hear Sarah comment to Irongron's serving wenches much later in the story that they were "still living in the Middle Ages"…before the realization hit her that they were doing just that!

Linx, the first Sontaran we see in **Doctor Who** (they reappear in 1975's *The Sontaran Experiment*, 1977's *The Invasion Of Time*, and 1985's *The Two Doctors* before making numerous appearances in fan films and the new series), is also the best of his kind. Later Sontaran characters just didn't seem quite as invulnerable as Linx did, and even the standards of the frog-like Sontaran makeup seemed to decrease with each successive appearance. The Sontaran seen here was truly cool and very, very alien.

INVASION OF THE DINOSAURS

The Doctor and Sarah Jane Smith return from their medieval adventure, but when they arrive in modern-day London, the streets are bare, the people are nowhere to be seen, and dinosaurs stalk the streets. Like everyone else, the Brigadier and UNIT have gone underground, hiding from the enormous reptiles while they try to figure out what suddenly brought them to the present day. The Doctor and Sarah soon discover that it's the product of an illegal time experiment designed to restore Earth to simpler, less polluted, less corrupt times – and it has come about thanks to a startling betrayal by one of the Brigadier's most trusted officers.

Jon Pertwee	. . . .	The Doctor	
Elisabeth Sladen	. . . .	Sarah Jane Smith	
Ben Aris	. . . .	Shears	
Brian Badcoe	. . . .	Adam	
Colin Bell	. . . .	Bryson	
John Bennett	. . . .	General Finch	
George Bryson	. . . .	Ogden	
John Caesar	. . . .	Soldier	
Dave Carter	. . . .	Duffy	
Nicholas Courtney	. . . .	Brig. Lethbridge-Stewart	
Timothy Craven	. . . .	Robinson	
Richard Franklin	. . . .	Captain Yates	
Pat Gorman	. . . .	UNIT Corporal	
Martin Jarvis	. . . .	Butler	
Noel Johnson	. . . .	Charles Grover	
Trevor Lawrence	. . . .	Lodge	
John Levene	. . . .	Sergeant Benton	
James Marcus	. . . .	Peasant	

UNIT

This story has been released on DVD

written by Malcolm Hulke
directed by Paddy Russell
music by Dudley Simpson

Part 1 aired on January 12, 1974
Part 2 aired on January 19, 1974
Part 3 aired on January 26, 1974
Part 4 aired on February 2. 1974
Part 5 aired on February 9, 1974
Part 6 aired on February 16, 1974

Peter Miles	. . . .	Professor Whitaker	
Gordon Reid	. . . .	Phillips	
Carmen Silvera	. . . .	Ruth	
Martin Taylor	. . . .	Corporal Norton	
Terry Walsh	. . . .	Looter	
Terence Wilton	. . . .	Mark	

BEHIND THE SCENES: The "spaceship" aboard which Sarah finds herself is furnished with futuristic – and no doubt expensive – set pieces from Barry Letts' and Terrance Dicks' between-seasons-of-**Doctor Who** one-off series Moonbase 3. The first episode of this six-part story was simply titled *Invasion*, in an attempt to preserve the surprise of the story's chief nemesis (this despite extensive advance promotion of the dinosaurs' presence in such publications as the Radio Times). However, during a routine purge of 1960s B&W videotapes that the BBC felt would no longer be needed (I leave you to cringe at the impact this has had on the **Doctor Who** archives on your own time), the master color videotape of part one of this story was erased along with all eight video master tapes of the 1968 Patrick Troughton/Cybermen story *The Invasion* (page 89). A B&W copy was recovered at a later date, and remains the best copy available. An attempt to process that B&W copy through the Chroma-Dot color recovery process – used to spectacular effect for the restoration of part 3 of *Planet Of The Daleks* – failed to produce an acceptable new color copy, though the somewhat blurry results *can* still be viewed as an "Easter egg" on the *Invasion Of The Dinosaurs* DVD.

The conventional wisdom passed down from many a fan is that you're not missing much if you haven't seen this one, complete or otherwise. To be fair, the dinosaurs are only slightly more effective than the goofy guy-in-a-dinosaur-suit thunder lizards seen in *Doctor Who And The Silurians*. There are some interesting historical firsts, including the first appearance of the Jon Pertwee-commissioned, flying-saucer-shaped Whomobile car (never referred to by that name onscreen), and to be honest, there is something compelling surrounding the character development of UNIT turncoat Mike Yates – easily the most character development bestowed upon any member of UNIT until *Battlefield* came around in 1989, and probably the closest thing that '70s **Doctor Who** has to the noticeable character "story arcs" that would later be bestowed upon Ace in the late '80s and virtually every new series companion since 2005. With that kind of reputation, it was little wonder that *Invasion Of The Dinosaurs* was relegated to the dubious distinction of being the *last* full **Doctor Who** story ever to be commercially released on videotape by the BBC in the early 2000s – complete with that hard-to-find first episode.

But should everyone be so quick to dismiss it? The subpar dinosaur effects seem to have disguised the strengths of what was yet another cleverly political storyline from the pen of Malcolm Hulke. The real fireworks here aren't in the "dinosaur puppets sort-of-stomping through superimposed London landmarks" scenes, but in the B-story of Sarah stranded aboard a spaceship set to colonize a new world with specially chosen humans. The story not only makes excellent use of Sarah's deductive reasoning skills as a journalist, but asks the sharply pointed question "Who, if anyone, has the right to *force the rest of the population* to live by their ideals?" Such questions may be even more valid now than they were in 1974, making *Invasion Of The Dinosaurs* surprisingly forward-thinking and influential (compare Sarah's plight to the *almost identical* storyline of the **Star Trek: The Next Generation** episode *Homeward*).

DEATH TO THE DALEKS

The TARDIS brings the Doctor and Sarah to Exxilon, but not by choice – an enormous sentient city on the planet drains so much energy from everything around it that the TARDIS is quickly rendered powerless. And the Doctor is not the only unwelcome visitor on Exxilon: an expedition of humans is there mining a substance necessary to cure a plague on Earth, though their ship is now useless. And soon, a ship full of Daleks arrives, on a mission to deprive the humans of that same precious drug – and their exterminating weapons are also left without power. Two factions of native Exxilons complicate this dilemma further, a group of superstitious traditionalists who worship the living city, and a smaller group of rational rebels, led by Bellal. Bellal befriends the Doctor and Sarah, and soon finds himself joining the Doctor on a hazardous journey into the city. But if the Doctor disables the city's defenses, it means the Daleks will regain their power and exterminate everyone on the surface.

Jon Pertwee . . . . The Doctor
Elisabeth Sladen . . . . Sarah Jane Smith
John   Abineri   .   .   .   .   Railton
Mostyn   Evans   .   .   .   .   High   Priest
Julian   Fox   .   .   .   .   Hamilton
Murphy   Grumbar   .   .   .   .   Dalek
Joy   Harrison   .   .   .   .   Jill   Tarrant
Roy   Heymann   .   .   .   .   Gotal
Steven   Ismay   .   .   .   .   Zombie
Duncan   Lamont   .   .   .   .   Galloway
John   Scott   Martin   .   .   .   .   .   .   Dalek
Neil   Seiler   .   .   .   .   Stewart
Cy   Town   .   .   .   .   Dalek

This story has been released on DVD

written by Terry Nation
directed by Michael E. Briant
music by Carey Blyton

Part 1 aired on February 23, 1974
Part 2 aired on March 2, 1974
Part 3 aired on March 9, 1974
Part 4 aired on March 16. 1974

Terry   Walsh   .   .   .   .   Spaceman / Zombie
Michael   Wisher   .   .   .   .   Dalek   voices
Arnold   Yarrow   .   .   .   .   Bellal

A.K.A.: John Abineri (1928-2000) was a veteran British TV actor who seemed to show up in nearly everything, given the chance. In the science fiction genre alone, he appeared on **Blake's 7** as Blake's uncle (*Hostage*, 1979), **Red Dwarf** as Rimmer's disapproving father (*Better Than Life*, 1989), **Robin Of Sherwood** as Herne The Hunter, and had a recurring role in the final season of Terry Nation's post-apocalyptic series **Survivors**. This was the second of three **Doctor Who** appearances for Abineri, who had already appeared as General Carrington in 1970's *The Ambassadors Of Death*, and would return in 1978 as Ranquin in *The Power Of Kroll*. He landed roles in major movies as well, but television ubiquity at home in England didn't translate to Hollywood star power: he had a very minor role in *The Godfather, Part III* (1990), and went uncredited for a brief appearance in the James Bond film *Diamonds Are Forever* (1971).

Probably the best Dalek show of the third Doctor's era, *Death To The Daleks* actually involves the Daleks in the story instead of assigning them a spokesperson or marginally more agile henchmen (both of which happened in *Day Of The Daleks*) or dragging things out for the sake of dragging things out (*Planet Of The Daleks*). At just four episodes long it's an ideal length: both the Daleks and the Exxilon setting would wear thin after that. The Exxilon city is a fascinating bunch of sets, and many of the "brain game" tests were repeated in *The Five Doctors*.

One of the most bizarre things about this adventure is the strange music, with the almost-whimsical sound of an electronically-modulated sax quartet. Though the Daleks are reduced in power by the story (otherwise they'd simply exterminate their way through every other character they meet in short order), the music robs them of even *more* menace, though the arpeggiated saxophones may have been an attempt to musically suggest the Daleks' staccato speech pattern. An interesting musical notion if that was the case, though the jury would seem to be out on whether or not it made for effective accompaniment to the story...

THE MONSTER OF PELADON

The Doctor brings Sarah to the planet Peladon, a world he last visited with Jo Grant in tow. But it's a place still plagued by trouble. Queen Thalira, the daughter of the young King that the Doctor met on his previous visit, is facing an uprising among Peladon's mineworkers. Little does she know, there are also worse threats ahead if the miners shut off Peladon's export of a vital mineral. Alpha Centauri is still serving as an ambassador, trying to smooth things over, but someone is working against the Queen and the miners – and the mighty beast Aggedor may be unable to stop them. This time, are the Doctor's instincts about the Ice Warriors correct?

Jon Pertwee	. . . .	The Doctor
Elisabeth Sladen	. . . .	Sarah Jane Smith
Alan Bennion	. . . .	Azaxyr
Sonny Caldinez	. . . .	Sskel
Ysanne Churchman	. . . . voice of	Alpha Centauri
Michael Crane	. . . .	Blor
Graeme Eton	. . . .	Preba
Roy Evans	. . . .	Rima
Max Faulkner	. . . .	Miner
Stuart Fell	. . . .	Alpha Centauri
Frank Gatcliffe	. . . .	Ortron
Donald Gee	. . . .	Eckersley
Nick Hobbs	. . . .	Aggedor
Rex Robinson	. . . .	Gebek
Gerald Taylor	. . . .	Vega Nexos

This story has been released on DVD

written by Brian Hayles
directed by Lennie Mayne
music by Dudley Simpson

Part 1 aired on March 23, 1974
Part 2 aired on March 30, 1974
Part 3 aired on April 6, 1974
Part 4 aired on April 13. 1974
Part 5 aired on April 20, 1974
Part 6 aired on April 27, 1974

Nina Thomas	. . . .	Queen Thalira
Terry Walsh	. . . .	Captain
Ralph Watson	. . . .	Ettis

BEHIND THE SCENES: This was the final appearance of the Ice Warriors in the original series. Though they continued to appear in other media such as audio dramas, comics and novels, their next TV appearance was in 2013's *Cold War.*

It's hard to follow up on a bona fide classic like *The Curse Of Peladon*, even if you're the same person who wrote it. *The Monster Of Peladon* is a bit more of a straightforward political allegory, and somehow just doesn't have the atmosphere of the original. The lack of more concrete links to *Curse* hurts things here – perhaps it would've been nice to see an aged King Peladon, even if only as a background character while his daughter was at the forefront of the story. Having lost Jo as the Doctor's companion in the interim may be a point against *Monster* as well, as she would've served as the ideal point-of-identification for the audience, pointing out for us what's changed and what connection the new has to the old. Instead, we wind up with what may be Sarah Jane Smith's weakest story of her first season. She's already gotten far too accustomed to traveling with the Doctor (considering that this is only her fourth story of the season and the series), and for someone in an alien environment that has less connection to modern-day Earth than any of her previous adventures (with the possible exception of Exxilon), she's a little too headstrong about interjecting herself into the proceedings.

A nice try at repeating a previous success, but too many of the key ingredients have changed.

PLANET OF THE SPIDERS

Past events catch up with the Doctor in an unexpected way. A race of evil giant spiders on Metebelis 3 is looking for one of their planet's perfect blue crystals to complete a crystal "web" that will broadcast the will of their leader, the Great One, across the entire universe. But the Doctor stole that crystal during a previous visit without realizing its significance, and his actions have drawn unwanted attention to Earth. The spiders use a monastery in the English countryside as their gateway to Earth, taking over the minds of a criminally-minded man named Lupton whose meditations have failed to turn him into a better person. In the end, the Doctor is obliged to return the crystal to prevent Earth from being overrun by the spiders – but the personal cost will be very high.

Jon Pertwee	. . . .	The Doctor
Elisabeth Sladen	. . . .	Sarah Jane Smith
Ralph Arliss	. . . .	Tuar
Christopher Burgess	. . . .	Barnes
Ysanne Churchman	. . . .	Spider voice
George Cormack	. . . .	K'anpo
Nicholas Courtney	. . . . . .	Brig. Lethbridge-Stewart
John Dearth	. . . .	Lupton
Kismet Delgado	. . . .	Spider voice
Max Faulkner	. . . .	Second Captain
Carl Forgione	. . . .	Land
Richard Franklin	. . . .	Mike Yates
Pat Gorman	. . . .	Soldier
Gareth Hunt	. . . .	Arak
John Kane	. . . .	Tommy
John Levene	. . . .	Sergeant Benton
Jenny Laird	. . . .	Neska
Kevin Lindsay	. . . .	Cho-Je
Terence Lodge	. . . .	Moss
Joanna Monro	. . . .	Rega

UNIT

This story has been released on DVD

written by Robert Sloman
directed by Barry Letts
music by Dudley Simpson

Part 1 aired on May 4, 1974
Part 2 aired on May 11, 1974
Part 3 aired on May 18, 1974
Part 4 aired on May 25. 1974
Part 5 aired on June 1, 1974
Part 6 aired on June 8, 1974

Geoffrey Morris	. . . .	Sabor
Maureen Morris	. . . .	The Great One
Chubby Oates	. . . .	Policeman
Michael Pinder	. . . .	Hopkins
Walter Randall	. . . .	Captain
Cyril Shaps	. . . .	Professor Clegg
Andrew Staines	. . . .	Keaver
Terry Walsh	. . . .	Man with boat

A.K.A.: This was **Kismet Delgado**'s only role in **Doctor Who**, though it's fair to say that she probably could've gotten a role in the series anytime she wanted: she was the wife of the late Roger Delgado.

NEW WHO CONNECTIONS: The Doctor is subjected to lethal doses of radiation in the crystal chambers of the Great One; his tenth incarnation would later suffer a similar fate in part 2 of *The End Of Time* (2010). For all of the Doctor's many mentions, in any of his incarnations, of visiting Metebelis 3, this is the only full adventure in the entire series that takes place there; an artifact from it later resurfaces in *Hide* (2013).

Though it falls victim to the typical ailments of the six-part **Doctor Who** story – namely, being one or two parts too long – *Planet Of The Spiders* is an adventure that moves toward an inevitable conclusion, the Doctor's third regeneration. Some regeneration stories try to build the entirety of their suspense from the viewer's knowledge that the Doctor will use up one of his precious lives by the end of the show – 1980's *Logopolis* is perhaps guiltiest of this – while others, such as this one, actually do tell a story that would work with or without the Doctor's regeneration at the end.

Parts four and five, which take place on Metebelis 3 (a planet whose exterior scenes usually consist of actors blue-screened over retouched photos of Wyoming), drag on a bit long and seem to center upon the Doctor and Sarah being captured, escaping, and being captured again, and in the end it's not really made clear how, if at all, the Doctor's actions in the final moments of the show will make life better for the oppressed humans living on Metebelis 3. And early on in the story there's an extended chase scene over land, sea and air that could have easily been trimmed as well.

On the good side, Sarah (Elisabeth Sladen) displays enough independence to get herself in trouble while still uncovering useful information, and Mike Yates, after his discharge from UNIT in *Invasion Of The Dinosaurs*, turns up as a civilian with an interesting new direction in his life. Also amusing is a scene in which we learn that the Brigadier has – or had – some kind of life out of uniform involving "a young lady named Doris," a throwaway bit of dialogue which later turned into a major character in the Brigadier's final original series appearance, 1989's *Battlefield*.

The Fourth Doctor
(Tom Baker: 1974-81)

In the wake of the announcement that Jon Pertwee would be relinquishing the role of the Doctor, **Doctor Who** producer Barry Letts mounted an extensive search for the fourth actor to play the role. At one point, actor and children's show presenter Richard Hearne was a strong contender, and stories for **Doctor Who**'s 12th season were mapped out with an older, almost elderly Doctor in mind. Having impressed Letts in season 10's *Carnival Of Monsters*, actor Ian Marter was drafted back into service as Dr. Harry Sullivan, a UNIT **Doctor Who** would treat the newly-regenerated Time Lord - and would then join the Doctor and Sarah in the TARDIS. Harry Sullivan was designed specifically to provide a younger male counterpart to an older Doctor, taking on some of the more physical tasks - including fighting - that Hearne would be incapable of.

And then Richard Hearne had a change of heart. Having spent years establishing himself as a children's show host named "Mr. Pastry," Hearne was considered by many to have lost himself in the role. He was concerned with the show's content, and - by one account - even told Letts that he didn't think "Mr. Pastry would be right for the part." Letts continued his search, until a fortuitous call from a BBC executive led him in the direction of a little-known actor named Tom Baker.

As only the luckiest actors have the luxury of being in demand year-round, Baker was laying bricks at a construction site when he was contacted by the BBC. Letts felt the interview was promising, and upon seeing some of Baker's film work, decided that he was right for the part, his eyes conveying the otherworldliness of the Doctor effectively. Happy to not only be offered a job, but a job that was almost guaranteed to continue for as long as he wanted to work, Tom Baker happily signed the contract.

In the 12th season, the fourth Doctor - with Sarah Jane Smith (Elisabeth Sladen) and Harry in tow - faced off against an array of classic villains, from the Sontarans (introduced in Pertwee's final season opener) to the Daleks to a curiously diminished platoon of Cybermen, a villain not seen since Patrick Troughton's era. The Doctor's eccentricity was played to the fore, and his new incarnation was more playful and yet more philosophical than the third Doctor. This Doctor was capable of defending himself in physical combat, but usually chose to outwit his enemies. The unanticipated change of lead actor left the character of Harry Sullivan at a loose end, but he was quickly retooled into a foil for Sarah, though without even a hint of sexual tension. The Doctor's physical prowess also landed Baker in an extremely painful situation, as a fall on the location shoot for *The Sontaran Experiment* sidelined the actor with a broken collarbone. For much of this two-part story (the first story of that abbreviated length since 1964's *The Rescue*), stuntman Terry Walsh played the Doctor in wide-angle shots, while close-up dialogue scenes were staged with a painfully propped-up Baker, his costume covering a neck brace.

Terry Nation returned to the fold with the surprising *Genesis Of The Daleks*, a six-parter in which the Daleks appeared only briefly. As the title implied, the story took the Doctor, Sarah and Harry to the Dalek homeworld of Skaro just before the Dalek terror was unleashed, where a Time Lord agent assigned the Doctor to prevent the metal monsters from ever coming into existence. The chief villain of the story was Davros (Michael Wisher), a gnarled husk of a scientist developing a protective casing for the mutants that his people would become after decades of atomic warfare. In a thought-provoking scene, the Doctor refused to disrupt established history - a timeline replete with unlikely alliances and peace treaties forged in the face of Dalek aggression - and merely set the Daleks' exodus from Skaro back by several years.

Season 13 brought the TARDIS team back to modern-day Earth for *Terror Of The Zygons*, which would also see Brigadier Lethbridge-Stewart's final appearance in the 1970s. And with his whole purpose in the series sidelined with the arrival of Tom Baker, Ian Marter left the cast as well, though he would return to play Harry Sullivan in a one-off appearance later in the season. Sarah continued her travels with the Doctor through some of the best stories in the Tom Baker era, crafted by the new team of producer Philip Hinchcliffe and script editor Robert Holmes. Both fans of gothic horror, Hinchcliffe and Holmes aimed to make the Doctor's adventures more mature and his enemies more sinister. With such stories as *Pyramids Of Mars* and *The Brain Of Morbius*, they succeeded brilliantly, though the increased violence - even often implied more than seen - was noticed by watchdog groups as well. Mary Whitehouse, notorious in some circles for her constant open criticism of nearly everything on television at the time, became a fixture of news stories about **Doctor Who**, and Hinchcliffe secretly reveled in it - every time she issued a public statement complaining about the show's content, ratings increased as casual viewers tuned in to see what the fuss was all about.

The Mary Whitehouse connection persisted into season 14, particularly in a four-part story called *The Deadly Assassin*, in which the Doctor travels alone to his home planet of Gallifrey in an attempt to thwart the assassination of the President of the Time Lords. In a Gallifreyan virtual reality construct known - curiously enough - as the Matrix, the Doctor fought the assassin in a variety of tense situations, most of them requiring the application of brute force. Episode 3's cliffhanger concluded on a shot of the assassin holding the Doctor's head underwater. Mary Whitehouse again complained, but the stark realism of that scene caused others to take note, and the BBC brass quickly earmarked producer Philip Hinchcliffe for a transfer to an adult police drama the network felt was more suited to that level of gritty violence.

But the rest of the season had already been completed by that time, and Hinchcliffe's final stories were broadcast as written and edited, including the following story, *The Face Of Evil*, introducing Leela, a scantily-clad savage who took great pride in her skill killing enemies with her dagger or a dart made from her home planet's deadly Janis thorn. Though Hinchcliffe and Holmes had already made decisive moves toward a running theme of the Doctor trying to "civilize" Leela a la Pygmalion, not everyone took to the new character - least of all Tom Baker, who took every opportunity to voice his objections to Leela: during rehearsals, during script read-throughs, during filming...

The 15th season of **Doctor Who** saw a new producer - Graham Williams - and a new direction for the show, one which would come back to haunt it for years to come. Williams was under orders to tone down the level of violence and horror introduced by Hinchcliffe, and to steer the series toward family viewing. The second story of the season, *The Invisible Enemy*, firmly pointed the TARDIS in that more whimsical direction by introducing a new companion in the form of a robot dog named K-9. Stories like *The Horror Of Fang Rock* and *Image Of The Fendahl* didn't reduce the violence as much as the BBC would have liked, and earned Williams a tap on the shoulder from his bosses. In the last story of the season, *The Invasion Of Time*, Leela was written out of the show, remaining on Gallifrey to marry a Time Lord security guard after fighting alongside him during a Sontaran invasion.

For the 16th season, Graham Williams and script editor Antony Read began to plan a season of stories linked by a single theme - the Doctor's quest to recover the Key To Time and restore balance to the universe. Initially, Williams wanted to make the unprecedented move of bringing back a previous companion, but when Elisabeth Sladen turned down the chance to play Sarah Jane Smith again, the character of Romana - a young female Time Lord selected to help the Doctor on his quest - was created. The second story of the season, *The Pirate Planet*, was written by a relatively unknown but enthusiastic radio writer named Douglas Adams; Adams' future claim to fame, **Hitchhiker's Guide To The Galaxy**, had yet to air at the time his first **Doctor Who** script was commissioned. But Douglas Adams' mix of humor and speculative SF made him not only a shoe-in for the show's writing pool, but a script-editor-in-training when Antony Read decided to move on.

The final story of the Key To Time season, *The Armageddon Factor*, would see Romana out after only six stories. Despite earning nearly universal fan acclaim for her portrayal of the brilliant and glamorous Time Lady, Mary Tamm was ready to move on. Williams and Adams realized that this didn't mean the end of the character, however: Romana, like the Doctor, could simply regenerate. And so she did, into actress Lalla Ward (an *Armageddon Factor* guest star whose performance had impressed the show's makers), in *Destiny Of The Daleks*, the season 17 opener. But Romana wasn't the only returning character in that story: Davros, the Daleks' creator, appeared as well (with a new face of his own - under the mask at least), and began to take center stage in the Dalek mythos, to the degree that, as with *Genesis Of The Daleks*, the titular Dalek menace got less screen time than the Daleks' fictional creator.

With Adams' humor now driving the scripts, Tom Baker was now making less of a fuss, though the same couldn't be said of Adams now that Baker was driving rehearsals. The actor had a growing tendency to play the part of the Doctor for laughs, something that Adams disagreed with. Adams professed a liking, on more than one occasion, for a style of storytelling that would follow bizarrely improbable plots to their logical extremes, however terrifying those may be. Adams' dark comedy was sacrificed to Baker's tendency to milk the scripts for every tongue-in-cheek verbal or visual gag possible. But Baker had now surpassed Jon Pertwee as the most prolific, longest-lived Doctor to date, and the series was riding a wave of consistently high ratings. Adams was still an unknown radio writer, and not yet an international multimedia superstar. Baker almost always won any disagreements about interpretation of the material.

Next up was *City Of Death*, one of the highlights of the entire Baker era, with a witty and yet plausible script written by Douglas Adams, writing under a pseudonym when another writer's assignment fell through at the last minute. Filmed on location in Paris, and featuring an all-star cast including Catherine Schell (**Space: 1999**), John Cleese (**Monty Python**), and Eleanor Bron, *City Of Death* was a stylish adventure with just the right amounts of comedy and drama and science fiction. By comparison, the remainder of season 17 faltered: *The Creature From The Pit* and *The Horns Of Nimon* were graced with low production values and scripts that went too far in the direction of a tongue-in-cheek interpretation, while *The Nightmare Of Eden* combined those already unfavorable elements with a ineffectual, dead-on-arrival anti-drug message. It wasn't unknown for moral messages to be written into the fabric of a **Doctor Who** story, but seldom did those parables misfire as miserably as they did in that case. And the final story of the season, a six-parter by Douglas Adams called *Shada*, became an enigma by virtue of never being completed. A strike at the BBC's production facilities meant that many vital scenes were never filmed, and as a result *Shada* was never aired. If he had remained as producer, Graham Williams might have been able to campaign for finishing *Shada*, but Williams was keen to move on, and his production unit manager, John Nathan-Turner, was eager to move up to the rank of producer. The BBC promoted Nathan-Turner and allowed him to run the show, but brought back Barry Letts temporarily with the unprecedented title of executive producer, giving him the authority to approve or challenge the rookie producer's decisions.

And Nathan-Turner had many distinct ideas on things he wanted to change: he wanted to do away with the logo and opening sequence that had been in place since 1974, with an eye toward replacing it with a more futuristic/space motif. The new producer also wanted a new arrangement of Ron Grainer's immortal theme music, and wanted this new theme and all of the incidental music to be handled by the synth wizards of the BBC Radiophonic Workshop. He also wanted to change the Doctor's costume, but after much debate, it was decided to keep the basic shirt--vest-overcoat-scarf combinbation that Baker had been wearing since his debut story, but change the color of all of these items to various shades of dark red. A question mark was added to each of the Doctor's lapels, a move Nathan-Turner felt would create a more identifiable and therefore marketable image for the character of the Doctor. He also wanted to do away with K-9, though leaks of this story to several newspapers resulted in an uproar among younger viewers, even before a single frame of Nathan-Turner's first season as producer had aired. According to some newspapers' polls, children would've been happier to see the Doctor leave his own series than K-9! But despite the outcry, John Nathan-Turner held fast: K-9 would be leaving the series, but would not be killed off, as some newspapers had reported. He also wanted to bring a more dramatic feel to the series, eliminating the tongue-in-cheek humor of Graham Williams' final stories.

It was this last change which didn't settle well with Tom Baker; he had been one of the architects of the show's shift toward humor, and through a series of meetings, it became increasingly apparent the Baker and Nathan-Turner could not see eye to eye. An agreement was struck in which Tom Baker would vacate the TARDIS at the end of his seventh year in the role. This would allow John Nathan-Turner to continue shaping the show to meet his requirements by recasting the Doctor himself, and the announcement of Baker's impending departure generated unprecedented publicity. Fans and the general public alike speculated on Baker's successor as the season began.

The new look, sound, and feel of **Doctor Who** was immediately apparent. With the advent of digital effects, the previously impractical shot of the TARDIS materializing as the camera appeared to zoom out to a wider view opened the season. Disabled in the season's first two stories, it appeared that K-9 would be benched until his exit. In the third story of the season, *Full Circle*, a new companion was introduced in the form of rookie teenage actor Matthew Waterhouse as Adric, an ill-mannered but brilliant math student from an alternate universe in which the TARDIS becomes trapped. That three-story arc, consisting of *Full Circle, State Of Decay* and the unusually abstract *Warriors' Gate*, also saw off Romana and K-9 - though by this time Lalla Ward and Tom Baker had become engaged and gotten married. The following story, *The Keeper Of Traken*, began a trilogy of another sort, introducing Sarah Sutton as another new young companion, Nyssa, and bringing back the corpse-like husk of the Master, a character who had only appeared once since Roger Delgado's death in 1973. At the end of *Traken*, the Master acquires a healthy new body - that of Nyssa's unfortunate father, played by Anthony Ainley, and Ainley then continued in the role of the Master, complete with a black suit and goatee reminiscent of Delgado.

The final story of the season, *Logopolis*, saw the Doctor and Master locked in mortal combat for the freedom of the universe, and introduced a third TARDIS crew member, Tegan Jovanka (played by Janet Fielding). At the end of part four, the Doctor sacrificed his fourth life to prevent the Master from enslaving the universe and regenerated into John Nathan-Turner's new choice for the role of the Doctor, actor Peter Davison. Already well-known on British TV for his portrayal of veterinarian Tristan Farnon on **All Creatures Great And Small**, Davison was a good bet in the bankable-celebrity department. But with the first new Doctor in nearly a decade (indeed, the first new Doctor ever in some young viewers' minds), a new cast of companions aboard the TARDIS, new music, a new look, and even a new Master...was this still the same show?

SEASON 12: 1974-75
ROBOT

The Doctor's regeneration and recovery come at an inopportune time for the Brigadier, who has to try to solve a series of crimes related to the top-secret plans for a disintegrator gun. Sarah, researching a story about the equally top-secret Think Tank organization, is introduced to a gigantic robot which could be the perpetrator of the thefts and killings – despite the scientists' horrifying demonstration that the robot could not kill Sarah. The Doctor, recovering slowly and aggravating the Brigadier with his unpredictable new personality, discovers that the Think Tank scientists are doing much more than research – they're planning on taking over the world and culling the human herd of those not up to genius standards.

Tom Baker . . . . The Doctor
Elisabeth Sladen . . . . Sarah Jane Smith
Ian Marter . . . . Harry Sullivan
Edward Burnham . . . . Professor Kettlewell
Nicholas Courtney . . . . Brig. Lethbridge-Stewart
Timothy Craven . . . . Short
Walter Goodman . . . . Chambers
Michael Kilgarriff . . . . Robot
John Levene . . . . RSM Benton
Alec Linstead . . . . Jellicoe
John Scott Martin . . . . Guard
Patricia Maynard . . . . Miss Winters

UNIT

This story has been released on DVD

written by Terrance Dicks
directed by Christopher Barry
music by Dudley Simpson

Part 1 aired on December 28, 1974
Part 2 aired on January 4, 1975
Part 3 aired on January 11, 1975
Part 4 aired on January 18. 1975

Tom Baker's first **Doctor Who** story isn't really the best measure of his future excellence in the role, though it is very similar to some of the seventeenth season's sillier moments. However, the Doctor's recovery from his regeneration makes for several memorable moments as well as allowing the other members of the cast to take center stage, particularly Sarah. And it's hard not to admire the design and sheer workmanship of the huge metal robot suit – and the strength and endurance of the poor soul (former Cyber Controller Michael Kilgarriff) who had to wear it. Ian Marter makes an excellent addition to the cast as Harry, who the Doctor later whisks away in the TARDIS. Considering the fact that the character of Harry was created to handle the action in the event that Jon Pertwee was followed by an older actor in the role of the Doctor, it's quite a feat that Marter was able to make the character endearing and useful, even though Tom Baker was able to handle most of the physical challenges that his new male companion was intended to handle.

This is, however, the beginning of the end for the Brigadier and the Pertwee-era backdrop of UNIT. Though present here, UNIT is reduced to cannon fodder for the robot as it grows to immense proportions (and let's not even go into the **King Kong** homage with Sarah Jane as the damsel in distress, or the infamous destruction-of-an-obvious-toy-tank scene). UNIT would make one further appearance in Tom Baker's era, and that would happen without Nicholas Courtney on hand to play the Brigadier. With verbal mentions in such later stories as *The Seeds Of Doom* and *Pyramids Of Mars*, UNIT ends up being talked about more than it's actually seen in action during this era – a further decisive step away from the Pertwee era's exile on Earth.

THE ARK IN SPACE

Several millennia in the future, heightened solar activity threatened to devastate the Earth, and mankind retreated into hibernation aboard an enormous space station, where the last surviving members of the human race are cryogenically preserved. The Doctor, Harry and Sarah arrive on the station, discovering that humanity has slept in by thousands of years thanks to unearthly saboteurs who intend to claim Earth in the absence of its original inhabitants...who are scheduled to become the main course.

Tom Baker . . . . The Doctor	
Elisabeth Sladen . . . . Sarah Jane Smith	
Ian Marter . . . . Harry Sullivan	
Stuart Fell . . . . Wirrn	
John Gregg . . . . Lycett	
Nick Hobbs . . . . Wirrn	
Brian Jacobs . . . . Dune	
Christopher Masters . . . . Libri	
Kenton Moore . . . . Noah	
Richardson Morgan . . . . Rogin	
Wendy Williams . . . . Vira	

This story has been released on DVD

written by Robert Holmes
directed by Rodney Bennett
music by Dudley Simpson

Part 1 aired on January 25, 1975
Part 2 aired on February 1, 1975
Part 3 aired on February 8, 1975
Part 4 aired on February 15. 1975

Gladys Spencer . . . . voices
Peter Tuddenham . . . . voices

A.K.A.: At least one of this episode's guest voice artists should sound familiar to afficionados of British science fiction: **Peter Tuddenham** (1918-2007) also provided the voices of all of the "hero" ships' computers in Dalek creator Terry Nation's late '70s/early '80s space opera **Blake's 7**, starting with the voice of the Liberator's built-in sentient computer system Zen, and then adding the cranky, almost-portable computer Orac to his weekly duties, in some cases performing "arguments" between the two characters in a single take with a single microphone (!). Tuddenham would provide more **Doctor Who** voices in *Masque Of Mandragora* (1976) and *Time And The Rani* (1987), and appears in person as a Time Lord in the fan-made video project *Devious*.

After the relative silliness of *Robot*, *The Ark In Space* is a wonderfully gloomy, scary four-parter which beat **Alien** to many of its punches by four years. (Interestingly enough, **Alien** director Ridley Scott was originally a designer for the BBC who alternated assignments with Dalek designer Raymond Cusick.) Some of the Ark characters occasionally get on my nerves with their preachiness (obviously a calculated character trait with the Biblically-derived names). And, considering the resources (or lack thereof) available to the BBC, the sets are some of the most amazing construction work that has ever been seen on **Doctor Who**, even if a lot of it is plastic, and even if you can, in fact, see the black electrical wiring that runs between all of the "stars" on the black...floor...of space outside the station's windows. The Nerva sets are wonderfully modular and functional-looking, so these few flaws are easily forgotten. It's a solid design that would do any SF project proud today, given some better-hidden wiring or lower lighting to hide the blackened stage beyond the station's "windows."

On a purely personal note, I always get an immense chuckle when the Doctor says that Harry, a Navy surgeon, is only qualified to work on sailors. It's one of the funniest lines in the history of the whole series.

THE SONTARAN EXPERIMENT

The Doctor, Harry and Sarah beam down to Earth from the space station to check the transmat receiver that will allow the repopulation of the planet. But they quickly find that they are not alone. A team of human colonists who left Earth long ago have come back to investigate a call that apparently came from there, but unfortunately for them, that call was a forgery transmitted by Sontaran soldier Styre, who is conducting experiments on the human being's resistance to Sontaran military might as a prelude to an invasion of Earth's solar system.

Tom Baker . . . . The Doctor
Elisabeth Sladen . . . . Sarah Jane Smith
Ian Marter . . . . Harry Sullivan
Donald Douglas . . . . Vural
Brian Ellis . . . . Prisoner
Glyn Jones . . . . Krans
Kevin Lindsay . . . . Styre / The Marshal
Peter Rutherford . . . . Roth
Terry Walsh . . . . Zake

This story has been released on DVD

written by Bob Baker & Dave Martin
directed by Rodney Bennett
music by Dudley Simpson

Part 1 aired on February 22, 1975
Part 2 aired on March 1, 1975

Peter Walshe . . . . Erak

BEHIND THE SCENES: For this story only, Sontarans suddenly have four fingers and a thumb; in other classic series appearances, and their new series appearances to date, all other Sontarans have two fingers and a thumb. Presumably Field Major Styre was born in the isolated cloning facility on the island of misfit Sontarans.

The only two-parter in Tom Baker's reign as the Doctor, this story is famous for being the show that was halted in mid-production when Tom Baker fell and broke his collarbone. This was covered up by having Baker remain still for most of his dialogue shots, and by having stuntman Terry Walsh don a curly wig and the Doctor's costume to do battle with Styre in part two. Overall, *The Sontaran Experiment* is an effective story that would have suffered for being dragged out to even as many as four episodes, and this time, the Sontaran is much more menacing in a psychological sense than the brutish Linx from *The Time Warrior*.

GENESIS OF THE DALEKS

The Doctor, Sarah and Harry are waylaid by a secret arm of the Time Lords en route back to space station Nerva. A Time Lord has diverted them to Skaro, the Daleks' homeworld, on the eve of their creation, and the Doctor is under orders to prevent the creation of the Daleks in order to avoid a future in which they could conquer the entire universe. An atomic war between the Kaleds and the Thals has reduced both of Skaro's superpowers from the nuclear age to the stone age, with the exception of the radiation-deformed Kaled genius Davros, who not only anticipates the mutation of his people that the war will cause, but embraces it as their future. Davros has devised armored life support systems to encase the shriveled mutants that the Kaleds will become after centuries of atomic bombardment — and he christens these devices Daleks. The Doctor, Harry and Sarah stumble into the Kaled city, and find that Davros has sympathizers as well as horrified opponents among his own people. And when the moment comes, despite the evil and hatred that Davros is building into his creations, the Doctor finds that there may be a just reason to allow the Daleks to run their destructive course through history.

Tom Baker . . . . The Doctor
Elisabeth Sladen . . . . Sarah Jane Smith
Ian Marter . . . . Harry Sullivan
Keith Ashley . . . . Dalek
Jeremy Chandler . . . . Gerrill
Dennis Chinnery . . . . Gharman
Max Faulkner . . . . Dalek
John Franklyn-Robbins . . . . Time Lord

This story has been released

written by Terry Nation
directed by David Maloney
music by Dudley Simpson

Part 1 aired on March 8, 1975
Part 2 aired on March 15, 1975
Part 3 aired on March 22, 1975
Part 4 aired on March 29. 1975

James Garbutt	. . . . . .	Ronson
Tom Georgeson	. . . . . .	Kavell
John Gleeson	. . . . . .	Thal soldier
Pat Gorman	. . . . . .	Thal soldier
Andrew Johns	. . . . . .	Kravos
Michael Lynch	. . . . . .	Thal politician
Peter Mantle	. . . . . .	Kaled guard
John Scott Martin	. . . . . .	Dalek
Peter Miles	. . . . . .	Nyder
Hilary Minster	. . . . . .	Thal soldier
Harriet Philpin	. . . . . .	Bettan
Richard Reeves	. . . . . .	Kaled Leader

on DVD

Part 5 aired on April 5, 1975
Part 6 aired on April 12, 1975

Ivor Roberts	. . . . . .	Mogren
Guy Siner	. . . . . .	Ravon
Roy Skelton	. . . . . .	Dalek voices
Cy Town	. . . . . .	Dalek
Michael Wisher	. . . . . .	Davros
Drew Wood	. . . . . .	Tane
Stephen Yardley	. . . . . .	Sevrin

NEW WHO CONNECTIONS: At the beginning of *Genesis Of The Daleks*, the Time Lords attempt to directly intervene in the future of the Daleks by enlisting the Doctor to essentially kill them in the crib; later in the story, the Doctor is forced to divulge details of the Daleks' future war campaigns (and how history records their defeats) to save Sarah and Harry. Russell T. Davies, who spun the vague web of mentions of the Last Great Time War throughout the eras of the ninth and tenth Doctors, has said that, for his purposes, **the Time War begins in** *Genesis Of The Daleks*. Aware that there's at least one Time Lord trying to alter their history to their disadvantage, and with Davros leading the charge as his vendetta against the Doctor becomes increasingly personal, it's inevitable that the Daleks would make it their mission to take on the Time Lords directly.

It sometimes seems to take ages to get there, but *Genesis Of The Daleks* is one of the most outstandingly intelligent and mature stories in the history of **Doctor Who**. Virtually every prior Dalek-related adventure took the stance that the Daleks were Evil incarnate, and therefore must be destroyed. But in this case, the Doctor realizes that resistance against the Daleks could have the beneficial side-effect of causing enemies to settle their differences and fight the Daleks as allies. Though the price of that truce may be thousands or even millions of lives, the resulting peace might just be worth it. Would any of us make the same call? It's a concept that certainly begs for extended debate.

Genesis' other great contribution to the **Doctor Who** mythos is Davros, the creator of the Daleks. Horribly injured in previous nuclear attacks, Davros relies on a self-contained life support wheelchair for his survival – and that chair is remarkably similar to the bottom half of a Dalek casing. Davros takes a permanent position that had been filled in previous shows by puppet dictators, allies, and slaves of the Daleks – he can deliver the Dalek credo faster than fifteen words a minute. Michael Wisher does a fantastic job as Davros, and he set a standard of subtle menace that neither of his successors in the role ever quite lived up to. Peter Miles and Guy Siner also turn in impressive performances.

The plot seems to take a detour for the sake of padding the story out to six episodes when Sarah and a number of slaves are forced to haul rocket and arms components up a dangerous scaffolding, but it's worth it for the freeze frame cliffhanger in which Sarah plummets – briefly – from her perch.

SHORT HOPS

...in which the author takes Terry Nation's other creation for a grim spin.

Mere days after the episode six of *Genesis Of The Daleks* was first broadcast, another Terry Nation creation hit the airwaves courtesy of the BBC, as his post-apocalyptic-plague series **Survivors** premiered. For years, one of the main sources of Nation's notoriety was that he had created the Daleks. With **Survivors**, he brought things back down to Earth with a multi-part, modern-day (for 1975) musing on the interdependence of human society. When a virulent plague wipes out most of the human race, except for scattered survivors who have an inexplicable immunity, human civilization ceases to exist (aside from a few pockets of folks who uselessly try to preserve the accoutrements and entitlements of their social class because they simply don't know how to process the world without them). Way ahead of his time, Nation casts a female lead as the organizing force behind a benign collective, who's also searching for her son (who may or may not be dead) and occasionally battling another collective who see themselves as the ideal – no, *only logical* – replacement for the now-extinct British government.

As you can probably imagine, **Survivors** is *not* a lot of laughs. If things aren't grim enough, the show posits the idea that, in the absence of authority, the least savory elements of society – whether due to mental illness or just pure human evil – have a new canvas on which to paint whatever color of chaos best suits them. Several episodes into the first season, one member of our heroine's shambling mobile commune of (presumed) do-gooders reveals his true colors as a serial rapist/murderer: a completely shocking topic to focus even part of an episode of *anything* on in early '70s television. And yet Nation and his writers go there, for the whole hour, even to the point of our heroes *executing the wrong suspect* and only later discovering the truth.

And yet **Survivors** had a kind of genteel, middle-class not-quite-grittiness to it. For all of the discussion of electricity and mass-produced foods being a thing of the past, *nobody ever runs out of cigarettes* or ways to light them. That'd just be *uncivilized*. (And then again, there's perhaps an unintended message to be squeezed out of what was probably just the show sticking to the norms of '70s TV: the things that are mass-produced the most may well be that which we need the *least*.)

There are numerous instances of cross-pollination between **Survivors** and **Doctor Who**, both in front of and behind the cameras. Aside from the obvious (Nation himself), there are numerous frequent-flyer directors (Pennant Roberts) and familiar actors (Terry Scully, John Hallett, Glyn Owen), many of whom also appear in **Doctor Who** or in Nation's later, more solidly sci-fi-oriented series, **Blake's 7**. Perhaps the most familiar face of all, ironically, is the one that has *never* appeared in **Doctor Who** (at least as of this writing): Carolyn Seymour, the first season's female lead, went on guest star in **Space: 1999**, **Babylon 5** (as the senator who informs Captain Sheridan that turncoat President Clark is dead), and did three very memorable guest turns on **Star Trek: The Next Generation** (*Contagion, First Contact* – the episode, not the movie – and *Face Of The Enemy*) before going on to be underutilized as a short-lived recurring holodeck character on **Star Trek: Voyager**. Like W. Morgan Sheppard, she's a great example of a British actor who has jumped the Atlantic and found no shortage of work – you've almost certainly seen her in *something*.

A remake of Nation's series launched in 2008, heavily publicizing Freema "Martha Jones" Agyeman's appearance – even though, as it turned out, she was one of the first plague victims in the first episode! (A similar fate awaited Shaun Dingwall, who was also still a recent fixture in **Doctor Who** fans' memory as Rose Tyler's dad.) The remake ran only two seasons, rocketing through the main plot points of the first 4-5 original series episodes in the *first hour* alone and differing significantly in that it went on to concentrate the storyline on the search for the creators of the virus.

The original **Survivors** ran for three seasons, 38 episodes total, though Nation was largely absent for the show's last year on the air (setting a pattern that would again occur with **Blake's 7**). A series of disagreements with producer Terence Dudley – who would both write **Doctor Who** (*The King's Demons*, *Black Orchid*, **K-9 & Company**) and direct episodes of it (*Meglos*) in later years – led Nation to abandon his own show. The final season's shifting focus – solving some of the "missing authority" problems and restoring the status quo to middle-class drama – may show what exactly Nation *didn't* want to write for the final season. In any case, as **Survivors** drew to a close in 1977, Nation was already busy coming up with stories for his next project, **Blake's 7**, a show with perhaps closer ties to **Doctor Who**.

REVENGE OF THE CYBERMEN

The Cybermen are out to pulverize the planetoid Voga, a small body rich in gold. As we learn here for the first time, gold is one of the only substances capable of shutting down the Cybermen, and Voga's wealth of the precious metal was key to the defeat of the Cybermen in the "Cyber Wars" (evidently, the Cybermen are acquainted with Usenet flame-fests too). The Cybermen's plan to destroy Voga hinges on the elimination of a manned satellite that stands sentinel near the planetoid – a satellite that will later become the Nerva space station that will preserve the human race. But the Cybermen don't count on the arrival of the Doctor, Sarah and Harry – or on the willpower and ability of the Vogans to defend their homeworld.

Tom Baker . . . . The Doctor
Elisabeth Sladen . . . . Sarah Jane Smith
Ian Marter . . . . Harry Sullivan
David Collings . . . . Vorus / Wilkins
Brian Grellis . . . . Sheprah
Melville Jones . . . . Cyberman
Ronald Leigh-Hunt . . . . Stevenson
William Marlowe . . . . Lester
Christopher Robbie . . . . Cyberleader
Kevin Stoney . . . . Tyrum
Alec Wallis . . . . Warner

This story has been released on DVD

written by Gerry Davis
directed by Michael E. Briant
music by Carey Blyton

Part 1 aired on April 19, 1975
Part 2 aired on April 26, 1975
Part 3 aired on May 3, 1975
Part 4 aired on May 10. 1975

Jeremy Wilkin . . . . Kellman
Michael Wisher . . Magrik/Colville/Vogan voice

NEW WHO CONNECTIONS: This was the first – and only – 1970s Cybermen story, but it would cast a long shadow over the Cyber-mythos with the introduction of the Cybermen's vulnerability to gold, an element which would arise in nearly every Cyber-story in the 1980s and then go completely ignored by the new series Cybermen stories; perhaps the "Cybus" Cybermen don't share the gold weakness due to their alternate universe origins (created by John Lumic rather than converted by technology from Mondas or Telos, which may be the source of that weakness).

For whatever reason, despite the fact that the team of the fourth Doctor and his two original companions made for some of the best character dynamics in the history of **Doctor Who**, this particular story never really excited me. For those lucky enough to have seen it in its original format of four 25-minute episodes (sadly, the original commercial video release is a "movie" comprised of all four parts edited together), you'll remember that the first part is actually reasonably interesting and tense, with the morgue atmosphere aboard the space station building a sense of dread. But the appearance of the Vogans, with their all-too-familiar political in-fighting subplot, never fails to slow things down, and even the Cybermen themselves – in their only appearance in the 1970s (after almost too many "guest villain of the week" turns in the 60s) – don't appear to be much of a threat to our heroes. In one scene, the Doctor and Sarah are subdued by a couple of Cybermen who seem to be giving them vicious shoulder rubs. Another detriment is Jeremy Wilkin, who plays Kellman with little or no subtlety whatsoever, practically telegraphing to the viewer that this guy is up to no good. (Wilkin was called upon by *Revenge Of The Cybermen* director Michael Briant to provide a similar characterization in the first episode of **Doctor Who**'s late '70s sci-fi stablemate, **Blake's 7**.)

Other than that, *Revenge Of The Cybermen* comes off as a simply average adventure for the fourth Doctor and company – a bit of a letdown at the end of a season that contained such superlative stories as *The Ark In Space* and *Genesis Of The Daleks*.

SEASON 13: 1975-76
TERROR OF THE ZYGONS

Recalled to Earth by the Brigadier via time-space telegraph, the TARDIS brings the Doctor, Sarah and Harry to the Scottish moors, not far from where offshore oil drilling platforms have been subjected to a series of attacks from the sea – but UNIT can find no traces of attacks from either a boat or a submarine. In the nearest village, the Doctor uncovers evidence that someone there may be behind the attacks, and Harry is shot while trying to help a man washed ashore from the latest attack.

Tom Baker . . . . The Doctor
Elisabeth Sladen . . . . Sarah Jane Smith
Ian Marter . . . . Harry Sullivan
Nicholas Courtney . . . . . Brig. Lethbridge-Stewart
Bernard G. High . . . . Corporal
Angus Lennie . . . . Angus McRanald
John Levene . . . . RSM Benton
Hugh Martin . . . . Munro
Robert Russell . . . . The Caber
Tony Sibbald . . . . Huckle
Lillias Walker . . . . Sister Lamont
Bruce Wightman . . . . Radio Operator
John Woodnutt . . . . Duke of Forgill / Broton

UNIT

This story has been released on DVD

written by Robert Banks Stewart
directed by Douglas Camfield
music by Geoffrey Burgon

Part 1 aired on August 30, 1975
Part 2 aired on September 6, 1975
Part 3 aired on September 13, 1975
Part 4 aired on September 20, 1975

NEW WHO CONNECTIONS: The Zygons don't reappear on TV until the 2013 50th anniversary special, *Day Of The Doctor*, though they are name-checked in a number of Matt Smith-era episodes.

Sometimes, Tom Baker-era **Doctor Who** was at its best when dropping a fairly traditional story into the middle of a previously unexplored setting (see also *The Talons Of Weng-Chiang* and *The Horror Of Fang Rock*), and *Zygons* is a fine example of that genre – effective and very creepy. The Zygons, one of the thankfully few shapeshifting alien species to appear in classic **Doctor Who**, were among the show's most effective adversaries and it's a wonder they didn't come back during the original series.

Zygons also bids farewell to Harry Sullivan as a regular companion; he makes a further one-off appearance in *The Android Invasion*, but as of *Zygons* he remains on present-day Earth and resumes his duties with UNIT. Really a bit of a pity, as Ian Marter was outstanding in the role, and together with Elisabeth Sladen was responsible for one of the best TARDIS companion "teams" in the series' history. Marter later died of complications from diabetes in 1986 after transforming his acting career into a writing career that included numerous well-received **Doctor Who** novelizations.

PLANET OF EVIL

On the planet Zeta Minor, an expedition from a neighboring planet is doomed. Their ship is unable to lift off from the surface, and something is stalking and killing the crew one by one. The TARDIS arrives and the Doctor and Sarah offer their help, but they're also suspected of causing the difficulties. The Doctor discovers that an attempt to bring a sample of antimatter back has attracted the unwelcome, but instinctively protective, attention of Zeta Minor's native antimatter life forms. Worse yet, Professor Sorenson, hell-bent on keeping the sample aboard, continues his experiments with antimatter, slowly transforming himself into a hybrid matter-antimatter creature with no control over his actions.

Tom Baker . . . . The Doctor
Elisabeth Sladen . . . . Sarah Jane Smith
Melvyn Bedford . . . . Reig
Terence Brook . . . . Braun
Prentis Hancock . . . . Salamar
Frederick Jaeger . . . . 2 . . Sorenson
Mike Lee Lane . . . . Monster
Louis Mahoney . . . . Ponti
Tony McEwan . . . . Baldwin
Ewen Solon . . . . Vishinsky
Graham Weston . . . . De Haan
Michael Wisher . . . . Morelli
Haydn Wood . . . . O'Hara

This story has been released on DVD

written by Louis Marks
directed by David Maloney
music by Dudley Simpson

Part 1 aired on September 27, 1975
Part 2 aired on October 4, 1975
Part 3 aired on October 11, 1975
Part 4 aired on October 18, 1975

A.K.A.: You might notice **Space: 1999**'s **Prentis Hancock** taking a break from his Moonbase Alpha duties — he was a friend of this story's director and made numerous appearances on **Doctor Who** (*Spearhead From Space, Planet Of The Daleks, The Ribos Operation*) both before and after his stint on the mid-1970s Gerry Anderson space saga, in which he co-starred as Moonbase Alpha's second-in-command, Paul Morrow. This was his only **Doctor Who** appearance *during* his **Space: 1999** gig, however.

You're might have to ignore the not-quite-airtight "science" of this four-parter's novel approach to antimatter as a story device, but *Planet Of Evil* contains some of the best cliffhangers of the early Tom Baker era. You'll just have to take it for granted, to give one example, that exposure to antimatter doesn't rip a man made of normal matter to parts in a moment of mutual annihilation, but instead just makes him a mad, hairy beast — as in just-this-side-of-werewolf hairy. The special effects are right out of the Pertwee era, and yet it all works — it's got a nice atmosphere of growing dread to it. The exotic jungle "exteriors" are actually all studio-bound — a rare example of the BBC set and scenery designers and builders really getting to show off on something other than a reproduction of period architecture.

PYRAMIDS OF MARS

In 1910, Egyptologist Marcus Scarman makes his greatest find ever — a crypt said to be the tomb of the god Sutekh. It is also Scarman's last find. His life as he has known it ends and his body becomes an obedient servant to the still very-much-alive Egyptian god Sutekh, in fact an alien consciousness trapped on Earth.

The TARDIS brings the Doctor and Sarah to Britain that same year, after a close call in the time vortex and the appearance of Sutekh's face in the console room — a psychic breach of the time machine's most important defenses. The Doctor follows the source of the interference to Scarman's mansion, where strange things are afoot — including the shadowy appearance of walking mummies. With Scarman's brother Lawrence in tow, the Doctor and Sarah stumble upon the force behind the unusual happenings: Sutekh is planning a strike, from Earth, against a mechanism on the surface of Mars which hold him captive on Earth. Even the primitive state of rocketry isn't holding Sutekh's effort back: he's lending Scarman and his robot mummies advanced technology. Sutekh hopes to dominate the Earth with his immense willpower and then take revenge upon his fellow Osirans on Mars — even if it means wiping out the human race to avenge his centuries of captivity.

Tom Baker . . . . The Doctor
Elisabeth Sladen . . . . Sarah Jane Smith
Bernard Archard . . Professor Macrus Scarman
Melvyn Bedford . . . . Mummy
Michael Bilton . . . . Collins
Nick Burnell . . . . Mummy
Peter Copley . . . . Dr. Warlock
Peter Mayock . . . . Namin
Kevin Selway . . . . Mummy
Michael Sheard . . . . . . Laurence Scarman
Vik Tabian . . . . Ahmed
George Tovey . . . . Ernie Clements

This story
has been
released
on DVD

written by Lewis Griefer
(pseudonym for Robert Holmes)
directed by Paddy Russell
music by Dudley Simpson

Part 1 aired on October 25, 1975
Part 2 aired on November 1, 1975
Part 3 aired on November 8, 1975
Part 4 aired on November 15. 1975

Gabriel Woolf . . . . Sutekh

NEW WHO CONNECTIONS: In *The Waters Of Mars* (2009), the Tenth Doctor mentions that the sentient water life form known as the Flood toppled a mighty empire on Mars. He neglects to mention if that empire was the Osirans, the Ice Warriors, or perhaps the Ambassadors of Death.

AUDIO WHO CONNECTIONS: Another Osiran with immense mental abilities gives the fifth Doctor and an Ice Warrior delegation trouble in the Big Finish audio story *The Bride Of Peladon* (2008).

SARAH JANE CONNECTIONS: Sarah Jane remembers the pyramids of Mars — and she uses her computer, Mr. Smith, to conceal their existence from a NASA Mars probe in *The Vault Of Secrets Part 1* (2010).

Atmospherically speaking, *Pyramids Of Mars* may be one of the best **Doctor Who** stories ever. Combining tales of ancient evils and mummy myths, the story quickly gets the idea across the Something Really Bad is going to happen to us all if the Doctor doesn't engage in his usual brand of interference. Following the James Earl Jones dictum of casting the right voice for the ultimate evil, this story gives us one of the creepiest **Who** villains ever in the form of Sutekh, who doesn't move much but sounds like the voice of death itself, courtesy of actor Gabriel Woolf.

Pyramids is also a fine example of the Tom Baker era at its best: the Doctor is *not* infallible here. In a showdown of psychic willpower, Sutekh comes close to laying the smackdown on our favorite Time Lord. It doesn't diminish the Doctor in any way, either — he's brave to be standing nose-to-nose with a badass entity to whom ancient Earth lore gave the name "Satan." It's sad that this kind of storytelling was phased out later in Baker's era, really — the Doctor almost not devoting that much concern to his enemies' schemes diminished him far more than it did to see him momentarily overcome by Sutekh's power.

THE ANDROID INVASION

The Doctor and Sarah arrive near a village that Sarah recognizes as Devesham, but it's immediately apparent that something is very wrong. Spacesuited robot guards patrol the countryside, firing guns built into their fingers at any intruders they see (including the time travelers), and they watch helplessly as a UNIT soldier bolts straight toward a cliff, and over the edge to his death. And yet he shows up later at the village pub, alive and well — and zombielike, until the clock strikes a certain hour. The Doctor has theories about the strange behavior, but nothing accounts for all of the variables until he realizes he's not on Earth. Sarah is captured by androids disguised as UNIT troops, and taken to a ship manned by Kraal invaders, who have copied everyone from the villagers to Harry Sullivan as part of their plan to take over Earth.

Tom Baker . . . . The Doctor
Elisabeth Sladen . . . . Sarah Jane Smith
Dave Carter . . . . Grierson
Heather Emmanuel . . . . Tessa
Max Faulkner . . . . Adams
Stuart Fell . . . . Kraal
Martin Friend . . . . Styggron
Milton Johns . . . . Guy Crayford
John Levene . . . . RSM Benton
Hugh Lund . . . . Matthews
Ian Marter . . . . Harry Sullivan
Patrick Newell . . . . Faraday
Roy Skelton . . . . Chedaki

UNIT

This story
has been
released
on DVD

written by Terry Nation
directed by Barry Letts
music by Dudley Simpson

Part 1 aired on November 22, 1975
Part 2 aired on November 29, 1975
Part 3 aired on December 6, 1975
Part 4 aired on December 13. 1975

Peter Welch . . . . Morgan

One of Terry Nation's final **Doctor Who** scripts (and his last before production commenced on his own creation, **Blake's 7**), *The Android Invasion* coasts through its first two episodes on creepy atmosphere alone, with seemingly normal places and people obviously dangerously amiss. But even when we get to the real Earth, things still seem odd – Colonel Faraday seems impossibly dense for someone who's had enough UNIT experience to fill in for the Brigadier (unless the character was intended to be a regular Army officer who hasn't had any experience dealing with UNIT's usual extraterrestrial fare). Still, the atmosphere keeps things going nicely, but ultimately it's atmosphere and setting standing in for plot – this story could have been told in three episodes, if not two.

If there's a real triumph to this story, it's the Kraals, easily one of the best-designed alien races of Tom Baker's era. Their mouths don't move much, but they're a wonderful invention, truly alien, and very individual – the different characters even have differing facial hair on their rhino-like faces to distinguish them. The way the actors playing them stand even hints at a physiology completely different from humans. From the masks to the costumes to the physical performance, it all adds up to something that, quite frankly, unlike a lot of **Doctor Who** aliens, just screams "alien." Somewhat less successful is the attempt at hinting, through the set designs of their ship, that the Kraals may lean on organic technology, but the characters themselves are memorable. Why they haven't appeared again (outside of novels and audio stories) is beyond me.

Android Invasion marks a number of farewells, though it's handled in a very low-key way. Ian Marter makes his last appearance here as Harry Sullivan, though he would continue his association with the show as the writer of numerous novelizations based on classic episodes, until his death in 1986. This is also the last official appearance in **Doctor Who** proper of John Levene as RSM (formerly Sergeant) Benton of UNIT; he'd make one last in-character appearance in the fan film *War Time* over a decade later. Nicholas Courtney was unavailable for filming, so what could've been UNIT's send-off instead comes off as a bit underwhelming.

THE BRAIN OF MORBIUS

On the planet Karn, the Doctor and Sarah happen upon a castle, home to a driven scientist named Solon and his disfigured manservant Condo. Though the time travelers are welcomed at first, the visit quickly becomes less cordial when Solon poisons the Doctor and Sarah's wine; he intends to use the Doctor's head to house the brain of his latest experiment in life extension. The being Solon is trying to keep alive, however, is Morbius, one of the most feared renegades ever produced by Time Lord society. Even without the interference of Solon, Condo, and the enigmatic Sisterhood of Karn (quietly planning to put an end to Solon's experiments), the Doctor may be no match for Morbius' evil power.

Tom Baker . . . . The Doctor
Elisabeth Sladen . . . . Sarah Jane Smith
Sue Bishop . . . . Sister
Gilly Brown . . . . Ohica
Colin Fay . . . . Condo
Stuart Fell . . . . Morbius monster
Cynthia Grenville . . . . Maren
Janie Kells . . . . Sister
Philip Madoc . . . . Solon
John Scott Martin . . . . Kriz
Gabrielle Mowbray . . . . Sister
Veronica Ridge . . . . Sister
Michael Spice . . . . voice of Morbius

This story has been released on DVD

written by Robin Bland
(pseudonym for Terrance Dicks)
directed by Christopher Barry
music by Dudley Simpson

Part 1 aired on January 3, 1976
Part 2 aired on January 10, 1976
Part 3 aired on January 17, 1976
Part 4 aired on January 24, 1976

NEW WHO CONNECTIONS: Is the soothsayer employed by Rassilon in the last days of Gallifrey a member of the Sisterhood of Karn (*The End Of Time*, 2010)? The Sisterhood reappears in the 2013 mini-episode *The Night Of The Doctor*.

AUDIO WHO CONNECTIONS: Morbius and the Sisterhood of Karn battle the eighth Doctor in the two-part Big Finish story *Sisters Of The Flame* and *The Vengeance Of Morbius* (2008).

It's hard for me to be really objective about *The Brain Of Morbius*, for it was **the first Doctor Who story I ever saw**, and I was hooked immediately. (I think having a huge crush on Elisabeth Sladen probably helped cement that fixation, though I stuck around even after she left the series.) *Morbius* may "borrows" quite heavily from Frankenstein, but as always, that Gothic horror feel works particularly well in **Doctor Who**. I'd say *Morbius* is an example of the atmosphere making the story what it is, but that threatens to shortchange the performances, which are off-the-scale for the duration of this story. The actresses portraying the Sisterhood of Karn throw themselves at those roles with utter conviction, while Philip Madoc magnificently portrays Solon's barely-kept-in-check madness and Colin Fay makes more of his role than a mere simpleton manservant. When Sarah is temporarily blinded, Elisabeth Sladen may well be doing one of the best jobs of "acting blind" that any sighted actor has ever managed.

THE SEEDS OF DOOM

The Doctor is called in to help identify a vegetable pod found buried in the Antarctic tundra. But another party has already learned of the pod's presence – the eccentric botanist Harrison Chase, who sends one of his hired guns and one of his scientists to procure the pod by any means necessary. At the south pole, the Doctor makes two dreadful discoveries: the pod is a Krynoid, an alien species of omnivore plant life which has been known to destroy all animal life on entire planets, and the overeager scientists at the Antarctic base have revived the Krynoid pod with ultraviolet light, causing it to open and take over the mind and body of one of them. Noting that Krynoid pods always arrive in pairs, the Doctor quickly finds another specimen of the deadly plant in the nearby ice just as Chase's men arrive under false pretenses, taking the second pod and leaving the scientists, the Doctor and Sarah for dead. Help arrives, and the Doctor and Sarah track the pod down to Harrison Chase, who is delighted at the discovery of a breed of meat-devouring plant life – for he prefers plants to the company of humans. Under Chase's obsessed care, the Krynoid soon grows to enormous proportions, ready to consume all animal life on Earth unless the Doctor can stop it.

Tom Baker . . . . The Doctor
Elisabeth Sladen . . . . Sarah Jane Smith
John Achson . . . . Major Beresford
Keith Ashley . . . . Secretary
Michael Barrington . . . . Sir Colin Thackeray
Ray Barron . . . . Sgt. Henderson
Tony Beckley . . . . Harrison Chase
John Challis . . . . Scorby
Alan Chuntz . . . . Chauffeur
Sylvia Coleridge . . . . Amelia Ducat
Ian Elliott . . . . Guard
Ian Fairbairn . . . . Dr. Chester
Harry Fielder . . . . Guard
Kenneth Gilbert . . . . Dunbar
John Gleeson . . . . Charles Winlett
Seymour Green . . . . Hargreaves
Mark Jones . . . . . Arnold Keeler / Krynoid voice

This story has been released on DVD

written by Robert Banks Stewart
directed by Douglas Camfield
music by Geoffrey Burgon

Part 1 aired on January 31, 1976
Part 2 aired on February 7, 1976
Part 3 aired on February 14, 1976
Part 4 aired on February 21, 1976
Part 5 aired on February 28, 1976
Part 6 aired on March 6, 1976

David Masterman . . . . Guard
Michael McStay . . . . Derek Moberly
Hubert Rees . . . . John Stevenson

AUDIO WHO CONNECTIONS: Again, the eighth Doctor gets a rematch against the Krynoids in the 2009 Big Finish audio story *Hothouse*.

One of the more incongruous elements of *The Seeds Of Doom* is the atypically high degree to which the Doctor employs physical violence. He throws punches, he pulls a gun on Harrison Chase, and nearly breaks Scorby's neck with his bare hands. He also gives a rare full endorsement to a military air strike on the Krynoid, and finally, after escaping a powerful mechanical composter, doesn't exactly fight too hard to keep its owner from being mulched. Now, I will grant that the Doctor was fighting to save the entire human race, sometimes from the Krynoid and sometimes from itself, but rarely has he resorted to such tactics – before or since.

Harrison Chase is underrated in the annals of **Doctor Who** villains. His dangerous eccentricity and preference for plants – in one scenes, he complains that the cultivation of bonsai trees is equivalent to mutilation and torture of vegetation – is pushed over the edge into blind madness when he comes into the possession of the Krynoid pod. But in the end, his allegiance to plant life isn't enough to keep the Krynoid from considering him nothing more than another animal to be devoured. He was very well played, and the character's motivation is much more simple and credible than, for example, trying to take over the entire universe or even just one world from a single location.

SEASON 14: 1976-77
MASQUE OF MANDRAGORA

During an aimless tour of the endless depths of the TARDIS, the Doctor introduces Sarah to the ornately wood-paneled secondary control room, which duplicates the functions of the master console room. When he fires up the secondary control room's instruments, the Doctor discovers that the TARDIS is headed for the Mandragora Helix, a spaceborne vortex of malevolent energy. Forced to the land within it briefly, the Doctor is helpless to prevent a fragment of the Helix's energy from boarding the TARDIS. After escaping from the vortex, the Doctor is surprised when the TARDIS brings them to late 1600s Italy, where Sarah is promptly kidnapped by a band of hooded figures. While trying to find her, the Doctor realizes that the Mandragora Helix has come to Earth. The local Duke has died, and his young, idealistic son Giuliano now holds his power, though the local population is under the tyrannical thumb of the boy's uncle, Count Federico. And Sarah is about to be sacrificed by a murderous cult which will find a great ally in the unearthly newcomer which the Doctor has unwittingly brought with him.

Tom Baker . . . . The Doctor
Elisabeth Sladen . . . . Sarah Jane Smith
James Appleby . . . . Guard
Gareth Armstrong . . . . Giuliano
Antony Carrick . . . . Captain Rossini
John Clamp . . . . Guard
Peggy Dixon . . . . Dancer
Jack Edwards . . . . Dancer
Brian Ellis . . . . Brother
Stuart Fell . . . . Entertainer
Alistair Fullarton . . . . Dancer
Pat Gorman . . . . Guard
Robert James . . . . High Priest
Norman Jones . . . . Hieronymous
John Laurimore . . . . Count Federico
Jay Neill . . . . Pikeman

This story has been released on DVD

written by Louis Marks
directed by Rodney Bennett
music by Dudley Simpson

Part 1 aired on September 4, 1976
Part 2 aired on September 11, 1976
Part 3 aired on September 18, 1976
Part 4 aired on September 25, 1976

Tim Piggott-Smith . . . . Marco
Michael Reid . . . . Dancer
Peter Tuddenham . . . . Mandragora voice
Peter Walshe . . . . Pikeman
Kathy Wilfit . . . . Dancer

NEW WHO CONNECTIONS: The TARDIS "keeping old console rooms on file" (*The Doctor's Wife*, 2011) is nothing new; the Doctor and Sarah wander into the wood-paneled pre-steampunk "secondary console room" in this story, which the show's producers actually intended to permanently replace the more familiar gleaming white control room set. The new console room set, while very atmospheric, proved to be just as problematic to break down, store and set up, so the more familiar white console room would return the following season. The secondary console room has a spiritual successor in the magnificent control room of the seventh and eighth Doctors' TARDIS in the 1996 TV movie, though certain steampunk-inspired elements have appeared in the TARDIS console since the series' 21st century rebirth.

COMICS CONNECTIONS: The seventh Doctor and Ace find themselves up against the Mandragora Helix again in the Doctor Who Magazine comic *The Mark Of Mandragora* (1991), which was included in, and lent its name to, the first **Doctor Who** graphic novel in 1993.

AUDIO WHO CONNECTIONS: This story sets a chain of events in motion that goes unseen for centuries, and then comes back to haunt Sarah Jane in the 21st century during the second "season" of the Sarah Jane Smith audio series produced by Big Finish (a short series of audio releases that predated the character's reappearance in modern **Doctor Who**).

Possibly the most fun one can have in watching *The Masque Of Mandragora* is in spotting the elements used from *other* shows. Peter Tuddenham, later the voice of Zen, Orac, and Slave in **Blake's 7**, provides the voice of the Mandragora Helix (well, maybe more of a throaty laugh than an actual voice) for this four-parter. And though the local foliage has grown considerably and the buildings are visibly more aged, sharp-eyed viewers will note that many of the location scenes were shot in Portmeiron, also known as the inescapable Village from **The Prisoner**; this is most obvious early in episode two, as the Doctor runs from the Count's guards.

The setting and the atmosphere of the superstitious middle ages does a lot to help along a story which seems a bit standard-issue. There are a lot of chases, captures, escapes, and more chases, accompanied by the old action series standby of people being repeatedly knocked unconscious with little or no ill effects when they wake up. The sets, costumes and location filming lend *Masque* a lot of its credibility.

SHORT HOPS

...in which the author nominates some 1970s Doctor Who adventures as fuel for the Satellite Of Love.

The Pertwee years are rife with material worthy of the **Mystery Science Theater 3000** treatment. Not only was **Doctor Who** now in color, but depending on the set and costume designers' preferences, it was IN COLOR - in the same way that the passage-of-time interstitial scenes in That '70s Show or the Austin Powers movies are IN COLOR. The series also started edging toward campiness in some segments, making for some inadvertently funny stories.

The Claws Of Axos, not a bad story in and of itself, is one of those stories that's IN COLOR. The freak-out scenes as Jo and the Doctor try to escape not only the physical body but the psychic presence of Axos are so '70s: you could almost make a T. Rex video out of that sequence. Somewhere between the golden Axon bodysuits, the tentacled monsters and the wobbly phallic internal "eye" of Axos, there's room for high hilarity.

The Time Monster is similarly trippy, without quite hitting the excesses of *Axos*. You've got Greeks, Dave "before he was Darth Vader" Prowse in a giant Minotaur head, and people saying "TOM-TIT" every few minutes. If that's not a recipe for snickering under your breath, you need a better cookbook.

From Pertwee's final season, *Invasion Of The Dinosaurs* is such a tempting target - *too* obvious, actually, with its slightly suspect dinosaur puppetry. No, from this season, *Death To The Daleks* takes home the (somewhat dubious) prize. With its Dalek who becomes suicidal upon failing to carry out its orders, robed critters performing underground ceremonies, and yet another noodly appendage (this time emerging from the city itself), it's almost perfect. Plus, a 'bots vs. Daleks death-match is a must.

The Tom Baker era is almost an embarrassment of riches. *Robot* is ripe for riffing, and *The Android Invasion* is a no-brainer for all-too-easy "pull my finger" gags. *The Invisible Enemy* and *Underworld* are also strong contenders for **MST**-ification. But I refuse to nominate anything between *Underworld* and *Meglos* for **MST**ie material – not because it's sacrosanct in some way, but because the show was reaching a point where even its star wasn't taking things seriously. It'd be *too* easy to poke fun at.

Keep your eyes open, we'll be lighting up the Movie Sign later on.

THE HAND OF FEAR

The TARDIS arrives in a desolate, rocky landscape – which the Doctor and Sarah realize, only too late, is actually a rock quarry. Sirens go off to signal imminent blasting, and the time travelers fail to get far enough away from the blast. The Doctor and Sarah survive, but Sarah finds something unusual and perhaps even alien: something which appears to be a petrified severed hand. Though she was only slightly injured by the blast at the quarry, Sarah soon begins to exhibit strange and dangerous behavior, even walking into the core of a nuclear reactor. As it turns out, she has been possessed by an entity known as Eldrad, whose quest for revenge upon her native world of Kastria is boundless – and who won't hesitate to sacrifice the lives of everyone around her to achieve that aim.

Tom Baker . . . . The Doctor
Elisabeth Sladen . . . . Sarah Jane Smith
Roy Boyd . . . . Driscoll
John Cannon . . . . Elgin
Robin Hargreave . . . . Guard
Glyn Houston . . . . Professor Watson
Judith Paris . . . . Eldrad
Roy Pattison . . . . Zazzka
Frances Pidgeon . . . . Miss Jackson
David Purcell . . . . Abbott
Libby Ritchie . . . . Hospital Nurse
Rex Robinson . . . . Dr. Carter
Renu Setna . . . . Intern

This story has been released on DVD

written by Bob Baker & Dave Martin
directed by Lennie Mayne
music by Dudley Simpson

Part 1 aired on October 2, 1976
Part 2 aired on October 9, 1976
Part 3 aired on October 16, 1976
Part 4 aired on October 23, 1976

Roy Skelton . . . . Rokon
Stephen Thorne . . . . Eldrad

BEHIND THE SCENES: Since the new **Doctor Who** series has made such a big deal out of Sarah Jane being *the* original series companion to beat, how indispensible did the makers of **Doctor Who** think she was? **Here's a pretty good measure of how important she had become: the next two producers of Doctor Who tried to entice Elisabeth Sladen to come back to the show.** In preparation for the "Key To Time" season in 1978, producer Graham Williams tried to woo Sladen back into the TARDIS; surely, to ensure the Doctor's success in finding the Key, the White Guardian would reunite the Time Lord with his most trustworthy sidekick. When she declined, the character of Romana was created. In 1980, Williams' successor, John Nathan-Turner, tried to lure Sladen back to the show to ease the blow (for the audience) of the Doctor's impending regeneration, and again she turned the offer down, leading to the creation of Tegan and the promotion of Nyssa – an intriguing one-off guest character – to full companion status. Sladen did reprise the role of Sarah Jane in the 1981 special **K-9 & Company**, 1983's *The Five Doctors* and the fan-made 1995 direct-to-video movie *Downtime*, all long before returning to **Doctor Who** in 2006 and then her own Sarah Jane spinoff the following year.

AUDIO WHO CONNECTIONS: Apparently Eldrad is pretty handy with making an escape as well – he makes an unlikely comeback in 2013's Big Finish audio story *Eldrad Must Die!*

So much has been written about cheap sets and cheap location work in **Doctor Who** that I have to point this four-parter out as an example of a show which doesn't *need* Industrial Light & Magic to pour on a thick atmosphere of doom and gloom. And for once, the rock quarry location was actually posing as a rock quarry, not an alien planet!

Elisabeth Sladen's swan song as a series regular gives her quite a bit to do, a fate which has befallen many an outgoing companion, from Adric to Romana to Jo Grant and beyond – their outgoing story tends to be their most involved. And for Ms. Sladen, that means a lot of creepy stuff, like single-handedly (ha!) taking over a nuclear power station and zapping anyone who stands in her way.

Special mention also needs to go to Judith Paris and Stephen Moore, who portrayed the two incarnations of Eldrad. Not a lot of the villain characters during this era of **Doctor Who** were very well rounded, and Eldrad is a fascinating exception, begging for further examination of the planet Kastria and its silicon-based life forms. The sets representing Kastria aren't shabby at all, and lend the story a good deal of credibility.

Finally, the extended departure scene for Sarah – and the end of what I always considered to be the best Doctor-companion pairing of Tom Baker's era, until his very brief solo journey with Adric – fits very well, and is played well by Baker and Sladen.

THE DEADLY ASSASSIN

The Doctor collapses in the TARDIS as it takes him back to his home planet of Gallifrey, experiencing a vivid premonition of the assassination of the President of the Time Lords' High Council – a vision in which he seems to play the part of the gunman. Since the Doctor's TARDIS is a stolen vehicle, he has to evade security guards upon his return to Gallifrey, trying to reach the President to warn him of his impending fate. When the Doctor tries to stop the assassin at the fateful moment, the only thing that any of his fellow Time Lords see is that he's the man with the weapon. The Doctor uses a legal loophole to buy enough time to find the real killer, who turns out to be his oldest enemy – but this time, the Doctor isn't the target. The Master, struggling at the end of his final regeneration, plans to take revenge on all of Gallifrey.

Tom Baker . . . . The Doctor
Peter Pratt . . . . The Master
Michael Bilton . . . . Time Lord
Helen Blatch . . . . Voice
Eric Chitty . . . . Coordinator Engin
John Dawson . . . . Time Lord
Bernard Horsfall . . . . Chancellor Goth
Angus Mackay . . . . Cardinal Borusa
Peter Mayock . . . . Solis
George Pravda . . . . Castellan Spandrell
Maurice Quick . . . . Gold Usher
Llewellyn Rees . . . . President

This story has been released on DVD

written by Robert Holmes
directed by David Maloney
music by Dudley Simpson

Part 1 aired on October 30, 1976
Part 2 aired on November 6, 1976
Part 3 aired on November 13, 1976
Part 4 aired on November 20, 1976

Derek Seaton . . . . Commander Hildred
Hugh Walters . . . . . . Commentator Runcible

NEW WHO CONNECTIONS: This marks the first appearance of the impossibly high-collared shoulder pieces that are now associated with almost any Time Lord other than the Doctor and the occasional insane Gallifreyan renegade. One of those costume pieces from this episode survived long enough to be used in 2007's *The Sound Of Drums* for a flashback sequence on Gallifrey.

Though this story is almost universally considered a classic these days, it wasn't received well by all **Doctor Who** fans when it was first broadcast. In previous episodes, the fleeting glimpses we'd caught of the home planet of the Time Lords gave the impression of vast, glittering spaces full of incredibly high technology (or whatever set pieces the BBC had at the time that gave the impression of such). But here, Gallifrey is a dark and gothic place, and though the Time Lords' world is still quite advanced, the look of their technology tends toward the ancient, and their culture, examined here for the first time in the series, is steeped in unyielding, age-old tradition: a society stuck in an unimaginative rut, unable to contemplate that someone on their world is ready to commit unthinkable acts, and unprepared to deal with the fallout when it happens.

Wisely, when it came to recasting the late Roger Delgado as the Master, the creative forces behind *The Deadly Assassin* went for a radical departure, portraying the character as a decaying husk instead of merely regenerating him into another actor. This was almost the only thing that could have been done that would have avoided disappointment for those members of the audience who recalled Delgado's portrayal. Peter Pratt plays the part well, but also plays it sparingly, since Goth does most of the dying Master's footwork. The scenes regarding the Eye of Harmony and the Doctor and the Master facing off once and for all – again – were echoed strongly in the 1996 TV movie.

I highly recommend this story for fans as well as newcomers. It's interesting to see Tom Baker's Doctor in a companion-less adventure, and it also **single-handedly created virtually the entire Time Lord/Gallifrey mythos**, though some other important pieces of that puzzle were to come in later stories set there.

THE FACE OF EVIL

The Doctor arrives on a distant world populated by two tribes, the Sevateem and the Tesh. He quickly bumps into a Sevateem woman named Leela, who has been banished from her village for denying the existence of Xoanon – an entity whom the Sevateem worship as a god. The Doctor can only stand by helplessly as the Sevateem mount a suicidal attack upon the more advanced Tesh. The Doctor soon realizes that these primitives are the descendants of an interstellar exploration detail: the survey team and the technicians. Both tribes recognize and revere him as the Evil One...but despite the bloodshed, no one will allow him to go near Xoanon, a sentient computer whose tyrannical rule is a result of the Doctor's past interference.

Tom Baker . . . . The Doctor
Louise Jameson . . . . Leela
Peter Baldock . . . . Acolyte
Leon Eagles . . . . Jabel
Rob Edwards . . . . voice of Xoanon
Mike Elles . . . . Gentek
Brett Forrest . . . . Guard
Anthony Frieze . . . . voice of Xoanon
David Garfield . . . . Neeva
Roy Herrick . . . . voice of Xoanon
Tom Kelly . . . . Guard
Victor Lucas . . . . Andor
Lloyd McGuire . . . . Lugo

This story has been released on DVD

written by Chris Boucher
directed by Pennant Roberts
music by Dudley Simpson

Part 1 aired on January 1, 1977
Part 2 aired on January 8, 1977
Part 3 aired on January 15, 1977
Part 4 aired on January 22, 1977

Brendan Price . . . . Tomas
Pamela Salem . . . . voice of Xoanon
Leslie Schofield . . . . Calib
Colin Thomas . . . . Sole

In some ways, *Face Of Evil*'s basic premise of a primitive society evolved from the remnants of a much more advanced, and yet doomed, civilization is almost Roddenberryesque. Similarly, I think Gene would've approved of the plot point of questioning one's deities (certainly writer and future **Blake's 7** script editor Chris Boucher had that in mind – the story originally had the far more provocative title *The Day God Went Mad*). It's actually a very **Trek**kish story overall (for **Doctor Who**). In **Who**-ish terms, though, the insane computer is a very old plot device – utilized by stories as old as 1966's *The War Machines* and as recent (for this 1977 adventure) as Jon Pertwee's 1973 battle with BOSS in *The Green Death*. *The Face Of Evil* is set apart by the Doctor's direct responsibility for Xoanon's insanity – a plot twist worthy of the late 80s' painted-heavily-in-shades-of-grey seventh Doctor adventures. The end of part three is one of the most disquieting cliffhangers of the entire series, then or now.

One sometimes inconsistent feature of this four-parter is the Doctor's stance on violence. One moment, he deplores Leela's habit of fatally felling any foe who crosses her path – and the next, he's holding two of her tribesmen at gunpoint with a crossbow as he tries to find an antidote to the janis thorn, the Sevateem's usually-deadly weapon of choice. (In the latter scene, he also threatens to break somebody's nose.) It's a worthwhile message, but also a muddled message. Leela herself actually gets a very good introduction, one which later stories betray by playing her as a simple savage. In this story, she knows enough to question whether or not Xoanon is a god, which is a sign of an intelligent skeptic, not a barbaric simpleton.

Produced one year before the first season of **Blake's 7**, *The Face Of Evil* is peppered with future Blake veterans – writer Chris Boucher became the script editor overseeing **Blake's 7**, while Leslie Schofield and Tom Kelly each had early major guest roles in that show's first season, and Pennant Roberts directed numerous early episodes.

THE ROBOTS OF DEATH

The Doctor and Leela arrive in a mobile sand refinery on a distant planet at precisely the wrong time – a murder has just taken place. Since they're the only newcomers among a bunch of paranoid miners who have been cooped up together for months, the Doctor and Leela are naturally the prime suspects, but even while they're under guard, members of the crew continue to turn up dead. The Doctor is the first to propose an outrageous theory – that the ships large complement of robots have somehow been programmed to override their built-in inability to harm human beings. But by the time he is able to convince anyone of the merit of this idea, most of the crew have fallen victim to the robots' onslaught – leaving the Doctor, Leela, and the surviving crew as the next victims.

Tom Baker . . . . The Doctor
Louise Jameson . . . . Leela
David Bailie . . . . Dask
David Collings . . . . Poul
Brian Croucher . . . . Borg
Gregory de Polnay D84
Rob Edwards . . . . Chub
Miles Fothergill SV7
Russell Hunter . . . . Commander Uvanov
Tania Rogers . . . . Zilda
Pamela Salem . . . . Toos
Tariq Yunus . . . . Cass

This story
has been
released
on DVD

written by Chris Boucher
directed by Michael E. Briant
music by Dudley Simpson

Part 1 aired on January 29, 1977
Part 2 aired on February 5, 1977
Part 3 aired on February 12, 1977
Part 4 aired on February 19, 1977

NEW WHO CONNECTIONS: The Sandminer's robots bear an unsettling resemblance to the Heavenly Hosts in 2007's *Voyage Of The Damned* – check out the very suspicious look the tenth Doctor gives the angelic robots aboard the spaceship Titanic. If both lines of robots are from the same manufacturer, I think a voluntary recall is in order.

AUDIO WHO CONNECTIONS: Though the Robots of Death return in the 2011 Big Finish audio story *Robophobia*, they've never been out of the limelight for long. Chris Boucher gave permission for Magic Bullet Studios to produce **Kaldor City**, an audio series set in the world of *Robots Of Death*, following Commander Uvanov back home only to find that the cutthroat politics on his planet make killer robots look amateurish by comparison. The series also included elements of **Blake's 7**, another BBC series with which Boucher was heavily involved, and which was once considered a contender for "shared universe" status with **Doctor Who**. The Doctor himself is up against the Robots once more in the Big Finish audio story *Robophobia* (2011).

Of the numerous times **Doctor Who** has tried its hand at an Agatha Christie style murder mystery – up to and including co-opting Christie herself as a character in 2008's *The Unicorn And The Wasp* – *Robots Of Death* is easily the most successful attempt. The atmosphere is appropriately gloomy, and the cast of characters are a bunch of gloomy people with their own skeletons in the closet. Almost every last one of them is a viable suspect at some point.

And the robots are indeed, as Leela describes them, creepy mechanical men, and strangely sculpted ones too. Their ever-calm voices are very unnerving, escpecially when they offer a reassuring "I only want to kill you" to their victims – as if that makes it all better! If only for the spooky atmosphere, this one is a must-see. It also contains, at the beginning, the Doctor's now-famous description to Leela of how the TARDIS can be bigger on the inside than out. A must-see.

THE TALONS OF WENG-CHIANG

The Doctor brings Leela to Victorian-era London to give her some exposure to what he considers civilization, though things quickly become less than civilized when a Chinese man makes an attempt on the Doctor's life. Relations between the natives of London and the city's growing Chinese population are equally strained elsewhere, as allegations of kidnapping surround stage magician Li H'sen Chang during his residence at a local theater, run by Henry Gordon Jago. Numerous men confront Chang with accusations that he hypnotized their wives and ladyfriends during his magic show – and every woman disappeared shortly afterward. The Doctor investigates Chang's magic show and discovers that the magician is using more than sleight-of-hand to accomplish his amazing feats – he is receiving technological help too advanced for the Victorian era, in exchange for which Chang is performing murderous services for his master – from the future.

Tom Baker . . . . The Doctor
Louise Jameson . . . . Leela
Conrad Asquith . . . . PC Quick
Trevor Baxter . . . . Professor Litefoot
Christopher Benjamin . . . . . Henry Gordon Jago
John Bennett . . . . Li H'sen Chang
Alan Butler . . . . Buller
Vaune Craig-Raymond . . . . Cleaning Woman
Stuart Fell . . . . Giant rat
Chris Gannon . . . . Casey
Peggy Lister . . . . Singer
Judith Lloyd . . . . Teresa
David McKail . . . . Sergeant Kyle
Deep Roy . . . . Mr. Sin
Patsy Smart . . . . Ghoul
Michael Spice . . . . Weng-Chiang

This story has been released on DVD

written by Robert Holmes
directed by David Maloney
music by Dudley Simpson

Part 1 aired on February 26, 1977
Part 2 aired on March 5, 1977
Part 3 aired on March 12, 1977
Part 4 aired on March 19, 1977
Part 5 aired on March 26, 1977
Part 6 aired on April 2, 1977

Tony Then . . . . Lee
Vincent Wong . . . . Ho
John Wu . . . . Coolie

AUDIO WHO CONNECTIONS: Jago & Litefoot were very briefly considered spinoff material soon after this story's broadcast, but they wouldn't continue their Victorian-era investigations of the incredible and unexplainable until they got their own audio series courtesy of Big Finish Productions in 2010, whose third "season" of adventures saw them rejoined by Leela. But even the road to an audio spinoff wasn't certain; the two characters featured in one of Big Finish's *Doctor Who* Companion Chronicles stories, *The Mahogany Murderers* (2009), as a sort of "backdoor pilot." Magnus Greel and Mr. Sin also return in an audio story, 2012's *The Butcher Of Brisbane*, a nickname for Greel mentioned in this story.

One of **Doctor Who**'s most atmospheric, tightly-plotted stories during the Tom Baker era, *Weng-Chiang* is a rare case of a six-parter that hangs a sharp left halfway through the story and doesn't fall apart or feel "padded" to fill out the time. One of the few complaints that can be lodged against the story is the laughable "giant rat" effects, and even that can be overlooked. Other aspects of the production – the period feel, the rich characterizations, an amazing cast and some very effective makeup for decidedly non-Chinese actor John Bennett as Chang – stand up to this day as some of **Doctor Who**'s finest. The characters of Jago and Lightfoot were even, at one point, considered for a non-science-fiction spinoff series that never got any further than the planning stages. (It would've been an enormously entertaining show, had the same actors been retained – as guest characters go, they were *that* good. Fortunately, Big Finish saw the potential that the BBC didn't.)

Even Leela's gritty demeanor comes into play, and it's good to see her kick and claw her way out of predicaments during which other companions might have screamed themselves silly. There's a subtle

"Pygmalion" gag in the subtext there, and it's just as well for the Doctor that he didn't succeed in "civilizing" Leela this time around…

SEASON 15: 1977-77
THE HORROR OF FANG ROCK

Leela is unimpressed when the TARDIS once again arrives on Earth, and on another foggy night to boot. But this time, she and the Doctor have landed near a lighthouse on a particularly treacherous rocky shoreline at the turn of the 20th century. The lighthouse's three-man crew is having trouble keeping their beacon lit, which leads to a ship running aground shortly after the Doctor and Leela make their presence known. But something else has made its presence known to at least one of the men – by killing him and assuming his shape. The survivors of the shipwreck make their way to the lighthouse, each with their own agenda blinding them to what could be the beachhead of an alien invasion. By the time the Doctor reveals the true nature of the threat to them, the alien visitor has claimed more victims.

Tom Baker . . . . The Doctor
Louise Jameson . . . . Leela
John Abbott . . . . Vince
Sean Caffrey . . . . Lord Palmerdale
Colin Douglas . . . . Reuben / Rutan voice
Rio Fanning . . . . Harker
Alan Rowe . . . . Colonel Skinsale
Ralph Watson . . . . Ben
Annette Woollett . . . . Adelaide

This story has been released on DVD

written by Terrance Dicks
directed by Paddy Russell
music by Dudley Simpson

Part 1 aired on September 3, 1977
Part 2 aired on September 10, 1977
Part 3 aired on September 17, 1977
Part 4 aired on September 24, 1977

NEW WHO CONNECTIONS: Never seen again in the original series, the Rutans are said to be engaged in an ongoing war against the Sontarans. A Rutan is seen in the direct-to-video fan-made production *Shakedown: Return Of The Sontarans* (1994), and another Rutan crops up, this time using its shapeshifting ability to wreak havoc at a critical juncture in history, in the 2011 PC Adventure Game *The Gunpowder Plot*.

Perhaps not really viewed as one of the quintessential Tom Baker stories – it's no *Genesis Of The Daleks* or *Talons Of Weng-Chiang* – *The Horror Of Fang Rock* succeeds in creating a tense enclosed atmosphere, a kind of setting that has provided **Doctor Who** with some of its finest hours (see also: nearly every story of the Troughton era). *Horror* tries to simulate a Victorian lighthouse with huge walls of bluescreen, and there are times when they just about pull it off – there's actually one brief shot of the Doctor clinging to the exterior of the lighthouse that's a very good piece of effects work – but there are at least as many times where the attempt at creating this setting comes off as fake. Considering that this was the first story to air after the theatrical premiere of **Star Wars** (the first episode was actually shot in the studio on the very day that movie debuted), it was a bold try…and a necessary one, since one can barely imagine filming in the light room of a real lighthouse at night, let alone getting permission to turn that light off at dramatically necessary junctures of the story!

Where *Horror* succeeds is in throwing a whole school of red herrings at the viewer to hold off the revelation of the real threat. Though I'm strongly tempted to label the various secondary plots as padding, they actually hold their own and provide a useful way to keep our heroes from calling for backup. It's doubly surprising that the motivations and portrayals that keep the secondary story strand going are as relatively adult as they are; I don't mean **Torchwood** adult here, but adult as in blackmail, con jobs, motivations for murder, and at least one utterance each of "hell" and "damn" at a time when **Doctor Who** was still widely considered a children's show. *Horror* marks the transition into the era of Graham Williams, the penultimate producer of the original series, whose reign is often criticized as the nadir of the show in the '70s, with Tom Baker's tongue-in-cheek tendencies becoming harder to repress. But this story feels like a part of the previous season – serious and scary. A change in tone was coming, though, and it would be rather sudden: the following story introduced K-9 and began to tone things down considerably.

Kudos also go to Louise Jameson. A lot of development for Leela is built into the dialogue, including her admission that she now trusts science more than superstition, but Jameson brings a naivete to the character that fits. She doesn't know how to handle a shovel, and doesn't know that there's anything wrong with starting to disrobe in front of someone she's just met so she can ditch her frilly clothes for something more utilitarian. On the other hand, she's completely oblivious to an attempt by one of the lighthouse crew to chat her up, but it doesn't break the character to do that.

THE INVISIBLE ENEMY

The TARDIS encounters a huge, fibrous mass in space, and as it attempts to pass through the obstruction, a violent discharge from the central console knocks the Doctor out. He manages to set a course for a medical outpost, the Bi-Al Foundation. Barely able to explain the Doctor's predicament, Leela leaves the Time Lord in the capable hands of Dr. Marius, a brilliant but eccentric pathologist (he has fashioned his portable computer in the shape of a dog and christened it K-9). But whatever affected the Doctor soon spreads to others at Bi-Al, and the Doctor is now clearly the center of a hive mind directing the actions of the infected. The fight to save the doctors and nurses at Bi-Al is a losing battle; the Doctor and Leela must take the fight to the source of the problem: inside the Doctor's body!

Tom Baker . . . . The Doctor
Louise Jameson . . . . Leela
Neil Curran . . . . Nurse
Pat Gorman . . . . Medic
Brian Grellis . . . . Safran
Roy Herrick . . . . Parsons
Frederick Jaeger . . . . Professor Marius
John Scott Martin . . . . Nucleus
John Leeson . . . . . . Nucleus voice / voice of K-9
Jim McManus . . . . Opthalmologist
Jay Neill . . . . Silvey
Elizabeth Norman . . . . Marius' Nurse
Edmund Pegge . . . . Meeker
Anthony Rowlands . . . . Crewman

This story has been released on DVD

written by Bob Baker & Dave Martin
directed by Derrick Goodwin
music by Dudley Simpson

Part 1 aired on October 1, 1977
Part 2 aired on October 8, 1977
Part 3 aired on October 15, 1977
Part 4 aired on October 22, 1977

Michael Sheard . . . . Lowe
Roderick Smith . . . . Cruikshank
Kenneth Waller . . . . Hedges

AUDIO WHO CONNECTIONS: The seventh Doctor and his companions face the Nucleus of the Swarm (once again played by John Leeson, more commonly associated with the voice of K-9) once more in 2014's *Revenge Of The Swarm.*

A pale imitation of **Fantastic Voyage**, this four-parter is one big delirious chase scene. If anything, the best parts to watch for are those creepy scenes in the TARDIS before it materializes on the Bi-Al asteroid. (Kudos to the BBC's effects shop for the Bi-Al model work, by the way.) On the whole, **Doctor Who** utilizes the "lead character mentally possessed by alien baddies" plotline a lot less than, oh, say, any given **Star Trek** after the original series does. When it happens here, it's really a bit unnerving.

The producers weren't quite sold on the idea of K-9 yet, and planned to film two endings: one with K-9 remaining with Dr. Marius, and the one with K-9 boarding the TARDIS and joining the Doctor. I don't mind the mecha-mutt in small doses, and actually he's used quite effectively here.

Overall, a nifty little check-your-brain-at-the-door romp that is both surprisingly lightweight and dark and menacing. Now, if only they could explain why the Doctor has Greek architecture floating around in his head...

IMAGE OF THE FENDAHL

The TARDIS is sidetracked by a time anomaly, depositing the Doctor and Leela near a secluded priory which has been serving as the laboratory of Dr. Fendelman and his colleagues. The object of the scientists' study is what appears to be a human skull...which, according to dating, originated over eight million years before homo sapiens existed on Earth. But Fendelman isn't sharing the whole story with his fellow scientists – in fact, one of them has unknowingly become a channel through which something sinister is emerging. The Doctor tries to intervene as the body count mounts in the countryside, but Fendelman has his well-armed security guards lock the Doctor away. The Doctor recognizes the threat as one from Gallifreyan folklore: the Fendahl, a gestalt entity, was exiled by the Time Lords, its world time-looped for twelve million years. Fendelman knows that the skull is alien, and hopes that studying it will reveal new insights into the origins of man. But Fendelman's trusted assistant has other designs on the alien artifact, plans which involve black magic. And somewhere between science and black magic, the Fendahl will gain the power it needs to strike.

Tom Baker . . . . The Doctor
Louise Jameson . . . . Leela
Edward Arthur . . . . Colby
David Elliott . . . . Security Guard
Edward Evans . . . . Moss
Scott Fredericks . . . . Max Stael
Daphne Heard . . . . Martha Tyler
Geoffrey Hinsliff . . . . Jack Tyler
Denis Lill . . . . Dr. Fendelman
Derek Martin . . . . Mitchell
Roy Pearce . . . . Security Guard
Graham Simpson . . . . Hiker

This story has been released on DVD

written by Chris Boucher
directed by George Spenton-Foster
music by Dudley Simpson

Part 1 aired on October 29, 1977
Part 2 aired on November 5, 1977
Part 3 aired on November 12, 1977
Part 4 aired on November 19, 1977

Wanda Ventham . . . . Thea Ransome

A.K.A.: Wanda Ventham would reappear (as a different character, naturally) in the first seventh Doctor episode, 1987's *Time And The Rani*. Denis Lill made a comeback slightly sooner, in 1984's *The Awakening*, and would later menace the **Red Dwarf** crew as a Borg-inspired enemy Simulant in the Emmy-winning 1993 fan favorite episode *Gunmen Of The Apocalypse*.

Well, hey, they had to figure out *some* way to re-use the giant maggots from *The Green Death*. This early horror effort from the oft-criticized Graham Williams era may not be quite up to the gorier stories of the Philip Hinchcliffe years, but it is helped by a crisp Chris Boucher script. There's a lot of wit among the nearly-nonsensical pseudoscience and occult plot points. There are also some major additions to **Doctor Who**'s Time Lord mythos – one throwaway reference in particular, to the Superstitious Disconnect in Gallifreyan society, led to numerous major developments in the New Adventures novel series (which may have also impacted the modern **Doctor Who** series – see *The End Of Time*). It's also one of the first instances of Time Lord interference which wasn't personally handled by the Doctor, something which seems to surprise him (he describes it as "criminal").

In the Something Cool I'll Bet You Didn't Notice category, when a certain structure implodes violently (represented by film of explosions running backwards), note that Dudley Simpson thoughtfully provided a piece of incidental music which would also run backwards, but musically speaking would progress forward.

THE SUN MAKERS

The TARDIS comes to an unexpected stop on a world that the Doctor hasn't explored before, but moments after he and Leela step out of the TARDIS and onto the top of an immense building, Leela spots a man moments away from committing suicide. The time travelers stop him from jumping off the building and try to learn what has brought him to the brink. They learn that they're actually on Pluto, which is now surrounded by artificial suns and colonized by the Company – which also employs virtually everyone who lives on Pluto, and taxes them into poverty. Cordo, stuck with a debt he'll never be able to afford to repay after failing to pay in full the tax on his father's death, sees only despair, until he remembers stories of the Others, a group of underground rebels who fight against the Company's taxes and bureaucracy. With the help of the Doctor, Leela and K-9, Cordo finds the rebellious Others and pledges to join them, only to discover that sticking it to the man could make him a dead man.

Tom Baker . . . . The Doctor
Louise Jameson . . . . Leela
John Leeson . . . . voice of K-9
Adrienne Burgess . . . . Veet
Derek Crewe . . . . Synge
Carole Hopkin . . . . Nurse
Michael Keating . . . . Goudry
Tom Kelly . . . . Guard
Richard Leech . . . . Gatherer Hade
Roy Macready . . . . Cordo
Colin McCormack . . . . Commander
David Rowlands . . . . Bisham
Jonina Scott . . . . Marn

This story has been released on DVD

written by Robert Holmes
directed by Pennant Roberts
music by Dudley Simpson

Part 1 aired on November 26, 1977
Part 2 aired on December 3, 1977
Part 3 aired on December 10, 1977
Part 4 aired on December 17, 1977

William Simons . . . . Mandrel
Henry Woolf . . . . Collector

A.K.A.: Actor **Michael Keating** made such an impression here that director Pennant Roberts recommended him for a regular role in the Terry Nation space opera **Blake's 7**, a series where Roberts was also frequently engaged as a director. Keating played the part of Vila, a thief with strong survival instincts, and was the only member of that show's cast to appear in all 52 episodes between 1978 and 1981. In early episodes, Keating was joined by **Tom Kelly** as a young member of **Blake's 7** who doesn't live very long. Keating would return to **Doctor Who** in a 2002 audio story, *The Twilight Kingdom*.

A great many books on the subject of **Doctor Who** have elevated *The Sun Makers* to a Swiftian parody of the British tax system, but what I discovered, rewatching it years later, is that it's incredibly uneven. There's a grim grittiness to the first episode, what with its fleecing of innocent taxpayers and a man driven almost to suicide, that is completely hijacked by the time part 4 unspools, by which time it's become a classic example of the campiness that was creeping into the series. The rough-and-tumble rebels who seem prepared to kill to avenge the downtrodden in part 1 seem like light comedy characters by the end of the story. Even their adversary, Gatherer Hade, who seems all too ready to tax a man to death in part 1, becomes a buffoonish blowhard by the time he gets his comeuppance.

There are quite a few good moments here for Leela, though many of them seem to be a case of Louise Jameson making lemonade out of the lemons she was given; the script all but reduces even the regulars to caricature. This is very surprising when one considers that the whole thing is written by Robert Holmes, generally considered one of **Doctor Who**'s best writers, old series or new – and he'd done quite well with the character of Leela in *The Talons Of Weng-Chiang*. *The Sun Makers* is certainly entertaining, but only if you can overlook a lack of consistency of tone from the story's beginning to its end.

SHORT HOPS

...in which the author admits to a deep and abiding love for Blake's 7.

It's not uncommon to run into **Doctor Who** fans who are also fans of the BBC space opera **Blake's 7**, created by Terry Nation, who had of course created the Daleks in 1963. Still hot property, and now best known for anything *but* his former career (comedy writing), Nation had met with mixed success in his post-Who TV endeavours. A 1960s attempt to launch the Daleks in their own series led to nothing except the Daleks' near-total absence from late '60s **Doctor Who**, and Nation had a serious falling-out with Terence Dudley, the producer of his 1975 series Survivors, leading to Nation abandoning that series at the end of its second season.

Nation's new adventure was still post-apocalyptic in a way, but decidedly more "sci-fi": **Blake's 7** chronicled the misadventures of a band of criminals – some wrongly accused, others quite rightly headed to prison – fighting against a totalitarian Earth-based regime. With a cast led by Gareth Thomas (later the voice of Kalendorf in Big Finish's Dalek Empire audio series, and a guest star in the *Ghost Machine* episode of **Torchwood**) and Paul Darrow (**Doctor Who And The Silurians**, *Timelash* and several Big Finish audio stories), **Blake's 7** was an excellent venue in which to see **Doctor Who** actors – both guests and regulars – playing other parts (Colin Baker once appeared as a scenery-chewing villain in head-to-toe black studded leather). Though it was occasionally outrageously campy (particularly in the latter half of its four-year run), **Blake's 7** was always enjoyable. Like **Doctor Who**, it cruised along at full speed on the back of committed performances rather than Hollywood production values. (And, much to the show's misfortune, **Blake's 7** had the bad timing to premiere mere months after *Star Wars* – unlike **Doctor Who**, **Blake's 7** was a series that took place in space, aboard spaceships, and as such couldn't rely on the going back in time, something that the BBC found a bit easier to do than cruising through space.)

Behind the scenes, the two shows were always competing for resources, including the expertise of the same small pool of inventive effects artists at the BBC. A friendly rivalry developed, though there was a bit of a tipping point in that rivalry when the cash-strapped **Blake's 7** grabbed a Sea-Devil costume to use as a random alien monster; **Doctor Who** producer John Nathan-Turner was *not* amused.

Though occasionally derided by **Doctor Who** fans who felt that it was a drain on production resources that should have been allocated to Who alone, **Blake's 7** was always hugely enjoyable, and frequently aired on American PBS outlets in the late '80s alongside **Doctor Who** – the BBC's syndication arm recognized the sudden hunger for any kind of British sci-fi and often offered both shows, along with others like The Tripods, to the same stations.

But the two shows *almost* shared more than special effects wizards and audiences.

How you know you'll forever be a "single" fan: you own 45RPM singles of the shows' *theme music.*

The second season finale of **Blake's 7** features the discovery of a gigantic force field, a huge wall at the edge of the Milky Way galaxy at the point which is closest to the Andromeda Galaxy. The crew of the Liberator, trying to find the corrupt Federation's secret control center, stumbles upon the control center that powers this force field and promptly sabotages it, blissfully unaware that they're about to knock a hole in a dam that's kept alien invaders from overrunning human space. Now Blake and his band of rebels had to join forces with the Federation fleet they often fought against, joining forces against a common enemy.

At one point, in constructing this thrilling cliffhanger, **Nation actually considered making the Daleks that all-conquering invasion force.** This would've been a game-changer for both shows: it would have said, in no uncertain terms, that **Doctor Who** and **Blake's 7** took place in the same "universe." Some viewers were already convinced of that – after all, both shows already took place in a universe where spaceships were constructed from slightly wobbly BBC scenery flats – but there was something about the backstabbing, bloodthirsty **Blake's 7** millieu that was hard to square against much of **Doctor Who**.

Furthermore, **Blake's 7** producer David Maloney and script editor Chris Boucher (who had written such notable **Doctor Who** stories as *The Face Of Evil* and *The Robots Of Death*) out-voted Nation, overruling him on the inclusion of the Daleks; they had signed up to work on **Blake's 7**, not on a show that was suddenly going to declare itself to be a mere **Doctor Who** spinoff halfway through its run. The alien threat was transformed into a more amorphous one (literally – they were blobby shapeshifters), and the threat of Dalek invasion never again loomed over the universe of **Blake's 7**.

Another crossover possibility – that the fourth Doctor and Blake would briefly pass each other without comment – was brought up by Tom Baker and Gareth Thomas (probably at the pub) and was similarly laughed out of the room.

Chris Boucher, however, has had the last laugh: in 1999, he wrote a **Doctor Who** novel following up on *The Robots Of Death*, incorporating characters and elements from his **Blake's 7** scripts. That crossover element was taken on board by Magic Bullet Productions' series of Kaldor City audio plays, picking up where the book's story left off.

This author is not of the opinion that **Blake's 7** shares anything more than DVD shelf space with **Doctor Who**, and so it won't be covered in any volume of VWORP! as a spinoff. But **Blake's 7** is a fun show, one which I love on an almost equal footing with **Doctor Who** – both of them, together with **Star Trek: The Next Generation**, got me through some very tough times in my life by providing a thought-provoking, imaginative escape from what was really going on around me. I'd strongly consider a separate Blake book, if there wasn't already a damn-near-definitive one out there already (Liberation: An Unofficial Unauthorised Guide to **Blake's 7**, Telos Books, 2003, by Alan Stevens and Fiona Moore). But in the absence of that, I recommend **Blake's 7** to **Doctor Who** fans – both shows tickle the same BBC-sci-fi gene, and that's something I think we can agree on them sharing.

UNDERWORLD

The Doctor and Leela find themselves at the edge of a galaxy, near an enormous nebula that could wreak untold damage on the TARDIS. To avoid this, the Doctor forces his ship to materialize on a nearby spacecraft. When he announces himself to the ship's crew, they regard Leela as a threat (and harmlessly quell her bloodlust with their pacification beam), but they regard the Doctor as a god. He has come aboard a starship crewed by the last of the Minyans, a race who the Time Lords aided and augmented – and who then destroyed themselves with the aid of their new technology, the incident that caused the Time Lords to withdraw into their non-intervention policy. Unlike Time Lords, the Minyans can regenerate thousands of times, with enough control over the process that they seem to simply become younger again when their bodies wear out, and they've been on this flight for thousands of years. Their quest is to find the P7E, a lost Minyan sister ship whose cargo of genetic material could revitalize the species. Their obstacle is that they can't seem to find the P7E, until the Doctor discovers that the missing ship is now the core of a forming planetoid – and that the descendants of its crew have taken on a new form entirely, a society that the Minyan searchers can't even recognize – a society that could kill them all before they reach their goal.

Tom Baker . . . . The Doctor	
Louise Jameson . . . . Leela	
John Leeson . . . . voice of K-9	
Imogen Bickford-Smith . . . . Tala	
Jimmy Gardner . . . . Idmon	
Godfrey James . . . . Tarn	
Frank Jarvis . . . . Ankh	
Alan Lake . . . . Herrick	
James Marcus . . . . Rask	
James Maxwell . . . . Jackson	
Jay Neill . . . . Klimt	
Jonathan Newth . . . . Orfe	
Christine Pollon . . . . voice of the Oracle	
Richard Shaw . . . . Lakh	

This story has been released on DVD

written by Bob Baker & Dave Martin
directed by Norman Stewart
music by Dudley Simpson

Part 1 aired on January 7, 1978
Part 2 aired on January 14, 1978
Part 3 aired on January 21, 1978
Part 4 aired on January 28, 1978

Stacey Tendeter . . . . Naia
Norman Tipton . . . . Idas

Underworld has accumulated a less-than-stellar reputation in fan circles for featuring tons of dodgy bluescreen shots as a substitute for real sets or locations. But considering that numerous scenes of the new series have featured entirely virtual or mostly virtual sets, perhaps all that *Underworld* is truly guilty of is being nearly 30 years ahead of its time.

The money for this episode simply ran out, leaving the production crew to stage huge chunks of the action against bluescreen, which would later be used to show elaborately-built scale model backgrounds. As cheesy as this may sound, there was obviously some thought put into it – many of these early virtual sets include exits that characters duck into, obstacles that the characters must navigate, and so on; all of this requires careful planning and coordination from the pre-production stage straight through post-production. Conspicuous in the end credits is A.J. Mitchell, a BBC visual effects wiz who is also credited with single-handedly inventing the complex animated teleport effect for **Blake's 7**. The Beeb's best and brightest were in on this – but **the technology to really build a set around an actor performing in front of a blank wall just wasn't there yet.** So while it has been a laughing stock for many years, *Underworld* isn't that risible in the present context; it's a noble attempt and a flawed experiment, and the first tentative step toward the kind of elaborate effects that we now see in the modern series on a regular basis. Little did anyone know this four-parter was, in fact, pointing the way forward.

The acting is above par for this point in the series' history, as this was when things were descending firmly into constantly tongue-in-cheek territory. There are a few of what I'd describe as unfortunate costuming choices when it comes to the story's antagonists – namely some laughably almost-phallic robot heads that it's incredibly difficult not to find a double meaning for (and spacesuit helmets to match, for our Minyan heroes), but even though they provide a hearty (if unintended) laugh, they don't detract from the story much. And as for that whole "thousands of regenerations" thing... my bet was that, if the revived television series lasted long enough the that "13 regeneration limit" on Time Lords became a stumbling block, we'd be hearing about Minyos again.

Give it a shot if you get the chance. In the present context of **Doctor Who**, *Underworld* is long overdue for a reassessment.

THE INVASION OF TIME

The Doctor returns, unbidden, to Gallifrey, claiming the Presidency of the High Council. Leela knows something is wrong, as she has witnessed his meetings with a shadowy group of aliens prior to returning to his homeworld. The Time Lords are aghast at the Doctor's breach of their power structure, to say nothing of him bringing an alien among them. But when the aliens Leela saw earlier materialize in Gallifrey's Capitol, all hell breaks loose – the Doctor orders many Time Lords, including his old mentor Borusa, expelled to the harsh surface of Gallifrey beyond the city domes. Leela is also thrown out, though she finds herself quite at home with the primitive nomadic tribes of homeless non-Time Lords known as the Shobogans. Leela rallies both Shobogans and exiled Time Lords to mount a resistance against the Doctor and his shady Vardan allies, but when the invasion is put down, everyone discovers that it was a ruse to allow a far more powerful enemy to slip into the heart of Gallifrey.

Tom Baker . . . . The Doctor
Louise Jameson . . . . Leela
John Leeson . . . . voice of K-9
Milton Johns . . . . Kelner
John Arnatt . . . . Borusa
Stan McGowan . . . . Vardan Leader
Chris Tranchell . . . . Andred
Dennis Edwards . . . . Gomer

This story has been released on DVD

written by Anthony Read & Graham Williams
directed by Gerald Blake
music by Dudley Simpson

Part 1 aired on February 4, 1978
Part 2 aired on February 11, 1978
Part 3 aired on February 18, 1978
Part 4 aired on February 25, 1978

UWORP!

Tom Kelly	Vardan
Reginald Jessup	Savar
Charles Morgan	Gold Usher
Hilary Ryan	Rodan
Max Faulkner	Nesbin
Christopher Christou	Chancellery Guard
Michael Harley	Bodyguard
Ray Callaghan	Ablif
Gai Smith	Presta

Part 5 aired on March 4, 1978
Part 6 aired on March 11, 1978

Michael Mundell	Jasko
Eric Danot	Guard
Derek Deadman	Stor
Stuart Fell	Sontaran

NEW WHO CONNECTIONS: Clara Oswald is seen to have intervened to thwart a previously unknown attempt on the Doctor's life by the Great Intelligence during this adventure in *The Name Of The Doctor* (2013). The story of Leela's life on Gallifrey is picked up in the Gallifrey audio spin-off series by Big Finish Productions.

K-9 CONNECTIONS: Early publicity material for the K-9 spinoff series stated that Leela's K-9 — the one inherited from Professor Marius — was the K-9 model who would appear in the robot dog's show. This, however, seems a bit unlikely: the regenerative technology that allows K-9 to assume a new form in the spinoff series would be much more in line with Gallifreyan technology than something devised by Professor Marius, which makes K-9 Mark II — introduced in the next season of **Doctor Who**, built from the ground up by the Doctor and inherited by Romana — a far likelier candidate.

Trying (perhaps a little too hard) to reclaim that bizarre mixture of wizardry, science, retro-tech and wonder that made *Deadly Assassin*, the original Gallifrey/Time Lords episode, so compelling, *The Invasion Of Time* is a real exercise in contrast. It's quite fascinating in what it reveals about the Time Lords and their history, though it's also quite exasperating in those scenes where the action is obviously being padded out for time.

But sometimes that Time Lord backstory/backgrounding is enough to balance it out. The hint at a subclass power struggle is very interesting, as is the realization, once and for all, that all Time Lords are Gallifreyans, but not all Gallifreyans are Time Lords. Various elements of *The Invasion Of Time* have been expanded on or jettisoned at the whims of later novelists, TV writers and audio playwrights, but in its own right it's interesting…if you're willing to endure the sometimes interminable chase scenes.

From the devil's advocate department, I also like to point out that, in spite of the protests around this six-parter's original airdate that the TARDIS was too advanced to contain brickwork and lattice-gated lifts, what once seemed like an anachronism (and, truthfully, was necessitated by filming on location in a hospital) is actually validated by the Jules Verne-style TARDIS interior seen in the 1996 TV movie, which seemed to say, once and for all, that the TARDIS can contain *anything*.

THE KEY TO TIME

SEASON 16: 1978-79
THE RIBOS OPERATION

The Doctor's TARDIS is diverted to an unknown place. Upon landing, the Doctor meets the White Guardian, a being more powerful than even the Time Lords, who has chosen the Doctor to retrieve the six missing segments of the Key To Time, which will supposedly restore time and space to a more balanced state. With a new version of K-9 up and running, the Doctor is keen to undertake this adventure alone, but again, the Guardian chooses a new companion for the Doctor, a Time Lady named Romanadvortrelundar.

The search for the first of the Key to Time's six segments leads the Doctor, K-9 and Romana to an unlikely place for such an item: the backwards planet Ribos. The natives are wrapped up in superstition and tradition, and they're largely unaware that their planet is being targeted for takeover by the mad exiled warlord Graff Vynda-K. But even the Graff is being targeted on Ribos by a pair of con men who hope he'll pay handsomely for directions which will supposedly lead him to a lost mine containing enough of the mineral jethrik to fund his operation. And when everyone's plans are exposed, they believe the Doctor and Romana are the responsible party.

Tom Baker . . . . The Doctor
Mary Tamm . . . . Romana
John Leeson . . . . voice of K-9
Timothy Bateson . . . . Binro
Iain Cuthbertson . . . . Garron
Prentis Hancock . . . . Captain
Robert Keegan . . . . Sholakh
Cyril Luckham . . . . White Guardian
Nigel Plaskitt . . . . Unstoffe
Paul Seed . . . . Graff Vynda-K
Ann Tirard . . . . Seeker

This story has been released on DVD

written by Robert Holmes
directed by George Spenton-Foster
music by Dudley Simpson

Part 1 aired on September 2, 1978
Part 2 aired on September 9, 1978
Part 3 aired on September 16, 1978
Part 4 aired on September 23, 1978

A classic Robert Holmes script full of double acts and wry humor, *The Ribos Operation* was originally just another story before producer Graham Williams — tired of the Doctor's aimless wanderings and irresponsibility — decided to create a season-long story arc to give the Time Lord more purpose. *Ribos* was rewritten accordingly, the most striking change being the addition of the White Guardian's introductory scene and the resulting removal of several scenes later in the story to compensate for the new material.

Also arriving in this story is Romana, in the form of the glamorous Mary Tamm. It's quite a gear shift to go from Leela to the first incarnation of Romana; she's not the subservient screamer that so many of her female sidekick predecessors became, but the air of arrogance — toned down later in the season — was both a bit off-putting, and perfectly in character. And fortunately, K-9 is used sparingly here, serving as *deus dog ex machina* only once or twice in the entire four-part adventure.

The Ribos Operation is not a story you can semi-watch while it's on in the background. A load of background information and things vital to the plot are imparted in the course of an extremely wordy (and witty) script, and you've got to pay attention. This is helped considerably by one of the best lineups of guest actors a **Doctor Who** story has ever sported. Almost all of the key guest players are paired off into double-acts with other characters, so there's a lot of lively banter in between the sparing bits of action.

THE PIRATE PLANET

The Doctor and Romana learn that the second segment of the Key to Time is on Calufrax, a planet described by the Doctor as an uninviting place. After the TARDIS inexplicably fails to land, it brings them to a world which is nothing like Calufrax — instead, it's inhabited, prosperous (at least on first glance), and unbelievably rich. But the prosperity is a thin charade; the Captain lords over the planet with an iron fist, while repeatedly bringing his subjects new epochs of prosperity with alarming regularity. And a group of rogue telepaths called Mentiads wander the wilds of the planet, drawing the wrath of the Captain and suspicion from everyone else. The Doctor discovers that this world is hollow. And whether it is by his own hand in the name of restoring the Key to Time, or by the hand of the Captain – who isn't as in charge of the situation as it appears – the planet Calufrax is doomed.

Tom Baker . . . . The Doctor
Mary Tamm . . . . Romana
John Leeson . . . . voice of K-9
Clive Bennett . . . . Citizen
Vi Delmar . . . . Queen Xanxia
Bernard Finch . . . . Mentiad
Adam Kurkin . . . . Guard
Rosalind Lloyd . . . . Nurse
Ralph Michael . . . . Balaton
Bruce Purchase . . . . Captain
Andrew Robertson . . . . Mr. Fibuli
David Sibley . . . . Pralix

This story has been released on DVD

written by Douglas Adams
directed by Pennant Roberts
music by Dudley Simpson

Part 1 aired on September 30, 1978
Part 2 aired on October 7, 1978
Part 3 aired on October 14, 1978
Part 4 aired on October 21, 1978

Primi Townsend . . . . Mula
David Warwick . . . . Kimus

NEW WHO CONNECTIONS: In *The Stolen Earth* (2008), the planet Calufrax Minor – presumably a leftover satellite of Calufrax or another planet in its solar system – is mentioned as one of the planets "stolen" by Davros and the Daleks. Whatever solar system Calufrax is a part of, it's not a very lucky one.

Douglas Adams' first contribution to **Doctor Who** can't quite decide if it's going to be serious or comical, though this problem may be one caused by the actors and director instead of the writer. Tom Baker in particular plays the Doctor as if he's virtually invulnerable to anything, which goes a long way in destroying any dramatic tension in the script. Mary Tamm also picked up some of this tone, and plays Romana so casually that she seems almost not to care about what's happening around her. K-9, the only character responding to any sense of danger, is repeatedly shushed by the Doctor, who then falls victim to whatever danger K-9 tried to warn him of.

Since this script is from the same period during which Douglas Adams wrote the original radio scripts for **The Hitchhikers' Guide to the Galaxy**, there was a sneaky crossover between the two fictional universes in the form of throwaway dialogue: the Doctor mentions the planet Bandraginus Five, which in Hitchhikers' lore is fabled for its mineral water. The plot point of Queen Xanxia's last moments of life being held at bay by a "time dam" was also lifted – even the character's name – in the first Hitchhiker's Guide novel.

THE STONES OF BLOOD

The search for the Key to Time brings the Doctor and Romana to modern-day England, very close to a stone circle being studied by Professor Amelia Rumford and her friend Vivien Fey. Romana is alarmed to see real evidence that a live animal may have been sacrificed at the stones very recently, but is told by Professor Rumford that it's probably just the work of an overenthusiastic local group of Druid recreationists. But it's not just would-be Druids who are moving around the circle – Professor Rumford is convinced that the stones themselves are moving. The Doctor and K-9 witness this for themselves, as an unknown force uses an apparition of the Doctor to lure Romana over the edge of a cliff. The stakes are higher now than anything that the Druid afficionados could imagine – one of the galaxy's most feared criminals is hiding out on Earth, using the rock-like Ogri to enforce her will…and hide her identity.

UWORP!

Tom Baker . . . . The Doctor
Mary Tamm . . . . Romana
John Leeson . . . . voice of K-9
Gerald Cross . . . . Megara voice
Judy Crowne . . . . Druid
Decima Delaney . . . . Druid
Susan Engel . . . . Vivien Fay
Elaine Ives-Cameron . . . . Martha
Beatrix Lehmann . . . . Professor Rumford
David McAlister . . . . Megara voice
Nicholas McArdle . . . . De Vries
James Muir . . . . Druid
Mike Mungarvan . . . . Druid
Ian Munroe . . . . Druid

This story
has been
released
on DVD

written by David Fisher
directed by Darrol Blake
music by Dudley Simpson

Part 1 aired on October 28, 1978
Part 2 aired on November 4, 1978
Part 3 aired on November 11, 1978
Part 4 aired on November 18, 1978

James Murray . . . . Camper
Margaret Pilleau . . . . Druid
Shirin Taylor . . . . Camper

One of the most intriguing stories in the Key To Time cycle, *The Stones Of Blood* benefits from better than usual production values and the kind of black magic/ghost story that suited **Doctor Who** so well in the Tom Baker years. The production looks a little slicker than usual due to director Darrol Blake's insistence on using video instead of film for location shooting. There's still some pure goofiness, including the giant moving stones and the Megara, two floating clumps of lights – erm, sorry, "justice machines" – which figure heavily into the latter half of the story.

Much has been made of Beatrix Lehmann's guest appearance in this story, and while I personally can't vouch for the rest of her body of work, she's got to be one of the most perfectly-cast guest artists ever to show up in the series. Equally well-cast is Susan Engel as Vivien Fey, though she may have poured it on a little too thick, a little too quick – I doubt I'm spoiling anything for anyone by saying it's easy to spot her as the baddie all the way from orbit.

Overall, though, a very interesting twist on what seems like it's going to be a familiar story, one which hangs a sharp right about halfway through.

THE ANDROIDS OF TARA

The Doctor and Romana arrive on the planet Tara, searching for the fourth segment of the Key to Time, but this time around the Doctor feels he's entitled to some vacation time. Romana goes on to find the fourth segment herself while the Doctor does some fishing, but this places them both in danger. Romana encounters the conniving Count Grendel of Gracht, a duplicitous duke who aspires to Tara's throne, and he promptly takes her prisoner, apparently believing her to be an android. The Doctor, in the meantime, is found by a small band of men loyal to Prince Reynart, the rightful heir to the throne, who is in hiding due to Grendel's machinations. Reynart has one defense – a perfect android replica of himself – which isn't working. The Doctor accompanies Reynart's men and his newly repaired android to the prince's coronation while the prince himself waits in seclusion. But it gets much more complicated than that when each side tries to outfox the other with android replicas – and Count Grendel may hold the winning piece, for he intends to replace Princess Strella, unwilling to be forced into a marriage to Prince Reynart, with her identical twin: Romana.

Tom Baker	. . . .	The Doctor
Mary Tamm	. . . .	Romana
John Leeson	. . . .	voice of K-9
Lois Baxter	. . . .	Madame Lamia
Neville Jason	. . . .	Prince Reynart
Peter Jeffrey	. . . .	Count Grendel
Simon Lack	. . . .	Zadek
Paul Lavers	. . . .	Farrah
Martin Matthews	. . . .	Kurster
Declan Mulholland	. . . .	Till
Cyril Shaps	. . . .	Archimandrite

This story has been released on DVD

written by David Fisher
directed by Michael Hayes
music by Dudley Simpson

Part 1 aired on November 25, 1978
Part 2 aired on December 2, 1978
Part 3 aired on December 9, 1978
Part 4 aired on December 16, 1978

A dizzy double-crossing tale with more similarities to The *Prisoner Of Zenda* than you can count on both hands, *Androids Of Tara* is a case where the style and execution of the story have to outweigh the (borrowed) story itself. Michael Hayes' fluid direction and some gorgeous location shooting help do the trick here, and for once it actually helps that Tom Baker seizes the opportunity to ham things up a bit and give them character. There's also a curiously tentative swordfight between Baker's Doctor and Count Grendel – perhaps he's just stressing the alien nature of his character by not fighting all that viciously, but hey, the third Doctor would've been *all over* this guy.

An entertaining enough story, just not terribly original. Then again, when it's set against the framework of the Doctor looking for various pieces of what amounts to a kind of sci-fi Holy Grail, what is?

THE POWER OF KROLL

Arriving on the third moon of Delta Magna, the Doctor and Romana are forced to leave K-9 in the TARDIS as they explore the swampy marshes in search of the fifth segment. The Doctor runs afoul of human miners who seem to have mistaken him for the notorious gun runner Rohm Dutt, while Romana is abducted by the displaced indigenous population of Delta Magna. Dubbed the "swampies" by the employees of the human mining colony, the natives have contracted with Rohm Dutt for weapons and training, hoping to boost their fight to free themselves from servitude to the human interlopers. The swampies worship Kroll, an enormous, squid-like being measuring almost five miles across, though the miners don't believe a word of it...until it appears. When the Doctor and Romana learn that Kroll isn't holding the fifth segment, but is the fifth segment, to say that they have a large problem on their hands is a bit of an understatement.

Tom Baker	. . . .	The Doctor
Mary Tamm	. . . .	Romana
John Abineri	. . . .	Ranquin
Frank Jarvis	. . . .	Skart
John Leeson	. . . .	Dugeen
Philip Madoc	. . . .	Fenner
Grahame Mallard	. . . .	Harg
Neil McCarthy	. . . .	Thawn
Glyn Owen	. . . .	Rohm Dutt
Carl Rigg	. . . .	Varlik
Terry Walsh	. . . .	Mensch

This story has been released on DVD

written by Robert Holmes
directed by Norman Stewart
music by Dudley Simpson

Part 1 aired on December 23, 1978
Part 2 aired on December 30, 1978
Part 3 aired on January 6, 1979
Part 4 aired on January 13, 1979

For some reason, and maybe it was that five-mile-wide squid that pops out of the ocean at the end of episode two, *The Power Of Kroll* has always stuck in my mind. It is a nifty example of one thing I do like about **Doctor Who**, however – when the Doctor discovers that the humans are in the wrong, he promptly puts them in their place and helps the local population instead. But since the natives have hired a gun smuggler to further their cause of freedom… well, I'd say it muddies the waters a bit, but that goes without saying in a four-parter that takes place in a swamp.

It's nice to see John Leeson actually appearing instead of voicing K-9; since the robot dog had to be written out of the show because the wetland setting was inhospitable to a radio-controlled prop, and since Leeson was already on contract for the entire season, he got to go on camera for once. Speaking of knowing when to be on camera and when to be off, how about that giant squid? Seriously, the director seemed to have a good sense that his serial's monster might look *just a little* silly, despite the BBC's visual effects wizards' best shot, and kept the huge creature's first full appearance at the end of the second episode – in other words, all we see are some slimy tentacles dragging people off screen for the first half of the story. In some ways, that works better than if we'd been seeing that whole plate of calamari throughout the story.

When I lived in Green Bay in the late 1990s, I used to drive by a restaurant across from Lambeau Field, called Kroll's East, fairly close to my apartment. I never did work up the nerve to go in and ask if they served squid, lest something really big rise up out of Lake Michigan to answer my question.

THE ARMAGEDDON FACTOR

In one of the better stories of the late 1970s, the Doctor, Romana and K-9 stumble into the middle of a fierce interplanetary nuclear war. The Atrios war effort is faltering, its population demoralized, because unknown to them, the Zeon war machine lives up to its name in the most literal way. Zeos is controlled by a computer, and there are no Zeons, just remote controlled attack ships. Somewhere in the darkness between the two planets lurks a third party, pulling the strings of both sides in the war. The hand of the Black Guardian becomes visible in moving the pieces in this game, and the Doctor is horrified to discover that he will have to take an innocent life to complete the Key to Time.

Tom Baker	. . . .	The Doctor
Mary Tamm	. . . .	Romana
John Leeson	. . . .	voice of K-9
Iain Armstrong	. . . .	Technician
Stephen Calcutt	. . . .	Super Mute
John Cannon	. . . .	Guard
Valentine Dyall	. . . .	Black Guardian
Harry Fielder	. . . .	Guard
Pat Gorman	. . . .	Pilot
Davyd Harries	. . . .	Shapp
Barry Jackson	. . . .	Drax
Ian Liston	. . . .	Hero
Ian Saynor	. . . .	Merak
William Squire	. . . .	The Shadow
Susan Skipper	. . . .	Heroine

This story has been released on DVD

written by Bob Baker & Dave Martin
directed by Michael Hayes
music by Dudley Simpson

Part 1 aired on January 20, 1979
Part 2 aired on January 27, 1979
Part 3 aired on February 3, 1979
Part 4 aired on February 10, 1979
Part 5 aired on February 17, 1979
Part 6 aired on February 24, 1979

Lalla Ward	. . . .	Princess Astra
John Woodvine	. . . .	Marshal

NEW WHO CONNECTIONS: Look closely at the Marshal's ship when he takes off from Atrios. The "cockpit" at the nose of the ship was originally part of the System ships that recaptured the Liberator in the second season premiere of **Blake's 7**, which also aired in January, 1979.

A.K.A.: The imposing **John Woodvine** would go on to feature in *An American Werewolf In London* a couple of years after this story's premiere. Other genre credits include a recurring role in the second season of the BBC's adaptation of **The Tripods** in 1985, and the starring role as Prior Mordrin in the 1987 alternate-future series **Knights Of God**, which also starred Patrick Troughton in one of his final roles. He also guest starred in Russell T. Davies' non-genre series **Bob & Rose** in 2001, and was the Player King in the 2009 David Tennant/Patrick Stewart TV movie of **Hamlet.**

For most of this six-parter, the usual slightly tongue-in-cheek humor typical of the Graham Williams/Douglas Adams era is subdued in favor of dark atmosphere and real drama. Even K-9, usually the Doctor's trap door to avoid any plot complications, isn't invulnerable to the danger, and in some cases, K-9's fate is truly in question and cause for concern (as opposed to the usual treatment of him as an invulnerable machine). The opening scene, which pulls out from a close-up on an eye-rollingly soapy war propaganda film, revealing it to be playing on a screen in a crumbling medical ward, is a brilliant set-up for the entire show. Even the potentially silly character of Drax in part five has an edge of his own, with the possibility that he may be under the control of the Shadow, though the silliness factor intrudes on *The Armageddon Factor* when Drax breaks out his dimensional stabilizer gun for a round of "Honey, I Shrunk The Time Lords!" Other than that brief comical interlude, however, *The Armageddon Factor* ranks up there with *The Stones Of Blood* as the highlight of the Key to Time cycle.

SEASON 17: 1979-80
DESTINY OF THE DALEKS

The TARDIS brings the Doctor and Romana to a desolate wasteland of a planet, one whose atmosphere is so radioactive that it can be toxic even to Time Lords without proper precautions – the post-atomic-war Skaro, home world of the Daleks. When the two are separated, Romana is trailed by a disheveled human. Convinced that he means her harm, she runs right into a barely-buried chute that deposits her underground in the waiting arms of the Daleks themselves. The Doctor meets the attractive humanoid crew of a nearby space vessel, who call themselves Movellans. At war with the spacefaring Daleks for centuries, the Movellans have followed their enemies back to Skaro to prevent them from unearthing a "secret weapon": Davros, whose life support system was damaged but not disabled, has apparently survived in a dormant state. His more emotional, cunning strategies could give the Daleks the edge. The Movellans hope that the Doctor and Romana can give them the same edge – and worst of all, the two Time Lords aren't exactly being given a choice about replacing the Movellans' battle computers.

Tom Baker . . . . The Doctor
Lalla Ward . . . . Romana
David Brierly . . . . voice of K-9
Tim Barlow . . . . Tyssan
Toby Byrne . . . . Dalek
Penny Casdagla . . . . Jall
Suzanne Danielle . . . . Agella
David Gooderson . . . . Davros
Mike Mungarvan . . . . Dalek
Tony Osoba . . . . Lan
Roy Skelton . . . . Dalek voice
Tony Starr . . . . Dalek
Peter Straker . . . . Commander Sharrel

This story has been released on DVD

written by Terry Nation
directed by Ken Grieve
music by Dudley Simpson

Part 1 aired on September 1, 1979
Part 2 aired on September 8, 1979
Part 3 aired on September 15, 1979
Part 4 aired on September 22, 1979

Cy Town . . . . Dalek
David Yip . . . . Veldan

Destiny Of The Daleks has always been one of the Tom Baker stories I remembered best from my early years of being a **Doctor Who** fan. It's a nice follow-up to 1975's *Genesis Of The Daleks*, but there are some glaring holes at the same time. Davros was never quite the same from here on out. Despite his obvious trait of megalomania, at least in *Genesis* he had a cunning and deadly calculation that made him a force to be reckoned with. From *Destiny* forward, Davros was portrayed as lashing out wildly at anything, and wishing his creations to do the same.

The dialogue written for the Daleks and, to a lesser degree, Davros, was really rather amusing in places. "Seek! Locate! Exterminate! Do not deviate!" A few years before it became fashionable, the Daleks were rapping. Such phrases as "Let no opposition halt you!" seem too much like cheerleading for Daleks – it's a relatively encouraging thing to say, and therefore useless when bleated from one Dalek to another. For Davros' part, I cite "Weaponry so devastating that all matter will succumb to it," etc., as being nearly humorous. These odd phrases and others like them are really my biggest peeve.

Aside from that, it isn't bad. Contrary to what some may think, the Doctor's sometimes comical taunting of the Daleks was really refreshing. Sure, disposing of a Dalek by hanging his hat on its eyestalk isn't terribly believeable, but the Doctor slapping Davros' own hand onto the detonator button is priceless. The Movellans actually come across as more threatening than the Daleks (until everyone starts pitching the Movellans' belt batteries around), and it's really sad no one ever seemed to think of bringing them back except as a passing mention.

One of the larger plot holes, however, is how the Doctor knew that the Daleks were digging for Davros (sounds like a game show!). As he himself said, he had every reason to believe that Davros had been killed. Why not say something about the possibility that the Daleks would be searching for some notes or other invention that Davros had concocted before the events of *Genesis*?

CITY OF DEATH

The Doctor and Romana are paying a visit to Paris in 1979 when they both sense an interruption in time. Dismissing it as a freak occurrence, they visit the Louvre, where the Doctor suffers a dizzy spell as the result of another time interference. The Doctor also uncovers a plot to steal the Mona Lisa, attracting the attention of two parties: a bunch of armed thugs working for the obscenely rich Count Scarlioni, and another armed – though less proficient – thug, detective Duggan, who has been trailing Scarlioni on a hunch that the Count plans to lift the painting. Scarlioni's men kidnap the Doctor, Romana and Duggan to his mansion, where the Doctor realizes that Scarlioni is embarking on hazardous time experiments with technology that couldn't possibly exist on 20th century Earth. As it turns out, the alien being that calls itself Count Scarlioni is well on his way to stealing the Mona Lisa, but that is merely a diversion, the tip of the iceberg in a plot to revive his extinct alien species…at the cost of erasing the human race from history itself.

Tom Baker . . . . The Doctor		written by David Agnew
Lalla Ward . . . . Romana		(pseudonym for Douglas Adams
Eleanor Bron . . . . Gallery visitor		and Graham Williams)
Tom Chadbon . . . . Duggan		directed by Michael Hayes

John Cleese . . . . Gallery visitor
Kevin Flood . . . . Hermann
Julian Glover . . . . Scaroth / Scarlioni / Tancredi
David Graham . . . . Professor Kerensky
Peter Halliday . . . . Soldier
Catherine Schell . . . . Countess Scarlioni
Pamela Stirling . . . . Louvre Guide

This story has been released on DVD

music by Dudley Simpson

Part 1 aired on September 29, 1979
Part 2 aired on October 6, 1979
Part 3 aired on October 13, 1979
Part 4 aired on October 20, 1979

Easily my favorite **Doctor Who** story of Tom Baker's seven-year reign in the part, this is an immensely clever and well-thought-out time travel story that misleads the viewer into thinking that it will concern itself with nothing more than the theft of the Mona Lisa. The best aspect of this four-parter is the witty, verbose script by Douglas Adams and producer Graham Williams (credited to the fictional David Agnew — amazingly, written hastily to fill a gap left open by a script that didn't work out). The actors carry it off beautifully, visibly delighted to be working with the material at hand. Tom Chadbon is the perfect choice for Duggan, the bumbling Bogart-wanna-be whose main contribution to human history comes in the form of a right hook. Another excellent addition to the cast is veteran actor Julian Glover, who adds just the right menacingly charming touch to Count Scarlioni (but also hams it up a bit too much in the role of one of Scarlioni's forebears in the past). Dudley Simpson's music is romantic, urgent and surprisingly jazzy in all the right places, a rare standout musical score for late '70s **Doctor Who**.

Douglas Adams has been quoted as saying that he didn't enjoy his time as the script editor of **Doctor Who** because his attempts to inject wit and humor into the scripts were interpreted by the cast as free license to play the show like a comedy series. Despite a few moments of over-the-top levity from Tom Baker, *City Of Death* succeeds brilliantly in that it follows Adams' preferred formula for a slightly bizarre adventure which is funny but serious at the same time. **This is as good as Doctor Who got in the late Tom Baker era.**

THE CREATURE FROM THE PIT

The Doctor, Romana and K-9 follow an urgent distress call to the planet Chloris, whose ruler, Lady Adrasta, lords over the planet's resources and meets any challenge with a threat of war. But the greatest threat to Adrasta's empire is her own short-sightedness in imprisoning an ambassador from another world who only wishes to open a peaceful exchange between their two worlds. The Doctor could help to start the negotiations, but he has been consigned to the pit along with the ambassador.

Tom Baker . . . . The Doctor
Lalla Ward . . . . Romana
David Brierly . . . . voice of K-9
Morris Barry . . . . Tollund
Geoffrey Bayldon . . . . Organon
John Bryans . . . . Torvin
Philip Denyer . . . . Guard
Myra Frances . . . . Lady Adrasta
Edward Kelsey . . . . Edu
Tim Munro . . . . Ainu
Dave Redgrave . . . . Guard
David Telfer . . . . Huntsman
Terry Walsh . . . . Doran

This story has been released on DVD

written by David Fisher
directed by Christopher Barry
music by Dudley Simpson

Part 1 aired on October 27, 1979
Part 2 aired on November 3, 1979
Part 3 aired on November 10, 1979
Part 4 aired on November 17, 1979

Eileen Way . . . . Karela
Tommy Wright . . . . Guard Master

A.K.A.: An actor as well as a director, **Morris Barry** had been on the other side of the camera working on **Doctor Who** as well — he was the director of the 1967 Cyber-classics *The Moonbase* and *Tomb Of The Cybermen*, as well as 1968's *The Dominators*.

Though *Destiny Of The Daleks* and *City Of Death* each had their humorous moments, this is probably the first story in the seventeenth season of **Doctor Who** that merits the long-held fan criticism that the series had taken a fatally silly turn under the direction of producer Graham Williams and script editor Douglas Adams. And with the unintentionally funny cheapness of the huge, squishy, green, and obviously inflatable alien creature, to say nothing of the killer "wolfweeds" menacing K-9, there may have been some sound basis for these complaints. The basic story at the heart of this adventure was sound, but the production values — a lot of which seemed to be poured into an obviously artificial "outdoor" set in the studio when a location would have been much more convincing — failed to live up to the promise of the premise.

NIGHTMARE OF EDEN

Two spacecraft collide in hyperspace, one of them a passenger liner loaded with vacationers. The Doctor and Romana witness it all but, as they try to lend aid, they discover that something more sinister is happening: the captain of the passenger ship was, at the time of the accident, high on a potent and addictive narcotic called vraxoin. When the proper authorities arrive to investigate, they naturally point the finger of blame at the two most recent arrivals — the Doctor, Romana and K-9. But what the Doctor finds out is more disturbing than a mere drug ring. Vraxoin itself is created only from the residue left by the death of humanoid creatures called Mandrels — and someone is transporting live Mandrels undetected, intending to kill them to create more of the drug.

Tom Baker	The Doctor
Lalla Ward	Romana
David Brierly	voice of K-9
Barry Andrews	Stott
Richard Barnes	Crewman
Geoffrey Bateman	Dymond
Peter Craze	Costa
David Daker	Rigg
Lewis Fiander	Tryst
Robert Goodman	Mandrel
Billy Gray	Wounded passenger
Geoffrey Hinsliff	Fisk
Stephen Jenn	Secker
David Korff	Mandrel
Jennifer Lonsdale	Della
James Muir	Mandrel
Jan Murzynowski	Mandrel
Annette Peters	Passenger

This story has been released on DVD

written by Bob Baker
directed by Alan Bromly
music by Dudley Simpson

Part 1 aired on November 24, 1979
Part 2 aired on December 1, 1979
Part 3 aired on December 8, 1979
Part 4 aired on December 15, 1979

Maggie Petersen	Passenger
Eden Phillips	Crewman
Peter Roberts	Passenger
Pamela Ruddock	Computer voice
Lionel Sansby	Passenger
Sebastian Stride	Crewman
Derek Suthern	Mandrel

K-9 CONNECTIONS: The Mandrels are shown to be a race that Anubis and his people have enslaved in the **K-9** episode *The Curse Of Anubis* (2010). *The Nightmare Of Eden* was written by K-9 co-creator Bob Baker.

At the time *Nightmare Of Eden* was broadcast by the BBC, it was intended to be a **Doctor Who** object lesson about the dangers of smuggling, selling or using illegal drugs. With the benefit of almost 25 years' hindsight, though, we can see that *Eden* has all the anti-drug-message power of Nancy Reagan's celebrity guest shot on **Diff'rent Strokes**. Perhaps even less.

For starters, *Eden* is from the latter half of the Graham Williams / Douglas Adams era, which means it's incredibly jokey and tongue-in-cheek. Not a good tone to take for an anti-drug message. Whatever message there is manages to go AWOL pretty quickly as the comedic excesses of the era – including Lewis Fiander's dreadfully affected accent (I almost typed "accident" there, and you know, maybe that's closer to the mark). One of Tom Baker's all-time funniest gags happens here, as he walks into a virtual jungle, vanishes, and then is hear yelling "Oh, my arms! My legs! My everything!" as tattered bits of his clothing are ejected from the jungle while a horrified Romana watches. Funny as hell, but again, completely undermining the Helpful Moral Message.

Not **Doctor Who**'s finest hour by a long shot, and certainly not a milestone in getting an important message across to a young and impressionable audience. I would've been more satisfied with this story had it only concerned itself with, oh, say, two spaceships colliding in hyperspace. If someone tries to convince you that this is a **Doctor Who** story with a message… *just say no*.

THE HORNS OF NIMON

One of the last mighty battlecruisers of the Skonnon Empire is being used to ferry a load of young slaves from the planet Aneth, until its already overworked engines are pushed past the breaking point, stalling the ship in space. By coincidence, the TARDIS is also at a dead stop in space nearby while the Doctor disassembles the time rotor for an overhaul. But a singularity in this area of space is drawing both ships together…toward their doom. Despite his reservations about repairing a slaver's ship, the Doctor decides to err on the side of saving lives and repairs the ship – but as soon as he does, the surviving Skonnon co-pilot ditches the TARDIS and takes off with Romana still aboard. The Doctor and K-9 find themselves in the path of a massive planetoid being pulled into the singularity, but the Doctor manages to bounce the TARDIS off of the planetoid. On Skonnos, a sycophantic leader named Soldeed begs a creature called the Nimon for more time, as Soldeed's people continue to search for the missing slaver ship. Thanks to the Doctor's repairs, the ship does make its way back to Skonnos, where the young slaves – and Romana – are to be handed over to the Nimon as a "tribute." The Doctor manages to patch up the TARDIS and follow the ship to Skonnos, where he is promptly thrown into the complex of the Nimon. But the Doctor quickly discovers that there's more than one Nimon – and the tributes of slaves and material from Skonnos are merely helping the Nimon's own invasion plans.

Tom Baker . . . . The Doctor
Lalla Ward . . . . Romana
David Brierly . . . . voice of K-9
Bob Appleby . . . . Nimon
John Bailey . . . . Sezom
Graham Crowden . . . . Soldeed
Janet Ellis . . . . Teka
Simon Gipps-Kent . . . . Seth
Trevor St. John Hacker . . . . Nimon
Bob Hornery . . . . Pilot
Clifford Norgate . . . . Nimon voice
Michael Osborne . . . . Sorak
Robin Sherringham . . . . Nimon

This story has been released on DVD

written by Anthony Read
directed by Kenny McBain
music by Dudley Simpson

Part 1 aired on December 22, 1979
Part 2 aired on December 29, 1979
Part 3 aired on January 5, 1980
Part 4 aired on January 12, 1980

Malcolm Terris . . . . Co-pilot

NEW WHO CONNECTIONS: A creature related to the Nimon is found to be at the heart of *The God Complex* (2011).

The Horns Of Nimon is one of those stories that seems to be perennially held in very low regard. But if the character of the Doctor is about anything at all, he's about not going with the status quo, so with that in mind, I thought I would watch *The Horns Of Nimon* afresh for the first time in what is probably 20 years, just to see if it's *really* that bad.

One thing that the critics seem to latch onto is the sheer amount of silliness on display in *Nimon*'s four episodes. This story is the height of Tom Baker's flippancy toward anyone or anything that's meant to pose a threat to him, defusing just about any dramatic tension that the story might be attempting to generate. (See also: the stripped-down TARDIS console falling apart to a symphony of well-worn comedy sound effects.) It doesn't help that, aside from the almost laughably unwieldly Nimon creatures, the chief "threat" in Nimon is Graham Crowden as Soldeed, a villain who's so over-the-top that one would've been hard-pressed to take him seriously in a 1960s story.

However, there's one thing to consider: this story's timing. If you look at the broadcast dates, *The Horns Of Nimon* began airing just before Christmas and became the story that took **Doctor Who** into the 1980s. Keeping in mind the British tradition of the Christmas pantomime, should we even be attempting to take *Nimon* seriously? Any more seriously than, say, *The Runaway Bride* and its own over-the-top villain?

Nimon also wasn't intended to end the 17th season on the silly note that it did; it was meant to be followed by the slightly more dramatic *Shada*, a Douglas Adams six-parter which was never finished. Perhaps what's missing from *The Horns Of Nimon* isn't so much the qualities of other classic **Doctor Who** stories; whats missing is *context*. Whether designed that way or not, *Nimon* was a holiday story. In short, there isn't a lot I can necessarily say in *Nimon*'s defense… but in its proper context, I'm not sure the story's earned quite the large number of brickbats that it seems to have drawn over the years.

SHADA

The Doctor and Romana come to St. Cedds College, Cambridge, to visit an old friend named Professor Chronotis. He has an item that they've come to retrieve on behalf of the Time Lords, for Chronotis is himself a renegade Time Lord in hiding, and he's in possession of "The Worshipful Law of Ancient Gallifrey," a book containing immense secrets. But the Doctor and Romana quickly realize that they're not the only ones trying to find Chronotis and his stolen book. A ruthless criminal, Skagra, hopes to find the secret location of the Time Lords' prison planet, Shada, where he means to release one of the most dangerous Gallifreyans in the history of the galaxy and gain his secret for controlling the entire universe with his mind alone. When he realizes that there are already Time Lords on the scene trying to get the book for themselves, Skagra adds the Doctor and Romana to his list of targets. But not even Chronotis has the book – he accidentally loaned it to two of his students at the college, who then carbon-dated it to an impossible age; those students are also hunted by Skagra. Once the chase brings the Doctor and friends to Shada itself, they learn something even more horrifying: the most dangerous criminal in history, the man Skagra hoped to befriend, is no long imprisoned there. Instead, he's been with the Doctor all along.

Tom Baker . . . . The Doctor	
Lalla Ward . . . . Romana	
David Brierly . . . . voice of K-9	
Victoria Burgoyne . . . . Clare Keightly	
Gerald Campion . . . . Porter	
Denis Carey . . . . Professor Chronotis	
James Coombes . . . . Krarg voices	
Shirley Dixon . . . . Ship	
Harry Fielder . . . . Krarg Commander	
John Hallett . . . . Constable	
Daniel Hill . . . . Chris Parsons	
James Muir . . . . Krarg	

This story has been released on DVD

written by Douglas Adams
directed by Pennant Roberts
music by Keff McCulloch (video release)

Christopher Neame . . . . Skagra	
Derek Pollitt . . . . Caldera	
Lionel Sansby . . . . Krarg	
David Strong . . . . Passenger	
Derek Suthern . . . . Krarg	
Reg Woods . . . . Krarg	

BEHIND THE SCENES: *Shada* was never finished or broadcast, due to a series of industrial strikes at the BBC which pushed the final studio shooting sessions back until they fell off the schedule and the six-parter missed its broadcast date; this had the rather unenviable effect of making *The Horns Of Nimon* — considered by more than a few fans to be one of the lowest points in the series' history — the swan song of producer Graham Williams. Incoming rookie producer John Nathan-Turner looked into salvaging *Shada* for broadcast, possibly as a Christmas special, but was unable to secure additional funding for this, much less schedule all of the necessary cast members again at the same time. As such, **the public's first glimpse of *Shada* was in the form of clips incorporated into 1983's *The Five Doctors*, which served as "new footage" of the fourth Doctor to cover for Tom Baker's absence from that story. *Shada*'s existing studio and complete location footage later saw release on VHS in 1992, with Tom Baker narrating those scenes which hadn't been shot; the story was also completely re-recorded by Big Finish Productions — in audio form only — with Paul McGann as the eighth Doctor, with revised dialogue indicating that the Doctor and Romana's original visit to St. Cedds having indeed been interrupted by their capture in *The Five Doctors*. The late Douglas Adams, for whom *Shada* also would have been his final work on the show, later offered his view that the story wasn't that noteworthy or exceptional, except in the minds of the show's fans due to its mysterious "unfinished" status. A 2009 BBC Radio documentary, *Shelved*, contended that the BBC allowed *Shada* to be derailed to put pressure on the union involved in the strike.

A.K.A.: Actor **Christopher Neame** is a familiar face in science fiction TV on both sides of the Atlantic. He has appeared in episodes of **Blake's 7, Beauty And The Beast, The Flash, Babylon 5** (as the unnamed "Knight" who induces Commander Sinclair's flashback to the Battle of the Line), **Star Trek: Voyager, Earth 2, Sliders,** and **Star Trek: Enterprise.** As a voice actor for video games, he's even dipped his toes into the *Star Wars* universe in the games *Jedi Knight: Dark Forces II* and *Star Wars: The Old Republic.* Non-genre audiences may have also seen him in **Murder, She Wrote, MacGyver, Dallas, Dynasty,** and *Ghostbusters II.*

NEW WHO CONNECTIONS: *Shada*'s script called for a rogues' gallery of all-star foes behind bars. But if there's a Dalek locked up in the prison on Shada, what makes that one Dalek so much more dangerous to the Time Lords than the rest of them? Perhaps this would've been our first glimpse of a member of the Cult of Skaro (*Doomsday*, 2006).

In 1979, the grand finale of **Doctor Who**'s seventeenth year on the air was scheduled to be the six-part *Shada*, written by Hitchhiker's Guide To The Galaxy scribe Douglas Adams and starring Denis Carey and Christopher. Due to a strike at the BBC, *Shada* had to be cancelled with only a few days' more studio work required to complete the story. All of the location filming and one of three studio sessions were already in the can, and because of the labor disputes, that's where they remained. Two short excerpts of the location footage were used to represent the fourth Doctor in the 1983 twentieth-anniversary special, in which Baker declined to appear. Many elements of Douglas Adams' novel Dirk Gently's Holistic Detective Agency were lifted straight out of the **Who** script and became a little more surreal and humorous for the printed page, but *Shada* itself remained a total enigma for over a decade.

Blazing onto videotape in a dubious cloud of glory, one wonders if perhaps *Shada*'s legendary status among **Who** fans hasn't been attained merely because of the "long-lost" nature of the story. It might have retained its mysterious luster had it remained buried in the BBC's video vaults, but in the ever-increasing crunch for new and interesting material to put on the retail shelves, it was inevitable that *Shada* would finally arrive in the stores.

Where the actual *Shada* footage is concerned, it doesn't take a lot of close examination to tell that it would've been one of the better stories of the much-maligned 1979 season. Christopher Neame is always in fine form as a slippery bad guy, and Denis Carey, who has appeared in other episodes of **Doctor Who** and **Blake's** 7, contributes much to any of his guest appearances with his haunting voice alone. His portrayal of a doddering old Time Lord masquerading as a Cambridge history professor finally allows him to delve further into the physical aspect of his role than usual.

The existing *Shada* footage is slated for inclusion in one of the final DVD releases of the classic **Doctor Who** range.

SHORT HOPS

...in which the author ponders Douglas Adams' influence on Doctor Who.

Douglas Adams, the writer of the wildly successful science fiction comedy phenomenon that was The Hitchhikers' Guide To The Galaxy, was the script editor of **Doctor Who** for two seasons. Compared to other renowned **Doctor Who** script editors as Terrance Dicks, Robert Holmes, David Whitaker, Andrew Cartmel or Eric Saward, Adams was practically a short-timer, and in his own writings and interviews, Adams admitted to having his attention deeply divided between **Doctor Who** and Hitchhikers' Guide during the production of the 1979 season. All things Hitchhiker were taking off and achieving escape velocity with surprising speed, leaving Adams with little enthusiasm for such tasks as fighting to keep the director and cast of **Doctor Who** - particularly one Mr. Baker - from taking every available opportunity to interpret the scripts as broad farce instead of science fiction drama.

For all of the scientifically-correct-but-still-technobabblish jargon of the Christopher Bidmead era, one wonders what Adams could have done if he'd been guiding **Doctor Who** in the early to mid-1980s, when everyone finally seemed to agree once more that it was a dramatic series at heart. Adams' own acquaintance with real science and real issues was growing exponentially at that point in his career, and could have paid huge dividends aboard the TARDIS. Or he might have grown to feel the same annoyance with John Nathan-Turner that Eric Saward did, in which case things might have turned out the way they did anyway.

But for the stamp that he's often credited with leaving on **Doctor Who**, is Adams really that much of an influence on the show?

For starters, it seems entirely likely that *Shada* wouldn't have quite the mystique that it has if not for it being an unfinished Adams story. "Trying to finish *Shada*" has practically become a cottage industry, with BBC Books, Big Finish and the entity formerly known as BBC Video all trying to "complete" the story in their own way. Even incoming producer John Nathan-Turner, while eager to make his own stamp on **Doctor Who**, lobbied hard for the completion of Shada from his predecessor's final season. Failing that, he did at least give the public its first glimpse of the existing *Shada* footage in *The Five Doctors*, a story in which Tom Baker might not otherwise have appeared (except, possibly, in waxwork form).

But after *Shada*, Adams was done with **Doctor Who**. Story outlines originally developed for **Doctor Who**, such as the unproduced *Doctor Who And The Krikkitmen*, were retrofitted into Hitchhiker's Guide novels

(Life, The Universe, And Everything); even *Shada*, which Adams was sure would never be seen or heard from again, was recycled into the first Dirk Gently novel. The Hitchhiker's Guide To The Galaxy was obviously Adams' new meal ticket. He would still patiently field interview questions about his time with **Doctor Who**, but there was no going back. His era lasted all of two seasons, one of them not exactly revered by fandom.

Arguably the most Adams-esque adventure the Doctor has endured since then was 2005's *The End Of The World*, but that's more of an exception than the norm: it stuck out like a sore thumb in a season that tended to be more Earthbound. Attempts to graft surreal science fiction humor in Adams' style onto literary **Doctor Who** have proven to be a similarly mixed bag: neither Eric Saward's blatantly Hitchhiker-esque novelization of *The Twin Dilemma* nor the New Adventures novel Sky Pirates! topped anyone's book lists, then or now.

Did Adams and Hitchhiker's Guide influence **Doctor Who** at all, or do they both share some of the same basic DNA that attracts fans to British science fiction in general? Consider this: most American-written, space-based SF presumes that two forces will carry us into space: the military or the government (**Star Trek, Babylon 5**, the various **Stargate** series, **Space: Above And Beyond**, countless others), and/or massive mega-corporations (the *Alien* movies). A third strand common to American-originated SF is that we'll plunder advanced alien technology that's been left behind, or given to us (frequently with some sort of Trojan horse attached, or as the result of some Faustian bargain), or that we've taken by force (**Stargate** and **Babylon 5** again, **Earth: Final Conflict**). It's the same post-NASA mindset that has left much of the American public unable to grasp the idea of privatized spaceflight.

British SF reflects its roots: colonialism (**Moonbase 3, Space: 1999**), smaller-scale commercial enterprise (**Red Dwarf**'s Jupiter Mining Corporation), and the mundane, such as police work (**Star Cops, Space Precinct**), will take us into space. Eccentric and inventive individuals will be able to make their own way (Hitchhiker's Guide). Very seldom does British SF celebrate the notion of military dominance of space, and when it does, it's usually a less than flattering scenario (the corrupt Federation of **Blake's 7**) or outright parody, and massive corporate presence in space is usually not seen as a good thing (see Hitchhiker's entities such as Sirius Cybernetics Corporation, or InfiniDim Enterprises, the outfit which takes over publication of the Guide itself in Mostly Harmless).

Douglas Adams' influence on **Doctor Who** really doesn't loom that large – he is, however, probably the one writer in the show's history whose name is best recognized. As much as he railed against the strictures and style of the series, it was an association that Adams was ready to sever when the time came. He acknowledged on numerous occasions that the character, and character flaws, of Ford Prefect were a reaction against the Doctor's willingness to interfere in any event where the day needed to be saved. But both **Doctor Who** and Hitchhiker's Guide share enough of the same traditions of British SF that it's nearly impossible to deny that they tickle the same gene and draw the same kinds of followers.

SEASON 18: 1980-81
THE LEISURE HIVE

The Doctor and Romana, after an unsuccessful attempt at a Brighton vacation, pay a visit to the war-torn planet Argolis. Laid to waste by a war between the native Argolins and the reptilian Foamasi, Argolis is now not much more than a deadly environment whose sole artificial structure – the Leisure Hive – is a holiday resort with an anti-war theme. The Argolins themselves are sterile, and have been sponsoring tachyon experiments conducted by a human named Hardin. Hardin boasts that he can use tachyonics to reverse the aging process of the Argolins, but in truth he's nowhere close to that goal. The arrival of two Time Lords seems to coincide with a wave of violence, including a man who appears to have been strangled with the Doctor's scarf. But the presence of two seasoned time travelers also threatens to unravel a plan to sell the defective tachyon technology to the Argolins...and the Doctor and Romana soon become targets themselves. To make matters worse, the brash young son of the Argolins' leader has plans to lift his people from a dying, pacifist race to conquerors of the galaxy.

Tom Baker . . . . The Doctor
Lalla Ward . . . . Romana
David Allister . . . . Stimson
David Bulbeck . . . . Foamasi
John Collin . . . . Brock
Adrienne Corri . . . . Mena
Alys Dyer . . . . Baby
Martin Fisk . . . . Vargos
David Haig . . . . Pangol
David Korff . . . . Foamasi
Nigel Lambert . . . . Hardin
Andrew Lane . . . . Chief Foamasi
Roy Montague . . . . Argolin Guide
James Muir . . . . Foamasi

This story has been released on DVD

written by David Fisher
directed by Lovett Bickford
music by Peter Howell

Part 1 aired on August 30, 1980
Part 2 aired on September 6, 1980
Part 3 aired on September 13, 1980
Part 4 aired on September 20, 1980

Clifford Norgate . . . . Generator voice
Laurence Payne . . . . Morix
Harriet Reynolds . . . . Tannoy voice
Ian Talbot . . . . Klout

NEW WHO CONNECTIONS: Another of the Doctor's incarnations undergoes a rapid-aging process at the conclusion of *The Sound Of Drums* (2007); as with his visit to *The Leisure Hive*, the Doctor's condition is reversed quickly. It seems unlikely that the Foamasi, with their pantomime-dinosaur tails and bulbous heads, could successfully disguise themselves as humans, unless they borrowed or stole the same technology that allowed the Slitheen (*Aliens Of London / World War Three*, 2005) to do exactly the same thing.

The Leisure Hive is John Nathan-Turner's first outing as the final producer of **Doctor Who** on British television. Depending on whether or not you enjoyed the decade that JN-T spent in the producer's office, you might then consider *Leisure Hive* to be the dawn of a new era for **Doctor Who**, or the beginning of the end. One has to look at the 18th season's premiere in context, however. Season 17, produced by Graham Williams, started strong with *Destiny Of The Daleks* and *City Of Death*, and went downhill from there. Season 17 culminated in the phenomenally silly *The Horns Of Nimon*, which drowned an intriguing premise with lousy scripts and a cast who seemed to refuse to take the story seriously. After that disappointing conclusion to the previous year, and the cancellation of the 17th season's final story (*Shada*), *Leisure Hive* isn't a bad season opener. Actually, it's fairly good no matter how you slice it.

One of my favorite things about JN-T's single season with Tom Baker as the Doctor is that he seemed to be moderately successful in wrenching the show back toward a dramatic tone, as opposed to the humorous feel that pervaded Graham Williams' stint in the producer's chair. Tom Baker, when told point-blank to play the role of the Doctor in a dramatic fashion, can do a damned good job of it – and the end of part one is an excellent example, with the cliffhanging moment of the Doctor screaming in agony as he seems to be torn apart inside the tachyon chamber. The "old man" makeup job on Baker after the sudden aging of the Doctor was above average as well.

As for the guest cast…it almost goes without saying that Adrienne Corri's maginificent performance as Mena overshadows the rest of the visiting actors. She brings dignity to a part that could so easily have been overlooked beneath her bizarre Argolin hair and makeup job. That she shines so brightly in her role – from self-assuredness to being beaten and tired – lends a great deal of credibility to a sometimes hard-to-follow storyline. Nigel Lambert also provides an excellent performance in the role of Hardin, who gradually evolves into a man with a conscience and winds up providing a trump card that saves the day.

The production values of *The Leisure Hive* are a huge step up from the previous season, but for a budget increase that was meant to bring **Doctor Who** into the age of *Star Wars*, it really only serves the bring the show neck-and-neck with a 1980 TV contemporary – the American-produced series **Buck Rogers In The 25th Century** – in terms of visual effects and the overall look of the production. Still, having said that, there's something fitting about the corrugated metal millieu of Argolis – it smacks of an artificial, prefabricated environment. I actually like the sets in this story quite a bit.

There are moments, however, when the attempts to put all of that money on the screen backfire. How many times do we have to see that shuttle landing? Or the point-the-camera-directly-into-a-studio-light sunrise? Some shaky camera work – very jumpy zooms and such – also detract from some moments meant to be intensely dramatic. Peter Howell's underscore – the first musical score created completely in-house at the BBC Radiophonic Workshop since 1972 – is effective in many places, but in a few places it's just as over-the-top and cheesy as some of the visuals…even when taking the style of the time into account.

It was good to see Tom Baker strutting his stuff as a dramatic Doctor instead of a woefully comedic Doctor. The previous few years' tongue-in-cheek performances had made me forget just how good an actor Mr. Baker can be.

MEGLOS

A power crisis in the underground habitat of the planet Tigella revives an age-old debate between science and religion. Tigella's scientists want to examine their power source, the otherworldly Dodecahedron, more closely to see if it can help to avert the impending crisis that would force the Tigellans back to their planet's uninhabitable surface. But the planet's religious faction, led by Lexa, refuses to allow anyone access to the Dodecahedron, which they claim is a sacred relic. Zastor, Tigella's leader, comes up with an unorthodox compromise: call for the Doctor's help. But just as the TARDIS responds to the call, another plan is set into motion: Meglos, the last surviving member of the cactus-like Zolpha-Thuran race, has enlisted the aid of Gaztak pirates to take over the physical form of a hapless human. Once Meglos has this ability, he uses it to impersonate the Doctor, go to neighboring Tigella, and steal the Dodecahedron for himself. To ensure that the real Doctor doesn't interfere with his plan, he traps the TARDIS in a chronic hysteresis – a time loop – from which the Doctor and Romana have to devise an ingenious escape. But by the time the real Time Lords arrive, the damage is done – the Dodecahedron is missing, and the Doctor is arrested for the gravest crime possible on Tigella.

Tom Baker . . . . The Doctor / Meglos
Lalla Ward . . . . Romana
John Leeson . . . . voice of K-9
Bill Fraser . . . . Grugger
Colette Gleeson . . . . Caris
Jacqueline Hill . . . . Lexa
Crawford Logan . . . . Deedrix
Christopher Owen . . . . Earthling
Simon Shaw . . . . Tigellan Guard
Frederick Treves . . . . Brotadac
Edward Underdown . . . . Zastor

This story has been released on DVD

written by John Flanagan
and Andrew McCulloch
directed by Terence Dudley
music by Peter Howell
and Paddy Kingsland

Part 1 aired on September 27, 1980
Part 2 aired on October 4, 1980
Part 3 aired on October 11, 1980
Part 4 aired on October 18, 1980

A.K.A.: This marks the only time that a former companion has returned to televised **Doctor Who** in a completely different role. **Jacqueline Hill** was one of the three original TARDIS travelers, Barbara Wright, in the earliest seasons of the series. Guest star **Bill Fraser** made himself infamous by claiming, during the publicity for *Meglos*, that he only took the part of General Grugger on the condition that he would get to kick K-9 onscreen. Apparently he was such a good adversary for the robot dog that he took on K-9 without the Doctor around to stop him in **K-9 & Company.**

The least effective story of Tom Baker's final season by miles, *Meglos* is just a bit of a mess. It can't decide if it's going to be highly dramatic or completely silly a la season 17, and it seems to be humping the leg of The Hitchhiker's Guide To The Galaxy the whole time, with the almost **Monty Python**-esque Gaztaks and their human prisoner who just wants to get home in time for tea. (The musical score, composed in part by Paddy Kingsland – who created music for Hitchhiker's radio and TV incarnations – makes things even more obvious.) Somewhere in here, one gets the impression that there was the vague germ of an idea about the ongoing struggle between religious fundamentalism and science, but that concept is quickly submerged by the end of part two and never manages to come up for air again.

Special effects-wise, though, *Meglos* tries new approaches to the execution of a completely virtual set. A new technique tried out on this episode, called "scene synch", involved locking two motion-control cameras together: one focused on actors in an entirely blue-screened set, the other aimed at a miniature environment. Objects on the blue-screen set were built to match elements of the miniature model, so that actors could appear to step behind foreground objects, and the camera could move and follow the action and keep everything in proper perspective. This solves a lot of the problems that were so glaringly obvious with *Underworld* just a few seasons before, and while the technique wasn't in use for long, some elements of it – namely a fully three-dimensional set painted blue to allow for the entire environment to be generated elsewhere – are still in use today. In retrospeect, it looks like actors blue-screened in on top of (or behind) miniatures, but it was a bold experiment for the time.

Jacqueline Hill became the first **Doctor Who** companion to return in another role here – actually, where the original series was concerned, she was the *only* actor to do so – and this character is very different from Barbara, though she's not all that different from any other eye-rollingly over-the-top religious figure in this genre or any other. Still, she gives it her best here, and as with her original **Doctor Who** stint, she makes Lexa impossible to ignore or take lightly. In other companion news, K-9 – through a rushed repair job aboard the TARDIS – is reduced to two hours of action before he has to shut down and recharge, the latest instance of the robotic dog being gradually emasculated in usefulness to wean the show's writers away from him (per instructions from producer John Nathan-Turner).

For its other faults, *Meglos* may actually contain the most interesting verbal description of the Doctor that the original series ever produced: "**He sees the threads that hold the universe together, and mends them when they break.**"

Meglos isn't a complete train wreck – there are pieces that are very entertaining – but those pieces add up to an uneven whole that really seems to belong more to the previous season than to this one.

FULL CIRCLE

The Doctor and Romana are en route back to Gallifrey when something strange happens to the TARDIS. Though it takes time for them to realize it, the TARDIS has fallen through a kind of wormhole into the alternate universe of E-space. Instead of Gallifrey, the Doctor has arrived on Alzarius, a planet whose small humanoid population is threatened by the onset of a deadly mist. During the time of mistfall, legend has it that spiders emerge from the indigenous fruit and deadly creatures appear. A troubled kid named Adric is trapped outside during mistfall, but stumbles into the TARDIS and befriends the Doctor and Romana. The Doctor soon finds that the horrific creatures that roam Alzarius during mistfall are more closely related to the besieged humanoids than either party realizes.

Tom Baker . . . . The Doctor
Lalla Ward . . . . Romana
Matthew Waterhouse . . . . Adric
John Leeson . . . . voice of K-9
Norman Bacon . . . . Marsh child
George Baker . . . . Login
James Bree . . . . Nefred
Stephen Calcutt . . . . Marshman
Tony Calvin . . . . Dexeter
Graham Cole . . . . Marshman
Andrew Forbes . . . . Omril
Adrian Gibbs . . . . Rysik
Keith Guest . . . . Marshman
James Jackson . . . . Marshman
Steve Kelly . . . . Marshman
Barney Lawrence . . . . Marshman

This story has been released on DVD

written by Andrew Smith
directed by Peter Grimwade
music by Paddy Kingsland

Part 1 aired on October 25, 1980
Part 2 aired on November 1, 1980
Part 3 aired on November 8, 1980
Part 4 aired on November 15, 1980

Leonard Maguire . . . . Draith
Bernard Padden . . . . Tylos
June Page . . . . Keara
Alan Rowe . . . . Garif
Steven Watson . . . . Marshman
Richard Willis . . . . Varsh

NEW WHO CONNECTIONS: In *The Doctor's Wife* (2011), a distress signal from another Time Lord draws the Doctor and his TARDIS into a "bubble universe," which may be similar to E-Space.

When you put a very clever story together with tremendously effective location filming and some of the show's best rubberized monsters, and add a catchy, atmospheric and positively hummable musical score by Paddy Kingsland, you get a knockout like *Full Circle*. The Doctor, Romana and K-9 all have plenty to do in the story, and the guest characters are unusually well-rounded. This is also the story in which Adric joins the TARDIS crew, becoming one of the least-liked companions in the show's history – quite unjustifiably, since he's one of the most intriguing parts of this particular story.

Full Circle gets one of my highest recommendations of the Tom Baker era of **Doctor Who**, though sometimes I wonder why the E-space trilogy was deemed a necessity – all three of the stories under that umbrella would have worked just fine as stand-alones. This one is a testament to the occasional benefits of JN-T's policy of seeking out new talent, as the story was originally sent in by a teenage fan of the show.

STATE OF DECAY

Still trapped in E-Space, the Doctor, Romana, K-9 and – unbeknownst to them – stowaway Adric arrive on a planet whose nomadic people live in deference to a trio of well-dressed royals – but their rulers are, in fact, vampires who worship an even more powerful vampire known as the Great One. The Doctor knows of the Great One too, recalling passages of ancient Gallifreyan history involving a pitch battle between Rassilon and the vampire race. The Doctor also realizes that the pieces are in place here to defeat the Great One once and for all, but before he can put his desperate plan into action, he may have already lost Adric to the vampires.

Tom Baker	The Doctor
Lalla Ward	Romana
Matthew Waterhouse	Adric
John Leeson	voice of K-9
Dean Allen	Karl
Thane Bettany	Tarak
Stuart Blake	Zoldaz
Alan Chuntz	Guard
Rachel Davies	Camilla
Stacy Davies	Veros
Stuart Fell	Roga
Clinton Greyn	Ivo
Arthur Hewlett	Kalmar
Emrys James	Aukon

This story has been released on DVD

written by Terrance Dicks
directed by Peter Moffatt
music by Paddy Kingsland

Part 1 aired on November 22, 1980
Part 2 aired on November 29, 1980
Part 3 aired on December 6, 1980
Part 4 aired on December 13, 1980

Rhoda Lewis	Marta
William Lindsay	Zargo
Iain Rattray	Habris

Man, if *this* didn't open a can of worms later on. After *State Of Decay*, you could scarcely mention vampires in **Doctor Who** – whether on TV or in print – without bringing Rassilon into it. (That was one of the reasons I loved *The Curse Of Fenric* so much – not a single mention!) Though it's certainly atmospheric, there's really not much that's new or innovative in this four-parter. It's momentarily interesting to think that Adric might sell out his new friends because life among the bloodsuckers may offer more promise. (Actually, considering what happened when Adric later helped the Doctor fight the Cybermen, one wonders if the budding mathematical genius didn't miscalculate…) And yet the notion of Gallifrey, led by Rassilon, in a sustained armed conflict with another world, is intriguing (and is kept intriguingly vague – frustrated would-be historians of the Time War, take note!).

On a more macabre note, take a look at how thin Tom Baker is in this story, even moreso than usual. He was suffering from a digestive disorder at the time and lost an unhealthy amount of weight during the location shoot.

WARRIORS' GATE

The TARDIS is boarded in mid-flight – a virtually unthinkable event – by Biroc, a lion-like Tharil who seems to be on the run from something. He brings the TARDIS to the zero point – an intersection between E-space and N-space that could finally get the Doctor back to his home universe. This is also of interest to Rorvik, the captain of a space freighter carrying a load of Tharil slaves. Rorvik's ship has been stranded here for some time, and his plans for escaping are growing more desperate and impractical. A mysterious and seemingly ancient gateway appears as space at the zero point begins to fall in upon itself. Romana is determined to free the Tharils from slavery, even if it means missing the chance to escape from E-space… but the Doctor learns the oppressed were once the oppressors, and there may be no justice for either party this time.

Tom Baker . . . . The Doctor
Lalla Ward . . . . Romana
Matthew Waterhouse . . . . Adric
John Leeson . . . . voice of K-9
Kenneth Cope . . . . Packard
Freddie Earle . . . . Aldo
Jeremy Gittins . . . . Lazlo
David Kincaid . . . . Lane
Vincent Pickering . . . . Sagan
Clifford Rose . . . . Rorvik
Robert Vowles . . . . Gundan
Harry Waters . . . . Royce
David Weston . . . . Biroc

This story has been released on DVD

written by Stephen Gallagher
directed by Paul Joyce
music by Peter Howell

Part 1 aired on January 3, 1981
Part 2 aired on January 10, 1981
Part 3 aired on January 17, 1981
Part 4 aired on January 24, 1981

NEW WHO CONNECTIONS: Dwarf star alloy, used by Rorvik and his crew to contain the Tharils and Romana, is also used to imprison the eleventh Doctor in *Day Of The Moon* (2011), though in that case it *does* let a time traveler — namely the TARDIS — escape.

This story marks a world record – it's the *only time anyone thought to use the Doctor's own scarf to try to strangle him* (omitting numerous occasions on which the Doctor almost managed to achieve this on his own). *Warriors' Gate* is a strange, high-concept story which jumps around in an occasionally confusing, non-linear fashion. In the years since, it has emerged that the studio sessions for this already-mystifying story were made even more frustrating by the glacial pace at which the director worked, necessitating a production assistant stepping up and effectively second-unit directing parts of the story himself. That production assistant's name was Graeme Harper, and he would become one of very few directors to make his mark on both classic and modern **Doctor Who**.

Warriors' Gate, as a story, may well be ahead of its time, using some intricately-thought-out science fiction elements to tackle the issues of oppression, slavery, and the sine-wave paths some civilizations carve through history, alternating between victims and victors.

One minor goof – Adric seems to automatically know how to flip a coin, or toss a coin as K-9 tells him. This is the same kid who, when told by the Doctor to cross his fingers in *Logopolis*, made a cross as if he was warding off vampires (which might have come in handy in *State Of Decay*). It would have rung true, and would have been funnier, if Adric had tossed the coin across the room rather than instantly catching on to this distinctly Earthly expression.

THE KEEPER OF TRAKEN

The dying Keeper of the harmonious Union of Traken summons the Doctor to help his world as his reign comes to a close. Normally the Keeper would never summon outside help, but in this case an otherworldly evil is slowly preparing to take control of the Union, and otherworldly help will be needed to defeat it. But as betrayals and complacency allow a malignant alien to assume the Keepership – and with it enormous power – the Doctor is slow to realize that this particular adversary is known to him personally. Though he is able to preserve Traken's people, the Doctor is unaware that his greatest adversary has gained a new lease on life.

Tom Baker . . . . The Doctor
Matthew Waterhouse . . . . Adric
Anthony Ainley . . . . Tremas
Geoffrey Beevers . . . . Melkur
Denis Carey . . . . The Keeper
Roland Oliver . . . . Neman
Sheila Ruskin . . . . Kassia
Robin Soans . . . . Luvic
Sarah Sutton . . . . Nyssa
Margot Van De Burgh . . . . Katura
John Woodnutt . . . . Seron

This story has been released on DVD

written by Johnny Byrne
directed by John Black
music by Roger Limb

Part 1 aired on January 31, 1981
Part 2 aired on February 7, 1981
Part 3 aired on February 14, 1981
Part 4 aired on February 21, 1981

The Union of Traken is one of the most detailed and interesting alien cultures seen in the history of **Doctor Who**, and in some ways, the Source that provides the Keeper with his power is very similar to the Great Machine of Epsilon 3 in numerous episodes of **Babylon 5**, though there are numerous hints that the harmony that Traken enjoys is an extension of the will of the sitting Keeper; since the Master is able to force his will onto Kassia, Tremas and even the Doctor, this is not an unreasonable assumption. If this is indeed the case, it's a wonder that there hadn't been a corrupt Keeper in Traken's past – or perhaps there was, and that history has been carefully buried. Now you begin to see why it's sad that Traken was never visited in later stories (barring the Big Finish audio *Primeval*), but in any case, the entire Union was destroyed in *Logopolis*.

Anthony Ainley, who became the Master at the end of part four, was very good as Councillor Tremas, though Sheila Ruskin tended to overdo her role as his wife. Denis Carey's guest appearances are always welcome, whether on **Doctor Who** or **Blake's 7** (he previously appeared in *Shada*, though that story itself failed to appear, and later in 1985's *Timelash*), though he is covered in makeup and confined to a chair for most of *Traken*.

Perhaps *Traken*'s best feature is the far-too-short-lived pairing of Tom Baker's Doctor and Matthew Waterhouse as Adric. With the next story bringing back Nyssa, adding Tegan and then regenerating the Doctor at the end, the unique dynamic of this story – of a teacher with a very promising student in tow – became a one-off. Without Romana and K-9 around to make the bright lad look dim by comparison, Adric is a very enjoyable companion for the fourth Doctor. This story also forms the basis for a much later bit of continuity – the Master can take over someone else's body, displacing their mind completely and assuming their form permanently. This is vital to the plot of the 1996 TV movie starring Paul McGann.

LOGOPOLIS

After he takes complete measurements of a British Police Box, the inspiration for the exterior appearance of the TARDIS, the Doctor plans to visit Logopolis to seek the help of the mathematical geniuses there, whose near-mystic incantations of intricate mathematical formulas actually keep the universe from dying a premature death. Thanks to the interference of the Master, the Doctor becomes trapped, and an Australian stewardess named Tegan wanders into the TARDIS, assuming it to be a real Police Box. The Doctor also receives a distress call from Nyssa, whose father has gone missing on Traken. A mysterious ghostly figure appears and disappears, but the Doctor remains silent as to its identity, and the Master finally emerges from the shadows on Logopolis, poised to destroy the universe by eliminating its guardians. All the while, the TARDIS cloister bell counts down last remaining hours of the Doctor's fourth life.

Tom Baker . . . . The Doctor
Matthew Waterhouse . . . . Adric
Janet Fielding . . . . Tegan
Sarah Sutton . . . . Nyssa
Anthony Ainley . . . . The Master
John Fraser . . . . Monitor
Tom Georgeson . . . . Detective Inspector
Christopher Hurst . . . . Security Guard
Ray Knight . . . . Policeman
Peter Roy . . . . Policeman
Robin Squire . . . . Pharos Technician
Derek Suthern . . . . Policeman
Dolores Whiteman . . . . Aunt Vanessa

This story
has been
released
on DVD

written by Christopher H. Bidmead
directed by Peter Grimwade
music by Paddy Kingsland

Part 1 aired on February 28, 1981
Part 2 aired on March 7, 1981
Part 3 aired on March 14, 1981
Part 4 aired on March 21, 1981

NEW WHO CONNECTIONS: The Master's catchy address — "peoples of the universe, please attend carefully..." — is repeated in the closing moments of *The Sound Of Drums* (2007) as he reveals that, despite being full of hot air and crazy ideas like many politicians, he really *isn't* Prime Minister Harold Saxon.

SARAH JANE CONNECTIONS: The Pharos Institute, from whose radio telescope antenna the fourth Doctor falls at the end of Logopolis, is still operating in the 21st century. Sarah Jane Smith calls upon their expertise in the **Sarah Jane Adventures** episodes *The Lost Boy* (2007) and *Day Of The Clown* (2008).

It's been said that the 1980s were an area of **Doctor Who** where style triumphed over storytelling substance, and I suppose that this argument could be made for *Logopolis*. It might just be that I've never been terribly fond of math, but at times *Logopolis* is quite simply incomprehensible. One of the worst faults is the concept that the Master would even contemplate trying to hold the *entire universe* hostage. This is a silly idea even when applied to taking over the world, but the thought of taking the entire cosmos hostage (and worse yet, broadcasting a "ransom note" from a radio telescope) is pure B-movie fodder.

Janet Fielding and Sarah Sutton make their first appearances as companions, Sutton having already appeared in *The Keeper Of Traken*, but the most interesting dynamic, over the first two episodes, is the relationship between the Doctor and Adric, a quirky mentor-and-student routine which ended with this episode. I think that more people would have appreciated the oft-maligned Adric (and actor Matthew Waterhouse) had this combination been explored more.

Given the abstract nature of the story, what atmosphere there is can probably be credited to yet another catchy (though, in this case, a bit repetitive) Paddy Kingsland musical score, and the viewer's knowledge that this is Tom Baker's final appearance as the Doctor. Unlike previous outgoing-Doctor stories that trundled along at their own pace, *Logopolis* is the first that really depends on the audience's awareness – in advance – that this is the incumbent Doctor's final story. (Contrast that with *The Tenth Planet*, or even the shock faux regeneration ending of *The Stolen Earth*, both of which were far stealthier surprises.)

The Fifth Doctor
(Peter Davison: 1982-84)

Faced with the unenviable task of replacing a character actor who had become nothing short of a national institution, producer John Nathan-Turner elected to go with someone he'd worked with before, someone he knew to have an even temperament, a good sense of fun and also a good sense of when to get down to work. Prior to working on **Doctor Who** as a unit production manager, Nathan-Turner had served in that capacity on the popular series **All Creatures Great And Small**, based on James Herriot's popular book series, where he met Peter Davison. Struck by the actor's professionalism, Nathan-Turner called on Davison again to replace Tom Baker as the Doctor, and Davison's initial reaction was to say that he felt he was too young for the part. Nathan-Turner's persistence finally brought Davison on board. At this point, Davison sought out Tom Baker for advice on playing the part, but in many interviews since, Davison says all he got were two words shouted across a pub: "Good luck!"

Nathan-Turner, Davison, and new script editor Eric Saward set about sketching out a character for the fifth Doctor. Nathan-Turner and Saward were keen on the idea of dispensing with Baker's near-infallible cool, making the new Doctor a little less certain of whether or not he could control a given situation. They both felt that the suspense of the series' legendary cliffhangers was undermined by Baker's wink-and-a-nod approach to the job, which seemed to tell the audience that no matter what happened, the Doctor and friends would escape unscathed. To that end, Saward wrote a script of his own which would point out the Doctor's vulnerability in the most essential way: one of his companions would die in the course of an adventure.

For the new Doctor's image, and indeed that of the new trio of companions introduced at the very end of Tom Baker's reign, John Nathan-Turner wanted readily-identifiable, marketable looks. Having remembered Davison's penchant for after-filming cricket games, Nathan-Turner wanted the Doctor costumed in Edwardian-era cricket garb, but again with the question mark lapels that had been introduced in Tom Baker's last season. Davison wasn't opposed to the idea, but later voiced some concerns that it made him too conspicuous. Airline hostess Tegan would be sticking with her flight uniform, and Adric and Nyssa wore the costumes from their debut adventures full-time.

The first season of Davison's Doctor would also pose another new challenge: the BBC scheduled it on Monday and Tuesday nights, instead of its traditional Saturday evening time slot. Just shy of its 20th anniversary, new episodes of **Doctor Who** would now be broadcast during the week for the first time ever. This also effectively cut the suspense of the show's multi-episode stories in half, as Monday cliffhangers were only 24 hours away from being resolved, instead of a week.

Davison's first season was well-received by audiences. *Four To Doomsday* and the challenging philosophical drama of *Kinda* were indicative of the new direction Nathan-Turner had wanted for the show when he started, and *The Visitation* - a Saward script submitted the previous year when the script editor was just another freelancer - was typical of the new approach to historical settings: some extraterrestrial influence would frequently been seen as the cause for historical events (in this case, the Great Fire of London). Following this, Nathan-Turner and Saward pulled off a major coup with *Earthshock*, a story introducing a reinvigorated, all-conquering new style of Cybermen. Nathan-Turner had closed this story's studio filming sessions off to anyone not directly involved with production, and had even declined a chance to get front cover exposure for the Cybermen's return in the <u>Radio Times</u>, the BBC's TV listings magazine. As a result, the venerable adversaries' return was a complete surprise to the audience - as was the death of Adric at the end of part four. Matthew Waterhouse, upset at being written out of the show so permanently, was still under contract for another story: he appeared as Adric's ghost in the season closer, *Time-Flight*. That story also seemed to do away with Tegan, though she would return the following season despite being left behind on Earth by the Doctor.

For the 20th anniversary season, Nathan-Turner was adamant on reflecting the series' past in each story. In some cases, this was quite a stretch - *Mawdryn Undead* was intended to bring back Ian Chesterton, one of the original companions from the Hartnell era, while *Arc Of Infinity* referred back to the tenth anniversary story, *The Three Doctors*, by bringing back its villain, Omega. Some of these other continuity references were less far-reaching: a trilogy of stories late in the season would reintroduce the Black and White Guardians from Tom Baker's Key To Time season, and *Snakedance* was a direct sequel to a very recent story, *Kinda*. And the season was designed to close with Eric Saward's *Sentinel*, pitting the fifth Doctor against the Daleks for the first time.

Not all of these plans went off without a hitch. William Russell was unavailable to reprise his role, so *Mawdryn Undead* was rewritten to include Nicholas Courtney as Brigadier Lethbridge-Stewart - now retired, and now teaching math at a boys' school (a relic of the original plotline - the Ian Chesterton character had always been a teacher since the series' inception). Industrial strikes within the BBC also canned *Sentinel*, robbing the season of its climactic story, but the BBC had other plans as well. International co-funding deals had been secured to mount a special, feature-length 20th anniversary story - and now John Nathan-Turner and Eric Saward had to create that story out of the blue, as none of the already-commissioned scripts were suitable for the occasion.

But first they had plans for the remainder of the season. Sarah Sutton wanted to opt out of the series about halfway through the season, so plans were made not only for her exit, but for her replacement. A new male companion was devised, and he would be introduced under less-than-ideal circumstances: he would be on the losing end of a shady bargain with the Black Guardian, on a mission to kill the Doctor. This story arc was intended to play out over three successive stories, with the new companion's redemption being part of the third story.

The first story of the season, *Arc Of Infinity*, brought Tegan back into the fold and took the Doctor back to Gallifrey, where it is discovered that someone is trying to take over his body - a possibility grave enough to merit summary execution. Curiously enough, the captain of the guard on Gallifrey was played by an actor named Colin Baker, who would come to figure prominently in the history of **Doctor Who** just a year later. *Snakedance* revisited the events of *Kinda*, but also raised the same confused response from some viewers as this also meant revisiting that story's Buddhist overtones and internalized drama. The Brigadier's reintroduction and the arrival of Turlough, the new male companion, occurred as planned in *Mawdryn Undead*, which also featured a flashback montage of footage dating back to the Troughton era as the Brigadier regains his memory of the Doctor's adventures. Nyssa departed at the end of the following story, *Terminus*, and Turlough was redeemed and somewhat uneasily continued his TARDIS travels after helping the Doctor defeat the Black Guardian in *Enlightenment*. With *Sentinel* struck from the schedule, the season closed on the two-part *The King's Demons*, involving the Master trying to prevent the signing of the Magna Carta. That story also introduced another new companion - a talking, shapeshifting robot called Kamelion.

Originally demonstrated to John Nathan-Turner by its creator, Kamelion was an engineering marvel capable of movement and speech. But just before *The King's Demons* could be filmed, the man responsible for creating the robot and its hardware died - and no documentation for its more detailed functions could be found. In its first story, Kamelion was therefore spoken for by actor Gerald Flood, and made very little movement. Its future appearances would be cut back drastically in planning for the next season.

Now John Nathan-Turner and Eric Saward had to crunch to get a 20th anniversary special ready for November. Both agreed that a full-scale reunion of surviving Doctors and companions and villains was in order, though there were some practical hurdles to this task: William Hartnell had died in 1975, and every actor's schedule had to be considered. Little did they know that, compared to some obstacles that would appear later, the death of the show's original lead actor would almost prove to be minor. Knowing that crafting a story around so many pre-existing elements would be a challenge, Saward's first choice to write the script for the special was a favorite of his from the Pertwee era: Robert Holmes.

Holmes took his best shot at a multi-Doctor script, even incorporating an android version of the Hartnell Doctor; John Nathan-Turner had spotted an actor named Richard Hurndall in a fourth-season episode of **Blake's 7**, playing the part of an old man with mannerisms somewhat similar to the first Doctor. By making the first Doctor a decoy, Holmes could account for the fact that the portrayal would be different. But ultimately, Holmes informed Saward that he couldn't weave all of these elements into a coherent, single 90-minute story. Saward turned to another reliable known quantity from **Doctor Who**'s past, former Pertwee-era script editor Terrance Dicks. Dicks turned in a script titled *The Five Doctors*, pitting the fifth Doctor against the Master in Gallifrey's notoriously inescapable "Death Zone", while the fourth Doctor weathered political intrigue within the High Council of the Time Lords, and the other three incarnations worked their way through the Death Zone for a final confrontation. For the first time in the show's history, Cybermen, Daleks, Yeti and other menaces would combine their forces to destroy the Doctor. (A sequence featuring the first appearance of the Autons since 1971 was dropped at a late stage.)

But as the start of production on *The Five Doctors* drew near, an unexpected complication arose: Tom Baker didn't want to reprise his role. Dicks literally got the call to rewrite his script at 2:00am while attending a science fiction convention in New Orleans. Nathan-Turner had tried and failed to talk Baker into returning, but the actor had decided to put the part behind him permanently. *The Five Doctors* would now be reduced to four, but clever use of the never-aired footage from the unfinished *Shada* provided a way to work "new footage" of Baker into the show. Otherwise, the special went off without a hitch - Patrick Troughton, in particular, was happy enough during filming to plant the idea in John Nathan-Turner's ear for another story bringing the second Doctor into the series' present. *The Five Doctors* aired in November to a rapt reaction from the fans, the primary complaint being that it actually aired in America a few days earlier - and on the actual November 23rd anniversary date.

Planning for the 21st season was now underway as well, though Peter Davison had made it clear that he was ready to bow out of the role at the end of his third year (he later attributed this time limit to advice given to him by Patrick Troughton). As with the 20th season, there were numerous elements from **Doctor Who**'s past woven into the stories: the season opener, *Warriors Of The Deep*, brought back the Silurians and Sea Devils, both of whom hadn't been seen since Jon Pertwee's era. Eric Saward's *Sentinel* script was dusted off and retitled *Resurrection Of The Daleks*. Both Mark Strickson and Janet Fielding announced their own plans to move on, so Turlough and Tegan would each receive a farewell story (in Tegan's case, it was written into the end of *Resurrection Of The Daleks*). Turlough would bow out in the following story, *Planet Of Fire*, which also saw off Kamelion (now almost entirely immobile) and introduced Nicola Bryant as Perpugilliam "Peri" Brown, the new companion. For the role, Bryant affected an American accent, as Nathan-Turner wanted to buck the tradition of what he referred to as "Earth-UK companions" (in fact, the last such companion had been Sarah Jane Smith).

The following story, *Caves Of Androzani*, sported a thickly-plotted Robert Holmes script and the fifth regeneration of the Doctor, but it wasn't the last story of the season. Nathan-Turner wanted to give viewers an entire adventure with the new Doctor before the series took its customary break for the rest of the year - and thus Colin Baker made an early debut as the sixth Doctor.

SEASON 19: 1982
CASTROVALVA

Chaos ensues in the wake of the Doctor's regeneration. Security guards at the Pharos Project arrest Tegan, Nyssa and Adric, who are just beginning to try to comprehend what has happened to the Doctor, let alone help him. They manage to divert the guards and get the Doctor back to the TARDIS, but at the last moment, the Master's TARDIS appears, blocking Adric's escape. The Master then disappears again, and Adric returns to help the Doctor, who is trying to find the recuperative Zero Room. Adric has also gotten the TARDIS underway to its next destination – which turns out to be the explosive event which created the Milky Way. The Doctor, still experiencing sudden changes of personality, is barely able to help Tegan and Nyssa evade disaster by jettisoning parts of the TARDIS, and Adric is nowhere to be found. But when the Zero Room is accidentally blasted away in the emergency, the Doctor's friends must find a place where he can recover. And all too conveniently, the relaxing planet of Castrovalva is at the top of the list.

Peter Davison . . . . The Doctor
Janet Fielding . . . . Tegan
Sarah Sutton . . . . Nyssa
Matthew Waterhouse . . . . Adric
Anthony Ainley . . . . The Master
Dallas Cavell . . . . Head of Security
Souska John . . . . Child
Michael Sheard . . . . Mergrave
Derek Waring . . . . Shardovan
Frank Wylie . . . . Ruther

This story has been released on DVD

written by Christopher H. Bidmead
directed by Fiona Cumming
music by Paddy Kingsland

Part 1 aired on January 4, 1982
Part 2 aired on January 5, 1982
Part 3 aired on January 11, 1982
Part 4 aired on January 12, 1982

The fifth Doctor's first adventure is, like *Logopolis* before it (written by the same writer), a strange exercise in mathematical concepts as the complication of the plot, but the story is at least interesting, if only for the first two episodes. It's still more than a little baffling as to what Adric is being forced to do, and how the Master is forcing him to do it – remember, Adric hadn't heard of the "block transfer computation" method of altering the physical universe through pure mathematics until just the previous story, which led directly into this one, so when did he gain the proficiency necessary to create an entire planet and its people with his mind, to say nothing of changing the course of the TARDIS?

Peter Davison's "post regeneration mental breakdown" is an inspired performance, but one which is the tip of the iceberg of one of the big problems with the John Nathan-Turner era: somewhere, someone became convinced that what fans wanted to see was a constant stream of reminders of the show's past. The reminiscing in *Castrovalva* goes no further than Davison's fleeting, manic impersonations of the Doctor's previous incarnations (no better and no worse than Matt Smith's similar performance in 2011's *The Almost*

People), but in some later adventures the callbacks would become all-consuming, seeming to assume an audience well-versed in **Doctor Who** lore.

Janet Fielding and Sarah Sutton carry the first two episodes, since the Doctor is tucked away into a cabinet made from pieces of the TARDIS much of the time, and Adric is in the clutches of the Master, and they're certainly up to the challenge of being competent companions. Sadly, especially for Tegan, these two companions weren't given many more chances to shine in later stories.

FOUR TO DOOMSDAY

The Doctor, trying to return Tegan to Heathrow Airport, manages to get the TARDIS to the correct time and date – but in the wrong place, landing aboard a vast spaceship which is slowly making its way toward Earth. The Doctor and his friends eventually meet Monarch, ruler of the alien Urbankans, who are preparing to visit Earth on what Monarch claims is a mission of peace. But it seems that the Urbankans have already paid Earth a visit – representatives of various periods and cultures in the planet's past. But none of it is real – the "abductees" aren't really human, and Monarch's mission is one of conquest, not peace.

Peter Davison . . . . The Doctor
Janet Fielding . . . . Tegan
Sarah Sutton . . . . Nyssa
Matthew Waterhouse . . . . Adric
Nadia Hammam . . . . Villagra
Stratford Johns . . . . Monarch
Burt Kwouk . . . . Lin Futu
Annie Lambert . . . . Enlightenment
Philip Locke . . . . Bigon
Illario Bisi Pedro . . . . Kurkutji
Paul Shelley . . . . Persuasion

This story
has been
released
on DVD

written by Terence Dudley
directed by John Black
music by Roger Limb

Part 1 aired on January 18, 1982
Part 2 aired on January 19, 1982
Part 3 aired on January 25, 1982
Part 4 aired on January 26, 1982

An interesting story is let down by some of the Davison era's worst character writing. Where *Four To Doomsday* sinks the lowest is in its portrayal of the Doctor's three companions. Though Adric has some distinct personality problems, and Doctors and companions had bickered and would continue to argue before and after this story, this was really the low point in terms of writing Tegan, Nyssa and Adric. In the second half of the story, Tegan and Nyssa actually fight each other physically, and a hysterical Tegan even hijacks the TARDIS, leaving the Doctor, Nyssa and Adric stranded on Monarch's ship in a hostile situation. While she does have a good reason to try to move the TARDIS – she's trying to reach Earth to warn them of the impending invasion – her endangerment of the only people who could stop that very invasion is almost inexcusable. And, between this story and *State Of Decay*, Adric's vulnerability to the lure of power makes him a liability as well. All of these things don't exactly make Tegan and Adric sympathetic characters that the audience would enjoy watching on a regular basis, not to mention the average viewer wondering why the Doctor would allow them to keep traveling with him in the first place.

There's also the time-filling argument between the three companions in the TARDIS in part one as the Doctor explores outside. For no readily apparent reason, Adric bleats a number of sexist insults, again taking him down several notches in the audience empathy department.

Still, it's not all bad. As science fiction concepts go, *Four To Doomsday*'s basic premise is sound, and there's a very interesting zero-G sequence where the Doctor is trying to reach the TARDIS — it may not be *Apollo 13*, but for the BBC, it's very good indeed. Though it may seem like a strange thing to focus on, this story's sets were very interesting too, very functional-looking and chunky, with doors that would light up internally when they opened.

KINDA

On the planet Deva Loka, an investigation team studies the primitive native Kinda people, and are rather alarmed when the Doctor and Adric are rounded up by an automatic security device. The Doctor has brought the TARDIS to Deva Loka so Nyssa can rest and recover from her expeiences aboard Monarch's ship. Tegan, in a nearby forest, drifts off to sleep and is visited by the Kinda, and her body is inhabited by an evil spirit from their lore, the Mara. The Doctor learns that, pending the final report from the increasingly unstable investigators, the Kinda could be displaced by human colonization of their world…unless all of them are destroyed by the Mara first.

Peter Davison	. . . .	The Doctor
Janet Fielding	. . . .	Tegan
Sarah Sutton	. . . .	Nyssa
Matthew Waterhouse	. . . .	Adric
Lee Cornes	. . . .	Trickster
Nerys Hughes	. . . .	Todd
Adrian Mills	. . . .	Aris
Roger Milner	. . . .	Anicca
Mary Morris	. . . .	Panna
Sarah Prince	. . . .	Karuna
Simon Rouse	. . . .	Hindle
Jeffrey Stuart	. . . .	Dukkha

This story has been released on DVD

written by Christopher Bailey
directed by Peter Grimwade
music by Peter Howell

Part 1 aired on February 1, 1982
Part 2 aired on February 2, 1982
Part 3 aired on February 8, 1982
Part 4 aired on February 9, 1982

Richard Todd	. . . .	Sanders
Anna Wing	. . . .	Annatta

SARAH JANE CONNECTIONS: The Trickster who appears here is obviously <u>not</u> the terrifying extradimensional being who makes several attempts on Sarah's life in **The Sarah Jane Adventures** (*Whatever Happened To Sarah Jane?*, 2007; *The Temptation Of Sarah Jane Smith*, 2008; *The Wedding Of Sarah Jane Smith*, 2009), tries to change Donna's destiny (*Turn Left*, 2008) or tries to interfere with American history (**Torchwood:** *Immortal Sins*, 2011).

Kinda is a radical departure from the typical structure of a **Doctor Who** adventure, including an extremely rare foray into the externalization of internal dialogue in the scenes where Tegan, standing in a black void, is confronted by the old couple, the Trickster, and finally herself. (This device has since been used *ad nauseum* in other genre shows.) This also gives Janet Fielding a rare chance to shine, since talent is usually submerged well beneath the dreck of the usual scenes where Tegan gripes at her fellow TARDIS travelers. But just to make sure we don't miss that aspect of the series, there was yet another senseless squabble between Adric and Tegan toward the end.

The mental instability of Sanders and Hindle is a truly scary random factor of the story, and all of the guest stars are excellent. A highly recommended adventure…despite the Cheesy Giant Snake in part four! If you like *Kinda*, you may also want to watch the 1983 sequel story, *Snakedance*, which is the last we've seen of the Mara — one of the very few "repeat offenders" villains invented during the '80s — on television to date.

THE VISITATION

The Doctor finally lands the TARDIS at Heathrow – in the 1600s, long before air travel – and immediately becomes the object of hostility from the locals, who fear for their lives since a falling star heralded the coming of a new and virulent plague. They befriend a rogue named Richard Mace, who is helpful as a guide, but is almost useless as a protector when they find an android lurking in an abandoned house. Tegan is stunned and Adric is taken prisoner, while the Doctor, Nyssa and Mace escape. Tegan and Adric are interrogated by a hideously wounded Terrileptil creature, the master of the android, and self-declared destroyer of mankind.

Peter Davison . . . . The Doctor
Janet Fielding . . . . Tegan
Sarah Sutton . . . . Nyssa
Matthew Waterhouse . . . . Adric
John Baker . . . . Ralph
Anthony Calf . . . . Charles
James Charlton . . . . Miller
Eric Dodson . . . . Headman
Valerie Fyfer . . . . Elizabeth
Richard Hampton . . . . Villager
Michael Leader . . . . Terileptil
Michael Melia . . . . Terileptil
Michael Robbins . . . . Richard Mace
John Savident . . . . Squire John

This story has been released on DVD

written by Eric Saward
directed by Peter Moffatt
music by Paddy Kingsland

Part 1 aired on February 15, 1982
Part 2 aired on February 16, 1982
Part 3 aired on February 22, 1982
Part 4 aired on February 23, 1982

David Summer . . . . Terileptil
Peter Van Dissel . . . . Android
Jeff Wayne . . . . Scytheman
Neil West . . . . Poacher

BEHIND THE SCENES: The Doctor's beloved sonic screwdriver is destroyed by a Terileptil in this story, but in reality the hit on the Doctor's signature tool was ordered by producer John Nathan-Turner, who felt the screwdriver had become a catch-all escape hatch for the Time Lord (and a lazy fallback for writers). Given what we've seen the new series sonic screwdriver accomplish since its comeback, one sometimes wonders if JN-T didn't have a point. (To be fair, the comeback actually happened in the 1996 Paul McGann TV movie, in which the seventh and eighth Doctors were seen to be in possession of a rebuilt sonic screwdriver modeled after the fourth Doctor's.) The sonic screwdriver was left for dead through the remainder of the fifth Doctor's reign and all of the sixth Doctor's reign; the seventh also operated without the device in all of his BBC-made episodes. The only Doctors never to have wielded the sonic screwdriver at all are the first and the sixth incarnations.

Lodged in between *Kinda* and *Earthshock*, *The Visitation* - future script editor Eric Saward's first contribution to **Doctor Who** – is interesting, but not as showy as its season 19 stablemates. Peter Davison grows ever more assured in the lead role, and spends much of this four-parter with Michael Robbins as the lovable rogue Richard Mace (though, truth be told, Mace isn't *that* lovable). The Doctor does, however, suffer from the script, which shows him leaving two of his companions to fend for themselves against a deadly alien menace – an action very unlike the Doctor in any of his regenerations.

The Terileptils are astonishing animatronic creations for a BBC TV series circa 1981/82. That so much effort was put into their elaborate alien appearance without a rematch is one of the biggest surprises of this era of the show; the Terileptils practically cried out for a return engagement, and never got one. (Given the acrimonious nature of writer and future script editor Eric Saward's exit from **Doctor Who** a few years later, however, the lack of a comeback isn't completely surprising.)

The Visitation is a simple story with a fair amount of action, but it's a story that would've been much better if told in two or three episodes as opposed to meandering through four half-hours.

BLACK ORCHID

The TARDIS brings the Doctor and his friends to a railway station in 1925, where a car is waiting for them – and the Doctor seems to be expected by name. He and his companions are taken to Lord Cranleigh's estate, where the Doctor turns the tide in a game of cricket. But as all the guests prepare for a fancy dress party, the Doctor's costume is stolen and his curiosity leads him down a hidden passage in the house. By the time the Doctor emerges, he is the prime suspect in at least two murders – and due to his own disappearance into the house's secret passageways, he has no alibi. Someone in the house does know who the real killer is, but if she tips her hand, other dreadful secrets could destroy the Cranleigh family.

Peter Davison . . . . The Doctor
Janet Fielding . . . . Tegan
Sarah Sutton . . . . Nyssa
Matthew Waterhouse . . . . Adric
Timothy Block . . . . Tanner
Michael Cochrane . . . . Lord Cranleigh
Brian Hawksley . . . . Brewster
Caron Heggie . . . . Ann's maid
Derek Hunt . . . . Footman
Ahmed Khalil . . . . Latoni
Gareth Milne . . . . George Cranleigh
James Muir . . . . Police driver
Barbara Murray . . . . Lady Cranleigh
Vanessa Paine . . . . Ann Talbot

This story has been released on DVD

written by Terence Dudley
directed by Ron Jones
music by Roger Limb

Part 1 aired on March 1, 1982
Part 2 aired on March 2, 1982

Ivor Salter . . . . Sergeant Markham
Andrew Tourell . . . . Constable Cummings
Moray Watson . . . . Sir Robert Muir
David Wilde . . . . Digby

Though it's a very short story by **Doctor Who** standards, and features virtually no science fiction elements, Black Orchid is a fascinating and charming little story. We find out that, despite the fact that she doesn't appear to be appreciably older than Adric and Nyssa, Tegan seems to be of legal drinking age (she orders a screwdriver, and Nyssa unwittingly asks for the same, which gets a quick "ahem" from the Doctor), and there is at least one scene that lends some credence to fan speculation that Adric has a bit of a crush on Nyssa. (It always surprised me, in fact, that this element wasn't played up more often.) When his host refers to "the master" (as in the master of the house), the Doctor is gripped by a momentary fear that this is a reference to the Master (as in Anthony Ainley), a rather humorous continuity non-sequitur (though it's actually a recycled gag from *The Evil Of The Daleks*).

All in all, this is a simple, enjoyable two-parter, just the right length for a show which avoids **Doctor Who**'s usual science fiction trappings, to great effect.

EARTHSHOCK

A 26th century geological expedition is ambushed underground, leaving only a single survivor. When she crawls her way back to the surface camp, she reports the massacre. A squadron of security troops arrives to investigate, but they also consider her a suspect. However, when the troops return to the subterranean caves to look for the evidence, they first find a pair of killer androids…and then they find four people claiming to be time travelers, who instantly become the prime suspects. But these travelers – the Doctor and his unharmonious trio of companions –

are more of a threat to the plans of the Cybermen. Fearing an upcoming conference of interplanetary superpowers that could spell the end to the Cybermen's war effort, the silver giants plan to slam a huge space freighter into the Earth, obliterating a large portion of the planet's surface. But when Adric manages to thwart the Cybermen's plans by accidentlly sending the freighter back in time (but still on the same trajectory), he's either helping to prevent the human race from coming into existence…or ensuring that event.

Peter Davison . . . . The Doctor
Janet Fielding . . . . Tegan
Sarah Sutton . . . . Nyssa
Matthew Waterhouse . . . . Adric
Suzi Arden . . . . Snyder
David Bache . . . . Cyberman
David Banks . . . . Cyberleader
June Bland . . . . Berger
Norman Bradley . . . . Cyberman
Michael Gordon Brown . . . . Cyberman
Anne Clements . . . . Trooper Bane
Clare Clifford . . . . Kyle
Graham Cole . . . . Cyberman
Mark Fletcher . . . . Crewmember Vance
Peter Gates-Fleming . . . . Cyberman
Mark Hardy . . . . Cyber Lieutenant
Ann Holloway . . . . Mitchell
Steve Ismay . . . . Cyberman
Barney Lawrence . . . . Android

written by Eric Saward
directed by Peter Grimwade
music by Malcolm Clarke

Part 1 aired on March 8, 1982
Part 2 aired on March 9, 1982
Part 3 aired on March 15, 1982
Part 4 aired on March 16, 1982

Steve Morley . . . . Walters
Beryl Reid . . . . Briggs
Alec Sabin . . . . Ringway
Carolyn Mary Simmonds . . . . Android
Mark Straker . . . . Trooper Carter
James Warwick . . . . Scott
Jeff Wayne . . . . Cyberman
Christopher Whittingham . . . Crewmember Carson

Along with *The Caves of Androzani*, *Earthshock* is one of the two definitive highlights of the fifth Doctor's era, offering a fantastic combination of relentless (and, given the BBC's standards and the show's budget at the time, *very* well-executed) action, surprise plot twists, and almost unbearable tension. The supporting cast is also top-notch, with comedienne Beryl Reid standing out in a perfectly credible dramatic performance as the captain of the hijacked space freighter. *Earthshock* also marks the first appearance of David Banks as the Cyberleader, a role he would continue to play through the last Cybermen episode of the classic series, 1988's *Silver Nemesis*.

To the surprise of many viewers at the time the show first aired, this was also the last live-in-the-flesh appearance of Matthew Waterhouse as Adric. (He later appeared as ghosts or visions of Adric in the following story, *Time-Flight*, and in *Caves Of Androzani*.) Despite the signature 1980s whining-companion syndrome that pervades the early TARDIS scenes, *Earthshock* is easily the best performance, not to mention the best narrative use, of Adric since his introduction in *Full Circle* just the previous season. In *Earthshock*, Adric is intelligent, petulant, compassionate, and ultimately sacrifices his life to save the planet for which the Doctor has demonstrated his concern and affection. His final scene in episode four, at least in my eyes, is worthy of a tear in the eye…but then again, I am very much in the minority in that I genuinely liked Adric as a character. Most of **Doctor Who** fandom doesn't care for the lad, but the writers didn't always have a clue how to use him, so I can see where that segment of fans is coming from. But the Adric of *Full Circle, The Keeper of Traken, Logopolis* and *Earthshock* is a character to be missed.

Malcolm Clarke's reverberating "metallic" electronic music for *Earthshock* is his first contribution to **Doctor Who** in the 1980s, and though some of his cues for Cyberman-related scenes recall the abstract music from 1972's *The Sea Devils*, he creates a downright hummable theme for the Cybermen – the best musical signature they've had since the 1960s episodes which tracked their appearances with the stock "Space Adventures" tune.

TIME-FLIGHT

The authorities at Heathrow Airport are suspicious when a Police Box appears in their terminal within moments of the disappearance of a Concorde aircraft in mid-air. The Doctor drops the name of UNIT and is allowed to help in the search for the whereabouts – or, he suspects, the whenabouts – of the missing plane. The Doctor, with Nyssa, Tegan and the TARDIS in tow, takes the next Concorde flight on an identical vector, and soon finds himself on prehistoric Earth, along with the passengers and crew of the other plane. A strange being called Kalid has hijacked the two planes into Earth's past to use their passengers and crew as slave labor for a sinister task – and Kalid is also very interested in the Doctor's TARDIS.

Peter Davison . . . . The Doctor
Janet Fielding . . . . Tegan
Sarah Sutton . . . . Nyssa
Anthony Ainley . . . . The Master / Kalid
Judith Blyfield . . . . Angela Clifford
Chris Bradshaw . . . . Terileptil illusion
Michael Cashman . . . . First Officer Bilton
Peter Cellier . . . . Andrews
Graham Cole . . . . Melkur illusion
Peter Dahlsen . . . . Horton
Keith Drinkel . . . . Flight Engineer Scobie
Richard Easton . . . . Captain Stapley
John Flint . . . . Captain Urquhart
Hugh Hayes . . . . Anithon
Barney Lawrence . . . . Dave Culshaw

This story has been released on DVD

written by Peter Grimwade
directed by Ron Jones
music by Roger Limb

Part 1 aired on March 22, 1982
Part 2 aired on March 23, 1982
Part 3 aired on March 29, 1982
Part 4 aired on March 30, 1982

Brian McDermott . . . . Sheard
Nigel Stock . . . . Professor Hayter
Matthew Waterhouse . . . . Adric illusion
Andre Winterton . . . . Zarak
Tommy Winward . . . . Security man

Despite a perfectly good first episode, this four-parter quickly takes a nose-dive and crashes, to coin a phrase. Setting aside the improbable proposition of a budget-addled BBC science fiction TV series portraying a Concorde traveling back in time and crashing on prehistoric Earth, the Master's elaborate charade is an utterly pointless one, and there's no need for him to even bother with his disguise until the Doctor arrives…and there's not much more point in continuing it even after he arrives. A common problem with the writing for the Master during the '80s also rears its head here, with his motivation for his evil activities shifting almost randomly in the second half of the story.

Some of the guest characters are endearing, and they almost make up for the lack of cohesive plotting later on. *Time-Flight* also sees one of the only instances of Nyssa ever being treated as an alien, exhibiting what seems to be a receptivity to telepathic influence (in previous stories, one could be forgiven for losing track of the fact that Nyssa isn't from Earth). It's a story that could have been interesting, but instead merely became an immense mess, and a dismal ending to what had otherwise been an enjoyable first season for the fifth Doctor. If the season had ended with *Earthshock*, season 19 could hold its own alongside the first season of Pertwee's and Tom Baker's eras as an example of **Doctor Who** firing on all cylinders and recovering from a change of leading man in fine style.

SEASON 20: 1983
ARC OF INFINITY

The Doctor and Nyssa's visit to a tranquil region of space known as the Arc of Infinity is cut short by a strange phenomenon – some kind of entity penetrates the TARDIS and tries to merge with the Doctor's body. The attempt is short-lived, and the Doctor escapes harm, but apparently the incident has been noticed – the Time Lords are recalling him to Gallifrey. With Nyssa in tow, the Doctor returns home only to discover that his biodata extract has been accessed by an unknown party – information that could be used to allow someone to take over his physical form. Fearing the ramifications of a Time Lord being taken over by an alien entity, the High Council – now led by the regenerated Borusa as Lord President – votes to have the Doctor executed. But a second attempt at a merge interrupts the execution, and the Time Lords find out that it's no alien entity at work, but one of their own.

Peter Davison . . . . The Doctor
Janet Fielding . . . . Tegan
Sarah Sutton . . . . Nyssa
Colin Baker . . . . Maxil
Andrew Boxer . . . . Robin Stuart
Ian Collier . . . . Omega
John D. Collins . . . . Talor
Alastair Cumming . . . . Colin Frazer
Neil Daglish . . . . Damon
Michael Gough . . . . Hedin
Elspet Gray . . . . Thalia
Guy Groen . . . . Second receptionist
Malcolm Harvey . . . . The Ergon
Max Harvey . . . . Zorac

This story has been released on DVD

written by Johnny Byrne
directed by Ron Jones
music by Roger Limb

Part 1 aired on January 3, 1983
Part 2 aired on January 5, 1983
Part 3 aired on January 11, 1983
Part 4 aired on January 12, 1983

Paul Jerricho . . . . Castellan
Leonard Sachs . . . . President Borusa
Maya Woolfe . . . . Hostel receptionist

NEW WHO CONNECTIONS: Clara Oswald is seen to have intervened to thwart a previously unknown attempt on the Doctor's life by the Great Intelligence during this adventure in *The Name Of The Doctor* (2013).

A.K.A.: It's not unusual, in modern **Doctor Who**, to see new companions show up in bit parts or guest roles (both Freema Agyeman and Karen Gillan played small guest roles prior to being cast as companions). But actor **Colin Baker** has both of them beaten: **he's the first actor in the history of the series to have shown up in a guest role before going on to play the Doctor himself!** The feat was repeated by **Peter Capaldi**, who guest starred in 2008's *Fires Of Pompeii* before taking over from Matt Smith as the Doctor at the end of *Time Of The Doctor* (2013).

The visual imagining of Gallifrey has never really been consistent in **Doctor Who** history. The amorphous spaces and techno-wizardlike Time Lords of *The War Games* and *The Three Doctors*, the ornate intricacy and intrigue of *The Deadly Assassin* (and, to a lesser degree, *The Invasion Of Time*), and then the garish look of the '80s: shiny and colorful and full of blinky lights…yes, this must be *the future*!

Arc Of Infinity does, at least, keep up with the forced, stilted political machinations of *The Invasion Of Time*, so there's some consistency. And speaking of forced, Tegan's abrupt departure in *Time-Flight*, followed up by her reintroduction in *Arc Of Infinity*, makes little sense and doesn't even advance the character significantly, if at all.

The Amsterdam location shooting is nice, though it doesn't have much to do with the story. Then again, what with giant gangly muppety birds shooting people in the sewers of Amsterdam, it's hard to say what does. If there's a highlight to *Arc*, it may well be some significant character development for Nyssa, in a script written by her creator. No longer a timid wallflower, life with the Doctor and witnessing countless deaths seems to have hardened her shell a bit. The girl from Traken is now unafraid to take up arms to save the Doctor's life, even attempting to instigate a hostage situation to save him (though she once again crumbles in the face of authority); it would've been fascinating to see this evolution explored further, perhaps asking the question if traveling with the Doctor really does make everyone a better person. Alas, she reverts to her original character in the following story, and such character investigation would have to wait for the 2008 season closer, *Journey's End*, with Davros gleefully shaming the Doctor by pointing out that his ex-companions have become something of an *ad hoc* army.

SNAKEDANCE

Having rejoined the TARDIS crew after their adventure with Omega in Amsterdam, Tegan begins experiencing recurring nightmares. The Doctor spots an even more pressing problem: someone has reset the TARDIS' coordinates, and it can only have been Tegan. The time travelers arrive on the planet Manussa…the homeworld of the evil Mara influence which possessed Tegan on Deva Loka. In this point in Manussa's history, the Mara has become a mere legend of an evil vanquished, and the cause for an annual celebration. But the Mara, now once again in control of Tegan's body, intends to possess the minds of every Manussan during the height of the festivities – unless the Doctor can find a way to stop it.

Peter Davison . . . . The Doctor	
Janet Fielding . . . . Tegan	
Sarah Sutton . . . . Nyssa	
George Ballantine . . . . Hawker	
John Carson . . . . Ambril	
Martin Clunes . . . . Lon	
Preston Lockwood . . . . Dojjen	
Brian Miller . . . . Dugdale	
Johnathon Morris . . . . Chela	
Colette O'Neil . . . . Tahna	
Hilary Sesta . . . . Fortune Teller	

This story has been released on DVD

written by Christopher Bailey
directed by Fiona Cumming
music by Peter Howell

Part 1 aired on January 18, 1983
Part 2 aired on January 19, 1983
Part 3 aired on January 25, 1983
Part 4 aired on January 26, 1983

Barry Smith . . . . Puppeteer

A very interesting story arc that seems positively subtle next to the continuity-heavy excesses of *Mawdryn Undead* and *Arc Of Infinity*, *Snakedance* is a bit less cerebral than the Mara's first appearance, more of a straightforward adventure, but it still manages to be damned creepy. Once again we can thank Janet Fielding for a lot of the impact of *Snakedance*, and she really seems to relish bringing "evil Tegan" to life yet again. This is also a particularly well-written script where the Doctor is concerned – the scene in which he points out the significance of a curious piece of headgear is one of Peter Davison's more priceless moments in the role.

MAWDRYN UNDEAD

A schoolboy named Turlough cons a classmate into "borrowing" a vintage roadster belonging to one of the teachers at his private school, naturally getting into an accident moments later. During a near-death experience, Turlough is forced into a deadly pact by the Black Guardian: Turlough's new mission is to kill a Time Lord known as the Doctor at any cost. Soon afterward, the Doctor lands the TARDIS on a seemingly derelict spacecraft orbiting Earth in both space and time, only to find that somehow, someone on board is still maintaining the vessel. The Doctor soon becomes a pawn in alien renegades' plot to end their pitiful immortality, and discovers that his old friend Brigadier Lethbridge-Stewart, now a math teacher at Turlough's school, is a pawn. It also soon becomes evident that Turlough is no ordinary schoolboy.

Peter Davison . . . . The Doctor
Janet Fielding . . . . Tegan
Mark Strickson . . . . Turlough
Sarah Sutton . . . . Nyssa
Lucy Baker . . . . Child Nyssa
David Collings . . . . Mawdryn
Nicholas Courtney . . . . . Brig. Lethbridge-Stewart
Brian Darnley . . . . Second Mutant
Valentine Dyall . . . . Black Guardian
Stephen Garlick . . . . Ibbotson
Sheila Gill . . . . Matron
Roger Hammond . . . . Dr. Runciman
Angus MacKay . . . . Headmaster

UNIT

This story
has been
released
on DVD

written by Peter Grimwade
directed by Peter Moffatt
music by Paddy Kingsland

Part 1 aired on February 1, 1983
Part 2 aired on February 2, 1983
Part 3 aired on February 8, 1983
Part 4 aired on February 9, 1983

Sian Pattenden . . . . Child Tegan
Peter Walmsley . . . . First Mutant

NEW WHO CONNECTIONS: In the 1993 New Adventures novel No Future, it is suggested that the Brigadier's mysterious nervous breakdown, alluded to in this episode, was caused by events he experienced with the *seventh* Doctor and friends in 1976.

BEHIND THE SCENES: This episode contradicts a supposedly key bit of **Doctor Who** continuity, and has resulted in an ongoing debate known in fan circles as the "UNIT dating conundrum." In the earlier episode *Pyramids Of Mars*, it is suggested that companion Sarah Jane Smith is from **1980**, though her first episode aired in 1974, which would presumably date *all* of the "present day" Earth stories from Jon Pertwee's last season in the *late* 1970s. Yet *Mawdryn Undead* tells us that it is now **1983** (the year the story was filmed), and that the Brigadier *retired* in 1977. All that fuss over two dating references written by different writers and filmed by different production teams and actors, eight years apart! No catch-all solution seems to have been accepted across fandom; I suggest filing this under "irreparable damage to the timeline."

Among other things, *Mawdryn* introduces us to Turlough (Mark Strickson), easily the most distinctive companion of Peter Davison's tenure as the Doctor. Now, admittedly, no one really knew how to handle Turlough after this story, but few companions have had as *interesting* an entrance as this. One of the two showpieces of **Doctor Who**'s 20th season (the other, in my opinion, being *Englightenment*, which closed the trilogy of Turlough/Black Guardian stories that begins in this serial), *Mawdryn Undead* succeeds in creating a very creepy atmosphere, and makes effective use of the beloved Brigadier, even though the original script called for math teacher Ian Chesterton – one of the Doctor's three original companions when the series launched in 1963 – to fill that role. Another neat element is the creepy "Someone just walked over my grave" sequence in which the Doctor helps the Brigadier regain his memory, accompanied by atmospheric music and numerous clips from various UNIT-related stories dating all the way back to 1967 – exactly the kind of continuity-themed touch that the entire season strove so hard to include, but so seldom succeeded on this level.

The music isn't just noteworthy in that scene alone, however – Paddy Kingsland, easily the composer with the most distinctive sound between 1980 and 1986 on **Doctor Who**, is responsible for a lot of the show's atmosphere, contributing numerous memorable, hummable cues throughout the four episodes. Though the complete score is available as an alternative audio track on the DVD, the soundtrack has never officially been released – a glaring omission.

TERMINUS

At the Black Guardian's bidding, Turlough interferes with the TARDIS internal systems enough to cause a critical failure: parts of the timeship's interior are now surrounded by a deadly haze, and those sections could be open to the time vortex at any moment. Nyssa's room is engulfed, and the Doctor performs an emergency merge with the nearest spacecraft in space-time to allow her to escape onto the other ship. When he stabilizes the TARDIS and then goes to retrieve Nyssa, however, the Doctor learns that he inadvertently sent his friend onto a plague-carriers' ship — and Nyssa, now infected, can never leave, nor does that transport's small crew seem even remotely inclined to help any of the people contaminated with Lazar's Disease.

Peter Davison	. . . .	The Doctor
Janet Fielding	. . . .	Tegan
Mark Strickson	. . . .	Turlough
Sarah Sutton	. . . .	Nyssa
R.J. Bell	. . . .	The Garm
Peter Benson	. . . .	Bor
Andrew Burt	. . . .	Valgard
Valentine Dyall	. . . .	Black Guardian
Liza Goddard	. . . .	Kari
Dominic Guard	. . . .	Olvir
Martin Muncaster	. . . .	Tannoy voice
Tim Munro	. . . .	Sigurd
Martin Potter	. . . .	Eirak
Rachel Weaver	. . . .	Inga

This story has been released on DVD

written by Stephen Gallagher
directed by Mary Ridge
music by Roger Limb

Part 1 aired on February 15, 1983
Part 2 aired on February 16, 1983
Part 3 aired on February 22, 1983
Part 4 aired on February 23, 1983

AUDIO CONNECTIONS: Big Finish Productions has released a series of audios reuniting the TARDIS crew of this era, based on the notion of a much older Nyssa rejoining the Doctor at some point after helping to eliminate Lazar's Disease.

A mixed bag of story elements, *Terminus* earns at least a few points for giving Nyssa the chance to exit the series with the promise of using her bio-engineering knowledge — knowledge which the character rarely exhibited beyond her debut story only two seasons before. On the downside, the story is padded out with loads of whiny dialogue between Tegan and Turlough, who are trapped in the far too clean and far too well-lit inner ductworks of the plague ship as an anything-but-menacing teddy bear-like creature stalks the corridors. Also be on the lookout for Liza Goddard in an embarrassingly clingy white spacesuit.

As companion exit stories go, it's an interesting concept, but somehow the visual presentation doesn't sell the story as well as it might, and as the middle chapter of the trilogy of stories introducing Turlough, it's fairly weak, eclipsed by the flashy nostalgia-fest of *Mawdryn Undead* and the conceptual boldness of *Enlightenment*.

ENLIGHTENMENT

The Doctor receives a very vague warning of danger from the White Guardian, but Turlough's interference — passed off as worrying that the TARDIS console would be damaged by the White Guardian's energy requirements — leaves the Doctor with only a shred of the information he needs. The TARDIS arrives on a vintage sailing ship, whose crew is not at all perturbed by the

Doctor's arrival, and whose officers are beings who live outside of time itself. The Doctor discovers that he is now taking part in a yacht race through the blackness of space, and the Eternals care nothing for the human sailors they've abducted. At the finish line lies the promise of everlasting enlightenment – or, if Turlough continues to fall under the sway of the Black Guardian, death for the Doctor.

Peter Davison . . . . The Doctor
Janet Fielding . . . . Tegan
Mark Strickson . . . . Turlough
Lynda Baron . . . . Captain Wrack
Keith Barron . . . . Striker
Christopher Brown . . . . Marriner
John Cannon . . . . Helmsman
Tony Caunter . . . . Jackson
Valentine Dyall . . . . Black Guardian
Leee John . . . . Mansell
Clive Kneller . . . . Collier
Cyril Luckham . . . . . . White Guardian

This story has been released on DVD

written by Barbara Clegg
directed by Fiona Cumming
music by Malcolm Clarke

Part 1 aired on March 1, 1983
Part 2 aired on March 2, 1983
Part 3 aired on March 8, 1983
Part 4 aired on March 9, 1983

James McClure . . . . First Officer
Byron Sotiris . . . . Critas

Enlightenment is one of the most remarkably atypical, high-concept stories ever attempted on **Doctor Who**, and it also holds the distinction of being one of only eight stories in entire run of the original series to have been written or co-written by a woman. *Enlightenment*'s sense of "heightened reality" is hugely enjoyable. Even performances which have been regarded by critics down through the years as disappointing don't faze me that much. It's one of the most boldly original entries from this era of the series.

The Doctor's other companion isn't shorted either; throughout this story, Turlough is seen at his most desperate, at one point even jumping overboard in a suicidal attempt to end his pact with the Black Guardian. This turns out to be an ill-timed move, since he is rescued by the Eternal captain of another ship, someone who turns out to be a servant of evil herself. Lynda Baron goes just over-the-top enough to make her mark as Captain Wrack, a menacing but also funny foil for our heroes. One question that remains is the almost naive trust with which the Doctor accepts Turlough even after learning about the boy's alliance with the Black Guardian. The final confrontation between the two Guardians is a satisfying conclusion, and even leaves things open for a follow-up (which never happened in the original TV series).

One of the best Peter Davison stories, and very, very highly recommended.

THE KING'S DEMONS

The arrival of the TARDIS coincides with a dangerous digression in Earth's history: King John announces he has no plans to sign the Magna Carta. The Doctor, Tegan and Turlough investigate and discover that his majesty is not all that he appears – King John has been replaced by an intelligent, shapeshifting android called Kamelion. But at the moment, Kamelion is merely a puppet, and his strings are held by the Master, who escaped from Xeriphas (bringing Kamelion, a Xeriphan invention, with him) and now hopes to unravel the entire history of western civilization.

Peter Davison . . . . The Doctor
Janet Fielding . . . . Tegan
Mark Strickson . . . . Turlough

written by Terence Dudley
directed by Tony Virgo

Anthony Ainley . . The Master / Sir Giles Estram
Isla Blair . . . . Isabella
Peter Burroughs . . . . Jester
Gerald Flood . . . . King John / voice of Kamelion
Michael J. Jackson . . . . Sir Geoffrey
Frank Windsor . . . . Ranulf
Christopher Villiers . . . . Hugh

This story has been released on DVD

music by Jonathan Gibbs

Part 1 aired on March 15, 1983
Part 2 aired on March 16, 1983

An interesting and fairly uncomplicated two-part episode, *The King's Demons* was intended primarily as a vehicle to introduce a new companion, Kamelion. As introduced to the press in publicity material and photo shoots, Kamelion really *was* a high-tech wonder, a remote-controlled robot "actor" capable of walking, moving its arms and hands, turning its head, and even moving its mouth. But when a tragic accident claimed the life of the special effects whiz who invented Kamelion, the character just as quickly disappeared from the show, to be featured in only one other story (which was hastily rearranged to show the now-crippled robot's exit). As a result, *The King's Demons* is a bit of a non-sequitur in the grand scheme of things.

While we're on non-sequiturs, the Master's increasingly improbable escape from his previous adventure is something of a Davison-era trademark. So too is the disguising of the Master's appearance in an attempt to preserve the surprise – in the Radio Times, the part of "Sir Giles Estram" was attributed to a fictional actor, "James Stoker"…or, slightly rearranged, "Master's joke." (A similar ploy, crediting "Neil Toynay" – an anagram of Tony Ainley – as Kalid, was used to keep the Master's appearance a surprise in *Time-Flight*.)

20th Anniversary Special: 1983
THE FIVE DOCTORS

The Doctor, Tegan and Turlough find themselves in no immediate danger for once, until the Doctor suffers from repeated, severe pain, claiming that his past is being altered in a way that could endanger him in the present. Somewhere on Gallifrey, long-abandoned machinery from the earliest days of the Time Lords is reactivated and its powers are brought to bear on each of the Doctor's first four incarnations, snatching each of them from their own timeline and depositing them in Gallifrey's infamous Death Zone, where the tomb of Time Lord founding father Rassilon stands. The fourth Doctor is trapped in the time vortex and never makes it to Gallifrey. As the various personae of the Doctor join forces, along with many companions, they find themselves fighting a variety of old adversaries for the future of Gallifrey itself, unaware that an old friend poses the greatest danger.

Peter Davison . . . . The Doctor
Jon Pertwee . . . . The Doctor
Patrick Troughton . . . . The Doctor
Richard Hurndall . . . . The Doctor
Tom Baker . . . . The Doctor
William Hartnell . . . . The Doctor
Anthony Ainley . . . . The Master
David Banks . . . . Cyberleader
Stuart Blake . . . . Commander
Nicholas Courtney . . . . . Brig. Lethbridge-Stewart
Janet Fielding . . . . Tegan
Ray Float . . . . Sergeant
Carole Ann Ford . . . . Susan

written by Terrance Dicks
directed by Peter Moffett
music by Peter Howell

Aired on November 23, 1983 (USA)
Aired on November 25, 1983 (UK)

John Leeson . . . . voice of K-9
John Scott Martin . . . . Dalek
Richard Mathews . . . . Rassilon
Stephen Meredith . . . . Technician

UWÛRP!

Richard Franklin	. . . .	Mike Yates	Wendy Padbury	. . . .	Zoe
Mark Hardy	. . . .	Cyber Lieutenant	David Savile	. . . .	Colonel Crichton
Frazer Hines	. . . .	Jamie	Dinah Sheridan	. . . .	Chancellor Flavia
Paul Jerricho	. . . .	Castellan	Roy Skelton	. . . .	Dalek voice
Caroline John	. . . .	Liz Shaw	Elisabeth Sladen	. . . .	Sarah Jane Smith
William Kenton	. . . .	Cyber Scout	Mark Strickson	. . . .	Turlough
Philip Latham	. . . .	Lord President Borusa	Lalla Ward	. . . .	Romana

This story has been released on DVD

NEW WHO CONNECTIONS: Rassilon looks nothing like Timothy Dalton (Rassilon from 2010's *The End Of Time*) or Don Warrington (Rassilon from Big Finish's **Doctor Who** audio plays), but hey, he's a Time Lord and he can regenerate. No matter the incarnation, he doesn't seem like much of a benevolent ruler. (But that myth was already being demolished by the second Doctor in this story anyway.) This story almost completely does away with the suspense of a Time Lord having only 13 "lives," established in *The Deadly Assassin*, by showing the High Council offering to effectively reboot the Master with a "complete new life cycle" of regenerations. (This piece of information may also explain how the Time Lords resurrected the Master, after his apparent inescapable death in the 1996 TV movie, to fight in the Time War, as the 2007 episode *The Sound Of Drums* claimed. *The Five Doctors* is also referenced in *The Time Of The Doctor,* which apparently sees the *Doctor*'s final incarnation granted a new series of regenerations.)

I still have a remarkably soft spot for *The Five Doctors*, the first story I ever saw that featured any Doctor other than Tom Baker (actually, I think *The Five Doctors* holds that distinction for a *lot* of American fans – the BBC's American syndication arm, sensing our affection for the tall guy in the long scarf, was terribly slow in rolling out anything *other* than Tom Baker stories well into the 1980s for most PBS stations). Baker gets a mention in this episode, and is even shown thanks to footage from the abandoned 1979 story *Shada*, which was never completed for broadcast, but *The Five Doctors* is so jam-packed with information and major developments that he isn't missed that much.

Patrick Troughton and Jon Pertwee fall right back into step as the second and third Doctors, not even missing a beat, though there is a question raised about both of them. The second Doctor remembers events surrounding his trial in 1969's *The War Games*, even though that is generally considered to be the point at which that incarnation of the Doctor ended, and the third one began. And the third Doctor seems to have some foreknowledge of what his fourth incarnation will look like – perhaps as a result of some untold tale, not unlike this one, in which the third and fourth Doctors meet. These, however, are minor details for which a variety of explanations have been offered by fans over the years. The first Doctor is brought back to life by Richard Hurndall, who was cast in the role after producer John Nathan-Turner saw him in a somewhat Hartnell-esque role in the 1981 *Assassin* episode of **Blake's 7**. And with all due respect to the late Mr. Hurndall, I think his guest shot on **Blake's 7** was much more first-Doctor-ish than his appearance in *The Five Doctors*. This may be due to the script, which emphasized his crabbiness over his whimsical sense of humor – a frequent misjudgement of Hartnell's take on the character, who could often verge on being quite amusing. The recasting did neither Hartnell nor Hurndall any great favors, especially since, again, this was the first "first Doctor" many American fans had met, the vintage Hartnell clip before the opening titles notwithstanding.

The various companions are good to see again, but my favorites among them are Lis Sladen as Sarah and Nicholas Courtney as the Brigadier, and it was interesting to see K-9 in Sarah's possession, which makes the 1981 **K-9 & Company** special "official" as a part of the **Doctor Who** storyline.

One welcome change seen in *The Five Doctors* is the return of Gallifrey to a slightly more gothic, sinister setting as seen in 1975's *The Deadly Assassin* – or parts of Gallifrey, at any rate. The gleaming, pretty sets that served as the Time Lords' home planet in the 1980s didn't suit its inhabitants as well as the darker, more ancient environs of previous Gallifrey shows, and it's interesting to see an acknowledgement of the "older" Gallifrey, hinting at a gleaming façade covering up a troubled past. (But covering it up for whose benefit?)

SEASON 21: 1984
WARRIORS OF THE DEEP

In the twenty-first century, the Doctor tries to show his companions Tegan and Turlough the shape of things to come on Earth. Unfortunately, their arrival coincides with a dangerous buildup of nuclear tensions between two unspecified superpowers, and the TARDIS brings them to an underground weapons platform manned by an edgy crew – particularly crewman Maddox, who has a computer interface implanted directly in his brain to allow him to fire the sea base's nuclear missiles with a single concentrated thought. Maddox, shell-shocked after months of unannounced battle drills, collapses and leaves the base defenseless. But the base isn't just prone to foreign attack – the repitile Silurians and Sea Devils, both ancient races which roamed the Earth freely before the evolution and rise of man, plan to launch the base's missiles, plunging Earth into an all-out nuclear war and destroying mankind so reptiles can once again be the masters of their world.

Peter Davison	. . . .	The Doctor
Janet Fielding	. . . .	Tegan
Mark Strickson	. . . .	Turlough
Tom Adams	. . . .	Vorshak
Stuart Blake	. . . .	Scibus
Mike Braben	. . . . . .	Sea Devil
Vincent Brimble	. . . . . .	Tarpok
Norman Comer	. . . .	Icthar
James Coombes	. . . . . .	Paroli
Christopher Farries	. . . . . .	Sauvix
Nigel Humphreys	. . . . . .	Bulic
Steve Kelly	. . . . . .	Sea Devil
Ian McCulloch	. . . . . .	Nilson
Martin Neil	. . . . . .	Maddox
Dave Ould	. . . . . .	Sea Devil

This story has been released on DVD

written by Johnny Byrne
directed by Ron Jones
music by Jonathan Gibbs

Part 1 aired on January 5, 1984
Part 2 aired on January 6, 1984
Part 3 aired on January 12, 1984
Part 4 aired on January 13, 1984

Ingrid Pitt	. . . .	Solow
Nitza Saul	. . . .	Karina
Jules Walters	. . . . . .	Sea Devil
Tara Ward	. . . .	Preston
Chris Wolfe	. . . .	Sea Devil

NEW WHO CONNECTIONS: This is the final appearance of either the Silurians or Sea-Devils in the original series; a significantly different species of Silurians would next emerge in 2010's *The Hungry Earth*.

It's not a bad storyline, perfectly in keeping with the aims of the Silurians and Sea Devils as previously seen in the episodes *Doctor Who and the Silurians* (1970) and *The Sea Devils* (1972), but numerous bizarre plot twists and distractions keep the viewer from focusing on that aspect. Among the strange events in question: at one point, after tripping the sea base's security systems, the Doctor decides to distract the security search parties by *setting the base reactor to melt down* (!!). On the plus side, the sets achieve a rare feel of great size, and the human characters' costumes are well-made and obviously not too cheap. Jonathan Gibbs contributes an eerily atmospheric synthesized music score that goes a long way in selling the story.

One of this episode's biggest disappointments is its presentation of the Silurians and Sea Devils. Both had been introduced in the early '70s Pertwee era as terrifying primal creatures, but here we see them as Guys In Rubber Masks. Gone is the clever and slimy organic technology the Silurians once used, and gone are their distinctive voices, replaced by a sped-up, processed voice treatment that sounds like nothing so much as Alvin and the Chipmunks under the influence of demonic possession. And let's not even discuss the Myrka creature, supposedly a warlike beast controlled by the Silurians, though in the end it looks more like a reject from a Sid & Marty Krofft children's series (it lacks enough credibility, apparently, that Solow thinks she can dispatch the Myrka with one of the most hilariously *badly* performed martial arts moves in the history of television). *Warriors Of The Deep* is an adventure into which the viewer must proceed with caution…and perhaps diminished expectations.

THE AWAKENING

The Doctor tries to steer the TARDIS to the present-day village of Little Hodcombe, where Tegan plans to visit her grandfather, Andrew Varney. But he has disappeared and something is amiss in the village – the annual medieval reconstructionists' wargames have taken a decidedly more hostile and sinister tone this year. In the nearby church, something terrible has taken hold of many of the villagers' minds, and it's manipulating them to create more fear and hatred – something the creature craves as psychic sustenance.

Peter Davison . . . . The Doctor
Janet Fielding . . . . Tegan
Mark Strickson . . . . Turlough
Jack Galloway . . . . Joseph Willow
Frederick Hall . . . . Andrew Verney
Glyn Houston . . . . Colonel Wolsey
Polly James . . . . Jane Hampden
Keith Jayne . . . . Will Chandler
Denis Lill . . . . Sir George Hutchinson
Christopher Saul . . . . Trooper

This story has been released on DVD

written by Eric Pringle
directed by Michael Owen Morris
music by Peter Howell

Part 1 aired on January 19, 1984
Part 2 aired on January 20, 1984

A neat little story wrapped up in two parts, *The Awakening* has the pleasant illuson of feeling like a meaty four-parter longer. That's not to say that it drags on, but it explores its characters well and gets off the stage at about the right time – before you have too much of a chance to find the appearance of the giant Malus face laughable instead of surprising.

The Awakening started out as a four-part script called *War Game* (which would have undoubtedly been changed in deference to the 10-part season 6 epic *The War Games*), but with all due respect to the writer and his original concept, *The Awakening* pans out nicely at two episodes. It's a pity that some of the clunkers from this area didn't have the good sense to get off the stage at the right time – else they might be remembered as fondly as *The Awakening*.

FRONTIOS

Quite by accident, the TARDIS brings the Doctor, Tegan and Turlough to Frontios, the home of the last surviving colony of the human race. A meteor storm brings the TARDIS tumbling out of orbit and right into the middle of the colony. The paranoid colonists, who have been enduring killer meteor showers for many years, believe the Doctor and his friends are responsible. The Doctor tries to lend a hand and is met only with suspicion, but soon he is as trapped as the colonists when another meteor shower appears to destroy the TARDIS. Tegan stumbles across evidence that there are more menaces to the population of Frontios than just rocks from the sky, and Turlough discovers that he has a terrifyingly intimate knowledge of that menace.

Peter Davison . . . . The Doctor		
Janet Fielding . . . . Tegan		
Mark Strickson . . . . Turlough		
Richard Ashley . . . . Orderly		
John Beardmore . . . . Captain Revere		
William Bowen . . . . Tractator		
George Campbell . . . . Tractator		
Jim Dowdall . . . . Warnsman		
Lesley Dunlop . . . . Norna		
John Gillett . . . . Gravis		
Peter Gilmore . . . . Brazen		
Hedi Khursandi . . . . Tractator		
William Lucas . . . . Range		
Michael Malcolm . . . . Tractator		
Raymond Murtagh . . . . Retrograde		

This story has been released on DVD

written by Christopher H. Bidmead
directed by Ron Jones
music by Paddy Kingsland

Part 1 aired on January 26, 1984
Part 2 aired on January 27, 1984
Part 3 aired on February 2, 1984
Part 4 aired on February 3, 1984

Maurice O'Connell . . . . Cockerill
Jeff Rawle . . . . Plantagenet
Alison Skilbeck . . . . Deputy
Stephen Speed . . . . Tractator

NEW WHO CONNECTIONS: This is the closest that the TARDIS comes to being completely destroyed in the original series, despite earlier stories asserting that the TARDIS is indestructible. (Perhaps it was still under warranty when those claims were made.) Barring unchronicled events in the Time War, the next time the TARDIS would take such a televised beating would be during David Tennant's turn at the wheel, during which the ship would be burned out (*Rise Of The Cybermen*, 2006), forcibly turned into an engine of destruction (*The Sound Of Drums / The Last Of The Time Lords*, 2007) and then subjected to the energy released by the Doctor's regeneration (*The End Of Time / The Eleventh Hour*, 2010).

Though a few things aren't explained as well as they could be in the course of the story, *Frontios* is a fairly interesting adventure for Peter Davison's Doctor, and especially for Mark Strickson, who has his first chance in a long time to make Turlough a fascinating companion again. As with *Mawdryn Undead*, Strickson displays a total command of essaying the emotion of sheer panic, but he does it so well that it's hard to fault him. It also turns a classic **Doctor Who** convention on its head, leaving a male companion stricken with panic while the female companion is notably stronger.

Though it really isn't explained all that well, an interesting notion is presented, that the TARDIS could be reduced to rubble leaving only a hat stand (which, amusingly, Turlough brandishes as a high-tech weapon against the terrified colonists for several scenes), and that the interior dimensions of the TARDIS could be scattered underground. But the Davison years did see a growing trend toward treating the TARDIS not as an extraordinary space-time machine, but as a fairly run-of-the-mill spaceship, mainly for the convenience of subjecting it to typical sci-fi plot devices.

RESURRECTION OF THE DALEKS

With the TARDIS caught in a time corridor upon leaving Frontios, the Doctor is surprised to find that he is being taken to some rather unremarkable London docks. His investigation into the origins of the time corridor lead him to a meeting with a group of hapless 20th century soldiers who can't even begin to imagine the traces of technology they've discovered in a nearby warehouse. The Doctor's arrival has been expected — in fact, carefully orchestrated — by the Daleks, who are in the midst of a plot that involves clones, biological warfare, and the rescue and revival of their mad creator, Davros.

Peter Davison . . . . The Doctor	
Janet Fielding . . . . Tegan	
Mark Strickson . . . . Turlough	
Chloe Ashcroft . . . . Professor Laird	
John Adam Baker . . . . Crewmember	
Rodney Bewes . . . . Stein	
Mike Braben . . . . Policeman	
Toby Byrne . . . . Dalek	
Maurice Colbourne . . . . Lytton	
Simon Crane . . . . Soldier	
Nicholas Curry . . . . Chemist	
Roger Davenport . . . . Trooper	
Jim Findley . . . . Mercer	
Leslie Grantham . . . . Kiston	
Sneh Gupta . . . . Osborn	
Del Henney . . . . Colonel Archer	
Michael Jeffries . . . . Policeman	
Pat Judge . . . . Man with metal detector	
Rula Lenska . . . . Styles	

This story has been released on DVD

written by Eric Saward
directed by Matthew Robinson
music by Malcolm Clarke

Part 1 aired on February 8, 1984
Part 2 aired on February 15, 1984

John Scott Martin . . . . Dalek	
Philip McGough . . . . Sergeant Calder	
Brian Miller . . . . Dalek voice	
Royce Mills . . . . Dalek voice	
Terry Molloy . . . . Davros	
Mike Mungarven . . . . Soldier	
William Sleigh . . . . Galloway	
Tony Starr . . . . Dalek	
Cy Town . . . . Dalek	
Linsey Turner . . . . Crewmember	

NEW WHO CONNECTIONS: The Daleks are infamous for their dangerous, inelegant time corridor technology, whether in this story or in new series episodes such as *Victory Of The Daleks* (2010). The Daleks are also seen to be aware of Gallifrey and the Time Lords here – possibly as a result of the Doctor's interrogation in *Genesis Of The Daleks* (1975) – and their plot to assassinate the High Council using duplicates of the Doctor and friends may be a strong indication that, whether the Doctor was aware of it or not, the Time War between Gallifrey and the Daleks was already in progress by this point in the series.

BEHIND THE SCENES: Due to coverage of the 1984 Olympic Games, *Resurrection Of The Daleks* was compressed into an unusual format – two extended-length, 50-minute episodes – presaging the series' move to that format in 1985 (a decision that had already been made at the BBC before *Resurrection* was re-edited) and its revival in a single-episode, 45-minute format in the 21st century. The hasty re-edit left out sound effects that were, in many cases, vital clues as to what was happening. The original, intended four-episode version was released on DVD, with all sound effects intact.

A fast-paced and sometimes confusing story, *Resurrection Of The Daleks* is actually a good outing for its titular adversary, giving them a stronger role and more menace than they've had in years, and even the reappearance of Davros – who, in the previous two Dalek stories, had come to overshadow his creations – doesn't diminish their effectiveness. Davros himself is brought back much more effectively by the script and by Terry Molloy's hateful portrayal.

There are several abrupt, out-of-left-field plot twists thrown into the mix that make this story difficult to follow. Lytton and his policemen – hired killers in disguise – aren't really explained, aside from establishing that they're bad guys for the purposes of this story. Lytton is later given a background in 1985's *Attack Of The Cybermen*, but even then his presence on 20th century Earth isn't fully explained. It almost smacks of a character being planted for a spin-off series that never happened. The Dalek plot to send programmed clones of the Doctor and his companions to Gallifrey to assassinate the High Council of Time Lords is brought up, and then nothing more is heard of it. It's a densely packed story that may be too densely packed for its own good, leaving unresolved plot threads trailing in its wake as it thunders along.

PLANET OF FIRE

The TARDIS has been set for a new course by Kamelion, who is attempting to go to the source of a distress signal which is overriding his every function. The Doctor manages to wrest control of the ship from Kamelion and lands the TARDIS on Earth to investigate. While the Doctor finds little of importance, other than a freshly uncovered batch of artifacts from an archaeological expedition, Turlough discovers the signal's source and immobilizes the TARDIS to avoid going there. Turlough also spots a drowning swimmer on the TARDIS scanner. He rescues the girl, discovering that she has stolen the oddest of the artifacts that the Doctor saw earlier. When the Doctor returns, the TARDIS again takes off without his control, and apparently with a new passenger on board. The mystery of the new passengers unravels quickly, as does the mystery of who has been controlling Kamelion. But why is Turlough so keen to avoid a colony from his own planet – a colony of outcasts of which he may be a member?

Peter Davison	. . . .	The Doctor
Mark Strickson	. . . .	Turlough
Nicola Bryant	. . . .	Peri
Dallas Adams	. . . .	Professor Foster
Anthony Ainley	. . . .	The Master
John Alkin	. . . .	Lomand
Max Arthur	. . . .	Zuko
Michael Bangerter	. . . .	Curt
James Bate	. . . .	Amyand
Jonathan Caplan	. . . .	Roskal
Gerald Flood	. . . .	voice of Kamelion
Edward Highmore	. . . .	Malkon
Ray Knight	. . . .	Trion

This story has been released on DVD

written by Peter Grimwade
directed by Fiona Cumming
music by Peter Howell

Part 1 aired on February 23, 1984
Part 2 aired on February 24, 1984
Part 3 aired on March 1, 1984
Part 4 aired on March 2, 1984

Barbara Shelley	. . . .	Sorasta
Simon Sutton	. . . .	Lookout
Peter Wyngarde	. . . .	Timanov

Though the rapid-fire changes in Kamelion's appearance and attitude are a bit confusing, there is a lot to like about this four-parter, whose main goal was to give Turlough (Mark Strickson) a send-off as enigmatic as his introduction. And in that regard, *Planet Of Fire* is a success, since we learn more about where Turlough is from, and how he was stranded on Earth in *Mawdryn Undead*, but not a great deal more about his culture. The Turlough in this story was once again the X-factor, sabotaging the TARDIS rather than allow it to take him back to his own people. After the running-around-scared-and-getting-captured of the previous two stories, it's quite a relief to see the ambiguous Turlough of old once more. His farewell scene was actually more emotional than I would have expected. It would be three years and two Doctors later before the series would be graced with such a complex and intriguing companion character.

Planet Of Fire's other primary goal was to introduce Nicola Bryant as the new companion, Perpugilliam "Peri" Brown. There's no denying that Nicola Bryant is a very attractive actress, but *Planet Of Fire* and *Caves Of Androzani* offered her two of her best outings in the show before she was relegated to well-endowed-damsel-in-distress status for much of the Colin Baker era. I'm reminded of Adric's very short reign as Tom Baker's only companion – Peri played off of the fifth Doctor much better than the sixth, and she showed a great deal of independence in the short span of these two stories.

Kamelion is also given the boot in this story, barely even showing up as a blip on the radar. Anthony Ainley reprises the Master for his final full confrontation with the fifth Doctor, and though his fate is a bit nebulous – does he or does he not burn to death in the garish blue glow of superimposed natural gas flames? – he's much more menacing than he's been in a long time, and his motives make more sense than they did in, say, *Time-Flight*.

THE CAVES OF ANDROZANI

The Doctor and Peri find themselves on Androzani Major, a world embroiled in a bloody war over the drug spectrox, which prolongs the human life span. While exploring some seemingly uninhabited caves, the Doctor and Peri fall into a foreign substance which has the immediate effect of causing an unpleasant rash, and are then captured by a platoon of soldiers who accuse them of smuggling weapons. While awaiting summary execution for this crime, the Doctor and Peri are then rescued – or perhaps kidnapped – by Sharaz Jek, a disfigured madman who hoards the planet's supply of spectrox and oversees the real weapons smugglers. The soldiers, Jek, the gun-runners and a treacherous corporate mogul with an eye on the presidency are all battling for control of the spectrox supply, and none of them will let anything stand in their way – especially not two innocent bystanders who are dying anyway.

Peter Davison . . . . The Doctor
Nicola Bryant . . . . Peri
Anthony Ainley . . . . The Master
Colin Baker . . . . The Doctor
Martin Cochrane . . . . Chellak
Janet Fielding . . . . Tegan
Gerald Flood . . . . voice of Kamelion
Christopher Gable . . . . Sharaz Jek
Robert Glenister . . . . Salateen
Keith Harvey . . . . Android
Roy Holder . . . . Krelper
Barbara Kinghorn . . . . Timmin
John Normington . . . . Morgus
David Neal . . . . President
Maurice Roeves . . . . Stotz
Andrew Smith . . . . Android

This story has been released on DVD

written by Robert Holmes
directed by Graeme Harper
music by Roger Limb

Part 1 aired on March 8, 1984
Part 2 aired on March 9, 1984
Part 3 aired on March 15, 1984
Part 4 aired on March 16, 1984

Stephen Smith . . . . Android
Ian Staples . . . . Soldier
Mark Strickson . . . . Turlough
Sarah Sutton . . . . Nyssa
Colin Taylor . . . . Magma Creature
Matthew Waterhouse . . . . Adric

NEW WHO CONNECTIONS: The Doctor returns to the Androzani system under even stranger – and slightly more festive – circumstances in 2011's *The Doctor, The Widow And The Wardrobe*.

This dark, doom-laden adventure is one of the all-time best **Doctor Who** stories – in fact, many fans rank it as *the* best, hands down. The tension and atmosphere are heightened by the fact that the Doctor will regenerate at the end, meaning that anything could happen in the meantime. And perhaps most terrifying of all, there are *no* sympathetic parties in the story. The closest we come to anyone even being helpful is the real Salateen, who brings Peri back to the military base – but even he doesn't give a damn about her beyond whether or not she lives long enough to help the military find Sharaz Jek. The suspense of all three cliffhangers is greater than usual, and no doubt the script was written to take advantage of the fact that the audience would be aware of the inevitable ending.

The acting by all involved is far above par, though John Normington as Morgus occasionally chews right through the scenery and swallows the fourth wall when he turns right into the camera and drops hints of his suspicions and paranoia to the audience! Christopher Gable must very nearly top the list of villains in the 1980s, his voice and eyes alone conveying a great deal of menace. Maurice Roeves also steals the show as mad gun-runner Stotz.

Given the enormous weight of nostalgia and emotion that loaded down Tom Baker's regeneration into Peter Davison, the regeneration scene in part four of *Androzani* had an enormous example to live up to – but it surpassed the finale of *Logopolis* by a huge margin: for my money, **it's the definitive regeneration scene of the entire series, old or new**, and it defines the Doctor's character: he's making the supreme sacrifice to save *one person, not* an entire world, with no witnesses to his heroism. The closest that modern Doctor has come to this was with the tenth Doctor's sacrifice to save Wilf (*The End Of Time*, 2010), though nowhere in *The Caves Of Androzani* does this Doctor even so much as find time to have a momentary emotional breakdown over his impending doom.

If you see no other adventures from Peter Davison's period as the Doctor, see this one.

The Sixth Doctor
(Colin Baker: 1984-86)

Tapped to fill the role of the Doctor by John Nathan-Turner after holding court and entertaining guests at the wedding of a mutual friend, Colin Baker quickly got attention for various ambitious claims (including that he intended to outlast Tom Baker in the role), outrageous quips (that the show's violence didn't go far enough for his tastes) and jokes, some of which didn't go over well (in early TV interviews and convention panels, he stated that his favorite monster from **Doctor Who** was...Tom Baker). Notoriety was nothing new to Colin Baker (who, for the record, is not related in any way to Tom). He had played the amoral, swindling Paul Merroney on the popular soap opera **The Brothers** in the mid 1970s, and prided himself on playing a character viewers "loved to hate." And Baker's Doctor was given an unusual amount of early exposure to **Doctor Who** fans, as his debut story, *The Twin Dilemma*, came not at the beginning of season 22 but the end of season 21.

In hindsight, the greater gap that would have been afforded by waiting until the new season to introduce the new Doctor might have helped. John Nathan-Turner and Colin Baker had decided on several parameters for the Doctor's sixth persona early on: that he should be so unpredictable as to be almost unlikeable at times, that the character's alien nature should be emphasized more than before, and that he should seem a little more arrogant and aloof than the departing Peter Davison's portrayal. But *The Twin Dilemma*, in which the Doctor donned a clashingly colorful patchwork coat, and later tried to strangle Peri (Nicola Bryant) in a bout of post-regenerative dementia, was met with consternation from casual viewers and diehard fans alike.

The 22nd season of **Doctor Who** was, for the most part, a great improvement over *Twin Dilemma*, but the making of that season posed problems of its own. For one thing, the series faced its first major format change in many years. The previous winter, due to a scheduling crunch arising from coverage of the 1984 Winter Olympics, the four 25-minute episodes of the Peter Davison story *Resurrection Of The Daleks* were consolidated into two 50-minute installments. Even before this unusual reformatting, however, the BBC had already instructed John Nathan-Turner to plan a season of 13 **50-minute** episodes, spread out among six stories. The new format eliminated two cliffhangers from each story - or, in the case of *The Two Doctors*, it robbed the story of a third cliffhanger. Saward wasn't happy with the idea of losing some of the show's trademark suspense, but the BBC left him little choice.

Attack Of The Cybermen kicked off the new season, combining continuity-heavy homages to episodes from the 1960s with the somewhat topical approach of Halley's Comet. Written by Paula Moore, *Attack* was actually an Eric Saward creation, but internal BBC rules - designed to prevent script editors from writing every episode of a series themselves - forced him to turn his plot outline over to a fellow writer. Philip Martin's *Vengeance On Varos* was up next, gaining considerable criticism for its depictions of violence - despite the fact that it was an allegory about the mind-numbing effect of overexposure to violence on TV. The Master, in the person of Anthony Ainley, returned in *The Mark Of The Rani*, a story designed to introduce a new Time Lady villain, the Rani, played by Kate O'Mara. Intended to be a recurring character, the Rani proved to be unavailable for a rematch when Aaron Spelling lured O'Mara to the United States to play Joan Collins' sister on **Dynasty**.

The next story, the three-part *The Two Doctors*, marked the return of writer Robert Holmes and actors Patrick Troughton and Frazer Hines. Having enjoyed reprising their roles in *The Five Doctors*, Troughton and Hines were up for a rematch of their own, this time with Colin Baker (who had once shared a house with Troughton's son). With the new episode structure, this story was equivalent to a six-parter from the 70s - and it was the first story of that length to air since *The Armageddon Factor*. It too contained numerous violent scenes, including the Doctor having to resort to smothering a pursuer with cyanide to save his own life. This made it all too convenient for the controller of BBC1, Michael Grade, to announce during the airing of this story that he was cancelling **Doctor Who**.

Once the announcement was made, John Nathan-Turner hastilty organized an elaborate campaign to rally the British press and the public behind a single cause: reversing the cancellation. Nathan-Turner had to use contacts he had built up in the course of publicizing the show to mount this effort without taking any credit, as it would have put him in a very bad position career-wise to be seen or heard challenging the BBC's decision. Fans around the world offered to raise money from their own pockets to get **Doctor Who** back in front of the cameras. Finally, after a great deal of pressure, Michael Grade backpedaled and declared the cancellation a "hiatus" - it would be back, he announced, but only after much consideration of the content of recent episodes. The fans breathed a sigh of relief, but it would still be 18 months before the Doctor was on their screens again after the current season.

The 22nd season closed with *Timelash*, guest starring **Blake's 7** star Paul Darrow, and Eric Saward's own *Revelation Of The Daleks*, the latter of which was criticised for numerous graphically violent scenes, again lending credence to Grade's claims that **Doctor Who** was due for an overhaul. The final scene of the episode, originally written to hint at the already-planned season 23 opener, was trimmed before air, as behind-the-scenes changes unraveled the stories that were already being written for the 1986 season. These stories would remain unmade until Big Finish Productions adapted them for audio in 2009 and 2010.

Unseen and unmade: Target novelizations of the never-produced season 23 stories
Mission To Magnus, The Ultimate Evil and *The Nightmare Fair.*

Grade's instructions to John Nathan-Turner were clear: the violence in **Doctor Who** had to be toned down, or the show would not return. Like Graham Williams almost a decade before, Nathan-Turner had to switch gears between gritty action and comedy. He and Saward devised a season-long story arc that would see the Doctor put on trial by his own people - a trial that would cost him his life if he lost.

Something that *was* lost was an entire season of stories written by some of the show's alumni and rising newcomers as well: Graham Williams' *The Nightmare Fair* was to have put the Doctor up against the Celestial Toymaker, an adversary from the Hartnell era, while *Mission To Magnus* would have seen the return of the Ice Warriors for the first time since Pertwee's reign; appearing alongside them in the Philip Martin two-parter would have been the slimy Sil from *Vengeance On Varos*. Wally K. Daly's *The Ultimate Evil* would have centered around a creature whose machine could drive an entire planet's population mad with violent urges, while another epic three-parter, Robert Holmes' *Yellow Fever And How To Cure It*, would have brought back the Master and, again from the third Doctor years, the Autons. In any event, the finished scripts - only a week away from filming - were nixed by the BBC's demand for a rethink of the series; some were reworked into novels several years later.

Eric Saward, though he liked using "classic" villains such as the Cybermen and Daleks, was beginning to chafe at the preponderance of returning enemies from the show's past - and at John Nathan-Turner's habit of "stunt casting" prominent roles to gain publicity from the appearance of famous actors. And in the long break between seasons, Saward himself wrote the only official **Doctor Who** adventure to air during the hiatus: a "Pirate" Radio 4 drama called *Slipback*, starring Colin Baker and Nicola Bryant as the Doctor and Peri.

When season 23 finally did premiere, it launched BBC1's fall schedule in September 1986. The 50-minute experiment had been brought to an end, but with mixed results: instead of thirteen 50-minute episodes, the BBC would now only produce fourteen 25-minute episodes. There would be a longer stretch of episodes to schedule, but in truth the show's season had been chopped in half. Only four stories would make up the new connected story arc called *The Trial Of A Time Lord*. Robert Holmes returned yet again to write the season premiere, referred to nowadays as *The Mysterious Planet* (episodes 1-4), while Philip Martin came back - and brought Sil with him - for *Mindwarp* (episodes 5-8), which saw Nicola Bryant exit the series.

Pip and Jane Baker, a husband-and-wife team of writers who had submitted prior unproduced **Doctor Who** scripts (but had written professionally for such SF series as **Space: 1999**), penned the third story, *Terror Of The Vervoids* (episodes 9-12), which introduced Melanie, a feisty new companion devised by John Nathan-Turner specifically so he could cast stage star Bonnie Langford in the role.

With the two-part story concluding *The Trial Of A Time Lord*, however, a problem arose unlike any other in the show's history. After writing episode 13, Robert Holmes succumbed to a long illness and died. Distraught over Holmes' death and tired of arguing with John Nathan-Turner, script editor Eric Saward walked off the job - and took a hastily-written draft of episode 14 with him, the only ending that the season had after Holmes died. John Nathan-Turner went back to Pip and Jane Baker, meeting with them under unusual circumstances (an attorney had to be present to ensure that details of Saward's withdrawn script were not discussed) and giving them the script for Robert Holmes' 13th episode. It was now up to the Bakers to finish the season. They quickly wrote the season finale, bringing the Trial to an end and finishing the season on upbeat note. (Originally, as has been disclosed since, Saward's story would have seen the Doctor and his arch-nemesis during the trial, supposedly an embittered, evil future incarnation of himself known as the Valeyard, locked in mortal combat in an unresolved, **Blake's** 7-style cliffhanger - Saward's reasoning being that it could either end the show, or be resolved if **Doctor Who** managed to escape cancellation.)

The ratings for the 23rd season were, generally speaking, unimpressive; beaten out largely by a contemporary American import, **The A-Team**, **Doctor Who** was now in an unenviable position where a case could be made to cancel it due to poor viewership. Instead, and perhaps mindful of the outcry from the 1985-86 cancellation, Michael Grade informed John Nathan-Turner that the show would go on in 1987 - but that a new Doctor would have to be found. Told that three years in the part was enough (in fact, he had only played the part for two seasons plus one story at the end of Peter Davison's final season), Colin Baker became the first Doctor in the show's history to be dismissed. Nathan-Turner argued that Baker's services should at least be engaged for the first story of season 24, to allow for a proper regeneration story to take place, and somewhat surprisingly his department heads at the BBC granted this request. But when Nathan-Turner approached Baker with the idea, his hopes were dashed - the actor was infuriated at his treatment and declined the offer of one more trip in the TARDIS. The series would go on - but now its producer had to find a new lead actor, a new script editor to guide his adventures, and start anew, very much aware that the axe could fall at any time.

THE TWIN DILEMMA

The seemingly harmless Professor Edgeworth abducts Romulus and Remus Sylvest, twin boys whose immense mathematical prowess is closely guarded for fear that it could become a powerful weapon in the wrong hands. Edgeworth's paymaster is Mestor, the giant gastropod, who plans to have the boys calculate a way to plunge the Jacondan solar system into chaos — all for the sake of hatching thousands of giant larvae containing a future swarm of gastropods. Edgeworth is the alias of Azmael, an outcast Time Lord who is reluctantly working for Mestor, but unknown to him, a fellow Time Lord is about to come crashing into Mestor's plan for universal domination — a Time Lord who is suffering from a severely traumatic regeneration, and whose actions and moods cannot be predicted, not even by a companion who now fears for her life.

Colin Baker . . . . The Doctor
Nicola Bryant . . . . Peri
Helen Blatch . . . . Fabian
Dennis Chinnery . . . . Sylvest
Andrew Conrad . . . . Remus
Paul Conrad . . . . Romulus
Maurice Denham . . . . Edgeworth / Azmael
Seymour Green . . . . Chamberlain
Dione Inman . . . . Elena
Kevin McNally . . . . Hugo Lang
Roger Nott . . . . Prisoner
Edwin Richfield . . . . Mestor
Oliver Smith . . . . Drak

This story has been released on DVD

written by Anthony Steven
directed by Peter Moffatt
music by Malcolm Clarke

Part 1 aired on March 22, 1984
Part 2 aired on March 23, 1984
Part 3 aired on March 29, 1984
Part 4 aired on March 30, 1984

Barry Stanton . . . . Noma
John Wilson . . . . Guard

Featuring some of the most disjointed writing and some of the least effective sets and costumes of the 1980s, *The Twin Dilemma* was a daring way to introduce a new Doctor, putting him through a period of mental instability that left the audience with no point of identification other than Peri. And somehow, after the dramatic magnus opus that was *The Caves of Androzani*, it almost seems inappropriate to chase the monumental changes in the series down with a story about two children (who aren't entirely convincing in their roles) being chased around by a large slug who commands even larger legions of strange-looking bird people who look only marginally more convincing than the San Diego Padres' Dancing Chicken mascot. There *is* a good side, though — Maurice Denham's portrayal of Edgeworth as tired and beaten effectively builds up our sympathy for him, and the revelation that he is an old Time Lord friend of the Doctor's builds this even more, making it a truly sad moment when he dies.

UWARP!

Much like the Doctor's new costume, it's hard to just avoid *The Twin Dilemma*, or act like it's not there, given its pivotal place in **Doctor Who**'s fictional and real-life history. But do take it with a great many grains of salt. (After all, nothing's better when you're dealing with giant slugs.)

SEASON 22: 1985
ATTACK OF THE CYBERMEN

The Doctor wanders right into a Cyberman scheme to alter their own history. When he first encountered them, the Doctor engineered the destruction of the Cybermen's home planet in order to save Earth. Now, the Cybermen – operating from their base on Telos – plan to divert the course of Halley's Comet circa 1985, so Earth won't be there to interfere in Cyber-history. Left behind after the attempted Dalek invasion, Lytton is up to no good on Earth, but his attempt to curry favor with the Cybermen in exchange for a ticket off of Earth turns into a deal with the devil that he can't survive. And on Telos itself, a pair of renegade slave laborers tries to steal a Cyberman timeship, and the original inhabitants of Telos, who cannot survive in anything but sub-zero temperatures, enlist help in their own fight against the Cybermen.

Colin Baker . . . . The Doctor
Nicola Bryant . . . . Peri
John   Ainley   .   .   .   .   Cyberman
Michael   Attwell   .   .   .   .   Bates
David   Banks   .   .   .   .   Cyberleader
James   Beckett   .   .   .   .   Payne
Sarah   Berger   .   .   .   .   Rost
Faith   Brown   .   .   .   .   Flast
Stephen   Churchett   .   .   .   .   .   .   Bill
Maurice   Colbourne   .   .   .   .   .   .   Lytton
Jonathan   David   .   .   .   .   .   .   Stratton
Esther   Freud   .   .   .   .   Threst
Brian   Glover   .   .   .   .   .   .   Griffiths
Pat   Gorman   .   .   .   .   .   .   Cyberman
Sarah   Greene   .   .   .   .   .   .   Varne
Michael   Kilgarriff   .   .   .   .   .   .   Cybercontroller

This story has been released on DVD

written by Paula Moore
directed by Matthew Robinson
music by Malcolm Clarke

Part 1 aired on January 5, 1985
Part 2 aired on January 12, 1985

Thomas   Lucy   .   .   .   .   Cyberman
Ian   Marshall-Fisher   .   .   .   .   .   .   Cyberman
Terry   Molloy   .   .   .   .   Russell
Brian   Orrell   .   .   .   .   .   .   Cyber   Lieutenant
Roger   Pope   .   .   .   .   Cyberman
Stephen   Wale   .   .   .   .   David

In this bizarre and slightly confusing tale, the Doctor wanders into a Cyberman scheme to alter their own history, and the viewer needs a crash course in **Doctor Who** history to understand the most basic points of the plot. Few of the B-stories are given any time to develop. Arguably, the main story isn't given time to develop either. It's all smashed together into a kind of plotline pate and it's up to the viewer to digest it – whether or not you've got the pre-requisite **Doctor Who** continuity memorized is up to you.

Some stories with several complex plot threads running simultaneously can bring it all together at the end, giving the viewer a satisfying conclusion. But *Attack Of The Cybermen* keeps all of its disparate storylines at a huge distance from each other, with many of the key characters in the drama never even meeting one another, and whether this happened at the writing or the editing stage, the juxtaposition of scenes doesn't give the viewer a chance to keep up, much less catch up.

Colin Baker does the best he can with the role of the Doctor in his first full post-regeneration story, but that's not saying much. I also feel sorry for Nicola Bryant – in this segment, more than any other, she spends half of the show wearing an embarassingly tight leotard, and several scenes of her running after the Doctor through London, and then having to run ever faster to catch up when the Doctor makes a U-turn without warning, seem to exist for no other reason than to meet some kind of "jiggle" quota. Though Ms. Bryant had to endure a couple of other skimpy costumes in this season, this had to be the worst example. As a viewer who was a teenage boy at the time I first saw *Attack Of The Cybermen*, my reaction was predictably favorable, but as someone trying to make sense of the story, even then, it's an incredibly impractical costume.

The idea of the Cybermen trying to better their own history using Halley's Comet –a big news item in 1985 and 1986 – is very intriguing. And it certainly should've gotten a better treatment than this.

VENGEANCE ON VAROS

The TARDIS stalls in deep space, drained of one of its power sources. The Doctor is able to nudge the TARDIS toward the planet Varos, the galaxy's only known natural deposit of zeiton-7 ore. But the rightful governor of Varos is under the thumb of Sil, a sinister profitmongering alien who plans to take over Varos and strip-mine it dry with no regard for the natives of the planet. Life on Varos is so bleak that executions and elections are both broadcast publicly, and they're not exactly two different things – anytime one of the governor's referendums fails to meet with the approval of the public, the governor himself suffers at the mercy of a disintegration beam, and naturally it's on the air. The Doctor and Peri arrive right in the middle of just such an execution, setting a condemned prisoner free and setting in motion a chain of events that could free Varos from Sil's murderous business dealings.

Colin Baker	. . . .	The Doctor
Nicola Bryant	. . . .	Peri
Geraldine Alexander	. . . .	Areta
Nicholas Chagrin	. . . .	Quillam
Forbes Collins	. . . .	Chief Officer
Jason Connery	. . . .	Jondar
Graham Cull	. . . .	Bax
Martin Jarvis	. . . .	Governor
Hugh Martin	. . . .	Priest
Jack McGuire	. . . .	Madman
Sheila Reid	. . . .	Etta
Nabil Shaban	. . . .	Sil
Bob Tarff	. . . .	Executioner

This story has been released on DVD

written by Philip Martin
directed by Ron Jones
music by Malcolm Clarke

Part 1 aired on January 19, 1985
Part 2 aired on January 26, 1985

Owen Teale	. . . .	Maldak
Keith Skinner	. . . .	Rondel
Alan Troy	. . . .	Madman
Stephen Yardley	. . . .	Arak

NEW WHO CONNECTIONS: The tenth Doctor again mentions the TARDIS' all-important zeiton crystals when the TARDIS suffers a major breakdown in *Time Crash* (2007).

A couple of years before Gene Roddenberry conceived the Ferengi, the **Doctor Who** production team gave us Sil, a slimy green slug with a disturbing laugh and a bloodlust exceeded only by his lust for money. With a potentially brilliant satire of television's effects on society, *Vengeance On Varos* could have been one of the best and most socially relevant **Doctor Who** stories ever, but there were so many distractions that it fell a little short of the mark. In a surprisingly adult reference, there was even a very brief mention of pornography, but not much of a message – just enough to register with an older audience. (I must admit, it went over my head for several years.)

On the good side, Nabil Shaban outshines the rest of the cast – including the regulars – as slimy Sil, who is easily the sixth Doctor's most distinctive and enduring companion. Sil returned in the second segment of 1986's *Trial Of A Time Lord*, though that appearance lacked the menace that the character displayed here, and its storyline was even *less* focused and coherent; on *Varos*, however, Shaban steals the show to such a degree that his performance alone merits repeat viewing. On the downside, a trend is carried over from the Peter Davison years, as the TARDIS continues to be treated as a very ordinary spaceship so the writers can foist occasionally ridiculous plot twists on the Doctor and Peri – in this case, the TARDIS runs out of fuel. They might as well have said the Doctor needed new mercury for the fluid links.

THE MARK OF THE RANI

The TARDIS is diverted to England at the dawn of the industrial revolution, a particularly sensitive point in human history that could be derailed by one careless time traveler – but in this case, there are no fewer than three careless time travelers. The Master is hatching a plot – yet again – to do away with the Doctor and destroy the Earth, while the Rani, a female Time Lord with a talent for sinister biochemical experiments, uses humans as her guinea pigs. This puts the Doctor and Peri in double jeopardy as the Master and the Rani interfere with each other's plans, and both of the evil Time Lords couldn't be less concerned about their effects on Earth's development.

Colin Baker	The Doctor	written by Pip & Jane Baker	
Nicola Bryant	Peri	directed by Sarah Hellings	
Anthony Ainley	The Master	music by Jonathan Gibbs	
Terence Alexander	Lord Ravensworth		
Gary Cady	Luke Ward	Part 1 aired on February 2, 1985	
Peter Childs	Jack Ward	Part 2 aired on February 9, 1985	
Cordelia Ditton	Older Woman		
Gawn Grainger	George Stephenson		
William Ilkley	Tim Bass	Richard Steele	Guard
Sarah James	Young Woman	Alan Talbot	Tom
Nigel Johnson	Josh	Martyn Whitby	Drayman
Hus Levant	Edwin Green	Kevin White	Sam Rudge
Kate O'Mara	The Rani		

This story has been released on DVD

Boasting some outstanding location filming, my favorite feature of this episode is Colin Baker's performance as the Doctor, honed to perfection in the first relatively straightforward script of his era. Baker's Doctor is a much more formidable match for the Master than Peter Davison was, and even though the Rani's motivations aren't quite clear, Kate O'Mara gives the new character a sinister edge. Even Peri gets to show some initiative and uses her knowledge of botany, a nice change from the constant argument scenes.

Also, some credit is due to the set designer, who took the basic concept of the Doctor's TARDIS, turned it up a few notches and put it in an art deco context, and created the very cool and expensive-looking set for the Rani's TARDIS. On the other hand, it's never made clear why she has a bunch of embryonic dinosaurs in glass jars perched precariously upon easily-toppled pedestals in the TARDIS, other than to set up the unnecessary cliffhanger for the Rani and the Master in the second half. One thing which was sadly never followed up was the vaguely disturbing flirtation between the Master and the Rani. The Rani could not possibly have shown less interest, while the Master seemed to think she'd go for a fey, mincing, wimpy villain like himself. In one wonderful scene, the Rani comments that the Master would get dizzy walking in a straight line – a very accurate criticism of the way the Master was written in the 1980s. It didn't take much imagination to see that the Rani established herself here as the more dangerous adversary.

THE TWO DOCTORS

The second Doctor and Jamie are sent on a mission by the Time Lords to ask a team of scientists, as diplomatically as possible, to bring their time travel experiments to an end. The Doctor is unable to convince the head scientist, Dastari, to heed the Time Lords' warnings; Dastari is far too busy admiring his own work, including his genetic "improvement" of Chessene, a savage Androgum. But Chessene's augmentations have simply given her the ability to apply her violent primitive impulses on a grander scale – such as a collusion with the Sontarans to use the new time travel device as a weapon of conquest. The Doctor is captured by the Sontarans and taken to their secret base of operations on Earth – and his sixth incarnation will have to find him to avoid the corruption of his entire timeline.

Colin Baker . . . . The Doctor
Patrick Troughton . . . . The Doctor
Nicola Bryant . . . . Peri
Frazer Hines . . . . Jamie McCrimmon
Aimee Delamain . . . . Dona Arana
Nicholas Farcett . . . . Technician
Carmen Gomez . . . . Anita
Clinton Greyn . . . . Stike
Fernando Monast . . . . Scientist
Laurence Payne . . . . Dastari
Jacqueline Pearce . . . . Chessene
Tim Raynham . . . . Varl

This story has been released on DVD

written by Robert Holmes
directed by Peter Moffatt
music by Peter Howell

Part 1 aired on February 16, 1985
Part 2 aired on February 23, 1985
Part 3 aired on March 2, 1985

James Saxon . . . . Oscar
John Stratton . . . . Shockeye

NEW WHO CONNECTIONS: This marks the final appearance of the Sontarans in the original series; they would later return to do battle with the Doctor and the people of Earth in 2008's *The Sontraran Stratagem*. The Sontarans were also fixtures in the '90s fan-made video productions that helped to tide fans over after **Doctor Who** had been cancelled by the BBC; Sontarans appeared in *Mindgame, Mindgame Trilogy* and *Shakedown: Return Of The Sontarans*.

For Patrick Troughton's swan song to **Doctor Who**, it was fitting that this was probably the most straightforward of the "multiple Doctor" stories, focusing on only two incarnations of the character instead of three or five or more. *The Two Doctors* is also the only story of the 1980s to reach the length of the frequent six-part format of the 1970s. Though there are many good plot ideas in the show, they're jumbled pretty badly. Jackie Pearce almost gives a retread performance of Servalan from **Blake's 7** here as Chessene, but the real show-stealer is John Stratton as the vicious (and hungry) Shockeye. Many people have complained that, in terms of violence, the sixth Doctor crossed the line in the climactic scene where he mothballed Shockeye with cyanide...but Shockeye was such a deliciously nasty character, any lesser resolution for him would've been a cop-out, and he was the kind of character that couldn't be left alive, because he'd only use his "second chance" to kill again.

I have to single out the music here as well, easily the best score of Colin Baker's era, provided by Peter Howell. There's a lot of nice Spanish guitar work to emphasize the Spanish location photography, but the percussive battle theme for the Sontarans is a very cool piece of electronic music that fits the Sontarans like a glove. (Ironically, of course, the Sontarans are probably at their weakest here in the entire series, not to mention that the actors cast were simply too tall, and the art of making the Sontaran makeup convincing had apparently been lost since their previous appearance in 1977.

TIMELASH

Rebellion is in the air on Karfel, a planet whose native population is enslaved by the Borad – a being which used to be one of them, but has now become a horrible genetic mutant. Tyranny is not the Borad's only gift to Karfel – he has also brought the Timelash, a device that allows political prisoners to be "executed" by dumping them into a time corridor. The Borad has also brought Karfel to the brink of war with the Bandrils, a race of peaceful hand puppets. In the midst of this bleak landscape, the Doctor and Peri arrive, and find themselves racing against time to save the Karfelons from their own esteemed leader.

Colin Baker . . . . The Doctor
Nicola Bryant . . . . Peri
Robert Ashby . . . . The Borad
David Ashton . . . . Kendron
Dicken Ashworth . . . . Sezom
Denis Carey . . . . Old Man
David Chandler . . . . Herbert
Jean Anne Crowley . . . . Vena
Paul Darrow . . . . Tekker
Eric Deacon . . . . Mykros
Martin Gower . . . . Tyheer
Dean Hollingsworth . . . . Android
Christine Kavanaugh . . . . Aram

This story has been released on DVD

written by Glen McCoy
directed by Pennant Roberts
music by Elizabeth Parker

Part 1 aired on March 9, 1985
Part 2 aired on March 16, 1985

Steven Mackintosh . . . . Gazak
James Richardson . . . . Guardolier
Peter Robert Scott . . . . Brunner
Tracy Louise Ward . . . . Katz

A.K.A.: Paul Darrow returns to **Doctor Who** for the first time since 1970, though his guest starring turn as Tekker seems to owe a lot to his career-making stint on the BBC science fiction series **Blake's 7** (1978-81). **Denis Carey** was last seen in *The Keeper Of Traken* during Tom Baker's final season, and also appeared in the Douglas Adams six-parter *Shada*, though *Shada* itself failed to appear because production was never completed.

One of the *worst* **Doctor Who** stories of the 1980s, *Timelash* is saddled with ridiculously low production values, including the pyramid full of Christmas tinsel that passes for the Timelash itself, the dull sets (which are given a token explanation in the script), and of course, the Bandril character which is barely a step away from being a sock puppet.

The guest stars are also uniformly bad as well, which is sad when the guest players include Paul Darrow (Avon of **Blake's 7** fame) and Denis Carey (who guest starred in the aborted *Shada* in 1979). Many of the younger actors seem to stumble through their roles with little enthusiasm, though it's just possible that, as with the audience, the cast were hopelessly confused by the script. It's hard to blame them. Many critics single Darrow out for ridicule here, but it seems much more likely that either the story's director, or someone higher up (such as the producer) asked him to "just play this like you did Avon." The wig and robes don't help in that respect. *Timelash* is actually something of a **Blake's 7** reunion: Pennant Roberts directed several episodes, while Denis Carey, Dicken Ashworth and Colin Baker all guest starred in different episodes.

The concept of H.G. Wells traveling with the Doctor and encountering the inspiration for some of his classic tales is actually a nice one, but that basic plot idea would be carried off with much more skill (and Charles Dickens instead of H.G. Wells) in 2005's *The Unquiet Dead*.

REVELATION OF THE DALEKS

The Doctor arrives on the planet Necros, whose chief industry is funeral services, to pay his final respects to an old friend. But Necros isn't what it used to be. It's now run by The Great Healer – in reality, Davros, creator of the malevolent Daleks – who is using Necros as cover for his experiments to convert human beings into mindless Dalek operators. The head of the funeral industry, Kara, has hired an assassin to dispose of Davros, but her hired gun quickly realizes that he's being paid to act as cannon fodder. The Doctor discovers that his arrival has been anticipated, but he doesn't suspect that the Daleks are involved until he falls into their clutches.

Colin Baker	The Doctor
Nicola Bryant	Peri
Ken Barker	Mutant
Eleanor Bron	Kara
Toby Byrne	Dalek
Trevor Cooper	Takis
Stephen Flynn	Grigory
William Gaunt	Orcini
Penelope Lee	Computer voice
Alec Linstead	head of Stengos
Bridget Lynch-Blosse	Natasha
John Scott Martin	Dalek
Royce Mills	Dalek voice
Terry Molloy	Davros
John Ogwen	Bostock
Alexei Sayle	DJ

This story has been released on DVD

written by Eric Saward
directed by Graeme Harper
music by Roger Limb

Part 1 aired on March 23, 1985
Part 2 aired on March 30, 1985

Roy Skelton	Dalek voice
Colin Spaull	Lilt
Tony Starr	Dalek
Clive Swift	Jobel
Jenny Tomasin	Tasambeker
Cy Town	Dalek
Hugh Walters	Vogel

NEW WHO CONNECTIONS: Davros' appearance in the 2008 two-parter *The Stolen Earth / Journey's End* takes this story into account, giving Davros a robotic hand to replace the one shot off by Orcini. The robotic hand was also depicted on the cover artwork of the Big Finish audio story *The Juggernauts* (2004), which predated the 2008 season finale by several years and yet anticipated many of the details of its appearance.

A.K.A.: Colin Spaull has a habit of consorting with the Time Lord's other greatest foes. His next **Doctor Who** appearance took place alongside the Cybermen, in 2006's two-parter *Rise Of The Cybermen / The Age Of Steel* - also directed by Graeme Harper, who was behind the camera for his second **Doctor Who** adventure here after 1984's *Caves Of Androzani*. Alexei Sayle, best known as one of **The Young Ones**, was brought to **Doctor Who** for a memorable piece of one-off stunt casting.

Possibly the most atypical Dalek story of the original series, this story's title trumpeted their presence and then barely showed them; Davros was really the focus here, and in that respect the Daleks are almost superfluous. (It would've been bolder to do a Davros story with *no* Daleks, but that would have to wait for a 2003 audio story, *Davros*, released by Big Finish, which pitted Colin Baker and Terry Molloy against each other for a rematch.)

Graeme Harper was back in the director's chair for this one, but his fast-cutting, gritty style jars against the new languid pace dictated by the 50-minute episode length of this season. But his casting choices still make for an array of memorable guest characters, from the pathetic Tasembeker to the loathsome Jobel, and the heavily-armed double-act of Orcini and Bostock, two characters who seem to have such a rich history that it's amazing they haven't gotten their own audio spinoff series. It all adds up to an interestingly off-format adventure – it doesn't follow the usual script for **Doctor Who**, or for a **Doctor Who** tale featuring the Daleks.

THE TRIAL OF A TIME LORD
SEASON 23: 1986
THE MYSTERIOUS PLANET
THE TRIAL OF A TIME LORD, PARTS 1-4

A huge space station drags the TARDIS out of time and space, depositing the Doctor in a Gallifreyan courtroom where a Time Lord tribunal accuses him of meddling in the history of the galaxy. The ruthless prosecutor, the Valeyard, presents events from the Doctor's past as evidence of his transgression of the Time Lords' non-interference laws. In the adventure shown, the Doctor and Peri – who is curiously absent from the courtroom – discover that the planet Ravolox is actually Earth, two million years hence, and somehow moved into another solar system. Two rogues from another galaxy are hunting down copies of a huge databank which have found their way into the possession of a robot which lords over the last remaining humans on Earth. The source of these copies also turn the Time Lords themselves into suspects in the crime of the eon – the disappearance of Earth.

Colin Baker . . . . The Doctor
Nicola Bryant . . . . Peri
Lynda Bellingham . . . . The Inquisitor
Michael Jayston . . . . The Valeyard
Adam Blackwood . . . . Balazar
Roger Brierly . . . . Drathro
Tom Chadbon . . . . Merdeen
Billy McColl . . . . Humker
Glen Murphy . . . . Dibber
Sion Tudor Owen . . . . Tandrell
David Rodigan . . . . Broken Tooth
Tony Selby . . . . Glitz

This story
has been
released
on DVD

written by Robert Holmes
directed by Nicholas Mallett
music by Dominic Glynn

Part 1 aired on September 6, 1986
Part 2 aired on September 13, 1986
Part 3 aired on September 20, 1986
Part 4 aired on September 27, 1986

Joan Sims . . . . Katryca
Timothy Walker . . . . Grell

After the 1985 season, the BBC took a very cool attitude toward **Doctor Who**, citing excessive violence as its major fault and effectively cancelling the show. Fan outcry forced the BBC to retract that move, and producer John Nathan-Turner was told to tone down the violence and increase the humor, and it was over a year before the Doctor was seen on television again.

This is probably the best of the four installments that made up the *Trial Of A Time Lord* season, and that's not really saying much – the *entire season* was a missed opportunity. Still, there are entertaining things in this particular segment. Glitz, who later appeared in *The Ultimate Foe* and *Dragonfire*, is at his best here. In those later stories, Glitz is bumbling comic relief, but here he's mad, bad and dangerous to know – and still funny at the same time, an obvious homage to such roughish characters as Han Solo. Dibber balances Glitz's character nicely, and it's a shame that Dibber didn't return in *Dragonfire* (admittedly, there wouldn't have been room for Dibber in *The Ultimate Foe*). Glitz and Dibber are at their best when serving as the mouthpiece for some typically hilarious Robert Holmes dialogue. The trial idea itself is a cleverly satirical swipe at the fact that **Doctor Who** as a series was very much on trial in 1986, and this is the only story of the season to comment on that, with the Valeyard charging that the Doctor has often been at the center of violent events.

My biggest gripe with the *Trial Of A Time Lord* stories is that none of them were terribly interesting or well told. Throughout each of them, the action is interrupted by more scenes of Colin Baker – whose command of the role of the Doctor improved tremendously in this season – and Michael Jayston as the slippery Valeyard bickering at one another. In some cases – particularly in the following segment, *Mindwarp* – the narrative flow of the story was jettisoned altogether, with the trial being used as an excuse to make a quantum leap forward in the plot. This device could have been used very inventively, but instead it was used to cover some very poor plotting logic.

Another glorious missed opportunity in this season could have been to intersperse some real past adventures in with the "new" past adventures presented as evidence. Numerous episodes of individual stories, especially from the first two Doctors' eras, are missing, but some of the "orphaned" episodes – survivng half-hour segments of incomplete stories – could have been used to great effect as smaller individual bits of "evidence" in the trial. With the four new stories presented, either the Doctor or the Valeyard was already verbally setting up the action with some backstory, and they could have done the same to fill in the gaps of missing shows. But paying the artists involved for the reuse of their material would have been cost-prohibitive…and using those old episodes in the midst of the new stories might have drawn unwanted attention to the inferior nature of some of the new material.

On a purely trivial note, you may note that Glitz and Dibber brandish some familiar artillery – their heavy-duty guns in part four would later get much more screen time as the bazookoid weapons aboard **Red Dwarf**, the show which eventually supplanted **Doctor Who** as the BBC's flagship science fiction series. On a similar note, the well-executed opening special effects scene of the TARDIS being drawn toward the Time Lords' space station was included in the promos and "electronic press kit" for the 1996 **Doctor Who** TV movie. This was the sole piece of footage from the original BBC series which was included in Fox's publicity.

.

MINDWARP
THE TRIAL OF A TIME LORD, PARTS 5-8

The Valeyard presents another adventure as evidence of the Doctor's meddlesome nature. During this escapade, the Doctor and Peri arrive on Thoros Beta, the home planet of their old enemy Sil. Kiv, the leader of Sil's people, faces a painful death unless a way can be found to transplant Kiv's mind into a physically larger brain. When the Doctor and Peri are captured by the guards, the Doctor is subjected to an experiment wiith the mind transplantation equipment and becomes mentally unstable. Peri escapes with the help of King Yrcanos, a warrior from neighboring Thoros Alpha, whose people are enslaved by Sil. But the Valeyard's evidence seems to show the Doctor betraying Peri to save his own skin, despite the Doctor's insistence that these events never occurred. But even the Doctor is stunned into silence when he finally learns why Peri is not present to defend him at his trial.

Colin Baker . . . . The Doctor	
Nicola Bryant . . . . Peri	
Lynda Bellingham . . . . The Inquisitor	
Michael Jayston . . . . The Valeyard	
Brian Blessed . . . . King Yrcanos	
Thomas Branch . . . . The Lukoser	
Richard Henry . . . . Mentor	
Trevor Laird . . . . Frax	
Alibe Parsons . . . . Matrona Kani	
Patrick Reycart . . . . Crozier	
Christopher Ryan . . . . Kiv	
Nabil Shaban . . . . Sil	
Gordon Warnecke . . . . Tuza	

written by Philip Martin
directed by Ron Jones
music by Richard Hartley

Part 5 aired on October 4, 1986
Part 6 aired on October 11, 1986
Part 7 aired on October 18, 1986
Part 8 aired on October 25, 1986

A.K.A.: Trevor Laird would return to **Doctor Who** several times in its 2007 season, appearing as Martha's father. **Christopher Ryan**, Mike of **The Young Ones** fame, would get over his headache here as the only other member of Sil's race that we ever meet; he returned to **Doctor Who** beginning in 2008 to play a number of Sontaran roles (*The Sontaran Stratagem / The Poison Sky*, *The Pandorica Opens*). This is Sil's final appearance in television **Doctor Who**, though **Nabil Shaban** returns to the role for the Big Finish audio adaptation of the abandoned 1986 script *Mission To Magnus*. **Brian Blessed** has appeared in **Blake's 7**, **Space: 1999**, **I, Claudius**, and **Blackadder**, in addition to providing the voice of Gungan overlord Boss Nass in *Star Wars Episode I: The Phantom Menace*, but admit it, you know him best as Prince Vultan of the Hawkmen from the 1980 big-screen version of *Flash Gordon*.

Despite an interesting first episode, the second four-part story of the *Trial Of A Time Lord* season could well be the worst of the sixth Doctor's short run. Colin Baker had a few other turkeys to tackle, including *Timelash* and *The Twin Dilemma*, but those two in particular look like taut, well-plotted thrillers in comparison to *Mindwarp*. Philip Martin's earlier opus, *Vengeance On Varos*, may not have been the fantastic biting satire that so many fawning critiques have made it out to be, but it was far, far better than this. (It's also worth noting that after this installment, Philip Martin's name never again appeared on an episode of **Doctor Who**, though he would later return to the TARDIS in the realm of audio.)

Nabil Shaban and Christopher Ryan, as Sil and Kiv respectively, turn in the best performances of the show, while Brian Blessed delivers his trademark over-the-top performance. Colin Baker utterly fails, for the first and only time in his stint as the Doctor, to play the character with any kind of coherence or conviction. The moment the Doctor is subjected to the mind transfer device, Baker seems to take this as his cue to make funny noises, stagger around drunkenly, and generally annoy anyone who's watching and trying to make sense of it all. (The DVD extras reveal considerable confusion between the story's writer, script editor Eric Saward, and the director, which naturally trickled down to the cast.)

There's also a great deal of confusion as to what some of the Doctor's more questionable actions represent. Temporary brain damage? Manipulation of the evidence? Or just an incoherent script? (I think we have a winner.) Though *Mindwarp* has some scenes which are vital to the *Trial Of A Time Lord* plotline, it also has the dubious distinction of being the one sixth Doctor story which I consistently avoid if at all possible.

TERROR OF THE VERVOIDS
THE TRIAL OF A TIME LORD, PARTS 9-12

The Doctor finally gets his chance to present his defense in his trial. He presents an adventure from his own future, in which he and new companion Melanie are summoned to a posh space luxury liner by an anonymous distress call. While the ship's captain — who has met the Doctor on a previous occasion — and the incompetent chief of security initially regard the Doctor and

Mel as stowaways, they find themselves with other problems when murders begin to occur aboard the ship, and three scientists are being very secretive about their hydroponics experiment in the ship's cargo deck. As more passengers die mysteriously, the ship's captain asks the Doctor to help – but, according to the evidence, the Doctor isn't really all that helpful…which isn't how he remembers the story.

Colin Baker	. . . .	The Doctor
Bonnie Langford	. . . .	Melanie
Lynda Bellingham	. . . .	The Inquisitor
Michael Jayston	. . . .	The Valeyard
David Allister	. . . .	Bruchner
Bob Appleby	. . . .	Second Vervoid
Hugh Beverton	. . . .	Guard
Honor Blackman	. . . .	Professor Lasky
Peppi Borza	. . . .	First Vervoid
Michael Craig	. . . .	Commodore Travers
Leon Davis	. . . .	Ortezo
Denys Hawthorne	. . . .	Rudge
Arthur Hewlett	. . . .	Kimber
Sam Howard	. . . .	Atza
Mike Mungarvan	. . . .	Duty Officer

This story
has been
released
on DVD

written by Pip & Jane Baker
directed by Chris Clough
music by Malcolm Clarke

Part 9 aired on Novemeber 1, 1986
Part 10 aired on November 8, 1986
Part 11 aired on November 15, 1986
Part 12 aired on November 22, 1986

Yolande Palfrey	. . . .	Janet
Tony Scoggo	. . . .	Enzu / Grenville
Simon Slaters	. . . .	Edwardes
Malcolm Tierney	. . . .	Doland
Barbara Ward	. . . .	Ruth Baxter

Though it's a very paint-by-numbers, Agatha Christie-ish story, that actually helps this segment of *The Trial Of A Time Lord* – it's the *least* convoluted of the four shows that comprised the entire season! For once, things are made interesting by the obvious tampering with the story as the Doctor remembers it, though it's baffling to think that he would be allowed to preview his own future. There's also a far-too-obvious hint planted for the audience that practically screams "THE VALEYARD DID IT!" in ten-foot-tall neon letters. I think by this point in the trial storyline, the audience had already grasped, or at the very least guessed, this turn of events.

The biggest downer for this story is the latter half, in which an almost funny succession of murderers and plotters is exposed every few minutes - it almost seems that the only innocent people on board the liner were the captain and the stewardess. One or two killers would've been fine, but the entire hydroponics team is corrupt, the security officer has sold out, the alien passengers are trying to hijack the ship…it goes on and on, to the point where each additional unveiling of a new villain has the unintentional effect of being *comical*. (It's also worth noting that the scripts for this story went into production without any adjustment from script editor Eric Saward, who had walked off the job over disagreements about the show's direction with producer John Nathan-Turner.)

Much-maligned companion Melanie is given a strange introduction – meaning no introduction at all, really, since she's already traveling with the Doctor in his own future. And that part of the show still bothers me – how many of his own future escapades did the Doctor witness while searching for evidence in his defense? Does he carry that knowledge with him when he leaves the trial? If so, doesn't *that* violate the much-talked-about-but-seldom-specified laws of time?

THE ULTIMATE FOE
THE TRIAL OF A TIME LORD, PARTS 13-14

The Doctor is still on trial for his life, facing a new charge – genocide – levelled at him by the prosecuting Valeyard. The Doctor counters that the Valeyard has tampered with the evidence through the immense Gallifreyan information storage system known as the Matrix – but a Time Lord whose job is to tend the Matrix refutes this charge. Then, mysterious things begin happening. Two friendly witnesses arrive in the form of criminal Sabalom Glitz and future companion Melanie – with whom the Doctor has yet to travel at this point in his history. And then the Master appears from within the Matrix, admitting to providing these witnesses as part of his plan to help the Doctor and topple the High Council of the Time Lords at the same time. The Master also reveals that the Valeyard is, in fact, a future incarnation of the Doctor – a future incarnation gone mad and turned to evil. With this revelation the Doctor and the Valeyard plunge into the Matrix, aided and abetted by Glitz, Mel, and the Master, ready to fight the most dangerous battle between good and evil that any Time Lord has ever fought, where his mortal adversary is himself.

Colin Baker . . . . The Doctor
Bonnie Langford . . . . Melanie
Lynda Bellingham . . . . The Inquisitor
Michael Jayston . . . . The Valeyard
Anthony Ainley . . . . The Master
James Bree . . . . Keeper of the Matrix
Geoffrey Hughes . . . . Mr. Popplewick
Tony Selby . . . . Glitz

This story
has been
released
on DVD

Part 13 written by Robert Holmes
Part 14 written by Pip & Jane Baker
directed by Chris Clough
music by Dominic Glynn

Part 13 aired on November 29, 1986
Part 14 aired on December 6, 1986

If you've ever taken part in a courtroom trial, the one sentiment that everyone is able to express at the end, win or lose, is *thank God it's over.* That's eminently applicable here.

The potentially fascinating basic plotline of the Doctor facing genocide charges, and in general the entire trial itself, was one of the worst-handled stories in the history of **Doctor Who**. There are numerous vast gaps in logic. The Doctor is charged for the crime of genocide – yet the act upon which this charge is based takes place in his own future, making it *a crime he has yet to commit.* Not to say that the rest of the story is invalid from this point on: surely the Time Lords could now claim that they want the Doctor put away precisely so he *cannot* participate in the extinction of the vegetable Vervoid race, or perhaps to keep the event from happening at all, but instead he's somehow supposed to *sacrifice his remaining regenerations* to… a future self, which must by definition be one of the very regenerations he's meant to give up?

The Valeyard is treated as a second-rate copy of the Master, though it would be much more interesting if the Valeyard was clearly portrayed as a much more *competent* evil than the Master. This would explain the Master's initial wish to help the Doctor (another character twist which is soon disposed of). But in part 14, the Valeyard turns into a bumbler whose evil schemes are easily seen through by the Doctor. Certainly, if the Valeyard is indeed the Doctor in his final incarnation, he would be able to come up with much more menacing ways of threatening or blackmailing his sixth self. Perhaps the Valeyard could have tried to interfere with one of the sixth Doctor's past adventures. There are numerous possibilities which would've made much more sense than the story that was finally broadcast. And it was also **a bad idea, possibly the worst in the history of the series, to potentially lock the Doctor into a future in which he would become the Valeyard anyway.** It's an elephant in the room that has had a few peanuts fed to it by novelists and audio playwrights, but has been quietly ignored by every subsequent television adventure until the Valeyard was name-checked in 2013's *The Name Of The Doctor*.

This is also the story which marked seasoned **Doctor Who** writer Robert Holmes' final contribution to the series before he died. That the last episode was written by Pip and Jane Baker is unfortunate, because it is between these two episodes that the most inconsistencies in characters and continuity arise. The dialogue in the second episode also becomes ridiculous, with Melanie referring to an antiquated-looking "blinky lights" prop (but supposedly a very potent weapon) as a "megabyte modem," and the highlight, the Valeyard's supposedly ominous warning to the Doctor that "there's nothing you can do to prevent the catharsis of spurious morality." Does that actually *mean* anything?

A sad **Doctor Who** segment in many ways. Sad for being the swan song of series-defining writer Robert Holmes, sad that the final episode completed after his death was a flashy train wreck, sad for being a completely inadequate send-off for Colin Baker, and sad for being the final act in a season-long disappointment. *The Trial Of A Time Lord* was **Doctor Who** at its lowest ebb, and hardly a fitting thank you for a viewing public and a fan base that campaigned so hard to keep the show from being cancelled.

SHORT HOPS

...in which the author admits that his favorite Doctor and his favorite actor to have played the Doctor are not the same

I have a Batcave full of science fiction memorabilia and vintage video game goodies, many of which have immense sentimental value to me. Almost none of them are signed. I'm a terrible autograph seeker because I'm amazingly self-conscious about even *asking* for anything to be signed. On a purely practical level, if I actually met this person, the memory in and of itself is the real prize to be taken away from that meeting (of course, I am making the perhaps-foolish assumption that my synapses will continue to fire flawlessly, replaying that moment on command until I croak). Signatures do little for me, and probably do even less for the people doing the signing (aside from providing them with a further step on the road toward repetitive motion disorder from constantly signing their name). I am, however, terribly fond of one item which is signed (to me by name, no less).

I haven't met Colin Baker personally - I should point that out up front. A friend of mine who was lucky enough to go to the 2009 San Diego Comic Con (the year in which a variant figure of the sixth Doctor, and the first-ever action figures of the first two Doctors, were available as Comic Con exclusives, or, as I call them, perfect bait for geek traps) snagged them for me *and* got the sixth Doctor signed by Colin Baker himself, who happened to be in attendance.

The variant is significant: it's the first and, thus far, only time that the sprawling **Doctor Who** action figure range has acknowledge Big Finish Productions' **Doctor Who** audio series, which also happens to be where the sixth Doctor really reaches his full potential, including – as this figure portrays him – ditching his blindingly colorful outfit for a nearly-identical one in various shades of blue. (It's amazing how you can just change major costumes like that in an audio-only medium!)

Colin Baker may well be my favorite *actor* to have portrayed the Doctor.

That's an interesting distinction to have to make, simply because there are incarnations of the Doctor that I like better – at least in their TV versions. (VWORP!2 will cover the audio stories in which the sixth Doctor gradually comes into his own in a way that, due to the Machiavellian behind-the-scenes maneuvers at the BBC in the '80s, Colin Baker just didn't have a chance to bring to fruition on television.)

But in the years since he occupied the TARDIS, Baker has frequently made good use of the instant celebrity conferred upon any actor who pilots the time machine. After suffering the tragic loss of his son, he became a tireless campaigner and fundraiser for research into Sudden Infant Death Syndrome. His newspaper column in the Bucks Free Press – available online for those of us *not* living in Buckinghamshire – offer a window into his view of the world around him: compassionate, occasionally curmudgeonly, and wondering whatever happened to common decency, both among the public and their elected officials.

For someone who doesn't write for a living, he has an impressive and concise way with words. That he frequently lets his readers in on a few adventures in showbiz name-dropping is simply a bonus.

He occasionally talks about **Doctor Who**, too, but it's the fact that he doesn't talk about it constantly that makes Colin Baker seem like he must be a terribly interesting person to just sit around and chat with. (To be fair, surely *all* of the ex-Doctors must be fascinating people, but they just haven't built up years of archived newspaper columns providing a handy answer to the question "Who are you when you're at home?" – it's hard to judge from endless interviews in which the subject is only asked about, of all things, **Doctor Who**.) He strikes me as someone whose time I could waste an awful lot of, talking about sociology, the role of government in its constituents' lives, useless laws, old cat stories, and judging by the waistlines of all involved, it's fair to say there would probably be a mandatory recipe swap.

If someone told me I'd be stepping into the fictional world and traveling with the Doctor, I can't honestly say I'd choose to accompany the sixth Doctor as seen on television. If, on the other hand, someone told me I'm going to be stuck in a room with one of the actors to have played the part, I have a gut feeling that the getting-on-one-anothers'-nerves potential would be the lowest with Colin Baker. Or at least I like to think so. He seems like a tremendously likeable person – and certainly not someone who deserved what has to be the *worst* treatment that the BBC has afforded to any of the Doctors to date.

The Seventh Doctor
(Sylvester McCoy: 1987-96)

Forced to find a replacement for Colin Baker, ousted forcibly from the role of the Doctor by the BBC's Head of Drama, producer John Nathan-Turner began auditions for the new **Doctor Who**.

Nathan-Turner had now occupied the producer's seat since 1980, guiding the show's destiny through high points and low ebbs. And he readily admitted that he was tired of the grind and the incessant and sometimes obsessive fan criticism of his work, and his enthusiasm was sapped by season 23's feud with script editor Eric Saward. He was ready to move on. But the BBC had other ideas: they wanted JN-T to stay put, and clearly implied that if he vacated **Doctor Who**, **Doctor Who** would likely vacate the BBC1 schedule shortly thereafter. JN-T stayed where he was, and began looking not only for a new face for the Doctor, but a new script editor to guide the series.

The latter search was resolved with the hire of Andrew Cartmel. Eager to return some mystery and menace to **Doctor Who**, Cartmel not only rewrote the ground rules for potential scriptwriters, he made Alan Moore's 2000 A.D. comic required reading to give prospective writers a sense of the tone he was after. The show's logo was revamped with comic book inspiration in mind as well, and would be unveiled in an unprecedented new title sequence rendered entirely in state-of-the-art computer animation.

After a lengthy search, Nathan-Turner also settled on his choice for the seventh Doctor: a versatile but little-known actor named Sylvester McCoy (actually a long-running in-joke of a stage name; McCoy's real name is Percy James Kent-Smith). McCoy's background included an eyebrow-raising range, from a small role in the 1970s feature film adaptation of *Dracula* to a long stint with Ken Campbell's Roadshow, where his repertoire included hammering nails up his nose and dropping a live ferret into his pants. Nathan-Turner was convinced McCoy was right for the role, and was consciously modeling aspects of the new Doctor on Patrick Troughton - an actor whose deceptively impish qualities McCoy echoed in his portrayal.

Cartmel had been hired late in the game, so McCoy's first season, premiering in late 1987, was drawn primarily from a slush pile of scripts originally commissioned by Eric Saward for Colin Baker's Doctor. These stories were also written under the BBC's more-humor, less-violence dictum, and didn't reflect the direction Cartmel hoped to take. Despite the opening story, *Time And The Rani*, featuring the return of Kate O'Mara as the evil Time Lady, fans seemed largely nonplussed by the stories in season 24 - and, by extension, some of them didn't seem impressed with the new Doctor either. In the last story of the season, Nathan-Turner and Cartmel began redirecting the series toward their renewed vision of menace and mystery; Bonnie Langford's Mel was written out of the series at the actress' request, and Sophie Aldred was introduced as Ace, a brash teenager with a penchant for home-made explosives and other forms of antisocial behavior.

The 25th anniversary season premiered with Ben Aaronovitch's complex *Remembrance Of The Daleks*, McCoy's first brush with the mechanical monstrosities, and the audience's first taste of the new, multi-layered approach to **Doctor Who**. The Doctor was hatching plans within plans, manipulating events on a massive scale, and thoroughly entrapping the Daleks in an elaborate snare designed to eliminate them once and for all. Ace was deployed almost like a chess piece in the Doctor's plan, sometimes stalling his enemy, sometimes sniffing out betrayals from within. Fans were stunned by the difference a few months had made, and it seemed that **Doctor Who**'s renaissance was underway. But there were also still complaints about an overly silly tone to the rest of the season - *The Happiness Patrol*, actually a rather clever parody of a fascist society, was undercut somewhat by the appearance of its chief villain, the Kandyman - a robot comprised of what appeared to be enormous pieces of candy. The story given the actual 25th anniversary airdate, *Silver Nemesis*, was a less-than-cohesive final outing for the Cybermen, and one which rehashed many of *Remembrance*'s mystery-of-the-Doctor's-identity plot points. *Greatest Show In The Galaxy* literally put the Doctor in the midst of a circus controlled by the corrupt Gods of Ragnarok.

Dapol of the Doctor: The 25th anniversary brought the first Doctor Who toys made in the 3¾ "
"*Star Wars* scale", including this special anniversary set putting K-9 in the TARDIS alongside
the seventh Doctor and Melanie, and (accidentally) making the TARDIS console five-sided.
(The "bottle cap TARDIS walls" were made by your author, not by Dapol.)

But the 25th anniversary wasn't just celebrated by a new season of **Doctor Who**. Amateur filmmaker Keith Barnfather, who had already made a name for himself with a popular series of interview videos called Myth Makers, embarked on a first: a non-BBC made original video drama using elements from the **Doctor Who** mythos. Securing the rights to use the UNIT characters, Barnfather directed *Wartime*, a short video production delving into the past of UNIT regular Sergeant Benton, with guest appearances by Nicholas Courtney as the Brigadier (at least as a voice over a walkie-talkie) and Michael Wisher, who had originated the role of Davros in the 1970s and now played Benton's father. *Wartime* was fairly well received in fan circles, and paved the way for many other video projects in the future - projects that would become as close to TV **Doctor Who** as one could find in the 1990s.

John Nathan-Turner again intended for the 25th anniversary season of **Doctor Who** to be his last, but again the BBC brass forced his hand. Planning began for the 26th year of the show, with Andrew Cartmel enlisting a close circle of writers (including Ben Aaronovitch) to construct a running theme for the entire year. The 26th season would explore Ace's past, the first time such attention had been lavished on a companion, and Sophie Aldred was even consulted. The three-story arc, consisting of *The Curse Of Fenric*, *Ghost Light* and *Survival*, would examine Ace's family history, her juvenile delinquent past, and her maturing attitude toward life. As it happened, a juggling of the schedule meant that *Ghost Light* aired before the other two, but the arc wasn't so tightly constructed as to make this a jarring change. The season was opened by Aaronovitch's *Battlefield*, bringing back retired Brigadier Lethbridge-Stewart and introducing a new character, Brigadier Winifred Bambera, to head up more modern-day UNIT stories. Where the previous season had seen the Doctor plotting far in advance of his adventures, this story put him in the bizarre position of dealing with the fallout of an unspecified <u>future</u> Doctor's exploits.

Battlefield was originally intended to write Lethbridge-Stewart out of the series by killing him off in a blaze of glory, but producer John Nathan-Turner backed off of this shocking plot point - and fans who had already heard leaked rumors of the Brigadier's demise were relieved to be proven wrong. *Fenric* added new depths to the Doctor-as-master-manipulator format, and paved the way for the Doctor's future adventures in ways that couldn't have been imagined. *Survival*, the final story of the season and the series, brought back the Master for the first time since *Trial Of A Time Lord*, this time with a new costume and a decidedly more desperate and maniacal portrayal from Anthony Ainley. The script was originally written - and filmed - to include the climactic revelation that - in his own words - the Doctor was "more than just a Time Lord." Again, Nathan-Turner balked at this development and struck it from the finished product. Aired second but filmed last, Marc Platt's *Ghost Light* was derived from Platt's earlier freelance submission, *Lungbarrow*, detailing the Doctor's return to his ancestral family home on Gallifrey. The series' producer again erred on the side of caution, asking Platt to shift the setting to 18th century Earth and the emphasis to Ace.

Late in 1989, during the airing of one of the season's early episodes, it became clear to Nathan-Turner and Cartmel that the BBC had no intention of picking the show up again. Only this time, the cancellation would hit with a whimper, not a bang of publicity. Tired of fighting the good fight, Nathan-Turner did not arrange for an outcry this time; he quietly allowed the production office's activity to wind down as Sylvester McCoy and Sophie Aldred were informed that they were now out of a job. McCoy was called in to record a short speech as a coda for *Survival*, giving the series some sense of closure, and that was that.

Fans weren't giving up on bringing the Doctor back to TV, however - though they had every right to lose hope. While fan-made video productions of a surprisingly high quality kept track of the Time Lord's companions and sometimes adversaries, plans for a full-scale, direct-to-video movie were afoot. Written by fan and author Adrian Rigelsford, and with Graeme Harper (*The Caves Of Androzani, Revelation Of The Daleks*) confirmed as director, *The Dark Dimension* would reunite almost all of the surviving Doctors, with an emphasis on the seventh Doctor and the fourth Doctor. A divergence in the timeline would have kept the fourth Doctor alive past the events of *Logopolis*, accounting for Tom Baker's readily apparent aging. Links to the New Adventures were also built into the story, including the brief appearance of a woman named Summerfield (though no one had sought the permission of Virgin Publishing or author Paul Cornell as yet). But not all of the show's past lead actors were happy with the script, which relegated them to cameo appearances, and ultimately the entire project was scrapped when the budget proved to be too much. Even with an international video release, *The Dark Dimension* didn't stand a chance of recouping its costs. Fans, who had been told that the movie was all but a done deal, were disheartened. The 30th anniversary was instead marked by *Dimensions In Time*, a bizarre all-star crossover skit with the cast of the BBC soap EastEnders, aired as part of a charity telethon. With all of its stars having donated their services, *Dimensions In Time* is contractually forbidden from an official video release. Despite featuring such moments as the seventh Doctor and Ace traveling with K-9, and the sixth Doctor meeting the Brigadier (a meeting that had never taken place in the actual series), *Dimensions* is considered by some fans to be the *Star Wars Holiday Special* of **Doctor Who**.

The fans weren't the only ones pining for the return of the TARDIS, however. Since the early 1990s, Philip David Segal, an expatriate British TV producer based in Los Angeles, had been trying to set the wheels in motion for the return of **Doctor Who** to television - and now, it seemed, he was finally succeeding, with a shooting date set, a script finalized, and even a new Doctor selected in the form of Paul McGann. Segal fought seemingly endless battles with the BBC – who, as the rights holders of **Doctor Who**, had the ability to approve or veto creative decisions – over the regeneration scene in his project. Though not an admirer of 1980s **Doctor Who**, Segal insisted on strict adherence to the show's established lore and wanted to show McCoy regenerating into McGann; in what was perhaps the best barometer yet of how the BBC regarded **Doctor Who**'s final decade on the air, the movie's BBC producer fought equally hard to have *Tom Baker* regenerate into Paul McGann, which would have nullified the Davison, Colin Baker and Sylvester McCoy eras…or at least introduced an alternate timeline to a series whose ongoing continuity was already complex enough as it was. In the end, Segal won the argument, but the BBC firmly vetoed any attempt to bring Ace back.

With his original costume in hand – including the "question mark" vest and umbrella which were ultimately left unused – Sylvester McCoy was en route to Vancouver to hand the keys of the TARDIS over to Paul McGann.

SEASON 24: 1987
TIME AND THE RANI

The TARDIS crash-lands on Lakertya with such force that the Doctor is forced to regenerate. He is promptly removed from the TARDIS by the evil female Time Lord biochemist known as the Rani, who is behind his rough landing. Melanie, also knocked out by the landing, is kidnapped by Ikona, a birdlike Lakertyan whose people are behind forced to cooperate with the Rani's scheme. In the meantime, the Rani gives the newly-regenerated Doctor a drug-induced bout of amnesia, trying to use him to help her complete her latest experiment – but she doesn't count on the rebellious nature that the Doctor carries through all of his incarnations.

Sylvester McCoy	. . . .	The Doctor
Bonnie Langford	. . . .	Melanie
Karen Clegg	. . . .	Sarn
Richard Gauntlett	. . . .	Urak
Mark Greenstreet	. . . .	Ikona
Kate O'Mara	. . . .	The Rani
Donald Pickering	. . . .	Beyus
John Segal	. . . .	Lanisha
Peter Tuddenham	. . . .	Voice
Wanda Ventham	. . . .	Faroon
Jacki Webb	. . . .	Voice

This story has been released on DVD

written by Pip & Jane Baker
directed by Andrew Morgan
music by Keff McCulloch

Part 1 aired on September 7, 1987
Part 2 aired on September 14, 1987
Part 3 aired on September 21, 1987
Part 4 aired on September 28, 1987

BEHIND THE SCENES: Though the new series almost always has a teaser scene before the opening credits, this wasn't a common practice in the original series. Part 1 of *Time And The Rani* is one of only *four* original series episodes with a pre-credits teaser scene – mainly because the new title sequence, which prominently features Sylvester McCoy's face, would have made no sense prior to the Doctor's regeneration!

NEW WHO CONNECTIONS: The Doctor gives his age here as 953 years old, though the new series seems to contradict this with numerous mentions of the Doctor being only 900 years old. (It's probably best to take *any* mention of the Doctor's age, new *or* original series, with a pinch of salt, if not the entire shaker, as the Doctor's age has varied from 900 to 1,000 years at various points since the Jon Pertwee era.)

The seventh Doctor's first adventure is easily his weakest, stemming from a muddled script, which itself was a victim of the BBC's directive to tone down violence in the series. *Time And The Rani* suffers from a goofy atmosphere more suited to a show aimed overtly at children, especially in the first two episodes, and though this improves later once the Rani's ridiculous charade to jog the Doctor's memory ends, the second half of the story is muddled by some of the worst pseudo-scientific gibberish in the entire history of **Doctor Who** (and I say this knowing full well that **Doctor Who** has never tried to be as scientifically accurate as, say, **Babylon 5**). The strange matter plot device is plausible enough, but what exactly the Rani plans to do seems to change from moment to moment. Does she want the Doctor's knowledge of time? Does she want the Doctor to help her work out technical glitches in her master plan? Does she want the Doctor to join the gestalt of her silly giant brain to work out how to turn a planet into one vast time machine? Or does she just want to kill him? And did she *really* expect him to fall for her attempt to disguise herself as Mel?

There are actually moments of charm in this show, however. When the Doctor first awakens in his seventh persona, he immediately leaps into action with no mental hindrances whatsoever, and it's a great preview of how McCoy will play the part for the next three years. To turn around and snatch this promising character away for the next two episodes, however, is a cheat to the audience, though there is a reward in the nice scene when the Doctor and the (real) Melanie finally recognize one another again. The now prerequisite costume-choosing scene was carried out with a minimum of finesse, unnecessarily repeating *The Twin Dilemma*'s gag of the Doctor going through some of his previous costumes. *Time And The Rani* also marks the first musical contributions – in the form of the new theme music arrangement as well as the episode score – from Keff McCulloch. Keff's later musical scores included a lot of dance music elements, and this story's music is the best that he provided for the series – despite the fact that he had very short notice on which to compose and produce it.

All the same, Sylvester McCoy's Doctor in this season is wonderfully funny and compassionate, with an underlying eruption of righteous indignation awaiting anyone who oppresses others or collaborates with an oppressor, whether it's the Rani, Beyus, Gavrok, or Kane. It lays the groundwork for the darker and more dangerous character the Doctor will become later, but much of that is evident in this episode, even if the rest of the plot falls down around him. Perhaps some consideration should've been given to a hitherto unthinkable plot twist, such as simply starting the story with the seventh Doctor at full speed, explaining that he'd regenerated already. That kind of daring maneuver would have to wait until Christopher Eccleston's first appearance as the Doctor.

PARADISE TOWERS

The Doctor and Mel arrive to do a little vacationing in the lush artificial paradise known as Paradise Towers, only to find that the huge structure has fallen into disrepair - and furthermore, its inhabitants have descended into savagery. The Kangs, warring factions of girl gangs, struggle for survival among the rule-bound Caretakers, the cannibalistic Rezzies, and another force which lurks in the shadows, using the mechanical cleaning robots to murder members of all of these groups. The Doctor is captured by the Caretakers, who believe him to be the Great Architect of Paradise Towers and sentence him to death, while Mel befriends Pex, mighty in his own mind and weak of stomach. The Doctor discovers that the Great Architect is indeed still lurking in his masterpiece of construction, killing off its residents before they foul Paradise Towers by living in it.

Sylvester McCoy . . . . The Doctor
Bonnie Langford . . . . Melanie
Julie Brennon . . . . Fire Escape
Richard Briers . . . . Chief Caretaker
Brenda Bruce . . . . Tilda
Simon Coady . . . . Video commentary
Howard Cooke . . . . Pex
Judy Cornwell . . . . Maddy
Catherine Cusack . . . . Blue Kang Leader
Clive Merrison . . . . Deputy Chief Caretaker
Astra Sheridan . . . . Yellow Kang
Elizabeth Spriggs . . . . Tabby

This story has been released on DVD

written by Stephen Wyatt
directed by Nicholas Mallett
music by Keff McCulloch

Part 1 aired on October 5, 1987
Part 2 aired on October 12, 1987
Part 3 aired on October 19, 1987
Part 4 aired on October 26, 1987

Joseph Young . . . . Young Caretaker
Annabel Yuresha . . . . Bin Liner

NEW WHO CONNECTIONS: If you think *Blink* was the first **Doctor Who** episode to mention the medium of the DVD, look closely at *Paradise Towers*: the Towers' illustrated prospectus was apparently pressed on DVD (obviously the prop was simply a CD, but even so, that's rather prescient for a production made in 1987).

This surreal four-parter could have been a wonderfully dark, **Twilight Zone**-esque tale, since the underlying premise had all those ingredients, but in keeping with the previous story of the twenty-fourth season, it was given a very comedic treatment, which quickly did away with any tension that could have helped the story along. Only the Rezzies have any kind of sinister air to them, friendly old ladies who welcome you into their homes and then proceed to eat you. But the Kangs really don't convey any sense of being criminally hardened gang members – they look more like stunt doubles from a Bangles video. And the Caretakers, particularly Richard Briers' Chief Caretaker, are too bumbling to take seriously. The creature in the basement of Paradise Towers is ridiculously represented by two neon lights in the shape of eyes. Even the music is underwhelming, not much more than a series of dance grooves, a bit of a disappointment after Keff McCulloch's score for *Time And The Rani* – but also very much a product of its era.

One of the most baffling elements of the story is Pex. He dodged a war more because of his cowardice than any pacifistic beliefs, but the Doctor later convinces him to give his life for the cause. This is the same **Doctor Who**, just one season later in *The Happiness Patrol*, establishes *himself* very firmly as a pacifist. It's a curious inconsistency of character that can probably be blamed on the fact that this first season of stories was commissioned with no clear direction of the future of the show, to say nothing of who the lead actor would be.

DELTA AND THE BANNERMEN

The Doctor and Melanie land at a toll booth in space, but instead of needing to dig into their pockets for exact change, they wind up winning a trip to Earth in 1959 for being the ten billionth visitors to the station. Joining the chartered trip is Delta, queen of the Chimeron - the last of her race who hasn't been hunted down by genocidal Gavrok and his army of Bannermen. Gavrok's forces trail the tourists to Wales, intent on killing Delta, who carries with her an egg that will soon hatch the first child in a new generation of Chimerons. Billy, a local boy with rock 'n' roll aspirations, falls in love with Delta, while the Doctor tries to prepare the Welsh locals for a mercenary attack from space.

Sylvester McCoy . . . . The Doctor
Bonnie Langford . . . . Melanie
Robin Aspland . . . . Band Member
Laura Collins . . . . Chimeron Princess

written by Malcolm Kohll
directed by Chris Clough
music by Keff McCulloch

UWORP!

Clive Condon	. . . .	Callon
Richard Davies	. . . .	Burton
Morgan Deare	. . . .	Hawk
Johnny Dennis	. . . .	Murray
Ken Dodd	. . . .	Tollmaster
Martyn Geraint	. . . .	Vinny
Anita Graham	. . . .	Bollit
Sara Griffiths	. . . .	Ray
Don Henderson	. . . .	Gavrok
Brian Hibbard	. . . .	Keillor
Carley Joseph	. . . .	Chimeron Princess
Stubby Kaye	. . . .	Weismuller
David Kinder	. . . .	Billy
Hugh Lloyd	. . . .	Goronwy
Belinda Mayne	. . . .	Delta

This story has been released on DVD

Part 1 aired on November 2, 1987
Part 2 aired on November 9, 1987
Part 3 aired on November 16, 1987

Keff McCulloch	. . . .	Band Member
Jessica McGough	. . . .	Young Chimeron
Leslie Meadows	. . . .	Adlon
Richard Mitchley	. . . .	Arrex
Justin Myers	. . . .	Band Member
Amy Osborn	. . . .	Young Chimeron
Ralph Salmins	. . . .	Band Member
Jodie Wilson	. . . .	Band Vocalist
Tracy Wilson	. . . .	Band Vocalist

A.K.A.: *Delta And The Bannermen* boasts one of the most star-studded casts that late '80s **Doctor Who** ever assembled on-screen. Stubby Kaye (1918-1997) was a fixture on Broadway, appearing in big-screen adaptations of the plays in which he had roles (*Guys And Dolls, Li'l Abner*). He was a frequent guest star on American TV in the 1960s and '70s, showing up on everything from **Laverne & Shirley** to **The Monkees** to **Adam-12** to **The Alfred Hitchcock Hour**. After completing this **Doctor Who** serial, he went on to play doomed cartoon movie mogul Marvin Acme in 1988's *Who Framed Roger Rabbit?* Don Henderson (1932-1997) also appeared in the obscure UK alternate-future-history series **Knights Of God** alongside ex-**Doctor Who** Patrick Troughton, which, despite being filmed in 1985, wasn't broadcast until 1987 — actually running alongside this season of **Doctor Who**. Henderson has also appeared as a stimulant in the **Red Dwarf** episode *Beyond A Joke*, but most sharp-eyed genre fans will recognize him as General Tagge, the Imperial officer who questions the Emperor's dissolution of the Senate in *Star Wars* (1977).

Though it's probably the most deliberately, shamelessly goofy **Doctor Who** installment in the history of the series, I love *Delta And The Bannermen*. More than any other segment his first year in the role of the Doctor, Sylvester McCoy truly shines in this three-parter, especially in the scene where he magnificently confronts Gavrok, accusing him of genocide. It's also the best use of Bonnie Langford's Melanie, a character that never really developed any distinguishing features aside from her spunky attitude, a perfect match for this story. The guest stars are also notable, including American theater veteran Stubby Kaye, Sara Griffiths as the wistful Ray, and especially Don Henderson as Gavrok. Contributing a perfectly fitting '50s style rock music score, complete with covers of several oldies, is Keff McCulloch, who also puts in a cameo appearance as a member of Billy's band.

Some die-hard fans don't like *Delta And The Bannermen* because it has a number of humorous elements and a rather simplistic love story, but those are among the very reasons that some of us find it so enjoyable. Highly recommended, especially for those who want to initiate younger kids into the world of **Doctor Who**.

DRAGONFIRE

The Doctor and Mel pay a visit to Svartos, an ice planet with an enormous habitation complex which extends far above the surface. Though it seems innocuous enough on the surface – the TARDIS materializes in a frozen goods store – a chance encounter with Sabalon Glitz, bumbling intergalactic treasure-seeker not-so-extraordinaire quickly leads the Doctor into trouble, and introduces him to Ace, a sarcastic teenager from Earth who inexplicably found herself on Svartos and now works as a waitress. Glitz has obtained a map of the caverns beneath the planet's surface, where a dragon is rumored to lurk, guarding a priceless treasure. The Doctor agrees to accompany Glitz on his search, more curious about the dragon itself than what it may be guarding. Mel, left behind with Ace, finds herself in very deep trouble when the younger girl runs afoul of the authorities and brings herself to the attention of Kane, an alien who cannot leave the sub-freezing portions of the complex. Little do the Doctor and Glitz realize that the dragon is all that stands between the people of Svartos and Kane's plans for a bloody reign of terror.

Sylvester McCoy . . . . The Doctor
Bonnie Langford . . . . Melanie
Sophie Aldred . . . . Ace
Sean   Blowers   .   .   .   .   Zed
Miranda   Borman   .   .   .   .   Stellar
Stephanie Fayerman . . . . McLuhan
Lynn   Gardner   .   .   .   .   Announcer
Chris   MacDonnell   .   .   .   .   Arnheim
Ian   Mackenzie   .   .   .   .   Anderson
Leslie   Meadows   .   .   .   .   Creature
Nigel   Miles-Thomas   .   .   .   .   Pudovkin
Stuart   Organ   .   .   .   .   Bazin
Tony   Osoba   .   .   .   .   Kracauer
Daphne   Oxenford   .   .   .   .   Archivist

This story has been released on DVD

written by Ian Briggs
directed by Chris Clough
music by Dominic Glynn

Part 1 aired on November 23, 1987
Part 2 aired on November 30, 1987
Part 3 aired on December 7, 1987

Edward   Peel   .   .   .   .   Kane
Patricia   Quinn   .   .   .   .   Belazs
Tony   Selby   .   .   .   .   Glitz
Shirin   Taylor   .   .   .   .   Customer

NEW WHO CONNECTIONS: Clara Oswald is seen to have intervened to thwart a previously unknown attempt on the Doctor's life by the Great Intelligence during this adventure in *The Name Of The Doctor* (2013).

Many regard this as the best story of the 24th season, and it's also historically important for **Doctor Who** fans because it introduces Ace, the companion who truly sharpened and defined Sylvester McCoy's tenure as the Doctor. Bonnie Langford leaves the show in episode three, having really accomplished all that she could with a character that was created with a kinder, gentler stint with Colin Baker's Doctor in mind. Mel would have been *astoundingly* out of place in McCoy's later, darker seasons, and Ace opened the door to for the writers to do some intense character development that was unprecedented for one of the Doctor's companions. Still, despite my feeling that Mel exited at the right time, the character never seemed to get on my nerves as badly as she did other fans' – well, except for that line about the megabyte modem in *Trial Of A Time Lord*, but Bonnie Langford didn't write the line, she just said it!

Tony Selby returns as Glitz, who also originated in *Trial Of A Time Lord*, though the character is softened considerably. Where Glitz's first appearance took great pains to note for the audience's benefit that this was a character who was capable of murder if it helped him achieve his goals, here Glitz was a bumbling idiot. There was almost a hint of the old Glitz when, after his ship is destroyed, he looks up and growls Kane's name. It at least demonstrated that Tony Selby had the skills needed to play the character as originally intended. Incidentally, Glitz's ship seems to be an homage to the prison ship London from the first season of **Blake's 7**.

Dominic Glynn's atmospheric music sets a new standard after the season's three previous stories of Keff McCulloch's dance-music club beats, paving the way for further excellent orchestral-style scores (Glynn's own later *Happiness Patrol* and *Survival*, and Mark Ayres' three scores).

And I'm not even going to try to explain the bizarrely literal cliffhanger where Sylvester McCoy climbs over a railing and dangles over a precipitous drop, hanging from the railing via his umbrella. Why he does this is never really made clear; somebody must have thought it was a good sight gag, but instead it's silly. If you're looking for one singular scene to point out as the nadir of McCoy's era, the "cliff hanger" is a good bet.

SEASON 25: 1988
REMEMBRANCE OF THE DALEKS

Daleks have converged on a junkyard in 1963 London, hot on the trail of a renegade Time Lord who possesses an amazingly powerful weapon from ancient Gallifrey. The Daleks' quarry has left Earth after being discovered by a pair of curious humans, but unknown to the aliens, that same Time Lord has returned to conclude his business, six lives hence. The Doctor and Ace quickly join up with Group Captain Gilmore and his team of soldiers and scientists, who have discovered the Daleks and are trying to flush them out of hiding. Gilmore begins accepting the Doctor's strategic advice, which is devised largely to keep the human race out of trouble – but the Daleks have already found like-minded allies on Earth, in the form of a group of fascist sympathizers led by Mr. Ratcliffe. The Daleks themselves are divided along a line of loyalty or disloyalty to the Emperor Dalek – who, as the Doctor discovers, has changed a little bit over the years too. The Doctor is actually playing a dangerous game, trying to ensure that the Hand of Omega *does* fall into the wrong hands – but which faction of the Daleks is actually worthy of this kind of power?

Sylvester McCoy . . . . The Doctor
Sophie Aldred . . . . Ace
Norman Bacon . . . . Dalek
Ron Berry . . . . Gravedigger
Kathleen Bidmead . . . . Mrs. Smith
Jasmine Breaks . . . . The Girl
Peter Hamilton Dyer . . . . Embery
John Evans . . . . Undertaker
Harry Fowler . . . . Harry
Karen Gledhill . . . . Allison
Peter Halliday . . . . Vicar
David Harrison . . . . Dalek
Derek Keller . . . . Kaufman
Richie Kennedy . . . . Mailman
John Leeson . . . . Dalek voice
Joseph Marcell . . . . John
Dursley McLinden . . . . Mike
Royce Mills . . . . Dalek voice
John Scott Martin . . . . Dalek
Brian Miller . . . . Dalek voice
Terry Molloy . . . . Emperor Dalek / Davros

This story has been released on DVD

written by Ben Aaronovitch
directed by Andrew Morgan
music by Keff McCulloch

Part 1 aired on October 5, 1988
Part 2 aired on October 12, 1988
Part 3 aired on October 19, 1988
Part 4 aired on October 26, 1988

Pamela Salem . . . . Rachel
George Sewell . . . . Ratcliffe
Michael Sheard . . . . Headmaster
Roy Skelton . . . . Dalek voice
Hugh Spright . . . . Dalek
Tony Starr . . . . Dalek
William Thomas . . . . Martin
Cy Town . . . . Dalek
Nigel Wild . . . . Dalek
Simon Williams . . . . Gilmore

NEW WHO CONNECTIONS: *Remembrance Of The Daleks* is a prime candidate in the category of "original series episodes that were part of the Time War," what with Davros' ranting about mounting an all-out Dalek attack on Gallifrey and the Time Lords. Interestingly, a new series episode – *The End Of Time* Part 2 (2010) – provides a solution to *Remembrance*'s one big problem, namely the destruction of Skaro in the middle of a complicated Dalek chronology whose future includes plenty of events yet to come on Skaro (*The Daleks, The Evil Of The Daleks*). Many a fan writer has postulated the colonization of a "Skaro 2" to solve this problem, but *The End Of Time* keeps it simple, mentioning that during the Time War, entire civilizations were wiped out and then resurrected by the combatants' constant changes to the established history. The Daleks could have easily made the destruction of Skaro "un-happen" during the Time War. The Doctor's actions here don't seem to be part of the Time War, incidentally, but more a case of him "going rogue." Who knows what he set into motion here? This story's unprecedented depiction of the Emperor Dalek as Davros reduced to a head in a casing is also troublesome: what about the Emperor Daleks seen in such stories as *The Evil Of The Daleks* (1967) and *The Parting Of The Ways* (2005)? Were these also Davros in some form, or was this a case of the Dalek creator making an illegitimate grab for the throne?

The definitive seventh Doctor story, *Remembrance Of The Daleks* is a seminal chapter in **Doctor Who** in the same way that *The War Games* and *Terror Of The Autons* colored everything that came after. This story defines the seventh Doctor as the master manipulator, and lays the first hints into the series that the Doctor may, in fact, have a much more mysterious and sinister history than he's ever revealed. Why is he stockpiling Time Lord weapons such as the Hand of Omega and validium (the living metal from the later *Silver Nemesis*) that seem to originate from the birth of Time Lord society itself? And did the first Doctor actually know the Daleks, even though, in 1963's *The Daleks*, he appeared *not* to know them? The air of mystery is wonderfully palpable.

Ace also becomes a vital part of the show in this story, gaining an endearing sense of indignation at the plight of others, healthy sarcasm, and just a hint of teenage hormones. The petulant sulkiness she displays in *Dragonfire* is thankfully toned down at this point. Ace also becomes an action heroine here, repaying years of companions-screaming-at-the-Daleks scenes by going after the aliens with an electrified baseball bat, an activity that almost gets her killed in part two. And even the Daleks are given character development, hints of internal ethnic-cleansing wars which actually justify the previous two Dalek stories. The Daleks are also seen in a more menacing form than they have ever been portrayed, and are easily at their best since the sixties – although the bulb-headed Emperor Dalek is nearly funny until we find out what's inside. If *Remembrance* fails on any count, it is the music – Keff McCulloch zips back and forth between nicely atmospheric bits of mood music and, mainly in action scenes, more distracting dance music. (Hint: Daleks don't dance.)

And for those wishing to get more from the story, you may wish to track down the novelization written by Ben Aaronovitch, printed by Target Books in 1990. Along with Ian Briggs' *The Curse Of Fenric* book, Aaronovitch added a great deal of material to his basic story and laid the groundwork that Virgin's early New Adventures novels would follow for at least a year.

THE HAPPINESS PATROL

The Doctor brings Ace to the planet Terra Alpha, a planet whose dark secrets are barely concealed by a thin coat of bright, playful colors. The megalomaniacal Helen A keeps her subjects happy by enforcing happiness itself – any public display of grief, doubt or disapproval are punishable by summary execution. Ace, with her almost permanent scowl, is quickly arrested by the Happiness Patrol, while the Doctor meets a fellow alien named Earl Sigma and has a near-fatal encounter with the robotic, psychotic Kandyman. A census representative from Earth has uncovered evidence that Helen A's regime has caused the unspecified "disappearance" of thousands of people. The Doctor has one night to stir a revolution in the streets of Terra Alpha…but Helen A's downfall may be caused by someone closer to her than she expects.

Sylvester McCoy	. . . .	The Doctor
Sophie Aldred	. . . .	Ace
Tim Barker	. . . .	Harold V
Rachel Bell	. . . .	Priscilla P
Jonathan Burn	. . . .	Silas P
Mark Carroll	. . . .	Sniper
Lesley Dunlop	. . . .	Susan Q
Ronald Fraser	. . . .	Joseph C
Ryan Freedman	. . . .	Wulfric
Georgina Hale	. . . .	Daisy K

This story has been released on DVD

written by Graeme Curry
directed by Chris Clough
music by Dominic Glynn

Part 1 aired on November 2, 1988
Part 2 aired on November 9, 1988
Part 3 aired on November 16, 1988

John Normington . . . . Trevor Sigma

Sheila Hancock	. . . .	Helen A	David John Pope	. . . .	Kandy Man
Mary Healey	. . . .	Killjoy	Tim Scott	. . . .	Forum Doorman
Annie Hulley	. . . .	Newscaster	Richard D. Sharp	. . . . . .	Earl Sigma
Harold Innocent	. . . . . .	Gilbert M	Steve Swinscoe	. . . .	Sniper
Philip Neve	. . . .	Wences			

NEW WHO CONNECTIONS: If you thought the Doctor unseating Prime Minister Harriet Jones with just six words in *The Christmas Invasion* (2005) was impressive, try *The Happiness Patrol* on for size: in just *one night*, the Doctor and Ace topple Terra Alpha's *entire planetary government*. All in a night's work.

Though it's near-incoherent in places, I have a soft spot for *The Happiness Patrol*, mainly because of its simple message – happiness can't be enforced. I couldn't agree more, and though many fans railed against the seemingly childish trappings of this story, they were almost necessary to tell a story with such an elementary psychological center; recent admissions by script editor Andrew Cartmel and the production team have revealed that the carnival-like atmosphere was there to help obfuscate a blatantly anti-Thatcher-administration message. There's also a scene in which the Doctor single-handedly talks two snipers out of their urge to kill, a defining moment – in my mind, at least – of the seventh Doctor's character. Dominic Glynn also provides a fantastic musical score, darting back and forth between the blues-driven harmonica theme that opens the story and the carnival-like theme for the Kandyman. It's a shame that Glynn's music for this story has never been released.

At the same time, *The Happiness Patrol* just as often lacks clear direction because of the numerous distractions – the Pipe People (whose processed voices are almost impossible to understand), the omnivorous Fifi, and a few seconds of backstory for Gilbert M which seem like they should've occurred two episodes earlier. There's also the incongruous sight of the Doctor jamming with Earl Sigma while Ace is in great danger elsewhere. Had the story been told with more directness, *The Happiness Patrol* would probably be much more fondly remembered today, but it still nets my recommendation.

SILVER NEMESIS

The Doctor is horrified when Nemesis, a statue carved from a living metal from the world of the Time Lords, arrives on Earth in 1988, falling from an orbit into which the Doctor launched it 350 years ago. At the same time, a creepy neo-Nazi group led by De Flores (Anton Diffring) plans to take control of the Nemesis, as does Lady Peinforte, a 17th century would-be sorceress which concocts a potion for time travel. The spearhead of a Cyberman invasion fleet also arrives, also looking for the statue. Its destructive power will be granted to whoever returns the Nemesis' bow and arrow, and it seems unlikely that the Doctor himself would have any use for that kind of power – unless, as Lady Peinforte claims, the Doctor has his own dark agenda.

Sylvester McCoy . . . . The Doctor	
Sophie Aldred . . . . Ace	written by Kevin Clarke
David Banks . . . . Cyberleader	directed by Chris Clough
Paul Barrass . . . . Cyberman	music by Keff McCulloch
Danny Boyd . . . . Cyberman	This story has been released on DVD
Tony Carlton . . . . Cyberman	Part 1 aired on November 23, 1988
Chris Cherin . . . . First Skinhead	Part 2 aired on November 30, 1988
Anton Diffring . . . . De Flores	Part 3 aired on December 7, 1988
Leslie French . . . . Mathematician	
Dolores Gray . . . . American Tourist	
Mark Hardy . . . . Cyber Lieutenant	John Ould . . . . Walkman

ЦШ0ЯЯ!

Symond Lawes	. . . .	Second Skinhead	
Vere Lorrimer	. . . .	Tour Guide	
Bill Malin	. . . .	Cyberman	
Scott Mitchell	. . . .	Cyberman	
Ernest Mothie	. . . .	himself	
Gerard Murphy	. . . .	Richard	
Brian Orrell	. . . .	Cyberman	
Dave Ould	. . . .	Walkman	

Courtney Pine . . . . himself
Martyn Read . . . . Security Man
Adrian Reid . . . . himself
Mary Reynolds . . . . Her Majesty the Queen
Frank Tontoh . . . . himself
Fiona Walker . . . . Lady Peinforte
Metin Yenal . . . . Karl

NEW WHO CONNECTIONS: The Cybermen have a hard time getting an insurance policy on their space fleets with the Doctor around: he destroyed their entire spacefaring war capability in both part 3 of *Silver Nemesis* and in 2011's *A Good Man Goes To War*. To top things off, in the latter episode, he blows their entire fleet to smithereens in the episode's *teaser*, no Nemesis required!

Following a theme very similar to *Remembrance Of The Daleks*, a story which first aired mere weeks before this one, *Silver Nemesis* is fun to watch, but presents a muddled mess of a story. A less convoluted story would have been more enjoyable – most of Lady Peinforte's role is comical, and indeed many of her scenes wound up on the cutting room floor prior to broadcast, restored only upon the release of the VHS tape. The Nazis also play a minor role, and the Cybermen – arguably the major villains of the piece – put in their weakest appearance since 1975's *Revenge Of The Cybermen*. Perhaps replacing one or two of these parties with a much more competent menace would have made the show more memorable. On the plus side, Gerard Murphy is almost the only believable guest star, in his role as Peinforte's manservant. He constantly pleads with her to return to the 17th century, and offers a humorous take on three centuries of change in the meantime. There's also a hammy American tourist character – also cut from much of the original broadcast – who comes across as a bit of a stereotype, but a harmlessly amusing one.

Keff McCulloch's score again dates itself by breaking into synthesized dance rhythms for action cues, though some of his more eerie pieces of music are very well-done and unnerving. The stylistic choices involved are a little baffling to me, but be prepared for a little annoyance in the course of watching this three-parter.

THE GREATEST SHOW IN THE GALAXY

The TARDIS is invaded – not by Daleks, Sontarans or Cybermen, but by a satellite delivering junk mail to any passing vessels. This particular satellite brings good tidings from Segonax, home of the Psychic Circus, and the Doctor is intrigued – while Ace is repulsed, primarily by the thought of circus clowns. The Doctor decides to go anyway, and finds Segonax less inviting than its sales pitch promised. From the curious variety of other circusgoers, to the abandoned bus manned by a homicidal robot tram conductor, to the mysterious explorer known only as the Captain and his exotic sidekick Mags, the Doctor immediately senses that something is wrong. Upon arriving at the Psychic Circus at last, the Doctor discovers the truth: those coming to visit the circus are not there as spectators, but as the entertainment – and the penalty for failing to entertain the unusual audience, a seemingly bland family of three, is death.

Sylvester McCoy	. . . .	The Doctor	
Sophie Aldred	. . . .	Ace	
David Ashford	. . . .	Dad	
Christopher Guard	. . . .	Bellboy	
Janet Hargreaves	. . . .	Mum	
Dean Hollingsworth	. . . .	Bus Conductor	
Chris Jury	. . . .	Deadbeat	

This story has been released on DVD

written by Stephen Wyatt
directed by Alan Wareing
music by Mark Ayres

Part 1 aired on December 14, 1988
Part 2 aired on December 21, 1988
Part 3 aired on December 28, 1988

Kathryn Ludlow . . . . Little Girl
Deborah Manship . . . . Morgana
Jessica Martin . . . . Mags
T.P. McKenna . . . . The Captain
Peggy Mount . . . . Stallholder
Daniel Peacock . . . . Nord
Ian Reddington . . . . Chief Clown

Part 4 aired on January 4, 1989

Ricco Ross . . . . Ringmaster
Dee Sadler . . . . Flowerchild
Gian Sammarco . . . . Whizzkid

In a season that featured one instantly-renowned classic (*Remembrance Of The Daleks*), a wildly surreal story the likes of which **Doctor Who** had never done before (*The Happiness Patrol*), and a disjointed Cyber-caper (*Silver Nemesis*), it's hard to imagine what anyone expected from the season's final story. Perhaps closer in style to *The Happiness Patrol* than to anything else in season 25, *The Greatest Show In The Galaxy* was a product of sheer desperation and inventiveness. With a full-scale shutdown of the BBC's studio facilities to comply with an official order to remove asbestos from the premises, *The Greatest Show In The Galaxy* went from being planned out and ready to start filming, to being homeless. Determined not to lose a story that was in danger of being cancelled outright, wasting the effort that had already gone into props and costumes, director Alan Wareing and producer John Nathan-Turner hurriedly moved filming to a real circus tent erected in the parking lot of the BBC's Elstree facilities. This turned a story that was meant to save money by staying almost entirely within a studio into an exercise in filming it by any means necessary.

The thing is, **it actually rings more true for this rushed location filming than it would have by staying in a studio.** The surface of a large tent, like a circus tent, never stays still: it undulates with the slightest breeze. A studio set probably wouldn't have gotten that minor detail right; the location filming does. The "desert" location - as usual for **Doctor Who**, a rock quarry (and the same one used by the same director for *Survival* in the following season) - is actually very effective. Much like 1970's *Spearhead From Space*, which was forced out of the studio and onto location due to a strike, *The Greatest Show* actually benefits from the change of venue.

Debate still rages to this day about the characters and the subtext of the story; it's frequently interpreted as a skewed look at the recent history of **Doctor Who** itself, with the brash, violent Nord as an analog of Colin Baker's Doctor, the well-traveled, been-there-and-seen-that Professor as a symbol for "professional" **Doctor Who** fandom that published its own magazines (and stuff like, well, this book), and the geeky Whizzkid as a stand-in for the hopeless geeks among fandom - he's gotten all the books and they're all signed, you know. It's an interesting interpretation, but it may well be one that was completely unintended by those making it.

The seventh Doctor scratches another notch into his bedpost in the "fighting godlike beings" department. The Gods of Ragnarok, though basically statues, are seen to be in command of awesome powers. The Doctor allows himself to be drawn into their midst just so he can do battle with them. (The scenes leading up to this feature an impressive array of tricks of the trade Sylvester McCoy learned as a circus entertainer himself.) Ace, thoroughly creeped out by the clowns and other trappings of the circus, wants none of it, which is significant in itself: this is a girl who chased after Daleks with an electrically charged baseball bat, and held Cybermen at bay with a slingshot full of gold coins... but a *childhood fear* can still throw her. This concept carries over into the next season's *Ghost Light*.

The Greatest Show In The Galaxy also marks, after a long series of unsolicited demo tapes and audition pieces, the debut of **Doctor Who** music composer Mark Ayres. For someone who only scored three **Doctor Who** adventures of the original series, he throws a long shadow into the **Doctor Who** soundscape: every restored music soundtrack released on CD, every lovingly catalogued sound effect from the BBC Radiophonic Workshop, and every classic **Doctor Who** DVD with remastered audio is his doing. (He also composed the criminally underrated score to a British crime drama called *The Innocent Sleep* in the

1990s, proving that, given the right resources, Ayres could've been the man to grace **Doctor Who** with a full orchestra, long before Murray Gold or the 1996 TV movie's all-synth orchestra.)

SHORT HOPS

...in which the author implores you not to shoot the showrunner.

Good grief, but we science fiction fans are a contentious bunch.

In the late '80s, I spent an inordinate amount of money on stuff from a science fiction specialty mail-order outfit in Dunlap, Tennessee called Star Tech. It was run by a lovely guy named William Anchors who had self-published mountains of material that he'd collected on his favorite show, **Lost In Space** - and he had to self-publish the hard way, doing the bulk of the work over his own photocopier. He had a pretty healthy selection of **Doctor Who** items in the Star Tech catalog, and I think some of it might have even been officially licensed by the BBC. This was one of those enterprises where fandom was doing what fandom is supposed to do best: be inspired to make cool stuff and share it with one other.

On one occasion, Star Tech reduced back issues of the British fanzine Doctor Who Bulletin to fire sale prices, and I picked up a stack of them. My issues arrived in the mail, and then I realized I wasn't the only one with issues.

I'd been operating in a bit of a vacuum where **Doctor Who** fandom was concerned (see also: living in Arkansas). I was 15 going on 16, and I watched the show - even if it was a rerun I'd already seen - and I bought the Target novelizations by the dozen, and I avidly scanned the table of contents of every new issue of Starlog to see if they were covering **Doctor Who** at all that month. But that didn't really provide one with any of the behind-the-scenes dirt.

DWB did. The 'zine's editorial position seemed to be almost the photo-negative opposite of what I set out to do with this book. I can find some charm, even if it's just embarrassing effects work giving me a belly laugh, in nearly any installment of **Doctor Who**. DWB, on the other hand, seemed to be latching on to anything they could *hate*.

At the center of it all, in the crosshairs of DWB's ire, was John Nathan-Turner, the producer of **Doctor Who**. Long before the term "showrunner" came to be in vogue, JN-T *was* the showrunner. He personally saw to much of the show's publicity and promotion, trying his best to deploy these things strategically.

DWB, on the other hand, dissected everything about the show in an effort to prove that JN-T wasn't up to the task. A then-recent tell-all interview with disgruntled script editor Eric Saward, originally appearing in Starburst Magazine, was cited relentlessly as proof of the editorial position of this 'zine: *JN-T had to go.*

What a dreary way to "enjoy" something. Years later, the same phenomenon rippled through the internet. The names of the show (**Star Trek: Enterprise**) and the showrunners (Rick Berman & Brannon Braga) were different. The incredibly nasty attitude was the same.

Fan angst, 1980s style: <u>Doctor Who Bulletin</u>, from the beginning of the Colin Baker era to the beginning of the Sylvester McCoy era.

We science fiction fans are a contentious bunch.

One of the reasons I've stayed on the outskirts of fandom like I have is that there's only so much time in the day to devote to hobbies and leisure activities. Especially if you're a parent. These leisure activities are like a cool glass of water in the middle of the desert. If you're a stay-at-home parent, hobbies are like a cool glass of water floating in the center of a shaded Olympic-size swimming pool in the middle of the desert.

Why spend that time on stuff that it sounds like you hate? It's natural to have likes and dislikes. But sometimes you get so wrapped up in something that you need to back off and take a break from it.

What would I have to say to John Nathan-Turner today if he was still around? I'd probably buy him a round of drinks of the man's choice, listen to some of his stories from the inside, and thank him for the thankless task of carrying **Doctor Who** on his back for over 1/3 of its original run. He didn't always hit it out of the park. Some of the series' *worst* seasons, in fact, happened on his watch - thanks in no small part to BBC management imposing their own outmoded vision of what the show was supposed to be like.

Oh, and I'd mention my admiration for all those loud Hawaiian shirts he used to wear. Hawaiian shirts are cool. In the late '80s, I was probably the most flamboyantly dressed straight man anyone in my circle of friends had ever known. I'd bet another round of drinks that JN-T, like myself, had some stories about that particular fashion choice.

Let's check the score here. Which era of the show has Big Finish spent so much of its time extending? The

JN-T era, leaning heavily on the three Doctors that he cast during his tenure (Davison, Colin Baker and McCoy) and the companions that he cast as well. When **Doctor Who** was cancelled after its 1989 season, which Doctor/companion team did the comics and novels follow? The seventh Doctor and Ace - JN-T's final pairing of regulars. When the 1996 TV movie was shot, despite the BBC wanting the familiar face of Tom Baker to suddenly be Paul McGann's predecessor, who did producer Philip Segal fly to Vancouver? Sylvester McCoy, the seventh Doctor. And when the *Time Crash* charity special was filmed in 2007, who was the first "past" Doctor to appear in new **Who**? Peter Davison, the fifth Doctor. All products of the JN-T era.

Doctor Who under JN-T can't have been *that* bad.

It's time for a fair reassessment of John Nathan-Turner's "era" of **Doctor Who**. It wasn't perfect - no stretch of the show under any producer has been - but it also wasn't the unmitigated disaster that, some "fan wisdom" seems to remember it to be. Here's to you, JN-T.

SEASON 26: 1989
BATTLEFIELD

The Doctor and Ace arrive in Britain in the late 90s, near a stranded UNIT convoy carrying a nuclear missile. Strange weather and power outages seem to be taking place all of a sudden, and the Doctor himself is mystified at the coincidences – especially since all of this is happening on the shores of the lake where, according to legend, the dying King Arthur returned Excalibur to the Lady of the Lake. The legend turns out to have a solid foundation in reality – but a different reality where one of the Doctor's future selves was trapped for a time, assuming the identity of Merlin. Now that warriors on both sides of the ancient battle are entering Earth's dimension, the Doctor must take on a role he doesn't even know how to play.

Sylvester McCoy . . . . The Doctor
Sophie Aldred . . . . Ace
Marek Anton . . . . The Destroyer
June Bland . . . . Elizabeth Rowlinson
Christopher Bowen . . . . Mordred
Angela Bruce . . . . Brig. Winifred Bambera
Noel Collins . . . . Pat Rowlinson
Nicholas Courtney . . . . Brig. Lethbridge-Stewart
Angela Douglas . . . . Doris
James Ellis . . . . Peter Warmsly
Marcus Gilbert . . . . Ancelyn
Robert Jezek . . . . Sergeant Zbrigniev
Jean Marsh . . . . Morgaine

(UNIT)

This story
has been
released
on DVD

written by Ben Aaronovitch
directed by Michael Kerrigan
music by Keff McCulloch

Part 1 aired on September 6, 1989
Part 2 aired on September 13, 1989
Part 3 aired on September 20, 1989
Part 4 aired on September 27, 1989

Dorota Rae . . . . Flight Lieutenant Lavel
Stefan Schwartz . . . . Knight Commander
Ling Tai . . . . Shou Yuing
Paul Tomany . . . . Major Husak

A.K.A.: Jean Marsh makes her third **Doctor Who** appearance here, having played a guest role in *The Crusade* (1965) and best known for her stint as short-lived companion Sara Kingdom, whose TARDIS travels took place entirely within the 12-part epic *The Daleks' Masterplan* (1965-66). This is **Nicholas Courtney**'s final appearance as Brigadier Lethbridge-Stewart in classic **Doctor Who** proper, though he would reprise the role for the 1993 charity sketch *Dimensions In Time*, fan-made direct-to-video productions (most notably 1995's *Downtime*) and for numerous Big Finish audio stories in the **Doctor Who** universe. Lethbridge-Stewart's next appearance in BBC-produced **Doctor Who** would take place in the spinoff series **The Sarah Jane Adventures** in the two-part story *Enemy Of The Bane* (2008); several episodes of that show's 2008 season were also directed by *Battlefield* director **Michael Kerrigan**. **Angela Bruce** was intended to appear as Lethbridge-Stewart's recurring replacement in future UNIT stories, a plan that was thwarted by the cancellation of **Doctor Who** at the end of this season. She had already carved out sci-fi TV immortality for herself in 1988 by appearing as the "female Lister" in **Red Dwarf**'s much-loved *Parallel Universe* episode.

Though it may be considered by many to be the weakest story of the final season, that is by no means to say that it's a bad show. In fact, **season 26 is the best season of Doctor Who in several years**, and easily the best of Sylvester McCoy's reign. If *Battlefield* does, in fact, have a weakness, it is that the entirety of the story seems to be a set-up for future events. The seventh Doctor has to contend with the mess left by one of his future regenerations, we're introduced to a new Brigadier (and she herself is introduced to Ancelyn), and there's always the lingering hint that Morgaine and Mordred will return to shake things up another day. Sadly, these various foundations were laid for stories that would never be told since the series was cancelled after this season. Still, with the Doctor now moving firmly into much darker waters, Sylvester McCoy plays the creepiness and shadiness of the character with great skill. It's almost scary at times, though it also gets silly – especially when he twirls round and round past the camera...oops, sorry, uh, "into an interstitial vortex."

Since this story was written as the farewell to Brigadier Lethbridge-Stewart, Nicholas Courtney had more to do here than he did in most of his past appearances. A lot of his character development, in fact, can be traced to *Battlefield* and 1983's *Mawdryn Undead*, the shows in which he had the least amount of prerequisite soldiering and skepticism to take up his screen time. The sight of him easing into old age and retirement – not to mention having gotten married! – is not only entertaining, it's also heartwarming in a way that **Doctor Who** rarely manages. (By the way, the entire character of Doris was based on a brief throwaway mention of a liaison between her and a much younger Brigadier in 1974's *Planet Of The Spiders*.)

The new Brigadier, played by Angela Bruce, is funny, smart and immediately likable. I also have to call attention to the Destroyer creature, in the running to be the best humanoid monster ever seen in the original series. The amount of craftsmanship that went into this creature is amazing, and it's certainly worthy of anything ever seen on an American science fiction series.

GHOST LIGHT

The Doctor brings Ace to a house called Gabriel Chase in the year 1883 – a house which a younger Ace firebombed in 1983, long before she joined the Doctor but long after anything had lived in the house. Gabriel Chase's original owner is a very unusual man named Josiah Samuel Smith, infamous in the 19th century for his controversial theories of evolution, and these theories have brought the Reverend Matthews to Gabriel Chase. But something else has brought the missing explorer Redvers Fenn-Cooper there – a offer of glory in exchange for an assassination. At the heart of all of these events lies a sinister secret of a far less earthly nature, something which could result in the destruction of Earth...but the Doctor's hands are already full when Ace discovers that he has brought her to her dreaded home town of Perivale a century before her birth.

Sylvester McCoy . . . . The Doctor
Sophie Aldred . . . . Ace
Michael Cochrane . . . . Redvers Fenn-Cooper
Sharon Duce . . . . Control
Carl Forgione . . . . Nimrod

written by Marc Platt
directed by Alan Wareing
music by Mark Ayres

Part 1 aired on October 4, 1989

UWURP!

John Hallam . . . . Light
Ian Hogg . . . . Josiah Samuel Smith
Brenda Kempner . . . . Mrs. Grose
John Nettleton . . . . Reverend Matthews
Katharine Schlesinger . . . . Gwendoline

This story has been released on DVD

Part 2 aired on October 11, 1989
Part 3 aired on October 18, 1989

Sylvia Syms . . . . Mrs. Pritchard
Frank Windsor . . . . Inspector Mackenzie

BEHIND THE SCENES: Filmed after both *The Curse Of Fenric* and *Survival*, *Ghost Light* has the dubious distinction of being the last **Doctor Who** production to be filmed at BBC Television Centre until the 2011 Children In Need charity sketch.

Though it's quite atmospheric, one almost needs the Target novelization of *Ghost Light* to tell what's going on. It almost seems as if it was originally intended to be a four-parter, but wound up being squashed into three parts instead. There's a considerable amount of narrative and wonderfully witty dialogue in those three parts, though, and it's worth the time it takes to watch it.

Sophie Aldred really comes into her own in *Ghost Light*, and quickly makes herself the most interesting person to travel in the TARDIS since Turlough. Fortunately, Ace was generally graced with far better scripts than Turlough, and Aldred rises to the challenge admirably. In sharp contrast to the usual portrayal of Ace – which had been seen as recently as *Battlefield* – she is given maturity and a much more realistic dose of teenage angst. These elements continued through the remainder of **Doctor Who**'s final season on the air, and it was a welcome change.

If *Ghost Light* provides just one major irritation, it is that the Doctor seems to know what's going on, and he remains tight-lipped on the subject. The unfortunate result here is that the *viewer* may not know what's going on. On the good side, there's yet another great musical score by Mark Ayres, which Silva Screen thankfully released on CD in 1993 (and re-released, in expanded form, in 2013).

THE CURSE OF FENRIC

The Doctor and Ace arrive at a soggy British naval camp in 1943, into which the Time Lord confidently strides, not even attempting to conceal his presence. He mingles with the base's disturbed commander and the brilliant but paranoid Dr. Judson, creator of the Ultima code-breaking device. The Doctor and Ace later encounter a small platoon of Russian commandos who plan to steal Ultima – a move which has been anticipated. In the background lurks a devious alien presence with whom the Doctor has an old score to settle – provided that the humans in the naval camp, merely pawns in a much more complex game, don't destroy their own world first.

Sylvester McCoy . . . . The Doctor
Sophie Aldred . . . . Ace
Christien Anholt . . . . Perkins
Marek Anton . . . . Vershinin
Joanne Bell . . . . Phyllis
Tomek Bork . . . . Sorin
Mark Conrad . . . . Petrossian
Peter Czajkowski . . . . Sergeant Prozorov
Aaron Hanley . . . . Baby
Janet Henfrey . . . . Ms. Hardaker
Marcus Hutton . . . . Sergeant Leigh
Joann Kenny . . . . Jean

This story has been released on DVD

written by Ian Briggs
directed by Nicholas Mallett
music by Mark Ayres

Part 1 aired on October 25, 1989
Part 2 aired on November 1, 1989
Part 3 aired on November 8, 1989
Part 4 aired on November 15, 1989

Dinsdale Landen . . . . Dr. Judson		Stevan Rimkus . . . . Captain Bates	
Alfred Lynch . . . . Commander Millington		Cy Town . . . . Haemovore	
Nicholas Parsons . . . . Reverend Wainwright		Raymond Trickett . . . . Ancient Haemovore	
Cory Pulman . . . . Kathleen Dudman			
Anne Reid . . . . Nurse Crane			

NEW WHO CONNECTIONS: Just as *Remembrance Of The Daleks* called the Doctor's age and origins into question with its hint that the Doctor was present to witness the birth of the Time Lords, *The Curse Of Fenric* again calls the Doctor's age into question, but on a much more vast scale. In his "evil since the dawn of time" rant, the Doctor seems to have intimate knowledge of the formation of the universe and matter itself, and *not* knowledge that can be explained away by his inadvertent proximity to those events (*Terminus*, 1983). Where *Remembrance* asked "how old is the Doctor, really?", *Fenric* begins to leave a breadcrumb trail of hints that the Doctor may be, or may have become imbued with, some elemental force of creation. The new series has occasionally dropped similarly tantalizing hints, but nothing so bold as this scene from *The Curse Of Fenric*.

Possibly the quintessential seventh Doctor story, this four-parter shows the Doctor at his darkest, having once again already planned the game that is played out across time and space, culminating in this confrontation in a seemingly out-of-the-way location. *The Curse of Fenric* also set the tone for Virgin Publishing's New Adventures series of novels which began publication in 1991 — in these books, as in this story, the Doctor uses Ace as both bait and bloodhound for the alien menace, regardless of her feelings. Another frequent plot device borrowed from *Fenric*, though it was used earlier in *Remembrance Of The Daleks* and *Silver Nemesis*, portrays the Doctor as a master manipulator against whom the alien menace never stood a chance. In its third recurrence in the TV series, this storyline was already becoming a bit predictable, but the first three years of the New Adventures books recycled the "Doctor-as-manipulator" element *ad nauseum*.

But that was in the future, and the fondness future writers showed for the *Fenric* "formula" is evidence of the powerful and mold-breaking nature of this story. The entire cast — with the possible exception of some of the Russian soldiers and the two delinquent girls — is remarkably convincing, and Sylvester McCoy and Sophie Aldred hit their stride outstandingly, again coloring future writers' portrayals of their characters. At times, however, the story seems to take quantum leaps forward. Some of these huge jumps in the plot are compensated by additional scenes included in the commercial video release which weren't broadcast due to time constraints, explaining some of the apparent gaps in the logic of the story.

Something else to seek out aside from the commercial video release of *Fenric* is Ian Briggs' novelization of his own scripts for Target Books, though the book may be hard to find outside of used bookstores. The novel, just one of the series of books based on the series, excels because of the wealth of related material which wasn't part of the original script. Some observers feel that the novelization of *The Curse of Fenric* set the pace for the earliest books in the New Adventures series; it also included a prologue, set well after the TV story's conclusion, with an older Ace who had long ago parted company with the Doctor — and such was the impact of the *Fenric* novel that later New Adventures writers went to great lengths to preserve this epilogue, which could just as easily have been considered unofficial.

SURVIVAL

The Doctor brings Ace to present-day Perivale to visit her friends, but she discovers that most of them have gone missing. Perivale is now a tense place where parents fear for their children's lives and Sergeant Paterson teaches self-defense classes in hopes that the residents of Perivale can help themselves when the time comes. Unusually vicious black cats stalk the streets, marking their territory in the deadliest ways. When Ace joins the ranks of the other missing teenagers, the Doctor follows her, finding himself on the planet of the feral Cheetah People, a hostile world whose inherent violence infects all who go there. The Master has also somehow become trapped here, enslaved by the Cheetah People's primitive bloodlust, and hoping to escape by using the new visitors from Perivale. The Doctor is left to face the dilemma: where is the Master more dangerous, on this alien world which will soon destroy itself, or running loose on Earth?

Sylvester McCoy . . . . The Doctor
Sophie Aldred . . . . Ace
Anthony Ainley . . . . The Master
Will Barton . . . . Midge
Kathleen Bidmead . . . . Woman
Lisa Bowerman . . . . Karra
Kate Eaton . . . . Ange
Gareth Hale . . . . Harvey
Julian Holloway . . . . Sergeant Paterson
David John . . . . Derek
Michelle Martin . . . . Neighbor
Sean Oliver . . . . Stuart

This story has been released on DVD

written by Rona Munro
directed by Alan Wareing
music by Dominic Glynn

Part 1 aired on November 22, 1989
Part 2 aired on November 29, 1989
Part 3 aired on December 6, 1989

Norman Pace . . . . Len
Sakuntala Ramanee . . . . Shreela
Adele Silva . . . . Squeak

NEW WHO CONNECTIONS: The Doctor's climactic hand-to-hand brawl with the Master, a more brutal depiction of their rivalry than the original series had ever attempted (the closest would be the relatively polite fencing match in 1972's *The Sea Devils*), is recalled in the tenth Doctor's face-to-face confrontation with the regenerated Master in *The Last Of The Time Lords* (2007), though it's a case where the newer episode, despite the more advanced production techniques at its disposal, lacks the intensity of the original scene. The Doctor's return "home" — to Earth — may also be explained by the eighth Doctor's claim to be half human (*Doctor Who*, 1996).

This was the last BBC episode of **Doctor Who**, and if it had been the Doctor's final televised adventure, it would have ended on a high note. *Survival* is one of the best Sylvester McCoy stories, if for no other reason than its break away from the long line of shows in which the seventh Doctor pulls the strings, hurts Ace's feelings, and knows what's going on all along. It takes a while for the Doctor to realize what the real danger is, and it's even a refreshing take on the Master, whose presence isn't made clear until the end of part one. That the Master isn't really in control of the situation or himself makes his character more interesting and dangerous than he had been in years, and Anthony Ainley really sinks those new pointed teeth of his into this new aspect of the Master.

The New Adventures books quickly dismissed the infection of the Cheetah Planet as a passing problem, which I've always thought was a big mistake. In *Survival*, it was established that once one had fallen under the planet's spell, one too many violent impulses could send one over the edge, past the point of no return. In the final confrontation, the Doctor prevents Ace from fighting, fearing that she's too close to that edge — and in his own final struggle with the Master, he himself almost goes too far. It would have made life much more interesting if the Doctor and Ace would have had to find ways to deal with this problem for a while longer, though I can see where it would've been limiting to make it a permanent condition.

Survival was the final outing for **Doctor Who** as a continuing television series until the 21st century. Sure, the death of the television show gave rise to the immensely creative series of original novels and audio plays that followed, and the seventh Doctor was brought back one last time in the 1996 TV movie, but the 26th season of **Doctor Who** demonstrated that the series was finally getting back on its feet after the missteps of the Colin Baker era; Sylvester McCoy, Sophie Aldred, the writers, and the production team were really hitting their stride, and the show was quickly heading for another epoch of sophistication and popularity, the like of which hadn't been seen since early in Tom Baker's tenure.

And then...**Doctor Who** was gone. For a very long time.

SHORT HOPS

...in which the author lights up an extra-colorful, garish, '80s-style Movie Sign.

On November 23rd, 1988, *Silver Nemesis* premiered on BBC1. On November 24th, 1988, **Mystery Science Theater 3000** premiered on a small independent TV station in Minneapolis. Coincidence? I think not!

Surely it was an omen. For, as staunchly as I was defending John Nathan-Turner's reign as producer of **Doctor Who**, I will also readily admit that the reign in question produced some outright howlers, of which *Silver Nemesis* is but one. Let's trawl through JN-T's tenure (or, as most of us call it, "the '80s") to see which stories could really have used as the means to torture the crew of the Satellite of Love.

From Tom Baker's final season, the real standout is *Meglos*. First off, you have strangely costumed space pirates running around, and a clueless captured Earthman. And if that's not enough to get you giggling: *Tom Baker, made up as a giant cactus.* I rest my case.

Peter Davison's reign usually boasted (if that's the right word) one noticeably subpar story per season. Season 19 gave us *Time-Flight*, whose Kalid character (spoiler: it's the Master in disguise for *no readily apparent reason*) makes me chuckle even without outside influences. Even season 20's best could be mined for a few laughs - the entire season, even the *good* stories, is up for grabs. Season 21's *Warriors Of The Deep*, with plot holes big enough to walk a Myrka through on a leash, is an early favorite for **MST**ification.

But Season 21 also saw out Peter Davison, and brought us Colin Baker in the head-scratchingly silly *The Twin Dilemma*. Giant slugs menacing the universe. I almost can't decide.

Colin Baker's first full season as the Doctor features *Timelash*, a story in which a hand puppet is the alien menace and a tank full of Christmas tinsel is a deadly gateway through time. If the hand puppet had been doing something less vaguely threatening, one could mistake the whole thing for an all-star variety show.

The Trial Of A Time Lord is another season where it's hard to decide which installments are most worthy of robot riffing. Surely Crow and Servo would chuckle at their robot brethren in parts 1 through 4 (*The Mysterious Planet*), but parts 5 through 8 (*Mindwarp*), with their utterly incoherent plot and Brian Blessed and Colin Baker acting as goofy as possible, would be almost too easy. Parts 9 through 12 (*Terror Of The Vervoids*) offer a similar embarrassment of riches, with strangely Muppet-ish killer plants offing an all-star cast, and as for parts 13 and 14? "Megabyte modem." *'Nuff said.*

Sylvester McCoy's first season is another bumper crop of silliness, though season 25 presents fewer obvious targets. *The Happiness Patrol* is a likely contender. The final season of the original **Doctor Who** gives us *Battlefield*, in which a time vortex is represented by a rotating column of glitter. As a general rule, it's hard to take something seriously as a threat if there's a better-than-even chance that a member of the Osmond family is going to pop out from behind it.

Mystery Science Theater 3000 went from being a strictly local Minneapolis phenomenon to being a national cult hit, just in time to plug the gap left by new episodes of **Doctor Who** in the lives of American fans. Its low-budget charm is rooted in the same keep-the-show-going-without-spending-any-money showbiz tradition upon which entire seasons of **Doctor Who** coasted. By suggesting installments of one to poke fun at on the other, I'm not trying to diminish **Doctor Who**. Rather, I'm just pointing out how neat it would've been to see the two collide, just once. (I'm not alone in this desire either; there's an entire fan venture, Mysterious Theatre 337, devoted to MST-ifying classic **Doctor Who** episodes at American conventions.)

Mystery Science Theater 3000 stopped just short of surviving into the 21st century. Looking at the media and cultural landscape we have now, in which it seems people are just *looking* for reasons to be offended, I put **MST3K** in the same category as **Doctor Who**: it was a great, smart show, one that didn't assume that its audience consisted of uncultured idiots, and *we've never needed it on the air more*.

DOCTOR WHO IN THE '90s
DIMENSIONS IN TIME

The Rani traps the Doctor's first two incarnations in the time vortex and makes unsavory plans for dealing with the others. The fourth Doctor is once again trapped and sends out a warning to his past and future incarnations. The seventh Doctor and Ace arrive in the east end of London, tracking the time disturbance caused by the Rani's activities, when suddenly they begin switching identities – the Doctor appears and sounds like his past incarnations, and Ace seems to be replaced by the Doctor's former companions (sometimes, inexplicably, *two* of his past companions). They find themselves interacting with the locals, some of whom also seem to be displaced in time, until the source of the time disturbance is found: the Rani herself, with an army of the Doctor's old enemies in tow.

Jon Pertwee . . . . The Doctor
Tom Baker . . . . The Doctor
Peter Davison . . . . The Doctor
Colin Baker . . . . The Doctor
Sylvester McCoy . . . . The Doctor
Sophie Aldred . . . . Ace
Nicola Bryant . . . . Peri
Nicholas Courtney . . . . . . Brig. Lethbridge-Stewart
Carole Ann Ford . . . . Susan
Richard Franklin . . . . Captain Yates
Louise Jameson . . . . Leela
Caroline John . . . . Liz Shaw
Ross Kemp . . . . Grant Mitchell
Bonnie Langford . . . . Mel
John Leeson . . . . voice of K-9
Steve McFadden . . . . Phil Mitchell
Philip Newman . . . . Kiv
Kate O'Mara . . . . The Rani
Mike Reid . . . . Frank

This story has been released on DVD

written by John Nathan-Turner
and David Roden
directed by Stuart McDonald
music by Dominic Glynn

Part 1 aired on November 26, 1993
Part 2 aired on November 27, 1993

Wendy Richard . . . . Pauline Fowler
Elisabeth Sladen . . . . Sarah Jane Smith
Pam St. Clement . . . . Pat Butcher
Nicola Stapleton . . . . Mandy
Sarah Sutton . . . . Nyssa
Gillian Taylforth . . . . Kathy Beale
Deepak Verma . . . . Sanjay
Lalla Ward . . . . Romana
Deborah Watling . . . . Victoria Waterfield
Adam Woodyatt . . . . Ian Beale

SARAH JANE CONNECTIONS: The Rani's somewhat silly threat, "You're going on a journey – *a very long journey!*", is echoed word-for-word in the opening teaser of part 1 of the **Sarah Jane Adventures** episode *Secrets Of The Stars* (2008). Given that *Dimensions In Time* hasn't faded into the obscurity that it really probably should have, and that the episode in question was written by longtime **Doctor Who** fan and novelist Gareth Roberts, it's almost certain that the homage was intentional.

BEHIND THE SCENES: This marks the only on-screen, in-character meeting between the sixth Doctor (Colin Baker) and Brigadier Lethbridge-Stewart (Nicholas Courtney), though one is hard-pressed to figure out exactly what they're saying to one another in his historic moment over the sound of the helicopter nearby. Big Finish would later give the two a proper adventure together fighting *The Spectre Of Lanyon Moor* (2000).

An all-star charity event marking the 30th anniversary of the first broadcast of **Doctor Who** (and missing the actual date by only three days), *Dimensions In Time* is sort of like the ***Star Wars Holiday Special*** of **Doctor Who**: everyone's seen it, usually by way of a downloaded copy that must have been sourced from a dilapidated VHS tape, everyone's had a polite chuckle at the actors who appeared in it, and moved on with their lives, never to devote even a moment's thought to considering it "official."

That's probably wise. With the first and second Doctors represented by sculpted heads shot against bluescreen, and the Rani hiding some kind of monstrosity behind every roundel in the walls of her TARDIS (so… most of the roundels are Japanese-style capsule hotels for **Doctor Who** monsters?), and no rhyme or reason to the "identity changes" of Doctors and companions, there's no story to be found here. Given that it was just a small part of a charity telethon, there was no reason to expect any different.

Lost on most American viewers is that *Dimensions In Time* includes an equal number of cameo appearances by cast members of the popular British soap **Eastenders**, and in the time-hopping spirit of their **Doctor Who** guests, there are both current and past **Eastenders** regulars on hand for the festivities. In the end, this was never going to be about bolting a proper new chapter onto the mythos of either show. *Dimensions In Time* is, however, a bit of fun showing how many stars from both **Doctor Who** and **Eastenders** were willing to give freely of their time and talent for a worthy cause. (Even outside of this episode, Jon Pertwee appeared in person to introduce the mini-episodes, took some good-natured ribbing, and gave as good as he got, which is almost as entertaining as *Dimensions In Time* itself.)

Some fans find it easy to dislike *Dimensions* simply for not being the epic direct-to-video **Doctor Who** drama (*The Dark Dimension*) that was in development for a 1993 release and then abandoned before production could begin, but for a chance to see some old favorites, it was better than nothing – and it was well-known at the time that something bigger and better was in development, maybe a movie, maybe a TV project, maybe with the involvement of Steven Spielberg, and maybe not. Crazy casting rumors – from Eric Idle to Leonard Nimoy to David Hasselhoff as the Doctor – were a dime a dozen in the British tabloids. As it turned out, the next real chapter of **Doctor Who** *would* be made on another continent after all, Hollywood *would* be involved, and a protégé of Spielberg's would be at the wheel.

None of which told anyone, at least until the resulting movie was broadcast in 1996, whether or not it'd be worth watching.

SHORT HOPS

…in which the author professes to know the identity of the only American actor who ever could have played the Doctor.

You heard me right. I'm openly admitting to heresy here: there *is* a Yank who could fly the TARDIS quite capably – or, at least, at one time there was.

In the years running up to the making of the 1996 movie, numerous publications claimed that the series' first American Doctor was in the offing, with names like David Hasselhoff (!) bandied about in the tabloids. All things considered… **Doctor Who** dodged a bullet or two with the casting of Paul McGann.

But there's one American actor who would have made a smashing **Doctor Who**, and for all intents and purposes had already done so… but not in anything even remotely connected to the **Doctor Who** universe.

Follow me here as I explain why one **Gene Wilder essentially played the Doctor** in 1971's *Willy Wonka And The Chocolate Factory*.

Skipping, for the moment, the foppish mode of dress (but it *wasn't* a million miles away from what Jon

Pertwee's Doctor was wearing at the time, was it?), Wilder-as-Wonka exhibited virtually all of the character traits that also marked out arguably the three most influential actors to pilot the TARDIS: Troughton, Tom and Tennant.

- The Doctor and Wilder's Wonka are both obviously eccentrics. Not just that-weird-guy-who-lives-across-the-street eccentrics, but *genuinely otherworldly* eccentrics who stand out like a sore thumb almost anywhere they go, at home only in their own carefully constructed worlds, be it an outdated TARDIS or a mammoth chocolate factory. And even given the massive exterior of the factory in *Willy Wonka And The Chocolate Factory*, there is no way, just *no way*, that all of what's shown could fit *inside* the edifice shown... unless, of course, one springs for the simplest possible explanation, that the factory is bigger inside than outside.

- The Doctor and Wonka both sit in stern but fond judgement of humanity. Yes, they seem to show little mercy in weeding out the bad apples, be they Adam of *The Long Game* fame or Veruca Salt, but the aim seems to be to improve humanity by skimming the gene pool. And the best of humanity – Jamie McCrimmon, Sarah Jane Smith, Rose Tyler or Charlie Bucket – gets to take off with the Doctor/Wonka in something that seems to be roughly the size of an elevator car, to serve not merely as companion, but as carefully-selected protégé. Neither of these men seems to have any problem playing God in his spare time.

- The Doctor and Wonka have no qualms associating with beings not of this Earth. Leela, Adric, Nyssa, Oompa-Loompas – neither of these men shows any bias against non-humans. Considering how much of Wonka's dirty work the Oompa-Loompas are shown to do, one can only assume that they like whatever arrangement keeps them employed at the chocolate factory and could leave at any time.

- Wilder's Wonka first appears with a cane and a limp, and then proceeds to do a somersault. Very much like most of the Doctor's incarnations, he's never quite what anyone expects. He also frequently quotes (and occasionally misquotes) classic literature whenever the mood takes him.

- Okay, I'll say it: ridiculously foppish outfit (though "in" at the time of production), amazingly curly hair, and a laser-like stare that cuts right through any pretenses that anyone might be trying to maintain... Wilder-as-Wonka practically *is* the Doctor, or may well be a renegade Time Lord in exile himself.

It's important to note that the character traits present in Willy Wonka are in the DNA of the character – both the original book <u>Charlie And The Chocolate Factory</u> and the screenplay of *Willy Wonka And The Chocolate Factory* were written by Roald Dahl, who, as Wonka's creator, had a firm grip on the character's strangeness and his fierce moral code (but the screenplay was also extensively reworked by David Seltzer, whose alterations weren't appreciated by Dahl). But credit also goes to Wilder, who wound up owning the character of Wonka as much as Dahl did (and in a way that, to be brutally honest, Johnny Depp never will). The movie Wonka was both gently reassuring and positively *terrifying* at times. You never quite knew if he had your best interests at heart, or, indeed, if you were ever getting even so much as a fraction of the whole story from him at any given point.

Gee, that reminds me of somebody. I wonder Who?

It's worth noting at this point that Jon Pertwee *was* considered for the part of Wonka, but, during 1971, was tied up with an ongoing TV series that demanded much of his time. Ron Moody was offered the part, but turned it down; he would later do the same when approached to be Pertwee's successor on **Doctor Who**.

Gene Wilder is now a bit too old to inhabit the Time Lord's skin, and truth be told, he was probably already too old to play the part by the time the casting call went out for Philip Segal's attempt to revive **Doctor Who**. But if we're going to debate whether or not an American actor could credibly play the Doctor, my argument is that one very capable American actor already *has* done so – and done so *brilliantly* – in every way but name.

Willy Wonka And The Chocolate Factory should almost be required viewing for **Doctor Who** fans: it hews closer to the character throughlines of the Doctor than the Peter Cushing films do.

That both the TARDIS and Torchwood have landed in Cardiff's Roald Dahl Plass is somehow fitting.

Ah, the 1990s: never had there been so little Doctor Who on TV, and yet never had there been so much *stuff*.
Clockwise from upper left: Doctor Who Missing Adventures <u>Goth Opera</u> novel, Doctor Who pinball backglass, <u>Radio Times</u> 1996 TV movie pull-out supplement, <u>Doctor Who Magazine</u>, Doctor Who: The Missing Episodes <u>The Ultimate Evil</u> novelization, Dapol Seventh Doctor action figure, Doctor Who New Adventures <u>Love & War</u> novel, *Dalek Attack* computer game, Dapol Time Lord action figure, Big Finish music soundtrack CD (technically released in 2000).
Photo of **Doctor Who** memorabilia from the author's collection.

"I CAN'T MAKE YOUR DREAM COME TRUE FOREVER,
BUT I CAN MAKE IT COME TRUE TODAY."

The Eighth Doctor
(Paul McGann: 1996)

Since the early 1990s, Philip David Segal, an expatriate British TV producer based in Los Angeles, had been trying to set the wheels in motion for the return of **Doctor Who** to television. He had prepared elaborate story treatments diverging wildly from the original series' premise - setting the Time Lord off on a quest to find his lost father, named Ulysses - but using such classic elements as the Daleks, Cybermen (renamed the Cybs and given an appearance more akin to *The Road Warrior*'s desert denizens). Originally developed at Steven Spielberg's Amblin Studio, the Americanized **Doctor Who** project eventually followed Segal off the Amblin lot when he left. With partner Peter Wagg (one of the guiding lights behind Max Headroom), Segal shopped the retooled **Doctor Who** around to various networks - with the BBC's blessing, of course. The project found a home at Fox, but only as a TV movie with the potential to spawn a series - not the up-front series order Segal had hoped for. A torturous international casting process ensued, with Segal pursuing actor Paul McGann to play the role. A Briton himself, Segal was keen to buck tabloid rumors of everyone from David Hasselhoff to Bill Cosby piloting the TARDIS by keeping the Doctor essentially British, even if the show would use American settings. Reluctant to take part, McGann finally agreed to take on the role, and fans were surprised - and relieved - when Segal's elaborate re-imagining of the **Doctor Who** mythos was reshaped into a direct continuation of the original series...complete with Sylvester McCoy making a cameo appearance to regenerate into the eighth Doctor.

In May 1996, **Doctor Who** returned to television at last, with Paul McGann immediately commanding the fans' loyalty as the eighth Doctor. Opinions of the movie were mixed, with many fans complaining that it was too Americanized, despite many familiar elements of the original series: the TARDIS' police box exterior, the Master, the Daleks, and many other deft touches that would have greater significance to longtime fans than to newcomers. But fan opinion was almost universally in favor of McGann's portrayal of the Doctor, an opinion that was only strengthened upon his next televised appearance in the role in 2013's short *Night Of The Doctor*. It was the second-highest-rated drama of the week of its premiere in the U.K., but in America, where the movie was scheduled opposite a pivotal episode of the sitcom Roseanne, it fared less well. Fox didn't pick up the series. Universal Studios, which had produced the movie for Fox and the BBC, had an option on the property until the end of 1997, but despite the participation of numerous personnel from Universal's popular Action Pack syndication package (the home of **Hercules** and **Xena**), Universal went nowhere with it. **Doctor Who** was once again in limbo.

1996
DOCTOR WHO

Before he is executed by the Daleks for crimes against them, the Master asks that his remains be given to the Doctor for transport to Gallifrey. En route in the Doctor's TARDIS, the Master's remains break free of their container, still pulsating with malevolent life. The Master sabotages the TARDIS, forcing an emergency landing in San Francisco on December 30, 1999. The moment he steps out of the TARDIS, the Doctor is caught in the middle of a gang shooting. One young survivor of the shootout, Chang Lee, calls an ambulance for the Doctor, unwittingly providing an escape for the Master as well. Cardiologist Grace Holloway ignores the X-rays which show the Doctor's two hearts and tries to operate on him. The operation and the anesthetics end the Doctor's seventh life. The Doctor regenerates in the morgue as the Master takes over the body of a paramedic. Grace resigns after losing her patient, but the newly reborn Doctor, suffering from amnesia, escapes the hospital and follows her home. After convincing Grace of his alien nature and regaining his memory, the Doctor discovers that his future regenerations are the Master's targets. Aided by Chang Lee and a hypnotized Grace, the Master captures the Doctor and tries to use the TARDIS' Eye of Harmony to transfer the Doctor's life energy into the paramedic's decaying body, but opening the Eye on Earth will destroy the planet at midnight on December 31. When Chang Lee rebels against the Master's dominance, the Master kills him and releases Grace to help him. Grace escapes and sets the TARDIS into motion, freeing Earth from danger. The Master's scheme fails, but he kills Grace after she releases the Doctor. The Master falls into the Eye of Harmony and vanishes from existence, while the TARDIS restores Grace and Chang Lee to full health. The Doctor brings his passengers back to Earth just after the dawn of the year 2000. Grace turns down the Doctor's offer to accompany him on his travels, and the Doctor departs in the TARDIS.

Paul McGann . . . . The Doctor
Eric Roberts . . . . The Master
Daphne Ashbrook . . . . Dr. Grace Holloway
Yee Jee Tso . . . . Chang Lee
Sylvester McCoy . . . . The Old Doctor
Darryl Avon . . . . Gangster
Jeremy Badick . . . . Gareth
Michael Ching . . . . Chang Lee's Friend
Dean Choe . . . . Chang Lee's Friend
Bill Croft . . . . Cop
Dolores Drake . . . . Curtis
Danny Groesclose . . . . Driver
Dave Hurtubise . . . . Professor Wagg
Dee Jay Jackson . . . . Security Guy
Ron James . . . . Motorbike Cop
Byron Lawson . . . . Gangster
Mi-Jung Lee . . . . TV Anchor
Catherine Lough . . . . Wheeler
Johnny Mam . . . . Gangster

This story has been released on DVD

written by Matthew Jacobs
directed by Geoffrey Sax
music by John Debney, Louis Febre
and John Sponsler

Aired on May 14, 1996 (US)
Aired on May 27, 1996 (UK)

John Novak . . . . Sallinger
Joanna Piros . . . . TV Anchor
Eliza Roberts . . . . Miranda
William Sasso . . . . Pete
Geoffrey Sax . . . . Dalek voice
Michael David Simms . . . . Dr. Swift
Gordon Tipple . . . . The Old Master
Joel Wirkkunen . . . . Ted
Paul Wu . . . . Gangster

CLASSIC CONNECTIONS: The seventh Doctor has rebuilt his sonic screwdriver, a device not routinely carried aboard the TARDIS since 1982's *The Visitation*.

NEW WHO CONNECTIONS: The Eye of Harmony is glimpsed directly in 2013's *Journey To The Centre Of The TARDIS*. Paul McGann returns as the eighth Doctor for the 2013 mini-episode *The Night Of The Doctor*, chronicling this incarnation's *final* adventure.

BEHIND THE SCENES: Writer Matthew Jacobs is the son of Anthony Jacobs, who guest starred along William Hartnell in 1966's *The Gunfighters*. This movie premiered exactly 30 years after the third episode of that story. Jacobs was not the first writer to take a swing at reviving **Doctor Who**; an elaborate series bible was written by John Leekley, who later went on to create such American series as **Kindred: The Embraced** and **Wolf Lake**. Leekley's concepts for the series took a much looser approach to continuity, rebooting the **Doctor Who** universe entirely and sending a younger Doctor on a quest to find his missing father. No one at the BBC objected to the changes, but this version of the story was eventually abandoned in favor of a more straightforward, open-ended adventure structure.

A.K.A.: Yee Jee Tso and Daphne Ashbrook have both continued their **Doctor Who** association by way of Big Finish's audio adventures, though not as their characters from this movie, who cannot be used in other **Doctor Who** media without permission from (and payment to) Universal Studios, who produced the TV movie for the BBC and Fox. Yee Jee Tso has also appeared in The 4400, Stargate SG-1, Stargate Atlantis, Battlestar Galactica, Highlander, and Dark Angel, while Ashbrook's career has stayed closer to Earth, with guest roles on JAG, NCIS, CSI, The O.C., and quite a few shows whose titles *aren't* abbreviations. Prior to her **Doctor Who** stint, her highest-profile genre role was a one-off guest shot in the Star Trek: Deep Space Nine episode *Melora*, as a Starfleet officer weakened by normal gravity. Will Sasso was one of the first cast members of another Fox series, the Saturday night sketch show MAD TV, and more recently played Curly in the big screen recreation of *The Three Stooges*. John Novak is a staple of SF series filmed in Canada, with appearances in Sliders, Strange Luck, Highlander, Poltergeist: The Legacy, the short-lived Babylon 5 spinoff Crusade, the '90s revival of The Outer Limits, First Wave, Relic Hunter, Stargate SG-1, Smallville, and Sanctuary. Dave Hurtubise has an extensive list of genre guest starring roles, including The Outer Limits, The X-Files, Millennium, Stargate SG-1, and Dead Like Me. Director Geoffrey Sax has worked with nearly every Doctor *since* McGann, directing Christopher Eccleston in the series Clocking Off, and Matt Smith in the TV movie *Christopher And His Kind*.

One of my missions with this book was to give a fair reassessment to some chapters of **Doctor Who** history that have been maligned by fandom, to the point that people who haven't seen some of the show's much-derided adventures just take it as a given that the story in question stinks. That's not the case here. From the moment I laid eyes on it, I was in love with the **Doctor Who** TV movie. I still do love it. **It's okay to love it.**

First and foremost, you have Paul McGann as the Doctor. Even producer Philip Segal's insistence on adhering to strict continuity and showing Sylvester McCoy regenerating into his successor was no guarantee of success. (Some of the movie's financial backers at Universal Studios and the BBC wanted to completely ditch continuity and depict McGann as the successor to the far more recognizable Tom Baker.) McGann's performance, however, instantly fits. That he only got to do this on TV once between 1996 and 2012 may be the biggest bummer of the entire exercise.

It's also a bummer that we didn't get more time with the solo-traveling, non-question-mark-clad, more circumspect seventh Doctor. In the wake of this movie, the authors of the then-still-ongoing New Adventures novels went out of their way to try to meet this portrayal of the seventh Doctor and show the evolution; the more seasoned and visibly older Doctor we see here is an intriguing character, and not at all how we left the Doctor in 1989. It's impressive that Segal fought tooth and nail to get McCoy flown to Vancouver instead of trashing the entire last decade of **Doctor Who** because the studio heads only had Tom Baker on the brain; for his efforts, we get one last, surprisingly long mini-adventure alongside the seventh Doctor.

Eric Roberts' Master is delightfully unhinged, and Roberts plays it to the hilt, even to the point of playing up the fact that a quintessentially British character is now stuck inside an American body (and voice). Whatever the Master has been through since we last saw him (though the snake/cat eyes in the movie's intro suggest, surprisingly, a direct link to 1989's *Survival*), it has taken him to the brink of madness and drop-kicked him over the edge. Some fans find fault with Roberts' over-to-top portrayal, but now that Roberts has successors, it all fits as part of a continuum. The Master isn't going to start out as evil and magically get better; he's going to lose more of his marbles with time. Roberts' performance is a nice halfway point between Anthony Ainley and John Simm.

Yes, there are plot holes. The whole "set the TARDIS clock running backward and time goes in reverse" was a bit convenient, and flew in the face of how the entire original series had handled time travel. And yes, I'm probably the one guy who wasn't even slightly fazed by the Doctor's out-of-left-field claim to being half-human (and I'm almost certainly the one guy who has never completely discounted it). The movie is flawed. But it went to such great lengths to give **Doctor Who** a new look and feel for a new decade – and so much of the new series' pacing and style can be traced back to this movie. It's the halfway house between old **Who** and new **Who**.

Should it have gone to series? Powerful forces were aligned against the Doctor on this occasion - more than simply the Master. The continued interest of Universal (the studio producing the movie) and Fox (the network showing it in the United States) were dependant upon blockbuster ratings... and with the movie scheduled against one part of a multi-week arc on the comedy series **Roseanne**, depicting Dan Conner (John Goodman) suffering a major heart attack, **Doctor Who** simply didn't stand a chance in hell. **Roseanne** was a juggernaut of American television at the time: it was a series whose huge audience now tuned in out of habit as much as loyalty. The Doctor wasn't going to win this fight.

But let's face it: even a series pickup would've been no guarantee of a new series of adventures worthy of the Time Lord. Fox has an abysmal track record with science fiction series. Incredibly promising shows such as **Space: Above And Beyond, Alien Nation**, and **Firefly** have gotten either only a single season, or were canned mere episodes into their first season. Few genre shows, most notably **The X-Files** and **Fringe**, have fared well on the Fox schedule. In any case, an ongoing **Doctor Who** series would've meant Universal sharing the profits with the BBC; Universal was more interested in the health of their alternate-universe series **Sliders**, which was developed in-house and owned outright by the studio. It may be that a Universal/Fox **Doctor Who** series would've done the character and the continuity no favors.

Doctor Who went back on ice for nearly a decade. The novelists, comic writers and audio dramatists took stock of the storyline changes introduced in the TV movie, quickly discarded the controversial "half human" line (even though it actually explains such things as the Doctor's frequent returns to Earth, and his return to Earth - and the TARDIS - as his "home" at the end of *Survival*), and moved on. The BBC had taken another swing at **Doctor Who**, and big ratings in England alone weren't sufficient to keep bankrolling production. The keys to the TARDIS were still in the hands of the fans.

Fox, Universal and the BBC couldn't make the dream of reviving **Doctor Who** come true forever, but they could make it come true for one night. Given the startling amount of mythology that has emerged from this single 90-minute movie, including a new Doctor and a beautiful new vision of the TARDIS interior that has influenced every TARDIS set since, it can't have been a total stinker. It's still hugely enjoyable.

SHORT HOPS

...in which the author deals with the Time Lord while on the clock.

I tried to send this one off in fine style. Damn, but I tried.

In 1996, I was in charge of promotions and production at a Fox TV station in Fort Smith - not exactly a huge American media market - and I was eagerly looking forward to the Paul McGann movie. I had been tracking the progress of the movie and was aware that it'd be landing as a movie of the week on Fox in May. This was my chance: I was well aware that **Doctor Who** had a following in Arkansas from its many years on AETN. It was a show that was remembered fondly, though it hadn't been seen on AETN in nearly a decade. I had that awareness to build from; I had a unique weapon in my arsenal that most promo producers at other Fox stations either weren't aware of or didn't think to use.

Perhaps I was overestimating the popularity of the Doctor in my home state.

Fox had created its own on-air spots for the movie, which surprisingly leaned heavily on imagery of the TARDIS from the dazzling opening shot of *The Trial Of A Time Lord*, but I wasn't content to use those. The electronic press kit provided was manna from heaven: I was going to make my own promos and play up the familiarity that the audience already had. (Virtually all of the elements of the EPK can be seen in the bonus features of the **Doctor Who**: *The Movie* DVD, so you can look through those and see what I had to work with.)

As I had just recently come into possession of a friend's huge stash of classic **Doctor Who** on VHS, I created an elaborate two-minute-long spot - intended to run late at night when paid advertisements weren't exactly filling out commercial breaks - which actually showed footage from the original BBC series, and all seven Doctors. *This was actually a big no-no*, but this was also a small media market in the south, and the spot containing the footage in question was in a late night/overnight rotation. Chances weren't good that the BBC would hear anything about it. (Now that we're in the YouTube generation, nobody could get away with this today.) The spots issued by the network ran during the day and early evenings, and I made sure they ran quite a bit.

The result, when we got the May Nielsen ratings book, was a surprisingly strong showing against the dreaded Roseanne sweeps episode – and by "surprisingly strong," I mean **Doctor Who** still soundly got pounded into the dust, but showed signs of putting up a fight. Not a great number (even if it had been, it wasn't a great number in Los Angeles, Chicago or New York, so *it really wouldn't have mattered*), but not as non-great a number as was expected against such competition.

Was I responsible for "rallying the troops" among the dormant **Doctor Who** fans out there?

Given the amount of time I put into my promo project, measured against the return it produced, at the very least I *was* responsible for losing perspective. But the thought of having some small hand in reviving **Doctor Who** was too irresistible to pass up. I knew the chances of the movie spawning a series were tiny; I just wanted to be that *one* promo guy at that *one* station that actually made a dent with it. It was a passion project if ever there was one.

1999
THE CURSE OF FATAL DEATH

The Doctor lures the Master to the planet Terserus, the home of an extinct race infamous for its method of communicating via flatulence. Perhaps feeling his half-human oats, the Doctor announces his intention to wed his pretty assistant Emma, something which disgusts the Master to no end – so it's fortunate that the evil Time Lord has prepared a series of nasty traps, to which he immediately and repeatedly falls victim himself. But the Master's allies, the Daleks, are rather less clumsy and have plans to take over the universe. The Doctor makes a final bid, for the love of Emma and the entire cosmos, to halt the Daleks' evil plans at the cost of not just one, but three of his precious lives…

Rowan Atkinson . . . . The Ninth Doctor
Jonathan Pryce . . . . The Master
Julia Sawalha . . . . Emma
Richard E. Grant . . . . The Tenth Doctor
Jim Broadbent . . . . The Eleventh Doctor
Hugh Grant . . . . The Twelfth Doctor
Joanna Lumley . . . . The Thirteenth Doctor
Roy Skelton . . . . Dalek voice
Dave Chapman . . . . Dalek voice

This story has **not** been released on DVD

written by Steven Moffat
directed by John Henderson
music not credited
(used from previous **Doctor Who** episodes)

Part 1 aired on March 12, 1999
Part 2 aired on March 12, 1999

NEW WHO CONNECTIONS: Writer Steven Moffat would later take over the reins of "real" **Doctor Who** when new series showrunner Russell T. Davies left the show in 2010. The Comic Relief charity was co-founded by Oscar-winning British writer Richard Curtis, who would also contribute to the 2010 season of **Doctor Who** with his script for *Vincent And The Doctor*.

This hysterically spot-on Comic Relief spoof brought **Doctor Who** back to the BBC in style, and made a mockery of the BBC's assertion that it no longer had the facilities to produce **Doctor Who**. In some scenes, with only three years for technology to march onward and bring the price down, the effects work seen in *The Curse Of Fatal Death* outclassed the 1996 Fox TV movie!

And I can't stress enough what a wonderful Doctor former **Blackadder/Mr. Bean** star Rowan Atkinson made. Other parodies have played the comedy to the hilt, but Atkinson and his co-stars wisely aim for understatement and deadpan humor, barely cracking so much as a smile until the lightning-fast succession of silly regenerations begins, at which point the proceedings become much more tongue-in-cheek. The funny thing is that I could actually imagine the Doctor calmly asking "how are things?" upon being reunited with the Daleks. Jonathan Pryce also makes a magnificent Master; a reunion of these two actors in these two roles in real, non-spoof **Doctor Who** would've been tremendous.

The rapid-fire regenerations barely give one a chance to get used to each resulting incarnation of the Doctor, but the point was to squeeze as many famous actors and comedians into as short a space as possible. Of the various Doctors, the best is easily – surprisingly – Hugh Grant, who was pooh-poohed by many fans when he was rumored to be in the running for the role in the 1996 Fox movie. He lasts all of a couple of minutes in *The Curse Of Fatal Death*, but Grant makes a passable Doctor. When he regenerates into Joanna Lumley, the show dives off the deep end into outrageous camp – but it's also almost over by that point.

The Curse Of Fatal Death was tremendously enjoyable, and while it was a parody, it wasn't a savagely critical one. Who could've guessed that **Doctor Who** would be back in just six years, and that the writer of *The Curse Of Fatal Death* would be among its creative forces?

UWORP!

THE NEW SERIES

2005-2011

The 21ˢᵗ Century Is When Everything Changes...

The 1996 TV movie came and went, establishing Paul McGann as a new Doctor loved by the fans, and setting him up as the star of a new era of **Doctor Who** comics and novels. But those other media, and later his return to the role in audio form thanks to Big Finish Productions, were seriously underground where the general public was concerned: *it wasn't new Doctor Who on TV*.

As 2003 approached, it was evident that the BBC was ready to put a little bit of effort into **Doctor Who**'s 40ᵗʰ anniversary, but despite persistent rumors (which, it must be said, had been circulating for years without coming true) of a new series, the anniversary seemed to focus entirely on classic DVD releases and new novels and audio stories. The BBC surprisingly announced an original new animated **Doctor Who** story, *The Scream Of The Shalka*, for "broadcast" on its popular BBCi web service.

For this new adventure, BBCi officially declared that Richard E. Grant, one of the participants in 1999's *Curse Of Fatal Death* spoof, would be portraying the ninth Doctor, and that his character would be official, carrying on into new novels and audio stories. Grant's Doctor was completely separate from the way he played the character in the spoof special, and the animation was handled by Cosgrove Hall. And that was the only surprise that the BBC *intended* to announce prior to the show's 40th anniversary on November 23, 2003 - until a slip of the tongue forced them to reveal more.

In September 2003, BBC1 controller Lorraine Heggessy let slip that a new season of a full live-action series revival of **Doctor Who** was in the works, due to be aired in 2005. The producer/writer behind the new series was Russell T. Davies, a well-known quantity in British TV and the creator of the original British version of **Queer As Folk**, among other series. Davies had also penned one of the final New Adventures novels for Virgin Publishing, Damaged Goods, so he was no stranger to **Doctor Who** - indeed, he was a fan, and brought fellow New Adventures writer Mark Gatiss - again a television veteran - aboard to assist in scripting duties.

The new **Doctor Who**, which fans worried might or might not be a continuation of the original series (Davies mentioned the possibility of a "reboot" of the show's mythology, only to downplay the likelihood of a radical revamp later), would be produced by BBC Wales, and a spread of thirteen 45-minute episodes was mooted early on, combining both self-contained stories and multi-part stories in a single season. Actors' names were bandied about en masse at the time of the announcement, with Bill Nighy having been mentioned on several occasions by Davies, though Paul McGann and Richard E. Grant were both said to be in the running as well. As the scripts weren't due to be written until early 2004, no firm news on casting was even remotely possible.

The BBC created **Doctor Who**, ardent fan writers and artists kept it alive, and now the circle was closing as a fan with distinguished professional credentials was finally poised to bring the Doctor back to the BBC.

The Ninth Doctor
(Christopher Eccleston: 2005)

After months of speculation by the press and the public, in March 2004 the BBC announced the casting of Christopher Eccleston as the ninth Doctor. Though recent reports - and even an erroneous, "Dewey Defeats Truman"-style headline courtesy of the Daily Mail - seemed to have actor Bill Nighy pegged as the new Time Lord, Eccleston - who had starred in Russell T. Davies' 2003 ITV miniseries *The Second Coming* - seemed to surprise many, with his penchant for serious roles (and, as he had recently appeared in Hollywood fare such as *Gone In Sixty Seconds*, big paychecks). A few weeks later, more rumors were laid to rest with the casting of Billie Piper - a former teen pop star who had made her own acting splash recently in the BBC's modernized version of Chaucer's *The Canterbury Tales* - was cast in the role of Rose Tyler, the Doctor's companion. The scripts were in progress, and production was due to start in July.

Elsewhere in the world of **Doctor Who**, the news of the new series was also having a ripple effect. Big Finish Productions made changes to their audio drama release schedule to bring a swifter close to the planned multi-year story arc of Paul McGann's eighth Doctor. The tightly interconnected stories that had characterized McGann's audio voyages since early 2001 would be wrapped up at the end of 2004, clearing the series of any ongoing storylines or major continuity references to make Big Finish's 2005 output more palatable to any newly-recruited fans of **Doctor Who**. Over half of 2004's Big Finish **Doctor Who** audio dramas would feature this rapid winding-down of McGann's convoluted voyages through the Divergent universe - somewhat akin to the brief cycle of E-Space stories in Tom Baker's final season on TV. Big Finish had no plans to retire the eighth Doctor, but simply needed to break him out of that storyline; as they renewed their own contract with the BBC, they found out what many fans were starting to hear through the grapevine: the BBC was considering the new **Doctor Who** a completely separate entity from everything that had gone before. Big Finish's renewal not only wouldn't allow them to use Christopher Eccleston, but the audio dramas could not refer to any of the new stories, even in ways that might serve to bridge the gap between the first eight Doctors' adventures and the ninth. The editors and writers of the BBC Books range of novels, which had recently pared its schedule down to one monthly release instead of two, found themselves under similar restrictions.

Filming began in Cardiff, Wales, the new production's home base, in July 2004, with the first block of location work covering the episodes *Rose, Aliens Of London* and *World War Three*, all directed by Keith Boak. In the 1980s, the **Doctor Who** Production Office had occasionally planted false information - one of the most famous incidents being a schedule board with the misleading "upcoming episode title" *The Doctor's Wife*, supposedly written by Robert Holmes - to try to figure out if any of the office help was leaking information to fanzines or the press. But in 2004, there was an entirely different beast to contend with: the internet. Within days of the start of production on the new series, fan-taken digital photos of the actors in costumes that had yet to be officially revealed made their way to the web, with rampant (and frequently way-off-base) speculation about what was in those photos following soon after.

The BBC, for its part, seemed to be savvy to the interest in the series, and also seemed to have paid attention to the official web presence for the recent *Star Wars* prequels. Like Lucasfilm, the BBC began publishing its own behind-the-scenes pictures on a daily basis, though ususally the pictures were close-ups of set dressing or props whose real significance wouldn't be known until later. (Not that this did anything to quell the speculation, mind you.) The fan photographers still scored a few firsts, however: pictures of the Doctor in costume and the redesigned Daleks leaked before the BBC officially revealed them. But while fandom was obsessing over photos, the BBC was obsessing over marketing the new series. The Corporation's internal marketing department later admitted that they looked to the successful promotion of the movies *Superman* (1978), *Batman* (1989) and, to some extent, the *Star Wars* prequels for guidance; each of these movies were new versions of an ongoing franchise, and used images that longtime fans would find familiar, but none of them necessarily set out to summarize their respective franchises for the uninitiated, instead treating them as a brand new story. The BBC followed that basic strategy in drawing attention to the new series: always mindful of the small but vocal long-time fan base, the promotion instead focused on drawing new viewers in for "the trip of a lifetime."

When the new series debuted on March 26th, 2005, it was a ratings success. Though it drew in an audience comparable in size to the viewers who watched the 1996 TV movie starring Paul McGann, the new series' premiere episode was competing in a new and constantly evolving broadcast environment: satellite and digital cable channels now competed with the familiar "terrestrial" broadcast outlets. With all of that competition, nine million viewers' eyeballs on a single channel was now considered a runaway success.

What no one expected to happen within a week of *Rose*'s broadcast, however, was that ratings were so promising that the show would be given an early pickup for a second season plus a one-hour Christmas special - or that Christopher Eccleston would announce his retirement from the TARDIS. Having completed filming on the first season, Eccleston found that the rigors of being the Doctor - appearing in nearly every scene, shooting at night, and then spending months afterward promoting the series - took over his life. The clues were even there for those watching **Doctor Who: A New Dimension**, a half-hour special shown immediately before *Rose*, in which Eccleston said "It's been my life for the past eight months." Only one episode into Eccleston's "era," if one can even call it that, the hunt was on for a new Doctor. Among fandom, casual viewers, television critics, and even actors who had played the Doctor in the past, Eccleston was lauded for his dynamic performance even while he was being sternly criticized for potentially endangering the new series. But as new episodes continued to air, the ratings held, either holding their own against, or soundly trouncing, ITV's competing variety show, **Ant & Dec's Saturday Night Takeaway**.

In terms of the fictional development of the series, there were both throwbacks to the past and major new developments in the show's mythos. As early as the first episode, *Rose*, we learn that the Doctor recently fought in a war; in the second episode, *The End Of The World*, the Doctor reveals that his home planet of Gallifrey, and all of the other Time Lords, had been eradicated in this Time War. As might be expected of a conflict involving a galactic superpower, it wasn't a quiet affair; the Time War had the unintended side-effect of almost wiping out the Gelth (*The Unquiet Dead*) and the Nestenes and Autons (*Rose*). In *Dalek*, we learn that the Time War pitted the Time Lords against the Daleks, and Gallifrey, along with all of the other Time Lords, burned in the conflict. The Doctor claims to have personally set the Daleks' defeat into motion, and the Time War passed into near-legendary status in future history (Captain Jack is aware of the Daleks' supposed extinction, but regards the Time War as a myth in *The Parting Of The Ways*; however, Jabe of the Forest of Cheem had heard of it and was aware of the Time Lords' destruction).

The TARDIS interior was radically different from any incarnation that had graced the screen before; the set was designed by comics artist Bryan Hitch, and incorporated more organic elements, doing away with the sleek, high-tech sets of the original series and the more Jules Verne-inspired set of the 1996 TV movie. The central console itself, while retaining the sky-high time rotor from the 1996 movie, was more of a rounded mushroom shape whose controls were cobbled together from such elements as a bicycle pump, a modern-day LCD monitor, and the wheel from a baby carriage. Moreso than ever before, the Doctor was seen having to coax the TARDIS into traveling at all (*Aliens Of London*), and for many of the ship's journeys the interior was seen to shake violently. In the original series (specifically, the seminal Time Lord story *The Deadly Assassin*), it was established that all TARDISes drew their energy from the Eye of Harmony, a black hole contained and stabilized on Gallifrey itself, and in the 1996 TV movie the TARDIS was shown to have its own Eye of Harmony, or at least a more direct physical link to it than was previously known to exist. With Gallifrey destroyed, there seemed to be clear hints that the Doctor's TARDIS was on its own for power; he parked his timeship in Cardiff in *Boom Town* specifically to recharge it from a rift of psychic energies left behind by the death of the Gelth over 100 years earlier (*The Unquiet Dead*). Also, the interface between the TARDIS and the outside world, rather than being seen as a "mystery alcove" somewhere between the original TARDIS' interlocking double doors and the Police Box exterior, was now seen to simply be the other side of the Police Box doors. And for the first time, many scenes looked into the TARDIS from the outside, either via green screen or a large photograph of the interior set propped up and lit within the Police Box prop (though, to be fair, this idea had been seen before, in the 1993 video documentary *More Than 30 Years In The TARDIS*).

The TARDIS demonstrated another unusual ability in both *Boom Town* and *The Parting Of The Ways*, as the ship's own psychic energy was seen to emanate from the console. In *Boom Town*, it enveloped a condemned Slitheen criminal and reverted her to the innocence of childhood; in *The Parting Of The Ways*, that energy literally took over Rose's body and she seemed to carry the TARDIS' essence outside the ship to save the Doctor, almost killing Rose in the process. The same energy gave Rose the ability to bring Jack back to life after he had been exterminated by Daleks, and that combined with the energy's incandescent appearance may mean that it's the same energy that brought Grace and Chang Lee back to life in the 1996 movie (a phenomenon that the eighth Doctor attributed to the TARDIS, commenting that it was a "sentimental old thing"). When the ninth Doctor regenerated into the tenth, this too was accompanied by a blinding burst of energy - and the ascending jet-engine-like whine/roar of the fifth Doctor's regeneration from 1984's *The Caves Of Androzani*.

While some fans spent considerable effort debating and speculating over the "Time War" storyline, some even comparing it to the ill-fated "Temporal Cold War" storyline in the recently-cancelled **Star Trek** spinoff series **Enterprise**, what many of them may not have known that the Doctor's recent involvement in a future war was a holdover from an early draft of the original series "format document" - something most producers now refer to as a "series bible." Quoted in The First Doctor Handbook by David J. Howe, Mark Stammers and Stephen James Walker, that 1963 document's description of the first Doctor, as written by C.E. "Bunny" Webber, included the following: "*He seems not to remember where he comes from but he has flashes of garbled memory which indicate that he was involved in a galactic war and still fears pursuit by some undefined enemy.*" And while this idea seems not to have come to fruition during Hartnell's tenure, it wasn't thrown out. Quoted in The Second Doctor Handbook, also by Howe, Stammers & Walker, a new format document was prepared by the show's makers for the beginning of Patrick Troughton's era. The authors of the revised document aren't identified, but probably included the then-current team of script editor Gerry Davis, producer Innes Lloyd, and writer David Whitaker, and it says of the Doctor's first regeneration: "*The metaphysical change which takes place every 500 or so years is a horrifying experience - an experience in which he relives some of the most unendurable moments of his long life, including the galactic war.*" The new series clearly insinuated that the Doctor was involved in the Time War before taking on his ninth form (*Rose* would seem to mark the first occasion that the Doctor has seen his ninth body in the mirror), so while Russell T. Davies was crafting his own storyline, it's interesting to note that the very idea of the Doctor's involvement in a war dated back to the development of the very first episodes ever broadcast.

As far as other elements of the series mythology, the Autons appeared much as they had in their previous appearances in *Spearhead From Space* (1970) and *Terror Of The Autons* (1971), though their creators, the Nestene Consciousness, had a new appearance not unlike an ever-morphing pool of molten lava. (The Nestenes in the '70s had appeared as large octopus-like life forms.) With the first appearance of the Daleks, although the basic design silhouette created by BBC staff designer Ray Cusick in 1963 was retained, the armored monsters were shown to have new abilities, ranging from a swiveling midsection to the use of their sucker-cup arm as a weapon, as well as a self-destruct mechanism (though at least one Dalek had previously been seen to self-destruct in 1974's *Death To The Daleks*, minus the flashy effects). CGI effects allowed the Daleks to fly effortlessly, thus conquering the age-old joke about beating them by running up a flight of stairs, but Daleks had been levitating on screen since 1985's *Revelation Of The Daleks* and even more visibly in 1988's *Remembrance Of The Daleks*. In *The Parting Of The Ways*, it is revealed that the new breed of post-Time-War Daleks have been created by harvesting dead humans; this isn't entirely a new practice either, as humans had been seen as fodder for Dalek conversion in *Revelation Of The Daleks*.

New aliens encountered in the course of the series included the bipedal-tree-based Forest of Cheem, along with several unnamed species, seen in *The End Of The World*, *The Unquiet Dead*'s gaseous Gelth, the Raxicoricalphalipatorians (of which the Slitheen were but a single family) from *Aliens Of London*, *World War Three* and *Boom Town*, and the Jagrafess lording over humanity in *The Long Game*. Chula technology was seen in *The Empty Child* and *The Doctor Dances*, though its owners weren't seen. One other alien race appeared, though it was from the original series - the "stuffed" head of an *Invasion*-era Cyberman in a trophy case in Van Statten's alien musuem in *Dalek*.

Russell T. Davies also seemed keen to introduce an ongoing story thread throughout the season, weaving it through the background of several episodes. As early as *Rose*, the words "Bad Wolf" could be glimpsed in London graffiti, and in later episodes it was seen on monitor screens, said aloud by various characters, spray-painted across the side of the TARDIS, and was even translated into Welsh for the name of a doomed nuclear reactor in *Boom Town* (Blaidd Drwg). Fans were quick to catch on to the references, and even began listening and watching intently for future occurrences; at least one was planted in every episode for those who were paying attention. Withheld from fandom and the public as late as possible, the penultimate episode of the season was, in fact, named *Bad Wolf*, though even the Doctor and Rose admitted that they too had noticed the recurring phenomenon in the previous episode, *Boom Town*. In this regard, especially later in the season when flashback montages became necessary to illustrate the various occurrences of "Bad Wolf," Davies seemed to be taking a page from **Babylon 5**'s book. Even before the Bad Wolf mystery was solved on screen, Davies hinted that a similar thread, again represented by a single word or phrase, would also recur in the second season, and that it would be heard once toward the end of the first season. (Early speculation, backed up by the BBC's registration of an Internet domain name, pointed toward "Torchwood," heard in Bad Wolf, which is also an anagram of "**Doctor Who**.")

In April 2005, the BBC announced that David Tennant would be taking over the TARDIS as the tenth Doctor. Regarded as a possible contender from the beginning, especially since Russell Davies had slyly mentioned that if Eccleston chose not to continue in the role that the producer would like Tennant to replace him, Tennant was known to be a serious **Doctor Who** fan in his own right, and had appeared in several Big Finish audio productions, starring as the lead character in Dalek Empire III, guest starring with Colin Baker in *Medicinal Purposes* and with Sylvester McCoy in *Colditz*, and with "Unbound" Doctors David Warner and Arabella Weir. Tennant had also narrated the half-hour **Doctor Who: A New Dimension** special. (He had also, coincidentally, appeared with Eccleston in the feature film *Jude*.) But it was none of these that had pegged him as the new Doctor; he had also starred in the charismatic and eccentric title role of Russell T. Davies' BBC2 miniseries *Casanova*, just as Eccleston had worked with Davies on *The Second Coming*. Without realizing it, Tennant had already turned in his audition piece.

Immediately after announcing his retirement from the series, a quote about typecasting was attributed to Eccleston by the BBC, which later admitted that the actor had not said any such thing. But sources within the BBC were now telling the press, under the condition of anonymity, that Eccleston was an extremely expensive Time Lord to have around - there seemed to be an implication that if the Doctor didn't regenerate, he might disappear from television again. With the naming of Tennant as Eccleston's successor, an unexpected *third* season renewal was announced, along with a second Christmas special.

The new series was, at least for the time being, here to stay - even if its new Doctor wasn't.

SERIES 1: 2005
ROSE

19-year-old Rose Tyler has a boyfriend, a department store job, and just enough curiosity to put her in harm's way. When she finds herself trapped in the basement level at work, surrounded by moving shop window mannequins who seem determined to crush her, she's snatched out of danger by a total stranger who calls himself the Doctor. While he saves her life, he doesn't do much to help her job when he completely destroys the department store, claiming that he's trying to halt an invasion by a force that can possess and control anything made of plastic - such as the mannequins. Rose is surprised when the Doctor reappears the next day at her home, looking for any of the plastic creatures that may have survived the explosion at the store, and she's even more surprised when he actually finds precisely that, namely a mannequin arm which tries to kill both of them before the Doctor disables it. Rose follows him, persistently trying to find out who he is, but the Doctor isn't inclined to give straight answers about his own identity. Rose walks away as the Doctor marches into an incongruous 1950s police call box in the middle of London and then turns around to find that the box has disappeared.

In an attempt to find out more about the Doctor, Rose winds up meeting with an internet conspiracy internet conspiracy theorist who says that the Doctor has been spotted throughout Earth's history. Waiting for her in a car outside, Rose's boyfriend Mickey is curious about a dustbin that seems to move on its own, but his curiosity turns into sheer terror as the bin engulfs him completely without a trace. When Rose returns to the car, her boyfriend has been replaced by a duplicate who seems unusually curious about her contact with the Doctor. When the duplicate becomes more aggressive in his line of questioning, the Doctor once again comes to the rescue, and the duplicate is exposed as yet another plastic creature, an Auton. The Auton attacks ferociously, but this time the Doctor is ready for it, disconnecting its head from its body. The headless Auton body still pursues the Doctor and Rose back to the police call box, and Rose is stunned to find that it's not a call box at all, but the TARDIS - the Doctor's time machine, bigger inside than outside and definitely not from Earth, not unlike the Doctor himself. Using the Auton's head, the Doctor follows the signal controlling the Autons to their source, and a confrontation with the Nestene Consciousness masterminding the Auton assault. But the Doctor alone can't prevent them from invading Earth.

Christopher Eccleston . . . . The Doctor		written by Russell T. Davies
Billie Piper . . . . Rose Tyler		directed by Keith Boak
Mark Benton . . . . Clive		music by Murray Gold
Nicholas Briggs . . . . Nestene voice		

Noel Clarke . . . . Mickey		
Camille Coduri . . . . Jackie Tyler		
Elizabeth Fost . . . . Auton		
Elli Garnett . . . . Caroline		
Paul Kasey . . . . Auton		
Adam McCoy . . . . Clive's son		
Helen Otway . . . . Auton		

This story has been released on DVD

Aired on March 26, 2005

Alan Ruscoe . . . . Auton
David Sant . . . . Auton

CLASSIC CONNECTIONS: The Nestene Consciousness and its plastic Auton minions repeatedly menaced Earth during the third Doctor's exile there, as chronicled in *Spearhead From Space* (1970) and *Terror Of The Autons* (1971).

A lovely little adventure to kick off the new series, *Rose* is almost giddy in its pacing - indeed, if a single thought crossed my mind while watching this premiere of a whole new generation of **Doctor Who** for the first time, it was that as much as fandom has taken to decrying the 1996 TV movie starring Paul McGann, the 2005 TV series starring Christopher Eccleston seems to owe an astounding amount of its basic style, and even several more specific elements, to that movie. There are other inspirations clearly on display as well: the all-out Auton attack at the end plays like a Devlin & Emmerich take on similar scenes from 1971's *Terror Of The Autons* - much faster-paced and appearing to play out on an almost incalculably grander scale by comparison. The Doctor's seemingly callous "alien" attitude hearkens back to several early Colin Baker stories, and the fact that, early on, he seems to be almost one step ahead of the Auton advance (and even has a weapon handy to deal with them) is reminiscent of the Sylvester McCoy era. Even though he winds up in real trouble at the end and needs Rose to bail him out, the Doctor's nonchalant attitude almost makes one think that, up to a certain point, thwarting this invasion started out as a milk run. But if I had to make more solid comparisons, even in Eccleston's lively portrayal of the Doctor, it all goes back to the McGann movie. Sure, there are certainly archetypal "Doctorish" things that have been around since Hartnell occupied the role, but there's so much tonal, stylistic and thematic influence from the 1996 movie that it's nearly impossible to avoid comparison.

One other element bears mention: the character of Clive, a web site "nutter" who has been tracking the Doctor's appearances throughout history. This was one of *Rose*'s most interesting elements: it was a clever way to deliver a lot of information about the Doctor while avoiding an obvious info-dump in the middle of the episode, and Mark Benton made quite an impression with such a brief appearance (he was also the nemesis of Eccleston's character in the Russell T. Davies-written 2002 miniseries *The Second Coming*). I'm sure some fans will be asking why the Doctor's other incarnations weren't in Clive's archive, but in a way it's much more plausible that Clive wouldn't know about the previous eight Doctors, and it simplifies things helpfully for a new audience. The scene when he realizes what the Autons are - and clearly knows what it means when one of them points an open hand at him point-blank - is priceless. (Kudos to the production team for tracking down the original Auton sound effects, too.)

Doctor Who was back on TV, with glossy location shooting, an obvious increase in budget, and creative talent that, for the most part, seemed unabashedly proud to be on board. The show got a real publicity blitz from the BBC, not the low-key, almost-apologist publicity of the late 1980s and 1996. With these things as a foundation, **Doctor Who** kicked off with a public profile that the original series' makers could never have dreamed of.

THE END OF THE WORLD

To do away with Rose's skepticism about the TARDIS' ability to travel through time, the Doctor takes his new companion to the year 5,000,000,000 – on the very day that the Sun expands into a red giant and swallows its innermost planets, including Earth. The TARDIS lands aboard Platform One, a shielded space station placed in a temporary orbit around Earth so special guests may bear witness to the planet's demise in complete safety. Rose isn't prepared for the guests to be alien though – from the enormous Face of Boe, which has to be kept in a protective tank, to the hooded Adherence of the Repeated Meme, to the sentient tree people represented by the lovely Jabe, to a being claiming to be "the last pure human" – in reality a face and a brain connected to a flat membrance of skin after hundreds of plastic surgeries to remove the rest of her "imperfect" body. But as the moment of Earth's death draws near, things begin to go wrong aboard Platform One – the Doctor discovers that a killer is slowly wiping out the guests and hospitality staff alike…and that someone else knows who he really is.

Christopher Eccleston . . . . The Doctor	written by Russell T. Davies
Billie Piper . . . . Rose Tyler	directed by Euros Lyn
Beccy Armory . . . . Raffalo	music by Murray Gold
Yasmin Bannerman . . . . Jabe	
Silas Carson . . . . Alien Voices	Aired on April 2, 2005
Camille Coduri . . . . Jackie Tyler	
Simon Day . . . . The Steward	
Sara Stewart . . . . Computer Voice	
Jimmy Vee . . . . The Moxx of Balhoon	Zoe Wanamaker . . . . Cassandra

This story has been released on DVD

A.K.A.: Red Dwarf fans may recognize **Yasmin Bannerman** (Jabe) as the air traffic controller who witnesses the Cat's amazing dancing feats in the season eight three-parter *Back In The Red*. Voice artist **Silas Carson** has been heard and seen in all three of the *Star Wars* prequels, portraying both Jedi Master Ki-Adi Mundi and the treacherous Nute Gunray. In *Star Wars Episode I*, he also portrayed Senator Lott Dod.

An almost surreal, science fiction romp, *The End Of The World* begins to examine what has long been an unexplored issue in **Doctor Who**: what kind of person would trade in a perfectly normal, non-violent, non-abusive existence for a life of danger alongside a man of mystery who travels through time in a police box? And furthermore, why should he take anyone on board at all? *The End Of The World* finally dishes out some answers, and even if they really only apply to the ninth Doctor and Rose, they're quite revealing.

An unabashedly space-based story that ate up one fifth of the entire effects budget for the first season, *The End Of The World* introduces a startling number of creatures and alien life forms for a single **Doctor Who** story. Not since the third Doctor's Peladon stories has the Doctor encountered such a wide variety of unusual creatures all in one place.

If there's anything that really prevents *End Of The World* from being a runaway success, it's pacing. It would have been lovely to see this one spread over two parts, perhaps giving some of the background characters more depth so that we feel a little something when some of them bite the dust. There's a hint of this in a scene where Rose meets one of the space station's maintenance workers, and to some extent with a major guest character who assists the Doctor later in the story, but it's hard to really gauge whether or not there's enough story to spread this story out over two parts. The episode excels at setting its quite surreal mood, however – from the Doctor getting down to the strains of "Tainted Love" (which, while cheesy, was lyrically right on the money for the scene in question) to the presentation of an ancient "iPod" to the archives – it's almost Douglas Adams-esque in places.

While Billie Piper continues to show new colors to Rose and her initial reactions to time travel, this episode is firmly about the Doctor. It drops a gob of information at our feet about who he is now, what's happened since he last left our screens (and as it turns out, a lot has happened in the show's mythology, including the destruction of Gallifrey and the Time Lords in a cataclysmic war, making the Doctor and his TARDIS the last of their kind). It turns out that other people know this too, which is interesting in and of itself. The guest cast is likeable, with Yasmin Bannerman making a good enough impression as Jabe that something about that character screams "companion material" for much of the episode.

The End Of The World may be a case of style not so much winning out over substance as style slightly obscuring substance. The substance is there – there's a scene at the end that really justifies what we've seen to that point and brings things into focus. The character-driven moments are spot-on, but the plot-driven component all happens so fast.

THE UNQUIET DEAD

Having demonstrated the TARDIS' ability to fast-forward through the pages of future history, the Doctor takes Rose into the past – Cardiff, Wales, on Christmas Eve, 1869 to be precise. Before the time travelers can immerse themselves in this time period, however, they encounter something very much out of place – a sign of alien interference in Earth's history. A recital of "A Christmas Carol" by Charles Dickens himself is brought to a halt by a walking corpse who exhales some kind of gaseous being into the theater. While the Doctor tries to make contact with the gas creature, Rose follows a local undertaker who retrieves the corpse – and winds up being kidnapped in the process. The Doctor and Charles Dickens give chase, eventually finding the undertaker's place of business and discovering that he is doing his best to contain the alien threat with the help of a psychic girl. The Doctor suggests establishing a more firm contact with these beings, but doing so could unravel Earth's timeline.

Christopher Eccleston . . . . The Doctor
Billie Piper . . . . Rose Tyler
Simon Callow . . . . Charles Dickens
Wayne Cater . . . . Stage Manager
Alan David . . . . Gabriel Sneed
Jennifer Hill . . . . Mrs. Peace
Eve Myles . . . . Gwyneth
Meic Povey . . . . Driver
Huw Rhys . . . . Redpath

This story has been released on DVD

written by Mark Gatiss
directed by Euros Lyn
music by Murray Gold

Aired on April 9, 2005

Zoe Thorne . . . . The Gelth

A.K.A.: Welsh actress **Eve Myles** would later land a much more visible role in the **Doctor Who** universe as Gwen Cooper of **Torchwood**; the fourth-season **Doctor Who** episode *Journey's End* would even hint that Gwyneth and Gwen were distant relatives. Writer **Mark Gatiss** was one of the driving forces behind the popular comedy series **The League Of Gentlemen**, but also wrote several **Doctor Who** novels, starting with the New Adventures book Nightshade in 1992. As an actor, Gatiss has also gotten in on the Time Lord's travels (sort of) – he took the part of an old enemy with a new disguise in the **Doctor Who** Unbound audio play *Sympathy For The Devil* in 2003, acting under the anagrammatical pseudonym of "Sam Kisgart". With his League of Gentlemen cohorts, Gatiss also provided "additional Vogon voices" for the 2005 feature film version of *The Hitchhiker's Guide To The Galaxy*.

TORCHWOOD CONNECTIONS: The site visited by the Doctor and Rose becomes a hotspot of temporal energy known as the Rift, and that makes it the natural place to build Torchwood Three some time later.

What starts out as a deceptively lightweight romp into history quickly turns into a creepy – but still lightweight – exercise in a historical horror story. On the one hand, it's nice to see a historical setting in **Doctor Who** again, and it's a treat to see it executed as beautifully as was done here, bringing Christmas to Cardiff in late summertime. On the other hand, as fun as it is, from a storytelling standpoint, *The Unquiet Dead* can't seem to decide if it's about Charles Dickens or the Gelth, a race of gaseous entities who can inhabit and reanimate human corpses as new host bodies. Either one would've been interesting on their own, but Dickens plus the Gelth seem to be trying to elbow each other out of the spotlight in 45 minutes. Simon Callow makes for a great Dickens, and it's fun to see the Doctor completely star-struck for once, though when that admiration gives way to almost-crass condescension, the Dickens side of things fades into the background and we deal with the more supernatural story. This is actually a case where the series' old format of four 25-minute episodes might have given both the Dickens and Gelth angles the time and space they both needed to develop properly.

The Unquiet Dead has all the makings of a great classic **Who** story – a historical figure playing a part in the proceedings, a scary ghost/possession/seance story with all the hallmarks of classic "black magic" stories from the series' past, and a great setting – but despite some sparkling dialogue, the story seems rushed.

ALIENS OF LONDON

The Doctor brings Rose back to Earth, promising that as far as anyone there is concerned, she's only been gone for 12 hours. As it turns out, though, the Doctor's control of the TARDIS is somewhat erratic – Rose has, in fact, been gone for 12 months, making her mother's life a living hell and making her boyfriend Mickey a murder suspect. Just as things seem to calm down after her arrival, an alien spaceship plummets through the skies over London, crashing right through Big Ben and coming to rest in the Thames. The Doctor seems optimistic at first that perhaps this is humanity's first contact with aliens, but his curiosity takes him to a hospital near the crash site, where the body of the ship's pilot is being kept. He quickly discovers that all is not as it seems, and that aliens have, in fact, been on Earth for some time, but even the Doctor doesn't suspect how deeply they've entrenched themselves into society until the Slitheen reveal themselves.

Christopher Eccleston	The Doctor
Billie Piper	Rose Tyler
Annette Badland	Margaret Blaine
Matt Baker	himself
Jack Barlton	Reporter
Lachele Carl	Reporter
Navin Chowdhry	Indra Ganesh
Basil Chung	Bau
Noel Clarke	Mickey Smith
Camille Coduri	Jackie Tyler
Corey Doabe	Spray Painter
Elizabeth Fost	Slitheen
Ceris Jones	Policeman
Paul Kasey	Slitheen
Andrew Marr	himself
Fiesta Mei Ling	Ru

This story has been released on DVD

written by Russell T. Davies
directed by Keith Boak
music by Murray Gold

Aired on April 16, 2005

Naoko Mori	Doctor Sato
Eric Potts	Oliver Charles
Alan Ruscoe	Slitheen
Steve Spiers	Strickland
Rupert Vansittart	General Asquith
Jimmy Vee	Alien
David Verrey	Joseph Green
Penelope Wilton	Harriet Jones

TORCHWOOD CONNECTIONS: "Dr. Sato" is **Torchwood** computer expert Toshiko Sato, operating undercover. Torchwood's staff doctor, Owen Harper, was originally assigned the job of infiltrating the alien investigation, but had to send Toshiko instead (as recounted in the 2007 **Torchwood** episode *Exit Wounds*).

One of the first season's best episodes, *Aliens Of London* goes a long way toward addressing, head-on, what it means to be the Doctor's companion, and more importantly, what being the Doctor's companion means to the companion's own family. This has never really been addressed before, and it's always been a very convenient plot device to have a succession of orphans (Victoria, Adric, Nyssa, Tegan, Peri), people who were lost/missing to begin with (Ace, Steven, Charley), and/or targets of ostracism (Turlough) travel in the TARDIS. In short: nobody that anyone would miss, whether on the intimate level of family or in the broader picture of history. *Aliens Of London* hits that issue dead-on center, with emotional repercussions aplenty.

Aliens Of London also features an intriguing new take on the old alien invasion trope, and builds very firm links to **Doctor Who**'s past by showing us the modern face of UNIT (the covert agency for whom the third Doctor spent a lot of time investigating extraterrestrial threats in the early 1970s). This is accomplished smoothly, without bringing the story to a screeching halt to try to feed the audience a truckload of continuity from the original series – if you know that Jon Pertwee's Doctor worked for UNIT, that's fine and it adds a nice layer of background to the proceedings, but if you aren't aware of the series' long history, that's fine too. It's also interesting to see that his UNIT associations can now get the Doctor swept off to 10 Downing Street.

The guest cast gets a lot of screen time here, and there really isn't a badly-cast actor anywhere to be seen. Penelope Wilton as Harriet Jones (MP, Flydale North, in case you didn't know) is especially effective, though the performers playing the alien invaders are remarkably creepy when it comes right down to it. Noel Clarke gets to show Mickey as something other than a clueless coward, and Camille Coduri gets to add some much-needed *non*-comedic elements to Rose's mother. And we get the new show's first real cliffhanger, and it all adds up to something that just feels right.

WORLD WAR THREE

The Doctor escapes the Slitheen, but of all the experts on alien life forms called to 10 Downing Street, only he survives. Rose and Harriet Jones, an MP who was among the first to witness the aliens' true nature and survive, also barely escape the Slitheen, while Rose's connection to the Doctor even makes her mother and Mickey targets for Slitheen elimination. Unable to escape 10 Downing Street, the Doctor, Rose and Harriet manage to fight their way to the most secure room in the building and lock the Slitheen out – but that also means that help can't reach them. And when Mickey and Rose's mother manage to kill their own Slitheen pursuer with advice phoned in by the Doctor, humankind's first contact situation may become its last.

Christopher Eccleston . . . . The Doctor
Billie Piper . . . . Rose Tyler
Annette Badland . . . . Margaret Blaine
Lachele Carl . . . . Reporter
Noel Clarke . . . . Mickey Smith
Camille Coduri . . . . Jackie Tyler
Corey Doabe . . . . Spray Painter
Elizabeth Fost . . . . Slitheen
Morgan Hopkins . . . . Sergeant Price
Paul Kasey . . . . Slitheen
Andrew Marr . . . . himself
Alan Ruscoe . . . . Slitheen
Steve Spiers . . . . Strickland

UNIT
This story
has been
released
on DVD

written by Russell T. Davies
directed by Keith Boak
music by Murray Gold

Aired on April 23, 2005

Jack Tarlton . . . . Reporter
Rupert Vansittart . . . . General Asquith
David Verrey . . . . Joseph Green
Penelope Wilton . . . . Harriet Jones

UWURP!

Following straight on from *Aliens Of London*, *World War Three* spends the bulk of its time on advancing the plot. That's not to say that it has little in the way of character development, but it's not as involved in everyone's emotional states as the previous episode. If anything, the real development here goes to Jackie Tyler and Mickey. Jackie evolves further away from her portrayal in the first episode and her "concerned mother" side comes to the fore; Mickey also shows a little bit of guts, and a lot of honesty when he has to admit to the Doctor, upon receiving an invitation to travel in the TARDIS, that he hasn't quite got the guts for time travel. Harriet Jones is also developed into a likeable character who didn't show up as often as I would've expected in later installments given the build-up; it was natural to assume that Harriet was being set up so the Doctor would have friends in high places in future earthbound adventures, especially since UNIT's best and brightest are all apparently eliminated in this story. It's a little disappointing that they were suckered into such a trap, but on the other hand…it *was* the perfect set-up.

The one real problem I find with *World War Three* is that there seems to be a bit of a dichotomy: are the Slitheen a comic foil, or a force to be reckoned with? There are times when they're almost silly, and times when they're the most terrifying things the new **Doctor Who** had given us up to this point. In their human disguises, the Slitheen are almost comical, as if the audience needs to have it telegraphed to them that something's up. It's hard to know whether or not to take an alien menace seriously when it's awash in fart jokes.

World War Three was also quite a surprising topical little slice of **Who**, with the ersatz Acting Prime Minister demanding that the U.N. allow Britain to fire nukes at a fictitious alien invasion force whose "massive weapons of destruction" could be ready to devastate Earth "in 45 seconds" (in reality, the nukes are intended to destroy all life on Earth). Harriet wonders if anyone will fall for this gambit, and Rose replies, "They did last time." These barely-disguised references to the still hotly-debated case made by the U.S. in favor of going to war with Iraq lend the episode a bit of a sharp sting, but in any case, the topicality of *World War Three* extends no further than that.

DALEK

In a well-guarded underground complex in Utah, billionaire Henry Van Statten collects every type of alien artifact he can get his hands on, and money is no object: the head of a Cyberman from the 1968 invasion of London, the arm of a Slitheen, pieces of the alien ship crashed in Roswell, and more. Unknown to Van Statten, though, there's a new alien arrival in his hidden museum: the TARDIS arrives, and the Doctor's curiosity gets the best of him, setting off the security alarms. He and Rose are quickly rounded up and taken to Van Statten. Furious about the intrusion, Van Statten is at least impressed with the Doctor's knowledge of alien artifacts, and decides to show the Doctor his most prized exhibit. As Rose gets to know Adam, Van Statten's acquisition expert, the Doctor is locked into a dark room with the only living specimen of Van Statten's menagerie: a live Dalek, possibly the last one in the universe. When the Doctor discovers that the Dalek's weapon no longer works, he taunts his old enemy, reminding the Dalek that the Doctor destroyed the rest of its race even as the Daleks were laying waste to Gallifrey in the Time War. But the conversation quickly reveals that the Doctor is an alien as well, and Van Statten has the last Time Lord hauled off for examination. Rose visits the helpless Dalek, but when she touches its casing, it seems to draw strength from that contact, reactivating its weapon

– and its murderous urges to exterminate every non-Dalek in sight. But even when the Doctor takes measures to stop the Dalek by any means necessary, Rose won't let him.

Christopher Eccleston . . . . The Doctor
Billie Piper . . . . Rose Tyler
Steven Beckingham . . . . Polkowski
Nicholas Briggs . . . . Dalek voice
Jana Carpenter . . . . DeMaggio
Barnaby Edwards . . . . Dalek
Corey Johnson . . . . Henry Van Statten
Bruno Langley . . . . Adam
Joe Montana . . . . Commander
Anna-Louise Plowman . . . . Goddard

This story has been released on DVD

written by Robert Shearman
directed by Joe Ahearne
music by Murray Gold

Aired on April 30, 2005

John Schwab . . . . Bywater
Nigel Whitmey . . . . Simmons

A.K.A.: Nicholas Briggs and Barnaby Edwards are both key players in Big Finish Productions' series of Doctor Who audio stories. Briggs wrote, directed and played roles in many of the company's Doctor Who audios (including the inaugural adventure, *The Sirens Of Time*, in 1999), and took over creative control of the Doctor Who range upon the departure of Gary Russell (who left the audio world to take a script editing job with a science fiction series filmed in Cardiff – funny, that). Barnaby Edwards has directed and written several Doctor Who audio adventures as well. Anna-Louise Plowman appeared in numerous episodes of Stargate SG-1 as Dr. Sarah Gardner, an archaeologist who was taken over by a Goa'uld named Osiris; despite the accent, she's a New Zealand native. Corey Johnson didn't have to affect an accent as Van Statten: he was born in New Orleans and has worked steadily on both sides of the Atlantic, appearing in MI-5 (aired in the UK as Spooks), Casualty, Band Of Brothers, *X-Men: First Class*, *United 93*, *Hellboy* and *Saving Private Ryan*.

I have extremely mixed feelings about *Dalek*. Perhaps the strongest of those feelings is that this is a story that's been told before. Russell T. Davies heard Rob Shearman's Big Finish 2003 audio drama *Jubilee* and asked Shearman to write, more or less, the same story for television, except in less time – and then Davies carried out his own extensive rewrites, taking it further away from the source material. *Jubilee* was far more effective, thought-provoking and original than *Dalek* by far. *Dalek*, by comparison, boasts some of the new series' most striking action sequences, but then dives off the deep end at its conclusion.

This story's lone Dalek gets a lot of attention, and does a lot of things we've never seen a Dalek do before. Russell T. Davies stated quite openly that he wanted this episode to drive the little ones behind the sofa, just like the Daleks did in the 1960s, and even if it doesn't quite have that effect, this episode does restore the lone Dalek as a terrifying force to be reckoned with, even if in doing so it raises the question of why we've never seen a Dalek do any of these things before. Nicholas Briggs, having provided all of the Dalek voices in Big Finish Productions' audio dramas (including his own Dalek Empire spinoff series), was recruited to provide the Dalek's voice here, though it's fair to say this was an unusually emotional Dalek. Every Dalek story *before and after* this one flies in the face of this lone Dalek's extraordinary emotional evolution, so the wrap-up of *Dalek* is a surprise, to say the last. Having a Dalek emote like this is unprecedented. Even years later, I'm torn about this episode.

Dalek is well-executed from a production standpoint, but it's an oversentimental pale shadow of *Jubilee* (almost certainly not Shearman's fault, if the biting cynicism of the audio story is anything to go by) and its "guest star" behaves wildly out of character. As later Dalek episodes of the revived **Doctor Who** slowly backed off of the extraordinary battle capabilities and extraordinary emotional range of this episode's Dalek, it seems to take place in an alternate universe all its own.

THE LONG GAME

The Doctor, Rose and Adam, a brilliant young computer whiz rescued from Van Statten's underground stronghold, arrive in the year 200,000 aboard Earth-orbiting Satellite 5. But from the moment they step out of the TARDIS, the Doctor begins to suspect that something is wrong: human technology hasn't advanced to the level he would have expected, and he begins to suspect that someone's interfering in human history. The technology is more than enough to impress Adam, though, but his fascination takes a self-serving turn as he decides to take advantage of the opportunity to take knowledge of future history home – and cash in. The Doctor and Rose investigate the unusual buildup of heat within Satellite 5, following the trail to Floor 500, a closely-guarded secret rumored to be the headquarters of Satellite 5's best and brightest. In reality, it's the lair of an alien intelligence that has humanity in its thrall. It wants the secrets of time travel from the Doctor – and if the Doctor won't surrender those secrets, perhaps Adam will…

Christopher Eccleston . . . . The Doctor
Billie Piper . . . . Rose Tyler
Christine Adams . . . . Cathica
Tamsin Greig . . . . Nurse
Judy Holt . . . . Adam's Mum
Bruno Langley . . . . Adam
Anna Maxwell-Martin . . . . Suki
Simon Pegg . . . . The Editor
Colin Prockter . . . . Head Chef

This story has been released on DVD

written by Russell T. Davies
directed by Brian Grant
music by Murray Gold

Aired on May 7, 2005

CLASSIC CONNECTIONS: This may be the oldest script to go into production in the revived **Doctor Who** - a young Russell T. Davies submitted an early version of *The Long Game* to the makers of **Doctor Who** in the 1980s, only to receive a rather curt form rejection letter in return. Undeterred, Davies later went on to become a writer, illustrator and producer (and, infamously, one-time-only host) of the BBC children's show **Why Can't You?** in the late '80s, ultimately going freelance and creating the short-lived, science-fiction-themed children's dramas **Dark Season** and **Century Falls** in the early 1990s.

A.K.A.: Simon Pegg, an avowed fan of the science fiction genre, gets around: he's become Scotty for J.J. Abrams' "reimagined" big-screen *Star Trek* universe, and he provided the voice of Dengar in the CGI animated series **Star Wars: The Clone Wars.** He's written and starred in the sitcom **Spaced**, and movies such as *Shaun Of The Dead* and *Hot Fuzz.* He also "appeared" in the 2002 **Doctor Who** audio story *Invaders From Mars.*

The Long Game is the beginning of a build-up to the end of the season, introducing us to, if nothing else, the setting where everything will go down. Perhaps the most interesting aspect of it is "What if the Doctor brought the wrong person aboard the TARDIS?" To be fair, the Doctor himself didn't exactly pick Adam; Rose did. But it's an interesting character idea anyway, without being quite as jackhammer-subtle as the introduction of Turlough in 1983 was. Still, as much as I like his portrayal, Bruno Langley does get a little too "arch" in trying to show that Adam's wheels are turning. When the jig is up and he's confronted by the Doctor, we get to see that perhaps Adam has learned a little too much from Henry Van Statten. (That confrontation may well be Eccleston at his scariest – Adam comments that he thought the Doctor was going to throw him out of an airlock, and the thought does occur upon seeing the look on the Doctor's face…)

The Jagrafess, despite being a CGI construct where one can see the seams that connect it to the rest of the picture, is somewhat refreshing in at least one respect: it's a good old-fashioned **Doctor Who** monster, and at no point does anyone even try to psychoanalyze it or play devil's advocate for it. (Of course, the number of mostly-dead bodies manning the controls in the Jagrafess' lair speaks against the creature's goodwill automatically.) As the Editor, the human face of the oppression that the Jagrafess wields against humanity, Simon Pegg attacks his role with relish, again echoing a classic **Doctor Who** villain archetype: the mystery man with the evil laugh, watching the Doctor's every move on a monitor in a dark room. Even the surprisingly low-tech effect used when one character tries to kill the Jagrafess herself evokes classic, low-budget **Who**. Of all the episodes of this first season of the new series, *The Long Game* may well be the one that would fit most comfortably alongside the original series – not terribly above average, but just good, scary fun.

FATHER'S DAY

Rose persuades the Doctor to take her back to 1987 to witness her father's death; disturbed by stories that her father died alone, she wants to be with him, even if he doesn't know who she is. But when the time comes, she's paralyzed with emotion, and asks the Doctor to take her back again – only now, not only does she only have one more shot at being with her father when he dies, she has to avoid being seen by the versions of herself and the Doctor from mere moments ago. But instead of comforting her father as he dies, this time Rose leaps out and pulls him out of the ray of an oncoming car, saving his life and completely changing the timeline. The changes in time ripple forward, turning the TARDIS into nothing more than an empty Police Box and gradually decimating the population in the surrounding area. Enormous black dragon-like creatures – reapers – appear, consuming people one by one, beginning with the oldest they can find. The Doctor races to the church where Rose's feuding parents were attending a friend's wedding, where Rose's father was supposed to have died, and hustles everyone inside, hoping the old church will be at least a temporary safe haven. Outside the church's doors, the reapers destroy everything, attempting to rectify the divergent timeline that Rose has created. Only one reminder of the outside world remains – the car that should have hit Rose's father still circles the church at high speed, its driver still reacting to an unseen obstacle, an obvious clue as to what must happen to set time right.

Christopher Eccleston . . . . The Doctor
Billie Piper . . . . Rose Tyler
Robert Barton . . . . Registrar
Eirlys Bellin . . . . Bev
Camille Coduri . . . . Jackie Tyler
Shaun Dingwall . . . . Pete Tyler
Casey Dyer . . . . young Mickey
Rhian James . . . . Suzie
Natalie Jones . . . . Sarah
Julia Joyce . . . . young Rose

This story has been released on DVD

written by Paul Cornell
directed by Joe Ahearne
music by Murray Gold

Aired on May 14, 2005

Christopher Llewellyn . . . . Stuart
Frank Rozelaar-Green . . . . Sonny

CLASSIC CONNECTIONS: The reapers in *Father's Day* seem to exhibit similar behavior to the winged Kronos creature, a chronovore or "time eater" who appears in the 1972 story *The Time Monster*. Both the reapers and the chronovore appear when the fabric of time is disturbed, here by Rose's interference in history and, in *The Time Monster*, by the Master's experiments with time. The reapers in *Father's Day* seemed to be having trouble penetrating the church, but a *single chronovore* is apparently responsible for the destruction of Atlantis in *The Time Monster*.

I'm a huge fan of Paul Cornell's **Doctor Who** New Adventures novels. The best of the New Adventures helped to elevate the Doctor and his travels into truly mythic territory, and showed that deeply emotional stories could be at the core of a **Doctor Who** adventure. In the early 90s, I was literally about to give up on the novels until I read Cornell's <u>Love And War</u>, which made me a diehard fan of the books. Paul Cornell has been a seminal influence on **Doctor Who** storytelling in print, and arguably, the New Adventures were a critical influence on the new series. I was very excited to hear that Cornell would be writing for the new show. It just seemed like a perfect, things-coming-full-circle kind of moment.

Where Cornell's trademark stories of deep emotion are concerned, *Father's Day* does not disappoint. It left me with a lump in the throat, despite the fact that a few parts of the story really seemed to be rather obviously manipulating the audience into that emotional corner. And yet on another level, there's something awfully familiar about this story – right down to the way that time has to be set back on its proper course. Pete Tyler must die, and he must die in a manner not unlike Edith Keeler! Fans of the **Star Trek** episode *The City On The Edge Of Forever* will find some distinct similarities here, with a shift toward a doomed familial love instead of a romantic interest.

There are so many things that make this vintage Cornell **Who**. The conversation the Doctor has with the happy-couple-to-be, about how their seemingly ordinary lives are actually unique and extraordinary and therefore worth saving, is precisely the sort of thing Cornell used to have the *seventh* Doctor say, which helps to make Eccleston not just the ninth Doctor, but *the* Doctor, a vital part of the whole continuum of that character.

The guest cast is fine, with Shaun Dingwall making a particularly good impression in his portrayal of Rose's father, a well-meaning loser who, I gradually realized, would've made a great addition to the TARDIS crew. With his quirky inventiveness and off-kilter emotions, it's easy to draw parallels between Pete Tyler and the Doctor, and to see why Rose finds traveling with the latter so appealing. And all this despite the Doctor's recurring "stupid ape" schtick reaching what I have to say is an extremely unappealing crescendo here; I'm assuming that Davies put it in the script rather than Cornell, because it's so at odds with the Doctor who's trying to save the lives of the happy couple.

THE EMPTY CHILD

Tracking a space vehicle that's capable of limited time travel as it plummets toward Earth, the Doctor and Rose are unaware at first that they've arrived in Britain during the Blitz. The Doctor begins looking for the crashed spacecraft, while Rose, trying to reach a child she sees dangerously close to the edge of a tall building, puts herself in danger and is rescued by the handsome Captain Jack Harkness. Supposedly an American advisor to the Royal Air Force, Jack reveals himself to be a rogue former "time agent," and assumes from such things as Rose's cell phone that she is too. In the meantime, the Doctor has also encountered the mysterious child Rose saw earlier, wandering around London even in the midst of bombing raids and asking for his mother. He seems to be following a group of homeless children led by a young woman named Nancy, who fears the child and tells the Doctor to keep his distance from him. The Doctor discovers that the child isn't the only person in London asking for his mother. A plague has begun creeping through the population, especially close to the crash site of the spacecraft, disfiguring its victims with wounds identical to the little boy's and literally molding the flesh of their faces into the shape of a gas mask – just like the one the child wears. The Doctor catches up with Rose and Jack and discovers that Jack is responsible for bringing the alien ship – a Chula combat ambulance vessel – to Earth, and is thus responsible for the spreading plague.

Christopher Eccleston . . . . The Doctor		
Billie Piper . . . . Rose Tyler		
John Barrowman . . . . Capt. Jack Harkness		
Cheryl Fergison . . . . Mrs. Lloyd		
Robert Hands . . . . Algy		
Kate Harvey . . . . Night Club Singer		
Florence Hoath . . . . Nancy		
Brandon Miller . . . . Alf		
Jordan Murphy . . . . Ernie		
Dian Perry . . . . Computer voice		
Damian Samuels . . . . Mr. Lloyd		
Zoe Thorne . . . . voice of the Child		

written by Steven Moffat
directed by James Hawes
music by Murray Gold

Aired on May 21, 2005

This story has been released on DVD

Joseph Tremain . . . . Jim		
Albert Valentine . . . . The Child		
Richard Wilson . . . . Dr. Constantine		

CLASSIC CONNECTIONS: A visit by the eighth Doctor to the London Blitz was considered, and indeed a scene was written for potential Doctors' screen tests, as a setting what eventually became the 1996 **Doctor Who** TV movie. The scene involved the Doctor saving a girl named Lizzie from the Blitz and taking her aboard the TARDIS; part of Paul McGann's screen test involved an excerpt from that ultimately abandoned version of the script.

BEHIND THE SCENES: Along with *The Doctor Dances, The Empty Child* won the **Best Dramatic Presentation** (Shortform) **Hugo Award** in 2006.

A cracking good two-parter here, something that feels as much like classic **Who** as it does like new **Who**. While I may have liked *Aliens Of London* and *World War Three* better, it's hard to argue that *The Empty Child* and its second part, *The Doctor Dances*, may be the best written episodes of the season.

The big development here is the introduction of Captain Jack, the almost impossibly good-looking hero played by stage star John Barrowman. For everyone who was expecting Russell T. Davies to bring a bit of **Queer As Folk** to **Doctor Who**, this is about as close as it gets – apparently, in the future, everyone's bisexual, footloose and fancy free. (If you think about it, this makes about as much sense as everyone being able to copulate with any other humanoid life form, *a la* **Star Trek** and its many spinoffs.) While Jack's relentless flirtation with members of any sex continue for the remainder of the series as a gag, it really only appears as a plot point in *The Doctor Dances*, and really, at least for me, it fades into the background after a while. Speaking of gags and **Star Trek**, apparently **Star Trek exists in the Doctor Who universe**, if you take Rose's plea to the Doctor, "Could you give me just a little bit of Spock, just this once?" as evidence. (Then again, depending on how you interpreted a throwaway gag from 1988's *Remembrance Of The Daleks*, **Doctor Who** also exists in the **Doctor Who** universe. See what you can make of *that*.)

Rose's barrage balloon vantage point of the Blitz is one of the new show's flashiest effects sequences yet, though I felt that the more subtle and more horrific effect of a plague victim's face transforming into a fleshy gas mask was more striking, and certainly more disturbing. Played out only twice on screen, and hinted at by sound effects and reaction shots of other actors elsewhere, this effect is truly disquieting. In terms of hearkening back to the Hinchcliffe era's use of horror in the series, *The Empty Child* wins the prize for this season.

THE DOCTOR DANCES

Cornered by gas-masked mutants all asking "Have you seen my mummy?", the Doctor manages to bluff his way out of danger and, with the help of Rose and the still somewhat suspect Captain Jack, begins to learn the nature of the spreading plague. Jack's stolen Chula ship carried a cargo of highly adaptable sentient nano-genes, capable of performing instant surgery on an injured person to heal their wounds at the genetic level. But the nano-genes' first contact with a human – the dying little boy, mortally wounded in a bomb blast – left them with confused information as to what humans look like and how their bodies work. So now the genetic changes are remaking everyone in the dead boy's image, from the gas masks to his frantic search for his mother…and the changes will spread across the entire Earth as an unstoppable plague, unless the Doctor can somehow provide the nano-genes with more accurate information.

Christopher Eccleston . . . . The Doctor
Billie Piper . . . . Rose Tyler
John Barrowman . . . . Capt. Jack Harkness
Cheryl Fergison . . . . Mrs. Lloyd
Robert Hands . . . . Algy
Florence Hoath . . . . Nancy
Brandon Miller . . . . Alf
Jordan Murphy . . . . Ernie
Dian Perry . . . . Computer voice
Luke Perry . . . . Timothy Lloyd
Damian Samuels . . . . Mr. Lloyd
Zoe Thorne . . . . voice of the Child

This story has been released on DVD

written by Steven Moffat
directed by James Hawes
music by Murray Gold

Aired on May 28, 2005

Joseph Tremain . . . . Jim
Albert Valentine . . . . The Child
Richard Wilson . . . . Dr. Constantine

BEHIND THE SCENES: Along with *The Empty Child*, *The Doctor Dances* won the **Best Dramatic Presentation** (Shortform) Hugo Award in 2006.

The conclusion to the best-written adventure of the first season, *The Doctor Dances* is a refreshing story where there's no villain, and even the growing threat is the manifestation of a horrible misunderstanding. With no moustache-twirling baddie (though admittedly, the little boy continues to be incredibly creepy, making me think of the twins from **The Shining**), the story spends its time on action-filled escapes, humor, and character development, often all at the same time. The sequence where the Doctor and Jack are competitively reeling off the specs of their respective sonic devices is rather funny, the scene with the tape recording of the child is very unnerving (especially when it's pointed out that the tape has run out and yet we're still hearing the child's voice), and Jack's weary acceptance of his fate at the end of the episode says a lot about his character (though it was just a bit obvious that the TARDIS would arrive to rescue him moments later).

After spending so much of the season berating humanity as "stupid apes," the ninth Doctor redeems himself here with his frantic attempt to bring about a happy ending, almost by sheer force of will. Christopher Eccleston plays this scene – with the line "please give me a day like this!" – beautifully, and it's funny, when I think about a scene that sums up the ninth Doctor at his most Doctor-ish, *this* is the scene I keep coming back to.

BOOM TOWN

The Doctor parks the TARDIS in Cardiff, Wales, to recharge the ship via the residual energy remaining from the death of the Gelth. They meet up with Mickey, but the reunion is interrupted when the Doctor learns that Margaret Blaine, the Slitheen in human disguise who survived the attack on 10 Downing Street, is also in Cardiff – as its mayor. Margaret has apparently convinced her constituents to let her build a massive nuclear reactor in the heart of Cardiff. The Doctor,

Rose, Jack and Mickey try to corner Margaret at her office, but Mickey accidentally lets her escape until the Doctor thwarts her attempts to teleport herself to safety. After discovering that the reactor project is simply a cover story for a device that will help Margaret escape the solar system (at the cost of destroying Earth), the Doctor plans to return her to her home planet as soon as the TARDIS is ready to travel again, even if it means that she'll face the death penalty for crimes she committed there.

Christopher Eccleston . . . . The Doctor
Billie Piper . . . . Rose Tyler
John Barrowman . . . . Capt. Jack Harkness
Annette Badland . . . . Margaret
Noel Clarke . . . . Mickey
William Cleaver . . . . Mr. Thomas
Mali Harries . . . . Cathy
Aled Pedrick . . . . Idris Hopper
Alan Ruscoe . . . . Slitheen

This story
has been
released
on DVD

written by Russell T. Davies
directed by Joe Ahearne
music by Murray Gold

Aired on June 4, 2005

Unusually, this story starts out pitching a quiet little time in Cardiff, and that's what it ends up being (major earthquake and cosmic rays erupting from a Police Box notwithstanding). *Boom Town* is chiefly a character drama, with a little bit of a sci-fi event occurring at the end (not to downplay that though – it's referred to later in the season in a big way). At the heart of it is two relationships: Rose and Mickey finally calling it off, and the Doctor having to spend an evening with someone he intends to deliver to an executioner the next day.

Annette Badland gets full marks here, returning as Margaret Blaine with a little more depth and a little less villainous moustache-twirling. Some of the ways we're led to feel sympathy for Margaret do, admittedly, feel just a little bit manipulative on the writer's part, but Badland's performance sells the feelings better than the words alone could manage (and in any case, the "last meal of the condemned" angle vanishes as soon as the action kicks in). The other returning semi-regular is Noel Clarke, who finally gets across some of the frustration that one can only imagine he'd be feeling after watching his girlfriend take off in the TARDIS time and again. On a slightly more practical storytelling level, it clears the decks for Rose to have future romantic involvements (I almost can't believe I'm saying that about a **Doctor Who** character), though that same practical thinking has me wondering why the TARDIS' returns to Earth keep occurring in a straight temporal line, without even addressing the possibility that this visit with Mickey may have occurred after the next time we see him (if, indeed, that makes any sense whatsoever). That said, the teaming up of the Doctor, Rose, Jack and Mickey makes for an interesting dynamic, though I'm not sure if such a crowded TARDIS team would work outside of this story (though three companions aren't unprecedented, as the Hartnell and Davison eras demonstrate).

BAD WOLF

The Doctor awakens to find himself in the Big Brother house, in a future where reality television has become a law unto itself. His "house mates" can provide no clues as to how he has arrived here, or what happened to the TARDIS or his companions. Jack similarly awakens as a contestant in a makeover show whose robotic glamour experts seem to have fatal designs on his body. Rose finds herself in a similar predicament, playing a version of The Weakest Link where those eliminated from play are also summarily executed. The Doctor also learns that those evicted from the Big Brother house are done away with as well, and fights his way out of the house, discovering that it – and all the other games – are played out in enclosed studio environments aboard Satellite 5, a hundred years after his last visit. The Bad Wolf Corporation is behind the games, and the Doctor and Jack team up to save Rose from The Weakest Link's "Anne Droid," only to see the robotic host fire a beam of energy at Rose, leaving no trace. Furious, the Doctor and Jack fight their way to Floor 500, where the Doctor discovers three things. Rose is still alive and in the hands of Bad Wolf Corporation. The Bad Wolf Corporation is a front for the Daleks, who seem to have escaped the destruction of Gallifrey and now once again number in the millions. And the Daleks have Earth, and the Doctor, in their sights.

Christopher Eccleston . . . . The Doctor
Billie Piper . . . . Rose Tyler
John Barrowman . . . . Capt. Jack Harkness
Sebastian Armesto . . . . Broff
Jamie Bradley . . . . Strood
Nicholas Briggs . . . . Dalek voices
Dominic Burgess . . . . Agorax
Sam Callis . . . . Security Guard
Susannah Constantine . . . . voice of Zu-Zana
Martha Cope . . . . Controller
Barnaby Edwards . . . . Dalek
Abi Enjola . . . . Crosbie
David Hankinson . . . . Dalek
Paterson Joseph . . . . Rodrick
Jo Joyner . . . . Lynda
Paul Kasey . . . . Android
Kate Loustau . . . . Colleen

This story has been released on DVD

written by Russell T. Davies
directed by Joe Ahearne
music by Murray Gold

Aired on June 11, 2005

Davina McCall . . . . voice of Davina Droid
Nisha Nayar . . . . Female Programmer
Nicholas Pegg . . . . Dalek
Anne Robinson . . . . voice of Anne Droid
Alan Ruscoe . . . . Android
Jenna Russell . . . . Floor Manager
Jo Stone-Fewings . . . . Male Programmer
Karen Winchester . . . . Fitch
Trinny Woodall . . . . voice of Trin-E

The opening volley of a season-ending cliffhanger, *Bad Wolf* opens up very deceptively, with every indication that it's going to put the not-dying-fast-enough "reality" TV phenomenon in its place, Time Lord-style. But wisely, Russell T. Davies realized that **Doctor Who** has already done this – way back in 1985's *Vengeance On Varos*, long before unscripted television had become the all-pervading virus of the airwaves that it seemed to be in the early 2000s, and took a different course. So while there is some reality TV spoofing going on here – and well-observed parody at that, with Anne Robinson herself providing the voice of her robotic replacement – it's a massive red herring.

The cast continues to impress, with John Barrowman really coming into his own here as the action hero of the piece. (He also gets one of the funniest lines I've heard in a modern TV show from any country recently, involving rising ratings. You'll know it when you hear it.) The events of the story thunder along like a runaway train, and when Rose wakes up to the Dalek control room sound effect that has been in use since 1963, it's both scary and a giddy thrill because there's no lonely Dalek to be reasoned with, but the all-conquering swarms of Daleks that have been scaring kids behind furniture since the sixties. The promise of a showdown between Daleks and Doctor brought me a childlike chill.

Bad Wolf isn't a *great* episode of **Doctor Who**, old or new. It's not deep. It doesn't have an airtight, tragic Shakespearean plot. But it is the sum of a great many entertaining parts, which add up to a fun episode.

THE PARTING OF THE WAYS

With the help of the terrified (and mostly unarmed) broadcasters and civilians of Satellite 5, the Doctor and Jack mount what appears to be a frontal attack on the Dalek command saucer via the TARDIS, but then the Doctor feigns the TARDIS' destruction from a Dalek missile attack and materializes in the heart of the Daleks' command center, saving Rose. With the TARDIS projecting a shield around him, the Doctor emerges and finds that the Daleks have recovered their Emperor – an enormous mastermind Dalek the Doctor thought he had destroyed in the final battle of the Time War. The damaged Emperor escaped the carnage, however, and rebuilt the Dalek race – using dead humans as a replacement for now-extinct Kaled mutants. The Emperor has also risen to prophetic heights of megalomania, declaring itself the god of the Daleks and vowing to attack Earth and turn its population into billions more Daleks. The Doctor vows to stop the Emperor at any cost, though he discovers that the cost is horrific: his own defense could destroy humanity as thoroughly as the Daleks will.

Christopher Eccleston . . . . The Doctor
Billie Piper . . . . Rose Tyler
John Barrowman . . . . Capt. Jack Harkness
Nicholas Briggs . . . . Dalek voices
Noel Clarke . . . . Mickey
Camille Coduri . . . . Jackie
Barnaby Edwards . . . . Dalek
David Hankinson . . . . Dalek
Paterson Joseph . . . . Rodrick
Jo Joyner . . . . Lynda
Nisha Nayar . . . . Female Programmer
Nicholas Pegg . . . . Dalek

This story has been released on DVD

written by Russell T. Davies
directed by Joe Ahearne
music by Murray Gold

Aired on June 18, 2005

Anne Robinson . . . . voice of Anne Droid
Alan Ruscoe . . . . Android
David Tennant . . . . The Doctor

CLASSIC CONNECTIONS: The visuals accompanying the "heart of the TARDIS" escaping the console aren't too different from the "fairy dust" effect that brought Chang Lee and Grace back to life in the 1996 TV movie starring Paul McGann. The TARDIS is indeed a sentimental old thing. The sound effects heard during the final moments of the Doctor's regeneration are very much like the crescendo of sound heard as the fifth Doctor regenerated into the sixth in part 4 of *The Caves Of Androzani* (1984).

The Parting Of The Ways has a lot to accomplish. It has to wrap up a mammoth cliffhanger and deal with the Daleks' impending assault on Earth. It has to usher in a new Doctor. And, at long last, it has to explain the meaning of the constant sightings of "Bad Wolf" throughout the show's 13 episodes. No sweat, right? With all that to get done in 45 minutes, it's almost inevitable that at least one of those balls will be dropped.

The Dalek element doesn't disappoint. With millions of CG Daleks streaming through space, or swarming into rooms like a flood of water, *Parting Of The Ways* gives us the Daleks of old: their strength is in their overwhelming numbers and near-invincibility. When the Dalek Emperor starts going off about being the god of the Daleks, and a swarm of Daleks (voiced by Big Finish's own resident Dalek, Nicholas Briggs) shrieks "Wor-ship-him!" in unison, things get extremely strange – this isn't a way we've ever seen the Daleks portrayed before, a charge that could also be leveled at *Dalek* earlier in the season.

The biggest mess *Parting Of The Ways* gets us into is with the Bad Wolf/heart of the TARDIS angle. Having the characters openly make a big deal about Bad Wolf since *Boom Town*, Russell T. Davies is forced to pay it all off here – and the payoff isn't that satisfying. The season would've been just fine without the Bad Wolf element; the stories would have been the same, and we wouldn't have had this big buildup to something which turns out to be much ado about nothing. Most of Russell T. Davies' **Doctor Who** scripts hit the spot, but lack the build-to-a-big-finale finesse of, say, **Babylon 5**.

The regeneration is a classic moment of **Doctor Who** history. It's a very different regeneration from what we've seen before, though also very much in line with the final moments of the fifth and sixth Doctors. (Note that, in both of those cases as well as here, regenerations that take place in the TARDIS seem to be noisier-verging-on-explosive – keep that in mind during the Doctor's *next* generation – which becomes a blinding visual metaphor here. It seems like the regenerations that occur away from the TARDIS – Pertwee-into-Baker, Baker-into-Davison and McCoy-into-McGann – are quieter events where the Doctor's new features simply morph into place.) Down to his last moments, Eccleston's Doctor is engaging, intriguing and off-the-wall, and as much as I like the choice of David Tennant as his successor, I can only walk away from this episode feeling that Eccleston's time in the TARDIS hot seat was far, far too short – like Colin Baker, we didn't get to see whatever long-term plan might have been in place for this Doctor play out. Russell Davies may have done the impossible and gotten **Doctor Who** back on the air, but Eccleston and Billie Piper should be credited with compelling the public (and therefore the BBC) to keep it there with their performances.

The Parting Of The Ways is ultimately a very, very mixed bag – and perhaps a case of a five-pound bag trying to contain twenty pounds of story that very rightly could've been a three-parter – but its confused whole contains several very enjoyable parts. The first season of **Doctor Who**'s unexpectedly successful return to TV, overall, was a lot of fun – maybe not quite on a par with the stellar first seasons enjoyed by Jon Pertwee and Tom Baker's Doctors, but memorable and fun all the same. It almost reads, in hindsight, like a fan's wish list for a perfect season: a story arc connecting everything, the return of the Daleks, a hint of the Cybermen, big new developments for the Time Lords, and a regeneration to top it all off.

The Tenth Doctor
(David Tennant: 2005-2010)

It was an inevitable development for a show as long-lived as **Doctor Who**. Sooner or later, the actor playing the part of the Doctor would be someone who had been a lifelong fan of the show.

To be sure, Peter Davison had already broken that barrier somewhat; he was an avid fan of the show's Patrick Troughton years, and even before *The Five Doctors* was in the planning stages, Davison got to meet Troughton himself. The second Doctor gave his successor a single piece of advice: don't stay longer than three years. Though Davison heeded that advice where television was concerned, he probably still chuckles about that now and again on the way to the latest Big Finish recording session.

Tennant was a known quantity for Big Finish Productions as well. As early as 2001, he had jumped at the chance to appear in their **Doctor Who** audio plays, appearing with Sylvester McCoy in *Colditz* and then with Colin Baker in 2002's *Medicinal Purposes*. Tennant made two appearances as Colonel Brimmicombe-Wood of UNIT, a successor and rival to Brigadier Lethbridge-Stewart, and starred in the third series of Dalek Empire audio plays as Dalek-battling rebel Galanar. Big Finish also made him the star of their audio adaptation of Bryan Talbot's Luther Arkwright comics.

It was immediately before the recording session for his second and final guest shot as the turncoat UNIT colonel that Tennant received a personal invitation from Russell T. Davies to watch some of the first finished episodes of the new **Doctor Who**. He had already narrated a half-hour promotional preview special, and in a 2009 radio interview, Tennant said that he expected to be asked to guest star on the show, a gig he was more than interested in.

Instead, he was asked if he wanted to be the next Doctor.

To an actor who'd spent his childhood watching Tom Baker on television, and even standing in line to get an autograph from the man himself, could there have been a better job?

Within weeks of the abrupt announcement of Christopher Eccleston's departure from **Doctor Who**, the BBC went public with the news: Tennant would be the new Doctor, with Billie Piper staying on as Rose.

Tennant had already starred in the recent Russell T. Davies-produced *Casanova* miniseries for BBC2, unwittingly turning in his audition piece in the process. With the first season of new **Who** still in progress, there was ample time to figure out such details as characterization and costume. Tennant's first official duty was to put on Eccleston's leather jacket to film the regeneration scene that would top off the season finale, giving the audience their first glimpse of the tenth Doctor.

Tennant's first season was a runaway success, with **Doctor Who** enjoying the full promotional support of the BBC (a far cry from the late '80s, where it almost seemed that the network was apologizing for the series still being on the schedule) and the adulation of a favorable viewing public. ITV was dealing with a new problem on Saturday nights: while anything they scheduled opposite **Doctor Who** would certainly get the attention of that portion of the audience that wasn't in the mood for science fiction, at the end of the day, the ratings numbers would still show that ITV was being pounded. ITV had even cooked up an attempt at its own science fiction series, the short-lived **Eleventh Hour**. Created by SF novelist Stephen Gallagher (who had written the '80s **Doctor Who** episodes *Warriors' Gate* and *Terminus*) and starring former **Star Trek: The Next Generation** star Patrick Stewart, **Eleventh Hour** couldn't match the popularity of **Doctor Who**, and its creator abandoned the show only two episodes into its four-episode run over conflicts about his stories and concepts being "dumbed down."

Doctor Who had no such problem; it's safe to say that Russell T. Davies and his writers had a wide open canvas upon which to tell any story they wished. More elements from the show's past were brought back, to both critical and popular acclaim; the return of the Cybermen was mooted before the season even began, but it was the return of Sarah Jane Smith and the fourth Doctor's robot dog K-9 that captured the viewers' interest the most. It was also a useful barometer of how far into the past Davies could dip for inspiration: while Elisabeth Sladen was nervous about returning to the role on television (despite recently reprising Sarah for a series of audio adventures), the public needed no introduction. K-9's return met with a rapturous reception as well. The news that the public was less pleased with, however, was the inevitable departure of Billie Piper. She had decided to leave before the season began, giving Davies the opportunity to weave clues about her apparently tragic exit through the entire season.

That exit took place in a two-part finale that, for the first time on TV, pitted the Doctor's most notorious enemies against each other: after years of being the stuff of fan fiction and comics, the Daleks and Cybermen were about to collide head-on. The first part of this story featured actress Freema Agyeman, who quickly made an impression on the producers and went on to win the role of Martha Jones, the tenth Doctor's new companion. Concerned that viewers might not take kindly to the departure of Rose, the BBC launched an extensive promo campaign to introduce the character of Martha even before she appeared in the series proper. (The character Agyeman played in *Army Of Ghosts* was later said to be Martha's cousin.)

It was also in the gap between the second and third seasons of the new **Doctor Who** that spinoffs began to appear in a way that had never happened during the original show's run. **Torchwood**, greenlit after the first season of **Doctor Who**, would detail the adventures of a group of humans, operating from a secret base in Cardiff, gathering alien artifacts and fighting off alien invasions. The concept had started life before the **Doctor Who** revival, and with no **Doctor Who** connections, as a previously-shelved series concept Davies then called **Excalibur**. Perhaps even more surprising, though, was the announcement - following the huge success of *School Reunion* - that Sarah Jane Smith would be back, not on **Doctor Who** but in her own series. A spinoff centering around Elisabeth Sladen's character had first been attempted in 1981, under the title **K-9 & Company**, but had failed to produce anything more than a pilot episode. Astoundingly, it looked as though the spinoff would be getting a pickup order - a quarter century late.

After seeding cryptic clues throughout the third season, Davies brought back the classic series character of the Master in what was essentially a three-part story. At first portrayed by Sir Derek Jacobi, the Master regenerated into John Simm, the star of the BBC's successful time-tripping police series **Life On Mars**, and just as quickly seemed to be killed off at the conclusion of the season-ending trilogy. Martha also left the TARDIS, though the BBC reassured fans that the character would be back in the following season.

In the interim, the series stayed in the headlines with its latest charity sketch, a mini-episode called *Time Crash* which brought back, for the first time in new **Doctor Who**, one of the classic series Doctors. Peter Davison once again donned the fifth Doctor's cricketing gear for a brief encounter with the tenth Doctor.

The fourth season commenced with Catherine Tate reprising the role of Donna Noble from the 2006 Christmas special *The Runaway Bride*, and the promise that 2008's returning classic series monsters would be the Sontarans (not seen in **Doctor Who** since *The Two Doctors* in 1985), but major developments were afoot. It was announced that 2009 would be a year with almost no **Who**: Tennant was tied up with a long-running engagement with the Royal Shakespeare Company's production of <u>Hamlet</u>, and there simply wasn't a schedule that would allow him to fulfill his season with the RSC and make a new season of **Doctor Who.** There would be several "specials" made and shown throughout the year, but the Doctor would otherwise be taking the year off. The 2008 season concluded with the departure of Donna and the brief return of Dalek creator Davros. Rose also made a comeback (with several brief glimpses and cameos throughout the season hinting at her return), only to be returned to the alternate universe in which she'd been deposited in *Doomsday*.

Prior to the broadcast of the 2008 Christmas special, David Tennant made a public announcement that he would be leaving **Doctor Who** at the end of the "lean year" specials in 2009, and Russell T. Davies announced that he too would be leaving the series, as he was eager to explore storytelling possibilities beyond the **Doctor Who** universe (though he would remain in charge of both spinoffs, **Torchwood** and **The Sarah Jane Adventures**, until they ended). Multiple Hugo Award-winning writer Steven Moffat, who had penned some of the most popular and critically-acclaimed episodes since the series' revival, was quickly installed as Davies' successor, with his first order of business being the casting of the eleventh Doctor.

David Tennant's final appearance as the star of **Doctor Who** took the form of an epic two-part battle against not just the Master, but the rest of the Time Lords, determined to escape their inevitable destruction in the Time War. But the actor's final contemporary appearance in the role took place on **The Sarah Jane Adventures** for a crossover adventure that would air prior to his **Doctor Who** swan song. He didn't have a new gig lined up for 2010, but he'd spent the past five years going from being a relatively unknown actor to one of the most well-known faces on British television. His starring role in a pilot for NBC in America (though ultimately rejected) seemed to be a strong indicator that, now that his schedule was open, the work would find him. (He wasn't too busy, however, to return for the 50th anniversary special in 2013.)

SERIES 2: 2005-2006
THE NEW DOCTOR
(2005 CHILDREN IN NEED SPECIAL SCENE)

Forced to regenerate by absorbing the power of the time vortex before it kills Rose, the Doctor isn't feeling so well. Rose is shocked by what's happened, accusing the new Doctor of being a Gelth, a Slitheen, or some other manner of impostor. Even after he recalls a moment that only he and Rose were there to witness, the Doctor can't convince her that he's the same person in a new body, and guesses that she wants to go home. But even after he sets the TARDIS on a course back to Earth to return Rose on Christmas Eve, the Doctor coughs up more of the time vortex energy – his ordeal isn't over, and he says something is going wrong with his regeneration. When the chiming of the TARDIS' cloister bell begins to fill the console room, it's yet another signal that something has gone horribly wrong...

David Tennant . . . . The Doctor
Billie Piper . . . . Rose Tyler

written by Russell T. Davies
directed by Euros Lyn
music by Murray Gold

Aired on November 18, 2005

This mini-story has been released on DVD

BEHIND THE SCENES: This untitled special was originally transmitted as part of the annual Children In Need appeal. This was also the first **Doctor Who** television production since 1964's *Edge Of Destruction* to feature no one other than the show's current regular cast, and to take place entirely inside the TARDIS.

It's almost unfair to critique a three-minute sketch assembled to benefit the Children In Need charity, but there is a lot of material packed into this short space of time. Despite all the crises that the TARDIS saw during the ninth Doctor's brief reign, even that bit of business in Cardiff, it's interesting to note that the cloister bell never once sounded until now (this rather arcane "red alert" sounded by the TARDIS in times of extreme danger first appeared in *Logopolis* and was last heard in the 1996 TV movie). The Doctor's immediate post-regeneration behavior fits with what's been seen before, and whether deliberately or not, seems to most strongly echo Tom Baker's zany performance in *Robot*, what with the hopping gag and the Doctor's bizarre comments about his own new face.

THE CHRISTMAS INVASION

Jackie Tyler and Mickey Smith are going about their normal everyday lives, each quietly hoping on Christmas Eve that the TARDIS will bring Rose home, despite the chaos that usually follows. But when it finally does appear, tumbling out of the sky, Jackie and Mickey are stunned to see a man they've never seen before emerge from the TARDIS and wish them a merry Christmas before collapsing. Rose steps out and tells them that the stranger is the Doctor.

Powerless to do anything but wait for the Doctor to regain consciousness, Rose joins Mickey for a bit of Christmas shopping, getting on his nerves with her constant talk of life in the TARDIS. When a group of horn-playing figures in Santa Claus masks stop playing and begin following her, Rose is immediately suspicious; when the Santas reveal their instruments to be powerful weapons and open fire, Rose quickly deduces that she and Mickey are the targets. Awakened by Jackie, the Doctor saves the Tyler family from the attack, but cryptically warns that something is coming before passing out again.

Again helpless until the Doctor awakens, Rose, Jackie and Mickey watch a live broadcast, waiting for the British-launched Guinevere One probe's first pictures from Mars. Its first picture, however, certainly isn't of the red planet – a hideous, skull-like face appears, bellowing in an indecipherable language. At UNIT HQ, Prime Minister Harriet Jones – voted in by a landslide following the attempted Slitheen invasion – swings into action, feeding a cover story to the media to buy time. But UNIT's people are very worried – a gigantic spacecraft has been detected leaving Mars orbit on a beeline toward Earth. The next contact from the Sycorax leaves no doubt as to their intentions: the human race will submit to slavery, or be destroyed. But the Doctor is in no condition to defend the Earth this time, leaving a terrified Rose to step up, speak for all of humanity.

David Tennant . . . . The Doctor
Billie Piper . . . . Rose Tyler
Paul Anderson . . . . Jason
Sagar Arya . . . . Newsreader #2
Anita Briem . . . . Sally
Lachele Carl . . . . Newsreader #3
Sean Carlsen . . . . Policeman
Noel Clarke . . . . Mickey Smith
Camille Coduri . . . . Jackie Tyler
Daniel Evans . . . . Danny Llewellyn
Adam Garcia . . . . Alex
Sean Gilder . . . . Sycorax Leader
Sian McDowall . . . . Sandra

UNIT

This story
has been
released
on DVD

written by Russell T. Davies
directed by James Hawes
music by Murray Gold

Aired on December 25, 2005

Jason Mohammed . . . . Newsreader #1
Cathy Murphy . . . . Mum
Chu Omambala . . . . Major Blake
Penelope Wilton . . . . Harriet Jones

CLASSIC CONNECTIONS: The UNIT logo is the same one seen in the final UNIT adventure of the original series, 1989's *Battlefield*. Its predominantly young staff, however, doesn't seem to have seen action, much less seen the Doctor (though the Major points out that Martians look different from the Sycorax; presumably he has a least a little experience with either the Ice Warriors or the Ambassadors of Death). The TARDIS wardrobe would appear to have grown since it was last seen in 1987's *Time And The Rani*, when the seventh Doctor was looking for his new threads. It also seems to be a requirement that every newly-regenerated Doctor try on The Scarf at least once (see also: *Castrovalva*, *Time And The Rani*, 1996 TV movie). This also marks the first and *only* time we see any part of this version of the TARDIS other than the control room. The Doctor mentions Arthur Dent — the perpetually bewildered hero of the late Douglas Adams' Hitchhiker's Guide To The Galaxy novels — and says Arthur "was a nice man," dangling the tantalizing notion of Hitchhiker's Guide and **Doctor Who** co-existing in the same universe just to make the heads of both fandoms explode.

TORCHWOOD CONNECTIONS: The covert Torchwood group is mentioned openly here for the first time; at the time of broadcast, the first **Doctor Who** spinoff to receive a full series order was nearly a year away from premiering. This episode establishes that the Prime Minister can order them into action (despite the fact that Torchwood is so classified that she isn't even supposed to know about them), but UNIT can't.

So, all *The Christmas Invasion* has to do is reintroduce the concept of regeneration for a new audience, check up with Jackie and Mickey, tell a ripping adventure tale of its own, and finally bring us the tenth Doctor in full command of his faculties so we can see how he compares to the ninth incarnation. In one hour. No pressure.

Ironically, for the expanded length of the full-hour episode, we get to see more of Rose falling apart because the Doctor may or may not be dying. (For his part, David Tennant's portrayal of an unconscious man is exceptional.) For a holiday special, *The Christmas Invasion* is surprisingly heavy, and in places, heavy-handed. We get another potshot at current events (Harriet asks an underling to convey a message to the unnamed President of the United States that he's "not my boss" and "isn't going to turn this into a war"), and a lot of scenes of Rose sobbing. Far more fun are the all-too-brief scenes of a band of robotic-looking Santas converting their instruments into weapons, and the ultimate appearance of the Doctor himself. David Tennant wastes no time in making the part his own, and even though there are some elements carried over from Christopher Eccleston's era — the Doctor's patented tendency toward stream-of-consciousness rambling, the occasional flash of ruthlessness toward his enemies — the role very quickly becomes Tennant's.

Until Tennant makes his grand entrance as the fully-recovered Doctor, the episode really belongs to Noel Clarke as Mickey and Camille Coduri as Jackie. In both the scripts and the performances, a nice balance has been found between both characters' comedic elements as well as the layers of drama that were added to them in *Aliens Of London* and *World War Three*. They seem like fully-rounded characters at last, responding at least somewhat realistically to the events surrounding them.

UWÔRP!

NEW EARTH

The Doctor and Rose leave present-day Earth behind for adventures on a new Earth – namely, a planet called New Earth that the human race colonized following the destruction of humanity's homeworld. A mysterious message has brought the Doctor to ward 26 of a hospital operated by the catlike Sisters of Plentitude, but along the way he is separated from Rose. She is diverted to an underground hideaway, where she is subjected to a psychograft by none other than Cassandra, who she thought had died on Platform One. Cassandra is indeed still alive, but wants to resume life in a human body, even if Rose's is the best she can manage. The Doctor becomes suspicious about the hospital's seeming ability to conquer any disease, and with the strangely-behaving Rose back at his side, he discovers that the Sisters of Plentitude have bred a new kind of lab rat to help them cultivate and devise cures to these diseases. But the Doctor knows these unfortunate, caged creatures by another name: homo sapiens.

David Tennant . . . . The Doctor
Billie Piper . . . . Rose Tyler
Adjoa Andoh . . . . Sister Jatt
Noel Clarke . . . . Mickey Smith
Camille Coduri . . . . Jackie Tyler
Dona Croll . . . . Matron Casp
Michael Fitzgerald . . . . Duke of Manhattan
Sean Gallagher . . . . Chip
Anna Hope . . . . Novice Hame
Simon Ludders . . . . Patient
Lucy Robinson . . . . Frau Clovis

This story has been released on DVD

written by Russell T. Davies
directed by James Hawes
music by Murray Gold

Aired on April 15, 2006

Struan Rodger . . . . Face of Boe
Zoe Wanamaker . . . . Cassandra

CLASSIC CONNECTIONS: Adjoa Andoh would return in the next two seasons, minus the cat makeup, as Martha's mother.

New Earth is a fun little romp, but there is no way, no way at all, that if I happened to be sitting in an executive producer's chair, I would ever have chosen it to kick off a season of **Doctor Who**, especially not right after a regeneration. My complaint with this story is much that same as the one I leveled at whoever thought *The Naked Now* should be the second episode of **Star Trek: The Next Generation** – it fundamentally screws around with the basic nature of one of our two regular characters, throwing the audience off-balance as to who they really are. I'm not accusing the audience of being so thick that they need their hands held here, but c'mon, we'd just completely changed the Doctor. *New Earth* would've made more sense in the middle of the season.

I'm a little torn on the value of bringing back Cassandra, but I can let that go for the very odd time loop that it suggests: by taking Cassandra, stuck in Chip's dying body, back to meet herself in human form (Zoe Wanamaker in the flesh this time), the Doctor may very well have set in motion the hyper-vanity that led Cassandra to abandon her human form. This is barely even touched on in the epiosde, and yet it's such an interesting notion that it's hard to let it go. Another holdover from *The End Of The World* shows up, and this time it's the Face of Boe, and this time he's talking. "Textbook cryptic" is about right – he's suddenly turned into the Ambassador Kosh of **Doctor Who**.

TOOTH AND CLAW

In 1879, a band of warrior monks takes Torchwood House and its staff by force – a place which just happens to be Queen Victoria's next stop on a trip through Scotland. The monks bring a cage with them, containing an unearthly terror which they also hope to introduce to Her Majesty. The Queen's entourage happens upon the Doctor and Rose, who have only just arrived, expecting it to be 1979. Her Majesty brings the travelers with her to Torchwood House, where a trap has been waiting over two centuries to spring. On schedule, when moonlight falls upon the monks' cage, its passenger – a werewolf – breaks loose. Now the Doctor finds himself having to protect not only Rose, but Queen Victoria and perhaps the entire human race.

David Tennant . . . . The Doctor
Billie Piper . . . . Rose Tyler
Pauline Collins . . . . Queen Victoria
Ron Donachie . . . . Steward
Michelle Duncan . . . . Lasy Isobel
Ian Hanmore . . . . Father Angelo
Ruthie Milne . . . . Flora
Derek Riddell . . . . Sir Robert
Jamie Sives . . . . Captain Reynolds

This story
has been
released
on DVD

written by Russell T. Davies
directed by Euros Lyn
music by Murray Gold

Aired on April 22, 2006

Tom Smith . . . . The Host

Every episode of **Doctor Who** now starts with a pre-credits teaser, but this is one of the most gripping teasers the new series had given us up to this point, even if martial arts wire work isn't anything we haven't seen before plenty of times. The whole episode is well directed – with the werewolf being a CGI construct, Euros Lyn had to be choosy where such an expensive and time-consuming creation would be glimpsed, and he wisely takes a less-is-more approach, making the creature's actual physical appearances rather sparse, but its effects are vividly portrayed.

Of course, that's only good for an effects artist's demo reel unless the actors hold the rest of the story together, and *Tooth And Claw* comes up aces there too. Pauline Collins, who appeared in the swingin' sixties four-parter *The Faceless Ones*, does an outstanding job with Queen Victoria, fitting the profile almost perfectly and never losing sight of the dignity and absolute conviction required to have a fictional Queen Victoria come off as anything but a parody. If anything, when she dresses down the Doctor and Rose at the episode's end, it's very difficult not to sympathize with the Queen where these two interlopers are concerned. (There seemed to be a theme running through this season in terms of dealing with the consequences of the Doctor's presence in one's life – Cassandra in *New Earth*, Sarah Jane Smith in *School Reunion*, and other characters down the road as well.)

SCHOOL REUNION

After Mickey alerts them to strange goings-on near Deffry Vale High School, the Doctor and Rose each take a job there, the Doctor posing as a new physics teacher and Rose winding up as a dinner lady in the school's cafeteria. The new headmaster, Mr. Finch, has brought a new curriculum, a new lunch menu, and several new staff members with him. But original faculty members and even students are vanishing without a trace. Rose spots large barrels of a strange and apparently dangerously corrosive oil being moved around by the cafeteria staff, and the Doctor discovers that students who have been eating foods from Mr. Finch's new lunch menu, prepared with that oil, are demonstrating knowledge and learning ability far beyond 21st century humans. The Doctor is stunned when he learns that someone else is investigating these unexplained happenings – namely, reporter Sarah Jane Smith, his former traveling companion, with her now somewhat dilapidated K-9 in tow. While the Doctor and Sarah are cautiously eager to renew their friendship, it becomes apparent – especially to Rose – that traveling in the TARDIS and seeing the wonders of the universe carries a price.

David Tennant . . . . The Doctor
Billie Piper . . . . Rose Tyler
Rod Arthur . . . . Mr. Parsons
Caroline Berry . . . . Dinner Lady
Heather Cameron . . . . Nina
Noel Clarke . . . . Mickey Smith
Lucinda Dryzek . . . . Melissa
Anthony Head . . . . Mr. Finch
John Leeson . . . . voice of K-9
Joe Pickley . . . . Kenny
Elisabeth Sladen . . . . Sarah Jane Smith

This story has been released on DVD

written by Toby Whithouse
directed by James Hawes
music by Murray Gold

Aired on April 29, 2006

Benjamin Smith . . . . Luke
Clem Tibber . . . . Milo
Eugene Washington . . . . Mr. Wagner

AUDIO CONNECTIONS: Sarah Jane Smith has also appeared in two series of Doctor-less audio adventures from Big Finish, though in this case without K-9 (in the final story of the first "season" of her audio adventures, Sarah notes that K-9 has been incapacitated, though the nature of K-9's state of disrepair in the audio plays is a case of deliberate sabotage; it's unclear if this is the same damage that the Doctor seems to fix rather quickly). *School Reunion* likely takes place between the first two "seasons" of Sarah's audio adventures.

A.K.A.: Guest star Anthony Head – a.k.a. **Anthony Stewart Head** – starred as Giles in **Buffy The Vampire Slayer**. He's been linked several times to **Doctor Who**, including a contender for the role of the Doctor himself when the new series was first announced in 2003. He appeared as a cunning, immortal villain in the linked *Excelis* trilogy of Big Finish audio plays in 2001, though he did so without ever meeting any of his co-stars, since recording schedules forced him to record his dialogue alone without any other actors! He has thus "appeared" with previous Doctors Peter Davison, Colin Baker and Sylvester McCoy without actually working with them. He also had a small role in BBC Radio one-off **Doctor Who** story *Death Comes To Time*.

I was even more eager to see this episode than I was to see the much-publicized return of the Cybermen. Elisabeth Sladen was in the first episode of **Doctor Who** that I ever watched back when my age was but a single digit, and I distinctly remember being more alarmed by her departure than I was a few years later when Tom Baker turned into Peter Davison before my eyes. And here she returns in a story that's perfectly suited to her, ties the new and classic series together beautifully (and even makes room for the 1981 one-off attempt at launching a full-fledged **Doctor Who** spinoff series, **K-9 & Company**).

Elisabeth Sladen slips effortlessly back into her character here, obviously having moved on with her life but just as obviously missing her time traveling days; her reaction to finding the TARDIS is nothing short of spine-tingling, and such exchanges as "I can't believe it's really you. Okay, now I can!" are instant classics. John Leeson effortlessly re-creates K-9 here, though I should also note that both of these actors have been reviving their characters in their respective series of Big Finish audio dramas, so it's no surprise that they can deliver the goods.

And I'd be remiss if I didn't hand out kudos to Anthony Stewart Head as well, for guest starring as one of the new show's slickest villains. At times it almost seems like he's stuck with a part that was written for Malcolm McDowell, but Head pulls out all the stops and gives us a truly creepy villain. There is, in fact, something very comfortably and cozily Sylvester McCoy-era about *School Reunion* – the Doctor and Rose are already on the scene, undercover; in a barely civil face-to-face showdown, the Doctor calmly tells the story's villain that they're going down; and the Doctor later has to resort to somewhat extreme measures, sacrificing a companion to save the day. One could be forgiven for thinking that perhaps *School Reunion* came from the pen of one of the New Adventures authors.

Again, the season-long theme of learning the consequences of being in the Doctor's company appears; there's a scene between the Doctor and Rose which practically telegraphs this to the viewer, even if it does fall somewhat short of explaining why the Doctor does eventually part ways with all of his sidekicks. Speaking of companions, Mickey formally signs on for TARDIS duty here (I had actually hoped for this scene at the end of *World War Three* myself), having realized that in being "the tin dog," he's missing out on the real adventure. He once again proves that he's got the resourcefulness necessary for TARDIS travels here, even if he doesn't necessarily have the stomach for all that the companion's life entails. (Oh, Mickey…it gets *so much worse* than vacuum-packed rats.) This is the first real change to the TARDIS crew since Captain Jack was unceremoniously left behind in *Parting Of The Ways*, and it's a welcome one – sadly, it was short-lived and Mickey was sorely underused.

THE GIRL IN THE FIREPLACE

The Doctor, Rose and Mickey explore a strange, unoccupied starship, sitting at a dead standstill in deep space – with its engines operating at full power to punch several holes through the fabric of time. Several chambers within the ship open into pockets of Earth's past, specifically the history of France. The Doctor quickly discovers that the ship's occupants, elegant but deadly clockwork robots, are interfering with the history of a young girl who, in exhibits chronicling her young adulthood, becomes known as Madame de Pompadour. The Doctor repeatedly interferes with the robots' attempts to alter history, and unwittingly goes from being Madame du Pompadour's imaginary friend to her savior at several points in his history. But to save her from the robots' last attack, the Doctor may have to maroon himself thousands of years in Earth's past, leaving Mickey and Rose stranded in the future.

David Tennant	. . . .	The Doctor
Billie Piper	. . . .	Rose Tyler
Noel Clarke	. . . .	Mickey Smith
Jessica Atkins	. . . .	young Reinette
Angel Coulby	. . . .	Katherine
Gareth Wyn Griffiths	. . . .	Manservant
Jonathan Hart	. . . .	Alien Voice
Emily Joyce	. . . .	Alien Voice
Paul Kasey	. . . .	Clockwork Man
Sophia Myles	. . . .	Reinette
Ellen Thomas	. . . .	Clockwork Woman

This story has been released on DVD

written by Steven Moffat
directed by Euros Lyn
music by Murray Gold

Aired on May 6, 2006

Ben Turner . . . . King Louis

BEHIND THE SCENES: *The Girl In The Fireplace* won the **Best Dramatic Presentation (Shortform) Hugo Award** in 2007.

This episode is another atypical adventure for the Doctor, a bit of a romantic adventure with a time traveling twist. This is a good example of a story that would've worked well with some Doctors – I could see Paul McGann or perhaps even Peter Davison in this story – but certainly not with others (I can't envision Jon Pertwee or either of the fabulous Baker boys here), but it definitely works with David Tennant. Stealing the show for much of the story is Sophia Myles, who can switch gears from stately steel to an impish smile.

The addition of Mickey to the TARDIS team is almost glossed over here, as is Rose's awkward reaction to his sudden request to travel with the Doctor at the end of *School Reunion*. Both of them get some good moments, but the story clearly isn't theirs. It's all capped off with an ending that's almost ripped straight from the pages of the best New Adventures novel of them all, Human Nature – ironic since that book was adapted the following season (though minus the ending in question).

It may not be the most original **Doctor Who** stew ever cooked up, but it's at least entertaining. Steven Moffat reused the star-crossed-lovers-moving-through-time-at-different-speeds gag again and again during his tenure as showrunner, subjecting Amy and Rory to variations of this basic plotline more than once.

THE RISE OF THE CYBERMEN

The TARDIS plunges out of the time vortex and into a parallel universe, and the Doctor fears the last TARDIS in the universe has made her final flight. Trapped on a parallel version of Earth, the Doctor, Rose and Mickey quickly find out what's the same (they're in London) and what's different (Pete Tyler, Rose's dad, is still alive, well, and hawking energy drinks from interactive signs on every street corner). Zeppelins fill the sky, carrying the rich and powerful – one of whom, inventor John Lumic, is stricken with a terminal disease. Lumic invites the President of Great Britain to hear a pitch for the newest innovation from his corporation, Cybus Industries. Cybus has already made Lumic unimaginably rich with the sales of its ubiquitous "EarPods," devices which download news, sports, and even phone calls directly into their wearers' brains. Now Lumic wants to offer "the ultimate upgrade" to the British public – constant connectivity, and virtually indestructible exoskeletal armor, which will virtually transform humanity into a new species – one which Lumic calls Cybermen. The President forbids any further experimentation along these lines, but Lumic has already begun creating an army of Cybermen in secret. The President goes to the lavish Tyler home that night for Jackie Tyler's birthday party, but thanks to his ability to retrieve information from EarPod wearers, Lumic knows where he'll be. The Doctor loses control of both of his companions – Mickey goes to see if his grandmother, dead in his reality, is still alive in this world, while Rose insists on finding her family. Curious about the effect that the EarPods are having on humanity, the Doctor tags along with Rose to the Tyler home, but this just means they're present when Lumic's army of Cybermen attack, killing the President and anyone else who won't submit to Lumic's "voluntary upgrade."

David Tennant . . . . The Doctor
Billie Piper . . . . Rose Tyler
Noel Clarke . . . . Mickey Smith / Ricky
Paul Antony-Barber . . . . Dr. Kendrick
Nicholas Briggs . . . . Cyber voices
Camille Coduri . . . . Jackie Tyler
Shaun Dingwall . . . . Pete Tyler
Duncan Duff . . . . Newsreader
Helen Griffin . . . . Mrs. Moore
Mona Hammond . . . . Rita-Anne
Andrew Hayden-Smith . . . . Jake Simmonds
Paul Kasey . . . . Cyberleader

This story has been released on DVD

written by Tom MacRae
directed by Graeme Harper
music by Murray Gold

Aired on May 13, 2006

Roger Lloyd-Pack . . . . John Lumic
Adam Shaw . . . . Morris
Colin Spaull . . . . Mr. Crane
Andrew Ufondo . . . . Soldier
Don Warrington . . . . The President

CLASSIC CONNECTIONS: Cybus Industries' "front" company, **International Electromatics**, is a fixture in "our" universe as well; it appeared in the 8-part Cybermen story *The Invasion* in 1969, in which the unscrupulous Tobias Vaughn used it to cover the Cybermen's invasion of Earth, starting with London; fortunately, the Doctor (then in his second incarnation) and the newly-formed UNIT were on hand to thwart his plans.

BEHIND THE SCENES: Graeme Harper, the director of this story, is one of the few behind-the-camera creative personnel who was involved with both the new **Doctor Who** series and the original series; he also directed 1984's *Caves Of Androzani* and 1985's *Revelation Of The Daleks*, and was slated to direct the abandoned 1993 straight-to-video special *The Dark Dimension* before the plug was pulled on that production.

Easily the most eagerly awaited episode of the new series' second year, *Rise Of The Cybermen* filled in another check-box in many a classic series fan's laundry list of elements to bring into the new show. Surprisingly, the Cybermen's new look is somewhat retro, owing more to their appearance in *The Invasion* than to their last appearance in the 80s (or any post-original-series visualizations that updated them into even sleeker, often more Borg-by-way-of-H.R.-Giger-like forms, for that matter). The new Cyber-voice — provided by Nicholas Briggs, who has not only voiced but has also written Doctor-less Big Finish audio adventures of both the Cybermen and Daleks — also hearkens back to the '60s.

But it's a little disappointing, perhaps, that in order to bring the Cybermen back, we go back to the '90s for a **Sliders**-style sideslip into an alternate, what-if universe. The alternate universe sets up several things to be paid off in the season finale, but here, on its own, it just seems like a flimsy excuse to show all kinds of catastrophic things without having to worry about the consequences.

Noel Clarke gets a chance to shine, twice over, as both Mickey and his alternate-universe counterpart, Ricky. The two characters give him the chance to play comedy, drama, action hero and a bit of pathos as well, as we get more backstory on both Mickey and Ricky than we've previously had in the entire series. Camille Coduri gets to play an entirely different Jackie Tyler (and an altogether unpleasant one, it must be said), and between that and Shaun Dingwall's return as Pete Tyler, Billie Piper gets plenty to do here. Roger Lloyd-Pack makes a wonderfully vile villain, and Graeme Harper's direction restores the Cybermen from "guys in silver spray-painted wetsuits" to "truly terrifying." The Cybermen hadn't been this scary since *Earthshock* — or possibly even since the '60s.

THE AGE OF STEEL

The Doctor and his friends are trapped by Lumic's new breed of Cybermen. Using the last remaining power source from the TARDIS, the Doctor immobilizes the Cybermen with an energy beam, and the survivors of the Cyberman attack on the Tyler mansion are now on the run. Ricky, the alternate universe's battle-hardened version of Mickey, is killed by Cybermen while trying to escape. Pete and Rose try to infiltrate the Cyber-factory, using fake EarPods as a disguise, to find this universe's Jackie, only to discover that she has already been converted into a Cyberman. The Doctor and Mrs. Moore, a resistance fighter from Ricky's operation, discover an army of dormant Cybermen hidden beneath London. Mickey forms an uneasy alliance with Ricky's friend Jake to storm Lumic's zeppelin and try to find the controls Lumic uses to guide the Cybermen. Lumic, however, is no long in control — his enfeebled body is scheduled for an "upgrade" by the Cybermen, whether he wishes to remain human or not — and when he is in control, he is no longer Lumic. The Doctor still sees an opportunity to thwart the Cyberman invasion and return the TARDIS to its own universe, but not everyone who came with him will be making the return trip.

David Tennant . . . . The Doctor
Billie Piper . . . . Rose Tyler
Noel Clarke . . . . Mickey Smith
Nicholas Briggs . . . . Cyber voices
Camille Coduri . . . . Jackie Tyler
Shaun Dingwall . . . . Pete Tyler
Helen Griffin . . . . Mrs. Moore
Andrew Hayden-Smith . . . . Jake Simmonds
Paul Kasey . . . . Cyberleader
Roger Lloyd-Pack . . . . John Lumic
Colin Spaull . . . . Mr. Crane

This story has been released on DVD

written by Tom MacRae
directed by Graeme Harper
music by Murray Gold

Aired on May 20, 2006

AUDIO CONNECTIONS: The plot point of restoring the Cybermen's consciousness and self-awareness to them as a means of bringing them to their knees was taken from the Big Finish audio play *Spare Parts* (whose author, original series scriptwriter Marc Platt, received a "special thanks" credit in both *Age Of Steel* and *Rise Of The Cybermen*).

I love the atmosphere of this two-parter, but where pacing and storytelling are concerned, it's reminding me why the original series had four-part stories – it seems like there should've been a third episode here, rather than ramping things up to breakneck speed halfway through part two with revelations about the roles that the alternate Mickey and alternate Pete Tyler are playing in their universe, and culminating in Mickey's rather sudden change of heart at the end of the story. That the Doctor can just take a cell phone, jam it into a piece of electronic equipment and bring down this little corner of the Cybermen's empire is a massive plot convenience if you're being charitable, and massive plot contrivance if you're not.

There's something quite satisfying, however, about the fate of John Lumic, even though once again it falls under the "Davros already did it" category. It does, however, make one wonder about who the Cyber Controller (*Tomb Of The Cybermen, Attack Of The Cybermen*) and the Cyber Planner (*The Invasion*) were in the Doctor's "home" reality. The manner in which these Cybermen are disposed of goes against the grain of everything that we knew about the Cybermen before, but on the other hand, it came be argued that Lumic's new breed of Cybermen are not "true" Cybermen as we knew them before; their origins are different and they may be more primitive.

THE IDIOT'S LANTERN

Intending to go see Elvis perform live in the 1950s, the Doctor and Rose wind up in London instead, on the eve of the coronation of Queen Elizabeth II. Among the last-minute preparations, though, the time travelers witness an event that suggests that there's more going on than a celebration. Black cars are pulling up to homes, and men spill out to abduct someone and leave again. The Doctor and Rose, after being urged by one family to turn their backs and say nothing, instead invade that family's home under the guise of government inspectors to find out what's happening. The truth that emerges is horrifying: something in this part of London is robbing people not just of their consciousness, but their faces. As the Doctor discovers where the police are taking the victims, Rose visits an electrical store selling TVs at a ridiculously low price and finds out that an alien intelligence called the Wire is behind the strange occurrences – but she becomes the Wire's next victim moments later.

David Tennant . . . . The Doctor
Billie Piper . . . . Rose Tyler
Jean Challis . . . . Aunty Betty
Ron Cook . . . . Magpie
Sam Cox . . . . Detective Inspector Bishop
Christopher Driscoll . . . . Security Guard
Jamie Foreman . . . . Eddie Connolly
Debra Gillett . . . . Rita Connolly
Rory Jennings . . . . Tommy Connolly
Margaret John . . . . Grandma Connolly
Marie Lewis . . . . Mrs. Gallagher

This story has been released on DVD

written by Mark Gatiss
directed by Euros Lyn
music by Murray Gold

Aired on May 27, 2006

Maureen Lipman . . . . The Wire
Ieuan Rhys . . . . Crabtree

Another winner from the pen of Mark Gatiss, *The Idiot's Lantern* does a fantastic job of both creating a nostalgic period setting, and then delivering a suspenseful and scary story within that framework. The '50s atmosphere is a thing of beauty, and it's recreated wonderfully. Gatiss pokes some fun at the styles and mores of the era, and yet somehow remains almost reverent about it. I'm always impressed with how the **Doctor Who** production team turns pieces of Cardiff into London or somewhere else, but they outdid themselves here. The period props and costuming lend the whole thing a remarkable authenticity.

All of that wouldn't mean a thing if there wasn't a villain worthy of threatening the idyllic setting, and *The Idiot's Lantern* has that as well, with Maureen Lipman combining menace and innocuous charm to create one of the new show's most memorable villains to date. I'm really hoping we get a rematch with the Wire at some point, but only if there's a worthy story that makes good use of the Wire's unique nature without just parroting this story in a different setting. Something for the viral video age…

And just when you think one of the story's characters is about to be dismissed as irredeemable, there's a last-minute course change that portends a hopeful resolution for them as well. It's an unusually cheerful ending even for new **Who**, and overall this episode ranks up there as one of the best hours of the second season.

THE IMPOSSIBLE PLANET

This time, the TARDIS has gone too far – so far into the future that it doesn't know when or where it is. The Doctor and Rose do a bit of exploring and find that they're on Sanctuary Base 8, a human outpost built on a planet whose stable orbit around a massive black hole isn't just improbable, but should be absolutely impossible. Ancient writing on the base's walls is so old that even the TARDIS' gift of translation can't help the Doctor decipher it. The bedraggled human crew – including an officer who has had to step uncomfortably into a command role following the death of the expedition's captain – has found that some source of power under the planet's surface is keeping it at a safe distance from the black hole. Entire star systems fall past the planet and into oblivion, but inexplicably, the planet itself remains; but even then, the base isn't completely safe, as earthquakes rattle their delicate habitat (and one particularly violent tremor seems to swallow the TARDIS whole, trapping the Doctor and Rose on the base). The small human crew is supplemented by a servile race called the Ood, who don't seem to object to working for the humans. A member of the base's crew begins hearing voices, and then finds that he's covered with the same symbols as the alien writing. The Doctor joins a foolhardy expedition beneath the planet's surface, hoping to find out for himself what's keeping the planet in place – but that's a question that everyone there may soon regret asking.

```
David Tennant . . . . . . . . . . . . . . The Doctor
Billie Piper . . . . . . . . . . . . . . . . . Rose Tyler
MyAnna Buring . . . . . . . . . . . . . Scooti Maniska
Claire Burnbrook . . . . . . . . . . . . . . Ida Scott
Silas Carson . . . . . . . . . . . voice of the Ood
Ronny Jhutti . . . . . . . . . . . . . Danny Bartock
Paul Kasey . . . . . . . . . . . . . . . . The Ood
Shaun Parkes . . . . . . . Zachary Cross Flane
Will Thorp . . . . . . . . . . . . . . . . Toby Zed
Danny Webb . . . . . . . . . . . . . Mr. Jefferson
```

This story has been released on DVD

written by Matt Jones
directed by James Strong
music by Murray Gold

Aired on June 3, 2006

Gabriel Woolf . . . . voice of the Beast

CLASSIC CONNECTIONS: Actor **Gabriel Woolf** is an apt choice to give the Beast its voice — he also voiced Sutekh in the original series classic *Pyramids Of Mars*.

A dandy thriller in the same basic mold as *The Ark In Space*, *The Impossible Planet* scoots along and builds its mystery at a nice pace without having to resolve everything in one episode. The cast is convincingly worn-down and yet likeable, and their setting is superb – possibly the best representation of a space colony that **Doctor Who** has ever been able to afford, complete with the Ood, who may well be the most unsettlingly alien aliens that the new series has given us. With their unnaturally calm voices (provided by Silas "Ki-Adi Mundi" Carson) clashing with their grotesque appearance and their increasingly threatening behavior, the Ood are a nasty creation indeed.

The Impossible Planet spends a lot of time setting an intriguing stage for the second part's revelations, but in and of itself it's very enjoyable, and more than a little bit unsettling. It succeeds in giving us a claustrophobic setting where one door opening can send the crew to their deaths. And this time, it really doesn't look like a studio or a rock quarry (though the exterior scenes on the "planet surface" are precisely that, a time-honored **Doctor Who** tradition).

THE SATAN PIT

The Ood, under the control of the one they refer to as the Beast, close in on Rose and the crew of Sanctuary Base 8, while the Doctor and Ida Scott are stranded beneath the surface of the planet. The Doctor makes a reckless jump into the pit they've discovered there – a literal leap of faith – while Rose helps the survivors of the Sanctuary Base marshal their resources to save themselves. In the pit, the Doctor finds the Beast – its body, chained forever in the pit, rages aimlessly, seemingly unable to communicate with him. Little does Rose know that the Beast also is on the base with her – its disembodied intelligence inhabits the body of a young archaeologist, quietly helping the Ood whittle the crew down to just two men and Rose. But the crew manages to shut down the telepathic field controlling the Ood and, leaving the Doctor and Ida for dead (over Rose's objections), they flee the base in their only escape vehicle. Now, unless the Doctor and Rose take decisive action without being able to contact one another, the Beast's mind may escape into the civilized center of the galaxy to build its new army.

```
David Tennant . . . . . . . . . . . . . . The Doctor
Billie Piper . . . . . . . . . . . . . . . . . Rose Tyler
Claire Burnbrook . . . . . . . . . . . . . . Ida Scott
Silas Carson . . . . . . . . . . . voice of the Ood
Ronny Jhutti . . . . . . . . . . . . . Danny Bartock
Paul Kasey . . . . . . . . . . . . . . . . The Ood
Shaun Parkes . . . . . . . Zachary Cross Flane
```

This story has been released on DVD

written by Matt Jones
directed by James Strong
music by Murray Gold

Aired on June 10, 2006

Will Thorp . . . . Toby Zed   Gabriel Woolf . . . . voice of the Beast
Danny Webb . . . . Mr. Jefferson

CLASSIC CONNECTIONS: The Doctor mentions Draconia and Daemos as worlds that have an image of the beast. The third Doctor met the Draconians in 1973's *Frontier In Space*, and that species has continued to feature in **Doctor Who** print fiction and video productions; the latter is an interesting choice since it's the homeworld of Azal, a demonic creature who the third Doctor battled when it posed as the devil in 1971's *The Dæmons*, the Beast seen here might have been a much older and more powerful Dæmon, or something else entirely.

Successfully building on *The Impossible Planet*'s doom-laden atmosphere, *The Satan Pit* seems to be flirting with exploring the theology of **Doctor Who**, and that might even be intriguing if it had had the time to play out. The problem with any such attempt is that *The Dæmons* went there already, and in 1971 no less, with another demonic creature in another pit which may also have been the inspiration for numerous societies' stories of the devil. I'll grant you, the CGI creature seen here is a little bit more menacing than Stephen Thorne in goatskin pants, but in the case of either *The Dæmons* or *The Satan Pit*, the real drama lies with someone acting as the devil's spokesperson – in *The Dæmons* it was Roger Delgado as the Master at his most sinister, and here it's Will Thorp as Toby, and he effectively steals the show from the huge red critter that's green-screened in in front of David Tennant.

Here we see a Rose not seen since the previous season – she has learned from her travels with the Doctor, including how to inspire and lead others, and she's learned that sometimes a supreme sacrifice is necessary. She loses points for trying to hijack the ship momentarily, but even the other characters in the scene know she doesn't have the cajones to pull the trigger. When she does finally work up the nerve, she's doing something considerably nobler.

If there's really a problem here, it's that the story and the script waltz right up to the edge of getting into the Doctor's belief system. This isn't really something we absolutely need to know for the series to go on, but it's an interesting idea to explore. (I for one think it's at least interesting that, since his ninth persona, the Doctor has suddenly been saying things like "For God's sake, Rose, run!", something that his previous selves just weren't prone to change.)

LOVE & MONSTERS

Elton Page's path has been crossed by the Doctor on more than one occasion, but in the past couple of years the encounters have come with more and more frequency. Trying to find out what it all means, Elton meets a blogger named Ursula, who has seen the Doctor in person. The two of them become good friends, eventually finding out that there are others who share their fascination with the Doctor and the TARDIS, but their tight-knit group – which Elton names LINDA (the London Investigation 'N' Detective Agency) – evolves beyond that interest, giving all of its offbeat members a place to call home. That is, until Victor Kennedy arrives on the scene. With seemingly limitless resources, and an unusually intense interest in the Doctor's whereabouts, Kennedy begins assigning "homework" to Elton, Ursula and their friends. Some of the members of LINDA stop attending meetings without a further word, and finally Elton speaks up, refusing to do Kennedy's bidding any more. But when Kennedy reveals his true identity – a creature who absorbs not just the minds but the physical mass of its prey – Elton realizes that it may take the Doctor to save him again. But every time the Doctor appears in Elton's life, terrible things happen – and even this occasion will be no exception.

David Tennant . . . . The Doctor
Billie Piper . . . . Rose Tyler
Moya Brady . . . . Bridget
Camille Coduri . . . . Jackie Tyler
Kathryn Drysdale . . . . Bliss
Bella Emberg . . . . Mrs. Crook
Simon Greenall . . . . Mr. Skinner
Shirley Henderson . . . . Ursula Blake
Paul Kasey . . . . The Hoix
Peter Kay . . . . Victor Kennedy

This story has been released on DVD

written by Russell T. Davies
directed by Dan Zeff
music by Murray Gold

Aired on June 17, 2006

Marc Warren . . . . Elton Page

BEHIND THE SCENES: The author of this book happens to agree with Elton that you can't beat a bit of ELO. "Mr. Blue Sky," excerpted repeatedly in the episode, originally appeared on the 1977 album *Out Of The Blue,* as does "Turn To Stone" (heard in the Tyler household), while LINDA's song of choice is "Don't Bring Me Down," from *Discovery* (1979). The Abzorbaloff was created by William Grantham, a young Blue Peter viewer who participated in a competition during the first season to create a monster that would feature in the series itself. LINDA – not the same group, mind you, but the Liverpool Investigation 'n' Detective Agency – was originally invented in an episode of the children's show Why Don't You?, written by Russell T. Davies during his tenure as a producer on the show (1988-92).

This episode seemed to split fandom right down the middle, and fiercely so. For one thing, the Doctor and Rose don't make much of a showing. They're seen early in the episode, and then don't show up until it's nearly over. But this is Elton's story, and Elton's story is that of someone whose life has been touched by the Doctor without him even having an inkling of who or what the Doctor is. There's a running theme through the whole season of the consequences of the Doctor's travels, and it's perhaps in *Love & Monsters* that this theme really reaches its ultimate expression. We've seen that there can be consequences to traveling with the Doctor – whether it's being left behind like Sarah Jane, or discovering your courage like Mickey, or…well…just about any of Rose's personal trials since the new series began. This episode focuses on people who are left to sit still relative to the TARDIS – Elton and, to a lesser degree, Jackie.

Or is it really about fandom? 1988's *Greatest Show In The Galaxy* had a bit of a meta-narrative running through it, which has been dissected, analyzed and debated endlessly since that story aired; the general opinion seems now to be that *Greatest Show* doesn't really represent an especially fond view of fandom. On the flipside, *Love & Monsters* seems to say that fandom, or any participatory hobby where people can gather, can be a saving grace, giving the aggrieved, the lonely, and the socially awkward a family they didn't previously have.

And then in walks Victor Kennedy. But who or what does he represent? Is he a symbol of the forces that would organize fandom to an almost-regimented degree? Is he a warning against trying to make a profession out of an enjoyable hobby? Or is he nothing more than the creation of a Blue Peter viewer who entered a contest? Actually, he's *exactly* that, but I'm analyzing here, perhaps overanalyzing, and on a subject that's actually quite close to my own thinking on hobbies and fannish endeavours. I've got lots of hobbies (and quite by coincidence, one of them is indeed a loving devotion to the music of Jeff Lynne and the Electric Light Orchestra, just like Elton – on that front, I almost felt like this story was eerily speaking directly to me somehow), and one thing I've noticed in some of my hobbies – and not even necessarily SF fandom – is a tendency for an Organizing Force to arrive on the scene, channeling and focusing everyone's creative energies to best effect, occasionally creating something wonderful for all to enjoy…and then later trying to make a buck off the deal, coming to rely on those creative energies. What was once done for the love of the hobby becomes something more like a job, and people start to burn out, and meanwhile, the Organizing Force tends, more often than not, to begin to take credit for other people's work, and to demand that work from them.

In short, *Love & Monsters*, as silly as it seemed on the surface to so many people, got me thinking even after the show was over. Sure I'm not the only person who's latched onto that message. For that matter, it's not even necessarily limited to fandom and hobbies either – any force that draws people together can be perverted into something that it was never meant to be, and certainly something that its constituent members never would have knowingly signed up for (don't get me started on my thoughts on organized religion). And this is a lovely, warm, personal tale cautioning against letting that happen. (Actually, not only is it a lovely, warm, personal tale cautioning against letting that happen, but it's a lovely, warm personal tale cautioning against letting that happen and making absolutely brilliant use of select snippets of ELO music as both source music and underscore. So maybe I'm not the best person to ask for an objective opinion here.) An underrated gem of an episode, frequently dismissed because the Abzorbaloff happens to be a bit silly.

FEAR HER

Rose and the Doctor arrive in London just in time for the running of the torch to open the 2012 Olympic Games. But a pall hangs over the perfectly ordinary neighborhood where the TARDIS has materialized: posters for missing children, all of them having disappeared in the space of the week, are everywhere. An elderly woman named Maeve claims to feel an evil presence in the neighborhood, and seems to have known, just before each child disappeared, that they were about to vanish. A woman named Trish keeps a close eye on her daughter Chloe, not out of fear that she'll disappear next, but out of fear that Chloe may be behind what's happening. The Doctor and Rose come to that conclusion too, discovering that something evil is exerting its influence, having taken over Chloe's body. But can they stop more people from disappearing – possibly even the entire human race – and restore Chloe's true personality?

David Tennant . . . . The Doctor
Billie Piper . . . . Rose Tyler
Abisola Agbaje . . . . Chloe
Edna Dore . . . . Maeve
Huw Edwards . . . . Commentator
Erica Eirian . . . . Neighbour
Tim Faraday . . . . Tom's Dad
Stephen Marzella . . . . Police Officer
Richard Nichols . . . . Driver
Abdul Salis . . . . Kel

This story has been released on DVD

written by Matthew Graham
directed by Euros Lyn
music by Murray Gold

Aired on June 24, 2006

Nina Sosanya . . . . Trish

BEHIND THE SCENES: This episode made one prediction about the 2012 London Olympics that would come true: in a way, the Doctor *did* carry the Olympic torch for part of its journey in May 2012, though in this case it was Matt Smith carrying the torch through Cardiff. No tiny heat-activated spacecraft were involved.

A nifty, **Twilight Zone**-esque tale, *Fear Her* is something that wouldn't have been impossible to do on the original series' budget. Maybe scaled down a bit, sure, what with an entire Olympic stadium full of people vanishing, but not completely impossible. A lot rides on the performance of Abisola Agbaje, playing the parts of both the possessed child and the entity that has taken her over, and she manages to portray both well enough to make her a force for David Tennant's Doctor to reckon with. Not *Exorcist* scary, but unnerving enough.

Fear Her is a fun little story. It doesn't blow down any huge barriers in storytelling, but, much like *Love & Monsters*, it's a nice change of pace slotted in among some of this season's more overt attempts to be epic.

ARMY OF GHOSTS

The Doctor and Rose pay a visit to Jackie, only to find that ghosts are walking the surface of the Earth – and Jackie claims that, after the initial shock wore off, no one's been worried about it much and the apparitions have become a fixture of everyday life, appearing at regular intervals. Ever skeptical, the Doctor rigs up a device to "trap" one of the ghostly figures, which elicits an almost violent reaction from his prey. He finds the source of the power that's enabling the "ghosts" to appear, narrowing it down to a place known as the Torchwood Institute. Inadvertently bringing Jackie along, the Doctor and Rose go to investigate Torchwood, but the Doctor is startled to find that not only is his arrival expected, but Yvonne Hartman, the director of Torchwood, knows who he is and that he seldom travels alone. Once again accidentally bringing Jackie along instead of Rose, the Doctor learns Torchwood's mandate: to secure alien technology (including the TARDIS) and repel alien threats (a category into which they apparently feel the Doctor belongs), not for the good of the world, but to restore Britain to its imperial glory days. In the depths of Torchwood's secret headquarters, a strange sphere has been the subject of intense study – radiating no heat or energy, it doesn't appear to exist, and yet there it sits. The Doctor recognizes the sphere as a voidship, a vehicle capable of traversing parallel dimensions, and warns that it's an extremely dangerous artifact. Equally dangerous, he warns, are the "ghost shifts" Torchwood is deliberately setting into motion. Deep within the Institute, a force from another universe begins to take over Torchwood, even taking control of the ghost shifts. They are the Cybermen created by John Lumic, and they're not alone – every ghost seen in every city and country in the world is one of their soldiers, and if they can figure out how to increase the energy of the next ghost shift and bring the legions of ghostly Cybermen into corporeal existence, their takeover of Earth will be complete.

Except that the Cybermen aren't the only ones trying to take over.

David Tennant . . . . The Doctor
Billie Piper . . . . Rose Tyler
Derek Acorah . . . . himself
Freema Agyeman . . . . Adeola
Takako Akashi . . . . Japanese newsreader
Hajaz Akram . . . . Indian newsreader
Alistair Appleton . . . . himself
Dan Barratt . . . . Dalek
Nicholas Briggs . . . . . Dalek voices / Cyber voices
Noel Clarke . . . . Mickey Smith
Camille Coduri . . . . Jackie Tyler
Stuart Crossman . . . . Dalek
Maddi Cryer . . . . Housewife
Anthony Debaeck . . . . . . French newsreader
Barnaby Edwards . . . . Dalek
Paul Fields . . . . Weatherman
Hadley Fraser . . . . Gareth
Trisha Goddard . . . . herself
David Hankinson . . . . Dalek

This story has been released on DVD

written by Russell T. Davies
directed by Graeme Harper
music by Murray Gold

Aired on July 1, 2006

Raji James . . . . Dr. Rajesh Singh
Paul Kasey . . . . Cyberleader
Oliver Mellor . . . . Matt
Kyoko Morita . . . . Japanese girl
Tracy-Ann Oberman . . . . Yvonne Hartman
Nicholas Pegg . . . . Dalek
Anthony Spargo . . . . Dalek
David Warwick . . . . Police Commissioner
Rachel Webster . . . . Eileen
Barbara Windsor . . . . Peggy Mitchell

I'll admit, after a whole season of watching mentions of Torchwood being shoehorned into every nook, cranny and crevice where they'd fit (and one or two where they really didn't), I wasn't sure if I'd actually care about Torchwood when the thing was finally unveiled. As it turns out, once finally unveiled, Torchwood proved to be an interesting concept, and the episode introducing the organization once and for all is brimming with atmosphere. Which is really pretty nervy when the previous week's episode had flagged up the Cybermen's involvement, and in fact that element of the story had been leaked since before the season even started.

Very atypically, the resolution of the finale is foreshadowed in a first-person narration by Rose, over an episode-opening montage boasting some remarkable FX shots as well as one of the few glimpses back into Christopher Eccleston's era since the torch was passed. There's also plenty of goofy humor, from the "kidnapping" of Jackie to the Doctor singing the **Ghostbusters** theme, but it's the more introspective stuff that's interesting, from the red herring of Jackie's reminiscences of her father to the return of a recurring Russell T. Davies theme, viewing events through the eyes of the media (also see *Aliens Of London* or Davies' pre-**Doctor Who** miniseries, *The Second Coming*). We also see that Jackie actually might've made a decent TARDIS traveler, if an occasionally uncooperative one.

It's interesting to see Torchwood introduced here as an entity that the viewer is highly unlikely to find sympathetic; it seems like this poses a challenge for setting up the spinoff series to follow. Another thing that almost begs to be followed up on, however, is a genie that may have been best left in the bottle: this episode and *Doomsday* bring us an Earth that not only can't deny the existence of alien life (we rounded that corner in *The Christmas Invasion*), but an Earth devastated by an alien invasion. For all of Davies' talk about the frequency of contemporary Earth stories being necessary to tell a story that an Earthbound audience cares about, it seems like we're moving away from anything that we recognize as contemporary Earth and moving into an Earth in the aftermath of events that would rock human society back on its heels on every level from the economic to the political to the metaphysical. It seems like there's an excellent post-terrorism allegory waiting to happen here, but years later, no such allegory has materialized.

DOOMSDAY

Just as the Cybermen flash into existence all over the Earth, a new threat erupts from the voidship – a group of Daleks, known to the Doctor as a particularly dangerous bunch called the Cult of Skaro, emerge with an unknown device of Time Lord origin called the Genesis Ark. The Daleks are fiercely protective of the Ark, but despite its origins, the Doctor has no idea what it is. The Cybermen aren't the only visitors from a parallel world: Mickey Smith, Pete Tyler and the soldiers of an anti-Cyberman resistance force have tracked their prey to this world, but now find themselves outgunned as the Daleks and Cybermen launch a full-scale war against each other, with the human race trapped in the middle and Torchwood powerless to fight back. Worse yet, the Genesis Ark is activated and reveals its Time Lord nature: bigger inside than out, it is a prison for millions of Daleks captured during the Time War, who join the fight that's laying waste to the entire Earth. The Doctor works out a plan to send both of the alien armies back into the void. But even if he can save the world, this time he may not be able to save Rose – and even if her newly (if awkwardly) reunited family saves her, her TARDIS traveling days are numbered.

David Tennant . . . . The Doctor
Billie Piper . . . . Rose Tyler
Dan Barratt . . . . Dalek
Nicholas Briggs . . . . Dalek voices / Cyber voices
Noel Clarke . . . . Mickey Smith
Camille Coduri . . . . Jackie Tyler
Stuart Crossman . . . . Dalek
Shaun Dingwall . . . . Pete Tyler
Barnaby Edwards . . . . Dalek
David Hankinson . . . . Dale
Andrew Hayden-Smith . . . . Jake Simmonds
Raji James . . . . Dr. Rajesh Singh
Paul Kasey . . . . Cyberleader

This story has been released on DVD

written by Russell T. Davies
directed by Graeme Harper
music by Murray Gold

Aired on July 8, 2006

Tracy-Ann Oberman . . . . Yvonne Hartman
Nicholas Pegg . . . . Dalek
Anthony Spargo . . . . Dalek
Catherine Tate . . . . The Bride

Maybe a Daleks vs. Cybermen death match is a dream date for longtime fans of **Doctor Who**, but the question here is: does it make for a good story? At the very least, it makes for some mighty memorable moments – there are a couple of rather funny instances of Dalek-Cyberman smack talk that are worth the price of admission alone (in one instance, chased down by Mickey's one-liner that it's "like Stephen Hawking arguing with the speaking clock"). It's like **Wrestlemania** meets **Doctor Who** – there's a lot of shouting about who the baddest boys at the bar are, but when the shooting starts, it's like I always suspected: the Daleks can smoke the Cybermen without breaking a sweat.

All of the alternate-universe-hopping and the Doctor's neat solution to the problem are just gravy to tide you over between Dalek/Cybermen war scenes and until we get to the real point of this episode, Rose's departure. The way in which it fills the premonitory mandate of Rose "dying" is, perhaps not unexpectedly, a bit of a cheat, but it doesn't lack punch. This companion departure is milked for the melodrama and the tragic angle, but at the same time, this association with the Doctor has given her a gift that's far above and beyond what most of his sidekicks have gotten out of the deal: she's gotten her entire family back (after a fashion), something that never would've happened without her travels in the TARDIS. And yet the glimpses we get of her post-TARDIS life seem utterly joyless.

Which brings us to the big question: what did Rose's departure do to the series in general? Rose's personality having become such a major part of the show was leading to some rather formulaic development of both story and character. Don't get me wrong, Rose got to do cool stuff in season 2, but she also frequently fell back on her well-worn weepy and smug modes, both of which had already seen quite a bit of use in season 1. Of course, Rose the character does this because the writers (and Russell T. Davies) write her that way, and perhaps the worst thing about Rose's departure was that she never really left – she became the elephant in the room, constantly talked about without being physically present.

Doomsday's still good popcorn material – annoyed with Rose or not, there's something awfully satisfying about watching the Daleks and Cybermen duke it out.

SERIES 3: 2006-2007
THE RUNAWAY BRIDE

Still stunned from the loss of Rose, the Doctor is even more surprised when he finds someone else in the TARDIS – someone else who's wearing a bridal gown and insists that she was only moments ago at a church walking down the aisle. Her name is Donna, and she's neither impressed nor pleased to find herself in an alien time machine.

The Doctor whisks her back to Earth, but no sooner has she arrived again than trouble follows: the robot Santas return, but this time they're not homing in on the Doctor – they're after Donna. The Doctor discovers that Donna's body has been irradiated with a kind of energy that hasn't existed for billions of years, and sets about tracking down the cause of it, eventually finding an elaborate but abandoned Torchwood installation beneath the Thames. But that top-secret organization isn't behind the energy or the robots. The Empress of the spider-like Racnoss is, and she plans to use Donna to jump-start a diabolical plan to revive her nearly-extinct race...at the cost of the human race's extinction. If the Doctor can't find a way to flush this not-so-itsy-bitsy spider down the waterspout, Donna's TARDIS travels may have already come to an end.

David Tennant . . . . The Doctor
Catherine Tate . . . . Donna Noble
Krystal Archer . . . . Nerys
Howard Attfield . . . . Geoff Noble
Zafirah Boateng . . . . Little Girl
Trevor Georges . . . . Vicar
Don Gilet . . . . Lance Bennett
Paul Kasey . . . . Robot Santa
Jacqueline King . . . . Sylvia Noble
Rhodri Meiur . . . . Rhodri

This story has been released on DVD

written by Russell T. Davies
directed by Euros Lyn
music by Murray Gold

Aired on December 25, 2006

Sarah Parrish . . . . Empress
Glen Wilson . . . . Taxi Driver

CLASSIC CONNECTIONS: Despite numerous mentions that the planet of the Time Lords has been destroyed, this marks the first time in the new series that the name "Gallifrey" has been spoken on screen. (It's somehow fitting, given that the name wasn't invented until Jon Pertwee's final season, over a decade into the original series' run.) The "dark times" during which the Time Lords did battle with the Racnoss may or may not be the same dark times hinted at by Lady Peinforte in *Silver Nemesis* (1988).

A neat special episode that neatly splits the difference between getting some closure on the events of *Doomsday* and clearing the decks and just having a rollicking one-off adventure, *The Runaway Bride* may not be the greatest entry in the **Doctor Who** mythos that the new series has given us, but it certainly is fun.

Catherine Tate is simply sensational as a one-time-only sidekick for the tenth Doctor – so much so that, without wanting to prematurely judge Freema Agyeman or her character in the upcoming third season, I really wished she had stayed aboard the TARDIS. Donna has an attitude, she has guts, and she's smart – for all of her cluelessness about the Doctor's world, she certainly saw through his attempt to pass off huon particles as harmless. Perfect companion material; luckily the production team realized this too.

The script and David Tennant's more-subdued-than-usual performance manage to make it clear that the loss of Rose is still an open wound for the Doctor, and yet he seems to delight in the fact that's found a promising new prospect for a companion. There's also a nice scene, if a little bit of a throwaway, to remind us that while some of us may have enjoyed **Torchwood**, they're certainly not good guys in the Doctor's world. Also not being a good guy is Sarah Parrish as the Empress of the Racnoss; there's scarcely a surprising action in that character's repertoire, but she gets full marks for chewing right through the scenery and making it impossible to ignore her. She's literally a larger-than-life character, so why not? (Too bad no one saw fit to throw in some mention about the Doctor not having a good history with giant spiders.)

UWORP!

SMITH AND JONES

Medical student Martha Jones can tell that this isn't going to be an ordinary day, whether it's the black-suited figures at the hospital where she's studying, or the rainstorm that surrounds the hospital and nothing else in London, or the odd patient with two heartbeats, or the fact that her hospital appears to be transported shortly afterward to the surface of the moon. As towering, skyscraper-like spacecraft land near the hospital and platoons of armed aliens enter, at least two other aliens are making their presence known within the hospital: one is a refugee on the run, and the other is a Time Lord known as the Doctor. When the Doctor all but assumes command of the situation, Martha has any number of questions about who – or what – he is. But if any of the other life forms get hold of the Doctor, Martha may never get her questions answered.

David Tennant . . . . The Doctor
Freema Agyeman . . . . Martha Jones
Adjoa Andoh . . . . Francine Jones
Nicholas Briggs . . . . Judoon voices
Paul Kasey . . . . Judoon Captain
Trevor Laird . . . . Clive Jones
Roy Mardsen . . . . Mr. Stoker
Gugu Mbatha-Raw . . . . Tish Jones
Anne Reid . . . . Florence Finnegan
Kimmi Richards . . . . Annalise
Ben Righton . . . . Morganstern

This story has been released on DVD

written by Russell T. Davies
directed by Charles Palmer
music by Murray Gold

Aired on March 31, 2007

Vineeta Rishi . . . . Julia Swales
Reggie Yates . . . . Leo Jones

Similar in pacing and emphasis to *Rose, Smith And Jones* feels a bit different, not only for the introduction of a new companion, but the fact that it has to focus on her out of necessity. So much emphasis has been placed previously on the Doctor being choosy about his traveling companions that the new series, by its very nature, almost has to come to a full stop to show us this person, and show us why the Doctor would consider welcoming them aboard. Martha is a very different character from Rose; she has goals and a career path, and yet she's also very likeable.

Once again, the Doctor-already-in-the-process-of-investigating-something-strange chestnut is rolled out – further proof that the Sylvester McCoy era is more influential on the revived **Doctor Who** than I think anyone's really giving it credit for. The Doctor seems a little more eccentric than usual, even for his tenth incarnation, having spent an unspecified amount of time without a sidekick in the TARDIS. (That unspecified gap will no doubt be a boon to BBC Books novelists and audio authors somewhere down the road.) One chestnut that *doesn't* show up here is the mad, bad and dangerous to know Doctor – even though Tennant is more than capable of pulling it off – because the story almost demands it. Maybe it's a course correction from lessons learned from Rose, but remember, we also need to see why Martha would want to travel with the Doctor, let alone the other way around.

The Judoon are an inspired design, both makeup and costume-wise, with movie-quality prosthetics on a level that, subconsciously, I still almost can't mentally associate with **Doctor Who.** The scare factor in this episode was impressive: there were action and plenty of shocking moments, and I couldn't think of anything that really hurt the show or took me out of the story.

There were more than a few neat little background details, including Martha's story of her cousin's death (Freema Agyeman also played the part of an ill-fated Torchwood employee in last season's *Army Of Ghosts*), and the fact that the Doctor is now on at least his fourth sonic screwdriver (and seems to have no problem getting replacements these days).

THE SHAKESPEARE CODE

Promising her a single trip through time, the Doctor takes Martha to London in 1599, the TARDIS landing within walking distance of the Globe Theatre and William Shakespeare himself. But the Bard behaves oddly at the end of a performance of "Love's Labours Lost", making a sudden promise to his audience that the sequel, "Love's Labours Won", will debut the following night...despite this being the first that any of his loyal troupe of actors have heard of it. The Doctor introduces Martha to Shakespeare, and then the sudden deaths begin, always near Shakespeare. The Doctor gradually learns that the play isn't the only thing at the Globe – the unusually designed venue may have a more sinister purpose underlying its design. With a little bit of toil, the Doctor uncovers a lot of trouble – three alien "witches" are planning to wipe out humanity to claim Earth for their own exiled race...and the key to their plan will come from Shakespeare's own pen.

David Tennant . . . . The Doctor
Freema Agyeman . . . . Martha Jones
Andree Bernard . . . . Dolly Bailey
Linda Clark . . . . Bloodtide
Christina Cole . . . . Lilith
Robert Demeger . . . . Preacher
Jalaal Hartley . . . . Dick
Dean Lennox Kelly . . . . Shakespeare
Matt King . . . . Peter Streete
Chris Larkin . . . . Lynley
Amanda Lawrence . . . . Doomfinger
Stephen Marcus . . . . Jailer

This story has been released on DVD

written by Gareth Roberts
directed by Charles Palmer
music by Murray Gold

Aired on April 7, 2007

Sam Marks . . . . Wiggins
Angela Pleasence . . . . Queen Elizabeth
David Westhead . . . . Kempe

CLASSIC CONNECTIONS: In *City Of Death*, the fourth Doctor claimed that the handwriting on the original manuscript of <u>Hamlet</u> was *his, not* Shakespeare's, so presumably – earlier in the Doctor's life, but later in the Bard's – the two met up again. The first Doctor and friends observed Shakespeare at another pivotal point in his history via the Time-Space Visualizer in *The Chase*.

BOOK CONNECTIONS: This may not the first time that the Doctor has had only one heart beating in his chest; Sabbath, an agent of the "time traveling voodoo cult" Faction Paradox, left the eighth Doctor with only one heart for a time in the BBC novels.

Very much in the mold of the previous season's *Tooth And Claw*, *The Shakespeare Code* – written by longtime **Doctor Who** novelist Gareth Roberts, whose printed travels in the TARDIS date back to the early days of the New Adventures novels – takes an established and well-known historical character, finds some odd nook or cranny in that person's known activities, and finds an off-the-wall SF explanation for it. In this case, the mystery is what happened to Shakespeare's <u>Love's Labours Won</u>. The resulting explanation isn't quite as engrossing as *Tooth And Claw*, however, and the whole thing would get a bit messy if not for Dean Lennox Kelly's engaging portrayal of Shakespeare in his youthful prime and Christina Cole's over-the-top-when-appropriate guest turn as the lead witch.

Beginning a trend that bothered me all season long, this episode tacks on reminiscences of Rose that are not only extraneous to the story, but are just unfair to Freema Agyeman's Martha from a character development standpoint. The Doctor has seldom, if *ever*, been this moribund after the non-fatal loss of a companion, and while the '80s saw a trend of a recently-departed companion getting a single token mention in the following story (i.e. mentioning Adric in *Time-Flight*, mentioning Romana and K-9 in *The Keeper Of Traken* or mentioning Tegan in *Planet Of Fire*), that's small potatoes compared to the Rose-o-rama that is the new series' third season. I don't think that a companion who's no longer with the Doctor has *ever* gotten this much lip service in the history of the series, and in my mind it stole time that could've been spent on the story or on the development of Martha.

The period atmosphere – including filming on location in the actual Globe Theatre – almost makes up for it, as do numerous comedic moments throughout the script (from the Doctor quoting Dylan Thomas and then having to explain to Shakespeare that he can't appropriate that line, to a slightly tacked-on gag touching on whether or not the Bard might've been bisexual). Almost the most promising thing about *The Shakespeare Code* is its ending, where the Doctor winds up nearly paying the piper for some apparent misdeed that he has yet to commit by his own timeline (but will commit later; see *Day Of The Doctor*).

The Shakespeare Code is really a fine, fun little romp whose weakest points are by no means the fault of its author (whose work I've almost always enjoyed), but are imposed on it as part of the season's overall arc.

GRIDLOCK

The Doctor, despite his initial promise of only one trip in the TARDIS, takes Martha to the distant future, returning to New Earth in the year 5,000,053, some time after his last visit there. But instead of towering cityscapes, the time travelers find slums, where humans tolerate the bleakness of their existence with chemical help from a thriving network of drug-dealing "pharmacists." Martha is kidnapped by a couple and dragged into an airbus, leaving the Doctor behind. When he tries to enlist the help of another airbus pilot to track Martha down, the Doctor discovers that traffic moves at the rate of mere meters per year – New New York is trapped in a permanent traffic jam worthy of its namesake, and vehicles and their occupants have been disappearing at the lowest altitudes, never to be heard from again. And Martha may soon share that fate when the Doctor's rescue mission is abruptly cut short.

David Tennant . . . . The Doctor
Freema Agyeman . . . . Martha Jones
Georgine Anderson . . . . May
Nicholas Boulton . . . . Businessman
Lenora Crichlow . . . . Cheen
Lucy Davenport . . . . Pale Woman
Tom Edden . . . . Pharmacist #1
Jennifer Hennessy . . . . Valerie
Anna Hope . . . . Novice Hame
Daisy Lewis . . . . Javit
Erika MacLeod . . . . Sally Calypso
Judy Norman . . . . Ma
Ardal O'Hanlon . . . . Brannigan
Travis Oliver . . . . Milo
Graham Padden . . . . Pa

This story has been released on DVD

written by Russell T. Davies
directed by Richard Clark
music by Murray Gold

Aired on April 14, 2007

Simon Pearsall . . . . Whitey
Struan Rodger . . . . The Face of Boe
Gayle Telfer Stevens . . . . Pharmacist #3
Bridget Turner . . . . Alice
Natasha Williams . . . . Pharmacist #2

CLASSIC CONNECTIONS: The crab-like Macra threatened the second Doctor and his friends in the 1967 story *The Macra Terror*; he is quick to observe that they appear to have devolved into mindless beasts. (They also appear to have grown considerably in size – either that, or someone in the effects department made a macro error in judging the scale of this particular Macra terror.)

A.K.A.: Ardal O'Hanlon previously co-starred as Father Dougal McGuire in **Father Ted**, and as Thermoman (and his mild-mannered alter-ego, George Sunday) in the long-running comedy **My Hero**. He's been a fixture on the comedy circuit since the '90s, and has appeared on **Comedy Central Presents** in the US. The voice of Boe, **Struan Rodger**, has shown in face in plenty of movies (*Chariots Of Fire, Four Weddings And A Funeral, The Innocent Sleep*, and *Stardust*, to name but a few) and television series (Highlander, Law & Order UK, Midsomer Murders, and Lovejoy). Georgine Anderson previously appeared as another character named May — with the surname, incidentally, of Harkness — in Russell T. Davies's spooky 1993 series Century Falls.

A marvelous piece of atmosphere, if not necessarily a great example of concise, airtight plotting, *Gridlock* is a lot like ***The Fifth Element*** — its atmosphere and fascinating setting and pacing are intriguing enough that I can just about let the story structure go for now. In less than an hour, it creates an interesting, densely-layered universe that I would've been happy to spend one of the original series' four-parters exploring. Numerous interesting facets of the culture and mindset that have emerged in the years-long traffic jam are explored through the characters, including an almost inexplicably moving scene where every stranded motorist marks the passing of time by singing "The Old Rugged Cross" in unison, and it's one of those nifty little pieces of fiction that leaves the viewer wondering about other facets and other characters that might have emerged in the same scenario that we *didn't* see on screen. That all this was achieved relatively economically — all of the hovercraft stalled on the freeway are redresses of a single set — is a testament to the ingenuity of the new show's creative staff.

In fact, *Gridlock* may be densely packed with *too* many ideas for its own good. There seems to be a hint of a bookend concept about a society that doses itself with anti-depressants to avoid some of the more unpleasant inescapable truths of their existence, but this seems to run out of steam at around the same time the freeway runs out of passengers. The circumstances that led to the motorists being trapped in the first place is seemingly glossed over with a little bit of dialogue. And if that's not enough, we finally follow up on the Face of Boe's promise/threat to return once more with a secret of momentous import for the Doctor. Once again, Boe knows… how to sound like Ambassador Kosh of **Babylon 5** fame. Of course, Rose gets another mention, through refreshingly, Martha starts to rail against the Rose reminder of the week phenomenon. (*About time, too.*)

But the complaints are very minor indeed — it's more a case of over-egging the pudding than anything that screws up the core of the story. Overall, in hindsight, *Gridlock* may well be my favorite installment of the new **Who**'s third season.

DALEKS IN MANHATTAN

In the throes of the Great Depression, New York City's towering Empire State Building is erected even as able-bodied men eke out a barely-adequate existence in its shadow, unable to find work. But something other than poverty is stalking them — rumors circulate of pig-faced creatures who walk like humans and abduct unsuspecting people who are then never seen again. The TARDIS lands in the shadow of the Statue of Liberty, and the Doctor and Martha make their way to Manhattan, where they learn of the abductions and follow clues to the sewer tunnels beneath the city. The Doctor does indeed find the pig-like beings — humans who have been subjected to genetic experimentation and mutation — but he also finds an amoeboid life form whose origins he knows all too well: a failed attempt to create a new mutant to occupy a Dalek casing. By the time the Doctor and Martha find the Daleks' base of operations beneath the streets of New York City, the Daleks have already taken a terrifying new step in their own evolution.

David Tennant . . . . The Doctor
Freema Agyeman . . . . Martha Jones
Stewart Alexander . . . . Worker #2
Nicholas Briggs . . . . Dalek voices
Peter Brooke . . . . Man #2
Alexis Caley . . . . Lois
Ryan Carnes . . . . Laszlo
Barnaby Edwards . . . . Dalek
Andrew Garfield . . . . Frank
David Hankinson . . . . Dalek
Paul Kasey . . . . Hero Pig
Eric Loren . . . . Mr. Diagoras
Joe Montana . . . . Worker #1
Nicholas Pegg . . . . Dalek
Earl Perkins . . . . Man #1

This story has been released on DVD

written by Helen Raynor
directed by James Strong
music by Murray Gold

Aired on April 21, 2007

Ian Porter . . . . Foreman
Hugh Quarshie . . . . Solomon
Miranda Raison . . . . Tallulah
Anthony Spargo . . . . Dalek
Flik Swan . . . . Myrna
Mel Taylor . . . . Dock Worker

A.K.A.: Hugh Quarshie has dabbled with Duane Dibbley in **Red Dwarf** and protected Padme as Captain Panaka in *Star Wars Episode I: The Phantom Menace.*

BEHIND THE SCENES: This marks the first time that footage for episodes of **Doctor Who** has been custom-shot in the United States. In 1985, the Colin Baker story *The Two Doctors* was originally written to take place in New Orleans, but budget constraints forced the story to be rewritten to take place in Seville. The 1996 TV movie's shots of San Francisco were taken from stock footage (the movie itself was shot in Vancouver). For *Daleks In Manhattan* and *Evolution Of The Daleks*, director James Strong and a small camera crew from BBC Wales traveled to New York City and shot video and photos — much of which would be digitally touched up in post-production to "de-age" the city to the 1930s. Most of the footage, even the scenes that appear to be at the base of the Statue of Liberty, were still filmed in Cardiff. This paved the way for the first American location filming, with members of the regular cast, to take place for 2011's *The Impossible Astronaut.*

After all these years, TV **Doctor Who** brings us to America in a way that doesn't make me cringe. For a SF show made in Wales, *Daleks In Manhattan* certainly does a better job than, well, most UK productions I can think of in terms of making me feel like the story really is taking place in the United States. It certainly succeeds better than the first season's *Dalek*, but what's with the title? If we're going to give it away right after the opening teaser, then please, let's be classy about it and call it *The Daleks Take Manhattan.* *Daleks In Manhattan* just sounds like an unfortunate TV Guide log line. If they *took* Manhattan, the Daleks could at least be in the same league with the Muppets.

One thing that this two-parter makes me fear is that the new series is reaching toward its own overly-convoluted Dalek mythology, much like the Dalek stories of the Tom Baker era onward from the original series. Between Tom Baker's first season and Sylvester McCoy's last, there was a grand total of five Dalek stories (I'm not counting the brief non-sequitur appearance of a Dalek in *The Five Doctors* as one of them), and they were all tied into each other. Just a few episodes into the third season of the new series, *Daleks In Manhatan* tacked new evolutionary steps onto such things as the Cult of Skaro and the Time War. If someone had uttered the word "Movellan" into the bargain, my head would've exploded. I can keep track of it all, but I'm a fan — and thus far, the new series has done a nice job of dropping bread crumbs to the fans while preparing nice meals of story for the general viewing public.

The real star of this episode may be the musical number, which is a neat feat of choreography and lyrics that are borderline-naughty without ever quite making you clamp your hands over the kids' ears.

EVOLUTION OF THE DALEKS

Dalek Sec, transformed into a hybrid between a Dalek's mutant occupant and a human, terrifies not only the Doctor and Martha, but even its fellow Daleks. Fearing any evolution that could steer them away from being "pure" Daleks, the rest of the Cult of Skaro now treat their leader's orders with skepticism. The Doctor and Martha lead their fellow captives to the relative safety of Central Park, but with the realization that the Doctor is working against them, the Daleks follow, no longer worried about hiding. When Dalek Sec spares the Doctor from imminent extermination, the other three Daleks turn against him. With his one hope of reasoning with a new breed of Daleks gone, the Doctor is all that stands between Earth in one of its most defenseless junctures in history and the Daleks' hunger for conquest.

David Tennant . . . . The Doctor
Freema Agyeman . . . . Martha Jones
Nicholas Briggs . . . . Dalek voices
Ryan Carnes . . . . Laszlo
Barnaby Edwards . . . . Dalek
Andrew Garfield . . . . Frank
David Hankinson . . . . Dalek
Paul Kasey . . . . Hero Pig
Eric Loren . . . . Dalek Sec
Nicholas Pegg . . . . Dalek
Earl Perkins . . . . Man #1
Ian Porter . . . . Hybrid

This story has been released on DVD

written by Helen Raynor
directed by James Strong
music by Murray Gold

Aired on April 28, 2007

Hugh Quarshie . . . . Solomon
Miranda Raison . . . . Tallulah
Anthony Spargo . . . . Dalek

CLASSIC CONNECTIONS: Though it seemed to come out of nowhere here, the Daleks were no strangers to internal wars involving racial purity. Following Davros' rewriting of Dalek DNA in 1984's *Resurrection Of The Daleks*, an all-out war raged through the two remaining Dalek stories of the original series, *Revelation Of The Daleks* (1985) and especially *Remembrance Of The Daleks* (1988). Until now, there seemed to be little trace of that civil war in the new series (perhaps both sides settled their differences amicably so they could devote all available Dalek resources to the Time War). The next occurrence of Dalek killing Dalek happens in 2010's *Victory Of The Daleks*. There are also references to Dalekanium (*The Dalek Invasion Of Earth*, 1964) and — for the first time since the Peter Cushing films of the 1960s — the Daleks are heard to measure time in "rels."

A.K.A.: Andrew Garfield's career has skyrocketed since his **Doctor Who** appearance; after appearing in such movies as *The Social Network* and *The Imaginarium Of Doctor Parnassus*, Garfield succeeded Tobey Maguire as the webslinger in the reboot movie *The Amazing Spider-Man* (2012). American actor **Ryan Carnes** has appeared in **CSI: New York**, **General Hospital**, **CSI: Miami**, **Bones**, and **NCIS**, but is probably best remembered for a recurring role as Justin in the second season of **Desperate Housewives**.

As shocking as it tries to make itself seem, *Evolution Of The Daleks* isn't really that novel, though at the time it certainly boosted fan speculation (and I'm going to guess that this was a deliberate move for the sheer publicity of it) that Raymond Cusick's Dalek casing design was about to be abandoned permanently. It turns out to be a bit of a red herring, of course, but the implication that a new breed of Daleks would be less murderous is even more so, because down through the years, from the original series through the books and audio plays, the Daleks have already tried on various aspects of humanity and found they didn't fit. One of these days, you'd think they'd get the hint.

As with so many Dalek tales, *Evolution* really stays afloat on the strength of those cast members who portray humans (or at least agreeable human-pig hybrids). Hugh Quarshie is exceptional in both episodes, and while I'm not quite so enamoured of Tallulah, she provides a bit of comic relief. The Doctor's rabbit-out-of-the-hat that saves the day really strains the suspension of disbelief to the breaking point.

THE LAZARUS EXPERIMENT

Martha is crestfallen when the Doctor brings her home, announcing that this is where their travels together end. When she sees her sister in a TV press conference, however, Martha is intrigued. When he hears Professor Richard Lazarus announce the unveiling of an invention that will "change what it means to be human," the Doctor decides to investigate. He and Martha go to the public demonstration of Lazarus' new invention, which – after a near-overload is averted by the Doctor before it can destroy the entire building – apparently regresses the elderly inventor to his youth. But the Doctor, examining Lazarus' DNA, discovers that the transformation is only just beginning, and when the first corpse is found, the Doctor believes that Lazarus is mutating into something that feeds on living flesh. He sets out to put Lazarus' evolutionary experiment to an end, but can't do so without putting Martha in mortal danger. And that's when Martha's mother – who has apparently received confidential information about the Doctor directly from the office of Harold Saxon, a candidate for Prime Minister – decides that Martha's TARDIS travels must end.

David Tennant . . . . The Doctor
Freema Agyeman . . . . Martha Jones
Adjoa Andoh . . . . Francine Jones
Thelma Barlow . . . . Lady Thaw
Bertie Carvel . . . . Mysterious Man
Mark Gatiss . . . . Lazarus
Gugu Mbatha-Raw . . . . Tish Jones
Lucy O'Connell . . . . Olive Lady
Reggie Yates . . . . Leo Jones

This story has been released on DVD

written by Stephen Greenhorn
directed by Richard Clark
music by Murray Gold

Aired on May 5, 2007

CLASSIC CONNECTIONS: The Doctor seems to have some experience as an organist, as he demonstrates both here and in 1985's *Attack Of The Cybermen*.

A.K.A.: Actor **Mark Gatiss** has written several **Doctor Who** stories (including *The Unquiet Dead* and *The Idiot's Lantern*) for television, Big Finish's audio adventures, and numerous novels, and has lent his voice to such characters as the Master in Big Finish audios as well.

BEHIND THE SCENES: Harold Saxon doesn't appear here, but is mentioned in *The Runaway Bride* and *Smith & Jones*; "Vote Saxon" signs were seen in the backgrounds of those episodes, and even in the **Torchwood** episode *Captain Jack Harkness*.

Though there's an interesting hard SF concept in the background of *The Lazarus Experiment*, namely that human DNA contains material left over from abandoned evolutionary branches (an idea also explored in the **Star Trek: The Next Generation** episode *Genesis*), much of this episode is a set-up for events that will unfold later in the season, particularly with regards to Harold Saxon. In that respect, *The Lazarus Experiment* almost feels like half a story.

It redeems itself with some of the Doctor's lamentations on near-immortality, though this turns out to be one instance in the new series where perhaps the CG monster at the heart of the conflict just wasn't quite ready for prime time. Especially with its digitized Mark Gatiss face, the Lazarus monster seems awfully video gamey, and not quite up to the extremely high standards that the revived **Doctor Who**'s effects work has displayed. I give the Mill points for trying, but this is one CG creation that didn't quite meet the bar that has been set.

The interplay with Martha's family is interesting enough to mention here as well, though it ties into the Saxon arc. *Aliens Of London* this isn't, though there are lots of parallels (the Doctor even mentions that this isn't the first time he's been slapped by his traveling companion's mother). Martha's family isn't used in quite the same way that Jackie Tyler and Mickey were in season one, and the reasons to keep showing them from here on out are more plot-related than sentimental.

42

The Doctor is modifying Martha's cell phone for "universal roaming" when the TARDIS suddenly picks up a distress signal. The call for help comes from the cargo ship Pentallian, whose engines have just died, sending it on a slow but fatal trajectory straight into the sun. The moment the Doctor and Martha announce their presence, pressure doors seal them off from the TARDIS, and when the Doctor tries to open the door to evacuate everyone with his timeship, he learns that the temperature in that area has risen dramatically. The ship's auxiliary engines are controlled on the other side of the ship, and a crew member is suffering from an unknown infection. Martha and one of the remaining crew go to try to reach the backup engines, while the Doctor tries to get the main engines restarted, but the ill crew member soon proves to be even more important. Though heavily sedated, he proceeds to get up and utters the phrase "burn with me" over and over just before vaporizing the ship's doctor. He continues to pick off the crew one by one, leaving them with little chance of escaping their fiery fate – and before long, he's not the only one saying "burn with me."

David Tennant . . . . The Doctor
Freema Agyeman . . . . Martha Jones
Adjoa Andoh . . . . Francine Jones
William Ash . . . . Riley Vashtee
Matthew Chambers . . . . Hal Korwin
Michelle Collins . . . . Kath McDonnell
Elize Du Toit . . . . Sinister Woman
Anthony Flanagan . . . . Orin Scannell
Rebecca Oldfield . . . . Erina Lessak
Gary Powell . . . . Dev Ashton
Vinette Robinson . . . . Abi Lerner

This story has been released on DVD

written by Chris Chibnall
directed by Graeme Harper
music by Murray Gold

Aired on May 19, 2007

CLASSIC CONNECTIONS: The fourth Doctor once mentioned a "Pentallian drive" in the 1975 story *Revenge Of The Cybermen*, which was set further in the future than *42*; it may or may not have been related to the ship of the same name.

A **Doctor Who** take on the "story told more or less in real time" chestnut, *42* is a bit darker than some of the season's other fare, coming as it does from the pen of **Torchwood** story editor Chris Chibnall. Still, it's a good spooky story, even though the twist in its tail – the "living star" – isn't anything that couldn't have happened on, say, **Star Trek: The Next Generation**.

Production-value-wise, however, *42* is a real rarity for the new series: it's not just a space-based story, but one that's done well, with enough greasy grimy spaceship innards to make Ridley Scott envious. Now, to be sure, a lot of it is pure illusion – "sweat" can be sprayed on, and there's a lot of dry ice blown onto the sets in front of red lights, so it just *looks* hot. But it does a convincing job of it, and so does the cast. Perhaps betraying Chibnall's **Torchwood** sensibilities, there's a relationship among two of the crew that's twisted into something terrifying by the end of the story. David Tennant's "pain" acting may be just a little bit over the top, but it doesn't last too long.

The subplot tying Martha back to her family on Earth shows that the creative team behind **Doctor Who** has learned a bit of a lesson: find a really good reason to keep going back to the companion's home life. In this case, it's another bread crumb on the trail that leads us to Harold Saxon and the season finale...

THE INFINITE QUEST

The Doctor and Martha barge onto the bridge of a ship commanded by the armored Baltazar, who plans to destroy Earth. The Doctor sets off a chain reaction to destroy Baltazar's ship, but Baltazar escapes. The Doctor and Martha learn from Caw, a robotic bird freeds from captivity aboard the ship, that Baltazar now seeks the location of an ancient spaceship known as the Infinite. Caw provides the Doctor with the first clue to the Infinite's coordinates, leading the time travelers on a wild chase to find the rest of the clues. At every turn, there seem to be adversaries more than willing to kill them both. Baltazar is waiting when the last clue is discovered, and the race is on to find the Infinite. Whoever discovers the derelict ship will be granted their heart's desire, as legend has it, but with both the Doctor and Baltazar aboard, whose desires are more dangerous?

David Tennant	. . . .	The Doctor
Freema Agyeman	. . . .	Martha Jones
Paul Clayton	. . . .	Mergreass
Tom Farrelly	. . . .	Swabb
Stephen Greif	. . . .	Gurney
Barney Harwood	. . . .	Control voice
Anthony Head	. . . .	Baltazar
Lizzie Hopley	. . . .	The Mantasphid Queen
Toby Longworth	. . . .	Caw / Squawk
Steven Meo	. . . .	Pilot Kelvin
Dan Morgan	. . . .	Locke / Warders
Liza Tarbuck	. . . .	Captain Kaliko

This story has been released on DVD

written by Alan Barnes
directed by Gary Russell
music by Murray Gold

Part 1 aired on April 2, 2007
Part 2 aired on April 9, 2007
Part 3 aired on April 16, 2007
Part 4 aired on April 23, 2007
Part 5 aired on April 30, 2007
Part 6 aired on May 7, 2007
Part 7 aired on May 14, 2007
Part 8 aired on May 21, 2007
Part 9 aired on May 28, 2007
Part 10 aired on June 4, 2007
Part 11 aired on June 11, 2007
Complete story aired on June 30, 2007

The Infinite Quest aired in short segments as part of **Totally Doctor Who**, a short-lived behind-the-scenes series aimed at younger viewers.

CLASSIC CONNECTIONS: The Doctor's monologue about relics from the dark times of the universe echoes the seventh Doctor's anguished explanation about the origins of Fenric (*The Curse Of Fenric*, 1989); he also gives the Great Vampire (*State Of Decay*, 1980) its first mention in the new series.

NEW WHO CONNECTIONS: The skeletal crew members of the oil rig look — at least at first — suspiciously like the Vashta Nerada from the following season's two-parter *Silence In The Library / Forest Of The Dead* (2008), but they very quickly cease to *act* like the Vashta Nerada. The design of Baltazar's breathing mask is also very similar to the Hath from 2008's *The Doctor's Daughter*.

A.K.A.: Best known to American audiences as **Anthony Stewart Head** (Giles of **Buffy The Vampire Slayer** fame), the actor behind this story's chief villain appeared in the flesh in 2006's *School Reunion*. He also appeared in the *Excelis* audio stories for Big Finish Productions and the BBC audio drama *Death Comes To Time*.

Produced in the same style as the two animated episodes of the DVD release of the 1969 story *The Invasion*, the animation for *The Infinite Quest* veers between being beautiful and doing the story no favors. The characters are easily distinguishable, but rather like the animated Patrick Troughton in the re-animated missing *Invasion* episodes, they're not very expressive. Most of that is left to the actors' voices. It would've been a joy to see animation based on character designs by artist Lee Sullivan (who created illustrations for the BBC webcasts of *Death Comes To Time* and *Real Time*, prior to the live-action series revival). Where the animation for *Infinite Quest* does excel is in setting the stage with truly alien vistas (populated by truly alien – i.e. non-anthropomorphic – aliens) in a way that's still beyond the live-action series.

Refreshingly, there's not a single mention of Rose anywhere in the story; the mostly-buried running subtext of Martha's attraction to the Doctor gets a payoff when she is granted her "heart's desire," but this is just as quickly turned into something unnerving. For something that was initially designed to be part of **Totally Doctor Who**, a behind-the-scenes/promotional series aimed at the parent show's younger audience members, *The Infinite Quest* is surprisingly scary and violent in places. In fact, almost too much: the Doctor seems to take an abnormally nihilistic pleasure in leaving Baltazar to his fate, not once but twice. Even though we've already seen that the tenth Doctor is occasionally running low on mercy (*The Christmas Invasion, School Reunion, The Family Of Blood*), here he's depicted as being almost *devoid* of it.

Even in the full-episode-length "omnibus" edition of *The Infinite Quest*, which aired the same day as the third season finale, *The Last Of The Time Lords*, the mini-episodic nature of the original short segments is blindingly obvious. It feels like the most attention-span-challenged **Doctor Who** adventure since *Dimensions In Time*.

Animated **Doctor Who** isn't a bad idea – it's been suggested as far back as the "lean years" following the cancellation of the original series in 1989 – but the character artwork of *The Infinite Quest* doesn't live up to its expansive story.

HUMAN NATURE

The Doctor and Martha are on the run from alien pursuers, who have the ability to track the TARDIS. The Doctor stores his own knowledge and personality in a pocketwatch fashioned from Time Lord technology – as well as detailed genetic information – and turns himself, both physically and psychologically, into John Smith, history teacher, a perfectly ordinary human (with odd gaps in his memory) teaching at a boys' school in 1913, on the eve of the First World War. Martha is left to fend for herself, but stays close to "John Smith" in the guise of his maid and guards the pocketwatch containing his true essence with her life. In the process of discovering what it means to be human, the former Time Lord falls in love with a local woman who is attracted to his simplicity and gentle nature – but when the aliens come to Earth, discovering that they have done business with a Time Lord and trying to track down his regenerative DNA to save their dying race, "Doctor John Smith" must risk everything and everyone to protect his fellow humans.

David Tennant . . . . The Doctor
Freema Agyeman . . . . Martha Jones
Peter Bourke . . . . Mr. Chambers
Gerard Horan . . . . Clark
Jessica Hynes . . . . Joan Redfern
Harry Lloyd . . . . Baines
Tom Palmer . . . . Hutchinson
Thomas Sangster . . . . Tim Latimer
Derek Smith . . . . Doorman
Rebekah Staton . . . . Jenny
Pip Torrens . . . . Rocastle

This story has been released on DVD

written by Paul Cornell
directed by Charles Palmer
music by Murray Gold

Aired on May 26, 2007

Matthew White . . . . Phillips
Lauren Wilson . . . . Lucy Cartwright

BOOK CONNECTIONS: This episode and its second part, *The Family Of Blood*, were adapted by Paul Cornell from his own 1995 **Doctor Who** New Adventures novel of the same name. Numerous changes were made, including the omission of the book's meeting between the Doctor's companion and a "future" tenth Doctor (actually one of the aliens in disguise, and "future" since that book originally featured the *seventh* Doctor as played by Sylvester McCoy). In the original novel, the "family" didn't take over human host bodies, but were instead shapeshifters called Aubertides. One carryover from the book is the metafictional mention that "Sydney and Verity" were Smith's parents' names, a nod to the creator of **Doctor Who** and the show's first producer, **Sydney Newman** and **Verity Lambert**.

CLASSIC CONNECTIONS: A book of sketches by "John Smith" reveals the faces of all of the past Doctors, though they're not all clearly seen on screen; these sketches also put to rest the running fan debate about whether or not Paul McGann is "official" as the eighth Doctor (he is).

A.K.A.: **Harry Lloyd** went on to co-star as Will Scarlett in the BBC's 21st century attempt to revive **Robin Hood** on TV, and has appeared in **Game Of Thrones** as Viserys Targaryen. Under his full name, **Thomas Brodie-Sangster**, the actor behind would-be Time Lord Tim Latimer has also appeared in the Big Finish **Doctor Who** audio stories *The Mind's Eye* and *The Bride Of Peladon*, both starring Peter Davison. **Jessica Hynes** co-starred in and co-created the sitcom **Spaced** with Simon Pegg, and returns in a different role in the closing scenes of the final tenth Doctor episode, part 2 of *The End Of Time* (2010).

I'm so torn on this one, because it's one of those cases where I read the book first, and I fully understand why it has consistently remained at the top of the fan polls of 1990s **Doctor Who** print fiction. In its original form, Human Nature was an amazing, and amazingly touching, story – could it survive intact on television, crammed into two 45-minute episodes?

It must be said that the first half of this two-parter is closer to the details of the book than the second. Even then, it has the feeling of being incredibly compressed: John Smith's burgeoning interest in Joan seems to blossom quite suddenly, where it had some room to breathe in the novel. Chalk that up to the evil necessities of the medium of television. The nascent Martha-Smith-Joan love triangle doesn't help matters much, as it takes time away that could've been spent on furthering the Smith-Joan relationship at a more reasonable pace.

Taken on its own merits, *Human Nature* is still quite the atypical **Doctor Who** story, quite unlike anything that's come before, and that's the charm of the novel as well. It's based on quite simply the best **Doctor Who** story ever put on the printed page, so one can see why it was poached for the new series (even if it causes a continuity train wreck – how same the same stuff happen to the same Time Lord twice, to paraphrase Bruce Willis?) But even in the more faithful half of that adaptation, some of what made the original story so compelling was lost.

THE FAMILY OF BLOOD

Martha manages to turn the tables on the Family as they try to force John Smith to change back into the Doctor. Smith, Joan, Martha and the other villagers run for the safety of the school, where the call to arms is sounded ahead of an attack by the Family and their army of scarecrows. Tim, the schoolboy with the pocketwatch containing the Doctor's Time Lord essence, helps to distract the Family, and later, after Smith goes into hiding, brings the watch to him. With the English countryside under siege, even Joan is now convinced that Smith isn't what he seems, and that he can help to save the day...but now that he's found love and happiness in human form, will the Doctor's alter-ego choose to become a Time Lord again?

David Tennant . . . . The Doctor
Freema Agyeman . . . . Martha Jones
Gerard Horan . . . . Clark
Jessica Hynes . . . . Joan Redfern
Harry Lloyd . . . . Baines
Tom Palmer . . . . Hutchinson
Thomas Sangster . . . . Tim Latimer
Rebekah Staton . . . . Jenny
Pip Torrens . . . . Rocastle
Sophie Turner . . . . Vicar

This story has been released on DVD

written by Paul Cornell
directed by Charles Palmer
music by Murray Gold

Aired on June 2, 2007

Matthew White . . . . Phillips
Lauren Wilson . . . . Lucy Cartwright

Thomas Brodie-Sangster was excellent in both of these episodes as Tim, the kid who wound up with the Doctor's essence – there could've been a whole side-story there with him and we didn't spend nearly enough time with him. Following Tim from his youth to the battlefields of World War I to Remembrance Day is powerful and effective, and the Remembrance Day scene in particular may be about the only instance where the televised story actually manages to *exceed* the book. Both of them contained that scene, but it demands a certain visual power that it gained here in spades.

Martha also wins the day here, as it is she who has to save everyone's bacon, repeatedly – almost to the point that the clueless Smith shouldn't even have to ask what the Doctor needs her for as a companion. By that point, she's done enough that it should be plainly obvious. David Tennant does a great job of conveying Smith's angst and his fear of losing everything, but somehow, it's all so rushed, and so full of detours (such as the flashbacks to the tentative idyllic future that Smith risks giving up) that what should be a powerful performance barely has a chance to take root. Yet another intriguing concept, that Smith is a man of peace even without the Doctor's influence, comes and goes in the blink of an eye.

During the Russell T. Davies years, the new series of **Doctor Who** grew a track record of poaching the best of the "expanded universe" tales that were told during the wilderness years, whether they were New Adventures novels or Big Finish audio plays, and then seeming to lose track of the very thing that made the originals so memorable. I realize that only diehard fans are going to spot the retreads, but even when I try to take them on their own merits, the episodes spawned from other media pale next to the stories that inspired them.

SHORT HOPS

...in which the author painted the town red... or... at least... painted some triangles red.

Human Nature disappointed me on television. <u>Human Nature</u> thrilled me on the page. What happened, Russell T. Davies?

I still remember my first encounter with this pivotal entry in the **Doctor Who** New Adventures novels. I had been flown into Columbus, Ohio in early 1997 to interview for a job at a TV station there. The fact that I was flown in from Arkansas seemed to be a positive sign that I was a strong candidate for the job - though it could also have been that the station had sacks of money to throw around. I was staying at a hotel in downtown Columbus, and there was a Waldenbooks within walking distance, so I went there and found <u>Human Nature</u>. I knew nothing of the stellar reputation the book already had (in 1997, it wasn't exactly a new release, and I was also barely on the internet, so I hadn't seen any reviews), but the magic words "Paul Cornell" on the spine convinced me to drop six bucks out of the fifty or so (!) that I was able to cobble together for the trip. (I was really, really broke.)

I went back to my hotel room, cracked open the cover, and got sucked into it to the point that I finished the book in one night, with one break to leave the hotel to find something to eat.

Two things hit me that night, one during dinner and one after.

I was watching the station I was in the running to work for (always a good idea when you're in town for an interview in this business), and there was an upside-down red triangle in lower right hand corner of the screen. *What the hell was this?* It wasn't until I changed channels to spy on my prospective employer's competition that I realized that, in the collective mind of the station with whom I'd interviewed, this was how you indicated a tornado watch was in effect in central Ohio.

(It must have followed me from Arkansas. Probably sat three rows behind me on the plane.)

Strangely enough, the other stations in Columbus had county maps up, like the stations in Arkansas and Oklahoma do, but my would-be employer soldiered on with its upside-down red triangle - surely that was all the information that anyone really needed, right?

The thing that hit me after dinner - way after dinner, like sometime around 2 a.m. - was that <u>Human Nature</u> was, if not the best damned **Doctor Who** book I'd ever read, then at the very least it was tied with <u>Love And War</u>. The common denominator of Mr. Cornell's name on the covers of both was not lost on me. I already knew that, of the many names that appeared on the spines of the New Adventures, Cornell and Kate Orman were my favorites. But with <u>Human Nature</u>, the novel, Cornell captured the essence of the Doctor so well, and turned the McCoy incarnation's decidedly *un*romantic nature on its ear so surprisingly, that I was convinced the man was a genius. (Meaning the writer, not the character.)

That he's written so few **Doctor Who** scripts for audio and television - and has apparently since retired from anything to do with **Who** due to the intense, hypercritical scrutiny of the fans - is our loss. I genuinely wish he'd take another swipe at it, but I can understand his reasons for not wishing to do so. My disappointment with *Human Nature* on TV stems entirely from the fact that the heavily Russell-T.-Davies-revised scripts bore so little resemblance to the book that kept me up until two in the morning in the heart of tornado-or-triangle-fearing Ohio.

As for that TV station in Columbus, Ohio, I was flown back home on their dime and never did get the job at the station with the red triangle. A few months later, the entire department that I might have become a part of was dismissed and replaced: if I'd gotten the job in Columbus, I would've been hundreds of miles from home, and up the creek without a boat, let alone a paddle, in under a year. (Was it, perhaps, because of brilliant ideas like representing public safety alerts with vague heiroglyphics?) Human Nature was the best thing that I got out of that trip. Not really a bad deal, someone footing the bill for me to fly to a city I'd never visited before, sit in a nice hotel room, ponder the meaning of upside-down triangles, eat some Subway and read the best **Doctor Who** novel ever. Thanks, guys.

BLINK

Sally Sparrow's inquisitive nature, and eye for a good photo, leads her to a creepy abandoned house. Under the house's peeling wallpaper, Sally discovers a message – written to her by name – containing a warning from someone called the Doctor. When she returns to the house with her best friend, Sally is stunned when her friend vanishes – and then a man claiming to be her friend's descendant arrives at an appointed time with a letter from his ancestor…in the distant past. Sally goes to share the shocking news with her friend's brother Larry, and finds him obsessed over several DVD easter eggs, all of them containing cryptic (and occasionally incomprehensible) messages from a man called the Doctor. But the video messages from the Doctor are very clear on one thing: alien killers in the guide of weeping angel statues are stalking the Earth…and if Sally and Larry blink when they encounter the statues, they're dead. But why isn't the Doctor on hand to fight the aliens himself?

David Tennant . . . . The Doctor
Freema Agyeman . . . . Martha Jones
Richard Cant . . . . Malcolm Wainwright
Ian Boldsworth . . . . Banto
Lucy Gaskell . . . . Kathy Nightingale
Louis Mahoney . . . . Old Billy
Carey Mulligan . . . . Sally Sparrow
Thomas Nelstrop . . . . Ben Wainwright
Michael Obiora . . . . Billy Shipton
Finlay Robertson . . . . Larry Nightingale
Ray Sawyer . . . . Desk Sergeant

This story has been released on DVD

written by Steven Moffat
directed by Hettie MacDonald
music by Murray Gold

Aired on June 9, 2007

BOOK CONNECTIONS: This episode is based in part on Steven Moffat's short story "What I Did On My Christmas Holidays, By Sally Sparrow", which appeared in the 2006 Doctor Who Annual as a *ninth* Doctor story with a much younger Sally – and *no* Weeping Angels.

BEHIND THE SCENES: *Blink* won the Best Dramatic Presentation (Shortform) Hugo Award in 2008.

UWORP!

Maybe it's saying something when each season's "Doctor-light" episode – filmed with only minimal participation from David Tennant and whoever his sidekick is as the time – turns out to be among my favorites of the year. Previously, I waxed rhapsodic about *Love & Monsters*, an episode that most people seemed to dismiss as lightweight, but *Blink* is some serious old-school **Doctor Who**: familiar and yet unnerving and truly scary in places.

My kudos have to go to the cast of *Blink*, because they were convincing enough in their roles that I didn't feel like I was really missing Tennant and Agyeman for much of the hour. In a way, just knowing that you're in for an episode with very little involvement from the Doctor raises the stakes – the characters here are on their own. And at least in this instance, they're up against a jump-out-of-your-seat-and-hide-behind-the-sofa adversary. The funny thing is, the menace in *Blink* is incredibly simple in execution, but also incredibly effective – really one of the scariest things the new series has pulled off really well. (Now, the thought occurs that maybe one verbal mention could've tied the Melkur from *Keeper Of Traken* into things, but…nah. Not every vampire needs to be a sworn enemy of Rassilon.)

Quite enjoyable stuff, almost faultless among the best of the entire series, and best watched with the lights out.

UTOPIA

The Doctor once again brings the TARDIS to Cardiff to recharge the timeship's engines with energy from the interdimensional rift that runs through the city. When he spots Captain Jack running toward the TARDIS at full speed, the Doctor tries to dematerialize the TARDIS – but Jack, eager to seek the Doctor's help with his newfound immortality, leaps onto the time machine and clings to it as it tries to escape him. The TARDIS makes a rough landing on the eve of what could be the last night of humanity: the universe is collapsing, the stars and galaxies are dying, and the last remnants of humankind huddle in a rickety launch silo, awaiting their orders to board a rocket that will take them to a planet called Utopia. Trying to help ready the rocket, but making little headway, is the enigmatic Professor Yana, who seems to have a strange reaction to the Doctor and the TARDIS. A race called the Futurekind closes in on the last human settlement to feed, and Yana reveals that the rocket really won't work at all. As the Doctor and Jack try to help, Martha notices that Professor Yana has a pocketwatch similar to one which once hid the Doctor's personality and genetic information – a device of Time Lord design. But when the Doctor realizes that he isn't the last Time Lord in the universe, he faces the horrifying revelation that only one other member of his race could've had the drive to survive the Time War…

David Tennant . . . . The Doctor
Freema Agyeman . . . . Martha Jones
John Barrowman . . . . Capt. Jack Harkness
John Bell . . . . Creet
Abigail Canton . . . . Wiry Woman
Chipo Chung . . . . Chantho
Paul Marc Davies . . . . Chieftan
Robert Forknall . . . . Guard
Sir Derek Jacobi . . . . Professor Yana
Deborah MacLaren . . . . Kistane
Neil Reidman . . . . Lieutenant Atillo

This story
has been
released
on DVD

written by Russell T. Davies
directed by Graeme Harper
music by Murray Gold

Aired on June 16, 2007

John Simm . . . . The Master
Rene Zagger . . . . Padra

CLASSIC CONNECTIONS: Both this colony and the isolated human colony seen in *Frontios* (1984) are said to be the last human colonies in existence in the universe, though the implication is that Utopia is set much, much further in the future, during the twilight of the universe itself. During Professor Yana's moments of mental distress, sound clips of Roger Delgado and Anthony Ainley as past incarnations of the Master can be heard.

A.K.A.: Sir Derek Jacobi played the part of the Master in a one-off animated **Doctor Who** story, *Scream Of The Shalka*, as well as starring in a well-received **Doctor Who Unbound** audio story, *Deadline*.

TORCHWOOD CONNECTIONS: Presumably, Jack's chase after the TARDIS takes place immediately on the heels of his disappearance in the **Torchwood** episode *End Of Days* (and the Doctor remarks that the Cardiff rift has seen recent activity, possibly from the opening of the rift in that episode), although *End Of Days* strongly implies that the TARDIS materialized *inside the Torchwood hub*. (Maybe the scattered papers found by the rest of Jack's team were an indication of how fast he ran outside...)

A mish-mash of individual ideas that each could've served as the springboard for an interesting story, *Utopia* suffers a bit from idea overload – the end of the universe, the end of humanity, Jack's reunion with the Doctor, the return of the Master – and it all seems a bit crammed in. Some of these strands are resolved satisfactorily; others seem to get an *"oops, almost forgot to finish telling that part of the story"* wrap-up. Even those threads that *are* tied off here are carried over into the following two episodes, forming a trilogy.

The clear winner here, though, is the return of the Master. Cleverly using an element that was seeded into *Human Nature / The Family Of Blood*, we get possibly the scariest incarnation of the Doctor's arch enemy to walk a soundstage since the late, great Roger Delgado. Sir Derek Jacobi is essentially playing two parts here, and he essays them both magnificently. When Yana transforms himself into the Master, it's the contrast that makes Jacobi's performance so scary, and John Simm, while he claims the part for himself later, just isn't scary in the same way. I wish Jacobi could've stayed for another episode; his Master is far more formidable.

As adversaries go, the Futurekind aren't up to much – a potpourri mix of post-apocalyptic SF "devolution" tropes with a heavy dose of **Mad Max**. Another not-so-subtle element is the "you are not alone" / "YANA" refrain toward the end of the episode, something which made even some of **Babylon 5**'s most *un*subtle flashback sequences seem unobtrusive. Chantho is a far more interestingly developed alien creature than the Futurekind, though the implication that she has deliberately kept the Master from reclaiming his own identity is left a bit disappointingly unresolved.

And as much as I hate to slam the show's music, which I've enjoyed (I've happily paid to import all of the new series soundtrack CDs from the UK before they were available Stateside), I think by this point in the season it was almost blazingly obvious that only one or two pieces of action music had been composed for the entire year, and they had been tracked over everything from the 1910s setting of *Human Nature* to the futuristic settings of *42* and *Utopia*. I was much more impressed by the brassy cue toward the end, following the Master's regeneration – it tied in nicely with the "sound of drums" idea, and so naturally we don't hear it again in either of the following stories.

There's a lot of story in *Utopia*, both interesting (the Master and Jack) and uninteresting (the Futurekind); ultimately the episode seems to rocket through them (pun intended) without tying anything off.

THE SOUND OF DRUMS

The Doctor, Martha and Jack are barely able to escape their fate in the year 100,000,000,000, returning to present-day Earth only when the Doctor is able to modify Jack's teleportation device. But the England they return to is in the thrall of its new Prime Minister, the charismatic Harold Saxon – a man that the time travelers now realize is the Master's new incarnation. The three are declared high-risk enemies of the state, and Martha's family is rounded up and placed under arrest to bait her – and the Doctor – out into the open. Once in office, "Saxon" quietly kills off his entire Cabinet and then announces to the public that he will conduct first contact with an alien race in full public view. The newly elected American President flies to London to demand that Saxon's alien encounter take place with a more international presence, to which Saxon only reluctantly agrees. The Doctor, Martha and Jack teleport aboard the airborne UNIT aircraft carrier Valiant, where first contact will take place with the Toclafane – a name that the Doctor remembers from Gallifreyan children's stories, but not a name that he's ever heard connected to an actual alien species. When the Toclafane appear, they assassinate the President on Saxon's orders, and he then has the Doctor brought before him. Using a laser screwdriver modified with the anti-aging technology pioneered by Dr. Lazarus, the Master ages the Doctor by decades, and kills Jack (with the full knowledge that Jack will recover). Using Jack's teleport, Martha teleports away from the Valiant as millions of Toclafane burst into the Earth's atmosphere, murdering countless people on the ground. The reign of the Master has begun – and now Martha can count only on herself to bring it to an end.

David Tennant . . . . The Doctor
Freema Agyeman . . . . Martha Jones
John Barrowman . . . . Capt. Jack Harkness
Adjoa Andoh . . . . Francine Jones
Lachele Carl . . . . US Newsreader
Elize Du Toit . . . . Sinister Woman
Nicholas Gecks . . . . Albert Dumfries
Olivia Hill . . . . BBC Newsreader
Trevor Laird . . . . Clive Jones
Gerard Logan . . . . Sphere voice
Johnnie Lyne-Pirkis . . . . Sphere voice
Gugu Mbatha-Raw . . . . Tish Jones
Nichola McAuliffe . . . . Vivien Rook
Daniel Ming . . . . Chinese Newsreader
Alexandra Moen . . . . Lucy Saxon

This story has been released on DVD

written by Russell T. Davies
directed by Colin Teague
music by Murray Gold

Aired on June 23, 2007

Sharon Osbourne . . . . herself
John Simm . . . . The Master
Colin Stinton . . . . President
Zoe Thorne . . . . Sphere voice
Reggie Yates . . . . Leo Jones
Ann Widdecombe . . . . herself
McFly . . . . themselves

CLASSIC CONNECTIONS: For the first time in the new series, the Time Lords and their world are seen as the Doctor reminisces about Gallifrey. The description of Gallifrey having orange skies and silver leaves dates back to a verbal description given by the Doctor's granddaughter Susan of her home planet in the first season of the original series – the 1964 six-parter The Sensorites – though this is really the first time that the show's incumbent production team has gone out of its way to stick to that description. The flowing Time Lord ceremonial costume, first seen in 1976's The Deadly Assassin, was originally created by then-costume designer James Acheson, and the design is largely adhered to here. Also seen is a black-and-white garment which was seen on the Time Lords in their first screen appearance, 1969's The War Games. Here, there seems to be an implication that the black and white robes signify that the wearer is a novitiate or a Time Lord in training, which does not seem to have been the case in The War Games.

BOOK CONNECTIONS: The Master's "origin story" here has never before been recounted in the television series; different versions of the Master's origins – though perhaps not necessarily conflicting – can be found in the novel The Dark Path and the Big Finish audio story Master. The mention of Time Lord children being "taken from their families" may or may not conflict with the New Adventures novels' continuity, which states that Gallifrey is a sterile planet whose children are "woven" on looms of genetic material; the families from which the children are taken could just as easily be the novels' families comprised entirely of cousins. On the other hand, the novels' Gallifrey-as-sterile backstory may already have been invalidated by the eighth Doctor's memories of being on Gallifrey with his father (as recounted in the 1996 TV movie). The Time Lord practice of taking families from their children for training parallels a similar practice among the Psi Corps in the '90s SF epic **Babylon 5**, in which humans with telepathic ability are detected at a young age.

The most cohesive story of the new series' "Master Trilogy", *The Sound Of Drums* is a taut thriller with plenty of action and suspense, but again, no clear resolution. Everything is a setup for *The Last Of The Time Lords*, even when that setup makes little sense: why wouldn't the Doctor simply regenerate when enfeebled to such a degree? It's not that I was eager to see David Tennant go – quite the contrary, in fact – but it doesn't add up. (Although there is a precedent for the Doctor being hyper-aged within a single regeneration, in the Tom Baker story *The Leisure Hive*.) Another element that isn't paid off is Lucy Saxon. A lot of time is devoted to setting up that she's been hoodwinked, that her husband isn't who she thinks he is, and yet when it comes down to it – the Toclafane disposing of Lucy's interviewer, the assassination of the President, and the Master ruthlessly unleashing the Toclafane on a helpless world – she seems to be all but getting off on it. She seems to be a thoroughly amoral person, at best, and yet by the time we're done with the trilogy, we know no more about her and her character takes further strange turns (though these may also be the result of scenes left on the cutting room floor).

The performances do more to hold things together than the script does in many places. Tennant, Agyeman and Barrowman are a dynamite combination, and John Simm gives the Master an unnerving ability to switch from maniacal glee to something much more deeply disturbed (and disturbing) on a dime. This is the Master at the absolute end of his rope. Even in the 1996 movie, as unhinged as the Master was, there was more restraint. Here, there's something disturbingly childlike about him. The Gallifrey flashback that explains this state of mind is fascinating, visually engrossing, and it's the visual interpretation of Gallifrey that longtime fans have waited over 40 years to see…and yet, what that flashback really seems to be giving us is an excuse for the Master's behavior, a *rationale* for it. But in this adventure, more than any other, the Master has more blood on his hands than we have ever seen him to have before. It's a sign that he's not just misguided, he's *thoroughly evil*. And yet he's a strangely fey evil – he's a diabolical foil for David Tennant's Doctor, but I can't help but think that the ninth Doctor would've thumped Simm's Master without breaking a sweat.

THE LAST OF THE TIME LORDS

A year after the Master's takeover of Earth, the aged Doctor remains his prisoner aboard the Valiant. After an escape attempt with the help of Martha's family and Captain Jack, the Doctor is subjected to the Master's aging process again, this time winding up as an emaciated, tiny figure unable to regenerate. Still, he promises that he has only one thing to say to his fellow Time Lord – one thing which the Master is not interested in hearing. As for Martha herself, she has spent a year walking the Earth, spreading the word of the Doctor's heroics and planting instructions for an eventual uprising against the Master's rule. With the help of other resistance fighters, Martha discovers the horrifying true nature of the Toclafane, but is eventually captured by the Master and sentenced to death. Even in the face of execution, Martha remains defiant, because she holds the secret to restoring the Doctor to his full power – and then some. But just how far will the Master go to torment his nemesis?

David Tennant . . . . The Doctor
Freema Agyeman . . . . Martha Jones
John Barrowman . . . . Capt. Jack Harkness
Natasha Alexander . . . . Woman
Adjoa Andoh . . . . Francine Jones
Tom Ellis . . . . Thomas Milligan
Tom Golding . . . . Lad
Ellie Haddington . . . . Professor Docherty
Trevor Laird . . . . Clive Jones
Gerard Logan . . . . Sphere voice
Johnnie Lyne-Pirkis . . . . Sphere voice
Gugu Mbatha-Raw . . . . Tish Jones

This story
has been
released
on DVD

written by Russell T. Davies
directed by Colin Teague
music by Murray Gold

Aired on June 30, 2007

Alexandra Moen . . . . Lucy Saxon
John Simm . . . . The Master
Zoe Thorne . . . . Sphere voice
Reggie Yates . . . . Leo Jones

That's *it!?* Remember when "One Year Later" was such a new, shocking thing back when the 2000s revival of **Battlestar Galactica** did it (way before **Desperate Housewives** did it, by the way)? In this case, it just seems cheap – and truth be told, it's not a new device to **Doctor Who**. The novels have done it (Seeing I) and the audio plays have done it (*Return Of The Daleks*) with varying degrees of success; Seeing I made it an incredibly effective and truly shocking thing, while the aforementioned Big Finish audio story got through that year in mere seconds, making it a whiz-past-your-head, what-the-hell? kind of thing that wasted any opportunity that might potentially have existed there. *Last Of The Time Lords*, unfortunately, is more akin to the latter.

It's interesting to see Martha come to the forefront, but ultimately, despite Freema Agyeman's wonderful performance throughout the third season, the character's potential has been wasted by a whole season of episodes in which the Doctor either wished Rose was there, pined away for Rose, or was more than a little condescending to Martha because *she wasn't Rose*. I can see the narrative sense in having the Doctor mourn Rose's loss for one, maybe two stories following her departure. But the way the third season was structured, he was agonizing about it in *nearly every episode*. Martha lost out on valuable character development time because of it. Even after she literally saves everyone's bacon in this episode, her missing year of heroically walking the Earth and mounting a resistance against the Master's domination is glossed over. It's almost heartening in the end when she leaves – not because I dislike the character or the actress. I think the character and the actress were great. It's just that for her to stay, having endured what she's endured between saving the world and putting up with being the Doctor's "rebound girl", would make Martha into a doormat; that she finally worked up the self-respect and dignity to get the hell out of the TARDIS at least is consistent with the character's intelligence and poise from her introduction…moreso than some of the stuff that she'd said and done before in the episodes in between.

John Simm's Master continues to go right off the rails into insanity, but also shows colder, more calculating moments here. We're treated to a virtual reprise of the Doctor and the Master's last confrontation in the final original series story *Survival*, though the real treat is when the Master somehow manages to stave off his own regeneration just to spite the Doctor. The Master reborn is also the Master so far off his rocker that his own survival doesn't even matter – though somehow hinting at this earlier in the episode might have ratcheted the tension up considerably. It's a logical extension of how completely unhinged the Master had become by the time of the 1996 TV movie.

Last Of The Time Lords borrows so many iconic scenes from other media entities that it's just mind-boggling. From the Master's Viking funeral (shot almost identically to that of Darth Vader from **Return Of The Jedi**) to the **Superman: The Movie**-esque reversal of time to the too-obvious **Flash Gordon** "The End…?" gag in which someone takes the Master's ring, to say nothing of the *deus ex machina* that restores the Doctor to full health (and then some, with powers that we've never seen the character display before), this episode almost makes me wonder if Russell T. Davies wrote himself into such a tightly apocalyptic corner with his cliffhanger that the resolution had no chance of living up to it.

TIME CRASH
(2007 CHILDREN IN NEED SPECIAL SCENE)

The Doctor solemnly gets the TARDIS underway after he bids farewell to Martha Jones and leaves her with her family on Earth, but the quiet is shattered as his timeship lurches uncontrollably – and suddenly has another occupant, a man in full Edwardian cricket regalia. A very familiar man, as it turns out: the Doctor is at a loss to explain why his fifth incarnation is suddenly sharing his TARDIS with him, but both know instantly that it's not good news. Much like the Doctor, the TARDIS has collided with its earlier self, and it'll take more than an exchange of insurance information to prevent space and time from collapsing as a result...

David Tennant . . . . The Doctor
Peter Davison . . . . The Doctor

written by Steven Moffat
directed by Graeme Harper
music by Murray Gold

Aired on November 16, 2007

This story has been released on DVD

CLASSIC CONNECTIONS: There were numerous in-jokes on past **Doctor Who** adventures, including a mention of zeiton ore (something the sixth Doctor ran out of in *Vengeance On Varos*). If you're interested in making a donation to Children In Need, please visit **www.bbc.co.uk/pudsey/** to find out more about the charity, where the money goes, what's up with the little yellow bear, and how you can help.

BEHIND THE SCENES: *Time Crash* was a 7-minute scene written for the BBC's 2007 Children In Need telethon, with the actors, directors, and crew donating their time and talent. Technically, it takes place during the final moments of *Last Of The Time Lords*, **between** Martha's departure and the TARDIS' collision with the *Titanic*. Director **Graeme Harper** also directed Peter Davison's final adventure as the incumbent Doctor, *Caves Of Androzani*, in 1984 – so he *remains* Davison's last director as the Doctor on TV. Davison is now tied with Tennant for appearing in the most in-character **Doctor Who** Children In Need specials, having also appeared in 1993's *Dimensions In Time*; technically, *The Five Doctors* was originally shown as part of the Children In Need telethon in 1983, but unlike *Time Crash* and the 2005 Children In Need special, it was not specially made just for the event.

A fun little piece for the Children In Need charity event, *Time Crash* is one of the new series' most overt valentines to the original series. In the 2007 season, we heard mentions of Sea Devils and Axons, saw Time Lords in full ceremonial garb, heard Professor Yana having hallucinations that included the voices of Roger Delgado and Anthony Ainley, saw the Macra for the first time in 40 years, and saw the faces of all nine of David Tennant's predecessors sketched in John Smith's Journal of Impossible Things. 2007 was a year of crystal clear homages to classic **Who**, and *Time Crash* was the icing on the cake.

Peter Davison was one of my two favorite original series Doctors, next only to Sylvester McCoy, so that alone wins points. That he looks remarkably like he did in the early 1980s, give or take some very graceful aging, just makes his appearance that much more impressive. Davison didn't look so different that we needed the "time differential" explanation for his apparent aging. If anything, he looked great, and I dare say that an audience that's prepared to suspend its disbelief for a time-traveling police box can probably overlook one actor's very minimal signs of age – it's not something that needed attention drawn to it. If anything was distractingly different about his appearance, it was the abnormally huge stalk of celery (maybe he's just happy to see his future self).

There was something remarkably old-school about the technobabble crisis that the two Doctors needed to solve – something warm and comfortably Bidmead-esque about it. I suppose there's a potential can of worms opened by nailing down that the tenth Doctor saves the day simply by doing what his fifth incarnation remembers seeing him do, as this would seem to make a hash of every multi-Doctor story before it. We'll just file that one away with the multiple explanations for the fall of Atlantis – the Master destroyed it by unleashing Kronos, the Fish People destroyed it, Torri Higginson and Paul McGillion were sacked (no, sorry, I was thinking of **Stargate Atlantis** there), take your pick.

Speaking of technobabble, one thing I wish they would've left out was the "desktop theme" gag, explaining away the current interior appearance of the TARDIS as nothing more than user's choice. I found that to be a hugely disappointing development, especially when it's dropped in our laps as nothing more than a cheap gag. Since the new series started, I had interpreted the TARDIS' appearance as the result of massive damage from the Time War, with the Doctor being forced to strip the ship down to its organic heart (as per the many mentions that TARDISes are grown rather than built) and jerry-rigging stuff like the laptop screen and various dangling wires to the console to keep her flying. The notion that the Doctor has *chosen* for the TARDIS to look this dilapidated is a bit ridiculous. (Then again, perhaps the fifth Doctor was guessing wildly as to why the ship looks as it does, and the tenth simply said nothing to avoid contaminating his own foreknowledge of the future.)

SERIES 4: 2007-2010
VOYAGE OF THE DAMNED

The bow of the Titanic slices through the skin of the TARDIS, much to the Doctor's alarm, though he is able to pull the timeship out of the collision so it can repair itself. Landing within the Titanic, the Doctor is stunned to find alien life forms and helpful robotic angels mingling with the passengers…until he looks out a window and discovers that he's aboard a spacefaring cruise ship bearing the same name. He befriends a cocktail waitress named Astrid, who admits that she only signed up for the opportunity to travel through space, but before the Doctor has finished sizing her up as a new companion aboard the TARDIS, things start to go disastrously wrong. The Titanic's captain, in observation of Christmas being celebrated below on Earth, dismisses his bridge crew, disables the shields, and steers his ship into the path of oncoming meteors. Several direct hits ensue, causing many deaths and leaving the Titanic reeling out of its orbit. But instead of just burning up when it comes through the Earth's atmosphere, the ship's powerful engines will overload, destroying all life on the planet. The angelic robot servants on the ship begin to slaughter the few survivors aboard. The Doctor doesn't have much time to save the day, barely managing to keep Astrid and several passengers alive. But who has set the Titanic on a deliberate course for disaster in the first place?

David Tennant . . . . The Doctor
Kylie Minogue . . . . Astrid Peth
Ewan Bailey . . . . Alien voice
Debbie Chazen . . . . Foon Van Hoff
George Costigan . . . . Max Capricorn
Bernard Cribbins . . . . Wilfred Mott
Stefan Davis . . . . Kitchen Hand
Andrew Havill . . . . Chief Steward
Paul Kasey . . . . The Host
Bruce Lawrence . . . . Engineer
Jessica Martin . . . . voice of the Queen
Colin McFarlane . . . . Alien voice

This story has been released on DVD

written by Russell T. Davies
directed by James Strong
music by Murray Gold

Aired on December 25, 2007

Geoffrey Palmer . . . . Capt. Hardaker
Clive Rowe . . . . Marvin Van Hoff
Clive Swift . . . . Mr. Copper
Russell Tovey . . . . Midshipman Frame

Jason Mohammad . . . . Newsreader
Gray O'Brien . . . . Rickston Slade

Jimmy Vee . . . . Bannakaffalatta
Nicholas Witchell . . . . himself

CLASSIC CONNECTIONS: The Heavenly Hosts bear an uncanny resemblance to the equally helpful (and, ultimately, equally deadly) Vocs and Super Vocs from the Tom Baker story *The Robots Of Death*.

A.K.A.: Guest star **Bernard Cribbins** may well be the new series guest star with the longest association to the golden days of **Doctor Who** — he appeared as hapless police constable Tom Campbell in the 1966 film adaptation *Daleks: Invasion Earth 2150 A.D.*, starring alongside Peter Cushing as Doctor Who. Cribbins continued to appear as Wilfred throughout the fourth season and the 2009 specials. **Clive Swift** previously appeared as the loathsome funeral director Jobel in 1985's *Revelation Of The Daleks*. Those wondering whether or not there's werewolf blood in the royal family's bloodline (see *Tooth And Claw*), here's your answer: the voice of the Queen is provided by actress **Jessica Martin**, who played a female werewolf encountered by the seventh Doctor in 1988's *The Greatest Show In The Galaxy*. Though best known for co-starring in the series **As Time Goes By** with Dame Judi Dench, **Geoffrey Palmer** also appeared in classic **Doctor Who**, in the Pertwee-era stories *The Mutants* and *Doctor Who And The Silurians* (in which he played the unfortunate civil servant who spread the Silurian plague to the rest of the human race).

BEHIND THE SCENES: A dedication appeared at the end of the episode to **Verity Lambert**, the first producer of **Doctor Who**, who died on November 22, 2007 — one day before the 43rd anniversary of the series she was so instrumental in launching.

With the possible exceptions of *Blink* and *Gridlock*, *Voyage Of The Damned* is one of the best **Doctor Who** adventures of 2007. Astrid is written as possibly the strongest potential companion character that the new series has seen, even moreso than Rose or Martha, and Kylie Minogue rises to the occasion admirably.

Considering that her roots are in acting and her staggeringly successful pop music career came later, perhaps it's unfair to have expected anything less from Ms. Minogue, but I was pleasantly surprised by her appearance here. Without falling back on the trappings of her Earthly stage persona, she inhabits the character with skill and grace, and I was truly sorry that Astrid didn't get to join the Doctor aboard the TARDIS. After *The Runaway Bride* gave us a likely companion who turned the Doctor down, *Voyage Of The Damned* gives us someone who eagerly says "yes" to traveling through time — and then doesn't survive to take even so much as her first journey. I'm not sure why the Doctor has been laying a big smooch on every TV sidekick since Grace Holloway, but if there's one story where it was justified, this would be it.

PARTNERS IN CRIME

On Earth in 2008, the Doctor investigates a company called Adipose Industries, the makers of a diet pill that magically makes the fat "walk away," suspecting that there's something sinister to their miracle cure for obesity. Little does he know that his friend, former runaway bride Donna Noble, is also at Adipose, having just taken a job in health & safety. Also realizing that Adipose's claims are too good to be true, Donna begins her own investigation. Donna's family has criticized her for not sticking to any one job for any length of time since the mysterious circumstances around her not getting married, but what she can't explain to them is that she regrets not taking the Doctor up on his offer of travel in the TARDIS — and hopes she'll see him again someday. As she and the Doctor independently snoop around Adipose, they both learn of the more sinister agenda behind the miracle diet pill — and each other's presence. Just as quickly, they're both on the run, with Donna leaving no doubt that she expects to be off with the Doctor once the current crisis is over. There's just one problem: she's assuming that they'll both survive the wrath of the mysterious Mrs. Foster once the secret of Adipose is out.

David Tennant . . . . The Doctor
Catherine Tate . . . . Donna Noble
Martin Ball . . . . Roger Davey
Bernard Cribbins . . . . Wilfred Mott
Jessica Gunning . . . . Stacey Harris
Verona Joseph . . . . Penny Carter
Sue Kelvin . . . . Suzette Chambers
Jacqueline King . . . . Sylvia Noble
Sarah Lancashire . . . . Miss Foster
Billie Piper . . . . Rose Tyler
Chandra Ruegg . . . . Clare Pope

This story
has been
released
on DVD

written by Russell T. Davies
directed by James Strong
music by Murray Gold

Aired on April 5, 2008

Rachid Sabitri . . . . Craig Staniland
Jonathan Stratt . . . . Taxi Driver

CLASSIC CONNECTIONS: The Doctor's observation about how things can come and go through a catflap are nearly identical to a similar comment his seventh incarnation made in 1989's *Survival* – a story whose working title was *Catflap*.

BEHIND THE SCENES: The episode carries a dedication to **Howard Attfield**, the late actor who played the role of Donna's father in *The Runaway Bride*. He originally shot some scenes for *Partners In Crime*, but upon his death, the bulk of his dialogue was rewritten for Donna's grandfather, played by Bernard Cribbins.

A cheerfully light-hearted story with twists both fun and ominous, *Partners In Crime* does a great job of reintroducing Donna to the show and presenting her as, perhaps, a slightly more sympathetic character than she was in *The Runaway Bride*. That's not to say that she isn't still aggravating in her own uniquely endearing way, but it's a breath of fresh air after the Doctor's relationship with both of his previous companions became increasingly angsty.

This brings us to one of my favorite things in *Partners*: it addresses, in dialogue, on camera, that the Doctor (and, by extension, **Doctor Who**) is going to get away from the "companion has a crush on the Doctor" plot element that was a staple of the first three seasons of the new show. It was an unusual thing to do with Rose, but in having Martha *also* harbor unrequited love for the Time Lord, it became a cliché that didn't do any of the companion characters any favors. Here, it's stated up front that the Doctor isn't looking for anything more than a platonic relationship at most. The idea that Donna has put her life on hold *just in case the Doctor shows up again* is an interesting glimpse into her character; in that respect, she's a sadder case than Sarah Jane Smith. At least Sarah had traveled with the Doctor for a long time before returning to Earth and finding everyday life unfulfilling (at least until she got her own show). For Donna to have done that after just *one* adventure is very telling.

There's also a surprising sting in the tail with the appearance of Rose in the closing moments of the show. The show's makers had made no secret of the fact that Rose would be reappearing in the fourth season, and even if they had tried to cover it up, people had already seen Billie Piper filming scenes on the streets of Cardiff (and obviously not for **The Secret Diary Of A Call Girl**, unless Belle's suddenly packing a giant laser as an insurance policy).

The scene in which the Doctor and Donna have an extremely animated (but silent) conversation through two panes of glass was priceless, one of the best comedic moments the new **Doctor Who** has yet pulled off. I went back and watched it several times – it simply does *not* get old. Despite some fans decrying the casting of Catherine Tate as a regular, she clearly brings her whole bag of tricks to the table in this one, with both dramatic and comedic moments on display. Such a relief after all that unrequited love!

THE FIRES OF POMPEII

The Doctor brings Donna to ancient Pompeii, only to discover that they've arrived on the eve of the eruption of Vesuvius. A woman in red robes who immediately noticed the time travelers after their arrival reports to the rest of her order – the blue box foretold by prophecy has appeared. When the Doctor and Donna race back to get in the TARDIS and leave, the blue box is exactly what they don't find: one of the street merchants sold it as a piece of art. The Doctor finds it soon enough, but now there's a new problem: Donna doesn't want to leave without saving some of the people of Pompeii from their fate, something which the Doctor assures her is impossible. Trying to outdo some of the local soothsayers, Donna warns everyone she can about the volcano, but the red-robed sisterhood marks her for death for the crime of false prophecy. The Doctor discovers that one of the locals is apparently in possession of advanced computer circuitry, but doesn't know exactly what it is. Even if he saves Donna and tracks down the alien attempting to influence history, the Doctor still can't save the people of Pompeii.

David Tennant . . . . The Doctor
Catherine Tate . . . . Donna Noble
Sasha Behar . . . . Spurrina
Gerard Bell . . . . Major Domo
Lorraine Burroughs . . . . Thalina
Peter Capaldi . . . . Caecilius
Tracey Childs . . . . Metella
Phil Cornwell . . . . Stallholder
Phil Davis . . . . Lucius
Francesca Fowler . . . . Evelina
Karen Gillan . . . . Soothsayer

This story has been released on DVD

written by James Moran
directed by Colin Teague
music by Murray Gold

Aired on April 12, 2008

Francois Pandolfo . . . . Quintus
Victoria Wicks . . . . High Priestess

A.K.A.: Come along, Pond, it's volcano day! If the face-painted Soothsayer looks a little familiar, it's **Karen Gillan** – the future Amy Pond – making her **Doctor Who** debut. **Tracey Childs** had already appeared as an enigmatic time traveler with fascist leanings named Klein in an early Big Finish **Doctor Who** audio adventure, *Colditz* (which also marked David Tennant's first appearance in an official **Doctor Who** project); she reprised the role of Klein for several later Big Finish stories after guest starring in this episode. **Peter Capaldi** plays a much larger role in **Torchwood: Children Of Earth** (2009) as the morally conflicted public servant Mr. Frobisher, before being announced as the Doctor's thirteenth incarnation in 2013.

AUDIO CONNECTIONS: Pompeii in 79 A.D. was positively crawling with incarnations of the Doctor. Somewhere across town, the seventh Doctor and Melanie were also trying to escape the eruption of Pompeii in the audio story *The Fires Of Vulcan* – though they weren't trying to battle an alien influence.

Just before the fourth season of the new **Doctor Who** kicked off, I did a marathon viewing/listening of all the classic **Doctor Who** stories I either hadn't seen, or didn't remember well. One thing that I was surprised to find myself enjoying was the wide variety of treatments of historical subjects in the Hartnell days – ranging from deadly serious drama to broad farce, the '60s historical stories seldom had to resort to the kind of tired sci-fi macguffin that this episode does.

And what's really sad about that is that the rest of the episode is really fine – a lot is established here where Donna is concerned, with regards to how much she wants to help those in need and how much she'll stand up to the Doctor to accomplish that. We also get some nicely fleshed-out characters from Pompeii, who don't deserve the fate that awaits them, and I felt a little bit cheated by the end of the hour that more time wasn't spent on that element than on the CGI rock critter smashing everything in sight. The "lone alien crashed in an escape pod" gag is also past its sell-by date.

In short, there's a great story in *The Fires Of Pompeii*, but the sci-fi elements distract from the emotional throughline of the story, the actual location filming in Italy, and what could've been a new lease of life for purely historical stories in **Doctor Who**.

PLANET OF THE OOD

Donna's first visit to the future brings the TARDIS to a barren, snowy planet, where she and the Doctor find a dying Ood. But before it dies, it says "the circle must be broken" and then glares at them with red eyes – the same sign of malignant external mind control that the Doctor witnessed in his last encounter with the Ood. The Doctor and Donna spot signs of civilization, though Donna becomes less convinced of that when she discovers that it's a sales and distribution center for Ood slaves. Donna is disgusted that the advanced society that humanity has become is still relying on slave labor, but the Doctor is curious as to what is driving some Ood to calmly kill their masters, and what is causing others to fly into a deadly berserker rage. Then the time travelers discover the secret that is taken from the Ood before they are "processed" into docile servants…but that secret may die with them as the Ood revolt against all humans on the planet *en masse*.

David Tennant . . . . The Doctor
Catherine Tate . . . . Donna Noble
Silas Carson . . . . voice of the Ood
Paul Clayton . . . . Mr. Bartle
Ayesha Dharker . . . . Salana Mercurio
Roger Griffiths . . . . Commander Kess
Tariq Jordan . . . . Rep
Paul Kasey . . . . Ood Sigma
Tim McInnerny . . . . Mr. Halpen
Adrian Rawlins . . . . Dr. Ryder

This story has been released on DVD

written by Keith Temple
directed by Graeme Harper
music by Murray Gold

Aired on April 19, 2008

A.K.A.: Tim McInnerny was a regular throughout the run of **Blackadder**, though he sat out most of the third season. He's also appeared in **The Young Indiana Jones Chronicles**, *Erik The Viking, Johnny English Reborn*, and **MI-5**.

The Doctor is no newcomer to helping enslaved species throw off the shackles of servitude, but in *Planet Of The Ood* it all happens so quickly that you almost don't have time to think about what just happened. A story about helping an oppressed people escape slavery is worthwhile, but this story's treatment of that theme is surprisingly shallow and simplistic. Losing just a little bit of the breakneck-speed action sequences – running/shooting soldiers, and the warehouse chase with the lifting claw – could have allowed more time to be spent on building up the backbone of the story.

The Ood are one of the more interesting alien inventions of the new series thus far, so it is interesting to see them and to hear more about them. It's also refreshing to see how quickly Donna adjusts to the Ood's appearance (versus Rose's reaction in season two), and her strong streak of decency. But she also has to navigate a minefield of plot holes, not the least of which is the very quickly glossed-over (and rather graphic) transformation of a human into an Ood – an explanation is given which might as well be summed up as magic, and it's an implausible *deus ex machina* that rushes the story to its completion. Maybe this should've been a two-parter – or maybe it should've been a little more coherent so that the story was equal to the performances and characterization that are built up for the first ¾ of the episode.

THE SONTARAN STRATAGEM

A call from Martha brings the TARDIS back to Earth, just in time for Donna and the Doctor to witness a UNIT raid on the Atmos factory. Standard-issue in more than half the automobiles in the world, Atmos cancels out all harmful pollution emissions from any car – and the Doctor recognizes it as something far ahead of current human technology. But as everyone knows, Atmos is the invention of former teen prodigy Luke Rattigan, who now heads his own academy for developing young genius. A visit to Rattigan's academy reveals that he is in league with a Sontaran invasion force, a discovery from which the Doctor barely escapes alive. He decides to dissect an Atmos device for himself, only to accidentally trigger a weapon within it that emits toxic gas. Using a clone of Martha to keep UNIT's attention away from the real danger, the Sontarans activate all of the gas emitters in all of the Atmos-equipped cars worldwide…

David Tennant . . . . The Doctor
Catherine Tate . . . . Donna Noble
Freema Agyeman . . . . Dr. Martha Jones
Christian Cooke . . . . Ross Jenkins
Bernard Cribbins . . . . Wilfred Mott
Rupert Holliday Evans . . . . Colonel Mace
Rad Kaim . . . . Worker
Jacqueline King . . . . Sylvia Noble
Eleanor Matsuura . . . . Jo Nakashima
Christopher Ryan . . . . General Staal
Elizabeth Ryder . . . . Atmos voice
Ryan Simpson . . . . Luke Rattigan

written by Helen Raynor
directed by Douglas McKinnon
music by Murray Gold

Aired on April 26, 2008

This story has been released on DVD

Clive Standen . . . . Private Harris
Dan Starkey . . . . Commander Skorr
Wesley Theobald . . . . Private Gray

CLASSIC CONNECTIONS: The Sontarans last appeared with *The Two Doctors* (namely Colin Baker and Patrick Troughton) in 1985, though fanmade productions such as *Mindgame* and *Shakedown* revisited them after the cancellation of classic **Doctor Who**. This is the first episode to give, in dialogue, the revised name for UNIT – the *Unified* Intelligence Taskforce – which was changed from the original name, United Nations Intelligence Taskforce, for completely non-fictional legal reasons. Despite the change, dialogue elsewhere in the episode still says that UNIT gets its funding from the United Nations. Speaking of UNIT, a bit of fun is poked at the long-standing debate over whether the third Doctor's stint with UNIT took place in the 1970s or 1980s (see *Mawdryn Undead*) – and the issue certainly isn't resolved. The Sontarans are apparently aware of the Time War, but for whatever reason were "not allowed to take part in it." The reference to the human female's "weak thorax" is a riff on the 1975 story *The Sontaran Experiment*, in which Field Major Styre noted differences in the thorax between the human genders.

A.K.A.: **Christopher Ryan**, Mike of **The Young Ones** fame, previously appeared in parts 5-8 of the 1986 *Trial Of A Time Lord* season as the Mentor Kiv, whose radical brain surgery left the sixth Doctor's companion Peri with a killer headache.

For their handful of appearances in the classic series – a grand total of four stories – the Sontarans have certainly ignited the imagination of fandom down through the years, placing them in the upper echelons of favorite enemies from the original series. Their lust for war and their hyper-macho code of honor, and the cloned nature of their species, are interesting things to build on, along with their critical weaknesses. Perhaps moreso than any classic series villain revisited in the new series, the Sontarans are back, perfectly intact, and while their new costumes aren't exactly identical to those of the original series, they look and sound a lot like their 1970s and '80s counterparts.

That same fate isn't, however, shared by UNIT. In the **Torchwood** episode *Fragments*, there was a clear implication that a change had taken place in the organization that the Brigadier once headed with a stiff upper lip and as few uniformed extras as allowed; "indefinite detention of enemy combatants" was now a staple of UNIT's playbook. This episode makes that explicit with Donna's reference to Guantanamo Bay, but what bugs me even more is Martha's dialogue about changing UNIT for the better from the inside – in other words, she's doing exactly what Captain Jack has been doing with Torchwood. Only Torchwood *needed* that change to its mandate; when and where and how did UNIT become this way? Even one momentary snippet of dialogue attributing this drastic change to 9/11 would satisfy me, because that's the most likely answer; I guess now that we consider the post-*Doomsday* Torchwood to be good guys, UNIT's now in the unenviable position of being the poster child for heavy-handed military tactics. Falling into Trap One, indeed.

Martha's return is welcome, and it's nice to see her get along with Donna instead of a rehash of the snippiness between Rose and Sarah. Another nice reversal is Donna's return home, which is handled without the high drama of *Aliens Of London* or *The Lazarus Experiment*; instead, her absence has barely been noticed, and the scene where we're reminded that Donna's entire family has already met the Doctor in a variety of weird but completely unconnected circumstances is genuinely funny. Donna continues to be the best companion that the new series has given us yet, and her almost-huggable grandfather is the most sympathetic "companion's family" character we've seen since Jackie Tyler.

The Sontaran Stratagem reminded me of how much I liked the Sontarans way back when.

THE POISON SKY

A worldwide crisis is declared as Atmos-equipped cars across the globe poison the atmosphere with toxic gases. Meanwhile, the Sontarans' clone of Martha continues to undermine UNIT's preparations for all-out war against the invaders, but she's also been noticed by the Doctor, who uses her to find the real Martha and discover why the Sontarans – usually a race that craves all-out war – are sneaking around with tactics such as poisoning the atmosphere. But the TARDIS is not at his disposal: the Sontarans have teleported it to their ship, with Donna inside. As he uncovers the plan to terraform Earth into a world suitable for breeding more cloned Sontaran warriors, the Doctor has a life-or-death choice to make – and he has to offer one to the Sontarans as well.

David Tennant . . . . The Doctor	
Catherine Tate . . . . Donna Noble	
Freema Agyeman . . . . Dr. Martha Jones	
Leeshon Alexander . . . . Male Student	
Lachele Carl . . . . US Newsreader	
Christian Cooke . . . . Ross Jenkins	
Bernard Cribbins . . . . Wilfred Mott	
Rupert Holliday Evans . . . . Colonel Mace	
Meryl Fernandes . . . . Female Student	
Bridget Hodgson . . . . Captain Price	
Jacqueline King . . . . Sylvia Noble	
Billie Piper . . . . Rose Tyler	
Christopher Ryan . . . . General Staal	

written by Helen Raynor
directed by Douglas McKinnon
music by Murray Gold

Aired on May 3, 2008

This story has been released on DVD

Ryan Simpson . . . . Luke Rattigan
Clive Standen . . . . Private Harris
Dan Starkey . . . . Commander Skorr
Wesley Theobald . . . . Private Gray
Kirsty Wark . . . . herself

CLASSIC CONNECTIONS: The Brigadier gets his first mention in the new series, even though he isn't seen; apparently there's only one Brigadier serving in UNIT, since Colonel Mace seems to instantly know who the Doctor is talking about.

Rounding off the best classic series villain revival since the Autons showed up in *Rose*, *The Poison Sky* keeps the Sontarans on course and even justifies their unusually sneaky behavior – the dialogue even points up how oddly they're acting. These are the Sontarans of old, and it's good to have them back.

If there's anything that's a little bizarre, it's the extended conversation between Martha and her clone. The odd empathy that they feel for each other adds little to the story, and feels like a detour that was dropped into the script to pad it out. Where Donna continued to be a spectacular breath of fresh air in the first part, *Poison Sky* paints her in more traditional new-series-companion colors, getting weepy if the Doctor is even within throwing distance of thinking about sacrificing himself to defeat the menace of the week. UNIT continues to be a study in contrasts – heavy-handed militaristic enetity in part one, noble warriors with an eve-of-battle speech worthy of ***Independence Day*** in part two. The UNIT colonel's insistence that his Sontaran foe turn to face him before he pulls the trigger is an interesting facet; so much has been made, earlier in the episode, of the Sontarans' weakness in the back of their necks that you'd think that was coming into play.

Perhaps the most fascinating aspect of this two-parter, by the end of it, is the notion of turning every motor vehicle on Earth against the human race. With all of the focus on the Sontarans, I almost wonder if this concept might not have gotten more airtime (pun intended) with a new villain that didn't demand the focus that the Sontarans do. It's a fascinating idea that almost becomes window dressing at times.

THE DOCTOR'S DAUGHTER

The Doctor and Donna – with Martha along as an unwitting passenger due to the TARDIS' unexpected takeoff – arrive in a war-torn underground world where the Doctor is immediately held at gunpoint by soldiers and subjected to a mechanical tissue sampling process that uses his DNA to create a new soldier – a young girl with a brilliant mind, two hearts, and, like the rest of the human soldiers, a genetically-programmed knowledge of the long war between the humans and the fishlike Hath. She immediately joins in a pitched battle against the Hath, and winds up saving her human comrades – but not before the Hath have abducted Martha. The Doctor's "daughter" – to whom Donna gives the name Jenny – is locked up with the time travelers for fear that she's been swayed by the Doctor's promise to stop the humans from committing genocide against the Hath, and vice-versa. Jenny proves to be as resourceful, and ultimately as compassionate, as the Doctor herself...but when she becomes the key to ending the bloodshed, she may also find out whether or not she can regenerate.

David Tennant . . . . The Doctor
Catherine Tate . . . . Donna Noble
Freema Agyeman . . . . Dr. Martha Jones
Joe Dempsie . . . . Cline
Akin Gazi . . . . Carter
Paul Kasey . . . . Hath Peck
Olalekan Lawal Jr. . . . . Soldier
Ruari Mears . . . . Hath Gable
Georgia Moffett . . . . Jenny
Nigel Terry . . . . Cobb

This story has been released on DVD

written by Stephen Greenhorn
directed by Alice Troughton
music by Murray Gold

Aired on May 10, 2008

A.K.A.: Actress **Georgia Moffett** really *is* the Doctor's daughter – just not *this* Doctor. She's the daughter of Peter Davison, who played the Doctor from 1982 through 1984 (and in the Children In Need mini-episode *Time Crash*). She guest starred in one of Davison's Big Finish audios, *Red Dawn*, in 2000, and in 2004 she auditioned for the part of Rose Tyler. She lent her voice to the second and last animated tenth Doctor adventure, *Dreamland*. She married David Tennant after his departure from **Doctor Who**, so now she's the Doctor's wife too.

The Doctor's Daughter doesn't really break new ground in **Doctor Who** storytelling, though it does put on the record, at long last, the admission that the Doctor has had a family before (presumably including Susan, and almost certainly the lost family he discussed with Victoria in *Tomb Of The Cybermen*). That's a mildly important continuity note, and the idea of him starting a new family is intriguing. By the end of the episode, one gets the impression that the family ties will probably remain unmined as a story element. It seems unlikely that the Doctor, having learned that his cloned daughter has two hearts – like a Time Lord has – would leave her to her fate without waiting to see if she'll regenerate like a Time Lord does. This is the same Doctor who was so desperate to simply know that another Time Lord existed in the universe, he was practically trying to get the Master to regenerate by sheer force of will. This same man wouldn't stick around on the off chance that Jenny would regenerate?

And yet there are great moments – Donna talking about her travels (and talking about how she has no plans to jump ship from the TARDIS anytime soon), the Doctor declaring that the war is over, and Jenny's music-video-inspired gymnastic flip through one of the colony's security systems.

The Doctor's Daughter is a fine story with an interesting time twist that isn't the same as, say, *Dragonfire*, so that's rather refreshing. The Hath are interesting creatures – fishlike bipeds with obvious gills and canisters of whatever fluid sustains them strapped to their faces like gas masks – and I think that they merit a revisit down the road, much like the Ood did. It just needs to be in a story that winds up making a little more sense than this one.

THE UNICORN AND THE WASP

The TARDIS brings the Doctor and Donna to the 1920s, to an ordinary cocktail party with an extraordinary guest – murder mystery author Agatha Christie. And right on cue, a murder takes place at the party, and the Doctor tries to enlist the famed writer's help in narrowing down a list of suspects whose alibis have no witness to back them up. Donna searches for clues, and discovers quite a big one – a huge wasp at least as big as a human being. She narrowly avoids its deadly stinger, and at the same time, a jewel thief is at large in the house. But is the killer related to the jewel thief…or the wasp? And after solving a mystery whose perpetrator is not of this Earth, will Agatha Christie ever be the same again?

David Tennant . . . . The Doctor
Catherine Tate . . . . Donna Noble
Ian Barritt . . . . Professor Peach
Christopher Benjamin . . . . Colonel Hugh
Leena Dhingra . . . . Miss Chandrakala
Charlotte Eaton . . . . Mrs. Hart
Tom Goodman-Hill . . . . Reverend Golightly
Felicity Jones . . . . Robina Redmond
Felicity Kendal . . . . Lady Eddison
Daniel King . . . . Davenport
David Quilter . . . . Greeves

This story has been released on DVD

written by Gareth Roberts
directed by Graeme Harper
music by Murray Gold

Aired on May 17, 2008

Adam Rayner . . . . Roger Curbishley
Fenella Woolgar . . . . Agatha Christie

A.K.A.: Christopher Benjamin's first **Doctor Who** appearance was in *Inferno* (1970), but he's best remembered for playing theater impresario Henry Gordon Jago in *The Talons Of Weng-Chiang* (1977). The team of Jago and Litefoot proved so popular with fans that they eventually returned in audio form for their own spinoff series courtesy of Big Finish. **Fenella Woolgar** also went on to "appear" with the eighth Doctor (Paul McGann) in the 2009 audio adventure *The Company Of Friends*.

An unabashedly funny installment of **Doctor Who**, *The Unicorn And The Wasp* gently pokes fun at everything from the general style of Agatha Christie's mysteries to the conventions used in translating those mysteries to the screen. Part of me thinks that this is yet another based-on-historial-events story that might've been better off without the goofy macguffin (which, in this case, is pure SyFy Original Movie fodder), but in this case it's entertaining enough. Fenella Woolgar deserves special praise for bringing Agatha Christie to life, but Catherine Tate gets a shot at the spotlight too, once again making Donna a refreshing change of pace. David Tennant almost overdoes it in a scene where he's having to initiate his Time Lord body's defenses to being poisoned; it's a bit too close, in both script and performance, to *Smith And Jones*' "radioactive shoe" scene from the previous season.

Unicorn is a story that thrives more on its atmosphere and setting than on actually trying to make sense out of it. The macguffin mystery is a little too quickly and conveniently wrapped up – the only way it could've been wrapped up any more quickly would've been with a can of Raid – and I find myself more interested in the Agatha Christie mystery, which is a fun **Who**-ish attempt to explain a real amnesiac episode/disappearance that the author actually suffered. There are some elements of the "Doctor meets a famous author" plot which come dangerously close to what *The Unquiet Dead* did with Charles Dickens, and it almost seems as the production team is trying to draw attention to that, with a very specific reference to that episode.

Good fun, but nothing that'd tax your brainpower on the order of, say, an actual Agatha Christie novel.

SILENCE IN THE LIBRARY

The Doctor's psychic paper receives a distress call from a library so huge it takes up an entire planet. But when he and Donna arrive, the entire library is deserted – they're the only two humanoids there. The Doctor expands the sensors to detect other life forms, and this time millions of millions are picked up – but none that the time travelers can see. Another expedition arrives to solve the mystery of the empty library, and this provides another puzzle for the Doctor when he discovers that Professor River Song, the expedition's archaeologist, has apparently met him and knows him quite well – but she knows him in his own future, and can't say any more than that. An automated node in the library warns the Doctor and Donna to count the shadows – and then warns them to run. When two members of the expedition die, consumed by the shadows, the Doctor realizes what they're up against…but that realization comes too late to save Donna. Meanwhile, somewhere across the galaxy, someone else seems to know exactly what's happening in the library…

David Tennant . . . . The Doctor
Catherine Tate . . . . Donna Noble
Joshua Dallas . . . . Node 2
Mark Dexter . . . . Dad
O-T Fagbenle . . . . Other Dave

written by Steven Moffat
directed by Euros Lyn
music by Murray Gold

Aired on May 31, 2008

UWARP!

Alex Kingston . . . . Professor River Song
Eve Newton . . . . The Girl
Sarah Niles . . . . Node 1
Harry Peacock . . . . Proper Dave
Steve Pemberton . . . . Strackman Lux
Talulah Riley . . . . Miss Evangelista

This story
has been
released
on DVD

Colin Salmon . . . . Dr. Moon
Jessika Williams . . . . Anita

NEW WHO CONNECTIONS: This is the first time the Doctor meets River Song. This is the last time she meets the Doctor. Confused yet? Have a seat, we're just getting started.

A.K.A.: Alex Kingston is best known to American audiences for a stint on the long-running hospital drama ER. Colin Salmon took over the role of Avon in an audio drama revival/reimagining of the classic BBC science fiction series Blake's 7. Talulah Riley appeared in *The Boat That Rocked* (retitled *Pirate Radio* for American consumption) and *Inception.*

Airing just a matter of days after it was learned that Hugo-winning writer Steven Moffat would be taking over from Russell T. Davies as the creative dynamo of **Doctor Who**, *Silence In The Library* was a harbinger of things to come. Moffat, who also wrote the incredibly unnerving *The Empty Child, The Girl In The Fireplace*, and *Blink*, all of them Hugo winning episodes, is still on fine form with the first half of this two-part story, whose main adversary appears to be – quite simply – the dark.

Alex Kingston steals the show from just about everyone else here, mainly because the (slowly dwindling) guest cast winds up with a lot of screen time; the Doctor and Donna aren't quite to the point where they're incidental to the plot, but they don't wind up with the lion's share of screen time unless they're interacting with River Song. The rest of the cast does a serviceable job, but I have to especially give kudos to the actress playing Miss Evangelista – to be quite frank, the character's a stereotype, and not the most flattering one in the world, but she still manages to come across as sympathetic-going-on-tragic. The whole element of characters avoiding "spoilers" – and literally saying so out loud – is one of the biggest dents in the **Doctor Who** universe's fourth wall since **Torchwood** started dosing people with retcon, but it's a knowing wink that doesn't break the show.

FOREST OF THE DEAD

Snatched out of the TARDIS in mid-teleport, Donna finds herself in an artificial world, where she meets the man of her dreams, has children, and enjoys a normal life with no sign of the Doctor or the TARDIS...until he suddenly appears in the place of her therapist, Dr. Moon, who she seems to see quite regularly. In the library, the Doctor's attempts to detect his shadowy adversaries are being jammed by something, somewhere, and the ranks of the expedition are dwindling as more of its crew are consumed. Only the enigmatic Professor River Song can be of any real help to him, but the Doctor is still worried about how well she knows him – especially after she whispers one word to him that proves she knows him very well, and again when she proves that she's more than willing to sacrifice her life to save him. Donna runs into a familiar face in the virtual construct, another victim of the Vashta Nerada who clues her in to the true nature of her new life, and she begins to question everything as her artificial world starts to collapse on itself. The Doctor realizes that Donna – and almost everyone else who was in the library before the shadows fell – have been saved in the Library's massive computer core, but as the Vashta Nerada try to claim the library world and bring it to the brink of destruction, they may not leave him enough time to recover the survivors.

David Tennant . . . . The Doctor
Catherine Tate . . . . Donna Noble
Mark Dexter . . . . Dad
O-T Fagbenle . . . . Other Dave
Alex Kingston . . . . Professor River Song
Alex Midwood . . . . Joshua
Eve Newton . . . . The Girl
Harry Peacock . . . . Proper Dave
Steve Pemberton . . . . Strackman Lux
Jason Pitt . . . . Lee
Eloise Rakic-Platt . . . . Ella
Jonathan Reuben . . . . Man

This story
has been
released
on DVD

written by Steven Moffat
directed by Euros Lyn
music by Murray Gold

Aired on June 7, 2008

Talulah Riley . . . . Miss Evangelista
Colin Salmon . . . . Dr. Moon
Jessika Williams . . . . Anita

The second part of Steven Moffat's creepily effective thriller does indeed pay off all of *Silence In The Library*'s mysteries, even if it goes about it in a way that completely defies the viewer's attempt to figure out what's going on. The creepiness of the Vashta Nerada creatures – possibly the best "cheap" monster in the history of a series renowned for cheap monsters (all you have to do is position or move an extra light behind a given actor) – carries things along, and the weirdness factor is off-the-scale when the story follows Donna into a virtual world.

If there's one plot strand that gets let down in the end, rather surprisingly, it's River Song. To see the Doctor make the effort to ensure her survival, and yet trap her in the little girl's virtual world, is a bit unsettling. River gets her happy ending, but she's trapped. Sure, the virtual world she's trapped in is no longer a hellish construct with creepy characters like Dr. Moon paying a visit every few minutes, but she's still trapped there. Moffat has a habit of making sure that he doesn't crank up the body count in his stories – witness *The Doctor Dances* and its "Everybody lives!" scene (directly referenced in this episode), or *Blink* or *The Girl In The Fireplace*, which only sees characters deposited in a different time or dying of old age – but it almost would've been more effective if River had perished. This is a ghoulish flipside to the ending of *The Doctor's Daughter*: River is alive, in a virtual world, and she dare not manifest herself in the real world again because the Vashta Nerada will have overrun the library completely.

Catherine Tate gets to show her dramatic chops again here, with her quickly-experienced "normal life", but I couldn't help but feel that she came up a little bit short when her virtual children vanished. I'm a grown man with a young child, and let me tell you, even in an enclosed space with no other people around, if you turn around and the kid isn't where you left him and you can't immediately find him, you freak out a hell of a lot more than Donna did in that scene. Otherwise it's a nice performance, sure, but in that moment Tate didn't convince me that the character she was playing was a parent who had just lost her children. But the remainder of the episode saw her giving one of the best straightforward dramatic readings of Donna yet. I appreciated that this element of the episode, which bears just a little bit of a resemblance to the **Star Trek: The Next Generation** episode *The Inner Light*, wasn't glossed over at the end of the show – even as they prepared to embark on their next adventure, neither the Doctor nor Donna had completely recovered from this one yet.

MIDNIGHT

The Doctor is eager to take a trip to the uninhabitable planet of Midnight, whose sun's radiation renders the surface completely inhospitable to any known kind of life – or so the legend has it. Faced with the choice of either this or sunbathing next to an opulent swimming pool, Donna lets the Doctor go off on his own for once. The Doctor gets acquainted with fellow passengers along the way, but when the tour ship comes to a sudden halt, so does the camaraderie – especially when the pilots' cabin is wrenched away from the ship and something begins knocking on the hull from outside. One of the passengers is apparently taken over by some form of life which has defied expectations and evolved on Midnight, and in its new body it begins rapidly learning about human characteristics such as speech. But when the other passengers become terrified enough to discuss throwing the possessed woman out of the ship to certain doom, just to rid themselves of the alien life form, it appears that the being is learning some of humanity's darkest behaviors too. And this time, there's almost nothing the Doctor can do to stop the worst from coming out of everyone present.

David Tennant . . . . The Doctor
Catherine Tate . . . . Donna Noble
Ayesha Antoine . . . . Dee Dee Blasco
Rakie Ayola . . . . Hostess
Tony Bluto . . . . Driver Joe
Lindsey Coulson . . . . Val Cane
Duane Henry . . . . Mechanic Claude
Colin Morgan . . . . Jethro Cane
Billie Piper . . . . Rose Tyler
Daniel Ryan . . . . Biff Cane

This story has been released on DVD

written by Russell T. Davies
directed by Alice Troughton
music by Murray Gold

Aired on June 14, 2008

Lesley Sharp . . . . Sky Silvestry
David Troughton . . . . Professor Hobbes

A.K.A.: A few episodes after meeting the Doctor's daughter, this time around we meet the Doctor's son – in real life. **David Troughton** is the son of the second Doctor, Patrick Troughton, and played a minor role in the last second Doctor story, *The War Games*, in 1969. He played a much more visible role opposite the third Doctor in 1972's *The Curse Of Peladon*. Like his father, he's no relation to this episode's director, Alice Troughton, who has also directed installments of **Torchwood** and **The Sarah Jane Adventures**.

Since the new series began, we've had "Doctor-lite" episodes such as *Blink* and *Love & Monsters*, but in a way, this episode, with its wall-to-wall companion-less Doctor, is also format-lite: it's almost **Twilight Zone** or **Outer Limits**-esque in nature, with the Doctor being the only thing really tying it to **Doctor Who** (well, unless you want to count yet another background monitor shot of Rose yelling "Doctor!"). I tend to like it when shows briefly go off-format (witness **Star Trek: Deep Space Nine**'s *Far Beyond The Stars* installment, the archetype-exploring **Blake's 7** episode *Sarcophagus*, the original - and now oft-imitated - **Xena** musical *The Bitter Suite* or the **Babylon 5** "newscast" episode, *And Now For A Word*), and go figure, I liked this one too. *Midnight* reminds me of why a lot of us probably got hooked on British SF TV in the first place: you stick some great actors in one or two sets, let them loose on a well-written script, and pretty soon you forget whether or not there are special effects involved at all.

By stripping the Doctor of his support systems – the TARDIS, his companion of the moment, UNIT or any other Earthbound allies – *Midnight* renders him essentially defenseless. Even the trusty sonic screwdriver, which has seen the kind of overuse in recent years that led to John Nathan-Turner removing it from the Doctor's toolbox in the early '80s, only comes in handy once or twice here, for relatively inconsequential tasks. The Doctor is powerless to stop one of his fellow passengers from being taken over by an alien, he's powerless to do anything but try to talk the other passengers out of killing the new arrival, and ultimately, when he himself is attacked by the alien, he's powerless to stop the other passengers from killing *him*. Only one person, answering only to her conscience and making an ultimate sacrifice, saves his skin – and even more depressingly, no one remembers who she was before that sacrifice was made. (Even the end credits, which lavish the guest cast with first and last names, refer to her simply as "Hostess".) *Midnight* gives us a Doctor stripped of all of his defenses and allies, and when it comes right down to it, once he's singled out as Not One Of Us, he's suddenly viewed as nobody's friend.

In a way, this episode almost redeems Russell T. Davies for the Eccleston season's tirades against "stupid apes," because the Doctor has almost nothing to do with saving the day. Oh, he does more intelligent analysis of the problem along the way... or does he? It seems like an awful lot of that legwork is done by Dee Dee and even by Jethro. The Doctor buys time for the alien to show its true colors, but that's about it — and buying it that time puts everyone in more danger.

The performances are above par, because they have to be — the bulk of the story takes place on a single set as a sort of one-act play. Only framing cutaways with Donna, at the beginning and end of the show, and a brief visit to the tour ship's cockpit break this up. David Troughton is an inspired piece of casting, but I'll admit to being distracted by how closely his face and voice now resemble those of his late father. I thought Jethro was a great character — he's painted as a sullen teenage goth-wanna-be, but as the story progresses he shows moments of startling intelligence and then shows how easy it is to side with the nearest mob in a crisis.

Midnight is, in short, Russell T. Davies' best **Doctor Who** script in ages, and one of his best contributions to the entire series. Perhaps not coincidentally, **Torchwood**'s finest hour (well, okay, *five* hours), *Children Of Earth*, follows closely along the same thematic lines as *Midnight*.

TURN LEFT

During a visit to a futuristic Chinatown, Donna is lured into a fortune teller's booth, where her fortunes aren't so much predicted as changed drastically. She finds herself over a year in the past, at the moment when she decided to take a job her mother found for her instead of going to work as a temp at H.C. Clemens — where she was working when her path became inextricably linked with the Doctor's. History changes. Without Donna to convince him to show the Empress of the Racnoss some mercy, the Doctor's mission to stop the Empress becomes a suicide mission. UNIT finds the Doctor's body, having suffered too much damage to regenerate — the last of the Time Lords has died. Without the Doctor, history unfolds very differently, but few notice the divergence until the moment when the starship Titanic slams into Buckingham Palace and its reactor goes critical on impact, destroying London totally. Donna and her family are assigned to a home in Leeds in a besieged and increasingly xenophobic Britain, a world that they would never have chosen to live in. Further events that would have been stopped by the Doctor continue to drastically alter the world: America is laid to waste by the Adipose incident, while the Atmos devices choke millions across the globe. And with each disaster, a young woman named Rose appears to Donna, insisting that she is the most important woman in human history — Donna must go with Rose to fulfill her destiny and set history back on its rightful course. But why should Donna Noble believe a total stranger who claims to be from another dimension of reality?

David Tennant	The Doctor
Catherine Tate	Donna Noble
Billie Piper	Rose Tyler
Paul Richard Biggin	Soldier #2
Terri-Ann Brumby	Woman in doorway
Lachele Carl	Trinity Wells
Chipo Chung	Fortune Teller
Neil Clench	Man in pub
Bernard Cribbins	Wilfred Mott

UNIT

This story has been released on DVD

written by Russell T. Davies
directed by Graeme Harper
music by Murray Gold

Aired on June 21, 2008

Bhasker Patel	Jival Chowdry
Ben Righton	Morgenstern

UWORP!

Noma Dumezweni . . . . Capt. Magambo	Clive Standen . . . . UNIT Soldier
Jacqueline King . . . . Sylvia Noble	Lawrence Stevenson . . . . Soldier #1
Marcia Lecky . . . . Mooky Kahari	Loraine Velez . . . . Spanish Maid
Joseph Long . . . . Rocco Colasanto	Natalie Walter . . . . Alice Coltrane
Sanchia McCormack . . . . Housing Officer	Catherine York . . . . Female Reporter
Suzann McLean . . . . Veena Brady	
Jason Mohammad . . . . Studio Newsreader	

SARAH JANE CONNECTIONS: The Trickster is mentioned as being the architect of the beetle-like creature on Donna's back; though he isn't actually seen in this episode, the Trickster *did* feature prominently in **The Sarah Jane Adventures** story *Whatever Happened To Sarah Jane?,* in which he threatened to remove the Doctor from time; presumably *Turn Left* is where he tried to make good on that threat. Sarah Jane and her three young friends from that spinoff series, Luke, Maria and Clyde, are said to have been in the same hospital where Martha Jones worked (and, in this timeline, died), and in the absence of the Doctor, Sarah is said to have prevented the Earth from being blasted by an accelerated MRI machine (as seen in *Smith And Jones*), paying for that bravery with her life and the lives of her young friends.

TORCHWOOD CONNECTIONS: Captain Jack, Gwen and Ianto of **Torchwood** apparently prevent the Sontaran takeover of Earth (*The Poison Sky*) at the cost of their own lives.

A.K.A.: Chipo Chung guest starred in 2007's *Utopia* as Chantho, while Lachele Carl's American news anchor – after appearing in episodes since the first season and in the same role in **Torchwood** and **The Sarah Jane Adventures** – finally picks up a name: Trinity Wells. **Noma Dumezweni** returns as UNIT Captain Magambo in 2009's *Planet Of The Dead,* but the next time we see her, she's in the "home" timeline.

A second straight winner from the pen of Russell T. Davies, *Turn Left* brings the fourth season of the new **Doctor Who** down the home stretch, playing out initially as "It's Not Really Such A Wonderful Life." But more than simply demonstrating the effects on Earth of not having the Doctor around to save the human race time and again, *Turn Left* packs a gut-punch of a surprise: if you thought all of season one's themes were wrapped up and tied off, such as Bad Wolf, you're so wrong. **Torchwood** and **The Sarah Jane Adventures** are explicitly referenced here, almost surprisingly so – and the story does not slow down to hold your hand and explain itself slowly if you haven't kept up with the whole franchise.

At first glance, this spinoff-mania may seem to be strictly a background texture, with Rose mentioning Torchwood's suicide misson and a television news announcer mentioning the death of Sarah Jane and the kids from her series, but it's not all in the background. The mention of the Trickster character all but makes the **SJA** two-parter *Whatever Happened To Sarah Jane?* required viewing, and it raises the interesting possibility that *Turn Left* occurs, in its entirety, during a brief interval of *Whatever Happened.* Perhaps knowing that the entire **Doctor Who** universe has a rabid following that watches/reads/listens to every permutation emboldened Davies enough to take this uncompromisingly interlocked approach here; in any case, this is the kind of intricately interwoven universe that many SF fans, myself included, were disappointed that we *didn't* see with the simultaneous **Star Trek** series of the 1990s.

It's also interesting to note that the Doctor isn't really done away with by malicious means in the alternate timeline. No one comes up and shoots or stabs him and takes him out of the picture. With the manipulation of the timeline simply involving depriving the Doctor of a companion at a key moment, the Doctor's own nature – and his darker nature at that – seals his doom. This is quite possibly as dark as **Doctor Who** has gotten in the new series. As if killing Sarah Jane Smith and her juvenile sidekicks isn't dark enough, we here see a kind of "it couldn't happen here" Britain, complete with non-natives being shipped off to euphemistically labelled "labor camps", mass relocations, and martial law. Donna's grandfather Wilf, given a dramatic and non-comic reading by Bernard Cribbins at his best here, serves as the story's barometer for civilization going to hell in a handbasket: he sees Britain doing things that Britain's *enemies* did during World War II, and he challenges a particularly paranoid soldier who trains his gun on Donna. Like Catherine Tate, even though much of Bernard Cribbins' career is associated with comedy, he's got the dramatic chops for this story – and it helps that Davies has imbued his script with a sociopolitical message much more resonant and meaningful than, oh, say, Harriet Jones taking easy cheap shots at American foreign policy.

THE STOLEN EARTH

Confronted with the imminent arrival of Rose from the alternate universe, the Doctor and Donna make a quick jump to modern-day Earth, finding that everything is all right and returning to the TARDIS. But a sudden displacement of time and space leaves the TARDIS floating in space – without Earth. The Doctor flies into action to try to track the planet down, even going so far as to pay an unannounced visit to the Shadow Proclamation, an intergalactic law enforcement body, where he talks his way past Judoon guards and discovers that Earth isn't the only planet missing: the Shadow Proclamation has placed the entire universe on alert. Taking note of the mass and properties of the missing worlds, the Doctor hypothesizes that the planets may have been stolen to become components of a massive engine, generating energy on a scale not seen since the creation of the universe. The representatives of the Shadow Proclamation are prepared to go into battle, but only if the Doctor surrenders his TARDIS; he opts to go it alone instead.

On Earth, chaos has broken out. Night has fallen around the world, and the sky is now teeming with unfamiliar planets. At UNIT HQ in New York City, at Torchwood in Cardiff and at Sarah Jane Smith's home in Ealing, former companions of the Doctor are among the first to hear a message transmitted from an oncoming barrage of spacecraft: a Dalek voice endlessly repeating the word "exterminate". The Daleks attack the planet, concentrating their firepower on military installations or entities that have prior knowledge of the Daleks: Torchwood and UNIT are among the first targets. An unlikely ally unites Martha, Torchwood and Sarah, using a technology invented for an emergency in which the Doctor hasn't arrived to save the day. But the TARDIS does indeed make its way to Earth, finding the stolen planets time-shifted within the Medusa Cascade. The Doctor discovers that Davros, creator of the Daleks, has survived the Time War and bred a new race of Daleks to do his bidding. As the Doctor's former companions race to join up with him, Torchwood comes under Dalek attack and Gwen and Ianto are left to fend for themselves. Sarah finds herself at the mercy of the Daleks, and even when Rose finds the TARDIS, it may not be enough to save the Doctor when he finds himself in a Dalek's gunsights.

David Tennant . . . . The Doctor
Catherine Tate . . . . Donna Noble
Billie Piper . . . . Rose Tyler
Freema Agyeman . . . . Martha Jones
John Barrowman . . . . Capt. Jack Harkness
Elisabeth Sladen . . . . Sarah Jane Smith
Adjoa Andoh . . . . Francine Jones
Alexander Armstrong . . . . voice of Mr. Smith
Julian Bleach . . . . Davros
Michael Brandon . . . . General Sanchez
Nicholas Briggs . . . . Dalek voices
Lachele Carl . . . . Trinity Wells
Bernard Cribbins . . . . Wilfred Mott
Marcus Cunningham . . . . Drunk Man

written by Russell T. Davies
directed by Graeme Harper
music by Murray Gold

Aired on June 28, 2008

This story has been released on DVD

Kelly Hunter . . . . Shadow Architect
Paul Kasey . . . . Judoon
Jacqueline King . . . . Sylvia Noble
Thomas Knight . . . . Luke Smith
Gary Milner . . . . Scared Man
Jason Mohammad . . . . Newsreader

UWORP!

Gareth David-Lloyd	Ianto Jones	Eve Myles	Gwen Cooper
Richard Dawkins	himself	Paul O'Grady	himself
Barnaby Edwards	Dalek	Nicholas Pegg	Dalek
David Hankinson	Dalek	Anthony Spargo	Dalek
Andrea Harris	Suzanne	Penelope Wilton	Harriet Jones
Amy Beth Hayes	Albino Servant		

CLASSIC CONNECTIONS: Davros first appeared in 1975's *Genesis Of The Daleks*, and returned to terrorize each of the Doctor's successive incarnations until his final appearance in 1988's *Remembrance Of The Daleks*. Even the cancellation of the original series didn't slow him down, as he returned to do battle twice more in audio adventures with the sixth Doctor, and then with Paul McGann as the eighth Doctor in *Terror Firma*. Big Finish also gave the Dalek creator his own audio spinoff series, **I, Davros**. Apparently he's been missing since a battle during the first year of the Time War, which — just to drive fans crazy — remains unrecorded in TV, novel, or audio form.

A.K.A.: Actor **Julian Bleach** becomes the fourth actor to play Davros, having played the Ghost Maker in an episode of **Torchwood**'s second season. (Bleach would later complete his **Doctor Who** trifecta with an appearance in **The Sarah Jane Adventures**.) **Bernard Cribbins**, as Donna's grandfather, has come up against the Daleks before — 42 years before this episode's premiere, in the 1966 feature film *Daleks: Invasion Earth 2150 A.D.* starring Peter Cushing as Doctor Who. **Penelope Wilton** returns as former Prime Minister Harriet Jones, not seen since the then-newly-regenerated Doctor uttered six fateful words in *The Christmas Invasion*. Appearing as himself, evolutionary science advocate **Richard Dawkins** is the husband of former **Doctor Who** co-star Lalla "Romana" Ward; coincidentally, they were introduced by former **Doctor Who** writer and script editor — and Hitchhiker's Guide To The Galaxy author — Douglas Adams.

A sense of inevitability surrounds *The Stolen Earth* from the first frame, picking up from *Turn Left*'s rather surprising "Bad Wolf" refrain. At this point, we know that Rose is returning, the Daleks are returning, and Davros is returning. What role any or all of these will play, and how they all come together…that's the mystery. Right before the opening credits, it really seems like all-star night on **Doctor Who**, and the opening credits themselves then hit you with a barrage of familiar names.

Stolen Earth picks up *Turn Left*'s dark, fatalistic atmosphere. When the Daleks broadcast their message to Earth, we get reactions from all of the new series companions, with Jack and Sarah mourning the likely fate of their loved ones. It's almost frustrating that the Doctor is separated from the action for much of the story, but I quite liked the plot point that in this great gathering of the Doctor's friends, Rose is left out. Like the audience, everyone else has safely assumed that she's gone and won't be returning. Jack and Martha both know she was trapped in another universe, and if Harriet Jones tried to look her up, she likely would've seen Rose listed as a casualty of the battle of Canary Wharf (as seen in *Doomsday*). No one has any reason to expect Rose to show up and save the day. (I did, however, like the little fourth-wall-busting moment in which Sarah says that she's aware of Torchwood but doesn't approve of the ease with which Jack and his team unholster their guns in any given situation.)

Speaking of Harriet Jones, I would really have liked some build-up to her appearance here, somewhere else in the past two seasons. There's a whopping great gap between her post-*Christmas Invasion* fall from power and her cobbling together a super-sophisticated top-secret communications network in what appears to be her living room, and even a mention of her would have been sufficient to bridge that gap — especially with Saxon's ascendency to 10 Downing Street in the third season, during which there would've been a perfect opening for such a mention. While she mentions that her financial backer was Mr. Copper (from *Voyage Of The Damned*), it seems almost sad that she's been shacked up alone, bringing technical skills that we never knew she had to bear on her task.

Julian Bleach turns in a wonderful Davros, though he doesn't honestly have much to do in this episode except make grand pronouncements of victory. I was caught off guard by the Dalek civil war not being reintroduced here, though I suppose it makes sense that the Dalek factions, during the Time War, would have pooled their resources against the Time Lords and put the matter of loyalty to Davros on the back burner. And it makes just as much sense that, in desperation, the sole surviving Dalek in the universe would have hatched a mad plan to bring Davros into the present to preserve the species. The scene in which Davros graphically demonstrates how he did this is possibly the greatest moment of stomach-turning horror in **Doctor Who**'s history.

JOURNEY'S END

Caught by a glancing blow from a Dalek weapon, the Doctor's body is involuntarily beginning the regeneration process - until the Doctor is able to divert the energy into his severed hand, benefitting from the restorative effects without changing his appearance or personality. On Earth, Sarah Jane is saved from the Daleks by Mickey Smith and Jackie Tyler, who have returned from the alternate universe after losing contact with Rose. The Dalek attack on the Torchwood Hub is halted by a defense mechanism that the late Toshiko Sato was developing, locking the Dalek into a moment of frozen time - but also trapping Ianto and Gwen inside, safe but unable to escape. To Mickey's disgust and Jackie's horror, Sarah surrenders herself and both of them to the Daleks, reasoning that being taken to the Dalek mothership as hostages will put her closer to the Doctor, and in a better position to help. The TARDIS is brought about the mothership by the Daleks, and the Doctor, Rose and Captain Jack step out to meet their fate - but the TARDIS doors close, trapping Donna inside. Declaring the time machine and anyone who is still inside it a threat, the Dalek Supreme orders the TARDIS dumped into the neutrino core of his own ship, where it will dissolve and surrender its energy to the Dalek war effort. But when Donna reaches for the Doctor's severed hand, she sets other events into motion which the Daleks can't possibly have foreseen. Davros is planning the destruction of the entire cosmos, every universe, every alternate universe, and every dimension, to prove himself a god, and nothing the Doctor says can dissuade the mad Dalek creator from his plans. Martha, Sarah, Jack, Mickey and Jackie join forces to put an end to Davros' plan, but he has anticipated their interference. But he hasn't anticipated Donna's next move - and he certainly hasn't anticipated whose help she has.

David Tennant	. . . .	The Doctor
Catherine Tate	. . . .	Donna Noble
Billie Piper	. . . .	Rose Tyler
Freema Agyeman	. . . .	Martha Jones
John Barrowman	. . . .	Capt. Jack Harkness
Elisabeth Sladen	. . . .	Sarah Jane Smith
Adjoa Andoh	. . . .	Francine Jones
Alexander Armstrong	. . . .	voice of Mr. Smith
Valda Aviks	. . . .	German Woman
Julian Bleach	. . . .	Davros
Nicholas Briggs	. . . .	Dalek voices
Noel Clarke	. . . .	Mickey Smith
Camille Coduri	. . . .	Jackie Tyler
Bernard Cribbins	. . . .	Wilfred Mott
Gareth David-Lloyd	. . . .	Ianto Jones
Barnaby Edwards	. . . .	Dalek
David Hankinson	. . . .	Dalek
Shobu Kapoor	. . . . , .	Scared Woman

This story has been released on DVD

written by Russell T. Davies
directed by Graeme Harper
music by Murray Gold

Aired on July 5, 2008

Jacqueline King	. . . .	Sylvia Noble
Thomas Knight	. . . .	Luke Smith
John Leeson	. . . .	voice of K-9
Gary Milner	. . . .	Scared Man
Eve Myles	. . . .	Gwen Cooper
Nicholas Pegg	. . . .	Dalek
Michael Price	. . . .	Liberian Man
Anthony Spargo	. . . .	Dalek
Elizabeth Tan	. . . .	Chinese Woman

NEW WHO CONNECTIONS: Though he nonchalantly blows it off as a mere diversion of regenerative energy, the Doctor pays a high price for maintaining his tenth face: from this story through *The End Of Time*, we are technically seeing the Doctor's <u>twelfth</u> incarnation. This is revealed in *The Time Of The Doctor* (2013), in which we find out that the

Doctor usually regarded as the eleventh is truly the Doctor's thirteenth and final life. (The count is also thrown off by the Doctor's deliberately-forgotten ninth face, as revealed in *The Day Of The Doctor* (2013).

Journey's End is an obvious note of closure to the era, and the story threads, of outgoing **Doctor Who** showrunner Russell T. Davies, and as such, it encapsulates not only the overarching themes of his era, but both his strengths and weaknesses as the new series' chief storyteller.

There are a lot of convenient plot contrivances here, not the least of which is an "out" for *The Stolen Earth*'s regeneration cliffhanger which stops just short of making a mockery of virtually every regeneration in the show's history. Red herrings such as the Osterhagen Key and Sarah Jane's "warp star" are built up and come to nothing. Maybe it's all in the name of keeping the viewer guessing, but at times it seems like these dead-ends stole time from story and character development that needed more breathing room.

And yet there were moments of pure, series-defining beauty here, namely the moment where Davros takes the Doctor to task for never arming himself, and yet turning his companions into an army unto themselves: Rose, Sarah, Jack and Martha all arm themselves, over the course of this two-parter, with weapons of various destructive power, ranging from humongous guns to nukes strategically placed to destroy the Earth. Sad as it is to say, Davros has a point - but one of these is not like the others. I realize that Sarah is there to tie her own spinoff series into its parent show, but if we're going to talk about the Doctor's companions being prepared to employ violence, one word comes screaming into my head: Ace. I'd say Leela too, but presumably she died on Gallifrey when that planet was wiped out during the Time War. Ace could've made a very effective comeback here, and it really would've made more sense for her to be toting around an unearthly weapon of fantastic destructive power than to have Sarah Jane "I steer clear of you lot, too many guns!" Smith doing the same - and Ace could've recognized Davros just as easily as Sarah did. (This, of course, assumes that whenever Ace parted company with the seventh Doctor, she did so on present-day Earth – the New Adventures novels paint an entirely different picture which may invalidate this line of thinking.) A golden opportunity was missed here. Besides, even K-9 showed up for a couple of scenes - would Ace really have been companion nostalgia overkill?

I wonder if Russell T. Davies wasn't slipping us a sly message by way of the whole conversation about the Doctor's "army" of companions. As far back as *The End Of The World*, we had little hints that, in Davies' future, religion is up there with weapons in terms of things that you don't carry around with you without causing trouble. Is Davies possibly – perhaps not even consciously – dropping us a warning about following *anyone* around with such blind devotion, no matter how good the intentions, for fear that even the purest such following can be corrupted?

Going back to the 1996 TV movie, the presence of the "second" Doctor digs up that whole debate about the eighth Doctor's claim to being half-human. Far from really resolving that issue, *Journey's End* actually confuses it further. I've always considered that throwaway line in the McGann movie to mean that, while the Doctor is physically and psychologically a Time Lord, he has a direct ancestor who happens to be human. The reason I can't just completely discount and ignore the half-human line from 1996 is that it <u>does</u> explain *so* much - the Doctor's constant affinity for Earth and the fact that when he returned "home" from the Cheetah Planet in *Survival* (1989), he didn't suddenly appear inside the TARDIS - he appeared *outside the TARDIS, <u>on Earth</u>*. I wish this whole issue had been dealt with in a more straightforward manner, even if it meant that the tenth Doctor is now 100% Time Lord with his human traits all splintered off into the **Doctor Who** remained with Rose.

That Rose was unceremoniously deposited back into her alternate universe, along with Jackie and a more human Doctor, was one of the better thought-out parts of the ending. The Doctor points out that the human copy of him is more like his ninth incarnation: capable of violence and pettiness, and a ticking time bomb if left alone. I also liked the acknowledgement that the ninth Doctor was a head case - fandom has kind of quietly nodded and shifted uncomfortably in its collective seat on that issue, sort of like a family awkwardly avoiding any discussion of a troublesome relative, but here it was, cards on the table: the Eccleston Doctor was a seething ball of post-traumatic stress disorder probably waiting to become the Valeyard (from *The Trial Of A Time Lord*, 1986) a few incarnations too early until Rose came along. As for the other companions, Martha and Mickey are conveniently deposited into the care of Captain Jack, with not-too-subtle hints of upcoming appearances in **Torchwood**'s third season in 2009 (though this, too, turned out to be a red herring); similarly, Sarah is dropped off just in time for the second season of her own series.

That leaves Donna, who gets the most heartbreaking exit of any new series sidekick to date, even moreso than Rose's departure in *Doomsday*. Her fate is perhaps worse than death: she's been relieved of the memory of the fantastic things she saw, felt and accomplished in the Doctor's company. Far from the aggravatingly attitudinal companion that most (particularly those acquainted with Catherine Tate's comedy work) expected, her exit reveals the true tragedy of the character: she's been psychologically beaten down into thinking that she's not in any way special. Donna's tearful plea to remain in the TARDIS for the rest of her life, her grandfather's assertion that she was better for traveling with the Doctor, and the Doctor's snappy retort to her mother that she should do something to bolster Donna's self-esteem all paint the picture: Donna didn't come from a broken home or a cruel family, but her sense of self-worth was still taken from her, piece by piece. Too many of us have personally seen how this can happen in real life, how insidious it is, and how hard it is to undo or overcome the resulting damage. If this was Russell T. Davies slipping another message into the story, that message may well be the best parting gift he could leave us with. I wish Donna could have remained aboard the TARDIS, as she was the best companion creation of the new show so far, but I suppose that having her around longer before the big revelation would've made the parting even more painful (and the build-up perhaps more exasperating). Another thing to miss about Donna, aside from her being the most independent and intelligent of the TARDIS travelers created on Davies' watch, is her grandfather, Wilfred. Bernard Cribbins crafted a great character, at turns both sympathetic/dramatic and comedic, from what was in the show's scripts, and made it his own. Any chance to see Cribbins show up as Wilf again, even briefly, was a cause for celebration, because he was never anything less than entertaining.

Julian Bleach's brilliantly mad, off-the-rails Davros was terrifyingly unhinged. I suppose that if my lot in life was to look / feel like he does, I'd probably want to drop-kick reality too. I was stunned that, after all of it, the Doctor tried to offer Davros a berth on the TARDIS, even temporarily, but slyly enough, we were not shown a definitive death for the character - at least no more definitive than any of his other supposed demises. Apart from the Sontarans, Davros has been the best original series callback in the entire new series; thanks to the makeup and a studied performance, I could believe that this was the same character played by Michael Wisher, Terry Molloy and David Gooderson. There's an advantage there in that Davros involves a mile of makeup on top of whoever is playing him, but that won't hide a performance that doesn't ring true. Bleach did his homework and stole the show.

I'm satisfied that a complete story was told here without a *Last Of The Time Lords* "reset button," but one thing that I am beginning to wonder about the new series is this: is the Earth depicted in **Doctor Who** any longer relevant and relatable to our own? The public knowledge of aliens is a handy device that lets one get away with huge, cataclysmic invasions on our own turf (which can be shot on location easily, negating the necessity for expensive sets), but the collective human psyche would change *so much* from this, in ways that the series just hasn't devoted time to exploring. Perhaps that in itself is meat for future stories. As much as I hate reset button storytelling, perhaps Earth needs a reboot of some sort - the only other options are to take more stories off-world (which I would like), or to keep ramping up the scale of future invasions of Earth (and I'm not sure how much bigger one could get than this two-parter in that department). Between the Slitheen and the Sycorax and the Cybermen and the Adipose and the Sontarans and the Daleks, surely we'd all be living in a tightly-wound state of fear, worried that every previously undiscovered asteroid or meteor shower is terror raining down from above... *oh*. Wait. Maybe that *is* relatable to our world today, and Davies is even more clever than I've given him credit for. Never mind. (And just in case, "Copyright, Donna Noble.")

This episode ties off Davies' era thematically - none too late and none too soon. Even if you haven't been a fan of his work (and even I haven't always been - again, see *Last Of The Time Lords*), I think the man's earned a hearty round of applause. He brought **Doctor Who**, one of the best shows ever to grace British television (and, indeed, anyone's television) back from what seemed like an obscurity of "inside joke" novels and audio plays for the faithful, and against all odds, he made it a huge hit - enough so that there's no shame in admitting to being a **Doctor Who** fan, old or new. If that isn't cause to celebrate Davies' "era," I'm not sure what is.

MUSIC OF THE SPHERES

As he travels alone in the TARDIS, the Doctor is busying himself by composing an elaborate piece of music. But his muse vacates him temporarily when a Graske appears in the console room, supposedly only wishing to warn the Doctor of a gaping void that appears moments later inside his timeship. The Doctor peers through the void and sees, to his amazement, the audience at a BBC Proms concert in the Royal Albert Hall in 2008. He decides to take the opportunity to throw some of his sheet music into the void so that the orchestra can give his composition its premiere performance – music inspired by the cosmos itself. But the Graske still has a trick up its sleeve…

David Tennant . . . . The Doctor
Jimmy Vee . . . . Graske

written by Russell T. Davies
directed by Graeme Harper
music by Murray Gold

BEHIND THE SCENES: *Music Of The Spheres* premiered on July 27, 2008 as part of the BBC Proms concert devoted to the music of **Doctor Who**. Pre-filmed with David Tennant on the TARDIS set, this skit "interacted" with elements of the live concert, including the Graske running through the audience trying to escape from the Doctor! For the first time in the new series era, the closing credits use the original Delia Derbyshire arrangement of the **Doctor Who** theme rather than Murray Gold's version.

Music Of The Spheres may be right up there with *Dimensions In Time* for some, but it's actually a nice little one-off gag with a little bit of audience participation, written by Russell T. Davies for the BBC Proms performance of **Doctor Who** music by the series' resident maestro, Murray Gold. (Gold also contributed the cacophonous piece of music ostensibly being written by the Doctor.) *Spheres* is certainly nothing groundbreaking in storytelling terms, but it *is* a bit of lightweight fun which undoubtedly delighted the live concertgoers; though the video appeared later on the BBC's **Doctor Who** web site, it works better if you know, for example, that sheet music rained down on the orchestra moments after the Doctor was seen to throw it past the camera and into the void, and that the Graske "escaped" the video screen and appeared among the live audience. This, and the televised recording of the 2006 **Doctor Who** concert in Cardiff, is perhaps most useful as a reminder of how great it must be to be a kid, growing up with the new **Doctor**

Who in Britain right now. Not simply content to rake in the merchandising money, the makers of the series are keen on creating experiences like this for the younger crowd, and for that I can only praise them - and envy the kids.

THE NEXT DOCTOR

The TARDIS lands in London, 1851, at Christmastime, but before the Doctor can even be serenaded by carolers, someone is calling his name. He discovers a woman in an alleyway, but even though he's arrived to save the day, she doesn't stop calling for help until another man shows up — another man claiming that he is the Doctor. Some sort of Cyber-converted creature bursts out of a building, leading both Doctors on a wild goose chase until they lose track of it, but then the Doctor — and the Doctor who was already on the case in 1851 — encounter real Cybermen, apparently escaped from the Void. Curiously, this other Doctor remembers nothing of his tenth incarnation, who then discovers why: this Doctor isn't the man he says he is. But why does he think he's another incarnation of the Doctor, and what monstrous plans are afoot that involve the Cybermen enslaving the children of London?

David Tennant . . . . The Doctor
Matthew Allick . . . . Docker
Michael Bertenshaw . . . . Mr. Cole
Nicholas Briggs . . . . Cyber voices
Ashley Horne . . . . Lad
Paul Kasey . . . . Cyberleader
Edmund Kenie . . . . Mr. Scoones
Dervia Kirwan . . . . Miss Hartigan
Tom Langford . . . . Frederic
Neil McDermott . . . . Jed
Ruari Mears . . . . Cybershade
Jason Morell . . . . Vicar

This story has been released on DVD

written by Russell T. Davies
directed by Andy Goddard
music by Murray Gold

Aired on December 25, 2008

David Morrissey . . . . Jackson Lake
Jordan Southwell . . . . Urchin
Velile Tshabalala . . . . Rosita

CLASSIC CONNECTIONS: While Peter Davison reappeared as the fifth Doctor in *Time Crash*, and *Human Nature*'s Journal of Impossible Things showed sketches of all of David Tennant's predecessors in the role of the Doctor, *The Next Doctor* marks the first time that actual footage from the original series or the 1996 TV movie have been incorporated into the new series, with a brief clip of each Doctor. The potential inconsistency of the alternate universe/"Cybus" Cybermen having information about the Doctor's prior regenerations is avoided with the Doctor's conjecture that these Cybermen stole the information from the Daleks trapped in the Void (*Doomsday*), which also explains why few, if any, of the clips are from Cybermen stories (though they're not necessarily from Dalek stories either).

A.K.A.: David Morrissey co-starred with David Tennant in the 2004 series **Blackpool** (imported to American PBS outlets as **Viva Blackpool**).

As with most of the **Doctor Who** Christmas episodes, *The Next Doctor* isn't terribly deep — it's required to tell its story, get off the stage and clear the decks for the next story without leaving any dangling continuity for the new season to deal with. The story once again takes place at or on Christmas itself, though in this case we finally get out of modern times and do a period piece — a welcome change.

Some of the changes to *The Next Doctor*'s antagonists, however, are puzzling. The Cybermen spend the entire episode paying homage to, building, and finally powering up the "Cyber King" — a giant-mecha-by-way-of-steampunk vehicle which proceeds to trample through London, *Godzilla* style. The Doctor points out that it's purely a vehicle — perhaps the Cyber equivalent of *Star Wars*' AT-ATs — but that doesn't explain why the Cybermen spend much of the build-up to its appearance worshipping it, as if it is its own being. The Cyberleader chides Miss Hartigan for being a slave to her emotions, but then joins its fellow Cybermen in a display of, for lack of a better word, faith…which is surely as far from the cold logic of the Cybermen as anything can be.

One can't fault guest stars David Morrissey, Velile Tshabalala and Dervia Kirwan, though; their performances keep the whole story afloat, and Morrissey in particular makes a fantastic Doctor-who-isn't-the-Doctor. If he *had* turned out to be the Time Lord's next incarnation, I would not have been disappointed. Once he's freed of some of the limitations of actually being an incarnation of the Doctor, his emotional depth is believeable, and up until the minor complication of a certain missing family member appeared late in the story, I found myself thinking that Morrissey's character should be a new companion. He certainly has the right stuff.

Aside from my qualms about the odd treatment of the Cybermen, *The Next Doctor* is a fun, lightweight adventure that thunders along and frequently doesn't let up enough to think about the shortcomings that are there; and on Christmas day, one can't expect much more than that.

PLANET OF THE DEAD

The Doctor boards a double-decker bus in London, on the trail of a space-time disturbance somewhere nearby. But to his dismay, the bus drives straight through the disturbance: a wormhole that deposits the bus to a rough landing on a barren desert world. Among the assortment of passengers on the bus are a slightly psychic woman whose abilities have been enhanced by the trip through the wormhole, and a mysterious and surprisingly well-equipped woman named Lady Christina de Souza, who quickly teams up with the Doctor, if only because he seems to be the only one who knows what's going on – and she wants to know why. When a group of insectoid bipeds called Tritivores find the travelers, it becomes apparent that the double-decker isn't the only recent arrival on this distant world. There's another race on this planet as well – one which created the wormhole, and intends to widen the wormhole leading to London. Their objective is to feed on everything and everyone on whatever planet they swarm to; their only obstacle is a Time Lord and a resourceful woman who's almost as mysterious as he is.

David Tennant . . . . The Doctor
Victoria Alcock . . . . Angela
David Ames . . . . Nathan
Glenn Doherty . . . . Sgt. Dennison
Noma Dumezweni . . . . Capt. Magambo
Lee Evans . . . . Malcolm
Adam James . . . . D.I. McMillan
Daniel Kaluuya . . . . Barclay
Paul Kasey . . . . Sorvin
James Layton . . . . Sgt. Ian Jenner
Ruari Mears . . . . Praygat
Keith Parry . . . . Bus Driver

UNIT

This story has been released on DVD

written by Russell T. Davies & Gareth Roberts
directed by James Strong
music by Murray Gold

Aired on April 11, 2009

Michelle Ryan . . . . Christina
Ellen Thomas . . . . Carmen
Reginald Tsiboe . . . . Lou

CLASSIC CONNECTIONS: The Doctor's reference to an incident involving a giant robot was, in fact, the first adventure of the fourth Doctor (Tom Baker) in *Robot* (1974/75), which also involved UNIT. In some respects, the character of Lady Christina vaguely resembles the character outline for a feisty female burglar who would have been introduced in the never-made fourth season of Sylvester McCoy's era, had it gone into production in 1990. (The abandoned stories featuring that character, now named Raine Creevy, were eventually adapted into Lost Stories audio plays by Big Finish.)

A.K.A.: Michelle Ryan may be best known on both sides of the Atlantic for starring as Jamie Sommers in the short-lived NBC remake of **The Bionic Woman**. This marks the second appearance of **Noma Dumezweni** as UNIT's Capt. Erisa Magambo, first seen (in an alternate timeline) in season four's *Turn Left.*

BEHIND THE SCENES: Just as *Spearhead From Space* marked the beginning of a new era as the first color episode of **Doctor Who**, *Planet Of The Dead* is another turning point: it's the first **Doctor Who** episode filmed in high-definition (though the first **Doctor Who**-related HD production was actually the first season of **Torchwood**). The desert scenes were filmed in Dubai, though the plot point of the bus being heavily damaged was helped along a little bit by damage incurred during shipping of a real double-decker to the location.

With far too little **Doctor Who** hitting our screens in 2009, every story needed to count, and while *Planet Of The Dead* was a nicely atmospheric tale, it was a little short on plot. The desert filming location in the United Arab Emirates adds a lot to the proceedings: this is easily the most effective foreign location filming that **Doctor Who** has seen since 1979's *City Of Death*, and it really adds to the story rather than just telegraphing the message that the BBC just spent a lot of money to send cast and crew to a far-flung location without it really being reflected on-screen.

For all of *Planet Of The Dead*'s abundance of atmosphere, however, other elements are lost. The plot is just about the simplest "go get the sci-fi McGuffin so we can escape before the big bad arrives" story imaginable. The supporting guest stars do well enough, but unlike, say, *Midnight*, there isn't enough time to really get into either the characters or the guest stars' portrayal of them. The one guest star who can command any attention here is Michelle Ryan as Lady Christina, a cross between the prototypical Perfect TARDIS Companion and Lara Croft, and it's interesting to turn the usual Russell T. Davies **Doctor Who** holiday special trope on its ear. Rather than meeting an ideal traveling companion who can't sign on for a tour aboard the TARDIS, the Doctor is the one who won't take Lady Christina with him, not because doing so might help her to escape justice (he seems more than willing to do that), but because he's tired of watching his friends get hurt – or worse – just for the privelege of traveling with him. Whether or not Davies is aware of it, one wonders if co-writer Gareth Roberts drew Davies' attention to the fact that the extended **Doctor Who** universe already has one mischievous woman in a space-hopping London double-decker: Time Lady Iris Wildthyme.

Advance publicity drew attention to the Tritivore creatures, though I found them just a little bit of a letdown. Maybe it was necessitated by a tight budget, but their elaborate bug-head makeup was let down a bit by their simple, one-piece zip-up jumpsuits – jumpsuits whose zippers aren't suited to the hands that we're repeatedly shown early in the show. To cite a random example, the Hath from *The Doctor's Daughter* combined an elaborate makeup with a somewhat more interesting costume; the Tritivores just needed a little more style to make them visually interesting below their necks. It's not often that a costume stands out enough to make me take notice because it's that good or that bad, but c'mon – even the Autons, renowned for their boiler suits in the 1970s, have gotten more stylish than that.

THE WATERS OF MARS

The TARDIS materializes on Mars in 2059 near Bowie Base One, the first human settlement on the red planet. The Doctor's stroll across Mars is interrupted by an armed robot, which brings him back to the base at gunpoint. It's only when the Doctor meets Captain Adelaide Brooke and her crew that he remembers how history records the fate of Bowie Base One: the base is doomed to be destroyed when Brooke activates the self-destruct mechanism. Why she did it, or will do it, is still a mystery – one in which the Doctor is reluctant to get involved. But when other members of the Bowie Base One crew stop communicating with their crewmates, it seems that the Time Lord has no choice but to play a pivotal role in the events that will transpire. The Doctor soon discovers the truth: a living form of liquid is taking over the crew one-by-one and intends to force an evacuation so it can stow away aboard the escape vehicle and begin to take over Earth. But even knowing that, the Doctor hesitates to interfere – the death of Brooke and her crew is a pivotal event that sets the stage for humanity's eventual expansion into interstellar space, and not allowing them to die could undermine all of Earth's future history. But does the entire crew have to die? It's not as if anyone's around to enforce the laws of time if the Doctor decides to save them.

David Tennant . . . . The Doctor
Lily Bevan . . . . Emily
Max Bollinger . . . . Mikhail
Gemma Chan . . . . Mia Bennett
Charlie De'ath . . . . Adelaide's Father
Lindsay Duncan . . . . Adelaide Brooke
Sharon Duncan-Brewster . . . . Maggie Cain
Rachel Fewell . . . . young Adelaide
Michael Goldsmith . . . . Roman Groom
Paul Kasey . . . . Ood Sigma
Aleksandar Mikic . . . . Yuri Kerenski
Peter O'Brien . . . . Ed Gold
Alan Ruscoe . . . . Andy Stone

This story has been released on DVD

written by Russell T. Davies & Phil Ford
directed by Graeme Harper
music by Murray Gold

Aired on November 15, 2009

Cosima Shaw . . . . Steffi Sherlich
Chook Sibtain . . . . Tarak Ital
Anouska Strahnz . . . . Urika Ehrlich
Zofia Strahnz . . . . Lisette Ehrlich

CLASSIC CONNECTIONS: The Doctor mentions a mighty empire on Mars that may have contained and frozen the Flood; it's likely that he's referring to the Ice Warriors (not seen on TV since 1974's *The Monster Of Peladon* starring Jon Pertwee), though other Martian societies have been portrayed in **Doctor Who**, including the godlike Osirans and the Ambassadors of Death. The disturbing image of a human body spewing forth a seemingly endless spray of water dates back to the second Doctor serial *Fury From The Deep* - could *Fury*'s seaweed creature and its human minions be the result of a previous attempt by the Flood to gain a foothold on Earth?

A.K.A.: Lindsay Duncan's most prominent genre role prior to *The Waters Of Mars* may be as the voice of protocol droid TC-14 in the opening scenes of *Star Wars Episode I: The Phantom Menace*, but she's also been seen in **MI-5, Rome,** Tim Burton's 2010 live action version of **Alice In Wonderland, Merlin,** the brief 2012 revival of **Absolutely Fabulous,** and the TV movie *Christopher And His Kind* (with Matt Smith). Peter O'Brien has guest starred on **Time Trax, The Lost World, Relic Hunter, Gossip Girl,** and *X-Men Origins: Wolverine*.

BEHIND THE SCENES: A sign that *The Waters Of Mars* is a true product of the DVD/download age, the many "computer screens" depicting the crews' biographies can be read in full when paused. *Waters* is dedicated to **Barry Letts,** producer of **Doctor Who** from Jon Pertwee's second adventure through the first Tom Baker story, who died shortly before this special premiered. *The Waters Of Mars* won the **Best Dramatic Presentation (Shortform) Hugo Award** in 2010, the first time a **Doctor Who** episode *not* written by Steven Moffat won the Hugo.

A mixture of familiar, tried-and-true elements of both **Doctor Who** and sci-fi horror in general, *The Waters Of Mars* doesn't show the hand that it has truly set out to play until the very end. It all seems fairly standard-issue: the trapped-in-an-isolated-base-with-the-bad-guys setup dates back to every second or third story of the Troughton era (or further still to Hartnell's final story, *The Tenth Planet*).

And yes, even the notion that the Doctor sometimes takes his Time Lord powers too far is familiar to anyone who read the early New Adventures novels, in which the seventh Doctor expertly played his companions and allies as pawns in a game of chess. In this case, however, the tenth Doctor isn't playing out the endgame in a confrontation that's been going for a while; his ethical dilemma is spur-of-the-moment and it plays into a theme that Russell T. Davies has been hinting at since Christopher Eccleston was the Doctor. All the way back in *Dalek*, the ninth Doctor was ready to render that Daleks extinct single-handedly (and let's not forget that both the seventh and presumably the eighth Doctors had each come to a point where they thought they were wiping out the Daleks as well). The only thing stopping him was Rose. Similarly, the only thing stopping the tenth Doctor from wiping out the Racnoss with extreme malice was Donna, and the "human tenth Doctor" of *Journey's End* proved himself capable of near-genocide as well. Here, nothing stops the Doctor, though time does right itself at the end of the story, with tragic consequences.

Davies seems to be presenting us with an interestingly humanistic notion: what makes or made the Doctor superior to the rest of the Time Lords was only partly his own nature. What really makes him special is the fact that he travels with humans… or at least he did in the past. He stubbornly refuses to accept any new companions in the 2009 specials, and the culmination of that is *The Waters Of Mars*, in which he truly seems to lose his way. When he clearly states that the laws of time "will obey me," it's telegraphed to the audience: Gallifrey has produced a host of megalomaniacal loonies, from the Master to the Rani to Borusa to Rassilon himself. And the Doctor is no different: absolute power corrupts absolutely. The pressure valve that kept him from going off this deep end before was his human companions. Where the fourth and fifth Doctors were tempted with leadership of the Time Lords, the tenth Doctor has decided: to hell with it. They're not here, and he is, and despite that too many people still end up suffering. Why *shouldn't* he be in charge?

The absolute conviction of Lindsay Duncan does wonders to sell the whole story. This isn't to slight the rest of the cast, but they're busy being turned into somewhat damp zombies, or their scenes are dominated by interactions with Gadget; Duncan carries much of the story's gravitas, and she even blows Tennant off the screen in a conversation that's conducted entirely via viewscreen; publicity for *Waters* described Adelaide Brooke as the Doctor's "most strong-willed companion yet", but in the end, she's such a forceful personality that the Doctor is practically *her* companion. There's no way this relationship could've carried on beyond this episode.

It's clear by the time that an Ood shows up as the tenth Doctor's harbinger of doom (the fourth Doctor had a much easier time of it with a mummified figure of mystery announcing his imminent end) that *Waters* is simply setting into motion the events of *The End Of Time*. *Waters* on its own is an exceedingly traditional **Doctor Who** adventure – and there's plenty that's enjoyable about that too.

DREAMLAND

Undetectable by the primitive civilization on the planet below, alien spacecraft battle each other above Earth. One combatant survives; the other crashes near Roswell, New Mexico. The year is 1947.

Years later, the Doctor arrives in the TARDIS; strange sightings at Roswell have all but passed into the local folklore. Some, however, are still convinced that something sinister is afoot, including ranch hand Jimmy Stalkingwolf, who the Doctor meets at a diner. A piece of supposed UFO debris on display at the diner catches the Doctor's eye, and he inadvertently proves that it's the real thing – men in black suits arrive almost immediately to confiscate it. The

Doctor and his new friends run for it and discover that there really are aliens in and around Area 51. Some of them are helpless, and some of them are bent on conquering Earth – with the unwitting help of the U.S. military.

David Tennant . . . . The Doctor
David Tennant . . . . The Doctor
Lisa Bowerman . . . . Saruba Velak
Peter Guinness . . . . Mister Dread
Tim Howar . . . . Jimmy Stalkingwolf
Ryan McCluskey . . . . Soldiers
Stuart Milligan . . . . Colonel Stark
Georgia Moffett . . . . Cassie Rice
Clarke Peters . . . . Night Eagle
Nicholas Rowe . . . . Rivesh Mantilax
David Warner . . . . Lord Azlok

This story has been released on DVD

written by Phil Ford
directed by Gary Russell
music by Murray Gold

Part 1 aired on November 21, 2009
Part 2 aired on November 22, 2009
Part 3 aired on November 23, 2009
Part 4 aired on November 24, 2009
Part 5 aired on November 25, 2009
Part 6 aired on November 26, 2009

SARAH JANE CONNECTIONS: The alien ship would be studied and copied by alien criminal Androvax in The Sarah Jane Adventures two-parter *Prisoner Of The Judoon*, which actually premiered before *Dreamland*. Mr. Dread returns to pursue Sarah Jane and her friends in *The Vault Of Secrets*, this time played by actor Angus Wright.

AUDIO CONNECTIONS: *Dreamland* almost resembles a Big Finish audio production with animation. It was directed by former Big Finish producer Gary Russell and recorded at Big Finish's usual haunt, The Moat Studios.

A.K.A.: Cast members **David Warner** and **Peter Guinness** have been associated with audio **Doctor Who** in the past; Warner has been associated with much genre fare in the past, including *Tron, Time After Time, The Omen, The Time Bandits, Titanic, Star Trek V: The Final Frontier, Star Trek VI: The Undiscovered Country*, a high-profile two-episode guest shot on **Star Trek: The Next Generation** (in which he donned Cardassian armor to torment fellow Royal Shakespeare Company alumnus Patrick Stewart), and appearances on everything from **Twin Peaks** to **Babylon 5** to the animated **Batman** and **Spider-Man** series. For Big Finish, he has appeared in the **Doctor Who** audio stories *Deimos, Circular Time, Empathy Games*, and *The Children Of Seth*, and as an "alternate third Doctor" in two **Doctor Who Unbound** audio stories, *Sympathy For The Devil* and *Masters Of War*. **Georgia Moffett** appeared in an early Big Finish audio play, but is best remembered as *The Doctor's Daughter* from the fourth season of the new TV series. **Lisa Bowerman** has been heavily involved with Big Finish since the company formed to launch a series of Bernice Summerfield audio plays over a year before obtaining the **Doctor Who** license in 1999, starring as Bernice and directing several productions; she also appeared as Karra in the final episode of the original **Doctor Who** series, *Survival*. This is **Stuart Milligan's** first **Doctor Who** "appearance"; he would later play a much more iconic American role against Matt Smith as the eleventh Doctor in 2011's *The Impossible Astronaut* and *Day Of The Moon*.

Doctor Who has avoided wading into the oversaturated sub-genre of absorbing/adapting the Roswell UFO crash mythology into its own mythos, but I suppose it was bound to happen at some point. *Dreamland* tells the story stylishly, and for the most part it's an interesting take on Roswell… but it's not without its faults.

The ease and convenience of Colonel Stark's conversion from collaboration with the Viperox to fighting against them is jarringly sudden; the Colonel simply switches sides too quickly, with only the Doctor's word for it that he's on the wrong side. Fortunately, Stark doesn't completely lose his teeth for the remainder of the story, but for such a pivotal story development to happen in the blink of an eye strains credibility.

The cel-shaded CGI animation of *Dreamland* is very detailed, but a lot of details seem left by the wayside – the characters end up being not very expressive, and the fluidity of movement leaves something to be desired. *Dreamland* won't be declaring a truce for **The Clone Wars** anytime soon; there have, frankly, been better-animated video game cutscenes. Sadly, the stylized animation betrays the staggering amount of beautifully rendered detail in the backgrounds and in such objects as vehicles. Even the Doctor is recognizably a digital David Tennant, but the CGI Doctor doesn't have a chance of duplicating or even beginning to emulate Tennant's wide range of rapidly-changing facial expressions – virtually a visual trademark of that character.

I wasn't holding my breath for a **Doctor Who** treatment of Roswell, but the story was – for the most part – decent enough. In the end, however, it's let down a bit by the execution, which was itself probably the result of an extremely compressed production schedule that simply needed more time for R&D and fine tuning.

THE END OF TIME

Nightmares plague the human race; every nightmare features the same laughing face – the face of a man that the world once knew as Harold Saxon. Most people forget the nightmares and are vaguely troubled the next day, but one man retains his memory of each incident – Wilfred Mott, Donna's grandfather, who immediately begins to keep a watchful eye out for the Doctor's return.

The Doctor, on the other hand, seems to be in no hurry to rush to the rescue. After events on Mars, he's actively avoiding situations where he must save the day, but a visit to Oodsphere changes that. The Ood are also experiencing nightmares involving the Master, as well as a disjointed series of images of other people, including Wilfred and Donna. The Doctor returns to Earth and discovers that a cultish group of followers has resurrected the Master's body, and the twisted Time Lord is now more powerful than ever, with abilities far beyond those of a normal Time Lord, and a bottomless appetite as a result. But not all-powerful: the Master is abducted before the Doctor's eyes.

With Wilfred's help, the Doctor tracks the Master down to the mansion of billionaire Joseph Naismith, who hopes to enlist the Master's help to gain control over an alien artifact called the Immortality Gate. But the Master, even though he's working at the point of a gun, has his own plans for the Gate. The Master has twisted the Immortality Gate into his own weapon, projecting himself as a template onto every human on Earth: every human on Earth is now the Master. The two aliens working undercover in Naismith's operation are unaffected, and Wilfred is unaffected as well, stuck in the Master's isolation booth. But the only other human not possessed by the Master is Donna Noble, whose adventures with the Doctor are flooding back into her mind. Wilfred urges her to run, but soon the amount of information crowding her human brain causes her to collapse. The Master interrogates the Doctor, demanding to know the whereabouts of the TARDIS, but this grueling interrogation is soon interrupted by the two aliens, who teleport themselves, the Doctor and Wilfred to their ship in orbit.

An alien artifact arrives on Earth, a piece of the extinct world of Gallifrey, and only then does the Master realize what the drumbeat in his head is: the rhythm of a Time Lord's two hearts. The Master uses this piece of Gallifrey to establish a link, and the entire planet of Gallifrey materializes close enough to Earth that tidal forces begin tearing the smaller planet apart. The Time Lords, desperate to escape their imminent doom in the Time War, have broken free by sending their distress signal – the drumbeat – back in time. They retroactively created the Master and made him a madman, all to compel him to provide an escape route for Gallifrey. The Lord President and members of the High Council of the Time Lords arrive on Earth, where the Master demands their obedience and just as quickly discovers that the Lord President is ready to eliminate him: the Master has served his purpose where the Time Lords are concerned. The

Doctor cuts Gallifrey's link to Earth as the Master and the Time Lord President do battle; the planet of the Time Lords disappears again, taking the Master with it.

But it is only after the crisis is averted that the Doctor realizes that the prophecy of his own death has nothing to do with the Time Lords *or* the Master.

David Tennant . . . . The Doctor
Freema Agyeman . . . . Martha Smith-Jones
Krystal Archer . . . . Nerys
Allister Bain . . . . Winston Katusi
Teresa Banham . . . . Governor
John Barrowman . . . . Capt. Jack Harkness
Max Benjamin . . . . Teenager
Claire Bloom . . . . The Woman
Lacey Bond . . . . Serving Woman
Brid Brennan . . . . The Visionary
Nicholas Briggs . . . . Judoon voice
Lachele Carl . . . . Trinity Wells
Silas Carson . . . . voice of Ood Sigma
Noel Clarke . . . . Mickey Smith
Camille Coduri . . . . Jackie Tyler
Karl Collins . . . . Shaun Temple
Brian Cox . . . . voice of Elder Ood
Bernard Cribbins . . . . Wilfred Mott
Timothy Dalton . . . . Lord President
Joe Dixon . . . . The Chancellor
David Harewood . . . . Joshua Naismith
Barry Howard . . . . Oliver Barnes
Jessica Hynes . . . . Verity Newman
Tracy Ifeachor . . . . Abigail Naismith
Paul Kasey . . . . Ood Sigma
Sinead Keenan . . . . Addams
Jacqueline King . . . . Sylvia Noble

This story has been released on DVD

written by Russell T. Davies
directed by Euros Lyn
music by Murray Gold

Part 1 aired on December 25, 2009
Part 2 aired on January 1, 2010

Thomas Knight . . . . Luke Smith
Pete Lee-Wilson . . . . Tommo
Julie LeGrand . . . . The Partisan
Lawry Lewin . . . . Rossiter
Ruari Mears . . . . Elder Ood
Alexandra Moen . . . . Lucy Saxon
Billie Piper . . . . Rose Tyler
Dwayne Scantlebury . . . . Ginger
Sylvia Seymour . . . . Miss Trefusis
Elisabeth Sladen . . . . Sarah Jane Smith
John Simm . . . . The Master
Matt Smith . . . . The Doctor
Dan Starkey . . . . Sontaran
Catherine Tate . . . . Donna Noble
Simon Thomas . . . . Mr. Danes
Russell Tovey . . . . Midshipman Frame
June Whitfield . . . . Minnie Hooper

CLASSIC CONNECTIONS: The cackling Visionary, constantly reminding Rassilon and his advisors of their impending doom, however, is unlike any Time Lord character the series has ever presented us with - a relic of a far more superstitious age. **But is she even a Time Lord?** Her robes are somewhat similar to those worn by the Sisterhood of Karn (*The Brain Of Morbius, Night Of The Doctor*), which brings up an interesting development from the New Adventures novels. The New Adventures books of the '90s — specifically Cat's Cradle: Time's Crucible (1992), by Marc Platt — presented an elaborate look into Gallifreyan history, marked by an extended struggle between science and reason (a cause, ironically, taken up by a younger Rassilon) and superstition and witchcraft (in the person of the Pythia). At the end of this conflict, the Pythia and her largely female followers left Gallifrey and settled on Karn, evolving into the Sisterhood, while Rassilon introduced time travel and regeneration to a race that had suddenly become sterile. If the Visionary is indeed a Sister of Karn, it's a remarkable development showing that Rassilon has become desperate enough to ask for help from a force he once drove out of Gallifrey.

TORCHWOOD CONNECTIONS: Naismith says that the Immortality Gate was originally recovered and held by Torchwood, and that he acquired it after Torchwood fell; this could either be referring to the fall of the London branch of Torchwood in *Doomsday*, or the destruction of Torchwood Cardiff in *Children Of Earth*. The Time Lord President, unwilling to permit even the slightest disagreement, uses something that looks suspiciously like the resurrection gauntlet found by Torchwood (*They Keep Killing Suzie*) — or perhaps its opposite number — to deal with dissenters; one quickly gets that idea that his inner circle of advisors is routinely depopulated and repopulated — it's probably not a position that's viewed as an upward career move. Or a survivable one...

By turns both brilliant and banal, *The End Of Time* Part 2 is both a fond farewell to Russell T. Davies' "era" of **Doctor Who**, and a series of textbook examples of why the showrunner baton needed to be passed.

What's good about this episode: just about any scene where David Tennant and Bernard Cribbins have a one-on-one discussion. It's a pity that we waited this late to team the two up; as much as we loved Cribbins is Wilfred Mott, Donna's grandfather, getting to know him as something other than a one-off cameo or an ancillary character is great, and the rapport and respect between him and the Doctor instantly makes him one of the all-time great male TARDIS travelers, with loyalty which would rival that of Jamie McCrimmon himself. It's a shame that Wilf didn't board the TARDIS a lot sooner. Bernard Cribbins is able to milk many of his lines for a laugh, but it's in scenes where he more dramatic instincts are dead-on that he truly soars.

The fact that the Doctor's tenth life is sacrificed not to save the world, but simply to save Wilf, may well be the best part of the entire story. This really speaks to the heart of the Doctor's character and to the message of the show overall: at one point, Wilf even tells the Doctor to go and leave him to his fate, and in a much colder analysis, no one would know if the Doctor did walk away – there would be no witnesses. That the Doctor does save him, at the expense of his own life (or one of them at any rate), having survived the whole epic dance of saving the world yet again, makes this the most personal and heart-wrenching regeneration story in the series' history.

The Time Lords prove to be one of the most fascinating classic series callbacks that the new show has given us. The state that they're in – cowering and conferring in vast, dark chambers on a planet that's clearly seen better days – says a lot about the devolution of the Doctor's race, to say nothing of their reliance on prophecy to set war policy. The Time Lords are so utterly clueless at fighting or managing a war that they're looking for clues in tea leaves and entrails.

The real jaw-dropper which comes late in the episode is that *the Lord President may be Rassilon himself* (which may explain why the Visionary is still around after delivering so much bad news – if she is a surviving Gallifreyan from the oft-vaguely-mentioned Dark Times, Rassilon might harbor his own superstitions about getting rid of her). Considering that *Utopia* and *The Sound Of Drums* established that the Master – who was presumed dead after falling into the Eye of Harmony in the eighth Doctor's TARDIS – was somehow revived to serve as a last-ditch weapon in the Time War, it's plausible that such a decision might have been taken by a people who were desperate enough for leadership that they would revive Rassilon as well. (In the Big Finish audios, Rassilon is still on the loose after the extended Divergent Universe cycle of eighth Doctor stories, so it's also possible that Rassilon himself, in a regenerated form, could've seized on an opportunity to return to power and take charge of the Time War.)

The other major piece of mythology dropped into our laps here is that the Master became the Master because of Time Lord interference. When this obviously encompasses every incarnation of the Master we've ever seen, this is a positively *huge* development. I'm on the fence, however, when it comes to explaining away/excusing all of the Master's past transgressions, including numerous incidents of mass-murder, as symptoms of his victimization at the hands of Rassilon's desperate cabal of hawkish Time Lords.

What doesn't work here: the action scenes, while flashy and eye-popping, present ideas that just don't stand up to much scrutiny. The Master launches an entire arsenal of nuclear missiles at the alien ship being piloted to Earth at kamikaze speed by the Doctor, while Wilfred and one of the aliens man Millennium-Falcon-style laser cannons to fend off the missiles. So… we've detonated dozens of nukes over the oceans of Earth with no ill effects? Similarly, and I thought this was nearly funny given that the collective memory of regeneration stories that have come before will be bubbling to the surface, we're presented with the idea that the tenth Doctor can survive a parachute-less skydive, from a spacecraft moving at least at the speed of a jet plane, through a huge glass skylight dome and survive with what appears to be only moderate scratches and bruises and no broken bones… while a fall from a stationary radio telescope onto stationary grass from a lower altitude doomed the fourth Doctor? Sure, it all looked fantastic, a spectacular combination of visual effects and stunt work, but these things kept troubling me – a real case of style over substance.

At the end of the story, with the crisis abated, the Doctor manages to stave off his regeneration for a surprisingly long stretch, so he can go and see – and save – many of his old friends and companions one more time. These range from cute (Captain Jack in modern **Who**'s answer to the *Star Wars* cantina scene) to sobering (the Doctor saving Sarah Jane's son Luke) to sweet (Donna's wedding and a Rose return that I'll actually let them skate by with) to real what-the-heck!? moments (a gun-toting Martha and Mickey, now married and "freelancing" against Sontarans?!?). In the middle of it all, the whole thing grinds to a halt for a callback to *Human Nature / The Family Of Blood*, and even though I'm an ardent fan of the series, it took a couple of moments for it to click with me that this was what the show was referring back to. It just seemed like an oddly obscure refrain, but still an effective one.

The End Of Time kisses off the Davies (and David Tennant) years in considerably flashy style.

The Eleventh Doctor
(Matt Smith: 2010-2013)

With David Tennant ready to leave the TARDIS, the search was on for his replacement. **Doctor Who** had just replaced its showrunner with the Hugo-winning Steven Moffat, who claimed to be an avowed **Doctor Who** purist. This would be Moffat's first indelible stamp on the series: casting the eleventh Doctor.

So it came as a surprise to fandom, media critics and the general public when Moffat, who had originally set out to cast an actor around the 40-year-old mark, unveiled a new Doctor who wasn't yet out of his 20s. Masterfully kept under wraps by the BBC until unveiled on a special, heavily publicized episode of **Doctor Who Confidential** airing on January 3rd, 2009, the eleventh Doctor was almost-unknown young actor Matt Smith.

Born in 1982 (or, for context, the same year that Peter Davison started his run as the Doctor), Matt Smith had already embarked on a promising acting career, appearing in such BBC dramas as **Moses Jones** and **Party Animals** (and, amusingly enough, a guest shot on Billie Piper's series **Secret Diary Of A Call Girl**, as one of Belle's customers). He went in to audition for **Doctor Who**, flying in the face of Steven Moffat's casting call for late 30-something, early 40-something actors with otherworldly intensity – and on the first day of auditions, no less. Moffat and incoming producer Piers Wenger met the young actor, watched his audition, and sent him on his way. Surely someone better suited to the part would come along.

But weeks later, Moffat and Wenger compared notes: no one better suited *had* come along, and both of them still vividly remembered Matt Smith's audition.

Smith was offered the part in total secrecy, as Moffat and Wenger began searching for the actress to play the companion Moffat envisaged for his tightly-plotted season. The producers finally settled on Scottish actress Karen Gillan, who had played a small role in *The Fires Of Pompeii* during David Tennant's last full season as the Doctor. Filming began in 2009, with Alex Kingston along to reprise the role of River Song, an enigmatic character introduced in Tennant's last season. The fans and the press made it clear, usually on the internet, that the jury was still out on the youngest Doctor in the show's history.

Aware that Smith's casting (and the criticism thereof) marked a huge turning point in the network's most bankable television property, the BBC spent lavishly on promoting the new Doctor and his new companion, including a dizzying promo piece shown in 3-D in theaters. Though these promo pieces risked showing off too much of the new cast and the enemies who would be appearing that season (a motley bunch that was already known to include the Weeping Angels introduced in Moffat's Hugo-winning *Blink*, redesigned Daleks, and possibly even the Silurians for the first time since 1984), it was a calculated risk: David Tennant had become ingrained in the minds of much of the viewing public as *the* Doctor of the new series. (Christopher who?) The BBC was aware that there would be resistance to the recasting of the Doctor, and giving the audience a taste of his personality outside of the series itself would help keep them on board.

The season began over Easter weekend in 2010, featuring the first radical revamp of both the visual and musical elements of the main titles. The season unfolded to critical acclaim, the viewing public and the fans clearly pleased to have the writer who had won most of **Doctor Who's** Hugo Awards to date at the wheel. The BBC's investment in publicizing and smoothing the change of leading man had paid off, and **Doctor**

Who had entered a new era, again with the kind of promotional tender loving care that would've been unimaginable in the waning days of the original series.

SERIES 5: 2010
THE ELEVENTH HOUR

Following the Doctor's regeneration, the TARDIS plummets back to Earth, damaged and out of control. The time machine comes to rest in the 1990s, where the Doctor has to seek the help of the first person he finds – namely, a little girl named Amelia Pond who is home alone. In exchange for her help, the Doctor investigates something that's been troubling Amelia: a crack in her wall through which she says she can hear voices. It turns out that her fears aren't unfounded: the Doctor finds something from another dimension behind her wall, but he seals the crack and seems fairly sure he's solved the problem. He promises to return in five minutes; Amelia packs a bag and sits in her garden, waiting for the TARDIS and the mysterious Doctor to return...

The TARDIS rematerializes in the garden, but it's been only moments for the Doctor – he's just realized the significance of the crack in the wall. But 12 years have passed for Amy Pond – and for the being behind her bedroom wall. The Doctor finds a door where no door should be in Amy's house, containing a being known only as Prisoner Zero, which then escapes. As the Doctor works to find the dangerous escapee, Earth receives a signal from an alien race called the Atraxi: if the people of Earth cannot contain Prisoner Zero, the Atraxi will wipe out all life on the planet, just to make sure the escaped prisoner is dealt with. There are only 20 minutes left to save the world, and the Doctor isn't exactly in peak condition...

Matt Smith	. . . .	The Doctor
Karen Gillan	. . . .	Amy Pond
Caitlin Blackwood	. . . .	Amelia Pond
Perry Benson	. . . .	Ice Cream Man
Olivia Coleman	. . . .	Mother
Arthur Cox	. . . .	Mr. Henderson
Annette Crosbie	. . . . . .	Mrs. Angelo
Arthur Darvill	. . . .	Rory Williams
David de Keyser	. . . . . .	Atraxi voice
Tom Hopper	. . . .	Jeff
Marcello Magni	. . . .	Barney Collins
Eden Monteath	. . . .	Child 1

This story has been released on DVD

written by Steven Moffat
directed by Adam Smith
music by Murray Gold

Aired on April 3, 2010

Merin Monteath	. . . .	Child 2
Patrick Moore	. . . .	himself
Nina Wadia	. . . .	Dr. Ramsden
William Wilde	. . . .	Prisoner Zero voice

CLASSIC CONNECTIONS: The lightning and thunderclaps in the new opening titles hearken back to the very origins of **Doctor Who**; the unaired pilot version of *An Unearthly Child* featured thunderclaps in the theme music, though these were removed before the remount of the series' first-ever episode. The redesigned TARDIS exterior resembles the police box as seen in the two Peter Cushing **Doctor Who** movies in the 1960s, while the new set for the TARDIS console room includes elements that recall the early William Hartnell stories (the large metallic light fixture above the console), the Davison/Colin Baker era TARDIS (a sound effect that occurs several times in *The Eleventh Hour*'s final scenes) and even the TARDIS as seen in the 1996 TV movie (the scanner screen as an old TV hanging above the console).

A.K.A.: Caitlin Blackwood is a good fit as young Amy because she's Karen Gillan's cousin in real life, even though the two had never met prior to filming. Karen Gillan made her **Doctor Who** debut in 2008's *Fires Of Pompeii*.

The first moments of Steven Moffat's reign as **Doctor Who** showrunner has to pick up the pieces left over by the final scenes written by Russell T. Davies, but once the TARDIS is finished vaulting over the top of Big Ben, we're off to the races – and yet we're in very familiar territory too.

The alien threat in *The Eleventh Hour* almost seems tacked-on; every time the emphasis shifted from the Doctor and Amy to Prizoner Zero and the Atraxi, I found myself wanting the pendulum to swing the other way; I suppose it's unreasonable to hope for a story that's bold enough to not have the world under threat. We learn so little about the Atraxi and their prisoner that, by the time the Doctor sends both packing, it's difficult to care about the alien menace of the week. Perhaps the best thing to come from the Atraxi plotline is the neat little montage as the Doctor asks them three questions and then advises them in no uncertain terms to leave Earth alone; the Atraxi's visual review of Earth history owes a little bit to the extended ending of James Cameron's *The Abyss*, but the third and final question triggers a montage of the ten previous Doctors, and ends wonderfully as Smith walks through a floating image of David Tennant – an inspired way to hand off the torch for anyone still bemoaning Tennant's departure.

But even more inspired is the relatively quiet storyline building the Doctor's relationship with Amy. His recurring appearances at different points in her life smacks more than just a little bit of Moffat's Hugo-winning *The Girl In The Fireplace*, except that unlike that story's tragic ending, Amy gets to join the Doctor on his travels, something she's obviously been waiting her whole life to do. (As formidable a presence as Karen Gillan is on screen, I find little Amelia an even more indelible image: the scenes of her waiting in the garden for her time-traveling friend to return are simply heartbreaking, and yet we're talking about two very brief scenes with no dialogue – and they don't *need* dialogue either. It would've been interesting if Amelia had been a recurring image throughout the season.)

THE BEAST BELOW

The Doctor and Amy happen upon an enormous vehicle in deep space in the 29th century: the Starship UK, a spaceborne version of the entire country. But the Doctor instantly senses that something isn't right: the population of the Starship UK is silently living in fear. Amy discovers that something alive – and alien – is aboard the vessel, but she is then captured by robed monks and shown a history of the ship, a history which she is then asked to protest or forget. The Doctor arrives, and he and Amy discover that the survival of the British people in the future has come at a horrifying price to an innocent life form. But if Amy doesn't stop the Doctor from taking further action, the price may become even higher.

Matt Smith . . . . The Doctor		written by Steven Moffat
Karen Gillan . . . . Amy Pond		directed by Andrew Gunn
David Ajala . . . . Peter		music by Murray Gold
Jonathan Battersby . . . . Winder	This story	
Alfie Field . . . . Timmy	has been	Aired on April 10, 2010
Christopher Good . . . . Morgan	released	
Terence Hardiman . . . . Hawthorne	on DVD	
Ian, McNeice . . . . Churchill		
Sophie Okonedo . . . . Liz 10		Catrin Richards . . . . Poem Girl
Chris Porter . . . . voice of Smilers / Winder		Hannah Sharp . . . . Mandy

A.K.A.: Sophie Okonedo was nominated for an Oscar for her role in 2004's *Hotel Rwanda*, but **Doctor Who** fans may remember her best as the voice (and character model) of Alison Cheney, the reluctant companion of an animated ninth Doctor played by Richard E. Grant in the 2003 BBC webcast *Scream Of The Shalka*. (Following the announcement of the

TV series' revival, the BBC — having announced that Grant was the "official" ninth Doctor — quietly swept *Shalka* under the rug.) She's also appeared in **MI-5**, the live-action adaptation of *Aeon Flux*, and *The Martian Child*, a movie adaptation of SF writer David Gerrold's semi-autobiographical novel.

AUDIO CONNECTIONS: A space whale had been central to an unproduced story pitched repeatedly during the early 1980s, *Song Of The Space Whale* by frequent-flyer <u>Doctor Who Magazine</u> comics writer Pat Mills. The story was originally pitched during Tom Baker's era, and rewritten and resubmitted during both the Peter Davison and Colin Baker eras (at one point it was considered a contender to be the story that introduced the sixth Doctor). It was finally produced — by Big Finish Productions — as part of the Lost Stories range of sixth Doctor audios, retitled *Song Of The Megaptera*. The Doctor has apparently been saving the (space) whales for a long time.

Though it's a lot more like what I'd expect from Steven Moffat calling the shots — menacing and featuring what's almost a proper hide-behind-the-sofa monster in the Smilers — there's still something strangely simplistic about *The Beast Below*.

The moment where we're treated to the sight of the Doctor having to make a horrifyingly tough decision is a bit strange; he seems to be ready to leap instantly toward a choice that runs counter to his nature (he even says he'd have to choose a new name, because he wouldn't be the Doctor anymore), and yet *Amy* is able to figure out that there's yet another alternative. For the second episode in a row, we're treated to a montage that hits us over the head with what a character has seen or heard, which proves to be part of the solution: In *The Eleventh Hour* it made me think "Okay, well, that's different," but in *The Beast Below* it made me think "Oh no, not again." We get it: the devil's in the details. But give the audience a bit of credit for observation right alongside the Doctor's companion.

The atmosphere of the whole thing is the best part of *The Beast Below*: before the opening titles run, we have a very good picture of the extremely enclosed world that is the Starship UK. Within a few minutes after the opening titles, it has effectively become a real place — and then the rug is yanked out from under us when the Doctor and Amy discover that there's an entirely different and much more organic side to things. By this point, the Starship UK has acquired a real sense of place, which isn't something that every episode is able to establish with its setting.

VICTORY OF THE DALEKS

The Doctor is summoned to wartime London during the Blitz. None other than Winston Churchill himself has called the Doctor for help, but with the TARDIS' unreliability, it's taken the Doctor a month to answer that call — and in the meantime, Churchill has turned elsewhere for help in the war effort. Professor Bracewell has designed mobile war machines of immense power, capable of picking off German bombing formations before a single bomb can be dropped. Bracewell and Churchill call them "Ironsides," but the Doctor knows them all too well as the last remaining Daleks — and he's puzzled that Amy can't remember ever having seen a Dalek, even after Earth was invaded by them. But these Daleks insist that they are soldiers, here to protect Britain from the Germans. In order to get them to reveal their true plan, the Doctor will have to do something very dangerous indeed: provoke the Daleks into showing their true, deadly colors.

Matt Smith . . . . The Doctor
Karen Gillan . . . . Amy Pond
James Albrecht . . . . Todd

written by Mark Gatiss
directed by Andrew Gunn

UWORP!

Nicholas Briggs	. . . .	Dalek voice
Nina de Cosimo	. . . .	Blanche
Barnaby Edwards	. . . .	Dalek 2
Susanah Fielding	. . . .	Lilian
Ian McNeice	. . . .	Churchill
Bill Paterson	. . . .	Bracewell
Nicholas Pegg	. . . .	Dalek 1

This story has been released on DVD

music by Murray Gold

Aired on April 17, 2010

Colin Prockter	. . . .	Air Raid Warden
Tim Wallers	. . . .	Childers

CLASSIC CONNECTIONS: There seems to be a hint that the conflict between Davros' "Imperial" Daleks and the "Renegade" Daleks who have rejected him (as seen in 1988's *Remembrance Of The Daleks*) may still be ongoing; leftover Daleks from *The Stolen Earth* (2008), who were created/augmented with Davros' own DNA, cannot kick-start the progenitor device that creates the new Daleks. (And the newly-created Daleks from the progenitor immediately exterminate their forebears, although the older Daleks offer themselves up as willing sacrifices without a fight.) This isn't the first time that the Daleks have pretended to be servants of the human race; they launched a very similar scheme in the future on Vulcan, a human colony planet, in the first Patrick Troughton story, *Power Of The Daleks*; incidentally, their aim there was also to power up the production line on a new race of Daleks. This marks the first new series reference to the Doctor's TARDIS being a Type 40 model (a statistic dating back to the original series, first mentioned in *The Deadly Assassin* during Tom Baker's reign), as well as the first new series reference to the Daleks' time corridor technology (*Resurrection Of The Daleks*, 1984).

AUDIO CONNECTIONS: One of the new Daleks has a rather ominous title – the yellow **Dalek Eternal** – without much of a hint of what its function is. But what if we've already met a Dalek Eternal by a different name? The 2009 Big Finish audio story *Patient Zero* features a character called the Dalek Time Controller, whose job description seems to include carefully plotting Dalek temporal incursions and calculating their potential ramifications for the timeline.

A hectic, rushed story, *Victory Of The Daleks* seems to be here merely to provide a "reset switch" for the Daleks as a whole. During Russell T. Davies' tenure as the showrunner, it had been noted, as far back as their first new series appearance in *Dalek*, that the Daleks had been marginalized and all but rendered extinct by the Time War. Even when they did reappear in great numbers, the racial-purity-obsessed Daleks of the new series were mongrels: *The Parting Of The Ways*' Daleks had hybrid Dalek-human DNA, the Cult of Skaro (*Doomsday*, *Daleks In Manhattan*) were "tainted" by individuality to the point that Dalek Sec was willing to surrender his bloodline in order to evolve and survive, and the Daleks of *The Stolen Earth / Journey's End* were a stew of Dalek and Davros DNA. Even the last pure Dalek (*Dalek*) was evolving an emotional dimension and thus betraying its birthright of pure hatred. Davies' Daleks were compromised by the need to survive. Mark Gatiss hits the reset switch in this story: the pureblood Daleks are back and are prepared to repopulate their species. Davies had to come up with a way to generate a new Dalek race for nearly every story in which they appeared, stretching credulity with each successive Dalek episode (not unlike the miraculous string of completely unexplained escapes from certain doom that the Master pulled off in the 1980s). Gatiss and Moffat have eliminated the need for that: the Daleks are back, and are here to stay.

The rest of *Victory* is a bit of a muddled mess, however. It paints a skewed picture of World War II, with Churchill depicted as far more corpulent than he was in real life, surrounded by characters who seldom rise above the depth of characterization you'd expect from Biggles. The story really doesn't do much justice to these extraordinary events in British history, apart from a token mention of Churchill as a beacon of hope to the world. There are so many other missed opportunities here that the mind boggles: there's an intriguing hint that anyone harnessing the power of the Daleks, even someone like Churchill involved in a noble struggle, could be overcome by a lust for power, but it's taken no further than a hint. There was also a completely missed opportunity to go back to the Daleks' roots in the mind of writer Terry Nation, who created the Daleks as a sci-fi proxy for the Nazis; there's never been a better opportunity to make that (perhaps unsubtle) parallel, but instead we wound up with the Daleks fighting the Nazis. There were plenty of opportunities for subtext here, but instead we got a *Star Wars*-style space dogfight with Spitfires which were apparently retro-fitted (future-fitted?) for flight *outside of Earth's atmosphere* in the space of mere minutes.

Perhaps unshackling the Daleks from their increasingly convoluted, Davies-era continuity was a necessity, but surely it could've been done a bit more gracefully than this. As it is, *Victory Of The Daleks* has an interesting A-story that demands more room to breathe (the Dalek story), set against a B-story (London in the Blitz) riddled with historical inaccuracies, stereotypes and a kind of lightweight jingoism that does no favors to the memory of those who fought and died in a very real conflict between good and evil. (Ironically, there's been a Dalek audio story – *Jubilee* – that deals with reducing symbols of real evil to marketing imagery. Maybe it bears a fresh listen.) Perhaps Churchill should've been saved for another occasion. The end result is entertaining, but mainly on a check-your-brain-at-the-door level.

TIME OF THE ANGELS

An artifact in a museum catches the Doctor's eye: a message is written in the Old High Gallifreyan language on its surface, a message in an extinct language meant just for him. The message leads him to a set of coordinates in time and space where he has seconds to rescue River Song after she ejects herself from an airlock aboard the starship Byzantium – a ship she still wants to follow. When the TARDIS next materializes, it's on an alien planet where the Byzantium has crashed, killing all aboard... all except for a lone Weeping Angel. The Doctor only has moments to bring Amy up to speed on the Angel's deadly abilities, but it's already wreaking havoc. And as the Doctor and Amy join River's expedition to board the Byzantium and destroy the Angel, it soon becomes apparent that it is the expedition that's outnumbered.

Matt Smith . . . . The Doctor
Karen Gillan . . . . Amy Pond
David Atkins . . . . Bob
Simon Dutton . . . . Alistair
Troy Glasgow . . . . Angelo
Iain Glen . . . . Octavian
Alex Kingston . . . . River Song
Darren Morfitt . . . . Marco
Mike Skinner . . . . Security Guard
Mark Springer . . . . Christian

This story has been released on DVD

written by Steven Moffat
directed by Adam Smith
music by Murray Gold

Aired on April 24, 2010

CLASSIC CONNECTIONS: River Song returns in this episode; *Silence In The Library* and *Forest Of The Dead* are still in her future, but have already happened for the Doctor (in his tenth incarnation). She has, however, seen pictures of all of the Doctor's faces. The Weeping Angels make their first appearance since season 3's Hugo-winning *Blink*, along with *Silence / Forest*, *Blink* was written by Steven Moffat as a freelance writer during Russell T. Davies' tenure as showrunner. The Old High Gallifreyan language was first mentioned in 1983's *The Five Doctors*; all of the Doctor's incarnations have been fluent in it, and presumably he passed that knowledge along to River Song. Even upon its first mention in 1983, it's implied that the language had fallen into infrequent use even among the Time Lords themselves.

Now what could be better than Steven Moffat revisiting the two most intriguing concepts he brought to the latter half of Russell T. Davies' era of **Doctor Who**... *at the same time?* This is really where the season kicks into gear.

To start with, as already implied in *Silence In The Library*, the timeline of the Doctor's meetings with River Song is going to be complicated; *Library* basically sees her death happen within hours of her first meeting with the tenth Doctor. *Time Of The Angels* is the eleventh Doctor's first meeting with her in *his* time stream, but it may well be her *final* encounter with him in this form prior to *Library*. I suspect that it won't even stay this cut-and-dried for long, with every meeting being diametrically opposed on the other character's timeline.

The Weeping Angels were the real draw card here, however – let's not kid ourselves. *Blink* has been perhaps the most universally-praised episode of **Doctor Who** to come along since the series was revived, and with good reason; the audience's affection with the concept was Steven Moffat's to lose if the rematch didn't equal their first appearance. It's clear that Moffat was clever enough to know that, because the Angels upped their game here: anything carrying the image of an Angel can essentially allow it to use that image as a portal. And looking an Angel in the eye too long can be just as bad letting it catch you – in other words, even *not blinking* is no longer a defense. If that's not enough, these Angels are just going around either killing their victims outright (rather than sending them to live the rest of their lives in the past, as in *Blink*) or using them as a conduit to communicate with their next potential victim (poor Bob). The Angels get new layers of bad tacked on to the existing wealth of badness they represent, making them even more fearsome without the new developments eliciting even one "Oh, come *on*."

The creep factor of this episode's atmosphere is right off the scale, the callbacks from only a season or two ago are worthy additions to the mythology, and it all works really, really well.

FLESH AND STONE

Surrounded by an army of statues – decayed Angels who are reawakening and gathering strength from the leaking radiation of the Byzantium's main drive – the Doctor has to take drastic measures to keep River Song, Amy and the rest of the expedition alive, and the Angels are never far behind. A crack appears in the wall of the Byzantium's flight deck – the same crack seen in Amy's childhood bedroom – and the Doctor suspects that something is going horribly wrong with time itself. Amy begins unconsciously counting down from ten aloud, and the Doctor discovers that she has looked into the eyes of a Weeping Angel long enough for the Angels to use Amy's eyes to monitor the expedition's movements; this mental link is also killing Amy slowly, and the Doctor has to ask her to close her eyes and keep them closed, cutting the Angels off from the information they need and prolonging her own life. River Song's part in the expedition is revealed as well: she's not the expedition's leader, but a convicted killer (whose victim was the "best man" she's ever known) taking on a dangerous assignment to win a pardon from her sentence. The expedition soldiers begin vanishing one by one, consumed by the ever-expanding crack, from which Amy instinctively knows they won't be coming back. The Doctor fights to come up with a solution that will keep his friends and allies alive, and all the while, the army of Angels closes in…

Matt Smith	. . . .	The Doctor
Karen Gillan	. . . .	Amy Pond
David Atkins	. . . .	Bob
Iain Glen	. . . .	Octavian
Alex Kingston	. . . .	River Song
Darren Morfitt	. . . .	Marco
Mark Monero	. . . .	Pedro
George Russo	. . . .	Phillip

This story has been released on DVD

written by Steven Moffat
directed by Adam Smith
music by Murray Gold

Aired on May 1, 2010

Densely packed with information that doesn't necessarily pay off by the end of this story, *Flesh And Stone* is as much setup as it is resolution. We're rid of the Weeping Angels by the end – though they were disposed of rather too easily – but the air of mystery surrounding River Song has increased considerably by the end of the story.

It also becomes very obvious that Moffat is playing a a much more long-term game with this season's timeline than what we're used to. Fairly early in the story, the Doctor has to sacrifice his tweed jacket to escape the Angels, but at one point, when he's forced to leave Amy under the protection of the expedition's soldiers, he vanishes after being rather dismissive toward her and then reappears moments later, with his jacket on, behaving with much more obvious concern for Amy's welfare. It's obvious that this isn't the Doctor we're following through much of this episode: this is a very brief visit from the Doctor from some point in his future, who has looped back in time to try to change events. Given that, in *The Beast Below*, we saw a recorded message from a future Amy, it should be obvious by now that the time travelers are trying to rewrite their own history to avoid some terrible fate; what fate that is no doubt will be explained toward the end of the season. There's also the in-your-face hint that all but screams to the audience that River's murder victim may be the Doctor himself... as if their relationship wasn't already complex enough.

The scene of the Angels closing in, illuminated only by strobes of light from the soldiers' machine guns, is simply one of the best things that's been shown this season – a brilliant way of speeding up the usual seemingly glacial speed of an Angel attack.

VAMPIRES OF VENICE

The Doctor returns Amy to her own time, and decides to take her and her fiancee Rory on a romantic getaway – namely, Venice in 1580. But almost as soon as the TARDIS brings them there, it's obvious that something is amiss. Venice is under the thrall of the reclusive House of Calvierri, from whose elite school no pupil ever returns. The father of one girl who has been enrolled in this school is demanding to see proof that his daughter is alive and well, and his demands are met with threats of violence. The Doctor and Amy both see members of the Calvierri inner circle reveal vampire-like teeth, but the despite all the traditional signs of vampires – no reflections in a mirror, sharp teeth, drinking blood – the Doctor thinks these vampires are actually aliens. When he discovers a plan to repopulate a nearly-extinct species by transforming Earth into a suitable environment, the Doctor may be left with no choice but to ensure their extinction to save humanity.

Matt Smith . . . . The Doctor		written by Toby Whithouse
Karen Gillan . . . . Amy Pond		directed by Jonny Campbell
Alisha Bailey . . . . Isabella		music by Murray Gold
Elizabeth Croft . . . . Vampire Girl		
Arthur Darvill . . . . Rory	This story	Aired on May 8, 2010
Simon Gregor . . . . Steward	has been	
Helen McCrory . . . . Rosanna	released	
Gabrielle Montaraz . . . . Vampire Girl	on DVD	
Lucian Msamati . . . . Guido		Hannah Steele . . . . Vampire Girl
Michael Percival . . . . Inspector		Sonila Vieshta . . . . Vampire Girl
Alex Price . . . . Francesco		Gabrielle Wilde . . . . Vampire Girl

CLASSIC CONNECTIONS: This episode marks the first appearance of the ninth and tenth Doctors' psychic paper in the eleventh Doctor's possession. He also has a library card, under the name of Dr. J. Smith, bearing a photo of his first incarnation.

AUDIO CONNECTIONS: The Doctor has visited Venice in previous incarnation in a variety of audio stories; the fourth Doctor has a fateful encounter with alien insects there in *Hornets' Nest: A Sting In The Tale*, while the eighth Doctor visited Venice in the future in *The Stones Of Venice*.

BEHIND THE SCENES: With the exception of a few background shots, none of this episode was actually filmed in Venice itself. A city in Croatia proved to be a more cost-effective location, with a variety of lighting tricks and digital effects evoking the look of Venice. The documentary series **Doctor Who Confidential**, however, *did* take Matt Smith and writer Toby Whithouse on location to Venice.

Vampires are a tricky thing to pull off in **Doctor Who**. Long before **Buffy** and the *Twilight* series of movies and books make bloodsucking a popular pastime, the dean of **Doctor Who** script editors, Terrance Dicks, wrote a 1980 script which intertwined vampire mythology with Time Lord mythology, making vampires an alien race that Rassilon himself had beaten back into submission. Since then, it's hard to do a vampire story without having to somehow give a nod to *State Of Decay*. The audio stories squeaked by – barely – with *another* race of vampires in the gritty sixth Doctor story *Project: Twilight*, and short-circuited vampire mythology in *Son Of The Dragon*. And *The Vampires Of Venice* earns a handy exemption too, mainly by revealing that its vampires are not really vampires.

The show's pre-credits teaser is a bizarre morsel of awkwardness, offering further proof that the eleventh Doctor just doesn't have the same suave cool of his previous two incarnations. Matt Smith has settled into the role nicely, and this scene and numerous others in *Vampires* really begin to showcase the eleventh Doctor's distinct, brilliantly scatterbrained personality. The scene in which he produces an out-of-date library card by way of identification – out-of-date enough to bear William Hartnell's publicity photo! – and then demands "Tell me the whole plan!" is a gem. Anyone worried about Amy's attempt to bed the Doctor at the end of *Flesh And Stone* can rest easy too – she's genuinely happy to be reunited with Rory, and she fills out the job description of companion handily, chasing after a vampire rather than running *away* from it.

Rory, for his part, is petrified at the implications of what goes on in the Doctor's travels, and tries to stand up for Amy anyway; in this respect he reminds me a lot of the rapidly-maturing Joxer from season 3 onward of **Xena: Warrior Princess** – sure, he's comic relief, but you believe and, more importantly, *like* him as a person. I'm glad to see him staying aboard the TARDIS at the end of the show – maybe he'll get to surpass the untapped potential of Mickey Smith's all-too-brief stint as a TARDIS crew member.

This is one instance where the location filming really pays off (unlike, say, *Planet Of Fire* confusingly using Lanzarote as both an alien planet and Lanzarote, or the could-have-been-filmed-anywhere feel of some of *Fires Of Pompeii*'s Rome location shoot). With a good deal of digital trickery, Croatia is surprisingly effective as a stand-in for Venice, and *Vampires Of Venice* winds up with a unique look as a result. It's a nice stand-alone adventure, even with the hints of the season's larger story arc tacked on abruptly at the end of the episode.

AMY'S CHOICE

The TARDIS lands in upper Leadworth, outside the home of former TARDIS travelers Rory and Amy, who are now expecting their first child. The Doctor is pleased to see them both, they're both perplexed to see him, and the excitement of the impromptu reunion lulls them all to sleep. They wake up aboard the TARDIS, still traveling together and decidedly not expecting a baby, mystified by what must surely be a dream. A being called the Dream Lord appears, demanding that the three travelers choose between the reality they've just seen, and the reality of travel in the TARDIS. The time travelers slip back and forth disconcertingly between the increasingly strange earthbound setting and the Doctor's timeship, which is growing increasingly cold. The Dream Lord insists that time is running out... and the one person who can decide which scenario is real isn't the Doctor, but Amy.

Matt Smith . . . . The Doctor
Karen Gillan . . . . Amy Pond
Arthur Darvill . . . . Rory
Audrey Ardington . . . . Mrs. Poggit
Nick Hobbs . . . . Mr. Nainby
Toby Jones . . . . Dream Lord
Joan Linder . . . . Mrs. Hamill

This story
has been
released
on DVD

written by Simon Nye
directed by Catherine Morshead
music by Murray Gold

Aired on May 15, 2010

An interesting little stand-alone tale, this story by Simon Nye (creator and chief scriptwriter of **Men Behaving Badly** – the original UK version, *not* the watered-down American adaptation) has a fairy tale quality and an off-the-scale surreal feeling that reminds me of Doctor Who Magazine's comics in the 1980s. It's really not like anything else that the revived **Doctor Who** series has produced since its return, partly because the Doctor seems so utterly powerless throughout the story.

The revelation that the old people of Leadworth aren't what they seem – at least in the shared dreamscape – leads to some of the most unnerving moments of the Moffat era thus far. The alien menace – imagined or not – owes a little something to *Invasion Of The Body Snatchers* and *Alien*, and it's almost a letdown that the "old folks of the corn" are not the real villain of the piece.

That distinction goes to the Dream Lord, played as a sort of dark parody of the Doctor by Toby Jones, and all sorts of interesting hints are thrown out there about who this character might be (on first viewing, my money was on the Master of the Land of Fiction from *The Mind Robber*). Unfortunately, the real villain turns out to be some kind of psychic spore, and the Dream Lord is, disappointingly, a dark mirror image of the Doctor borne out of the Time Lords own fears and insecurities. That revelation is just so **Star Trek: The Next Generation** – and yet there seems to be a hint at the very end that perhaps the Dream Lord is more than just that. (Hello, Valeyard?)

A very intriguing episode let down by a somewhat lame excuse for the villain's origins. If it was my choice, the wrap-up would've been more intriguing and less reset-button-pushing.

THE HUNGRY EARTH

The Doctor tries yet again to take Rory and Amy on a romantic getaway, but instead of Rio, the TARDIS lands in Wales in 2020, near the site of a project to drill deep through the Earth's crust. One man has already vanished without a trace from the small drilling operation, and other strange things are happening as well, such as patches of blue grass appearing on the surface. The rig's owners hope this is a sign of a promising subsurface mineral deposit, but the Doctor can immediately tell it's something else. When Amy disappears, his suspicions are confirmed: the drill has awakened the Silurians, the bipedal reptiles who roamed Earth before the ascent of humankind... and they're more than wiling to take hostages to announce their presence prior to reclaiming their world. The Doctor and Nasreen Chaudrhy, the project's chief researcher, go underground in the TARDIS to recover Amy and the other hostages, while the one Silurian that the Doctor and Rory can capture has plans of her own. Unlike the Doctor's plan, her strategy doesn't involve the human race's better nature.

Matt Smith . . . . The Doctor
Karen Gillan . . . . Amy Pond
Arthur Darvill . . . . Rory
Samuel Davies . . . . Elliot
Neve McIntosh . . . . Alaya
Robert Pugh . . . . Tony Mack
Alun Raglan . . . . Mo
Nia Roberts . . . . Ambrose
Meera Syal . . . . Nasreen Chaudhry

This story has been released on DVD

written by Chris Chibnall
directed by Ashley Way
music by Murray Gold

Aired on May 22, 2010

CLASSIC CONNECTIONS: This isn't the first time that the Doctor has stumbled across industrial activity in Wales that uncovered something nasty: the third Doctor had to shut down Global Chemicals' operation in 1973's *The Green Death*, that incarnation of the Doctor also encountered the Silurians in *Doctor Who And The Silurians* (1970) and their aquatic relatives in 1972's *The Sea Devils*.

Long overdue for a return to the **Doctor Who** universe (numerous book and audio appearances notwithstanding), the Silurians are one of the most intelligently-concocted antagonists of the original series – mainly because they weren't really villains. The Silurians are the original owners of Earth, and according to the mythology established in their first appearance, they took to underground shelters to avoid a calamity that would soon befall the surface. Small pockets of Silurian civilization have awoken from time to time as human activity triggered their automatic defenses, never in enough numbers to declare full-scale war (and, consequently, never in enough numbers to break BBC bosses out in a cold sweat by requiring an army's worth of rubbery lizard suits). But on a purely conceptual level, the Silurians allow the show to address thorny topics such as the displacement of native cultures without invoking history and politics that the younger portion of the audience may know nothing about. Devised by Malcolm Hulke for their first appearance 40 years before *The Hungry Earth* aired, the Silurians are, in a word, characters with an Earthly agenda.

And it's that 1970 debut, *Doctor Who And The Silurians* (which also happens to be one of the author's all-time favorite **Doctor Who** television adventures), that *The Hungry Earth* evokes the most, with barely-glimpsed creatures skulking in the shadows, slowly chipping away at a small cast of human characters, and hatching schemes to reclaim the Earth. With its mad plan (on the part of the humans, naturally) to drill miles into the Earth's crust, there's also more than a slight nod toward the other shining gem of season 7, *Inferno* (another high point of Pertwee's era) – not a bad couple of stories to remind us of. But *The Hungry Earth* adds a delicious twist: the Silurians are counting on the psychology of the "apes" to guarantee a martyrdom which will lead to a war. There's an opportunity here for Rory to shine, showing some increased maturity after traveling in the Doctor's company, but not much is made of that.

I also have to admit to not being that impressed with the redesigned Silurians. I can accept the explanation that there are many tribes/subspecies in existence; even the New Adventures and Missing Adventures novels of the 1990s played with this idea, with one in particular, Scales Of Injustice, depicting a Silurian/Sea Devil hybrid in its cover artwork. But the new series Silurians diverge a little *too* much from what's come before. The returning enemies in the Davies era – Daleks, Cybermen, Sontarans – all had significant nods to the previous designs; not so much here. The original 1970 Silurians were unnervingly non-human (though the redesign for 1984's *Warriors Of The Deep* managed to botch that design); the 2010 models look like, in all honesty, something from **Star Trek: Voyager**... or, worse yet, when they don their strange masks, they look like Sleestaks.

Whatever my issues are with the Silurians, however, they're offset by a great cast of supporting human characters, with Meera Syal in particular raising the notion that it might be really interesting, sometime down the road, for Matt Smith's Doctor to be accompanied by a companion who's obviously older than the Doctor seems to be. To some extent, this has been done in the Big Finish audio stories with the sixth Doctor and Evelyn Smythe, but the age divide could be even more significant with the eleventh Doctor.

COLD BLOOD

Silurian warrior Alaya is counting on her human captors' animal bloodlust: she expects to be killed, and her resulting martyrdom will remove any objections among her own people to declaring war on humanity. Rory tries his best to keep a lid on the growing tensions between Alaya and the humans, but he can't guard her every moment, and soon enough Alaya gets her wish. Beneath the Earth's surface, the Doctor and Nasreen discover that Amy and the other vanished humans are alive and well, and that there are both sympathetic and warlike factions among the Silurians. He tries to get peace talks started between the two dominant species of Earth, but he may not be able to keep the warrior faction's ambitions quelled when Alaya's body is returned. Stopping an all-out war now will come at an agonizing cost.

Matt Smith . . . . The Doctor
Karen Gillan . . . . Amy Pond
Arthur Darvill . . . . Rory
Samuel Davies . . . . Elliot
Richard Hope . . . . Malohken
Neve McIntosh . . . . Alaya / Restac
Stephen Moore . . . . Eldane
Robert Pugh . . . . Tony Mack
Alun Raglan . . . . Mo
Nia Roberts . . . . Ambrose
Meera Syal . . . . Nasreen Chaudhry

This story has been released on DVD

written by Chris Chibnall
directed by Ashley Way
music by Murray Gold

Aired on May 29, 2010

As with *The Hungry Earth*, *Cold Blood* closely mirrors the structure (and the underlying message) of 1970's *Doctor Who And The Silurians*. What's surprising in this installment is that the Doctor steps back and lets the humans do their own talking. Rory is more or less left in charge on the surface, while Amy and Nasreen negotiate with the Silurian elders in their city. He doesn't do this without sternly explaining that everyone needs to be on their best behavior, but it remains an interesting and mature twist to the standard-issue way that Silurian stories unfold. Most of the time (*Doctor Who And The Silurians, Warriors Of The Deep*) the Doctor steps out of the way very late in the (attempted) peace proceedings, only to watch the humans he has championed slaughter the emerging Silurian population. And he even admits to that having happened here, a direct reference to the 1970 story (in Earth's history, *Warriors* still has yet to happen). Maybe he's learned that humanity will need to do its own talking for this to work.

Unfortunately, things of course do not go well, and Rory ends up not only paying for it with his life, but suffering a fate arguably even worse than death: the dreaded "crack" that has plagued the TARDIS crew all season long envelops Rory, wiping him from the timeline altogether. By the end of the episode, Amy has forgotten him (but the Doctor hasn't). This is the most upsetting departure of a TARDIS traveler that the new series has given us thus far (and that includes Rose's exit/exile to an alternate universe), and possibly the most disquieting fate for a companion since *The Trial Of A Time Lord*. It also occurs without a lot of last-episode signposting, so it's truly a shock to the system. But of course, nothing's that simple where time travel is involved…

VINCENT AND THE DOCTOR

At an exhibit of Vincent Van Gogh's artwork, the Doctor thinks he's spotted – in a painting – evidence that an alien creature that may have been stalking the Earth in Van Gogh's time. The next stop for the TARDIS is in Provence, where something has indeed been claiming the lives of numerous people – and Van Gogh, considered a crazy outsider, has been blamed for the deaths. The Doctor and Amy offer to help, but how can the Doctor save any lives when Vincent is the only one to actually see the alien creature? And will helping Vincent fight the beast change the painter's own future?

Matt Smith . . . . The Doctor	
Karen Gillan . . . . Amy Pond	
Andrew Byrne . . . . School Child	
Chrissie Cotterill . . . . Mother	
Sarah Counsell . . . . Waitress	
Tony Curran . . . . Vincent	
Nik Howden . . . . Maurice	
Bill Nighy . . . . Dr. Black	
Morgan Overton . . . . School Child	

This story has been released on DVD

written by Richard Curtis
directed by Jonny Campbell
music by Murray Gold

Aired on June 5, 2010

A.K.A.: Bill Nighy – whose name was not shown in the end credits of the episode – was considered a hot contender for the role of the ninth Doctor when the series' return was still in pre-production. He has featured in the *Harry Potter* film series and appeared as Slartibartfast in the 2005 film adaptation of *The Hitchhiker's Guide To The Galaxy.*

BEHIND THE SCENES: Oscar-nominated writer **Richard Curtis** penned the screenplays for *Four Weddings And A Funeral, Notting Hill* and *Love, Actually,* prior to his film career, however, Curtis wrote or co-wrote every episode of **Blackadder,** starring Rowan Atkinson, who would play *another* ninth Doctor in the 1999 Comic Relief spoof *The Curse Of Fatal Death* (written, coincidentally, by one Steven Moffat). Curtis also founded the Comic Relief charity.

A truly off-format episode, even by **Doctor Who** standards, *Vincent And The Doctor*'s alien-hunting plotline is almost incidental; it's very clear that the real meat of this episode is the interaction with Van Gogh. That part of the episode wears its heart on its sleeve unashamedly, and Tony Curran does such an outstanding job as Van Gogh, that I found myself growing annoyed when the "alien" plot distracted from these scenes.

Why can't modern TV **Doctor Who** grow the pair that Big Finish audio **Doctor Who** has had for many years, daring to tell "historical" stories with *no* science fiction elements other than the time travelers themselves?

The real treat of the Van Gogh scenes is that they don't skimp on depicting the man's anguish and mental disarray. That part of the show could've been even more powerful with no goofy sci-fi influence. Van Gogh's interactions with the Doctor and Amy have heart and have a strange kind of reality to them. No alien snipe hunt was necessary to drive it home that the only characters capable of even beginning to understand Van Gogh were the time travelers.

The unexpectedly charming and touching conclusion takes Van Gogh briefly into a future where his work is revered and he himself is regarded with sympathy. Amy expects, for some reason, that this revelation will change his future, but we're left to ponder the possibility that it may simply cement the tragic end that hovers over Van Gogh throughout the episode. Tony Curran's performance in these scenes is scene-stealing; Matt Smith is no slouch in this episode, and there's also an uncredited turn from Bill Nighy, but Curran simply blows everyone else off the screen by the episode's end. It's tempting to ponder the wonders of Van Gogh traveling on the TARDIS for an extended period of time, and then returning to his old life – a jarring return to humdrum normalcy that could, very conceivably, have driven him to the depths that awaited him.

In the face of all of this character development, the alien subplot – surprisingly for an episode of a science fiction series – winds up looking awfully superfluous.

THE LODGER

The TARDIS lands on Earth, only the Doctor isn't expecting it to land there. When he steps out the door, the TARDIS practically ejects him – and then dematerializes with Amy aboard. The Doctor is able to contact Amy and deduces that something is preventing the TARDIS from making a full landing. The Doctor decides to rent a room from an affable bloke named Craig, who spends most of his time trying to overcome his fear of telling his friend Sophie that he has romantic feelings for her. But that's far from the worst of Craig's problems: a slowly spreading stain on the ceiling accompanies a recurring series of strange noises from whoever is renting the upstairs room. The Doctor is convinced that whatever is making the noise and the stain is also keeping the TARDIS from landing. As he spends several days at the house, the Doctor impresses Craig's other friends, meets Sophie, and becomes a constant but still strange fixture in Craig's life. When Craig decides to throw caution to the wind and investigate the room upstairs, that life may come to a quick and unpleasant end if the Doctor can't intervene.

Matt Smith . . . . The Doctor
Karen Gillan . . . . Amy Pond
Babatunde Aleshe . . . . Sean
Kamara Bacchus . . . . Clubber
James Corden . . . . Craig
Owen Donovan . . . . Steven
Daisy Haggard . . . . Sophie
Karen Seacombe . . . . Sandra
Jem Wall . . . . Michael

This story has been released on DVD

written by Gareth Roberts
directed by Catherine Morshead
music by Murray Gold

Aired on June 12, 2010

CLASSIC CONNECTIONS: When the Doctor telepathically transfers his knowledge to Craig, his fifth, sixth and seventh incarnations are not shown (whereas it's the second appearance this season for the second Doctor, and the season's third visual reference to the first Doctor).

COMICS CONNECTION: This episode is based on a comic by the same name that appeared in an issue of Doctor Who Magazine, originally centered around the tenth Doctor and Mickey Smith (with a very brief appearance by Rose) and set shortly after *The Christmas Invasion*, in that version of the story, of course, the Doctor moved in with Mickey, who would've rather been spending more uninterrupted time with Rose.

Another great, way-off-kilter episode for the eleventh Doctor, *The Lodger* – despite a massive rewrite from the comic that inspired it – is further proof that Matt Smith's incarnation of the Time Lord may well work best in stories that don't feel like traditional **Doctor Who**.

The Lodger revisits some of the same territory as *The Eleventh Hour*, as it jams something extraordinary and more than a little scary into an ordinary situation populated by ordinary people. If anything, it actually does a better job of it than the season opener, mainly because the characters of Craig and Sophie have a dynamic that's nearly universal (friends who want to be more than friends, and yet don't want to ruin their friendship). Just about everyone has been there, and that – along with the portrayal of these characters as normal folks who just happen to like each other (a lot) who aren't the Beautiful People one so often winds up casting for TV – grounds *The Lodger*'s more bizarre moments.

The revelation, near the end of the story, that some alien race has had a go at replicating TARDIS technology is pretty shocking stuff, and it's actually surprising that it isn't addressed more directly. Of course, the fact that it's coaxed into leaving of its own accord helps. (I also couldn't help but notice that this craft was piloted by an emergency hologram, to whom the Doctor says "Please state the nature of the emergency!" – **Doctor Who** is just about the *last* place I ever expected to see a **Star Trek: Voyager** in-joke.)

It's becoming increasingly apparent that the eleventh Doctor doesn't just thrive, but *excels* in stories that aren't cut from the same overly epic cloth as the tenth Doctor's stories. In some ways, this season of **Doctor Who** is starting to feel like the 25th anniversary season of the original series: we still get occasional epics, but we also get completely off-the-wall stories like *The Lodger*, *Vincent And The Doctor*, *The Greatest Show In The Galaxy*, and *The Happiness Patrol*, which are hard to envision with any other incarnation of the Doctor at the helm, and are completely unlike what we'd been accustomed to from **Doctor Who** stories up to that point. *And that's not a bad thing.*

THE PANDORICA OPENS

A series of events ripples through time and space upon the completion of Vincent Van Gogh's latest painting depicting the fiery destruction of the TARDIS. Many of the Doctor's friends and allies encounter the painting through time, from Winston Churchill to Liz 10 to, finally, River Song. River draws the Doctor to Earth at the time of the Roman Empire to show him the painting, which she believes is a warning Van Gogh received in a vision. Within the painting itself is a time and a location, leading the Doctor, Amy and River to Stonehenge.

The Doctor finds a chamber beneath Stonehenge, containing a large, cubical object of alien origin: the Pandorica, something which River has mentioned before but the Doctor believed was a myth. But before the Doctor can investigate or open the Pandorica, dozens of alien ships descend into the sky over Stonehenge: many of the Doctor's enemies have come to call. While he bluffs his would-be captors into leaving, River attempts to move the TARDIS closer to the Pandorica, but the timeship begins behaving erratically and is flung violently through the time vortex. It begins to seem as though the Doctor is destined not to be at the controls of the TARDIS when it suffers the fate forseen by Van Gogh.

The Doctor's enemies return to Stonehenge, and only then does the Doctor realize the horrifying truth: the Daleks, Cybermen, Sontarans and many more have set aside their differences to conspire against their greatest enemy. With their combined forces against him, the Doctor may be doomed, and the universe along with him.

Matt Smith . . . . The Doctor
Karen Gillan . . . . Amy Pond
Simon Fisher-Becker . . . . Dorium Maldovar
Nicholas Briggs . . . Dalek/Cyber/Judoon voices
Chrissie Cotterill . . . . Madame Vernet
Tony Curran . . . . Vincent
Arthur Darvill . . . . Rory
Barnaby Edwards . . . . Dalek
David Fynn . . . . Marcellus
Joe Jacobs . . . . Guard
Paul Kasey . . . . Judoon
Alex Kingston . . . . River Song
Howard Lee . . . . Doctor Gachet
Ian McNeice . . . . Winston Churchill
Ruari Mears . . . . Cyber Leader

written by Steven Moffat
directed by Toby Haynes
music by Murray Gold

Aired on June 19, 2010

This story has been released on DVD

Marcus O'Donovan . . . . Claudio
Sophie Okonedo . . . . Liz 10
Bill Paterson . . . . Bracewell
Christopher Ryan . . . . Commander Stark
Clive Wood . . . . Commander

CLASSIC CONNECTIONS: River Song name-checks several classic **Doctor Who** aliens as part of the attack force gather over Stonehenge, including Drahvins (*Galaxy Four*, 1965) and Zygons (*Terror Of The Zygons*, 1976). In *The Time Meddler* (1965), a rival Time Lord known as the Monk claims to have played a part in Stonehenge's construction, so he may have had a hand in planting the Pandorica there as well.

BOOK CONNECTIONS: River also says that the Chelonians are part of the attack force. The Chelonians are a reptilian warrior race introduced in the New Adventures novels published in the 1990s (in the book The Highest Science). This marks the first time that an element specific to the New Adventures has been acknowledged by name in the new TV series.

BEHIND THE SCENES: This marks the first time Daleks, Cybermen and Sontarans have all shared the screen in anything other than a flashback. If one wishes to count flashbacks, however, the first time would have been during the flashbacks experienced by the fourth Doctor at the end of part 4 of *Logopolis*. Along with *The Big Bang*, *The Pandorica Opens* won the **Best Dramatic Presentation (Shortform) Hugo Award** in 2011.

The first half of Steven Moffat's two-part season finale takes off at thundering speed, rocketing through callbacks to many of the season's episodes and characters, connecting the dots and tightening the various loose plot threads of the season together. Moffat can construct a cracking cliffhanger. How can you beat the whole universe fading to black and suddenly going silent? (And more to the point, how do you recover from it and tell another episode's worth of story?)

Pandorica spends quite a bit of time on the re-introduction of Rory, only to bring our expectations for his inevitable reunion with Amy crashing down with the realization that he's not who we thought he was. Arthur Darvill gives his best performance yet in the role, getting to show a much more serious side of Rory than we've seen thus far. Maybe serious isn't the word — "tragic" fits the bill better. Also returning is Alex Kingston as River Song, though for much of this episode she really seems to be a plot device rather than a character in her own right, propelling the Doctor and Amy forward from one critical set of events to the next. There is some interesting stuff with River, such as the Stormcage containment facility, but the crime that landed her there is left off the menu for this outing. And for such a secure facility, she seems to have little trouble escaping from it.

The two major developments here are the alliance between the Doctor's many enemies and the strange twist that a great deal of the events of the season may have been directly influenced by Amy's own mind. The notion of Daleks, Cybermen, Sontarans, Autons and others joining forces to put the Doctor away forward is by far more interesting. (One minor quibble: we see Cybermen, or at least parts of one, do things that we've never seen Cybermen do before, and more to the point, they do things that were once part of the function of the classic series' Cyber*mats*, creatures that wouldn't return until the following season. Then again, these are still the "Lumic Cybermen," apparently not bound by the same rules as the classic series Cybermen.)

THE BIG BANG

Trapped in the Pandorica by his enemies, the Doctor is powerless to prevent the universe from ending. The collapse isn't instantaneous, and Earth is at the epicenter, growing cold and dark as every star in the universe vanishes. Young Amelia Pond remembers the stars, though, despite what everyone tells her as the changes ripple backward through time.

Freed from the Pandorica, the Doctor embarks on an elaborate attempt to manipulate the timeline; while Earth still exists, he can influence its history and make changes to the present. But he'll need help, and there's where the problem lies: Amy is dead, River has probably died in the cataclysmic explosion that has ripped the TARDIS apart, and Rory isn't who anyone thought he was. Time is running out, even for the Time Lord.

Matt Smith	. . . .	The Doctor
Karen Gillan	. . . .	Amy Pond
Frances Ashman	. . . .	Christine
Caitlin Blackwood	. . . .	Amelia
Nicholas Briggs	. . . .	Dalek voice
Arthur Darvill	. . . .	Rory
Barnaby Edwards	. . . .	Stone Dalek
Halcro Johnston	. . . .	Mr. Pond
Alex Kingston	. . . .	River Song
William Pretsell	. . . .	Dave

This story has been released on DVD

written by Steven Moffat
directed by Toby Haynes
music by Murray Gold

Aired on June 26, 2010

Susan Vidler	. . . .	Aunt Sharon
Karen Westwood	. . . .	Tabetha

CLASSIC CONNECTIONS: The Doctor tells Rory that he's a Nestene, but this is technically incorrect; the Nestenes are large, squidlike creatures who control the plastic-based Autons, so technically Rory is an **Auton**. The Doctor has known fezzes are cool since the 25th anniversary episode back in 1988: the seventh Doctor briefly donned a fez while exploring Buckingham Palace in *Silver Nemesis*. To give River and Amy credit where it's due, Ace was similarly nonplussed at the Time Lord's taste in headgear.

BEHIND THE SCENES: Along with *The Pandorica Opens*, *The Big Bang* won the **Best Dramatic Presentation** (Shortform) Hugo Award in 2011.

Strange even by **Doctor Who** standards, *The Big Bang* features a number of characters making supreme sacrifices for one another, and it answers a number of questions raised during the rest of the season, but leaves some very big ones open for next season – it would seem that Steven Moffat is planning on playing a longer game than the average season of **Doctor Who** under Russell T. Davies.

The all-star line-up of villainy from *The Pandorica Opens* evaporates fairly quickly here, with the exception of one very cranky, 1800+ year old stone Dalek who really serves as more of a nuisance than anything. And really, that's a good thing – having captured the Doctor, the pantheon of bad guys could either vanish from existence, having miscalculated rather spectacularly what the effects of eliminating the Doctor from time might be, or they could rampage through the second episode, which wouldn't even make a terribly appealing video game, let alone crowding an already complicated episode which runs almost ten minutes longer than the usual 45-minute running time of the modern series' episodes.

And though the resolution is epic – there's talk of "rebooting the universe," a concept which may or may not have much more drastic implications for the show's internal continuity down the road – the path leading to it is rather light-hearted. Those accustomed to RTD's apocalyptic season enders may find the degree of lightness off-putting, but again, it points toward what much of the latter half of this season reveals: Matt Smith's Doctor works better when he's not just being written as a generic Doctor. The eleventh Doctor's penchant for off-format stories continues here, and when things become more serious and emotional, he works well in those scenes too. At the end of his first year in the TARDIS, Matt Smith *is* the Doctor, in the vein of some of the show's great eccentric leading men (Troughton, Tom Baker and McCoy) – not bad company. It's also extremely refreshing, after the companion-for-a-season RTD era, to see the TARDIS take off for its next round of adventures with the same companions we've had for much of the season.

SERIES 6: 2010-2011
A CHRISTMAS CAROL

Rory and Amy's honeymoon takes an unexpected turn – a downward turn into the stormy atmosphere of an alien planet, as it happens. With the starship they're aboard just minutes away from a crash landing, Amy sends a distress signal to the Doctor. The TARDIS lands in the city below, where the Doctor tries to negotiate with the powerful Kazran Sardick, who has the ability to control the weather. Sardick cares nothing for the fate of anyone aboard the crashing ship, and doesn't have much regard for anyone else either. The Doctor decides to intervene, not technologically but psychologically, going into the past to change Sardick's own history beginning with his childhood. But even a youth and an adolescence spent having adventures aboard the TARDIS with the Doctor may not be enough to soften Kazran Sardick's heart.

Matt Smith . . . . The Doctor
Karen Gillan . . . . Amy Pond
Micah Balfour . . . . Co-Pilot
Leo Bill . . . . Pilot
Arthur Darvill . . . . Rory
Michael Gambon . Kazran Sardick / Elliot Sardick
Danny Horn . . . . adult Kazran
Katherine Jenkins . . . . Abigail
Nick Malinowski . . . . Eric
Laurence Melcher . . . . young Kazran

This story has been released on DVD

written by Steven Moffat
directed by Toby Haynes
music by Murray Gold

Aired on December 25, 2010

Tim Plester . . . . Servant
Pooky Quesnel . . . . Captain

Steve North . . . . old Benjamin   Laura Rogers . . . . Isabella
Bailey Pepper . . . . Benjamin   Meg Wynn-Owen . . . . old Isabella

BEHIND THE SCENES: Arthur Darvill's name appears in the opening credits for the first time here.

SARAH JANE CONNECTIONS: The Doctor mentions making up for Amy and Rory's curtailed honeymoon by sending them to an actual moon made of honey; this is where he says the newlyweds are in the **Sarah Jane Adventures** two-parter *The Death Of The Doctor*, so that story takes place after *A Christmas Carol*.

The first **Doctor Who** Christmas special under the Steven Moffat regime is a curious beast, deriving heavily from Charles Dickens' A Christmas Carol (even to the point of borrowing its title unapologetically). That Dickens doesn't get a co-writing credit is almost a shame – surely it'd be quite a publicity coup for **Doctor Who** to boast a writer of Dickens' caliber. Given time, that **Doctor Who** connection might buy him a cult following as large as Douglas Adams' fan base!

The episode has a unique look and feel, both among the other **Who** Christmas episodes and other episodes in general – the flying fish are a neat idea, and the foggy atmosphere and the alien planet whose seemingly human inhabitants exist in an approximation of a bygone Earth era are right out of the classic series. There are also a couple of casting coups to boot, with Michael Gambon and Katherine Jenkins raising the bar considerably. The Dickens-inspired darker tone is unusual for a Christmas episode: still more Christmassy than *The End Of Time*, but still surprisingly dark.

But it's the attempt to slavishly follow the Dickensian formula that causes some of *A Christmas Carol*'s biggest problems. The ghosts of Christmas past, present and future in Dickens' opus are somewhat omniscient beings, while the Doctor is basically attempting a last-ditch rewrite of history in order to save a ship full of people. There's some mileage in the notion of the Doctor – who is not omniscient – doing that, but instead what we get is a Doctor who basically does away with Sardick's free will entirely. The Doctor is reshaping Sardick's personal history to suit himself (admittedly with the aim of saving lives) in a way that flies in the face of everything the character stands for.

Consider: in *Enlightenment*, the fifth Doctor relies on Turlough to find the answer to his moral dilemma within himself, without any prodding or prompting, even though one of Turlough's choices could mean the Doctor's own death. And even in *Genesis Of The Daleks* and *Resurrection Of The Daleks*, the Doctor tries to persuade Davros to use his unique position to influence the evolution of the Daleks – but we never see the Doctor go into Davros' childhood to influence his own development. Surely, if one is going to break the laws of time to that degree, you're going to expend that effort on the big fish – Davros, the Master, the origins of the Cybermen, etc. – rather than wasting that sort of risky endeavour on a miserable old man whose power extends no further than his own planet. The Doctor has never been the type to completely erase anyone's free will.

SPACE / TIME

The Doctor enlists Rory's help in working on the TARDIS, but with Amy unwittingly providing a distraction, a near-disaster results: the TARDIS' outer police box shell materializes inside its own control room, spelling certain doom for its occupants unless they can find a solution. Fortunately, one by one, the Doctor's companions – from just a few moments into their own future – pop out of the police box to offer helpful suggestions. Unfortunately, the Doctor's companions now have to remember what their future selves have just said so they can remember to say exactly the same thing in just a few moments' time to save their own lives.

Matt Smith	. . . .	The Doctor	written by Steven Moffat
Karen Gillan	. . . .	Amy Pond	directed by Richard Senior
Arthur Darvill	. . . .	Rory	music by Murray Gold
			Aired on March 18, 2011

BEHIND THE SCENES: This was the **Doctor Who** franchise's contribution to the 2011 Comic Relief charity event; past **Doctor Who** and related Comic Relief appearances have included 2009's **Sarah Jane Adventures** mini-episode, a 2007 **Weakest Link** special featuring David Tennant and other cast members, and the 1999 spoof *The Curse Of Fatal Death*, which was technically the first televised **Doctor Who** adventure for current showrunner Steven Moffat. This adventure was presented as two mini-episodes — neither of them topping four minutes — titled, respectively, *Space* and *Time*.

Clocking in at under ten minutes total, this two-part adventure is the **Doctor Who** equivalent of what the producers of the various **Star Trek** spinoffs once called a "bottle show" — the entire thing takes place in the TARDIS' standing set, the only real prop is the ubiquitous police box, and the only characters who show up are the regulars, all donating their time and talent for a good cause.

But *Space* and *Time* **do** have a bit of a surprising precedent in the **Doctor Who** timeline — this is hardly the first time that the TARDIS has materialized inside itself, and it's also not the first time that this sort of event has been predicted to have a dire outcome for those aboard. In — of all things! — Tom Baker's 1981 swan song *Logopolis*, vast portions of the four-part story are spent depicting the Doctor and Adric enterting a police box in the TARDIS control room, only to find themselves in a more dimly-lit TARDIS control room with a police box in it… which they then, of course, enter, until they're standing in a TARDIS within a TARDIS within a TARDIS within a TARDIS *ad nauseum*, with the console room barely lit at all. All the while, the fourth Doctor muses about what a catastrophic event this is. Fortunately, *Space* and *Time* play it for laughs — and blessed brevity.

(It's also worth noting that the eleventh Doctor, Amy and Rory suss the whole thing out in mere minutes, a fraction of the time it takes for the Doctor's fourth incarnation and Adric — he of the badge of mathematical excellence! — to arrive at a solution.)

THE IMPOSSIBLE ASTRONAUT

2011: Amy and Rory (having settled into life on Earth following their honeymoon) and River Song (still in her stormcage prison) receive numbered invitations consisting only of a date and a place. The place is the American plains, where the Doctor — presumably the sender of the invitations — awaits. But to their horror, an astronaut — clad in a vintage Apollo spacesuit — emerges from a body of water and shoots the Doctor, triggering his regeneration. The astronaut then shoots the Doctor again, killing him before the regeneration is completed, and returns to the water. An elderly man named Canton Delaware III appears, bearing his own numbered invitation and convenient means for disposing of the Doctor's body. The Doctor's stunned companions then discover the Time Lord alive and well, blissfully unaware of what's just happened — in his own future, of which they can divulge nothing.

1969: A scant trail of clues leads the time travelers to the White House, mere months before the launch of Apollo 11. President Richard Nixon has been receiving strange phone calls, almost always on a phone line that happens to be nearest wherever he is, from a child terrified of a spaceman who has appeared nearby. Despite the Secret Service's lack of enthusiasm about the four apparently British visitors who have popped into the Oval Office without warning, the Doctor appoints himself the chief investigator of the case of the mysterious phone calls. He deduces the location from which the phone calls must be coming, and with a younger Canton Delaware III aboard the TARDIS, goes to find the child who's placing the calls.

At the White House, Amy sees a creature – a creature of which she saw only a glimpse in 2011. At the abandoned warehouse from which the calls are being placed, Rory and River both see the creatures as well. There's only one problem: they're fully aware of who the Doctor is, and of the fate he will suffer. And anyone who sees them, once they look away, doesn't remember having seen them. Are these the assassins who have killed the last of the Time Lords?

Matt Smith	The Doctor
Karen Gillan	Amy Pond
Arthur Darvill	Rory
Emilio Aquino	Busboy
Nancy Baldwin	Joy
Henrietta Clemett	Matilda
Paul Critoph	Charles
Mark Griffin	Phil
Chuk Iwuji	Carl
Stuart Milligan	President Richard Nixon
Adam Napier	Captain Simmons
Kieran O'Connor	Prison Guard

This story has been released on DVD

written by Steven Moffat
directed by Toby Haynes
music by Murray Gold

Aired on April 23, 2011

Mark Sheppard	Canton Delaware
William Morgan Sheppard .	old Canton Delaware
Marnix van den Broeke	The Silent
Sydney Wade	Little Girl

CLASSIC CONNECTIONS: The interior of the alien spacecraft was glimpsed last season in *The Lodger*. The TARDIS has landed as an invisible object before, in 1969's *The Invasion*, though the second Doctor was able to find both the time machine and its entrance a bit more gracefully in that story.

A.K.A.: Guest star **William Morgan Sheppard** – often credited as **W. Morgan Sheppard** in the US and as **Morgan Sheppard** in the UK – has guest starred on nearly every genre series under the sun, from several "generations" of **Star Trek**, **Babylon 5**, **seaQuest**, and more, to a memorable regular role on **Max Headroom** in both its British and American incarnations. He is the real father of actor **Mark Sheppard**, of whose character he portrays a much older version. Mark Sheppard is familiar to followers of such series as **Supernatural**, **Battlestar Galactica**, **The Middleman**, **Warehouse 13**, and **Firefly**. Where both the Sheppards were born in the UK, **Stuart Milligan** was born in Boston and has portrayed several Presidents of the United States during a career which has seen him do much of his television work in Britain. Milligan was also the voice of Colonel Stark in another Stateside adventure for the Doctor, the 2009 animated story *Dreamland*.

Having firmly established the key players and the atmosphere of his "era" of **Doctor Who**, showrunner Steven Moffat is playing on the audience's newfound familiarity with the characters and their relationships here by ripping the rug out from under everything. *The Impossible Astronaut* succeeds spectacularly at creating an atmosphere that's unusual even among other episodes of **Doctor Who**. The show has never put the Doctor's future in doubt in quite this way, and it's a novel element to have the Doctor's companions knowing more than he does about the long-range plot while he, as usual, dominates the immediate plot.

As has been heavily publicized prior to the episode's premiere, portions of *The Impossible Astronaut* were shot in Utah, with BBC America chipping in to bring a few key cast members to the States for a location shoot that was, at the time, unique in the series' history. There have been a few attempts in the past to set stories across the pond – from the 1996 TV movie (set in San Francisco, but shot in Vancouver) to 2007's *Daleks In Manhattan* – but this is the first time that the BBC has spent the money to send cast members to the US. There's no denying that the Utah locations are incredibly effective, but even for scenes set in the White House, it's back to business (in Cardiff) as usual.

As with the 2010 season's Winston Churchill episode, the show sticks its neck out by showing the Doctor associating with President Nixon. Stuart Milligan gets much of Nixon's verbal cadence down, but even with prosthetic makeup designed to emulate Nixon's jowled look, he doesn't quite manage to really look like Nixon. There's also the tightrope act of writing Nixon as a character: the real Nixon was seldom short of an opinion (including a few that that would keep modern Presidential candidates from getting past a primary), and he was seldom short of the gumption to express those opinions. Here, however, he's portrayed as gruff-but-basically-kindly-underneath – it's hard to imagine the real Nixon having much patence for repeated mysterious phone calls from an unknown child. In service of the need to portray Nixon as one of the Good Guys, the script takes some significant liberties with history.

Where it does succeed, however, is in creating one of the creepiest villains that the show has seen in recent years. The notion of a creature that one forgets as soon as one looks away from it is an interesting one, though if that's not enough to make the Silence scary as hell, they vaporize a hapless woman within the walls of the White House for good measure. The episode also introduces some very likeable good guys to do battle with the Silence, namely Canton Everett Delaware III, played by guest-star-in-every-show-imaginable Mark Sheppard (many fans will know him best as eccentric lawyer Romo Lampkin in later seasons of the new **Battlestar Galactica**). At the actor's suggestion, rather than aging him with makeup, his real-life father, W. Morgan Sheppard, was hired to play the elderly Canton; the elder Sheppard has, of course, appeared in just about every genre series imaginable – the best part of the American location shoot may, in fact, be the guest actors recruited for it. Mark Sheppard easily gets the best lines in the entire episode – something about him screams "potential future companion material."

DAY OF THE MOON

Amy, Rory and River are on the run after the Doctor is captured by the unknown, skull-faced aliens, who seem to have Canton Delaware under their control. But the Doctor and Canton are secretly working together, and stage the "capture" of the rest of the TARDIS travelers. The only way any of them have been able to remember anything about the aliens on Earth is to mark their own skin each time they see one – but no other information remains until Amy's cell phone photo of one provides the means to construct a hologram of one of the aliens inside the TARDIS. The Doctor equips each of his friends, including Canton, with recording devices, and is forced to take President Nixon into his confidence about the alien invasion. Even Nixon is hard-pressed to explain the Doctor's presence when the Time Lord is found rewiring the Apollo 11 capsule. The other time travelers try to discover where the missing girl came from, leading to an abandoned orphanage who doesn't seem to grasp that it's no longer 1967. Amy finds the girl – still in a NASA spacesuit – but is taken prisoner by the aliens.

Matt Smith . . . . The Doctor
Karen Gillan . . . . Amy Pond
Arthur Darvill . . . . Rory
Peter Banks . . . . Dr. Shepherd
Frances Barber . . . . Eye Patch Lady
Tommy Campbell . . . . Sergeant
Ricky Fearon . . . . Tramp

This story has been released on DVD

written by Steven Moffat
directed by Toby Haynes
music by Murray Gold

Aired on April 30, 2011

Mark Griffin . . . . Phil
Chuk Iwuji . . . . Carl
Alex Kingston . . . . River Song
Jeff Mash . . . . Grant
Stuart Milligan . . . . President Richard Nixon
Kerry Shale . . . . Dr. Renfrew
Mark Sheppard . . . . Canton Delaware

Marnix van den Broeke . . . . The Silent
Sydney Wade . . . . Little Girl
Glenn Wrage . . . . Gardener

CLASSIC CONNECTIONS: Dwarf star alloy is very handy for trapping time travelers; Rorvik and his crew landed a ship with an entire outer hull made of dwarf star alloy — said to be super-dense material — to enslave the time-hopping Tharils in 1981's *Warriors' Gate*, at least until the fourth Doctor and Romana helped to free them.

A.K.A.:   Guest star **Frances Barber** put in another surreal appearance in a 1989 **Red Dwarf** episode, the fan favorite *Polymorph.*

Not exactly picking up right where *The Impossible Astronaut* leaves off, *Day Of The Moon* milks a little more mileage out of its Utah location filming with a series of on-the-run vignettes before launching into a series of more studio-bound vignettes that, by virtue of the most flashbacks I've seen in anything since **Lost** went off the air, can be a bit confusing even if you are carefully following along.

A lot of the episode is spent wallowing in the externals of early space-age nostalgia, from the Doctor being discovered aboard the Apollo 11 command module, to Rory breaking the scale model of the lunar lander, to copious nods to the original television footage of the landing. Intriguing character hints drop during the improbably long interval between Amy's kidnapping and her rescue from the heart of the Silence's operation; we learn that the (presumably non-Auton) Rory does, in fact, remember the centuries he spent protecting the Pandorica cntaining Amy.

The most troublesome element of *Day Of The Moon*, really, is the implication of Moffat's otherwise well-thought-out comeuppance for the Silence. The notion that the single most-watched piece of television in history contains humanity's marching orders for wiping out the Silence is a nifty one... until you bother to think this through to its logical conclusion. Supposedly this message has been turning generations of humans into soldiers capable of killing the creatures behind the alien invasion, and equally capable of forgetting doing that deed. That in itself is a little bit disturbing. But let's keep following where this idea leads. Children have been shown the moon landing for generations now. Are they out there killing the Silents? Nobody whose brain is wired slightly differently has ever had some sort of breakdown or mental aberration from repeated exposure to these images? As disheartened as the tenth Doctor was at Davros' suggestion that his companions essentially became an army unto themselves (*Journey's End*), the eleventh Doctor is now okay with turning much of humanity into soldiers to fight off the invasion of the Silence? Sure, the human race in this scenario is defending its home planet, and sure, it's cute to send the Silence packing with humanity's boot up their collective backside, but there's an ends-justifying-the-means theme here that doesn't really feel quite right for **Doctor Who.**

THE CURSE OF THE BLACK SPOT

Captain Henry Avery and his pirate ship crew have fallen upon hard times, haunted by a deadly curse: any man among them who sheds so much as a single drop of blood sees a black spot appear on his hand, and the next time the seafaring Siren appears on the ship, that man will be destroyed by her. Worse yet, a large blue box is found in the hold, containing three stowaways who, despite their insistence that they're here to help, must be trying to take Avery's loot after waiting for the Siren to pick off the rest of his crew. Another stowaway is revealed: Avery's young son, convinced that his father is a fine, upstanding Naval officer and unprepared for the truth. When Rory's hand is cut and the black spot appears on his hand, the Doctor and Amy are fighting not just to keep the Siren from devouring Avery's crew, but one of their own as well.

Matt Smith	The Doctor	
Karen Gillan	Amy Pond	
Arthur Darvill	Rory	
Michael Begley	Mulligan	
Hugh Bonneville	Captain Henry Avery	
Lily Cole	The Siren	
Chris Jarman	Dancer	
Oscar Lloyd	Toby Avery	
Tony Lucken	De Florres	
Carl McCrystal	McGrath	
Lee Ross	The Boatswain	

This story has been released on DVD

written by Steve Thompson
directed by Jeremy Webb
music by Murray Gold

Aired on May 7, 2011

A nice diversion from the conspiracy-heavy season opener, *The Curse Of The Black Spot* is a rollicking good tale of piracy, something that **Doctor Who** has attempted few times on TV (and only once in audio form – as a musical, no less). But this isn't off-the-wall surreal like *Enlightenment*, or drawn-out like *The Smugglers* (William Hartnell's penultimate TV adventure) seemed to be. Buckles are swashed (by Amy, no less) in very short order, the Doctor gets to walk the plank, and there's a doozy of a creature for whom there's a perfectly rational explanation, once the Doctor shows up to dispel the superstition.

Once things go off the rails, the story becomes a stress test for Amy and Rory, as well as for Avery and his son. There's real weight in watching Avery's son put two and two together and realize that his father's chosen trade is not the honorable one he'd been told about, and the plot twist that makes the audience believe that no reconciliation between father and son will be happening is a kick in the gut. The kid could've been an intensely annoying character, but some very good casting and a child actor capable of delivering the characterization necessary steer clear of those waters.

The science fiction explanation behind all of the siren songs and apparent vaporizations is an interesting one, including the darkly humorous take on medical paperwork and bureaucracy (Amy having to prove that she's Rory's wife). The Siren – and whoever constructed her – join the pantheon of **Doctor Who** aliens about whom we wish we knew more, and yet knowing more might steal some of the mystique away. A fun, well-judged episode all around.

THE DOCTOR'S WIFE

A telepathic distress call-in-a-box – a technology used only by the Time Lords – tracks down the Doctor's TARDIS in deep space. Eager to find out if the sender of the distress call is still alive, the Doctor follows the call to its point of origin: an asteroid that exists outside the boundaries of the universe in its own "bubble universe". But upon making the trip, the TARDIS' energy – and, according to the Doctor, its soul – is drained, leaving the ship immobile. A very strange couple of humanoids, with a green-eyed Ood servant they refer to as "Nephew", occupy the living asteroid, while a woman named Idris exhibits wildly unusual behavior near the Doctor. The Doctor sends Amy and Rory back to the TARDIS for their own safety, and soon enough discovers that he's walked into a trap: the couple inhabiting the asteroid has several Time Lord distress call boxes stowed away, which they've used to lure many Gallifreyans to their deaths. The Doctor also finds that Idris' body is inhabited by another life form: his own TARDIS. The mind of the living asteroid is taking her place as the controlling force in his TARDIS, while the timeship's actual living essence is trapped in a human body never meant to hold it. Now his companions are trapped in the TARDIS with a malevolent entity, and time is running out to return the TARDIS' own energy to it.

Matt Smith	The Doctor	
Karen Gillan	Amy Pond	
Arthur Darvill	Rory	
Elizabeth Berrington	Auntie	
Suranne Jones	Idris	
Paul Kasey	Nephew	
Adrian Schiller	Uncle	
Michael Sheen . . . . voice of House		

This story has been released on DVD

written by Neil Gaiman
directed by Richard Clark
music by Murray Gold

Aired on May 14, 2011

CLASSIC CONNECTIONS: The Time Lord telepathic distress call boxes haven't been seen since the Doctor himself summoned the Time Lords with one in 1969's *The War Games*. This is the first new series episode to show areas of the TARDIS other than the console room or the wardrobe glimpsed in *The Christmas Invasion*. *The Doctor's Wife* was a title that the late producer John Nathan-Turner kept posted on a bulletin board in the **Doctor Who** production office in the 1980s, credited to writer Robert Holmes. There was never any such story in the planning: it was a ploy to try to discover the identity of a mole in the production office who was leaking advance information to fanzines.

A.K.A.: Suranne Jones previously appeared as an alien presence trapped within the Mona Lisa in the **Sarah Jane Adventures** two-parter *Mona Lisa's Revenge* (2009). Michael Sheen, providing a disembodied voice for the entity that tries to take over the TARDIS, has appeared in *Underworld, Underworld: Evolution, Frost/Nixon* (as legendary British TV personality David Frost), both parts of the Twilight movie adaptation *Breaking Dawn, Tron Legacy* (as the traitorous Castor), and Tim Burton's *Alice In Wonderland*.

BEHIND THE SCENES: The "junk TARDIS" console, like the Abzorbaloff before it (seen in 2006's *Love & Monsters*), was designed by a young Blue Peter competition winner, Susannah Leah.

A stand-alone episode we've been waiting for since it was delayed from the first Matt Smith season, *The Doctor's Wife* proves to have been worth the wait. Not only is it a fun romp with a slightly obvious plot twist, but **it calls the very origins of the series into question.** Not bad for 40-odd minutes of TV.

The obvious plot twist is that the Doctor's "wife" is the soul of the TARDIS itself. This writing has been on the wall for decades, ever since the show established that the TARDIS is a living thing with a symbiotic link to its pilot, but with the possible exception of the Big Finish audio story *Zagreus*, which gave the TARDIS its own voice (namely, the voice of the late Nicholas Courtney), the TARDIS has never gotten a chance to speak before. Suranne Jones makes the disheveled Idris an endearingly strange character – like Canton Delaware, there's "potential companion" written all over her, though she's best as a one-off. Giving the TARDIS a voice full-time would rob the Doctor's timeship of its mystery and would turn it into a steampunk KITT.

But Gaiman doesn't waste the TARDIS' precious few minutes with a voice with small talk. We learn that, where we previously accepted the explanation that the first Doctor, bored with Gallifrey, stole his TARDIS and left, the reverse may also have been true: the TARDIS was also bored, and needed a Time Lord "mad enough" to take it to see the universe. Little plot developments that retroactively rewrite the DNA of the show's early years without breaking everything that we know are nifty additions to the mythos, and very difficult to pull off without rewriting the show's backstory in huge broad strokes. Add to that the first TARDIS other than the Doctor's that we've seen on TV since 1986, complete with its console and walls that hearken back to the original series, and there's a *lot* for long-term fans to love in this episode.

The mythology of the current series doesn't go unaddressed either, with Amy and Rory enduring a nightmarish escape into the bowels of the TARDIS (something else we haven't seen since, at the very least, the 1996 movie, on whose 15th anniversary this episode was broadcast), and a reminder for the audience's benefit that the Doctor still hasn't learned of the fatal future seen in *The Impossible Astronaut*. It was interesting to see Rory agonizing over the apparent death of Idris – it's nice to have some character development going on with Rory that doesn't have anything to do with Amy.

Even though it's just one episode with no major connecting tissue to this season's story arc, *The Doctor's Wife* is an instant favorite – an episode that left me with the feeling that I'd just seen something magical in the Doctor's ongoing story. (Funny, I had the same feeling about Neil Gaiman's solitary episode of **Babylon 5**.) Gaiman says he has no immediate plans to write another episode of **Doctor Who**, but I hope he isn't completely writing off a return to the Doctor's world at any point down the road.

THE REBEL FLESH

A solar storm brings the TARDIS down on 26th century Earth, at an isolated castle which is now the site of a small team overseeing a large vat of Flesh – an acidic, sentient liquid which can shape itself into Gangers, perfect copies of any of the team members, capable of performing dangerous tasks without endangering the original human technician. The violent solar flare that forced the TARDIS to land will soon impact Earth, and the Doctor tries to offer his help to the castle's crew. When it arrives, however, the solar storm front impacts Earth more violently than expected, and everyone including the Doctor is knocked out cold before his plan can be put into action. When everyone comes around, something has changed: the Gangers have become aggressive, demanding that their existence is at least as valid and precious as the lives of the humans of whom they are copies. Worse yet, by coming into physical contact with the Flesh, the Doctor has inadvertently provided the template for a new Ganger, one with his intellect and instincts.

Matt Smith . . . . The Doctor
Karen Gillan . . . . Amy Pond
Arthur Darvill . . . . Rory
Frances Barber . . . . Eye Patch Lady
Mark Bonnar . . . . Jimmy
Raquel Cassidy . . . . Cleaves
Marshall Lancaster . . . . Buzzer
Sarah Smart . . . . Jennifer
Leon Vickers . . . . Dicken

This story has been released on DVD

written by Matthew Graham
directed by Julian Simpson
music by Murray Gold

Aired on May 21, 2011

Here's something I never thought I'd say about an episode of **Doctor Who**, old or new: I remember this plotline when it was on **Star Trek: Voyager**, and it was about holograms instead of fleshy clones.

Sadly, there is something awfully familiar about *The Rebel Flesh*, but to be fair, the general plot outline wasn't new when it was done in **Voyager**'s last season either: humans have created a form of artificial life to serve in their stead in situations that are simply too dangerous for flesh-and-blood people. Only in this case, the twist is that the clones have human "operators" who can control their clones from a safe location. When the inevitable uprising happens, not only do the creators have to look in the eyes of their creations, but there's an equally inevitable game of "is this the real person or is it a clone that's going to kill one of our heroes?"

The Doctor himself somes into contact with the fleshy goo that can replicate both his physical form and elements of his personality and intelligence. The setup for this, however, is more than a little strange – it's not terribly clear what draws the Doctor into contact with the Flesh. Even the Doctor's natural curiosity has to run into some common-sense limits now and then.

Rory gets a larger-than-usual share of the action, again using the nurse/caretaker angle to put him in harm's way; at least this time we get to see him operating independently of Amy. Now, this also means that Rory get clobbered by a clone who reverts to a vaguely Odo-esque face, but that goes with the job description.

THE ALMOST PEOPLE

Trapped in the castle with a group of hostile Gangers imitating the physical forms and personalities of the humans of whom they're copies, the Doctor is now faced with a copy of himself, though the Doctor's Ganger seems benign and helpful no matter how much suspicion he receives from the humans. An evacuation flight is dispatched to the castle, and the race is on to greet it when it lands. The Gangers, fighting for their right to continued existence rather than the inhumane "decommissioning" that usually awaits them, are content simply to wipe out their former masters. Despite the humans harboring much the same sentiment toward the Gangers, the Doctor – and his duplicate – try to maintain the possibility of a peaceful solution. But as the humans, even Amy, continue to ostracize the surplus Doctor, he begins to wonder if he's on the right side. And the Doctor and Rory make the horrifying discovery that there's one more Ganger in their midst than they realized.

Matt Smith	The Doctor
Karen Gillan	Amy Pond
Arthur Darvill	Rory
Frances Barber	Eye Patch Lady
Mark Bonnar	Jimmy
Raquel Cassidy	Cleaves
Marshall Lancaster	Buzzer
Edmond Moulton	Adam
Sarah Smart	Jennifer
Leon Vickers	Dicken

This story has been released on DVD

written by Matthew Graham
directed by Julian Simpson
music by Murray Gold

Aired on May 28, 2011

For every thing that *The Almost People* does well in an interesting way – such as its shock cliff"ganger" ending, or its exploration of prejudice and ostracization by way of Amy's less-than-pleasant interactions the Doctor's double – it does another thing in an off-the-rails way (the sudden revelation that the Gangers can open their mouths and consume their victims, *a la* Diana wolfing down a guinea pig in the original **V**, comes out of nowhere and really adds nothing but a cheap-horror-flick shock to the story). The Gangers have already shown that they're dangerous, and the clock's already ticking in the form of the "extraction team" that will rescue one team or the other from the isolated compound – in that respect, *The Almost People* is classic enclosed-base-under-siege **Doctor Who**, a subgenre that the series has specialized in since the Doctor's *second* incarnation was making bow ties cool.

Matt Smith steals the show handily here, portraying not only the Doctor we know but also a less certain creature who wants badly to be the Doctor, despite every human and Ganger around making it very clear that they expect him to fail to be the Doctor. That the story begins to make the audience wonder which one they're watching at any given moment actually indicates that the Ganger Doctor is doing better than he thinks – so well, in fact, that the real Doctor entrusts him with his sonic screwdriver. Speaking of real vs. ersatz Doctors, this episode marks the first time that the new series has seen the current Doctor impersonating his predecessors, as the Ganger Doctor, assimilating the real Doctor's memories of his past incarnations, briefly imitates Pertwee and Tom Baker. This is accomplished by quoting somewhat predictable cliched catchphrases – "reverse the polarity of the neutron flow" and "would you like a jelly baby?" – but it's no better or worse than Peter Davison breaking into a Troughtonesque "When I say run, run!" in part 1 of *Castrovalva*.

The ending, though, may be the biggest shock of the Steven Moffat era so far. It's also awfully strong stuff for family-hour viewing – basically, what we've got here is the real Amy, as somebody's hostage, about to give birth in captivity. There's no reassuring scene (as in the end of *Bad Wolf*) to let the kiddos know that the Doctor's going to rush to her rescue, opting instead to save those scenes for the next episode. It's pretty unsettling stuff, and may well be the most eyebrow-raising, "I-can't-believe-they-did-that-on-TV" cliffhanger the show's given us since the fourth Doctor's head was held under water in *The Deadly Assassin*. (But if you think *that's* bad, imagine how Rory feels – he's been spending his free time with a slimy clone since before the season started…)

A GOOD MAN GOES TO WAR

The Doctor and Rory hunt tirelessly through time and space to find the real Amy Pond: the Amy who has been aboard the TARDIS since the trip to America has been a Ganger all along. Enlisting the help of unlikely allies – a Sontaran pressed into service as a combat nurse, a Silurian at large in Victorian London, even a fleet of Cybermen – the Doctor gathers an army to help him rescue his kidnapped companion. Held captive by the mysterious Kovarian, Amy has already given birth to a daughter, Melody. Fully expecting the Doctor's arrival, Madame Kovarian has assembled an army of her own, with the deadly headless monks to strike fear into anyone who doubts their duties. Just when the Doctor thinks he's rescued Amy and her baby without any bloodshed, Kovarian springs her trap: the baby that the Doctor has rescued is a Ganger as well, and Kovarian has Amy's real baby: a human child with TARDIS-altered DNA that can be traced back to Gallifrey itself, a child Kovarian intends to raise as the perfect weapon to fight the Doctor. Little do the time travelers know that they've already met Melody Pond, all grown up.

Matt Smith . . . . The Doctor
Karen Gillan . . . . Amy Pond
Arthur Darvill . . . . Rory
Charlie Baker . . . . Fat One
Frances Barber . . . . Madame Kovarian
Hugh Bonneville . . . . Henry Avery
Nicholas Briggs . . . . voice of the Cybermen
Christina Chong . . . . Lorna Bucket
Annabel Cleare . . . . Eleanor
Simon Fisher-Becker . . . . Dorium Maldovar
Joshua Hayes . . . . Lucas
Dan Johnston . . . . Thin One

written by Steven Moffat
directed by Peter Hoar
music by Murray Gold

Aired on June 4, 2011

This story has been released on DVD

Neve McIntosh . . . . Madame Vastra
Danny Sapani . . . . Colonel Manton
Dan Starkey . . . . Commander Strax
Catrin Stewart . . . . Jenny
Richard Trinder . . . . Captain Harcourt

Damian Kell	. . . .	Dominicus	Henry Wood	. . . .	Arthur
Alex Kingston	. . . .	River Song
Oscar Lloyd	. . . .	Toby Avery

CLASSIC CONNECTIONS: The Doctor destroys Cybermen fleets with impeccable timing, whether it's in *The Wheel In Space* (1968), *Silver Nemesis* (1988) or this episode.

A classic example of a strong build-up to a decidedly strange ending, *A Good Man Goes To War* seems like it's building up to something huge, and even manages the neat trick of assembling a group of guest characters we've never seen before who seem like old friends by the end of the hour. The Doctor is back to being mad, bad and dangerous to know, and Rory's back in the ridiculous Roman gladiator outfit. What's not to love?

The episode does an awful lot of backtracking to make sure we know that we haven't really seen Amy this season – at all. Amy, in this season, has been a Ganger since somewhere between *A Christmas Carol* and *The Impossible Astronaut*, and we haven't seen the real Amy until the shock ending of *The Almost People*.

But the bad guys' reason for hatching such a grand scheme against the Doctor seems like a rehash of some Russell T. Davies-era material. They just assume that the Doctor will be the end of them unless they beat him to the punch, kidnapping Amy and Rory's child – who, since she was conceived aboard the TARDIS, apparently has Time Lord DNA – and programming her from infancy to track down and kill the Doctor. When we learn that the child will grow up to be one River Song, the rest of the season's story arc falls into place. But the strange cliffhanger ending practically has River seeing off the Doctor with a wink and a nudge before revealing her identity to her parents, resulting in what may be the most bizarre cliffhanger since Sylvester McCoy dangled over a sheer drop from his question mark umbrella in 1987's *Dragonfire*. It isn't much of a shocking, tune-in-next-time moment – the revelation and the Doctor's strangely relaxed exit suck any built-up tension right out of the story.

There's a lot to like in *A Good Man*, though, and oddly it's nothing to do with the main characters. An assemblage of guest characters turns out to be ridiculously appealing, almost to the point that I would rather have spent the episode learning more about their backstories. (When we spent two entire episodes setting up the Gangers, is this too much to ask?) The strange conundrum of a Sontaran pressed into service as a combat medic makes for a memorable character with scene-stealing lines, repeatedly stitching up human patients while reminding them that he'd happily see them dead on the field of battle. And one of history's darkest characters is dispatched humorously – and off-screen! – by a human/Silurian couple (and a lesbian couple, no less) living in Victorian times. The notion that the Silurian half of that couple has just gotten back from the small task of disposing of Jack the Ripper is one of the show's bigger laughs. These characters are all recruited by the Doctor to march into danger with him, and by the time they stand alongside him in the fight, it's easy to care what happens to them.

LET'S KILL HITLER

Amy and Rory use decidedly unconventional means to summon the Doctor for a progress report on his search for their daughter Melody, only to be interrupted by Melody herself – or at least one of her future incarnations, who has grown up alongside her own parents as a troubled child. She forces the Doctor and his friends to take her into the TARDIS with no more of a destination in mind than "let's kill Hitler." But when the TARDIS arrives in Berlin, 1938, there is already an alien presence among the Third Reich attempting to do away with the Fuhrer – an assassination attempt that the Doctor's arrival foils. Wounded in the ensuing firefight, Mels regenerates into River Song before her parents' eyes, but her new incarnation is mentally unstable. The self-proclaimed psychopath poisons the Doctor and continues to wreak havoc across Berlin, oblivious to any ripples she might be leaving in the timeline. Amy and Rory are taken into the custody of the alien police force which has now shifted its attention to River, and they now have two seemingly conflicting objectives: save the Doctor and somehow keep River alive when the authorities catch up with her.

Matt Smith . . . . The Doctor
Karen Gillan . . . . Amy Pond
Arthur Darvill . . . . Rory
Eva Alexander . . . . Nurse
Paul Bentley . . . . Professor Candy
Caitlin Blackwood . . . . Amelia Pond
Tor Clark . . . . Female Teacher
Amy Cudden . . . . Anita
Richard Dillane . . . . Carter
Davood Ghadami . . . . Jim
Maya Glace-Green . . . . young Mels
Elia Kenion . . . . Harriet
Mark Killeen . . . . German Officer

This story has been released on DVD

written by Steven Moffat
directed by Richard Senior
music by Murray Gold

Aired on August 27, 2011

Alex Kingston . . . . River Song
Philip Rham . . . . Zimmerman
Nina Toussaint-White . . . . Mels
Albert Welling . . . . Adolf Hitler
Ezekiel Wigglesworth . . . . young Rory

CLASSIC CONNECTIONS: The "state of temporal grace" – a long-standing piece of obscure **Doctor Who** continuity from the Tom Baker years that supposedly prevents weapons from being fired inside the TARDIS – is said to be fictitious here, although it did work at one point. The first time it failed to work was in the Peter Davison story *Earthshock* (after a Cyberman blasted the TARDIS console), and it's been consistently failing to work since then. The River Song we've seen so far is at least the *third* incarnation of Melody Pond. For the first time in Steven Moffat's tenure as showrunner, we see Rose, Martha and Donna, though they're familiar publicity photos presented as "holograms" by the TARDIS, which finally settles on the avatar of little Amelia Pond (still played by Karen Gillan's younger cousin) to interact with the Doctor.

A.K.A.: Hitler doesn't recognize the Doctor, who has regenerated four times since the two were uneasy allies during the events of the second New Adventures novel, Timewyrm: Exodus. Even without the changes in appearance, that book's alien interference in Hitler's mental state would account for his inability to remember the TARDIS, so the two adventures don't necessarily conflict.

Can we *not* kill Hitler and just *say* we did? Oh wait – *that's precisely what this episode does*.

This was where I firmly began to believe that **Doctor Who** was becoming a bit bogged down by the ongoing story strand of River Song. There was a time when any upcoming appearance of the character (and certainly the actress playing her) was something to look forward to; now each subsequent appearance of River is becoming loaded down with story baggage that demands an ever-larger share of each season's precious thirteen-episodes-plus-a-special. Alex Kingston never fails to bring the deliciously unhinged sexy to the show, but with each appearance of River, I found myself wishing that the episodes she dominated each season could be spent telling more original, less-convoluted stories.

And yet... there's a lot to like about the bizarrely-titled *Let's Kill Hitler*. The cheaply realized, jellyfish-like alien enforcement creatures are endearingly low-budget, and very old-school **Doctor Who** (complete with the calm spoken disclaimer that their victims will "experience a tingling sensation, and then death"). The idea of the alien law enforcement agency in miniature with its shapeshifting technology is a damn sight more intriguing than the notion of the Judoon trampling all over everything; I find myself wondering where these guys fit in with the Shadow Proclamation. And there's also the interesting idea, carried over from *The End Of Time*, of the slow-dawning realization that any rebirth of the Time Lords (via River) may not be in the universe's best interests. At the birth of Melody's "River Song" incarnation, she's as nutty – and about as dangerous – as the Master.

But what of Melody's parents? **Amy and Rory seem maddeningly *au fait* with the idea that, since there are multiple older versions of Melody out there, baby Melody must be all right**, or at least has to be allowed to be raised by her abductors in order to become River and thus preserve everyone's personal timeline. Never mind going against character, it just seems to go against human nature that Amy and Rory aren't turning the universe upside-down to recover their daughter, with or without the Doctor's help... or, at the very least, that they don't seem that upset by it all. Rory's grim determination from *A Good Man* carries forward into this episode, and he's finally throwing punches and kicking ass without the ridiculous Roman garb (about time!).

It's the lack of follow-through from *A Good Man* that's most aggravating here. The enemy force raised against the Doctor in that episode is not addressed here. The smaller but more righteously determined force raised by the Doctor to help him is not addressed here. Whatever larger force is pulling the strings behind the scenes to abduct Melody and use her as a weapon against the Doctor is not addressed here, nor is their motivation. We learn that the Silence is a religious order rather than a species, fearing its own extinction since the first question was ever asked in the universe (one can only assume that the answer is 42). There was a lot to like here, but it's easy to lose patience with the season's increasingly convoluted storyline.

NIGHT TERRORS

The Doctor receives an unlikely message – "save me from the monsters" – via his psychic paper, and follows it back to an apartment on present-day Earth, certain that it comes from someone very young. The source of the signal turns out to be a seemingly ordinary Earth boy named George, whose family situation, while loving, isn't quite ideal. The Doctor convinces George's father to let him find out what's causing George's monster nightmares, but this only reveals that George's imagined monsters may be very real and very dangerous. Amy and Rory are sucked into the child's nightmares, where they find other victims who have already fallen victim to the Dolls that stalk the darkest corners of George's psyche. In the end, it's not the Doctor, but George's father, who holds the key to freeing everyone from this nightmare world.

Matt Smith . . . . The Doctor	
Karen Gillan . . . . Amy Pond	
Arthur Darvill . . . . Rory	
Sophie Cosson . . . . Julie	
Emma Cunniffe . . . . Claire	
Leila Hoffman . . . . Mrs. Rossiter	
Daniel Mays . . . . Alex	
Jamie Oram . . . . George	
Andy Tiernan . . . . Purcell	

This story has been released on DVD

written by Mark Gatiss
directed by Richard Clark
music by Murray Gold

Aired on September 3, 2011

CLASSIC CONNECTIONS: The Doctor's mention of Snow White And The Seven Keys To Doomsday is a tongue-in-cheek reference to the 1974 stage play *Doctor Who And The Seven Keys To Doomsday*, which starred Trevor Martin as an alternative post-Pertwee Doctor fighting the Daleks. The play was written by '70s **Doctor Who** script editor Terrance Dicks, and was more recently revived in audio form by Big Finish Productions.

A nice departure from the slightly overblown mid-season saga, *Night Terrors* is a good old fashioned scary story that manages not only to return to some of the roots of **Doctor Who**, but is an almost-metafictional piece that any fan could love. After all, who wouldn't like a house call from the Doctor?

Mark Gatiss, who's been writing **Who** since the days of the New Adventures novels, turns in an almost perfectly-pitched script that, while it does feature an alien with extraordinary powers, really only uses that angle of the story as a vehicle to draw the Doctor's attention. Much like 2010's *Vincent And The Doctor*, *Night Terrors* need not have included an extraterrestrial story element at all (other than the Time Lord himself). It's good, scare-you-behind-the-sofa stuff, but at its heart it's basically about the fears that accumulate in the mind of a child when they pick up on signs that all is not well at home.

The whole thing could come crashing down without the right child actor as George, but in his first television role, Jamie Oram is a winner. He's not in every frame of the story, but when we do get to see him, it's easy to believe that this is a kid who fears the future so much that it's driving him nuts. Now, since he's technically an alien in human form, his fears are also generating physical manifestations that turn unsuspecting victims (folks he'd just like to go away, such as the landlord or a cranky neighbor) into creepy life-sized dolls that are scarier than most of the latex or CGI creations that have appeared in recent seasons. The first time another victim from the real world is transformed into one of the dolls, it's really one of the most disturbing moments in the already-well-stocked pantheon of **Doctor Who** shock/horror scenes – more disturbing, perhaps, than *The Empty Child*'s sight of gas masks morphing out of human flesh.

Night Terrors may not be the most original slice of SF ever to hit the screen – every other SF/horror anthology to hit a television has done some variation on the same basic plotline – but I did like the resolution at the end, where dad making it all better saves the day. Television in general has a nasty habit of depicting fathers as buffoons who'd rather be swilling beer and watching the game than having anything to do with their kids; I'm always happy to see an example that defies the stereotype and goes in the opposite direction.

THE GIRL WHO WAITED

Promising Amy and Rory a glimpse of the second most popular vacation destination in the universe, the Doctor miscalculates slightly, landing the TARDIS in the right place at the worst possible time: the planet is in the thrall of a global plague, and robotic medics have been mobilized to contain and treat those with the illness. A system of vast temporal engines has been set up to keep the victims alive by altering the speed of their timestreams. Amy is separated from the Doctor and Rory, and worse yet, when they go to rescue her, the Doctor can't step outside the TARDIS due to the brute-force temporal engineering taking place. Rory has to find Amy himself, and indeed he does: she has aged 36 years since she last saw her fellow TARDIS travelers, and she's not happy about it. The Doctor devises a plan to go back and undo this timeline, but the older Amy objects strenuously: if Amy Pond is going to resume her travels in the TARDIS, it'll be Amy in her fifties, not Amy in her twenties. The Doctor leaves it up to Rory to make the agonizing decision.

Matt Smith . . . . The Doctor
Karen Gillan . . . . Amy Pond
Arthur Darvill . . . . Rory
Imelda Staunton . . . . voice of Interface
Josie Taylor . . . . Check-In Girl

This story
has been
released
on DVD

written by Tom MacRae
directed by Nick Hurran
music by Murray Gold

Aired on September 10, 2011

CLASSIC CONNECTIONS: This episode summons memories of numerous iconic **Doctor Who** adventures past. The Doctor and his companions were accosted in a blank, all-white space by all-white robots in 1968's *The Mind Robber*, while the TARDIS toolbox (a fixture dating back to Tom Baker's era) was last seen in the 1996 TV movie starring Paul McGann. That movie was also the last time that the TARDIS was seen to have an alarm-clock-style split-flap display roaring backward or forward in time at full speed. The free-standing gateways to other dimensions are slightly reminiscent of the Iconian gateways in **Star Trek** lore (TNG: *Contagion*, DS9: *To The Death*), though anyone who's ever been to Narnia can attest that **Star Trek** was hardly the first SF or fantasy epic to use the device.

This episode would've been *amazing* in the 2010 season. The only problem with it appearing in the 2011 season is that, by now, we've already seen *Rory* wait two thousand years – in a goofy Roman centurion outfit, no less! – to be reunited with Amy in the 2010 season's two-part finale.

The episode really belongs to Arthur Darvill and Karen Gillan, with the Doctor sidelined in the TARDIS, and truth be told, it's a much more effective treatment of the "long wait through time" storyline than *The Pandorica Opens / The Big Bang* was. The robots are a stylish threat with an obligatory Moffat-style creepy repeated catchphrase ("This is a kindness!"), and the stark white settings accomplish the task of being unsettlingly surreal (just as it was in *The Mind Robber*). We've traded Roman Rory for Joan of Arc Amy in the obligatory strange costume choice. And the whole star-crossed-lovers-moving-through-time-at-different-speeds is an old favorite of Moffat's too, isn't it? Not just referring to last year's finale, but dating back to *The Girl In The Fireplace* in David Tennant's first season as the Doctor. (The similarities must be slipping past most people though: the same basic plotline keeps winning the Hugo Award.)

Not to crap all over *The Girl Who Waited* – it's actually the *best* version of this same basic story out of the three, by far, with a temporal paradox that plays the heart strings as skillfully as it tickles the geek gene. But when the same concept keeps recurring in a fairly short space of time, **Who** *a la* Moffat is in danger of seeming like it's got a very limited box of tricks.

THE GOD COMPLEX

The TARDIS brings the Doctor, Amy and Rory to a chintzy hotel, but their destination suddenly seems less relaxing when three people – two humans and one alien – burst into the hotel lounge with warnings about the hotel. No one who goes into a room alone comes out the same – those who survive chant "Praise him" and eventually meet a horrible fate. A monster stalks the halls, seeking its next victim and their worship. The surviving hotel guests warn that to go into a room alone invites one's worst fears to appear all at once, but what nightmares await time travelers who have survived the worst horrors the universe has to offer… and who demands their praise?

Matt Smith . . . . The Doctor
Karen Gillan . . . . Amy Pond
Arthur Darvill . . . . Rory
Caitlin Blackwood . . . . Amelia Pond
Dafydd Emyh . . . . P.E. Teacher
Roger Ennals . . . . Gorilla
Amara Karan . . . . Rita

This story
has been
released
on DVD

written by Toby Whithouse
directed by Nick Hurran
music by Murray Gold

Aired on September 17, 2011

UWARP!

Rashid Karapiet . . . . Rita's Father
Dimitri Leonidas . . . . Howie Spragg
Daniel Pirrie . . . . Joe Buchanan
Sarah Quintrell . . . . Lucy Hayward

David Walliams . . . . Gibbis
Spencer Wilding . . . . The Creature

NEW WHO CONNECTIONS: The Doctor peeks into Room 11, hears the TARDIS Cloister Bell, and says "Of course, who else?" and then closes the door again, without the camera ever revealing what he sees. In hindsight, he could be seeing the incarnation that he buried in his memory while attempting to forget his guilt over the Time War (*Day Of The Doctor*, 2013).

CLASSIC CONNECTIONS: The Doctor says the creature is related to the Nimon — the Minotaur-esque beasts behind *The Horns Of Nimon* (1979), which may well be the least-loved adventure of the fourth Doctor's era. The Doctor seems to have forgotten his previous encounter with the Minotaur of legend, during his third incarnation in *The Time Monster* (1972).

A.K.A.: David Walliams is either making his first or second **Doctor Who** appearance, depending on how you look at it. He starred alongside writer/actor Mark Gatiss in *The Web Of Caves*, a spoof of Hartnell-era **Who** that Walliams co-wrote with Gatiss for BBC2's **Doctor Who** Night in 1999. That same year, he and Gatiss also appeared in Gatiss' first **Doctor Who** audio story for Big Finish Productions, *Phantasmagoria* (the second story produced in Big Finish's long series of audio plays based on the Doctor's previous incarnations). With comedy partner Matt Lucas, Walliams is best known as one of the creators and stars of **Little Britain**.

As avant garde as it seems in places, *The God Complex* is one gigantic callback to the final season of the original **Doctor Who**. And they could've gotten away with it if not for us meddling kids — or, at the very least, if not for the fact that *The God Complex* borrows the central escape hatch of what may remain the seventh Doctor's most-revered, best-known story.

The crucial plot element of the Doctor needing to break Amy's faith in him in order to fend off the big bad is done in a low-key way. But add more histrionics, more World War II and more torrential rain, and you've got the exact same scenario from 1989's *The Curse Of Fenric*, in which the seventh Doctor had to cruelly dismiss Ace in order to stave off the power of the Ancient Haemovore. Granted, it's not like this story is borrowing a big twist from something terribly well-known like *The Ark In Space*, but it is sort of like a familiar song that never got past #26 on the charts landing on a greatest hits album.

And truth be told, most folks won't notice the rehash, since the emphasis is on imagery here. The horror in this episode is purely psychological, and it too falls back on an old chestnut, the room filled with horrors custom-made to fit the person walking in the door (if you're going to borrow from the best, it's a shame not to include Orwell in that list). Some of the horrors are oddly tame (a clown?), mildly creepy (ventriloquist dolls who laugh without an operator), not entirely surprising (a father's disappointment) and rather funny (Howie's fear of being confronted with a gaggle of teenage girls). Let's also add vague to that list (whatever the Doctor sees that involves the TARDIS' cloister bell). Other external influences on the story include an obvious **Star Trek** reference (It was all on the holodeck! And I don't mean that metaphorically: change those grid lines from blue to yellow, and it's the holodeck!).

All in all, it's a mix of familiar ingredients that adds up to something that's probably going to be new to younger viewers, and will creep everyone else out in the meantime. Worthy of praise indeed.

CLOSING TIME

Aware that the clock is counting down to his appointment with a killer astronaut in America, the Doctor pays a last visit to his friend Craig, discovering that Craig's become a dad – and a somewhat befuddled one at that. But no house call from the Doctor ever goes quite as smoothly as planned. Strange power outages have plagued the area, with a local department store at the epicenter of the disturbance. The Doctor does what he has to in order to investigate the store without raising suspicion: he gets a job there. Soon enough, between mentions of a "silver rat" roaming the store and a string of employees going missing, the Doctor discovers that Cybermen are lurking here. The Doctor's plans for a quiet visit with his friend are further complicated when Craig insists on involving himself in the Doctor's impending battle with the Cybermen. The lives of the Time Lord's companions are nearly always in jeopardy, but if the Doctor doesn't win this time, it could cost a baby his father.

Matt Smith . . . . The Doctor
Frances Barber . . . . Madame Kovarian
Lynda Baron . . . . Val
Nicholas Briggs . . . . voice of the Cybermen
James Corden . . . . Craig Owens
Arthur Darvill . . . . Rory
Seroca Davis . . . . Shona
Holli Dempsey . . . . Kelly
Karen Gillan . . . . Amy
Daisy Haggard . . . . Sophie
Paul Kasey . . . . Cyberman

This story has been released on DVD

written by Gareth Roberts
directed by Steve Hughes
music by Murray Gold

Aired on September 24, 2011

Alex Kingston . . . . River Song
Chris Obi . . . . George

CLASSIC CONNECTIONS: Craig and Sophie first appeared in the previous season's *The Lodger*. Cybermats first appeared in 1967's *Tomb Of The Cybermen*, and were last seen in 1975's *Revenge Of The Cybermen*; they've had some dental work done in the intervening years, and arguably need to go back for a second round.

A.K.A.: Lynda Baron makes her third **Doctor Who** appearance here: as pirate captain Wrack, she tried to make the fifth Doctor walk the plank in 1983's *Enlightenment*, while her first **Doctor Who** "appearance" was audio-only, as the unseen vocalist warbling the sung narrative throughout the first Doctor story *The Gunfighters* in 1966 – which also saw the Doctor wearing a Stetson.

I was a huge fan of *The Lodger* simply because it was so... *un*-**Doctor Who**, making the Doctor half of a blokey comedy duo – territory the show had simply never ventured into before. *Closing Time* follows up on that unlikely trip off the grid quite successfully, adding a new dimension via Craig's fatherhood. As was the case with the 2010 season, Moffat-era **Doctor Who** is at its best when it veers away from what's usually expected of **Doctor Who**, and *Closing Time* comes in right behind *The Doctor's Wife* as the best episode of 2011, with *Night Terrors* following close behind in third place. Perhaps it's not coincidental, but two out of the three episodes deal with fatherhood, and broadly speaking, all three deal with doing what must be done to take care of a loved one. There is indeed a theme to the 2011 season, one that resonates much more than the convoluted "Doctor's predicted death-date" running plot.

But hey, while we're on that, *Closing Time* services *that* running gag as well, and does it a damn sight better than the constant glancing at the TARDIS screen's death notice for the Doctor. Matt Smith plays the solemnity and acceptance of a doomed Doctor beautifully, though perhaps the best take on that is the scene where he's gently lecturing Stormageddon, the dark lord of all, that the real adventure is his now – and that life's pretty awesome when you're a kid and you're being taken care of. It's a charming, touching and honest scene – and it's not just a little bit metaphorical: the infant the Doctor is addressing is, by proxy, the whole human race that he's been coddling for untold hundreds of years (if not longer). The Doctor's putting the entire species on notice that, out of necessity, he won't be around to do the changing anymore.

The notion that Craig's paternal instincts could save him from Cyber-conversion doesn't hold water quite as well, and the script even knowingly winks at the audience and admits that failing in a nice bit of under-the-radar meta-interaction with the audience. To be fair, it's no more and no less cheesy than *The Age Of Steel*'s Cybermen who shut down when they get their emotions back, or the freshly-converted Cyberman crying oil out of the corner of its eye in *Doomsday*. The new series has really robbed the Cybermen of their teeth, and there isn't much point in crying foul on Moffat's writing team when the de-fanging began under the Davies "administration." (At least this episode shows us who's got the teeth in the Cyber-food-chain…)

Closing Time was a welcome diversion from this season's running plotline. Here's hoping that Craig gets a return visit next season. I don't think he'd work as a full-time companion, but these yearly visits are turning out to be some of the high points of the Matt Smith era.

THE WEDDING OF RIVER SONG

Rather than marching quietly to his date with death, the Doctor goes on a series of missions to find out why the Silence wants him dead. Every piece of information simply leads to another question, until finally he arrives in Utah with Rory, Amy and River – and then his death fails to happen, thwarted by river. But history records the Doctor's death at that moment, and when it fails to happen, history unravels, overlapping alternate histories with history as the Doctor and his friends know it. Amy, River and Rory now command a fighting force with orders to defend the Doctor from the Silence, and the mysterious Madame Kovarian has been captured – or has she really been pulling the strings all along? The Doctor's fate is inescapable – but this time, that's just how he wants it.

Matt Smith . . . . The Doctor
Karen Gillan . . . . Amy Pond
Arthur Darvill . . . . Rory
Frances Barber . . . . Madame Kovarian
Nicholas Briggs . . . . voice of the Dalek
Sean Buckley . . . . Barman
Katharine Burford . . . . Nurse
Simon Callow . . . . Charles Dickens
Emma Campbell-Jones . . . . Dr. Kent
Richard Dillane . . . . Carter
Simon Fisher-Becker . . . . Dorium Maldovar
Niall Grieg Fulton . . . . Gideon Vandaleur
Rondo Haxton . . . . Gantok
Richard Hope . . . . Dr. Malokeh
Alex Kingston . . . . River Song

This story has been released on DVD

written by Steven Moffat
directed by Jeremy Webb
music by Murray Gold

Aired on October 1, 2011

Ian McNeice . . . . Emperor Winston Churchill
William Morgan Sheppard . . . . Canton Delaware
Bill Turnbull . . . . himself
Marnix van den Broeke . . . . The Silent
Meredith Viera . . . . Newsreader
Sian Williams . . . . herself

A.K.A.: Emma Campbell-Jones returned in a different role in the fan-favorite 2013 minisode *The Night Of The Doctor* as someone who decided most emphatically that she did not need the eighth Doctor's help.

With the plotline from *The Impossible Astronaut* playing out at last, Matt Smith's second season wraps up with a mess that rivals *Let's Kill Hitler* for sheer disjointedness (I'm not even entirely sure that's a real word, but hey, maybe it's a real word in the alternate universe). Again, we're treated to a jumble of vignettes that might be nifty as funny DVD bonus scenes, but don't add up to a coherent story.

Amusing: Simon Callow reprising his role of Charles Dickens (from *The Unquiet Dead*) in a media-drenched alternate universe, the Doctor "looking rubbish" (Amy does have a point — with the longer, more-frazzled-than-usual hair, he looks like he should be the lead singer of an early '80s new romantic synth band), and the Doctor's swaggering search for the identity of his future executioners.

Less amusing: "Emperor" Churchill (I wasn't really crazy about the portrayal of Churchill in *Victory Of The Daleks*, and this is just silly), yet another alternate timeline for Amy and Rory, and showrunner Steven Moffat's insistence that the name of the series should now become an element of the plot (WOTAN was ahead of its time!).

The season's opening volley of "the Doctor's gonna die" was indeed an irresistible hook, but given that the show's *about the Doctor*, and the public knows the show's going to have at least two more seasons, the resolution of that plotline seemed awfully dragged out and ill-advised in the first place. The best episodes of the season (*The Doctor's Wife, Closing Time, Night Terrors*) were those stand-alone shows that gave us a merciful *break* from the sight of the Doctor morosely staring at his own obituary on the TARDIS monitor. The season's secondary theme — that we'd get all the answers about River — also wore thin very quickly. The character used to be a lot of fun to speculate about, but she became the center of a few episodes too many.

There's also the bizarre, clinically cold approach to characterization that would be so strange on its own, but after the occasionally over-emotional Russell T. Davies era, is an even colder dash of water in the face. Amy and Rory's calm acceptance of what has happened to their daughter is not only unreal, it's *unrealistic*. Exposure and experience with time travel or no, it cheapens them as characters and turns them into chess pieces that Moffat's scripts push around the board into clever corners, with no regard for the emotional stakes that would be in play if Amy and Rory were living, breathing people.

The Wedding Of River Song has a lot of fun pieces that somehow fail to add up to a cohesive whole.

DEATH IS THE ONLY ANSWER

An incident with a mini-time-vortex and a fez alerts the Doctor to a disaster in the making: Albert Einstein is conducting his own experiments in time travel. Even stranger than that is the celebrated scientist's sudden transformation into an Ood, with a cryptic, ominous warning for the Doctor.

Matt Smith . . . . The Doctor		written by the children of Oakley Junior School
Nickolas Grace . . . . Albert Einstein		directed by Jeremy Webb
Paul Kasey . . . . Ood		music by Murray Gold
		Aired on October 1, 2011

BEHIND THE SCENES: *Death Is The Only Answer* was a short script selected by Steven Moffatt as the winning entry in the "Script to Screen" contest that was part of series six of **Doctor Who** Confidential, challenging young writers to create a short adventure for the Doctor. The finished mini-episode, running just under four minutes, aired as part of the final episode of the behind-the-scenes series **Doctor Who Confidential**, which was cancelled shortly before the episode aired. There are no clues as to where this story happens chronologically, or if it can be considered official at all.

CLASSIC CONNECTIONS: *Death* opens up a huge can of chronological worms (timewyrms?) in the continuity of **Doctor Who**, rivaling the infamous UNIT dating conundrum (see *Pyramids Of Mars*) in its complexity. The Doctor mentions that Einstein once tried to steal the TARDIS — and in fact, we may well have seen the famous scientist contemplating just that, when the seventh Doctor rescued him from the Rani in 1987's *Time And The Rani*. But that Einstein already had wild hair, a look he apparently doesn't adopt until after *Death Is The Only Answer*. Then again, if anyone's going to be capable of remembering that time is relative, it's going to be Albert Einstein, right?

The very enjoyable result of a search for enthusiastic amateur writers, *Death Is The Only Answer* brings **Doctor Who** back to some roots that it's forgotten: a showcase for rising talent, not just whoever's on the producer or script editor's speed dial.

For once upon a time, no one had ever heard of Andrew Smith or Robert Holmes or Glen McCoy or Ben Aaronovitch. Each of them sent unsolicited "spec scripts" to **Doctor Who** and jump-started their careers. Well, maybe McCoy didn't — he wrote *Timelash*, poor guy. Still, it had to be a lot of fun. Even after the original TV series ended, whole careers were launched via the **Doctor Who** novels and audio plays: Paul Cornell, Kate Orman, Joseph Lidster, Paul Magrs… the list goes on. **Discovering new talent has always been something that Doctor Who does.** In what had to be one of the best things he did in the 2011 season, Steven Moffatt brought that back and sent would-be young TV writers across the UK scrambling to their word processors. Bravo! They should've made the *ten* best scripts, not just one.

2011 CHILDREN IN NEED SPECIAL

The Doctor, in trying to draw attention toward a worthy cause, offers the shirt off of his back, as well as a few things he wears on his front. The problem now is how to get back to the TARDIS without anyone seeing that he's just given up his clothes.

Matt Smith . . . . The Doctor

written by Steven Moffat
directed by Richard Senior
Aired on November 18, 2011

BEHIND THE SCENES: Written by Steven Moffat and shot at BBC Television Centre in London mere days before air, this brief (exactly two minutes) scene was part of the BBC's annual Children In Need charity event, of which **Doctor Who** has been a part for years (*Dimensions In Time*, the 2005 special scene, *Time Crash*). This was the first time **Doctor Who** had been before the cameras at Television Centre since the production of the Sylvester McCoy story *Ghost Light* wrapped in 1989.

Any attempt to actually try to tackle this short sketch on a critical level would be silly — in fact, it probably takes longer to read this than it actually takes to watch the whole thing. It's amusing to watch **Doctor Who** shamelessly flirting with breaking the fourth wall — almost a tradition in itself since William Hartnell directly wished the viewing audience a merry Christmas during *The Feast Of Steven* in 1965 (see *The Daleks' Masterplan*).

My only suggestion would've been to have the "holographic clothes" briefly glitch into some of his earlier incarnations' outfits just for giggles (they obviously still exist, as they're on display at the **Doctor Who** Exhibition), but that would probably have confused viewers as to precisely which costume was up for auction. After all, the Doctor has worn many a cool bow tie before.

THE DOCTOR, THE WIDOW AND THE WARDROBE

The Doctor sabotages a gigantic spaceship on a mission to destroy Earth, only barely getting a spacesuit on in time to ride to the planet's surface amid the ship's debris. Amazingly, he survives re-entry and the landing, but he has to enlist the help of a woman named Madge Arwell, who believes he's either a spaceman or an angel.

Three years later, Madge Arwell has completely forgotten the otherworldly visitor. Days before Christmas, she receives a telegram informing her of her husband's death in an RAF fighter during the World War II. Worse still, Madge and her children, Cyril and Lily, are evacuated to a country house to avoid the air raids. The Doctor is waiting for them, having renovated the house in his own unique way. Under the tree, a gigantic present awaits, but the Doctor insists that it remain unopened until Christmas. Naturally, Cyril opens it early and climbs in, finding himself in another world. When the Doctor learns of this, he and Lily follow, and the Doctor explains that it literally *is* another world, one where the trees grow their own organic Christmas ornaments. Huge footprints in the snow reveal that Cyril wasn't alone here. The Doctor and Lily find Cyril in a domed, castle-like structure where a king and queen carved from sentient wood are sizing the boy up as a host body for the collected consciousness of the forest outside – a forest which will soon be clear-cut by acid rain induced by human harvesters from Androzani Major. But Cyril isn't up to the task, and to his own surprise, the Doctor is judged unfit for the task as well.

That's when Madge Arwell shows up, having followed the Doctor and her children to this world through the gift-wrapped gateway. She's also managed to drive the crew from Androzani off-planet and commandeered their harvester. And the trees decide she is their ideal host, but she already has the weight of the world bearing down on her: she hasn't told her children that their father has died in the war, until it's revealed for her by the trees.

Matt Smith . . . . The Doctor	
Alexander Armstrong . . . . Reg Arwell	
Bill Bailey . . . . Droxil	
Paul Bazely . . . . Ven-Garr	
Maurice Cole . . . . Cyril Arwell	
Arthur Darvill . . . . Rory	
Holly Earl . . . . Lily Arwell	
Karen Gillan . . . . Amy Pond	
Paul Kasey . . . . Wooden Queen	
Claire Skinner . . . . Madge Arwell	

This story has been released on DVD

written by Steven Moffat
directed by Farren Blackburn
music by Murray Gold

Aired on December 25, 2011

Sam Stockman . . . . Co-Pilot
Arabella Weir . . . . Billis
Spencer Wilding . . . . Wooden King

⑩ CLASSIC CONNECTIONS: Androzani Major was the site of murderous political intrigue in 1984's *The Caves Of Androzani*, at the end of which the fifth Doctor was forced to regenerate. This story doesn't make clear if the forest snowscape is on Androzani Major or not.

❸ A.K.A.: Actor **Alexander Armstrong** has a long association with the **Doctor Who** universe, having provided the voice of Sarah Jane Smith's alien computer, Mr. Smith, for the entire run of **The Sarah Jane Adventures**. **Arabella Weir** also has a voice-only **Doctor Who** connection; she starred as the Doctor (!!) in Big Finish's continuity-busting **Doctor Who Unbound** story *Exile* in 2003.

A more intimate take on a **Doctor Who** Christmas story, *The Doctor, The Widow And The Wardrobe* isn't perfect, but it succeeds in ways that *A Christmas Carol* didn't – it gets back to inviting the viewer to invest deeply in the emotional state of its one-night-only protagonists, and avoids the timey-wimey stuff until the very end of the story. The 2010 Christmas special was so wrapped up in its own time-hopping that it interfered with that investment; this time, the tone's just about right.

The cast is top-notch here. Even the obligatory Light Entertainment guest stars are on fine form, with the three Androzani harvester crewmembers providing menace and comic relief at the same time. The obligatory alien creatures for this episode are spooky, but they're quite literally wooden, and don't seem to do much other than just looking creepy.

It would be easy to dock points from this episode for yet another "power of a parent's love" story, but I'll let this one slip through for the same reason I let *Closing Time* get by with its borderline-cheesy resolution. And frankly, being a Christmas episode, perhaps one shouldn't be expecting too much from *The Doctor, The Widow And The Wardrobe*. It's hard to make this annual special a vital part of the storyline when it may be the only time some viewers sample **Doctor Who** all year – it's got to be all things to all people. That there's even a hint of an ongoing plot thread – namely the return of Amy and Rory – is a bonus for those interested.

A fun little story with an almost-fairytale feel to it, *The Doctor, The Widow And The Wardrobe* made for an unexpectedly enjoyable Christmas present.

INDEX

UWURP!

BIBLIOGRAPHY

Doctor Who: Regeneration (2000, Harper-Collins) by Philip Segal with Gary Russell

Doctor Who: The Eighties (1996, Virgin Publishing) by David J. Howe, Mark Stammers & Stephen James Walker

Doctor Who: The Handbook - The First Doctor (1994, Virgin Publishing) by David J. Howe, Mark Stammers & Stephen James Walker

Doctor Who: The Handbook - The Second Doctor (1997, Virgin Publishing) by David J. Howe, Mark Stammers & Stephen James Walker

Doctor Who: The Handbook - The Third Doctor (1996, Virgin Publishing) by David J. Howe & Stephen James Walker

Doctor Who: The Handbook - The Fourth Doctor (1992, Virgin Publishing) by David J. Howe, Mark Stammers & Stephen James Walker

Doctor Who: The Handbook - The Fifth Doctor (1995, Virgin Publishing) by David J. Howe & Stephen James Walker

Doctor Who: The Handbook - The Sixth Doctor (1993, Virgin Publishing) by David J. Howe, Mark Stammers & Stephen James Walker

Doctor Who: The Handbook - The Seventh Doctor (1998, Virgin Publishing) by David J. Howe & Stephen James Walker

Doctor Who: The Inside Story (2003, Big Finish) by Benjamin Cook

Doctor Who: The Nth Doctor (1997, Virgin Publishing) by Jean-Marc Lofficier

Periodicals:

Doctor Who Magazine (Panini Publishing)

Audiovisual:

The John Nathan-Turner Memoirs (2004, Big Finish Productions) by John Nathan-Turner

Who & Me (2008, BBC Audio) by Barry Letts

Shelved (2009, BBC Radio) by Shaun Ley

"Production Notes Subtitles" from various **Doctor Who DVDs** (2001-2012, 2!entertain)

ACKNOWLEDGEMENTS & THANKS

No book is written in a vacuum (writers in a vacuum have a tendency to run out of ideas pretty fast, resorting to scribbling "more... air... *jdfgjblrgh...*"). Even if the writer is working solo, there's a whole support system operating around him.

Mine consists primarily of Jan and Evan, with an additional shout-out to our four-legged family members: Xena, Olivia, Oberon, Puck, Portia, Gabby, and Maria. Thanks also to Shawn, Jerry and Jane, Brett and Jennifer and Katie, Shane, Robert, and Kent.

For my family, sadly few of whom are still around to see this book land on a table in front of them with a resounding thud, thank you for shrugging and saying "Ah, let him sit and watch Doctor Who and Star Trek. At least he's not getting into trouble." Hear all these pages turning? That's the sound of me continuing to not get into trouble.

For inspiration, I thank my friends who are fellow writers: Rob O'Hara, Brett Weiss, Rob Strangman, Leonard Herman, Chris Cavanaugh, and H.D. Campbell. I don't know how they do what they do, as often as it seems like they do. I'm a slowpoke compared to these guys.

Second Edition thanks: thanks to Shane Vaughn for the text of the "Nigerian omnirumor spam", and thanks to Little E for the loan of his precious "solids" (also known as RPG dice – I seem to have misplaced mine)!

Over at theLogBook.com, there's been no shortage of encouragement from the small core of loyal forum denizens: Ubik, Steve W, Zloth, Flack, and Gapporin. Drop by and find out how you can join them in the forum, for it is a magical place. Well, okay, it's more like an aimless sci-fi convention populated by a handful of curmudgeonly old guys. But that's what makes it fun. A big thanks to Dave, Rob, Philip, and all the other past and present contributors to the site, and all of the site's readers and Facebook fans.

Rather than trying to present any kind of groundbreaking work of original research, the author has tried instead to present a synthesis of his own opinions and the existing research of others who have had direct access to the source material. VWORP!1 is aimed at a more entry-level audience without actually being egregiously wrong. This book is meant for casual fans who see the DVDs in the store and find themselves asking "Which ones should I get?" - in other words, it's a gateway drug for those already in love with the show, who want to see more. If I've actually gotten anything wildly, incomprehensibly wrong, drop me a line at earl@thelogbook.com and I will make the effort to correct future printings.

And more than that, I hope you liked it. It was fun an exhausting to put together, and now I've got about a year to hammer together a book of similar size on the subject of Star Trek. Wish me luck.

VWORP!1 is dedicated to the memories of

Earl Green Sr. and **Alison Green**

Edward L. Harvey and **Evelyn Eugenia Harvey**

and a friend and mentor gone far too soon

Bill Kunkel

About the Author

Earl Green has been watching **Doctor Who** since his age was in the single digits. An award-winning former TV promotions writer/producer, his freelance writing work has appeared in <u>All Game Guide</u> and <u>Classic Gamer Magazine</u>, and he was a fact-checker for Benbella Books' <u>Boarding The Enterprise</u> anthology (2006, edited by Hugo- and Nebula-winning authors Robert J. Sawyer and David Gerrold with Leah Wilson). He contributed material to the second edition of <u>Memoirs Of A Virtual Caveman</u> (2014, written and edited by Rob Strangman). He writes about science fiction, classic video games, soundtracks and music, action figures and more on his own site, theLogBook.com. He wrote, scored, and produced the popular *Phosphor Dot Fossils* and *Classic Gaming Expo* video game documentary DVDs (and ended up with his own Twin Galaxies trading card as a result!). He is currently working on more books (turn back a page and see!). He has also designed the cover artwork for several newly-programmed video games designed for classic console systems. He only sleeps on even-numbered Mondays, and could never get the hang of Thursdays.

About THELOGBOOK.COM

theLogBook.com is perhaps most famous for its science fiction episode guides, which originated in 1989 before most of us had heard of the Internet. Since then, theLogBook.com has become a diverse entertainment destination covering such things as TV, books, music, movies, and toys and collectibles. It has also become popular for the award-winning **Phosphor Dot Fossils** classic video game archive, covering many vintage favorites from the arcades of the 1970s and 80s to such home video game systems as the Atari 2600, Odyssey 2, ColecoVision, Intellivision, and others. New material is added frequently, including a daily podcast mashing up both science fiction and science fact, and the site has a small but talkative forum community. More multimedia projects are being spawned from the site's deep database of original content, stretching back a quarter century.

THE LOG BOOK .COM 25 YEARS 1989-2014

Made in the USA
Las Vegas, NV
28 February 2022